# THE PHŒNICIAN
# ORIGIN OF BRITONS
## SCOTS & ANGLO-SAXONS

*DISCOVERED BY PHŒNICIAN & SUMERIAN
INSCRIPTIONS IN BRITAIN, BY PRE-
ROMAN BRITON COINS & A MASS
OF NEW HISTORY*

BY

## L. A. WADDELL
LL.D., C.B., C.I.E.

Fellow of Royal Anthropological Institute, Linnean & Folk-Lore
Societies, Hon. Correspondt. Indian Archæological
Survey, Ex-Professor of Tibetan,
London University

*WITH OVER ONE HUNDRED ILLUSTRATIONS AND MAPS*

# Kessinger Publishing's
## Rare Mystical Reprints

### THOUSANDS OF SCARCE BOOKS
### ON THESE AND OTHER SUBJECTS:

Freemasonry * Akashic * Alchemy * Alternative Health * Ancient Civilizations * Anthroposophy * Astrology * Astronomy * Aura * Bible Study * Cabalah * Cartomancy * Chakras * Clairvoyance * Comparative Religions * Divination * Druids * Eastern Thought * Egyptology * Esoterism * Essenes * Etheric * ESP * Gnosticism * Great White Brotherhood * Hermetics * Kabalah * Karma * Knights Templar * Kundalini * Magic * Meditation * Mediumship * Mesmerism * Metaphysics * Mithraism * Mystery Schools * Mysticism * Mythology * Numerology * Occultism * Palmistry * Pantheism * Parapsychology * Philosophy * Prosperity * Psychokinesis * Psychology * Pyramids * Qabalah * Reincarnation * Rosicrucian * Sacred Geometry * Secret Rituals * Secret Societies * Spiritism * Symbolism * Tarot * Telepathy * Theosophy * Transcendentalism * Upanishads * Vedanta * Wisdom * Yoga * *Plus Much More!*

### DOWNLOAD A FREE CATALOG
### AND
### SEARCH OUR TITLES AT:

### www.kessinger.net

PLATE I

*a*          *b*          *c*

Aryan Phœnician inscriptions on Newton Stone of " Part-olon, King of the Scots," about 400 B.C., calling himself " Briton," " Hittite," and " Phœnician."

*a* Face.      *b* Semi profile.      *c* Profile.

*(From author's photographs.)*

# PREFACE

THE treasures of ancient high art lately unearthed at Luxor have excited the admiring interest of a breathless world, and have awakened more vividly than before a sense of the vast antiquity of the so-called " Modern Civilization," as it existed over three thousand years ago in far-off Ancient Egypt and Syria-Phœnicia. Keener and more personal interest, therefore, should naturally be felt by us in the long-lost history and civilization of our own ancestors in Ancient Britain of about that period, as they are now disclosed to have been a branch of the same great ruling race to which belonged, as we shall see, the Sun-worshipping Akhen-aten (the predecessor and father-in-law of Tut-ankh-amen) and the authors of the naturalistic "New" Egyptian art—the Syrio-Phœnicians.

That long-lost origin and early history of our ancestors, the Britons, Scots and Anglo-Saxons, in the " Prehistoric " and Pre-Roman periods, back to about 3000 B.C., are now recovered to a great extent in the present work, by means of newly discovered historical evidence. And so far from these ancestral Britons having been mere " painted savages roaming wild in the woods," as we are imaginatively told in most of the modern history books, they are now on the contrary disclosed by the newly found historical facts to have been from the very first grounding of their galley keels upon Old Albion's shores, over a millennium and a half of years before the Christian era, a highly civilized and literate race, pioneers of Civilization, and a branch of the famous Phœnicians.

In the course of my researches into the fascinating problem of the Lost Origin of the *Aryans*, the fair, long-headed North European race, the traditional ancestors of our forbears of the Brito-Scandinavian race who gave to Europe in prehistoric time its Higher Civilization and civilized Languages—

researches to which I have devoted the greater part of my life, and my entire time for the past sixteen years—I ascertained that the Phœnicians were *Aryans* in race. That is to say, they were of the fair and long-headed civilizing " Northern " race, the reality of whose existence was conclusively confirmed and established by Huxley, who proved that

"There was and is an *Aryan Race*, that is to say, the characteristic modes of speech, termed Aryan, were developed among the Blond Long-heads alone, however much some of them may have been modified by the importation of Non-Aryan elements."
("The Aryan Question" in *Nineteenth Century*, 1890. 766.)

Thus the daring Phœnician pioneer mariners who, with splendid courage, in their small winged galleys, first explored the wide seas and confines of the Unknown Ancient World, and of whose great contributions to the civilization of Greece and Rome classic writers speak in glowing terms, were, I found by indisputable inscriptional and other evidence, *not Semites as hitherto supposed, but were Aryans in Race, Speech and Script. They were, besides, disclosed to be the lineal blood-ancestors of the Britons and Scots*—properly so-called, that is, as opposed to the aboriginal dark Non-Aryan people of Albion, Caledonia and Hibernia, the dusky small-statured Picts and kindred " Iberian " tribes.

This discovery, of far-reaching effect upon the history of European Civilization, and of Britain in particular, was announced in a summary of some of the results of my researches on Aryan Origins in the " Asiatic Review " for 1917 (pp. 197f.). And it is now strikingly confirmed and established by the discovery of hitherto undeciphered Phœnician and Sumerian inscriptions in Britain (the first to be recorded in Britain), and by a mass of associated historical evidence from a great variety of original sources, including hitherto uninterpreted pre-Roman-Briton coins and contemporary inscriptions, most of which is now published for the first time.

In one of these inscriptions, a bi-lingual Phœnician inscription in Scotland of about 400 B.C., now deciphered and translated for the first time, its author, in dedicating a votive monument to the Sun-god Bel, calls himself by all three titles " Phœnician," " Briton " and " Scot " ; and

## PREFACE

records his personal name and native town in Cilicia, which is a well-known ancient city-port and famous seat of " Sun-worship " in Asia Minor.

This British-Phœnician prince from Cilicia is, moreover, disclosed in his own inscription in Scotland to be the actual historical original of the traditional " Part-olon, king of the Scots," who, according to the Ancient British Chronicles of Geoffrey and Nennius and the legends of the Irish Scots, came with a fleet of colonists from the Mediterranean and arrived in Erin, after having cruised round the Orkneys (not far distant from the site where this Phœnician monument stands) and colonized and civilized Ireland, about four centuries before the Roman occupation of Britain. And he is actually called in this inscription " Part-olon " by a fuller early form of that name.

This uniquely important British-Phœnician inscription, whilst incidentally extending back the existence of the Scots in Scotland for over eight centuries beyond the period hitherto known for them to our modern historians, and disclosing their Phœnician origin, at the same time rehabilitates the genuineness of the traditional indigenous British Chronicles as preserved by Geoffrey of Monmouth and Nennius. These chronicles, although formerly accorded universal credence in Britain and on the Continent up till about a century ago, have been arbitrarily jettisoned aside by modern writers on early British history, obsessed with exaggerated notions of the Roman influence on Britain, as mere fables. But the genuineness of these traditional chronicles, thus conclusively established for the period about 400 B.C., is also now confirmed in a great variety of details for other of these traditional events in the pre-Roman period of Britain.

This ascertained agreement of the traditional British Chronicles with leading ascertained facts of pre-Roman British History wherever it can be tested, presumes a similarly genuine character also for the leading events in the earlier tradition. This begins with the arrival of " King Brutus-the-Trojan " and his " Briton " colonists with their wives and families in a great fleet from the Mediterranean about 1103 B.C., and his occupation, colonization and civilization of Albion, which he then is recorded to have called after himself and his Trojan Briton followers " Brit-ain " or "Land of the Brits," after dispossessing a still earlier colony of kindred Britons in Albion. All the more so is this pre-Roman-British tradition with its complete king-lists and chronicles probably genuine, as the Ancient Britons, properly so-called, are now found to have been accustomed to the use of writing from the earliest period of their first arrival in Albion or Britain. And the cherished old British tradition that Brutus-the-Trojan and his " Britons " hailed from the Mediterranean coast of Asia Minor is in agreement with the fact that King Part-olon " the Briton " actually records his native land as being also on the Mediterranean coast of Asia Minor. And this tradition is now confirmed by the discovery that many of the prehistoric gravings and inscriptions on the rocks and monoliths in Britain are of the Trojan type.

Fully to appreciate the historical significance of these long-undeciphered Phœnician and Sumerian inscriptions in Britain, and their associated evidence, it is necessary to have some general acquaintance with the results of my researches into the racial origin and previously unknown early history and world activities of the Phœnicians for a period of over two thousand years beyond that hitherto known to our historians. I, therefore, give in the introductory chapter a brief summary of the manner in which I was led to discover that the Phœnicians were Aryan in Race, Speech and Script, and were of vast antiquity, dating back from the testimony of their own still existing inscribed monuments to about 3100 B.C.

My new historical keys to the origin and " prehistoric " activities of the Phœnicians in early Europe disclose these virile ancestral pioneers of the Higher Civilization as no mere dead figures in a buried past, but instinct with life and human interests, adventurously exploring and exploiting the commercial possibilities of the various regions along the unknown seas of the Old World; and indicating to us at the present day the paths which led to the propagation and progress of the Higher Civilization over the World.

Starting from the solid new ground of the positive, concrete, historical inscriptions, we are led by the clues thus gained to

## PREFACE

fresh clues which open up for us, as we proceed, new and unsuspected avenues of evidence, disclosing rich mines of untapped historical material, written and unwritten. These clues lead us from Britain back to the Phœnician and Hittite homeland of the Aryan Phœnician Britons in Syria, Phœnicia and Asia Minor of St. George of Cappadocia (and England), and there offer us the solutions to most of the long-outstanding problems in regard to the origin of the Ancient Britons and the source and meaning of our ancestral British folklore, national emblems and patron saints.

In this way we gain not only a fairly intimate knowledge of the personalities of the Early Aryan Phœnicians who, as the ancestral Britons and Scots, colonized and civilized Britain, and the historical reasons for their various waves of migration hither with wholesale transplantation of their cults, institutions and names on British soil. We gain at the same time a considerable new insight into the remoter origin and racial character of the pre-Briton, non-Aryan aborigines of the British Isles in the Stone Age and their relation to the Picts and Celts which unravels to a great extent the hopeless tangle in which the question of the aboriginal races in Britain has hitherto become involved.

In thus enlarging, not inconsiderably, the boundaries of Clio's domain in Britain, we are led into several provinces not hitherto suspected of connection with Britain, though the relationship now becomes obvious. This wider outlook on the parent-land, as well as its colony in Britain and their intercommunications, reflects fresh light on both the Ancient Britons and on their parent Phœnicians. Amongst the great variety of historical effects thus elicited by this new light may be mentioned the following :

Archæologically are disclosed the racial character, original homeland and approximate dates of our ancestral erectors of the prehistoric Stone Circles in the British Isles with the motive of these monuments, also the erectors of the prehistoric stone cists and long barrow graves of the " Late Stone Age." The discovery of the key to the script of the prehistoric " Cup-marks " engraved upon the rocks and monoliths unlocks the hitherto sealed messages of these prehistoric literary records of our ancestors, and gives us a vivid picture of the exalted ideals which already ruled their lives in those far-distant days. Relatively fixed data are obtained for the much-conjectured beginning of the Bronze Age in Britain, and of the race who introduced it and manufactured the Early Bronze weapons, implements and trinkets which are unearthed from time to time, and hitherto supposed to be " Celtic." The racial character and original homeland of the pre-Aryan aborigines of the British Isles in the Stone Age also become evident. And we discover that the hitherto inexplicable Unity in the essentials of all the Ancient Civilizations is owing to the original Unity of the Higher Civilization, and its diffusion throughout the world by its originators, the ruling race of Aryans, and especially by their sea-going branch, the Phœnicians.

Historically, besides recovering the approximate dates of the chief waves of Aryan-Briton invasions, and the political causes apparently leading to these invasions, we recover and establish the historicity, names, achievements and dates of a great number of the chief kings and heroes of the Ancient Britons in what has hitherto been considered " the prehistoric period." Amongst other results is the interpretation of the unexplained legends and the wholly unknown origin and meaning of the symbols stamped upon the very numerous coins of the Ancient Britons in the pre-Roman period, and now disclosed for the first time.

In British National Patron Saints and emblems of Phœnician origin are now found to be St. George of Cappadocia and England and his Dragon legend and his Red Cross ; also the Crosses of St. Andrew and St. Patrick, now forming with St. George's the Union Jack and the kindred Scandinavian ensigns, all of which crosses are found to have been carried by the Phœnicians as their sacred standards of victory and imported and transplanted by them in the remote past on to British soil. " Britannia " also is discovered to have been evolved by the ancient sea-going Phœnicians as their patronymic tutelary goddess, and under the same name and with substantially the same form of representation as the British " Britannia." And the Phœnician origin and hitherto unknown meaning of the Unicorn and Lion emblems in British heraldry are now disclosed for the first time.

Linguistically, we now find that the English, Scottish, Irish, Gaelic, Cymric, Gothic and Anglo-Saxon languages and their script, and the whole family of the so-called " Aryan " languages with their written letters, are derived from the Aryan Phœnician language and script through their parent, the " Hittite " or Sumerian ; and that about fifty per cent of the commonest words in use in the " English " Language to-day are discovered to be Sumerian, " Cymrian " or Hittite in origin, with the same word-form, sound and meaning. This fact is freely illustrated in these pages, as critical words occur incidentally as we proceed. And it is found that the English and " Doric " Scottish dialects preserve the original Aryan or " Sumerian " form of words more faithfully than either the Sanskrit or Greek. The Phœnician origin of the ancient sacred " Ogam " script of the pre-Christian monuments in the British Isles is also disclosed.

In Religion, it is now found that the exalted religion of the Aryan Phœnicians, the so-called " Sun-worship," with its lofty ethics and belief in a future life with resurrection from the dead, was widely prevalent in early Britain down to the Christian era. In this " Sun-worship," as it is usually styled by modern writers, we shall see that, although the earliest Aryans worshipped that luminary itself, they were the first people to imagine the idea of God in heaven, and at an early period evolved the idea of the One Universal God, as " The Father God," some millenniums before the birth of Abraham, and they symbolized him by the Sun. They further emblemized the Sun as " The Light of the World " by the True Cross, in the manner now discovered, and they carved the Cross, as the symbol of Universal Divine Victory, upon their sacred seals and standards, and sculptured it upon their monuments from the fourth millennium B.C. downwards ; and invented the Swastika with the meaning now disclosed. This now explains for the first time the very numerous Crosses and Swastikas carved upon the prehistoric stone monuments and pre-Christian Stone Crosses with their other solar and non-Christian symbols throughout the British Isles. It also now explains the solar " wheeled " Cross, the so-called " Celtic " Cross, and the Red Cross of St. George, the Fiery Cross of the Scottish clans, the Bel Fire rites still surviving in the remoter parts of these islands at the summer solstice, and the numerous True Crosses with solar symbols stamped upon the ancient Briton coins of the " Catti " and " Cassi " kings of the pre-Roman and pre-Christian periods in Britain.

Geographically, the topography of the " prehistoric " distribution of the early Aryan Phœnician settlements throughout Ancient Britain is recovered by the incidence of their patronymic and ethnic names in the oldest Aryan place, river and ethnic names in relation to the prehistoric Stone Circles and monuments, before the thick upcrop of later and modern town and village names had submerged or obscured the early Aryan names on the map. The transplantation by the Phœnician colonists of old cherished homeland names from Asia Minor and Phœnician colonies on the Mediterranean is also seen. The Phœnician source and meaning of many of the ancient place, river and mountain names in Britain, hitherto unknown, or the subject of more or less fantastic conjecture by imaginative etymologists, is disclosed. And a somewhat clearer view is, perhaps, gained of the line of Phœnician seaports, trading stations and ports of call along the Mediterranean and out beyond the Pillars of Hercules in the prehistoric period.

In Economics and Science, the Hitto-Phœnician Aryan origin of our ordered agricultural and industrial life becomes evident. And the old British tradition is confirmed that London was built as the commercial capital several centuries before the foundation of Rome.

In Art, a like origin is disclosed for many of the motives in our modern decorative art. The religious solar meaning of the " key-patterns " and spiral designs is elicited for the first time. And the art displayed by the Ancient Britons in the pre-Roman period is found to be based upon Hitto-Phœnician models, and to be of a much higher standard than in the Anglo-Saxon and "mediæval" period in Britain.

Politically, the newly discovered racial link, uniting the Western Barats or " Brit-ons " with the Eastern Barats (or "Britons") of India—still called "The Land of the Barats"—through the blood-kinship with the ruling chiefs of India now revealed and established, should favourably determine the latter, in these days of Indian unrest, to remain within the fellowship of the British Commonwealth, which is now shown to have retained the real "*Swarāj*" elements of the old progressive ancestral Barat Civilization in a much purer form than the Indian branch. And the intimate kinship of the Britons and British, properly so-called, with the Norse—the joint preservers of the ancestral Gothic epics, the Eddas—is now disclosed to be much closer and much more ancient than has hitherto been suspected; and long before the Viking Age.

Classic Legend and Myth is to some extent rehabilitated by finding that some of the great heroes and demi-gods of Homer had a historical human origin in the personalities and achievements of famous Early Aryan and Barat Kings whose actual dates are now recovered.

The Psychologist and Eugenist may probably find a somewhat clearer standpoint for observing the effect of the mixing of racial elements in the composite British Nation, and in regard to the question of the racial element making for real progress in the complex conditions of our modern National Life.

Amongst the many minor effects of the discovery of the Aryan racial character of the Phœnicians and their merchant princes now disclosed, it would appear that the beautiful painting by Lord Leighton which adorns the walls of the Royal Exchange in London, portraying the opening of the Trade era in Britain, now requires an exchange of complexions between the aborigines of Albion and the Phœnician merchants, as well as some slight nasal readjustment in the latter to the Aryan type.

In thus opening up for us lost vistas of history adown the ages, and lifting considerably higher than before the dense veil that hung so long over the origin and ancestry of the composite races now forming the British Nation, the new-found historical evidence suggests that the modern Aryan-Britons or British, more fully than the other descendants of the Phœnicians, have inherited the sea-faring aptitudes and adventurous spirit of that foremost race of the Ancient World; and that the maritime supremacy of Britain, under her Phoenician tutelary Britannia, has been mainly kept alive by the lineal blood-descendants of these Aryan Phœnician ancestors of the Britons and the Scots and Anglo-Saxons.

In traversing such wide and varied fields of research in so many different specialized departments of culture and civilization, wherein a great mass of the new uncoordinated knowledge, laboriously unearthed by countless modern archæologists working in separate water-tight compartments, now receives a new orientation, it is scarcely possible that one individual, however careful, in such a pioneer exploration for the path of Truth along this vastly complex problem, can escape falling into errors in some details. But no pains have been spared to minimize such possibilities, and it is believed that such errors of commission, if they do occur, are relatively few and immaterial, and do not at all affect the main conclusions reached, which are so clearly established by the mass of cumulative historical evidence.

The long delay in publishing these discoveries, which were mostly made many years ago, has been owing to the vast scope of this exploration over so many wide fields, with the re-orientation of much of the mass of knowledge unearthed by countless archæologists working in specialized but isolated and uncoordinated departments. To this has been added the necessity for my acquiring a working knowledge of the ancient scripts and languages in which the original ancient inscriptions and records were written, in order to revise at first hand the spelling of the proper names in the original records in the Cuneiform and its parent the Sumerian hieroglyphic script, also in the " Akkadian," Hittite, hieroglyph Egyptian, Cretan, Cyprian, Iberian, Runic Gothic, Ogam, and the so-called Phœnician Semitic, and its allied Aramaic and Hebrew scripts, in addition to the Indian Pali and Sanskrit. This has entailed the spending of many additional years in strenuous toil for the necessary equipment for this pioneer exploration from the Aryan standpoint, as disclosed by my new historical keys found embedded in the

## PREFACE

Indian Sanskrit Vedas and Epics. And it has been supplemented by actual visitation of some of the chief sites in the ancient homeland of the Phœnicians and Hitto-Sumerians in Mesopotamia and Syria-Phœnicia. It is for the unbiassed reader now to judge whether these many years of intensive study are justified by their results. Some of the outstanding historical results of these discoveries are indicated in the concluding chapter.

And here I gratefully acknowledge the great obligations I owe to my friend Dr. Islay Burns Muirhead, M.A., who from first to last has favoured me with his helpful candid criticism on many of the details of the discoveries, with not a few suggestive comments, some of which I have gladly incorporated in these pages, and whose unflagging interest in the progress of the work has been a constant source of encouragement. I am also indebted to the courtesy of the several authorities mentioned in the text, for replying to my enquiries and permitting the use of a few of the illustrations. A list of the chief authorities and publications referred to is given at the end of the work.

L. A. WADDELL.

*January*, 1924.

FIG. A.—Sun-horse of Phœnician Archangel Mikal (Michael) and his Cross vanquishing Dragon, inscribed *DIAS'* in Sumerian, with equivalent 5 " cup-marks."
From Hittite seal of about 2000 B.C.
(After Delaporte, D.C.O., pl. 89. 2.)

FIG. B.—Ancient Briton Coin of 1st or 2nd cent. B.C. of same scene, also inscribed *DIAS*.
(After J. Evans, E.C.B., pl. 6. 14.)
The Cross, Goat, and 5 " cup-marks " of Michael appear in others of these Coins. Thus see the 5 " cups " behind horse on the Briton coin on back of cover, and Figs. 3, 43A. 61, 64. 65, &c.

# CONTENTS

PREFACE . . . . . . . . V–XV

CHAP.

1. THE PHŒNICIANS DISCOVERED TO BE ARYANS IN RACE AND THE ANCESTORS OF THE BRITONS, SCOTS AND ANGLO-SAXONS . . . . 1–15

2. THE UNDECIPHERED PHŒNICIAN INSCRIPTIONS OF ABOUT 400 B.C. IN BRITAIN AND SITE OF MONUMENT . . . . . . . 16–20

3. THE INSCRIPTIONS ON NEWTON STONE AND PREVIOUS FUTILE ATTEMPTS AT DECIPHERMENT 21–25

4. DECIPHERMENT AND TRANSLATION OF THE PHŒNICIAN INSCRIPTIONS:
   *Disclosing Monument to be a votive Fire-Cross to the Sun-god Bel by a Phœnician Hittite " Brit-on," and the script and language Aryan-Phœnician or Early Briton* . . . . 26–32

5. DATE OF NEWTON STONE INSCRIPTIONS ABOUT 400 B.C.:
   *Disclosing special features of Aryan-Phœnician Script, also Ogam as sacred Sun-cult script of the Hittites, Early Britons and Scots* . . 33–37

6. PERSONAL, ETHNIC AND GEOGRAPHIC PHŒNICIAN NAMES AND TITLES IN NEWTON STONE INSCRIPTIONS AND THEIR HISTORIC SIGNIFICANCE:
   *Disclosing also Phœnician source of the " Cassi " title of Ancient Briton kings and their Coins* . . . . . . . 38–51

## CONTENTS

CHAP.                                                                                         PAGE

7. PHŒNICIAN TRIBAL TITLE OF "BARAT" OR "BRIHAT" AND ITS SOURCE OF NAMES "BRIT-ON," "BRIT-AIN" AND "BRIT-ANNIA":
   *Disclosing Aryan-Phœnician Origin of the tutelary Britannia and of her form and emblems in Art* . . . . . . . 52–66

8. PHŒNICIAN BARAT OR "BRIT" AUTHOR OF NEWTON STONE INSCRIPTIONS DISCLOSED AS HISTORICAL ORIGINAL OF "PART-OLON, KING OF THE SCOTS" AND TRADITIONAL CIVILIZER OF IRELAND ABOUT 400 B.C.:
   *Disclosing Hitto-Phœnician Origin of clan title "Uallana" or "Vellaunus" or "Wallon" of Briton Kings Cassi-Vellaunus or Cad-Wallon, &c.; and of "Uchlani" title of Cassi ruling Britons* . . . . . . 67–80

9. LOCAL SURVIVAL OF PART-OLON'S NAME IN THE DISTRICT OF HIS MONUMENT:
   *Disclosing Phœnician Origin of names Barthol, Bartle, Bartholomew, and "Brude" title of the Kings of the Picts* . . . . . 81–90

10. PART-OLON'S INVASION OF IRELAND ABOUT 400 B.C. DISCOVERS THE FIRST PEOPLING OF IRELAND AND ALBION IN THE STONE AGE BY MATRIARCHIST VAN OR FEN "DWARFS":
    *Disclosing Van or "Fein" Origin of Irish aborigines and of their Serpent-Worship, St. Brigid and Matrilinear Customs of Irish and Picts* . . . . . . . 91–110

11. WHO WERE THE PICTS?
    *Disclosing their Non-Aryan Racial Nature and Affinity with Matriarchist Van, Wan or Fein Dwarfs and as the aborigines of Britain in Stone Age* . . . . . 111–126

CONTENTS  xix

CHAP. PAGE
12. WHO WERE THE " CELTS " PROPERLY SO-CALLED ?
    *Disclosing identity of Early British " Celts "
    or Kelts and " Culdees " with the " Khaldis "
    of Van and the Picts* . . . . 127–141

13. COMING OF THE BRITONS OR ARYAN BRITO-
    PHŒNICIANS UNDER KING BRUTUS-THE-TROJAN
    TO ALBION ABOUT 1103 B.C. . . 142–167

14. ARYANIZING CIVILIZATION OF PICTS AND CELTS BY
    BRUTUS AND HIS BRITO-PHŒNICIAN GOTHS
    ABOUT 1100 B.C. :
    *Disclosing Phœnician Origin of Celtic, Cymric,
    Gothic and English Languages, and Founding
    of London and Bronze Age* . . 168–187

15. PHŒNICIAN PENETRATION OF BRITAIN ATTESTED
    BY " BARAT " PATRONYM IN OLD PLACE AND
    ETHNIC NAMES :
    *Disclosing also Sumero-Phœnician sources of
    " Cumber, Cymer and Somer" ethnic Names* 188–199

16. " CATTI," " KEITH, GAD AND CASSI " TITLES IN
    OLD ETHNIC AND PLACE NAMES EVIDENCING
    PHŒNICIAN PENETRATION OF BRITAIN AND ITS
    ISLES :
    *Confirming Hitto-Phœnician Origin of " Catti "
    and " Cassi " Coins of pre-Roman Britain* 200–215

17. PREHISTORIC STONE CIRCLES IN BRITAIN DIS-
    CLOSED AS SOLAR OBSERVATORIES ERECTED
    BY MOR-ITE BRITO-PHŒNICIANS AND THEIR
    DATE :
    *Disclosing method of " Sighting " the Circles* 216–235

18. PREHISTORIC " CUP-MARKING " ON CIRCLES, ROCKS,
    ETC., IN BRITAIN, AND CIRCLES ON ANCIENT
    BRITAIN COINS AND MONUMENTS AS INVOCA-

## CONTENTS

CHAP.                                                                      PAGE

TIONS TO SUN-GOD IN SUMERIAN CIRCLE SCRIPT BY EARLY HITTO-PHŒNICIANS:
*Disclosing Decipherment and Translations of prehistoric Briton inscriptions by identical Cup-marks on Hitto-Sumerian seals and Trojan amulets with explanatory Sumer script; and Hitto-Sumer Origin of god-names " Jahveh " or Jove, Indra, " Indri "-Thor of Goths, " St. Andrew," Earth-goddess " Maia " or May, " Three Fates or Sibyls " etc., and of English names and signs of Numerals* . 236–261

19. "SUN-WORSHIP" AND BEL-FIRE RITES IN EARLY BRITAIN DERIVED FROM THE PHŒNICIANS: *Disclosing Phœnician Origin of Solar Emblems on pre-Christian monuments in Britain, on pre-Roman Briton Coins, and of " Deazil " or Sunwise direction and Horse-shoe for Luck, etc., & John-the-Baptist as Aryan Sun-Fire priest*. . . . . . 262–288

20. SUN CROSS OF HITTO-PHŒNICIANS IS ORIGIN OF PRE-CHRISTIAN CROSS ON BRITON COINS AND MONUMENTS AND OF " CELTIC " AND " TRUE " CROSS IN CHRISTIANITY:
*Disclosing Catti, " Hitt-ite " or Gothic Origin of " Celtic " or Runic Cross, Fiery Cross, Red Cross of St. George, Swastika and " Spectacles," Crosses on Early Briton Coins, etc., and introduction of True Cross into Christianity by the Goths ; and ancient " Brito-Gothic " Hymns to the Sun* . . . . . 289–314

21. ST. ANDREW AS PATRON SAINT WITH HIS "CROSS" INCORPORATES HITTO-SUMERIAN FATHER-GOD INDARA, INDRA OR GOTHIC "INDRI"-THOR AND HIS HAMMER INTRODUCED INTO EARLY BRITAIN BY GOTHIC PHŒNICIANS:
*Disclosing pre-Christian worship of Andrew in Early Britain and Hittite Origin of Crosses*

## CONTENTS

| CHAP. | | PAGE |
|---|---|---|
| | on Union Jack and Scandinavian Ensigns; Unicorn and Cymric Goat as sacred Goat of Indara; Goat as rebus for "Goth"; and St. Andrew as an Aryan Phœnician | 315–337 |
| 22. | CORN SPIRIT "TAS-MIKAL" OR "TASH-UB" OF HITTO-SUMERS IS "TASCIO" OF EARLY BRITON COINS AND PREHISTORIC INSCRIPTIONS, "TY" GOTHIC GOD OF TUES-DAY, AND "MICHAEL-THE-ARCHANGEL," INTRODUCED BY PHŒNICIANS: *Disclosing his identity with Phœnician Archangel "Tazs," "Taks," "Dashap-Mikal," and "Thiaza," "Mikli" of Goths, "Daxa" of Vedas, and widespread worship in Early Britain; Phœnician Origin of Dionysos and "Michaelmas" Harvest Festival and of those names* | 338–362 |
| 23. | ARYAN-PHŒNICIAN RACIAL ELEMENT IN THE MIXED RACE OF THE BRITISH ISLES AND ITS EFFECT ON THE PROGRESS OF BRITISH CIVILIZATION | 363–378 |
| 24. | HISTORICAL EFFECTS OF THE DISCOVERIES | 379–384 |

## APPENDICES

| | | PAGE |
|---|---|---|
| 1. | CHRONOLOGICAL LIST OF EARLY BRITON KINGS, FROM BRUTUS ABOUT 1103 B.C. TO ROMAN PERIOD, COMPILED FROM EARLY BRITISH CHRONICLES OF GEOFFREY OF MONMOUTH AND SUPPLEMENTED BY RECORDS OF DR. POWELL, ETC., *and confirmed by testimony of Briton Coins, etc.* | 385–393 |

## CONTENTS

PAGE

2. Part-olon's Identity with "Cath-luan," First traditional King of the Picts in Scotland . . . . . . 394–396

3. "Catti" Place and Ethnic Names evidencing Phœnician Penetration in the Home Counties, Midlands, North of England, Ireland and Scotland . . . . . 397–403

4. Brutus-the-Trojan as the Homeric Hero "Peirithoos" . . . . . 404–406

5. Founding of London as "New Troy" (Tri-novant) by King Brutus about 1100 B.C. . . . . . . 407–410

6. Mor or "Amorite" Cup-marked Inscription with Sumerian Script on Tomb of Aryan Sun-Priestess, of about 4000 B.C., from Smyrna, supplying a Key to Cup-marked Script in Britain . . 411–412

7. The Amorite Phœnician Tin Mines of Cassiterides in Cornwall(?) referred to by Sargon I. of Akkad, about 2750 B.C.; & Kaptara or "Caphtor" as Abdara in Spain . . . . . . 413–415

ABBREVIATIONS FOR CHIEF REFERENCES . . 417–420

INDEX . . . . . . . 421–450

# LIST OF ILLUSTRATIONS

PLATE I. Aryan Phœnician inscriptions on Newton Stone of "Part-olon, King of the Scots" about 400 B.C., calling himself "Brit-on," "Hittite," and "Phœnician." (From author's photographs). (a) Face. (b) Semi-profile. (c) Profile . *Frontispiece*

## FIGURES IN TEXT.

FIG.                                                                                                               PAGE

A. Sun-horse of Phœnician Archangel *Dasap Mikal* (Michael) and his Cross, vanquishing the Dragon, inscribed in Sumerian *DIAS*, with his 5 "cup-marks." From Hittite sacred seal of about 2000 B.C. (After Delaporte) . . . xv

B. Two Ancient Briton coins of 1st or 2nd cent. B.C. of same scene also inscribed *DIAS*. (After Beale and J. Evans) . xv

1. Bel, "The god of the Sun" and Father-god of the Phœnicians. From a Phœnician altar of about 4th century B.C. (After Renan)   2

2. Swastika Sun-Crosses on dress of Phœnician Sun-priestess carrying sacred Fire. (After Di Cesnola) . . . 3

3. "Catti" Briton coin of pre-Roman Britain of about 2nd century B.C., with Sun and Cross symbols. (After B. Poste) . . 6

4. Early Khatti, "Catti" or Hittites in their rock-sculptures about 2000 B.C. (After Perrot and Guillaume) . . . 7

5. Phœnician coin of Carthage inscribed "Barat." (After Duruy)   9

5A. Briton prehistoric monument to Bel at Craig Narget, Wigtonshire, with Hitto-Phœnician Sun-Crosses, etc. (After Proc. Soc. Antiquaries, Scotland) . . . . . . 15

5B. Prehistoric Briton monument to Bel at Logie in Don Valley, near Newton Stone, with Hitto-Phœnician inscription and Solar symbols. (After Stuart) . . . . . 20

6. Aryan Phœnician inscription on Newton Stone . . . 29

7. Ogam Version of Newton Stone inscription as now deciphered and read . . . . . . . . . 30

8. Ogamoid inscription from Hittite hieroglyphs, on the Lion of Marash. (After Wright) . . . . . . 36

9. Phœnician inscription on Early Briton Coins found near Selsey. (After J. Evans) . . . . . . . 43

10. Cilician Gothic king worshipping "Sun-god." From bas-reliefs in temple of Antiochus I. of Commagene, 63-34 B.C. (After Cumont) . . . . . . . . . 46

11. Cassi Coin of Early Britain, inscribed "Cas" with Sun-horse. (After Poste) . . . . . . . . 48

12. Cassis of Early Babylonia ploughing and sowing under the Sign of the Cross. From Kassi official seal of about 1350 B.C. (After Clay) . . . . . . . . . 49

12A. "Cassi" Sun-Cross on prehistoric monument with Cup-marks at Sinniness, Wigtonshire. (After Proc. Soc. Antiquaries, Scotland) . . . . . . . . . 51

13. Phœnician patronymic titles of "*Parat*" and "*Prydi*" or "*Prudi*" on Phœnician tombstones in Sardinia . . . 53

## CONTENTS

| FIG. | | PAGE |
|---|---|---|
| 14. | Coins of Phœnician "Barats" of Lycaonia of 3rd cent. A.D. disclosing their tutelary goddess "Barati" as "Britannia." (After W. M. Ramsay) | 55 |
| 15. | Britannia on Early Roman coins in Britain. (After Akerman) | 56 |
| 16. | Phœnician Coin of Barati or Britannia from Sidon. (After Hill) | 57 |
| 17. | Brit-annia tutelary of Phœnicians in Egypt as *Bāirthy*, "The Mother of the Waters," *Nut* or "Naiad" (After Budge) | 60 |
| 18. | Egyptian hieroglyphs for Goddess *Bāirthy* of Phœnician sailors | 62 |
| 19. | Briton Lady of *Cat-uallaun* clan, wife of *Barates*, a Syrio-Phœnician. From sculpture of about 2nd century A.D. at South Shields | 73 |
| 20. | A prehistoric Matriarch of the Vans(?) of the Stone Age. From a Hittite rock-sculpture near Smyrna. (After Martin) | 93 |
| 21. | Van or "Biana," ancient capital of Matriarch Semiramis, and "The Children of *Khaldis*" on flanks of Ararat. (After Bishop) | 98 |
| 21A. | Sun-Eagle triumphs over Serpent of Death, from pre-Christian Cross at Mortlach, Banff. (After Stuart) | 110 |
| 22. | Three main racial head-types in Europe | 135 |
| 23. | Hitto-Phœnician war-chariot as source of Briton war-chariots. (After Rosellini) | 145 |
| 24. | "Trojan" solar shrine at Brutus' birth-province (Latium) with identical Hittite symbols as in Ancient Britain. (After Chantre) | 149 |
| 25. | Phœnician tin port in Cornwall, *Ictis* or St. Michael's Mount in Bay of Penzance. (After Borlase) | 165 |
| 25A. | Prehistoric Catti Sun-Cross and Spiral gravings on barrow stones at Tara, capital of Ancient Scotia or Erin. (After Coffey) | 187 |
| 25B. | Catti coin inscribed "*Ccetiyo*" from Gaul. (After Poste) | 215 |
| 26. | Phœnician Chair of 15th cent. B.C., with solar scenes as in Early Briton monuments and coins. From tomb of "Syrian" high-priest in Egypt. (After A. Weigall) | 221 |
| 27. | Sumerian Sighting Marks on Observation Stone of Keswick Stone Circle | 227 |
| 28. | Mode of Sighting Solstice Sunrise by Observation Stone at Keswick Circle | 230 |
| 29. | Mode of Sighting Solstice Sunrise by Observation Stone at Stonehenge | 230 |
| 30. | Prehistoric "Cup-markings" on monuments in British Isles. (After Simpson) | 237 |
| 31. | "Cup-markings" on amulet whorls from Troy. (From Schliemann) | 238 |
| 32. | "Cup-marks" on archaic Hitto-Sumerian seals and amulets. (From Delaporte) | 239 |
| 33. | Circles as diagnostic cipher marks of Sumerian and Chaldee deities, in "Trial" scene of Adam, the son of God *Ia* ("*Iahvh*" or Jove). From Sumer seal of about 2500 B.C. (After Ward) | 239 |
| 34. | Circle Numerical Notation in Early Sumerian, with values | 241 |
| 35. | Father-god *Ia* ("*Iahvh*" or Jove) or Indara, bestowing the Life-giving Waters. From Sumer seal of about 2450 B.C. (After Delaporte) | 245 |
| 36. | Dual Circles designate two-headed Resurrecting Sun. From Hitto-Sumer seals of about 2400 B.C. (After Delaporte) | 247 |
| 37. | Returning or Resurrecting Sun entering "Gates of Night." From Hittite seals of about 2000 B.C. (After Ward) | 248 |
| 38. | Returning or Resurrecting Sun in prehistoric Irish rock-gravings as Two-Cup-marks with Reversed Spirals entering Gates of Night. (Figs. after Coffey) | 249 |

## CONTENTS

| FIG. | | PAGE |
|---|---|---|
| 39. | Pentad Circles designate *Taśia*, the archangel Michael | 250 |
| 40. | Archangel *Taśia* (winged) invoked by Mother (4 Circles) for Dead (3 Circles). From Hittite seal of about 1500 B.C. (After Lajard) | 250 |
| 41. | Phœnician seal reading " *Taś*," Archangel. (After A. Di Cesnola) | 251 |
| 42. | Heptad Circles for Heaven. (After Delaporte) | 251 |
| 43. | Muru, Mor or " Amorite " archaic tablet of about 4000 B.C. from grave of Aryan Sun-priestess, in Cup-mark and Sumerian script, " Hoffman tablet." (After Barton) | 257 |
| 43A. | Tascio horseman, and horse of the Sun, on Briton coins of 1st cent. B.C., with Cross and circle (" cup ") marks. (After Poste) | 261 |
| 44. | Sun Symbols—Discs, Horse, Hawk, etc., on Early Briton coins. (After J. Evans) | 285 |
| 44A. | St. John-the-Baptist with his Sun-Cross sceptre or mace. (After Murillo) | 288 |
| 44B. | Ancient Briton coin with Corn Sun-Cross, Andrew's Cross, Sun-horse, etc. (After Poste) | 289 |
| 45. | Twin Fire-Sticks crossed in Fire-production, as used in modern India. (After Hough) | 292 |
| 46. | Sun Crosses, Hitto-Sumerian, Phœnician, Kassi and Trojan, plain, rayed and decorated, on seals, amulets, etc., 4000–1000 B.C. | 294 |
| 47. | Ancient Briton Sun Crosses derived from Hitto-Sumerian, Phœnician, Kassi and Trojan sources, on prehistoric pre-Christian monuments and pre-Roman Briton coins | 295 |
| 48. | " Gyron " Cross of British Heraldry is the " *Gurin* " Cross of the Hittites | 307 |
| 49. | Identity of Catti or Hittite Solar monuments with those of Early Britain, *re* Cadzow pre-Christian Cross | 308 |
| 50. | Swastika on Phœnician (or Philistine) coin from Gaza, disclosing origin of Scottish " Spectacle " darts | 310 |
| 51. | Swastika of Resurrecting Sun transfixing the Serpent of Death on Ancient Briton monument at Meigle, Forfarshire. (After Stuart) | 311 |
| 52. | St. Andrew, patron saint of Goths & Scots, with his Cross. (After Kandler) | 314 |
| 53. | Indara's X Cross on Hitto-Sumerian, Trojan and Phœnician Seals | 316 |
| 54. | " Andrew's " Cross on pre-historic monuments in Britain and Ireland and on Early Briton coins | 317 |
| 55. | Indara or " Andrew " slaying the Dragon. From Hittite seal of about 2000 B.C. (After Ward) | 319 |
| 56. | " Andrew's " X Cross is Indara's Bolt or " Thor's Hammer " on Ancient Briton monuments | 321 |
| 57. | Indara spouting water for benefit of mankind. From Hitto-Sumerian seal of about 2500 B.C. (After Ward) | 324 |
| 58. | Unicorn as sole supporter of old Royal Arms of Scotland, and associated with St. Andrew and his " Cross " | 329 |
| 59. | Goats (and Deer) as " Goths " of Indara, protected by Cross and Archangel *Taś* (Tashub Mikal) against Lion and Wolf of Death on Hitto-Sumer, Phœnician and Kassi seals. (After Ward, etc.) | 334 |
| 60. | Ancient Briton Goats (and Deer) as " Goths " of Indara, protected by Cross and Archangel *Taś* or *Tascia* (Michael) against Lions and Wolf of Death. (After Stuart, etc.) | 335 |
| 60A. | Ancient Briton " Tascio " coin inscribed *DIAS*. (After Poste) | 338 |
| 61. | *Tascio* or *Tascif* of Early Briton coins is Corn-Spirit *Ɽaś* or " Tash-ub " of Hitto-Sumerians. (Coins after J. Evans) | 339 |

## CONTENTS

FIG.                                                                              PAGE

62. *Tascio* or *Tascif* as " Tashub " the Hittite or Early Gothic Corn-Spirit. From archaic Hittite rock-sculpture at Ivriz in Taurus. (After von Luschan and Wilson) . . . . 340
63. Archangel *Taś* interceding with God Indara for sick man attacked by Dragon of Death. From Hittite seal of about 2500 B.C. (After Delaporte) . . . . . . . . 344
64. Archangel *Taś-Mikal* defending Goats (and Deer) as " Goths " with Cross and Sun emblems on Greco-Phœnician coins. (From coins in British Museum, after Hill) . . . 346
65. Archangel *Taś* defending Goats as " Goths " with Cross and Sun emblems on Early Briton coins. (From coins after J. Evans and Stukeley) . . . . . . . . . 347
66. *Taś* as " Michael " the Archangel, bearing rayed " Celtic " Cross, with Corn, Sun-Goose or Phœnix on Phœnician coins of Cilicia of 5th century B.C. (Coins in British Museum, after Hill) . 349
67. *Taś* or *Tascio* or St. Michael the Archangel on Early Briton pre-Christian coins. (Coins after J. Evans) . . . . 349
68. Phœnix Sun-Bird of Tas or Tascio with Crosses and Sun-discs from Early Britain cave-gravings and coins. (After Simpson, Stuart and J. Evans) . . . . . . . . . 350
69. " Tascio " in Egypt as Reŝef. (After Renan) . . . . 353
70. *Tascia, Dias* or *Tax* as " *Daxa*," the Indian Vedic Creator-god. (After Wilkins) . . . . . . . . . 353
71. Logie Stone Ogam inscription as now deciphered, disclosing invocation to Bil and his Archangel " *Tachab* " or " Tashub " 356
72. " Bird-Men" on Briton monuments, at Inchbrayock and Kirriemuir, Forfar. (After Stuart) . . . . . . 362
73. Early Bronze Age Briton button-amulet Cross. From barrow-grave at Rudstone, Yorks. (After Greenwell) . . 378
74. Ancient Briton " Catti " coin of 2nd cent. B.C., with Sun Crosses, Sun-horse, etc., and legend *INARA* (Hitto-Phœnician Father-god *Indara* or " Andrew "). (After Evans) . . 384
75. Tascio (Hercules) coin of *Ricon* Briton ruling clan. (After Poste) 385
76. Archaic Hittite Sun Horse with Sun's Disc and (?) Wings. From Seal at Cæsarea in Cappadocia (After Chantre) . . . 410
77. Pendant Phœnician Sun-Cross held in adoration. From Hittite seal of about 1000 B.C. (After Lajard) . . . . 420

## MAPS AND PLANS

Sketch-Map of Site of Newton Stone and its Neighbourhood in Don Valley . . . . . . . . . . . 19
Megalith Distribution in England. (After W. J. Perry) . . 217
Survey-plan of Keswick Stone-Circle, showing orientation of Observation-stone bearing Sumerian sign-marks. (After Dr. W. D. Anderson) . . . . . . . . . . 229
Map of Phœnician Empire in Western Asia, Mediterranean, and N.W. Europe, showing " Khatti " (or Hitt-ite), " Kassi " and " Barat " and " Phœnice " place-names in Phœnician colonies    At end

# THE PHŒNICIAN ORIGIN OF THE BRITONS SCOTS & ANGLO-SAXONS

I

THE PHŒNICIANS DISCOVERED TO BE ARYANS IN RACE AND THE ANCESTORS OF THE BRITONS, SCOTS & ANGLO-SAXONS

> "The able *Panch* ['Phœnicians'] setting out to invade the Earth, brought the whole World under their sway." — *Mahā,- Bārata* Indian Epic of the Great Barats.[1]
>
> "The *Brihat* ['Brit-on'][2] singers belaud Indra ... Indra hath raised the Sun on high in heaven ... Indra leads us with single sway—The *Panch* [Phœnic-ian Brihats] leaders of the Earth. Ours only, and none others is He!"—Rig Veda Hymn.[3]

IN the Preface it is explained that the most suitable starting point to begin unravelling the tangled skein of History for the lost threads of Origin of the Britons, Scots and Anglo-Saxons is from the fresh clues gained on the solid ground of the newly deciphered Phœnician inscriptions in Britain.

The chief of these Phœnician inscriptions, and the first to be reported in Britain, is carved upon a hoary old stone of about 400 B.C. (see Frontispiece), dedicated to Bel, the Phœnician god of the Sun (see Fig. 1), by a votary who

---

[1] M.B., Bk. i., chap. 94, sloka 3738.
[2] On "Brihat" as a dialectic Sanskrit variant of the more common "Barat", and the source of "Brit" or "Brit-on" see later.
[3] R.V. i., 7, 1–10.

calls himself therein by all three titles of " Phœnic-ian," " Brit-on " and " Scot," by ancient forms of these titles ; and whose personal appearance is presumably illustrated in the nearly contemporary sculpture from his homeland, Fig. 10 (p. 46). In thus preserving for us the name and titles of a " prehistoric " literate Phœnician king of North Britain upon his own original monument, it at the same time supplies a striking proof of the veracity of the ancient tradition cited in the heading, which the Eastern branch of Aryans has

FIG. 1.—Bel, " The God of the Sun " and Father-God of the Phœnicians.
From a Phœnician altar of about the fourth century B.C.
(After Renan, *Mission de Phénicie* pl. 32.)
Note rayed halo of the Sun.

faithfully preserved in their famous epic, " The Great Barats" (*Mahā Bārata*), in regard to the prehistoric worldwide civilizing conquests of the *Panch* or " Phœnicians," the greatest ruling clan of the Aryan *Barats*, or *Brihats*, who, we shall find, were the ancestors of the " *Brits* " or *Brit-ons*, our own ancestors. And the amplifying second quotation in the heading, from the Early Aryan psalms, also preserved by the same Eastern branch of the Aryan Barats or Brit-ons, discloses the Phœnician motive for erecting this inscribed monument in Early Britain to the God of the Sun with his special symbol of the Swastika Cross—an emblem embroidered on the dress of the priests[1] and priestesses of the Sun (see Fig 2), and figured freely with other solar symbols on Phœnician and Early Briton monuments and on pre-Roman Briton coins, as we shall see later.

This Brito-Phœnician inscription in Britain, in recording unequivocally the Aryan character of the Phœnicians, as well as the Phœnician ancestry of the Britons and Scots, merely confirmed the historical results which I had previously

FIG 2.—Swastika Crosses on dress of Phœnician Sun-priestess carrying sacred Fire.
From terra-cotta from Phœnician tomb in Cyprus. (After Cesnola, 30.)

elicited many years before, from altogether different sources, by discovering new keys to the Phœnician Problem. These unlocked the sealed stores of history regarding the origin and activities of the Early Phœnicians, and disclosed them to be the leading branch of the Aryan race, and Aryan also in speech and script, and the lineal parents of the Britons, Scots and Anglo-Saxons.

Before proceeding further, therefore, it is desirable to

[1] For Swastikas on dress of a Hittite high-priest, see Fig. in Chapr. XXII.

indicate briefly here what these new keys are, and the manner in which I was led to discover them.

In attacking the great unsolved fascinating Aryan Problem—the lost origin of our fair, long-headed, civilized ancestors of the Brito-Scandinavian and Ancient Greco-Medo-Persian race who gave to Europe and Indo-Persia their Aryan languages and Higher Civilization—a problem which had so completely baffled all enquiring historians that, after failing to find any traces of them as a race, they threw it up in despair about half a century ago, I took up the problem at its eastern or Indo-Persian end and devoted to it most of my spare time during over a quarter of a century spent in India.

There were some manifest advantages in attacking the problem from its eastern end. Philologists, ethnologists and anthropologists were generally agreed that the eastern branch of the ancient ruling Aryan race in India had presumably preserved in the Sanskrit dialect a purer form of the original Aryan speech than was to be found in the European dialects, from Greek to Gothic and English ; whilst they also preserved a great body of traditional literature regarding the original location, doings and achievements of the Early Aryans which had been lost by the western or European branch in the vicissitudes and destructive turmoil of long ages of migration and internecine wars. Besides this, the long prevalence in India of the rigid caste system, by restricting intermarriage between different tribes and the dusky aborigines, was supposed to have preserved the Aryan physical type in the ruling Aryan caste there, in relatively purer form than in Europe.

After acquiring a working knowledge of Sanskrit and the vernaculars, and studying the Indian traditions, written and unwritten at first hand, as well as all the reports of the archæological survey department on excavations, etc., and personally visiting all of the most reputed ancient sites, and making several fresh explorations and excavations at first hand, and measuring the physical types of the people, I eventually found that, despite all that has been written about the vast antiquity of Civilization in India, mostly

# HITTITES OR CATTI THE EARLY ARYANS

by theorists who had never visited India, there was *absolutely no trace of any civilization, i.e., Higher Civilization in India before the seventh century* B.C. Indeed, nothing whatever of traces of Civilization, apart from the rude Stone Circles, has ever been found by the scientifically equipped Indian Archæological Survey Department, in their more or less exhaustive excavations on the oldest reputed sites down to the virgin soil during over half a century, which can be specifically dated to before 600 B.C.

On the other hand, I observed, that historical India, like historic Greece, *suddenly* bursts into view about 600 B.C. in the pages of Buddhist literature, and in the Maha Barat epic, with a multitude of Aryan rulers speaking the Aryan language, with a fully-fledged Aryan Civilization, of precisely the same general type which has persisted down to the present day.

The question then arose: whence came these Aryan invaders suddenly into India about the seventh century B.C., with their fully-fledged Aryan Civilization, into a land previously uncivilized?

On analysing this early Aryan Civilization thus suddenly introduced into India, in regard to its culture, social structure, customs, folklore and religion, and the traditional topography and climate of its ancestral homeland as described in the Vedas—descriptions wholly inapplicable to India—I was led by numerous clues to trace these "Aryan," or as they called themselves "*Arya*," invaders of India back to Asia Minor and Syria-Phœnicia.

I then observed that the old ruling race of Asia Minor and Syria-Phœnicia, from immemorial time, were the great imperial, highly civilized, ancient people generally known as "Hitt-ites,' but who called themselves "*Khatti*" or "*Catti*," *which is the self-same title by which the early Briton kings of the pre-Roman period called themselves and their race, and stamped it upon their Briton coins*—the so-called "*Catti*" coins of early Britain (see Fig. 3). And the early ruling race of Aryans who first civilized India also called themselves "*Khattiyo*," as we shall see presently.

This ancient Khatti or "Catti" ruling race of Asia

Minor and Syrio-Phœnicia also called themselves "*Arri*" with the meaning of "Noble Ones." Now this was the identical racial title which was also applied to themselves by the Indo-Aryans or Eastern branch of the Aryans, who called themselves "*Arya*," the "*Ariya*" of the older Pali, which had also the literal meaning of "Noble," and which is the actual word from which our modern English term "Aryan" has been coined. And these ancient Khatti or "Hittites" are represented in their ancient sculptures in Gothic dress. Here then already I seemed to have found not only the origin of the Indo-Aryans, but also the original land of the Aryan Race, and the homeland of the Goths and of our own ancestral Britons and Anglo-Saxons. And further examination soon confirmed this.

FIG. 3. "Catti" Briton Coins of pre-Roman Britain of about second century B.O. with Sun symbols.
(After Poste.)
Note the Crosses around Sun-horse, and in second coin contraction of title into "ATT." The "El" between the face and back of coin = Electrum alloy of gold of which coin consists, and A = *Aurum* or Gold.

The civilization of this *Arri* (or Aryan) race of Khatti or "Catti" was essentially of the kind which is now called the Aryan type, and of the same type as that introduced into India by the Eastern branch of the Aryas or Aryans. In appearance also these Khatti, who were called "The White Syrians" by Strabo,[1] are seen in their own rock-sculptures and sculptured monuments of between 3000 and and 2000 B.C., to be of the Aryan type. They are tall in stature, with conical "Phrygian" caps and snow boots with turned-up toes, and garbed significantly in what is now commonly called the "Gothic" style of dress (see Fig. 4), for the reason, as we shall see later, that they were the primitive Goths, and the Goths were typically Aryan in race.

[1] S. 542, 12.3.6; 551-4.

# HITTITES OR CATTI THE EARLY GOTHS

The ruins of their great walled cities, built of cyclopean masonry and adorned with sculptures and hieroglyphic writing, are found throughout the length and breadth of Asia Minor and extend into Syria-Phœnicia; and the country is intersected by their great arterial highways, the so-called "royal roads," radiating from their ancient capital at

FIG. 4.—Early Khatti, " Catti " or Hitt-ites in their Rock-sculptures dating probably before 2000 B.C.
(After Perrot and Guillaume.)[1]

Note " Gothic " dress and snow-boots. The scene is part of a religious procession.

Boghaz Koi or Pteria in the heart of Cappadocia, the traditional home of St. George of England, and the country in which St. Andrew, the apostle and patron saint of the Scots, is reported to have travelled in his mission to the

---

[1] P.G.G., pl. 49. From bas-reliefs in the Iasili rock-chambers below Boghaz Koi or Pteria in Cappadocia.

Scyths[1] or *Getae*, the Greco-Roman form of the name " Goth " —the historical significance of this fact will be seen later.

These ancient imperial Khatti people of Asia Minor and Syria-Phœnicia, are the same ruling race which are now generally known as the " Hittites " ; for, although calling themselves " *Khatti* " and called also thus by the Babylonians and Ancient Egyptians, the Hebrews corrupted the spelling of that name into " *Heth* " and " *Hitt* " in their Old Testament, when referring to them as the ruling race in Phœnicia and Palestine on the arrival of Abraham there ; and the translators of our English version of the Hebrew text have further obscured the original form of the name by adding the Latin affix *ite*, thus arbitrarily coining the modern term " Hitt-ite."

The identity of these *Khatti Arri*, or " Hitt-ites " with the eastern branch of the Aryans who invaded and civilized (by Aryanizing) India, was now made practically certain by my further observation that the latter people also called themselves in their Epics by the same title as did the Hitt-ites. They called themselves *Khattiyo Ariyo* in their early Pali vernacular, and latterly Sanskritized it by the intrusion of an *r* into *Kshatriya*[2] *Arya* (in Hindi *Khattri Arya*), and these Indian names (*Khattiyo, Kshatriya*) have the same radical meaning of " cut, or ruler," as the Hittite *Khatti* has. Later I observed that the early Khatti or " Hitt-ites," as well as the Phœnicians, called themselves by an early form of *Barat, i.e.* as we shall see the original of " Brit " or " Brit-on," and that they also used that form itself (see Fig. 5 and later) ; and that their language was essentially Aryan in its roots and structure. This practically established the identity of the Khatti or Hitt-ites with the Indo-Aryans, and disclosed Cappadocia in Asia Minor as the lost cradle-land of the Aryans.

This now led to my discovery of the key, or rather the complete bunch of keys to the lost early history, not only of the Indian branch of the Aryans and its parent Aryan stock back to the rise of the Aryan race, but also to the lost history of the Khatti or Hitt-ites themselves, who have

[1] B.L.S. Novr. 594.    [2] Also spelt *Xatriya*, and " Hittite " is also spelt *Xatti*.

## CATTI OR HITTITES THE EARLY BRITONS

hitherto been known no earlier than about 2000 B.C.,[1] or still later.[2]

I had long observed that amongst the most cherished ancestral possessions which the Indian branch of the Khattiyo Ariyo Barats had brought with them from their old homeland to their new colony in India, like Æneas in his exile jealously bringing with him his " rescued household gods " from his old Trojan homeland,[3] were their treasured traditional lists of their ancestral Aryan kings, extending back continuously to the first Aryan dynasty in prehistoric times.

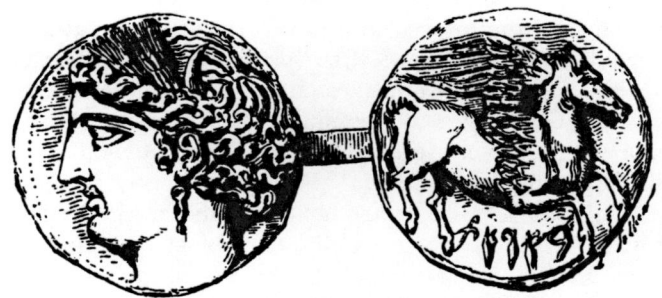

FIG. 5.—Phœnician Coin of Carthage inscribed "Barat."
(After Duruy *Hist. romaine.*)
Note the winged Sun-horse (Asva of the Catti Briton coins) and on obverse the head of *Barati* or "Britannia." See later.

Those treasured ancestral Aryan King Lists they embedded in their great epic the *Mahā Bārata* in summary; but in their " Older Epics " (the *Purāna*) they religiously preserved them in full detail. There they cover many hundreds of pages, recording in full detail the main line and numerous branch line dynasties from the commencement of the Aryan period down to historical times; and specifying the names and titles of the various kings, reproduced with scrupulous care, and citing in regard to the more famous of them their chief achievements, thus making the record something of a chronicle of the kings as well. These traditional Aryan kings are implicitly believed by all Brahmins and modern orthodox Hindus to be the genuine lineal ancestors of the present day ruling Indo-Aryan caste in

[1] G.L.H., 52.  [2] S.H. 16 and H.N.E. 199.  [3] Virgil *Æneid* 1. 382.

India. And often I observed, in my travels through the country, groups of villagers listening with wrapt attention and reverence as one of them read out the narrative of great achievements by some of these traditional early Aryan kings, who are confidently believed to be the genuine historical kings of the Early Aryans and the ancestors of the purer Aryan ruling princes in India to-day, some of whom trace their ancestry back to them.

But modern western Vedic scholars, without a single exception as far as I am aware, have summarily rejected all this great body of Epic literary historical tradition as mere fabulous fabrications of the Brahmin priests and bards—just as modern writers on British history have arbitrarily rejected the old traditional Ancient British Chronicles preserved by Geoffrey and Nennius. The excuses offered by Vedic scholars for thus rejecting these ancient epic traditional records are twofold. Firstly, they say that, as these voluminous King-Lists are not contained in the Vedas, and only a very few of the individual kings therein are mentioned in the Vedas, which books they assume to be the sole source of ancient Aryan tradition, these King-Lists must be fabulous. In making such an objection, they entirely overlook the patent fact that the Vedas are merely a collection of psalms, and not at all *historical* in their purpose, so that one would no more expect to find in them systematic lists of kings and dynasties than one would expect to find detailed lists of kings and prophets in the " Psalms of David." The second argument of Vedic scholars for rejecting these ancient Epic King-Lists is, as they truly say, that no traces whatever of any of these Early Aryan Kings can be found in India. But this fact is now disclosed by the new evidence to be owing to the very good reason that *none of these Early Aryan Kings had ever been in India,* but were kings of Asia Minor, Phœnicia and Mesopotamia centuries and millenniums before the separation of the Eastern branch to India.

Picking up these despised traditional Epic King-Lists of the Early Aryans, thus contemptuously rejected by Vedic scholars, I compared the names of their later main-line dynasties with the names of the later historical Hitt-ite kings of Asia Minor, as known from their own still extant monuments, as well as from the contemporary Babylonian and Assyrian records, and I found that *the father of the first historical Aryan king of India (as recorded in the Mahā-Bārata epic and Indian Buddhist history) was the last historical king of the Hitt-ites in Asia Minor*, who was killed at Carchemish on the Upper Euphrates on the final annexation of that last of the Hitt-ite capitals to Assyria by Sargon II. in 718 B.C. And I further found that the predecessors of this Hitt-ite king, as recorded in the cuneiform monuments of Asia Minor and in the Assyrian documents, back for several centuries, were substantially identical with those of the traditional ancestors of this first historical Aryan king of India as found in these Indian Epic King-Lists.[1]

Thus the absolute identity of the Indian branch of the Aryans with the Khatti or Hitt-ites was established by positive historical proof; and at the same time the Khatti or Hitt-ites were disclosed to be Aryans in race, and of the primary Aryan stock; and the truly historical character of the Indian Epic King-Lists was also conclusively established.

On further scrutinizing the earlier dynasties of these Epic King-Lists, I observed that several of the leading kings of the earlier Aryan dynasties in these lists bore substantially the same names, with the same records of achievements, and in the same relative chronological order as several of the leading kings of early Mesopotamia—the so-called " Sumerians " and " Akkads," as recorded in their own still extant monuments and in the fragmentary ancient chronicles of that land. Still further, I observed that isolated early kings of Mesopotamia, who are only known to Assyriologists from their stray inscribed monuments as solitary kings of unknown dynasty and unknown origin and race, were mostly recorded in my King-Lists in their due order and chronological succession in their respective dynasties with full lists of the Aryan Kings of these dynasties

[1] Full details, with proofs, in my forthcoming *Aryan Origins*.

who had preceded and succeeded them.[1] It thus became obvious that these Indian Epic King-Lists supplied the key to the material required for filling up the many great blanks in the early history of Ancient Mesopotamia in the dark and " prehistoric period " there.

Not only did these Epic King-Lists lighten up the dark period of Early Mesopotamian history, but they shed a similar illuminating light upon the dark period of Early Egyptian history and pre-history as well, and disclosed the wholly unsuspected fact that Menes and his " pre-dynastic " civilizers of Early Egypt were also of this race of Khatti or Hitt-ite " White Syrians " or Aryans.

The Phœnicians also were now disclosed to be Aryans in race and Khatti Arri or " Hitt-ite Aryans " by these new historical keys thus placed in my hand s. This, therefore, corroborated the fact found by anthropologists from the examination of Phœnician tombs that *the Phœnicians were a long-headed race, like the Aryans, and of a totally different racial type from the Jews,*[2] to whom they have hitherto been affiliated on merely linguistic arguments by Semitists. This eastern or Indian branch of the Aryans, the *Khattiyo Ariyo* Barats, call themselves in their epic, the Mahā Bārata, by the joint clan-title of *Kuru-Panch*(āla),—a title which turned out to be the original of " Syrio-Phœnician." These Kuru and *Panch*(-āla) are described as the two paramount kindred and confederated clans of the ruling Aryans; and they are repeatedly referred to under this confederate title in the Vedas. Now " *Kur*," I observed, was the ancient Sumerian and Babylonian name for " Syria " and Asia Minor of the Hitt-ites or " White Syrians " ; and it was thus obviously the original of the *Suria* of the Greeks, softened into " Syria " by the Romans.[3] Whilst " *Panch*(-āla) " is defined in the Indian Epics as meaning " The able or accomplished *Panch*," in compliment, it is there explained, to their great ability—

[1] See previous note.  [2] R.R.E., 387–389.
[3] " Suria " (or " Syria " ) was the name of Cappadocia in the time of Herodotus (i.72 and 76). And the Seleucid dynasty, which inherited Alexander's eastern empire called their Asia Minor Empire, extending from Ephesus on the Ægean to Antioch on the Levant, " *Suria* " on their coins. Compare B.H.S., ii, 115f; E. Babelon *Les Rois de Syrie*.

also an outstanding trait of the Phœnicians in the classics of Europe. This disclosed " *Panch* " to be the proper name of this ruling Aryan clan, whom I at once recognized as the " *Phœnic*-ians," the *Fenkha* or *Panag* or *Panasa* sea-going race of the eastern Mediterranean of the Ancient Egyptians,[1] the " *Phoinik*-es " of the Greeks, and the *Phœnic*-es of 'the Romans.

This " *Panch* " ruling Aryan clan was celebrated in the Vedas as the most ardent of all devotees of the Sun and Fire cult associated with worship of the Father-god Indra, as in the Vedic verses cited in the heading, and we shall see that the Hitto-Phœnicians were especial worshippers of the Father-god Bel (also called by them " *Indara* ") who was of the Sun-cult, and whose name is recorded in the early Briton monuments to be examined later on. The " Panch " Aryan clan was also significantly the foremost sea-going Aryan people of the ancient world in the Vedas, in which most, if not all, of the many Aryan kings, celebrated in the Vedic hymns as having been miraculously rescued from shipwreck by Indra or his angels, were kings of the *Panch* Aryan clan, and " a ship of a hundred oars " is mentioned in connection with them.[2] These Panch Aryans are also sometimes called " *Krivi* "[3] in the Vedas, which word is admitted by Sanskritists to be a variant of " *Kuru*,"[4] which we have seen means "of *Kur*" or " Syria." This confederate Vedic title for them and their kinsmen, the later Syrians, namely " *Kuru-Panch*(-āla)," is thus seen to be the equivalent of the later title for these two confederate Aryan ruling clans, the Syrians and Phœnicians, which is referred to in the New Testament as " *Suro-Phoiniki* " and Englished into " Syrio-Phœnician."[5]

Further, I found that the Early Phœnician dynasties in Syrio-Phœnicia or " The Land of the Amorites " of the Hebrews, as well as in Early Mesopotamia on the shores of the Persian Gulf (where Herodotus records that the Phœni-

---
[1] See later for the references to these names in Egyptian texts.
[2] R.V. i. 116. 5. Numerous Vedic and Epic references to these Aryan " *Panch* " (or Phœnicians) as the foremost seamen of the Ancient World will be found later on.
[3] R.V. viii, 20, 24 ; viii, 22, 12.   [4] M.K.I. i. 166f.   [5] Mark vii, 26.

cians were located before about 2800 B.C.),[1] also called themselves by the "*Khatti*" or "Hitt-ite" title and also by the early form of "Barat" in their own still extant monuments and documents, and dated back to about 3100 B.C.[2]

The Phœnician Khatti Barat ancestry of the Britons and Scots, and of the pre-Roman Briton "Catti" kings was then elicited and established by conclusive historical evidence in due course. The "Anglo-Saxons" also were disclosed, as we shall see, to be a later branchlet of the Phœnician-Britons, which separated after the latter had established themselves in Britain.

This identity of the Aryans with the Khatti or Hitt-ites was still further confirmed and more firmly established by further positive and cumulative evidence. In 1907, at the old Hittite capital, Boghaz Koi in Cappadocia, Winckler discovered the original treaty of about 1400 B.C. between the *Khatti* or Hittites and their kinsmen neighbours on the east, in Ancient Persia, the Mita-ni[3] (who, I had found, were the ancient Medes, who also were famous Aryans and called themselves "*Arriya*"). In this treaty *they invoked the actual Aryan gods of the Vedas of the Indian branch of the Aryans and by their Vedic names.* Significantly the first god invoked is the Vedic Sun-god Mitra (*i.e.* the "Mithra" of the Greco-Romans), as some of the later Aryans made separate gods out of different titles of the Father God. His name is followed by *In-da-ra*, that is the solar Indra or "Almighty," the principal deity of the Indo-Aryan Vedic scriptures, and as instanced in the verses cited in the heading, the especial god of the Barats or Brihats (or "Brits") and of their Panch or Phœnic-ian clan—and his image and title are represented on Ancient Briton monuments and coins. But even this striking historical evidence of itself did not induce either the Assyriologists or the Vedic scholars to seriously entertain the probability

[1] Herodotus i, 1 ; ii, 44 ; vii, 89.
[2] Some evidence of this is given in these pages; and the full details with proofs in my *Aryan Origin of the Phœnicia*,s.
[3] H. Winckler *Mittil. d. Deutsch. Orient-Gesellschaft* No. 35, Dec. 1907, pp. 30f; and review by H. G. Jacobi *Jour. Roy. Asiatic Soc.*, 1909, 721f.

# EARLY BRITONS WERE ARYAN PHŒNICIANS

that the Hittites were Aryans, obsessed with the preconceived notion that the Hittites, whatever their affinities might be, were certainly not Aryans.

The present work is the first instalment of the results disclosed by the use of my new-found keys to the Lost History of the Aryan Race and their authorship of the World's Higher Civilization. It offers the results in regard to the lost history of our own Aryan ancestors in Britain; and discloses them, the Early Britons and Scots and Anglo-Saxons, to have been a leading branch of the foremost world-pioneers of Civilization, the Aryan-Phœnicians.

FIG. 5A.—Briton prehistoric monument to Bel at Craig-Narget, Wigtownshire.
With Hitto-Phœnician Sun Crosses, etc.
(After Proc. Soc. Antiq. Scotland 10.59, by kind permission.)
Details explained in Chaps. XVIII. and XX.

## II

### THE UNDECIPHERED PHŒNICIAN INSCRIPTIONS OF ABOUT 400 B.C. IN BRITAIN AND SITE OF THE MONUMENT

> " That exhaustive British sense and perseverance, so whimsical in its choice of objects, which leaves its own Stonehenge or Choir Gaur to the rabbits, whilst it opens pyramids and uncovers Nineveh."—EMERSON on " Stonehenge."
>
> " We have no first-hand notice of Britannia until Julius Caesar landed there in 55 B.C."—Sir H. E. MAXWELL, 1912.[1]

THIS uniquely important and hitherto undeciphered inscribed ancient monument (see Frontispiece), bearing a " first-hand notice of Britannia " dating to about 400 B.C., and thus three and a half centuries earlier than Cæsar's journal, is now disclosed herein to have been erected by an Aryan-Phœnician Briton king ; and it offers us a convenient starting point for our fresh exploration for the lost history of our civilized ancestors—the Britons, Scots and Anglo-Saxons.

The monument now stands at Newton House in the upper valley of the Don in Aberdeenshire (see sketch-map, p.19), whence it derives its common modern name of " The Newton Stone." It has been known since 1803, by the opening up of a new road in its neighbourhood, as an antiquarian curiosity which has baffled all attempts of the leading experts at the decipherment and translation of its inscriptions.

It appears to be the first Phœnician document yet reported in Britain. Although tradition has credited the Phœnicians with long commercial and industrial intercourse with Cornwall in exploiting its tin and copper mines, and numerous

[1] *Early Chronicles relating to Scotland,* 1912, 1.

## PHŒNICIAN INSCRIPTIONS IN BRITAIN 17

traces of the extensive workings of these mines in " prehistoric " times are still abundantly visible near Penzance and elsewhere in The Duchy—many of which I have personally examined several times—no specific Phœnician inscription seems hitherto to have been reported either in Cornwall or elsewhere in the British Isles. Yet this unique ancient historical monument does not appear to be under the protection of the Ancient Monuments Act.

The following description of this rude stone pillar and its site and environments embodies the results of my personal examination of the monument itself and its neighbourhood, supplemented by local enquiry and the chief published references to the stone.

Its former, and presumably its original site where it stood before its removal to its present site about 1836, was recorded from personal knowledge by the famous archæologist Prof. J. Stuart as being at (see sketch-map) :—

" a spot surrounded by a wood, close to the present toll-gate of Shevack, *about a mile south of the House of Newton.* From its proximity to the Inn and Farm of Pitmachie it has occasionally been called the Pitmachie Stone. When the ground on which it stood was in course of being trenched several graves were discovered on a sandy ridge near the stone . . . graves made in hard gravel without any appearance of flags at sides or elsewhere."[1] This information was supplemented by the late Lord Aberdeen, who wrote that the Stone originally stood on an open moor . . . 'a few paces distant from the high road near Pitmachie turnpike of the Great Northern Road recently opened, the old road having been on the opposite side of the Gady."[2]

The spot, thus indicated (see sketch-map) by these authentic contemporary records, stands in the heart of a romantic meadow encircled by picturesque hills and dominated by the beetling crags of Mt. Bennachie, crowned with the ruins of a prehistoric fort, rising on the west. It is within the angle of the old moorland meadow (now part of the richly cultivated Garioch vale of old Pict-land) between the Shevack stream and the Gadie rivulet, which latter formerly,

---

[1] SSS i, 1–2.  [2] *Ib.* i, 2.

before the accumulation of silt, may have joined hereabouts with the Shevack and Urie tributaries of the Don.

This "Gadie" name for this vigorous rivulet, half encircling the Bennachie range, and in the direct line of the lower Don Valley, is highly suggestive of Phœnician influence, as we shall find that the Phœnicians usually spelt their tribal name of " Khatti " or " Catti " as " *Gad,*" and were in the habit not infrequently of calling the rivers at their settlements " *Gadi,*" or " *Gad-es,*" or " *Kad-esh.*"

This romantic Gadie glen of the Don, sequestered among the green groves and overhung by the purple slopes of the bold Bennachie, was presumably of ancient repute, as it is celebrated in a well-known old Scottish song with a haunting plaintive melody of ancient anonymous origin and the refrain :—

> " O gin I were where Gadie rins,
> At the back o' Ben-nach-ie."

In its stanzas, given by Dr. John Park over a century ago, it appears almost as if the Gadie contained a sacred ancient site of burial :—

> " O gin I were where Gadie rins
> Mang fragrant heaths and yellow whins,
> Or brawling down the bosky linns,
> At the back o' Ben-nach-ie.
>
> O aince, aince mair, where Gadie rins,
> Where Gadie rins, where Gadie rins,
> O micht I dee where Gadie rins
> At the back o' Ben-nach-ie."

And this vale, we shall find, was probably the actual site of the traditional sacred cemetery of the prehistoric royal erector of this monument that is celebrated in the early chronicles of the Irish Scots.[1]

The prehistoric antiquity of this district of the Don Valley as a centre of Stone Age habitation and of Early Civilization for the north of Britain is evidenced by its richness in

[1] BOI., 81f.

## PHŒNICIAN INSCRIPTIONS AT NEWTON 19

Stone Age implements and in "prehistoric" sculptured stones in the neighbourhood, with several Stone Circles[1]—the so-called "Druid" Circles, but which, as we shall see, were solar observatories of the Phœnicians and Early Goths, and essentially non-Druidical and anti-Druidical. So rich indeed is this Don Valley district in "prehistoric" sculptured monuments, most of which, I find, bear Phœnician

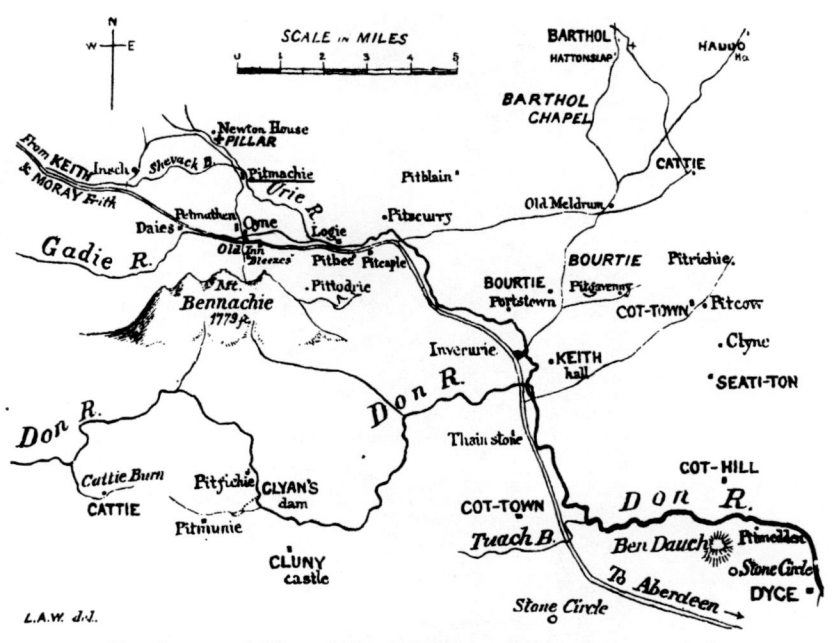

Sketch-map of Site of Newton Stone and its Neighbourhood.

and Sumerian symbols of the Sun-cult, that out of 150 of the ancient sculptured stones in the whole of Scotland, mostly "prehistoric" described and figured by Stuart in his classic survey, no less than 36 are located in the Don Valley, in which the Newton Stone stands. (For one of them see Fig. 5B.)

[1] S.S.S. i, 1. These local circles had already been removed by villagers within living memory at the time when Stuart wrote (*ibid.*). On the adjoining circle at Insch, see N. Lockyer in TBB., 85.

20 PHŒNICIAN ORIGIN OF BRITONS & SCOTS

The stone is an elongated, somewhat irregular, unworked, natural slab of boulder formation, of closely-grained quartzose gneiss, like other boulders lying on the surface in its neighbourhood. It stands about six and a half feet above the ground, and is about two feet broad. It bears inscriptions in two different kinds of script. These inscriptions now claim our notice.

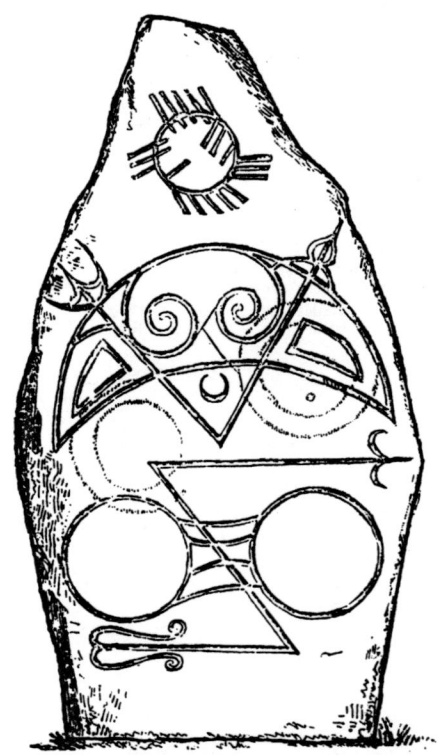

FIG. 5B.—Prehistoric Briton monument to Bel at Logie in Don Valley near Newton Stone.
With Hitto-Phœnician inscription and Solar symbols.
(After Stuart I. 3.)
(Deciphered and symbols explained in Chap. XXII.)

# III

## THE INSCRIPTIONS ON THE NEWTON STONE AND PREVIOUS FUTILE ATTEMPTS AT DECIPHERMENT

> "It is *provoking* to have an inscription in our own country of unquestionable genuineness and antiquity, which seems to have baffled all attempts to decipher it; and that, too, in an age when Egyptian hieroglyphs and the cuneative characters of Persepolis and Babylon and Nineveh have been forced to reveal their secrets to laborious scholars."—A. THOMSON.[1]

THE inscriptions on the Newton Stone pillar, of which the one in " unknown " script referred to in the heading has still remained hitherto undeciphered, are two in number, and in different scripts. That in the " unknown " script, also often and rightly so called the " main " inscription, is engraved on the upper half of the flattish face of the boulder pillar (see Frontispiece *a* and Fig. 6). It is boldly and deeply incised in six lines of forty-eight characters, with the old Swastika Sun-Cross exactly in the centre—twenty-four of the letters, including dots, being on either side of it. The other inscription is incised along the left-hand border of the pillar and overruns part of the flat face below (see Frontispiece *c*, also Fig. 7); and is in the old " Ogam " linear characters, the cumbrous sacred script of the Irish Scots and early Britons.

On the publication of a reproduction of these inscriptions about a century ago, some time after the monument first

[1] P.S.A.S. v. 224.

attracted modern notice,[1] innumerable attempts were made to decipher and translate them, with the most conflicting and fantastically varied results.

As the traditional key to the Ogam script has been preserved in the Book of Ballymote and in several bi-lingual Ogam-Roman inscriptions, and as it was surmised that the Ogam was presumably contemporary with and was a bi-lingual version of the "unknown" script, it was hoped that the Ogam version might afford a clue to the reading of that main script. But this expectation was admittedly not realized by the more authoritative experts.

Even respecting the Ogam inscription no two of the essaying translators were agreed in their readings. The disagreement between the various attempted interpretations of the Ogam version was owing to the unusual absence of divisions or spaces between most of its series of strokes, owing to their overcrowding through want of space; for different numerical groupings of these Ogam letter-strokes yield totally different letters. Indeed the prime authority on Ogam script, Mr. Brash, in publishing his final careful study of that version,[2] deliberately refrains from giving any translation of it, saying " I have no translation to give of it "[3]; because the letters, as tentatively read by him without any clues to the names therein, made up no words or sentences which seemed to him intelligible or to yield any sense.

The attempts at deciphering and translating the main or central inscription in the unknown script were even much more widely diverse. Some writers surmised that this unknown script was Celtic and the language Gaelic or Pictish, or Erse or Irish; others thought it was Hebrew or Greek or Latin, others Anglo-Saxon or Coptic or Palmyrene, and one suggested that it was " possibly Phœnician," that is the Semitic Phœnician, and attempted to read it back-

---

[1] An early engraving of the Stone and its inscriptions appeared in Pinkerton's *Inquiry into the History of Scotland*, 1814; and another by Prof. Stuart in 1821 in *Archaeologia Scotica* (ii, 134); and a more careful lithographic copy in Plate I of SSS. above cited.
[2] B.O.I., 359-362.    [3] *Ibid.* 362.

# ATTEMPTED DECIPHERMENT OF NEWTON STONE

wards. But all of them totally disagreed in their readings and translations, which most of them candidly admitted were mere "guesses," till at last its decipherment was thrown up in despair by the less rash antiquaries and palæographers.

The chief later attempts at deciphering this central inscription, since those made by Lord Southesk in 1882–5,[1] Sir W. Ramsay in 1892,[2] Whitley Stokes,[3] and Professor J. Rhys[4] in the same year, have been by Dr. Bannerman in 1907[5] and Mr. Diack in 1922.[6] These attempts, like most of the earlier ones, were on the assumption that the script and language were "Pictish" or "Celtic," although Dr. Stuart, a chief specialist in "Pictish" or "Celtic" script who edited one of the oldest real Picto-Celtic manuscripts,[7] confessed his inability to recognize the script as such, and expressly refrained from proposing the decipherment of a single letter. Professor Rhys, also an authority on Celtic script, similarly confessed his inability to decipher this inscription as he "cannot claim to have had any success," though he nevertheless ventured to hazard "a translation of part of both it and the Ogam script"—which latter he calls "non-Aryan Pictish"—with the apology that it was "purely a guess" and a mere "picking from previous attempts by others and by myself."[8] Yet this final attempt does not carry him beyond three words in the former and five in the latter.

The totally different results of these latest conjectural readings and "translations" will be evident when the readings are here placed alongside, and makes it difficult

---

[1] P.S.A.S., 1882, 21f; 1884, 191f; 1865, 30f.
[2] Academy, Sept. 1892 240–1.
[3] Ibid. June 4, and July 12, 1892.    [4] P.S.A.S., 1891–2, 280f.
[5] Ibid. 1907–8, 56f.
[6] *Newton Stone and other Pictish Inscriptions*, 1922. He surmises that the main inscription is in "Old Gaelic" language in "Roman" script, and construes it after the opening sentence still altogether different from previous attempts, and makes it the epitaph of two persons Ette and Elisios; and that the Ogam is not bi-lingual but added later as epitaph of a third person.
[7] Adamnan *Book of Deer* with life of St. Columba, edited and translated by J. Stuart.
[8] P.S.A.S., 1892–3, loc. cit., and 1898, 361f.

## 24 PHŒNICIAN ORIGIN OF BRITONS & SCOTS

to believe that the writers are dealing with the self-same inscriptions :—

| LATEST READINGS.[1] | LATEST TRANSLATIONS. |
|---|---|
| Lord Southesk : | |
| *Ogam* Aiddai qnn forrerr iph ua iossii. | " Eté Forar's daughter of the race of the sons of Uos |
| *Main* Aittai/furur/ingin sucl o uose urchn elisi/ maqqi logon-patr | " Eté Forar's daughter of the race of the sons of Uos, disciple of Eliseus, son of the priest of Hu (or Logh Fire-priest)." |
| Sir W. Ramsay : | |
| *Main* Edde/ecnunvaur | ......................................... |
| Whitley Stokes : | |
| *Ogam* eddar Acnn vor renni Pui h Iosir | ..................................... |
| *Main* edde/Ecnunuar hu-olocoso/cassaflisi maggi/lopouita | |
| Sir J. Rhys : | |
| *Ogam* Idda $\frac{\text{r hc}}{\text{i q}}$ nnn vorrem ip $\frac{u}{o}$ a $\frac{io}{i}$ iosir | " Lies here Vorr's offspring Iosif " |
| *Main* Aettae/Aecnun var svoho coto/caaelisi Unççi/hopovauta | " Lies here Vorr's " ......... ..................................... |
| Dr. Bannerman : | |
| *Main* : Ette/cun-anmain Maolouoeg un rofiis : I h-inssi/Loaoaruin | " Draw near to the soul of Moluag from whom came knowledge. He was of the island of Lorn." |
| Mr. Diack :[2] | |
| *Ogam* Iddaiqnnn vor-renni ci Osist. | " Iddaiqnnn son of Vorenni here Osist." |
| *Main* Ette Evagainnias Cigonovocoi Uraelisi Maqqi Noviogruta | " Ette son of Evagainnias descendant of Ci(n)go here. The grave of Elisios son of New Grus." |

[1] The locations of these readings are already cited.
[2] *Op. cit.*, pp. 9, 12, 14, and 16.

# NEWTON STONE REMAINED UNDECIPHERED 25

As a consequence of such irreconcilable attempts at deciphering and translating these inscriptions, and as at the same time their supposed contents were conjectured to be of little or no historical importance or significance, this ancient inscribed monument of such unique importance for Early British History has fallen practically into oblivion.[1]

---

[1] Thus it is not mentioned in the text of " The County Histories of Scotland " for Aberdeenshire, nor in " Early Britain " in The Story of the Nations series, nor in " Celtic Britain " by Rhys, nor in the modern county and district manuals for Aberdeenshire, except in Ward's popular "Aberdeen" book where the fact of its existence is noted in four lines with the remark that the inscription is " in Greek—varied and conflicting are the attempted readings."

## IV

### DECIPHERMENT AND TRANSLATION OF THE PHŒNICIAN INSCRIPTIONS ON THE NEWTON STONE

*Disclosing Monument to be a votive Fire-Cross to the Sun-god Bel by a Phœnician Hittite Brit-on and the script and language Aryan Phœnician or Early Briton.*

WHEN I first saw this "unknown" script of the central inscription on the Newton Stone many years ago, in the plates of Dr. Stuart's classic "Sculptured Stones of Scotland," I formed the opinion that that learned archæologist was right in his surmise that the writing was possibly in "an eastern alphabet." I further recognized that it was presumably a form of the early Phœnician script, cognate with what I had been accustomed to in the Aryan Pali script of India of the third and fourth century B.C.; and I thought it might be what I had come to call "*Aryan* Phœnician," which it now proves to be.

At that time, however, I did not feel sufficiently equipped to tackle the decipherment of this inscription in detail. But having latterly devoted my entire time for many years past to the comparative study at first hand of the ancient scripts and historical documents of the Hitt-ites, Sumerians, Akkads, Ægeans and Phœnicians, and the Aramaic, Gothic Runes and Ogams, I took up again the Newton Stone inscriptions for detailed examination some time ago. And I found that the "unknown" script therein was clearly what I term "Aryan Phœnician," that is true Phœnician, and its language Aryan Phœnician of the Early Briton or Early Gothic type.

By this time, I had observed that the early inscriptions of the Phœnicians were written in Aryan language, Aryan script, and in the Aryan direction, that is towards the right hand. The so-called "*Semitic* Phœnician" writing, on the other hand, with reversed letters, and in the reversed or left-hand direction, and dating mostly to a relatively late period, was, I observed, written presumably by the ruling Aryan Phœnicians for the information of their Semitic subjects at their various settlements : and by some of these Phœnicianized Semitic subjects or allies helping themselves to and reversing the Phœnician letters. It was obviously parallel to what we find in India in the third century B.C., where the great Aryan emperor of India, Asoka, writes his Buddhist edicts in reversed letters and in reversed or " Semitic " direction, when carving them on the rocks on his northwestern frontier in districts inhabited by Semitic tribes ; yet no one on this account has suggested or could suggest that Asoka was a Semite.

By this time also, I had recognized that the various ancient scripts found at or near the old settlements of the Phœnicians, and arbitrarily differentiated by classifying philologists variously as Cyprian, Karian, Aramaic or Syrian, Lykian, Lydian, Korinthian, Ionian, Cretan or " Minoan," Pelasgian, Phrygian, Cappadocian, Cilician, Theban, Libyan, Celto-Iberian, Gothic Runes, etc., were all really local variations of the standard Aryan Hitto-Sumerian writing of the Aryan Phœnician mariners, those ancient pioneer spreaders of the Hitt-ite Civilization along the shores of the Mediterranean and out beyond the Pillars of Hercules to the British Isles.

In tackling afresh the decipherment of the Newton Stone inscriptions, in view of the hopelessly conflicting tangle that had resulted from the mutually conflicting attempts of previous writers, which proved a hindrance rather than a help to decipherment, I wiped all the previous attempts off the board and started anew with a clean slate and open mind.

The material and other sources for my scrutiny of these Newton Stone inscriptions have been a minute personal examination of these inscriptions on the spot, the comparative study of a large series of photographs of the stone by myself and others, including the published photographs and eye-copies by previous writers, and the careful lithographs by Stuart from squeeze-impressions and photographs.

In constructing the accompanying eye-copy of the uniquely important central inscription, here given (Fig. 6), I scrupulously compared all available photographs from different points of view, for no one photograph can cover and focus all the details of these letters owing to the great unevenness and sinuosities of the inscribed surface of this rough boulder-stone. It will be seen that my eye-copy of this script differs in some minute but important details from those of Stuart and Lord Southesk, the most accurate of the copies previously published.

In my decipherment of this central script I derived especial assistance from the Cilician, Cyprian and "Iberian" scripts and the Indian Pali of the third and fourth centuries B.C. and Gothic runes, which were closely allied in several respects; and Canon Taylor's and Prof. Petrie's classic works on the alphabet also proved helpful.

So obviously *Aryan Phœnician* was the type of the letters in this central script, when I now took it up for detailed examination, that, in dealing with the two scripts, I took up the central one in this "unknown" script first, that is in the reverse order to that adopted in all previous attempts. I found that it was Aryan Phœnician script of the kind ordinarily *written with a pen and ink* on skin and parchment, such, as we are told by Herodotus, was the chief medium of writing used by the early inhabitants of Asia Minor; and the perishable nature of such documents accounts for the loss of so much of the original literature of the Early Aryans both in Asia Minor and in Britain.

On deciphering in a few minutes most of the letters in this Phœnician script with more or less certainty, I then proceeded to decipher the Ogam version in the light of the Phœnician. I thereupon found that *the strings of personal ethnic and place-names were substantially identical in both inscriptions, thus disclosing them to be really bi-lingual versions of the same.*

This fortunate fact, that the inscriptions on the Newton

# PHŒNICIAN INSCRIPTION DECIPHERED

Stone are found to be bi-lingual versions of the same historical record, is of great practical importance for establishing the certainty of the decipherment; for a bi-lingual version always affords the surest clue to an "unknown" script. It was a bi-lingual (or rather a tri-lingual) inscription which provided the key to the Egytian hieroglyphs in the famous Rosetta Stone. And the fact that the Ogam version of the Newton Stone inscriptions—the alphabetic value of the Ogam script being well known—agrees for the most part

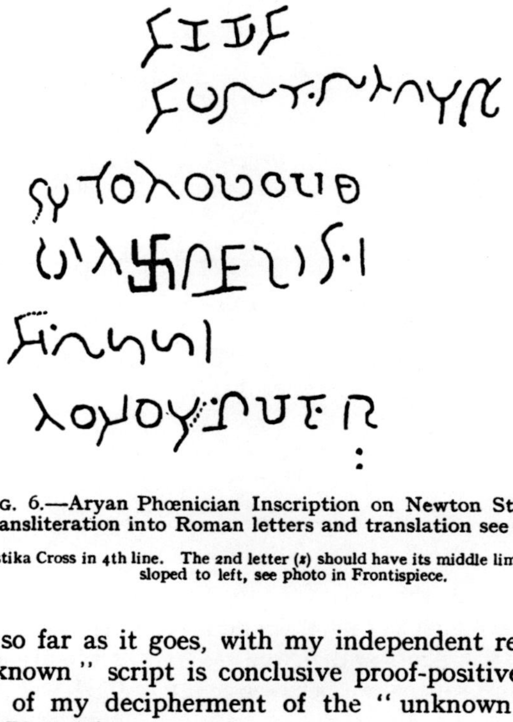

FIG. 6.—Aryan Phœnician Inscription on Newton Stone.
(For transliteration into Roman letters and translation see p. 32.)

Note Swastika Cross in 4th line. The 2nd letter (z) should have its middle limb slightly sloped to left, see photo in Frontispiece.

literally, so far as it goes, with my independent reading of the "unknown" script is conclusive proof-positive for the certainty of my decipherment of the "unknown" script as Aryan Phœnician.

Here I give my transcription of the main or Aryan Phœnician inscription (see Fig. 6.).

It will be seen by comparing this script with its modern letter-values given in my transliteration into Roman (on

p. 32) that most of the corresponding Greek and Roman alphabetic letters, and their modern cursive writing, are obviously derived from this semi-cursive Phœnician writing or from its parent.

My reading of the Ogam version, in Fig. 7, also will be seen to differ from that of Mr. Brash,[1] the most careful attempt of all previous ones, chiefly in regard to those letters, the signs for which, formed by a conventional number of straight strokes, were, on account of the limited space available on the stone, crowded together and not clearly separated from the other groups of conventional numbers

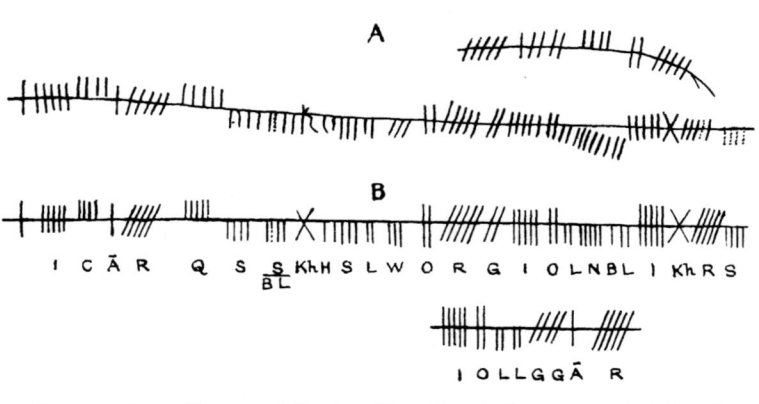

FIG. 7.—Ogam Version of Newton Stone Inscription as now deciphered and read.

*A.* As engraved on the stone.    *B.* Arrangement of the letter-strokes as now read with their values in Roman letters. The 9th letter is read as A.

of similar strokes, the separate grouping of which formed a different letter or letters in this cumbrous sacred alphabetic script of the Irish Scots and Britons.[2] It was the absence of any clue to this separation between many of the letter group-strokes, which led Mr. Brash to confess, after completing

---

[1] Mr. Brash's final reading of this Ogam inscription was (*op. cit.* 362) :—
    AIDDARCUNFEANFORRENNNEAI(*or*R)(S)IOSSAR

[2] On the origin and solar meaning of this cumbrous " branched " form of alphabet, see later.

# OGAM INSCRIPTION DECIPHERED

his tentative transcription of the text into Roman characters, that the result was so unsatisfactory that he could make no sense of it, and so abstained from attempting any translation whatsoever. With the clue, however, now put into my hands by the Phœnician version, the doubtful letters in this Ogam version were soon resolved into substantially literal agreement with the Phœnician version.

The full reading of this Ogam inscription requires the introduction of the vowels; for the Ogam script, like the Aryan Phœnician, Semitic Phœnician and Hebrew, and the Aryan Pali and Sanskrit alphabets, does not express the short vowel *a* which is inherent as an affix in every consonant of the old Aryan alphabetic scripts.[1]

I now place here side by side my transcript-readings and translations of the two versions of the inscription for comparison. And it will be seen that both read substantially the same. The slight differences in spelling of some of the names are due mainly to the poverty of the Ogam alphabet, which lacks some of the letters of the Phœnician (*e.g.* it has no *K* or *Z*, but uses *Q* or *S* instead); while the omission in the Ogam version of three of the titles which occur in the Phœnician was obviously owing to want of space; for the bulky Ogam script, even when thus curtailed, overruns the face of the monument for a considerable distance. The Phœnician script, it will be seen, like the Aryan Pali and Sanskrit, does not express the short affixed *a* inherent in the consonants, and, like them also, it writes the short *i* and the medial *r* by attached strokes or " ligatures." In my transliteration here, therefore, I have given the short inherent *a* in small type, and the consonants and expressed vowels in capitals, whilst the ligatured consonants (here only *r*) and ligatured vowels (namely *i* and *o*) are also printed in small type, not capitals.

---

[1] It will also be noted that the end portion of the Ogam inscription, which is bent round over the face of the stone, is read from its right border (*i.e.* in the reverse direction to the rest) with its lower strokes towards the right border of the stone, so that when the curved stem line is straightened out the lower strokes occupy the same lower position as in the rest of the inscription.

THE BI-LINGUAL INSCRIPTIONS ON THE NEWTON STONE, COMPARED IN TEXT AND TRANSLATION.

| Aryan Phœnician. | Ogam. |
|---|---|
| line<br>1  KaZZi                               Ka<br>(*This Cross*) *The Kazzi of* | + ICĀR QaS$_{\overline{B(i)L}}^{S^1}$   KhĀ<br>*This Cross Icar    Qass of* |
| 2  KĀST·        S(i)LUYRi<br>*Kast          of the Siluyr* | S(i)LWOR<br>*the Silur* |
| 3  GYĀOLOWONIĒ[2]<br>*the Khilani* (*or* Hitt-ite palace dweller) | GIOLN<br>*the Khilani* (*or* Hitt-ite palace-dweller) |
| 4  BĪL  ⌐⌐  PoENĪG.   Ī-<br>*to Bil* (*this*) *Cross the Phœnician Ī-* | B(i)L                            I-<br>*to Bil*                             I- |
| 5  -Kar                    SSSĪ-<br>-*khar*               *the Ci-* | $\frac{-Kha}{-Xa}$R          SIO-<br>-*khar*         *of*         *Ci-* |
| 6  -LOKOYr PrWT[3]   R :<br>-*lician, The* " *Brit,*" *raised.* | -LLaGGĀ         R<br>-*licia*         *raised.* |

Thus this bi-lingual inscription records that: " This Sun-Cross (Swastika) was raised to *Bil* (or Bel, the God of Sun-Fire) by the *Kassi* (or Cassi-bel[-an]) of *Kast* of the *Siluyr* (sub-clan) of the " *Khilani* " (or Hittite-palace-dwellers), the *Phœnician* (named) *Ikar* of *Cilicia*, the *Prwt* (or Prāt, that is ' Barat ' or ' Brihat ' or *Brit*-on)."

[1] The second *s* in " Qass " is somewhat doubtful, as the 4th stroke in the series of 4 strokes under the stem-line which conventionally form the letter *s* in Ogam script is doubtfully represented. If only 3 strokes are present they spell " B(i)l," which would give " Qas-b(i)l " or " Qas-b(e)l " ; but " Qass " is probably the proper reading, and in series with the *Kazzi* of the Aryan Phœnician.

[2] The third letter here is read Ā, which latter sometimes has a form resembling this, though different from the letter read Ā in second line, which is similar to the Ā in the later Phœnician inscriptions.

[3] The second detached letter read *W* from its head strokes may possibly be Ā, and thus give the form " Prāt " instead of " Prwt."

## V

### DATE OF NEWTON STONE INSCRIPTIONS ABOUT 400 B.C.

*Disclosing special features of Aryan Phœnician Script, also Ogam as sacred Sun-cult Script of the Hittites, Early Britons and Scots.*

THE date of these two inscriptions on the Newton Stone is fixed with relative certainty at about 400 B.C. by palæographic evidence, from the archaic form of some of the letters in the Phœnician script.

The hitherto " unknown " alphabetic script, in the face of the monument, I have called Aryan Phœnician, as it is written in the Aryan direction, like the English and Gothic and European languages generally, from the left towards the right, and not in the reversed or Semitic direction. This distinguishes it sharply from the later Semitic retrograde form of writing the later form of Phœnician letters which has hitherto been universally and exclusively termed " Phœnician." For I had found, as already mentioned, that the Phœnicians were really Sumerians, Hittites and Aryans; and that the Sumerian script, always written in Aryan fashion towards the right, was the parent of all the alphabets of the civilized world.

The cursive shape of the letters in this Aryan Phœnician script suggests that the Phœnician dedicator of this inscription had written it himself on the stone with pen and ink in his ordinary business style of writing for the mason to engrave —as the practical necessity for the Phœnician merchant-princes " to keep their accounts in order " must early have resulted in a somewhat more cursive style of writing than the " lithic " or lapidary style engraved on their monuments and artistic objects, a difference corresponding to that between modern business writing and print.

[The forms of the letters, whilst approximating in several respects the semi-Phœnician "Cadmean" or Early Greek, present several cursive archaisms not found in the later straight-lined lithic Semitic Phœnician; but this is not the place to enter into the technical details of these differences, which will be apparent to experts from the photographs and transcription. Here, however, must be mentioned an outstanding feature of this Aryan Phœnician script in its use of short vowels, and the frequent attachment of the vowels *i*, *e* and *o*, and the semivowel *r*, to the stems of the consonants—the so-called ligature. This feature is found in the ancient Syrian and Palmyrene forms of Phœnician. In the interpretation of these ligatured vowels I derived much assistance from comparing them with those of the affiliated Indian Pali script of the third and fourth centuries B.C. The value of *o* for the horizontal bottom stroke was thus found along with that of the other ligatured letters.]

On palæographic grounds, therefore, the date of this Aryan Phœnician inscription can be placed no later than about 400 B.C. This estimate is thus in agreement with what we shall find later, that the author of the inscription, Prat-Gioln, was the sea-king "Part-olon, king of the Scots" of the Early British Chronicle, who, in voyaging off the Orkney Islands about 400 B.C., met his kinsman Gurgiunt, the then king of Britain, whose uncle Brennius was, as we shall see, the traditional Briton original of the historical Brennius I. who led the Gauls in the sack of Rome in 390 B.C. The archaisms in script of that date were doubtless owing to the author having come from the central part of the old Hitto-Sumerian cradle-land; as it is found that the cuneiform and alphabetic script of Cappadocia and Cilicia preserve many of the older primitive shapes of the word-signs and letters, which persisted there long after they had become modernized into simpler forms elsewhere.

The fact that few examples of exactly similar cursive Aryan Phœnician writing have yet been recorded is to be adequately explained by the circumstance that, as Herodotus tells us, the usual medium for writing in Ancient Asia Minor was by pen and ink on parchments; and such perishable documents have naturally disappeared in the course of the subsequent ages. Moreover, there was wholesale exterminating destruction of the pre-Christian monuments and documents by the early Christian Church, as we shall see later.

The Language of this Aryan Phœnician inscription is essentially Aryan in its roots, structure and syntax, with Sumerian and Gothic affinities.[1]

The Ogam version is clearly contemporary with, and by the same author as, the central Phœnician inscription, as it is now disclosed to be a contracted version of the latter. This discovery thus puts back the date of Ogam script far beyond the period hitherto supposed by modern writers.

Ogam, or " Tree-twig " script, which is found on ancient monuments throughout the British Isles, though most frequently in Ireland, has hitherto been conjectured by Celto-Irish philologists to date no earlier than about the fourth or fifth century A.D., and to have been coined by Gaelic scribes in Ireland or Britain,[2] and to be non-Aryan.[3] This late date is assumed merely because some of the Ogam inscriptions occur on Early Christian tombstones, which sometimes contain bi-lingual versions in Roman letters in Latin or Celtic, which presumably date to about that period. But I observed that several of the letter-forms of this cumbrous Ogam script are more or less substantially identical with several of the primitive linear Sumerian letter-signs, which

---

[1] The *Ka* affix to " Kazzi " seems to be the Sumerian genitive suffix *Ka* " of," and the Sumerian source of the modern *Ka* " of " in the Indo-Persian and Hindi, and thus defines him as being " of the Kassi clan." This Sumerian *Ka* is also softened into *ge* (L.S.G. 131 etc.) which may possibly represent the *S* in Gothic. The final *r* in *Sssilokoyr* or " Cilician " seems to be the Gothic inflexive, indicating the nominative case. *R*, the concluding letter, is clearly cognate or identical with the final *R* in Gothic Runic votive and dedicatory inscriptions, and is sometimes written in full as *Risthi* " raised," or *Risti* " carved " (cp. P.S.A.S., 1879, 152 and V.D. 500). It is now seen, *along with our English word* " *Raise* " *to be derived from the Sumerian* RA " to set up, stand, stick up."

[2] Rhys surmised that Ogam script was " invented during the Roman occupation of Britain by a Goidelic grammarian who had seen the Brythons of the Roman province making use of Latin letters " (*Chambers' Encycl.* 7, 583). This, too, is the opinion of a later writer, J. MacNeill (*Notes on Irish Ogham*, 1909, 335) ; whilst the latest writer, G. Calder, cites a text saying that Ogam was invented in " Hibernia of the Scots " (C.A.N., p. 273).

[3] Rhys, in P.S.A.S., 1891–2, 282.

# 36  PHŒNICIAN ORIGIN OF BRITONS & SCOTS

possess more or less the same phonetic values as in the Ogam.' Such Ogamoid groups of strokes also occur, I observed, in ancient Hittite hieroglyph inscriptions devoted to the Sun-cult and containing Sun-crosses, as in the group here figured (Fig. 8).[2]

Now, however, as this Ogam script is here found in the earliest of all its recorded occurrences at about 400 B.C., at Newton and in the adjoining and presumably more or less contemporary pillar at Logie (see later), inscribed upon Sun-cult votive monuments in association with the Sun-Cross, just as quasi-Ogam letters are also found in Hitt-ite hieroglyph votive monuments of the Sun-cult, and also *accompanied by Sun-Crosses*, it seems to me, in view of these facts, that this bulky stroke-script, which possesses only

FIG. 8.—Ogamoid Inscription from Hittite Hieroglyphs on the Lion of Marash.
(Alter Wright.)

sixteen consonants, and thus presumably not intended for

---

[1] Amongst the similarities between the Ogam and Sumerian letter-signs which I have observed are the following :—

*I* in Sumerian is written by 5 perpendicular strokes, just as in Ogam script 5 perpendicular strokes form the letter *I*.

*E* in Early Sumerian is written by 4 parallel strokes on a double base-line, which compares with the Ogam 4 parallel strokes across the ridge-line for *E*; and the Sumerian sign for the god EA is absolutely identical with the Ogam E with its strokes extending on both sides of the ridge-line.

$\widehat{AO}$ diphthong of Ogam has precisely the same form of inter-crossing strokes as one of the three Sumerian signs all rendered tentatively as *U*, but one of which was suspected to be *O* or diphthong *Û* (compare Langdon, *Sumerian Grammar*, 35–37). It thus may, in view of the identical Ogam sign, have the value of *O*.

*B* in Ogam, written by a single perpendicular stroke, compares with the bolt sign in Sumerian for *Ba* or *Bi*.

*S* in Ogam, formed by 4 perpendicular strokes on the ridge-line, compares with the Sumerian *S* formed by 4 perpendicular strokes on a basal line, with stem below.

*X* or *Kh* in Sumerian generally resembles the letter X in Ogam, which is disclosed by the Phœnician version to have the sound of *Kh* or *X*.

[2] W.E.H., pl. 27, in lowest line between the paws of the Lion of Marash. This inscription significantly contains in its text a Sun-Cross.

ordinary secular writing, was a sacred script composed by later Aryan Sun-priests for solar worship and coined upon a few old Sumerian signs of the twig pattern. And we shall see later that the Sumerians and Hitto-Phœnicians symbolized their Sun-cult by the Crossed sticks or twigs by which, with friction, they produced their sacred Fire-offerings to the Sun, just as the ancient and medieval Britons produced their Sacred or "Need" Fire offering.

Moreover, this solar cult origin for the Ogam script seems further confirmed by its title of "Ogam." It was so named, according to the Irish-Scot tradition, after its inventor "Ogma," who is significantly called "The Sun-worshipper,"[1] and is identified with Hercules of the Phœnicians.[2] Such a pre-Christian and solar cult origin for the Ogam also now explains its use on the Newton Stone, as well as the Irish-Scot tradition that Ogam writing, which was freely current in Ireland in the pre-Christian period, especially for sacred monuments and tombstones, as attested by numerous surviving ancient monuments, was denounced by St. Patrick as "pagan" and soon became extinct.

We are now in a position to examine the rich crop of important historical, personal, ethnic and geographical names and titles preserved in this Brito-Phœnician inscription of about 400 B.C.

[1] BOI. 24.  [2] BOI. 25.

## VI

### PERSONAL, ETHNIC AND GEOGRAPHIC PHŒNICIAN NAMES AND TITLES IN NEWTON STONE INSCRIPTIONS AND THEIR HISTORIC SIGNIFICANCE

*Disclosing also Phœnician source of the "Cassi" title of Ancient Briton kings and their coins.*

> " One of the few, the Immortal Names
> That are not born to die."—F. HALLECK.

THE rich crop of personal, ethnic and geographical names recorded in these Newton Stone inscriptions of about 400 B.C. by their " Sun-worshipping " Phœnician-Briton author—whose personal appearance is illustrated in Fig. 10, p. 46—are of especial Phœnician significance. These names disclose, amongst other things, not only the Phœnician origin of the British Race, properly so-called, and their Civilization, but also the Phœnician origin of the names Brit-on, Brit-ain, Brit-ish, and of the tutelary name "Brit-annia." The patronymic origin of that title is seen in the Aryan tradition preserved by the eastern branch of the Barats in their epic cited in the heading on p. 52 as well as the old custom of the Aryan clans referred to in the Vedas[1] to call themselves after their father's name. And King Barat, after whom this ruling clan called themselves, was the most famous forefather of the founder of the First Phœnician Dynasty, which event, I find by the new evidence, occurred about 3100 B.C., according to the still extant contemporary inscriptions.[2]

Whilst calling himself a " Phœnician " and giving his personal name, the author of this Newton Stone inscription

---

[1] See heading on pp. 1 and 52.
[2] Details in *Aryan Origin of the Phœnicians*.

## TITLE OF PHŒNICIAN IN INSCRIPTION

also calls himself by the title of Briton and Scot, and "Hittite," "Silurian" and "Cilician," by early forms of these names, and records as the place of his nativity a famous well-known old capital and centre of Sun-worship in Cilicia. We shall now identify these names and titles in this uniquely important historical British inscription in detail.

His title of "*Phœnician*" first calls for notice. Its spelling of "*Poenig*" in this inscription equates closely with the Greek and Roman and other still earlier forms of that title. Thus it is seen to equate with the "*Phoinik*-es" of the Greeks, the "*Phœnic*-es" of the Romans, the *Panag Panasa* and *Fenkha* of the ancient Egyptians[1] (which latter sea-going people are referred to in the records of the Fifth Dynasty of Egypt); the *Panag* of the Hebrews,[2] and "The able *Panch*" of the Sanskrit Epics and Vedas. These different dialectic forms of spelling the name Phœnic-ian thus give the equation :—

| Newton Stone. | Egyptian. | Hebrew. | Sanskrit. | Greek. | Latin. | English. |
|---|---|---|---|---|---|---|
| *Poenig* = | *Panag Panasa Fenkha* = | *Panag* = | *Panch*(-ala) = | *Phoinik*-es = | *Phœnic*-es *Punic*-i | = Phœnic-ian. Punic |

The omission of this title in the Ogam version is obviously due to want of space, as that cumbrous script had already overrun the edge of the stone (its usual place) on to the face of the stone.

This title of "*Poenig*" or *Phœnic*-ian possibly survives locally at the Newton Stone in the name "Bennachie," for the bold mountain dominating the site of the monument, and celebrated along with the Gadie river in the old song already referred to. "Ben," of course, is the Cymric and Gaelic name for "mountain," but there seems no obvious Gaelic or Celtic suitable meaning for "Nachie" or "Achie." On the other hand, the letters *P* and *B* are always freely interchangeable dialectically, and as a fact "Phœnix" and "Phœnicos" were names for several mountains at Phœni-

---
[1] See B.E.D., 982a, wherein the affix *bu* of Panag-bu merely means "place of" (see *ibid.*, 213); and for Fankh or Fenkh, see *ibid.*, 995b, and H.N.E., 159 and 276.
[2] Ezekiel, 27, 17.

cian sites, such as in Caria (an early Phœnician colony) and in Lycia adjoining Cilicia, and in Bœotia in Greece.[1] It thus seems not impossible that Bennachie mountain may preserve the title of the famous " Pœnig" king who first civilized this part of Britain and erected his votive pillar at its foot, and who presumably was buried beside it under the shadow of the beautiful Bennachie. Or there may have been a Sun-altar on its topmost peak or at its base, dedicated by this Phœnician king or his descendants to the " Phœnix " Sun-bird emblem of Bil or Bel. (See later).

In this regard also, the name of " *Bleezes* " for the old inn at the foot of Mt. Bennachie (now a farm house) is suggestive of former Bel Fire worship here. " Bleezes," "Blaze," Blayse, or Blaise, was the name of a canonical saint introduced into the Early Christian Church in the fourth century, from Cappadocia, like St. George,[2] and, like the latter, has no authentic historical Christian original, but is evidently a mythical incorporation of the Bel Fire cult introduced for proselytizing purposes. He was made the patron-saint of Candlemas Day, 2nd (or 3rd) February—the solar festival of end of winter and beginning of spring, mid-way between Yule or Old-time Christmas, the end of the solar year and the spring equinox ; it is still the common name for the beginning of the Scottish fiscal year.[3] He is represented in art as carrying " a lighted taper, typical of his being a burning and a shining light."[4] So popular was his worship in Britain in the Middle Ages that the Council of Oxford in 1222 prohibited secular labour on that day.[5] It was till lately the custom in many parts of England to light bonfires on the hills on St. Blazes' night.[6] Norwich still observes his day, and at Bradford in Yorkshire a festival is held every five years in honour of St. Blaze.[7] He was specially associated with the text in Job v., 23 " thou shalt be in league

[1] Strabo, 410 ; 651 ; 666.
[2] The traditional place of his massacre was at the old Hittite city of Savast. Y.M.P., 1, 43.
[3] On a " Candlemas *Bleeze* " tax, *cp.* H.F.F., 85.
[4] B.L.S., Feb., 49.
[5] *Ib.* 48.
[6] *Ib.* 48 ; and Percy, *Notes on Northumberland*, 1770, 332.
[7] B.L.S., Feb., 48.

with the Stones of the Field,¹" which is perhaps a reference to the sacred stones of natural boulders, such as were used in the Bel Fire cult ; so that this local name of " Bleezes," under Bennachie and in sight of our monument, may preserve the tradition of an ancient Phœnician altar blazing with perpetual Fire-offering to Bel.

His title of " Cilician " occurs in two forms of spelling. In the Phœnician script it is spelt " *Sssilokoy*," and in the Ogam, which possesses fewer alphabetic letters, it is written " *Siollaggā*." This clearly designates the " Cilicia " of the Romans, the " Kilikia " of the Greeks and the " Xilakku " or " Xilakki " of the Babylonians,² the maritime province of eastern Asia Minor bordering the north-east corner of the Mediterranean (see map). Situated on the land-bridge connecting Asia Minor and the west with Syria-Phœnicia, Egypt, Mesopotamia and the east, and of great strategical importance, it was early occupied by the Phœnicians, and contained one of their early seaports, namely Tarsus, the " Tarshish "³ of the Hebrew Old Testament, famous for its ships. That city-port was also significantly named " Parthenia "⁴ or " Land of the *Parths*," that is, as now seen, a dialectic variant of the Phœnician eponym " Barat ," in series with the " Prat " on our Newton monument.⁵ Significantly also it was an especial centre of Bel worship, and was under the special protection of the marine tutelary goddess *Barati* who was, as we shall see, the Phœnician prototype of our modern British tutelary " Britannia."

So intimately, indeed, were the Phœnicians identified with Cilicia, that later classic Greek writers, when the exact relationship of Cilicia to the Phœnicians had become forgotten, still make the Cilicians to be " the brothers " of the Phœnicians. *Phœnix* and King Cadmus-the-Phœnician

¹ *Ib.*, 48.
² See M.D., 314.
³ Tarshish is generally arbitrarily identified with Tartessus in Spain, which was also a Phœnician colony. But Rawlinson (R.H.P., 98) inclines to identify it with Tarsus in Cilicia, and rightly so, as my new evidence shows later.
⁴ R.C.P., 135.
⁵ Cilicia was occupied later by the Parthians (S., 669), who, we shall find, were a branch of the Barats.

are called the sons of Agenor, the first traditional king of the Phœnicians, and their brother was *Kilix*,[1] that is the eponym of Cilicia, the "Kilikia" of the Greeks. And the ancient Phœnician colonists from Cilicia proudly recorded their Cilician ancestry, like the author of our monument, and like the apostle Paul who boasted, saying "I am a Jew of Tarsus, a city of Cilicia, a citizen of no mean city."[2] They thus not infrequently recorded their "Cilician" ancestry on their sacred monuments and tombstones in foreign colonies[3], but also transplanted their cherished name "Cilicia" to some of their new colonies.

Cilician colonists, like the author of our Newton inscription, were in the habit of not returning to their native land, Strabo tells us;[4] and patriotically they sometimes transplanted their homeland name of "Cilicia" to their new colonies. Thus they name one of their colonies on the Ægean seaboard of the Troad, south of Troy, "Cilicia."[5] This now leads us to the further discovery of an early-Phœnician Cilician seaport colony in South Britain, at Sels-ey or

---

[1] Apollodorus of Athens (abt. 140 B.C.), 3, 1–4.
[2] Acts, 21, 39.
[3] Just as some of the historical Briton kings were in the habit of occasionally adopting the Sun-God's title of Bel as a personal name (S.C.P., 15, 16, and 434), so their Phœnician ancestors had previously often called themselves after Bel, and sometimes adding the locality of his chief centre of worship, presumably because it was their own native home. Thus Bel was sometimes called "Bel Libnan" (Bel of Lebanon), "Bel Hermon" (Bel of Hermon), and similarly "Bel of Tyre, Sidon, Tarsus," etc. (*cp.* R.H.P., 325). In this way "Bel *Silik*" or "Bel of Cilicia" was a not uncommon personal name recorded on the tombstones and votive monuments to Bel in Phœnician colonies outside Cilicia, and presumably by Phœnicians of Cilician ancestry. Thus in Phœnician tombstones in Sardinia, where we shall find one of the deceased bears the title of "*Part*" or "*Prat*" (*i.e.*, as we shall see, "Barat" or "Brit-on"), another is recorded as "Son of Bel of *Silik*" (C.I.S. No. 155 and L.P.I. No. 1); and a trilingual inscription gives the Grecianised form as "Sillech" (C.I.S. Vol. I, 72). This same name, I observe, is borne by many other Phœnicians on votive monuments and tombs in Carthage (*ib.* Nos. 178, 205, 257, 286, 312, 358, 368); and "Silik," in combination with the divine Phœnician title of Ásman, is borne by Phœnicians in Cyprus and Carthage (*ib.* Nos. 50, 197). Here and elsewhere, the name of the Phœnician Father-god when occurring, in the "Semitic" Phœnician I transliterate "Bel," as the middle letter is a solitary "ayin," which is often rendered *e*, though with unwarranted licence it is usually rendered in this word *aa*, and arbitrarily given the form "Baal," to forcibly adapt it to the Hebrew "Baal."
[4] S. 673, 14, 5, 13.
[5] S. 585: 13, 1, 17, etc.

## CILICIANS IN EARLY BRITAIN 43

" Island of the Sels."[1] A hoard of pre-Roman coins of Ancient Britain, mostly gold, were found on the sea-shore between Bognor and Selsey, the latter being the name of the ancient Briton sea-port town of the peninsula offlying the Briton " Caer Cei " city, the Chichester of the Romans.[2] These coins are of archaic type with solar symbols (see later) and bear an inscription hitherto undeciphered, and described by the leading numismatist as " a number of marks something like Hebrew characters, which is, however, undecipherable."[3]

Now, this inscription on these Ancient Briton coins from Selsey (see Fig. 9) is, I find, stamped in clear Aryan Phœnician writing, with letters generally similar to those of the Newton Stone, and, like it, reads in the usual Aryan or *non*-Semitic direction.[4] It reads " $SS(i)L$," which seems a contraction

Fig. 9.  Phœnician Inscription on Early Briton Coins
found near Sels-ey.
(After Evans.)[5]
Note Inscription reads " $SS(i)L$," a contraction for " Cilicia."

for the fuller " Sssilokoy " or " Cilicia " of the Newton Stone Phœnician inscription ; for it is the rule in Early Briton coins, also followed in modern British, to use a contracted form of place and other names for want of space. Topographically, this Sels-ey was precisely the sort of island

---

[1] The *ey*, or *ay* or *ea* affix in British place-names such as Chelsea or Chelsey, Battersea, Rothesay, Orkney, Alderney, etc., is admittedly the Gothic and Norse *ey* " an island " (*cp*. V.D. 134). And significantly the Phœnician word for " island " or " sea-shore " was *ay* (Hildebrand), a word also adopted by the Hebrews in their Old Testament for " Isles of the Gentiles " and places beyond the sea.
[2] C.B., i, 267 ; and B.H.E., 13.
[3] E.B.C., 94–5.
[4] This direction is clearly indicated by the third or last letter, which is turned to the left, *i.e.* in the opposite direction to the retrograde " Semitic " Phœnician letter *L*.
[5] E.B.C., pl. E., Fig. 10.

or peninsula, offlying the mainland marts, as at Tyre, Sidon, Gadesh, St. Michael's Mount, etc., which the Phœnician sea-merchants were in the habit of selecting, for defensive purposes, as a mercantile seaport, before they established themselves on the mainland. And its name on these coins implies that the Phœnicians at that old city-state here had a mint established for the issue of these coins. That old city is unfortunately now, through subsidence of the coast, submerged in the channel.[1] On the adjoining mainland, a few miles from Sels-ey, stands the old pre-Roman city-port of Chichester (with an ancient Briton-paved highway to London called " Stane Street "), with prehistoric earthworks and remains of prehistoric villages and Bronze Age implements[2] implying early habitation. And at *Sil*-chester to the north of Sels-ey and Chichester on the ancient road from Chichester via Winchester to London, and the pre-Roman capital of the Segonti clan of Britons, and said to have been also called " *Briten*-den " or " Fort of the Britons,"[3] with prehistoric and early Iron Age remains,[4] and a temple with a Roman inscription to " Hercules of the Segonti Britons "[5] —a fact of Phœnician import—there also exists an inscription in Ogam script,[6] which we have seen is of Phœnician origin or influence.

This discovery that the ancient Phœnician origin of the name of Sels-ey or " Island of the *Sels* or Cilicians," now suggests that the name " Sles-wick " or " Abode of the *Sles*," for the home of the Angles in Denmark, presumably also represents this softened dialectic form of the name " Cilicia " in series with that on the Newton Stone and the Sels-ey coins, and thus appears to indicate the foundation of Sles-wick by a colony of Phœnicians from Cilicia. The " Silik " form of " Cilicia " of the Phœnicians seems also to be probably the source of the " *Selg*-ovæ " tribal title, which was applied by the Romans to the people of the Galloway

---

[1] " It is clear and visible at low water " C.B., 1, 268.
[2] W.P.E., 248.
[3] C.B., i, 171.
[4] W.P.E., 248, 279.
[5] C.B. i, 204. The Segonti Britons are mentioned by Cæsar (D.B.G. 5, 21).
[6] Nicholson, *Keltic Researches*, 16.

coast of the Solway, who seem to have been the same warlike tribe elsewhere called by the Romans "Atte-Cotti," which, we shall see, is obviously a tautological dialectic form of "Catti" or "Atti" or Hitt-ite. The substitution of the soft sibilant *C*, with the sound of *S* for the hard *K*, is seen in the Roman spelling of "Cilicia" for the Greek "Kilikia" and in "Celt" for the earlier Kelt, as well as in the modern "Cinema" for "Kinema," etc. Now we resume our examination of the further significant titles borne by this Cilician Phœnician upon his votive monument at Newton.

His "*Kāst*" (or "*Kwast*") title also is clearly a geographical one. It designates him as a native of the famous *Kasta*-bala, a sacred Cilician city[1] and the ancient capital of Cilicia about 400 B.C., that is at the actual period of the Cilician Phœnician author of this monument at Newton.

Kastabala on the Pyramus River of Eastern Cilicia (see Map), and commanding the caravan trade-route to Armenia, Persia, Central Asia and the East, and the route by which Marco Polo travelled overland to Cathay,[2] was still the capital of Eastern Cilicia at the occupation of Asia Minor by the Romans in 64 B.C., who confirmed its Hitto-Syrian king Tarcondimo and his dynasty in the sovereignty. On account of its sacred ancient shrine (where Diana was called *Perathea*[3] who, we shall find, was "*Britannia*,") it was called Hieropolis or "Sacred City" by the Seleucid emperor, Antiochus IV., about 175 B.C.,[4] which name occurs on its coins and other documents from that date onwards; and some of its coins figure its deity carrying a Fire-torch,[5] implying the solar Fire-cult, and others bear an anchor as evidence of its sea-faring trade.[6] Moreover, the upper valley of the Pyramus, above Kastabala, was called by the Greco-Romans "*Kata*-onia" or "*Cata*-onia," that is, "Land of the *Kat* or *Cat*," which title, we shall see,

---

[1] Its site is fixed at Budrum by local inscriptions. See M.H.A., 189; R.H.G., 342*f*., 376*f*., H.C.C., ci, cxxix.
[2] Y.M.P., 1.
[3] Strabo, 573; 12, 2, 7.
[4] S. 12, 2, 7; B.H.S., 2, 157.
[5] H.C.C., pl. 14, 3 and 4.
[6] *Ib.* pl. 39, 8 and nos. 2-4.

is a dialectic form of "Catti," the title of the Ancient Britons as found stamped on their coins, and a title of the Phœnician Barat rulers.

This identification of the Kast of our inscription with Kastabala in Cilicia now gives us the clue not only to the Cilician source of the Sun-cult imported into North Britain by this Phœnician Barat prince, but it also supplies a clue to his own personal appearance and dress. Amongst the remains of the Sun-cult monuments in ancient Cilicia, which was a chief centre for the diffusion of the Sun-cult of "Mithra"

*a*        *b*

FIG. 10. Cilician Gothic King worshipping "Sun-god." From bas-reliefs in temple of Antiochus I. of Commagene, 63-34 B.C.
(After Cumont.)

Note: These two representations of same scene, which are partly defaced, complement each other. The king who is shaking hands with the Sun-god (with rayed halo in *a*) presumably illustrates dress and physique of the Sun-worshipper, King Prāt or Prwt, who also came from the same region.

in Roman Europe through the Roman legionaries stationed there,[1] are in Upper Cilicia two bas-reliefs from the Sun-temple of King Antiochus I. of Commagene, on the Upper Pyramus, 63-34 B.C. (see Fig. 10).[2] In these, which represent

[1] See C.M.M., 41-3.
[2] These reliefs are from a Sun-temple on the Nimrud range near the eastern frontier of Cilicia, reproduced in *Ctesias apud Athen.*, 10, 45, and in *Textes et Monuments* by Cumont, p. 188.

## HIS SUN-CULT & "KASSI" TITLE

the same scene, the king is seen shaking hands by the right hand with the image of the Father-God of the Sun, as part of the old Sumerian ceremony of coronation, when the solar kings assumed the title of " Son of the Sun-god," a title also adopted from the Aryans by the pharaohs of Egypt. This ancient Sumerian ceremonial seems referred to in the Vedic hymn to the Sun-god Mitra which says :

" When will ye (Mitra) take us by both hands, as a dear sire his son ?"[1].

And even more significantly it was evidently practised by the Goths in Ancient Britain, as recorded in the Eddas:

" The Sun wrapped its sunshine o'er the assembly of men,
His Right hand (was) caught in the House of Heaven."[2]

In this way, as our Barat king, in his votive inscription to the Sun-god at Newton, tells us that he was a native of this region, he presumably resembled this king generally in dress and physique. This king, it will be noticed, is attired in *Gothic* dress, and the Sun-god with the rayed halo (*a* in Fig.) wears the Gothic or Phrygian cap, and is also clad in Gothic dress.

His " *Kazzi* " or " *Qass* " title is clearly and unequivocally a variant dialectic spelling of " *Kāśi,*" an alternative clan title of the Phœnician Khatti Barats.

[z is a frequent dialectic variant in spelling s; for example, the Hebrews spelt " Sidon " and " Sion " as " Zidon " and " Zion " ; and Q is habitually used for *K* in the Ogam, which does not possess the letter *K*. And Tarsus in *Cilicia* was spelt Tarz.]

Kāśi was an eponym title adopted, we find, by some of the early Aryan Phœnician Barats and their successors, from the name of a famous grandson of King Barat, named *Kaś*, or *Kāś*. It is applied in the Vedas to one or more kings of the First Panch(-āla) Dynasty, as well as in the Indian Epic King-Lists, some of which apply it to the whole of that dynasty as well as to their descendants. And on arrival in India, the Kāśi Dynasty, significant of their maritime sway,

---

[1] R.V., 1, 38, 1. Mitra is named in v. 13 as chief deity and invoked through his angel Maruts.
[2] Volu-Spa Edda v. 5.

## 48   PHŒNICIAN ORIGIN OF BRITONS & SCOTS

held the river-way up the Ganges, at their capital of Kāśi, the modern Benares, bordering the Panch(-āla) province of Ancient India.

"*Kassi*" (or "*Cassi*") was the title used by the First Phœnician Dynasty about 3000 B.C., as attested in their still extant inscriptions.[1] It was the title adopted by the great dynasty of that name in Babylonia which ruled the Mesopotamian empire for about six centuries, from about 1800 B.C., and who are now generally admitted to have been Aryans. And *Kaśi* also occurs as a personal name of Phœnicians in inscriptions in Egypt.[2]

This *Kāśi* title is thus now disclosed as the Phœnician source of the "Cassi" title borne by the ruling Briton Catti kings of pre-Roman Britain down to Cassivellaunus (see later), who minted the "Cas" coins bearing the Sun-horse and other solar symbols (see Fig. 11).

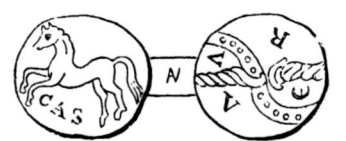

FIG. 11.   Cassi Coin of Early Britain inscribed "Cas" with Sun-horse.
(After Poste.)[3]

The Early Aryan Kāśi are referred to in Vedic literature as offerers of the sacred Fire and the especial protégés of Indra. And in Babylonia the Kaśśi were ardent "Sun-worshippers" with its Fire offering; and were devotees of the Sun Cross, which is very freely represented on their sacred seals and monuments, in the various forms of St. George's Cross, the Maltese Cross (see Figs., Chap. XX). This fact is well seen in the engraving on the sacred official seal-

---

[1] Details with proofs in my *Aryan Origin of the Phœnicians*.
[2] C.I.S., 112b, etc.
[3] P.B.C. 45. Two of these "Cas" Briton Coins, of different mintages, and including this one, are figured by Dr. Stukeley in his *oins of the Ancient British Kings*, Lond. 1765, plates 4, 2, and 3. This particular coin is also figured in Gibson's ed. of Camden (Pl. II, 4); but Evans, in referring to the "Cas" legend (E.C.B., 231), appears to confuse it with a different coin having no Cas legend, namely Beale's pl. iii, Fig. 7.

## KASSIS PLOUGHING UNDER THE CROSS 49

cylinder here reproduced (see Fig. 12). This shows the pious *Aryan Cassis of Babylonia about* 1350 B.C. *ploughing and sowing under the Sign of the Cross,* which, we shall find later, was their emblem of the Aryan Father-God of the Universe, as the Universal Victor.

This now explains for the first time the hitherto unaccountable fact of the " prehistoric " existence of the Cross, which is sculptured on this Newton Stone and on the many still surviving pre-Christian monuments with solar emblems in the British Isles, as we shall see later ; and also the Cross symbol with other solar emblems on the pre-Roman coins of the Catti and *Cassi* kings of Early Britain. It also now

Fig. 12. Cassis of Early Babylonia ploughing and sowing under the Sign of the Cross.

From a Kaśśi official seal of about 1350 B.C.
(After Clay.)

Note the plough is fitted with a drill, which is fed by the right hand of the sower from his bag, and the corn seed passes down directly into the fresh furrow opened by the plough.

explains the " Cassi " title used by these pre-Roman Briton kings—a title in series with "*Écossais*" for " Scot," as seen later—as well as the " *Kazzi* " and " *Qass* " title of the Phœnician author of this votive Cross at Newton and his Aryan racial origin. It also illustrates the fact, as we shall find later, that husbandry, with the settled life, formed the basis of the Higher Civilization of the Aryans, as the Aryans were the introducers of the Agricultural Stage in the World's Civilization. Indeed, so obviously " Aryan " was the language of these Kassis of Babylonia, that most modern Assyriologists now admit that the Kassis were Aryan in race as well as speech. But yet, although Assyriologists mostly admit that these Kassis were apparently affiliated to the Khatti or Hittites, they nevertheless refuse the logical inference that the latter also were presumably Aryans.

His personal name "*Ikhar*," "*Ixar*," or "*Icār*," also significantly confirms his royal Kassi ancestry. This name was borne not infrequently by Kassis of Babylonia in their still extant legal and business documents, etc., of the second millennium B.C. It occurs therein in the varying dialectic spelt forms of *Ikhar* or *Ixar, Ikhur, Ikkaria, Igar, Akhri, Agar, Agri, Ekarra,* and *Ekur*[1]; and amongst the Hittites of the fourteenth century B.C., as "*Agar*."[2] These vagaries in the phonetic spelling of the name, reflected also in the variation in spelling it on the Newton Stone itself, are merely in keeping with the notorious vagaries in the phonetic spelling of personal names, even by the individual himself, down to modern times, until printing has nowadays stereotyped the form of spelling. Thus we have the well-known instance of Shakespeare, who is said to have spelt his own name over half a dozen different ways in the same document. The meaning of this personal name possibly has an especial Phœnician significance. The land of Phœnicia and the Amorites was called by the Babylonians, who not infrequently interchanged the vowels, *Akharri* or *Axarri* or "Western Land."[3]

The title of *S(i)luyri* or "*S(i)lwor*," suggests the ethnic name of "Silur-es" applied by some late Roman writers to the people of South Wales bordering the Severn. But these Silures, described by Tacitus as dark-complexioned and Iberian,[4] were clearly non-Aryan; and there is no suggestion in the Ancient British Chronicles to connect the author of these inscriptions with Wales. This title, therefore, is probably the designation of his subclan; though it may possibly

---

[1] C.P.N., 45, 50, 51, 78, 85, 149, 152.
[2] *Ib.* 45.
[3] M.D., 30.
[4] Tacitus, *Agricola* ii.

# CASSI SUN-CROSSES IN BRITAIN

designate a Silurus district in Spain,[1] from which country he is traditionally reported to have come immediately, as we shall see, on his way to Britain.

His further titles of " Prat " or Prwt " and " Gyaolownie," or " Gioln " are of such great historical significance as to require a separate chapter.

Fig. 12A. "Cassi" Sun Cross on prehistoric monument at Sinniness, Wigtonshire.
(From Proc. Soc. Antiquaries Scotland, by kind permission.)
For many other examples of "Cassi" Crosses in Britain see Chap. XX.

---

[1] " Silurus " was the name of a maritime mountain in Ancient Spain (Festus Avienus, *Ora maritima* 433).

## VII

PHŒNICIAN TRIBAL TITLE OF "BARAT" OR "BRIHAT" AND ITS SOURCE OF NAMES "BRIT-ON," "BRIT-AIN" AND "BRIT-ANNIA"

*Disclosing Aryan Phœnician Origin of the tutelary Britannia and of her form and emblems in Art.*

> "And King *Ḃarat* gave his name to the Dynastic Race of which he was the founder; and so it is from him that the fame of that Dynastic People hath spread so wide."—*Mahā Bārata*.[1]
> "Like a Father's Name, men love to call their names."—*Rig Veda*.[2]

THE title of "*Prāt*" or "*Prwt*," borne by our colonizing Phœnician Cassi prince on his British monument at Newton, is now seen to be clearly a dialectic form of the patronymic title "Ḃarat" or "Brihat" used by the Aryan Phœnicians as recorded in the Indian epics and in the Vedic Hymns, as cited in the heading, the Phœnicians being, as we have seen, a chief branch of the Barats, or the descendants of King Barat, and they are systematically called "Ḃārat" in the Indian epics and Vedas. And this Aryan Phœnician title of "Barat" or "Brihat" is now disclosed to be the Phœnician source of our modern titles "Brit-on," "Brit-ain," and "Brit-ish."

[As explaining the various spellings of this name "Barat," it is to be noted that the interchange of the labials *B* and *P* is a not uncommon dialectic change in all languages, and it is especially frequent at the present day in the highlands of Scotland and in Wales. It already occurs to some extent even in Sumerian; and in the Indian Vedas and epics, this particular word "Ḃarat" is also sometimes spelt *Pritŭ* or *Prithu* and

---

[1] M.B., i ch. 94, verse 3704; and *cp.* M.B.R., i, 279.
[2] R.V., 10, 39, 1. Kaegi's translation, 140.

*Brihat* (as seen in the heading on p. 1) and *Brihad*.[1] This latter form, whilst thus equating with the Cymric Welsh " *Pryd*-ain " for " Brit-on," also illustrates the further common dialectic interchange of the dentals *t* and *d*, in the spelling of this name. It also shows that the early pronunciation of this name varied considerably, and that the *i* came early into " Brit " or " Briton."]

The Cassi kinsmen of our Cassi Phœnician Briton in Babylonia and Syria-Phœnicia also used this patronym of Barat freely as a personal name or title, in the various dialectic forms of Barata, Biriitum, Paratum, Baruti, Burattu, Burta, Biriidia, Piradi, and Piritum.[2]

The later Phœnicians also, whilst spelling this title " Barat " on their coins (as we have seen in Fig. 5, p. 9) that is, in its full orthographic form, also spelt it, I find, with

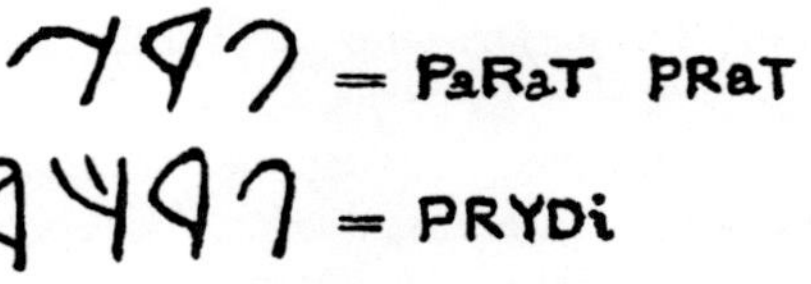

$$ ⟁ = PaRaT \ PRaT $$
$$ ⟁ = PRYDi $$

FIG. 13. Phœnician Patronymic titles "*Parat*" and "*Prydi* "or" *Prudi* " on Phœnician tombstones in Sardinia.[3]

an initial *P* as " *PRT*," thus giving practically the identical form on the Newton Stone ; and they also spelt it as " *Prydi*," or " *Prudi*," thus giving the same form as in the Cymric. Thus, for example, in the old Phœnician grave stones in Sardinia, an ancient colony of the Phœnicians, I find that, in two out of a series of eight tombstones, the Phœnician persons are so designated (see Fig. 13) ; and that in a script, closely allied to that of the Newton Stone, but written in the reversed direction with reversed letters, presumably, as already noted, for the information of a Semitic population accustomed to read their writing backwards like the Hebrews. And it is further significant that the name by which these

---

[1] Details in *Aryan Origin of the Phœnicians*.
[2] C.P.N., 32, 65, 106, etc.
[3] L.P.I., Nos. 4 (line 1), 7 (line 1) and 8 (line 3) on gravestones from Nora, and now in the museum at Cagliari.

F

Phœnicians call their graves, "*Khabr*," appears to be essentially the same as the Gothic term "*Kubl*," applied in Runic inscriptions to the funereal barrows of the Goths—the liquid semi-vowels *r* and *l* being freely interchangeable, as in Ha*l* for Ha*rr*y, co*r*onel for co*l*onel and the cockney "a*r*f" for "ha*l*f."

This Phœnician spelling of the Barat title as *PRT*, in which the short vowels are unexpressed, as usual in Phœnician, just as they are similarly unexpressed in our Newton Stone inscription, and in the Indo-Aryan, Pali and Sanskrit, and in Hebrew, etc., thus gives a little variety in its reading. It may read either *PaRaT* or *PaRT* or *PRaT*, thus giving all the three forms of *Parat* (the equivalent of Barat), or *Part*, or *Prat*, as in the Newton Stone, and the equivalent of "Brit." In regard to this latter form of *Prat* or *Prwt* on the Newton Stone, we shall find later that the famous Ionian navigating geographer Pytheas who circumnavigated and surveyed Britain as far as Shetland about the middle of the fourth century B.C., that is, about the time of our Newton Stone inscription, also spelt the name of Britain with an initial *P*, calling the British Isles "*Pret*-anikai"; and "*Pret*-anoi" continued to be the name used by Ptolemy and other Greek writers for Britain and the Britons.

But, although the later Phœnicians of Cilicia, like those of Sardinia above-noted, whilst using *P* for *B*, in calling their chief city-port Tarsus, by the name of "*Parth*-enia" or "Place of the Parths," their remnant or their Aryanized and Phœnicianized successors thereabouts, so late as about the third century A.D., nevertheless continued to call themselves "*Barats*," as seen in their coin here figured. (Fig. 14).

The first of these coins tells us that it was a coin of the "Barats of Lycaonia," which was the ultramontane portion of Cilicia to the north of the Taurus, and contained, besides the capital city of Iconium (the modern Turkish capital Konia, a city which was visited more than once by St. Paul)[1], also the ancient city of Barata, to the south of which (at Heraclea, the modern Ivriz), on the ancient Hittite highway from

---
[1] Acts 14, 1 and 21 ; 16, 2.

## BRITANNIA OF PHŒNICIAN ORIGIN

Ephesus and Troy to Tarsus and the Cilician Gates of the Taurus, are famous herculean Hittite sculptures and hieroglyphs, resembling those on Briton coins (see Fig. 62 in Chapter XXII.). The Lycaonians in the Roman period were still confederated with their kinsmen of Cilicia. The legend stamped on this coin is " The Commonwealth of the Lycaon *Baratas* " (Koinon Lukao *Baratcōn*) ; and the Early Phœnician empire, we shall see later, was held together as a commonwealth by the confederation of home and colonial city-states.

FIG. 14. Coins of Phœnician " Barats " of Lycaonia, of third century A.D. disclosing their tutelary goddess " Barati " as " Britannia." [1]

*a*. From Barata City. *b*. From Iconium City. Note she has the Sun-Cross or St George's - Red Cross as shield.

These coins, with others of the same type elsewhere, are of immense historical importance for recovering the lost history of the Britons in Britain and in their earlier homeland, as they now disclose the hitherto unknown origin of the modern British marine tutelary " Britannia," and prove her to be of Hitto-Phœnician origin.

Usually the head only of this goddess is figured on Phœnician coins, and it is of a fine Aryan and *non*-Semitic type ; see for example the Phœnician " Barat " coin from Carthage (Fig. 5, p. 9), and Phœnician coins generally. In these coins of Lycaonia the general resemblance to Britannia

[1] *a* and *b*, after R.C.P., 368 and 415 ; and *cp.* photos in H.C.C., pl. 1, Fig. 3 and 9. Coin *a* is ascribed to the period of the Roman governor Otacilia Severa, 249 A.D.

will be noticed—Britannia hitherto being supposed to have been first invented by the Early Romans in Britain in the 2nd century A.D. (see Fig. 15) in practically the identical form still surviving on our modern British penny.

FIG. 15.—Britannia on Early Roman Coins of Britain.
(After Akerman.)
*a*. Coin of Hadrian (117—137 A.D.).   *b*. Coin of Antonine (138—161 A.D.).

In these Barat Lycaonian coins Barati is seated in the pose of Britannia, in the first upon a rock, and in the second on a chair (of a ship) amidst the waves, the latter being personified by a semi-submerged water-nymph, as was the conventional method of representing rivers and the sea, after the nereid model of the Lycians, in the Roman art of the period to which this coin belongs. She holds a cornucopia or horn of plenty and in her right hand, in one of the coins, an object which may be a sceptre, as is figured in her representation on many of these coins; and in the other she holds the tiller of a rudder, indicating her marine tutelarship; and beside her chair on board ship is the shield-like Sun Cross or St. George's Cross within the Sun's disc, designating her to be of the solar cult. This latter emblem is now seen to be the origin of the shield bearing the Union Jack which is figured in the modern representations of Britannia, but which cannot date earlier than the Union of England and Scotland in 1606 A.D., and was previously presumably the St. George's Red Cross or the rayed Cross or the rayed Sun itself, as in these coins. In other coins of Cilicia, Lycaonia, Phœnicia and other Phœnician

# BRITANNIA ON PHŒNICIAN COINS

colonies she sometimes holds a sceptre[1] or a standard Cross (see Fig. 16), or a caduceus,[2] which latter ensigns of authority were presumably the source of the Neptune trident now given to her in her modern British representation. And she sometimes carries a torch [4] as in the representation of the "Sun-god" Mithra, the torch of the Sun, which explains the lighthouse figured beside Britannia on the old pennies

FIG. 16.—Phœnician Coin of Barati or Britannia from Sidon.
(After Hill.)[3]
Note she holds a *Cross* as standard and a rudder amongst the waves.

This beneficent marine and earth tutelary goddess of Good Fortune has not usually her name stamped on the coins bearing her effigy, and has been surmised by modern numismatists to be the late Greek goddess of Fortune (Tychē), the "Fortuna" of the Romans, a goddess unknown to Homer,[5] and who first appears in Greek classics in the odes of Pindar (about 490 B.C.). In this regard it is interesting to note that the first traditional statue of this goddess of Fortune (or Tychē) is reported to have been made for the people of

[1] H.C.P., 116, 297 ; H.C.C. on a " Barata " coin she carries a palm branch of Victory and ears of corn. Pl. 1, Fig. 1.
[2] H.C.P., 116.
[3] H.C.P., 297 ; H.C.C. xxvi, 68, No. 14 ; in Pl. 1, Fig. 2, she carries a spear.
[4] *Coins of Syracuse*, Brit. Museum, post-card series, xxiv. 5a reverse. Syracuse was an ancient colony of the Phœnicians.
[5] She does not appear in the Iliad and Odyssey, but only in the apocryphal Hymn to Demeter Ch. 4, 7–20 ; and see P.D.G. 4, 30 ; and Liddell and Scott, *Greek Dict.* under Tychē.

Smyrna[1]—that is, an ancient Hittite seaport of the Ægean with rock-cut prehistoric Hittite hieroglyphs in the neighbourhood.

Her proper name is now disclosed by the Vedic hymns of the Eastern branch of the Aryan Barats to have been *Bárati*, meaning " Belonging to the Barats." She is also called therein " *Brihad*-the Divine " (Brihad-divā) ; and she seems identical with *Pritvi* or " Mother Earth." Her especial abode was on the " *Saras*-vati River," which, I find, was the modern *Sarus* River of Cilicia which entered the sea at Tarsus, the " *Tarz* " of its own coins (see Figs. later) or Parth-enia, which appears to have been the first seaport of the Barat homeland. In these Vedic hymns all the attributes of Britannia are accounted for ; her tutelarship of the waters and of ships, her lighthouse on the sea, her Neptune trident (as well as the origin of Neptune himself and his name), her helmet and shield, her Cross on the shield, as well as the cornucopia, which she sometimes bears upon the Phœnician and Greco-Roman coins, taking the place of the corn-stalk on the Briton coins.

In the Vedic hymns she is called " The great Mother (Mahī)" [2] and " Holy Lady of the Waters " [3] and is hailed as " First-made mother " in a hymn to her son " *Napat* the Son of the Waters "[4] who has a horse [thus disclosing the remote Aryan origin of the the name and personality of the old Sea-god, Neptune, and his horses, and accounting for Neptune's trident in her hands]. She is a " Fire-Priestess "[5] and " shows the Light "[6] [thus accounting for the Lighthouse on the older British coins with Britannia]. She is personified Fire[7] and sits upon the sacred Fire[8] [thus accounting for the St. George's Cross which, we shall find later, symbolizes Fire of the Sun]. She is associated with the twin horsemen of the Sun (Aswin or Dioscorides), represented on the Briton coins,[9] and coins of Syracuse (an ancient Phœnician

---

[1] P.D.G., 4, 30.
[2] R.V., 1, 13, 9, etc. Frequently she is triplicated by treating her two other commoner titles as separate personalities, called her " sisters," namely the personified Saras-vati River, on which she specially dwelt, and personified Food or Oil (Ilā) ; but in other hymns these three are identified as one with her. R.V., 2, 1, 11, etc.
[3] R.V., 2, 355 ; 3, 56, 5.   [4] R.V., 2, 35, 6.   [5] R.V., 2. 1, 11.
[6] R.V., 10, 110, 7-8.   [7] R.V.., 2, 1, 11.   [8] R.V., 2, 31, 4 ; 10, 59, 9.
[9] See, for example, Figs. 61, etc., and E.B.C., Pl. G. 2 and 3.

## BRITANNIA IN THE VEDAS, ETC. 59

colony)¹ etc. She is " Lady of Health," and " The Food-bestower "² [thus accounting for the cornucopia and heads of corn on the coins]. She " shelters, protects and aids her Barat votaries "³ [thus accounting for the " Saviour " (sōter) title of the Greco-Roman goddess of Fortune], and she " bestows good mornings."⁴ She is " slayer of the leviathan brutes (vritra),"⁵ [thus accounting for her warrior's helmet of Hittite pattern and shield] ; and she " speeds forth our cars." ⁶

The name " Fortuna," by which the Romans called this Barat tutelary goddess of Good Fortune,⁷ as well as the English word " Fortune," now appear to be coined from her title of " Baratī "—the letter F being interchangeable dialectically with P and B, as we have seen in the Egyptian " Fenkha " for " Phœnic " and in the Greek *Pyr* for *Fire*, and P with *B* ; and its affix *una* or " one " is now disclosed to be derived from the Hitto-Sumerian *ana* (" one "), thus giving the title of " The one of Barats " (or " Fortune "). The *o* came in dialectically like the *w* in Pr*w*t on the Newton Stone and the *u* in Br*u*t, the name of the first Briton king in the Ancient British Chronicles, as we shall see later. " Fortuna " was figured in identical form and symbols with Barati and Britannia and in the same associations with water.⁸

Further striking positive inscriptional proof of this *Bāratī* title for the Aryan marine tutelary (Britannia) and also of her Phœnician origin is now gained from the records of Ancient Egypt and Mesopotamia, both of which lands are now disclosed in these pages to have derived their Civilization from the Aryan Phœnicians.

¹ *Coins of Syracuse*, Brit. Museum post-cards xxiv, Figs. 1, 2, 7, and 9 ; and see below, note 6.
² R.V., 2, 3, 1, 4, as Brihad-the-Divine.
³ R.V., 1, 22, 11.    ⁴ R.V., 3, 6, 23.    ⁵ R.V., 2, 1, 11.
⁶ R.V., 2, 31, 4. This speeding of cars she is said to perform in association with the Aswins (or Dioscorides), solar horsemen, thus explaining her representations on the Syracuse coins (see footnote 1), as well as figures holding the rudder, and standing on the prow of ships in the coins.
⁷ The special temple to Fortuna in Italy was at Præneste, on a tributary of the Tiber, not far from where the exiled Trojan Æneas, the traditional ancestor of the first Briton king, established his Latin capital.
⁸ As " Fortuna," inscribed Roman altars to her were found in the baths on Roman wall at Castlecarry and at Bowes in Yorks (G. Macdonald *Roman Wall, in Scotland*, 343,) ; and there are others to her as "*Britanni*" (*Ib.* 329).

## 60 PHŒNICIAN ORIGIN OF BRITONS & SCOTS

Amongst the deities of Ancient Egypt is a protective goddess named, "*Bāīrthy*,[1] *goddess of the Water*," whose name and functions are thus seen to be precisely those of the Aryan tutelary Bāratī (or Britannia). She is one of several deities in the Egyptian pantheon who are called by Egyptologists "foreign," or imported from Syria and elsewhere, notwithstanding that several of the leading "indigenous Egyptian" deities, such as the Sun-god Horus, Osiris and Isis are also admittedly imported, also from "Syria" in certain traditions; and, according to Egyptian myth, this particular "Goddess of the Waters" (Bāīrthy) herself was "the mother" of the above-cited triad.[2] And under her title, in the inscription below, as "Goddess of the Waters," she is also of the solar cult and supports "the Boat of the Sun-god."[3] She is represented in art, moreover, by the ancient Egyptians (see Fig. 17) as a seated queen in the same general form and pose as in the Asia Minor coins of

FIG. 17. Brit-annia tutelary of Phœnicians in Ancient Egypt as *Bāīrthy*, "The Mother of the Waters" (*Nut*) or "Naiad."

(After Budge.)

Compare the horns on her head with those of "Barat" on her coin from Carthage Fig. 5, p. 9.

[1] This is the spelling of the Egyptian hieroglyphs of her name (see Fig. 18 below) by the generally recognized phonetic transliteration; but it is rendered "*Bāirtha*" in B.G.E., 2, 281. In the spelling of her title "*Nut*" or "Goddess of the Waters"—which appears to be a variant of "Naiad"—the determinative sign for "Sky" is sometimes, as here, omitted; see B.G.E., 2,108.
[2] B.G.E. 2, 109.      [3] *Ibid.* 2, 99, and Fig. there.

Barati (Fig. 14, p. 55), and bearing a similar pitcher on her head (symbolizing the Waters) and holding a long spear-like sceptre and the handled Cross-sceptre, corresponding to the Cross on the throne of Barati and on the shield of Britannia.

She is further entitled " The Lady Protector of *Zapuna*,"[1] a seaport city which is usually identified with the " Zephon-by-the-sea " of the Hebrew Old Testament account of the exodus of the Israelites from Egypt to the Sinai desert.[2] But this name, usually transliterated " Zapuna," reads in full in the Egyptian hieroglyph texts ZA-PUNAQ(m),[3] and thus appears to mean " The Sailings of the *Punaqs* (i.e., of the Phœnicians) "[4] (see Fig. 18 for the hieroglyphs of her name and title).

But the more important and presumably original city or district of " Za-Puna(q)," with its temple to its protective tutelary, of which the Suez one appears to have been only a transplanted namesake, was situated significantly in *Northern Phænicia*.[5] This Phœnician place is also mentioned by an Assyrian king about 950 B.C. under the title of " The country of Bi-'i-li Za-Bu-na(or Za-pi-na) " designating it as under the protection of the Lady of Bil or Bel,[6]

[1] See f.n. 3.
[2] Exod. 14, 2. Near Suez and thus presumably a port of the Phœnicians who were the chief mariners of the Egyptian coast and Red Sea, and who in the time of Solomon had two ports in the other northern arm of the Red Sea (1 Kings, 9, 26, etc.) and who still had several river-port settlements in Egypt so late as the time of Herodotus.
[3] Budge, *op. cit.* 2, 281 spells it " Tchapuna " by transliterating the letter Z as *Tch*, and by omitting the last hieroglyph which has the value of *Qm* or *Q*. This latter sign was used in later times as a " determinative " (or sign to fix the meaning of a word) for foreign tribes and cities; but " in the Old Kingdom " its use as a "determinative" was very limited (G.H. 52); and when so used it is not usually used by itself as here, but is followed by the sign for country or people, neither of which occur here. Yet even if it be treated as this foreign tribal affix to the name " *Puna*," the latter may still represent the Egyptian *Pa ag* or *Fenkha* or " Phœnician," because the Egyptians were in the habit of dropping out the final G or Q or *Kh* of this name, as seen in their " Bennu " for the " Phœnix," Sun-bird of the Phœnicians, and the Roman *Pun* (or " Punic ") for Phœnician; and the Egyptians were in the habit, as we shall see, of substituting Q for G, K and Kh.
[4] *Za* = " to travel, to sail; " see P.V.H., 731–2 under " Tá "; and B.E.D., 894 under " Tch."
[5] Müller *Asien und Europa*, 315.
[6] In an inscription of Tiglath Pileser II. for which the cuneiform is cited by B.G.E., 2, 282 with transliteration as " Ba-'-li Sa-pu-na."

the Father-god and Lord of the Sun. Moreover, this " Lady Protector [Bāīrthy] of Za-pu-na [-gu?]"[1] is invoked by a Babylonian emperor about 680 B.C. as " *a Phœnician god across the Sea* " to bring down upon the ships of his enemies at sea an evil wind to destroy them and their rigging[2]—that is precisely the especial function of the Aryan Phœnician Barati.

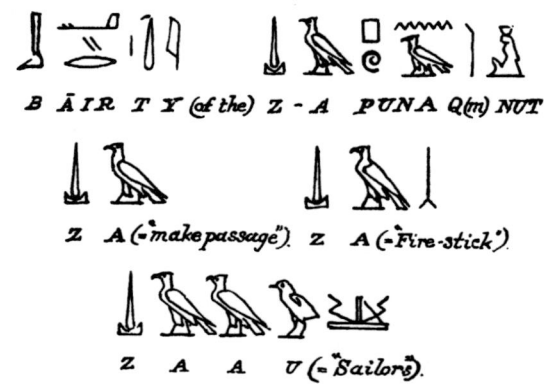

*B Ā I R  T Y (of the)  Z - A  P U N A  Q(m) N U T*

*Z  A (= "make passage")   z   A (= "Fire-stick")*

*Z   A   A   U (= Sailors).*

FIG. 18. Egyptian hieroglyphs for the Goddess Bāīrthy of the Phœnician sailors.

Moreover, the hieroglyph sign employed for spelling this word *Za* is not the usual serpent-viper sign, but it *is the Fire-drill* (see the sign above the letter *z* in Fig. 18). This picture-sign—whilst giving us the picture of the later-developed form of the two sticks of the Fire-drill for producing the sacred fire by friction for Sun-worship, in which the lower one is the matrix and the upper one the revolving stick, which was rapidly rotated between the palms of the operator until fire resulted—appears to be of special Phœnician import, to designate that land of Bāīrthy as the Land of Phœnicia, for the Phœnicians freely used the Fire-drill symbol for the Sun, as we shall see. *Za*, spelt by the same signs as in the above (Fig. 18), not only means " to sail, make

[1] The cuneiform text (see next note) has two signs after *na*, the first of which is possibly *gu*, which would give Za *Punagu*, wherein the latter name would be " Phœnicia."
[2] Kuyunjik fragment Brit. Museum Cuneiform Text, No. 3,500, Col. 4, l. 10.  B G.E. 2, 282. The cuneiform word therein rendered " river " primarily means " Sea."

passage";[1] but also "Fire-drill or Fire-stick;"[2] and this name is also spelt more fully in the Ancient Egyptian as *Zax* with the determinative sign for "wood."[3] Now this is the literal Sumerian word for Fire-brand (*Zax*)[4] with the synonym of *Bil* (or *Gi-Bil* The Great *Bil* or god Bel), and *it also is pictured in Sumerian writing by a Fire-Drill*, with the revolving stick in the palm of the hand; thus disclosing again *the Sumerian origin of an ancient Egyptian fundamental cultural word*. And *Za-hī* was an actual Egyptian title for the whole Phœnician coast;[5] and thus presumably designated it as "The Land of the Fire-cult."

Thus the tutelary Bāīrthy of the Ancient Egyptians and Assyrio-Babylonians appears to have been designated by them as "The Warrior Water-goddess of the Sailor Phœnicians of the Land of the Fire-drill cult." The significance of this Fire-cult of the Phœnicians for this votive Sun-monument of the Phœnician Barat at Newton and elsewhere in Early Britain will appear later.

Besides being the original of Britannia, this Phœnician tutelary *Barati*, or *Brihad*-the-Divine, is now seen to be presumably the *Brito-Martis* tutelary goddess of Crete, an island which, we shall see, was early colonized and civilized by the Phœnicians, who are now disclosed as authors of the so-called "Minoan" Civilization there. This goddess Brito-Martis was a Phœnician goddess, according to the Greco-Roman legends.[6] She was the divine "daughter" of Phoinix, the Phœnician king of Phœnicia, and was armed like Diana, with whom she was latterly identified,[7] with weapons for the chase, as she is also represented on Early Hittite seals,[8] and like the tutelary goddess *Parthenos*, a form also of

---

[1] B.E.D., 849.     [2] *Ib.*, 894b, see under *Tcha*.
[3] *Ib.* 894a, and *Za-tu* also means "Fire, Burn," 900b.
[4] See Br. 4577 and P.S.L., 362.
[5] Maspero *Hist. anc. de l'Orient*, cited by P.V.H., 736.
[6] Callimachus' *Hymn to Artemis*; and Antonius Liberalis. *Metamorphoses* ch. 30.
[7] S., 478, 12.
[8] C.S.H., 1922. Pl. 1, Fig. 1, and p. 17. The place of origin called "Lulubi," we shall see, is Halab or modern Aleppo in Syria-Phœnicia.

Diana.[1] She sailed from Phœnicia to Argos in Southern Greece, with its cyclopean masonry buildings of Hitto-Phœnician type at its old capital Tiryns. Thence she sailed to the adjoining island of Crete, where, pursued by the unwelcome attention of her admirer, Minos, she escaped by retreating to the sea—that is to the element of Barati and Britannia and the Barats. She then sailed to Aegina, an island in the Ægean off Athens, and disappeared there at the spot where stands the temple of Artemis or Diana.

The British bearing of this identity of Barati and Brito-Martis with Diana is, as we shall see later, that the first king of the Britons had Diana (who bore also the title of " *Pera-then* " or " Britannia ") as his tutelary, and on arrival in Britain is reported to have erected a temple to Diana on Ludgate Hill (on the site of the modern St. Paul's), and vestiges of this pre-Christian Diana temple there have survived. Indeed this Brito-Martis myth of the martial Bāratī of the Phœnicians seems to have been imported also by the Phœnicians with their Sun-cult into Britain, and to be presumably the source of the old popular phrase, still floating about in provincial Britain, of " O my eye and Betty Martin !" This phrase now appears to preserve possibly an old traditional invocation to the martial tutelary of the Britons, Barati or Britannia, wherein her name is shortened into Betty like the Irish " Biddy " for Bridget and couched in the popular and once common dog-latin form of the invocations in the Romish Church liturgies : "O mihi Brito-Martis "; if the first part of the sentence does not actually preserve an invocation to her under her old title of *Mahī* or " The great Earth Mother," the *Maia* of the Greeks and Romans, and the goddess " May " of the British May-pole spring festival.

---

[1] " *Parth*-enos " as a title for Diana and Athene appears to have been coined by the Greeks from that of Barati. It is used by Homer for a stately young wife (Iliad 2, 514), and for a maid or virgin (Iliad 22,127, etc.). A siren rock amid the sea near Sicily was called " *Parth*-en-op" (S. 1, 2, 13) wherein *op*, we shall see, was a Hitto-Phœnician affix for a "high" site. And the *Parth*-enios River in the Paphlagonian coast of the Euxine flowing from Midas city with Hittite remains, and inhabited by Trojan allies, *Cauc*-ones [Cassi ?] and Heneti or Veneti (S. 543) who accompanied Æneas in his flight from Troy, and the significance of which for Britain history will appear later, was a traditional abode of Diana or *Parth*-enos.

# ORIGIN OF NAMES BRITON AND BRITAIN 65

The names " Brit-on " and " Brit-ain " and " Brit-ish " also are derived from this Early Phœnician " Barat " title. The former two names, we are told in the Ancient British Chronicle, as seen later, were given to the people and the country by the first king of the Britons in Britain, after his own patronymic name. The original form of the name " Brit-on " is now disclosed to have been " *Barat*-ana " or " *Brihad*-ana." The affix *ana* in Hitto-Sumerian means "one" and is now disclosed as the primitive Aryan-Sumerian origin of our English word " one " and of the Scottish " ane " (which latter is seen to preserve more faithfully the *a* of the original Sumerian word) as well as the Sumerian source of the Greek and Roman ethnic affix *an* or *ene*.[1] Thus " Barat-ana " or " Brihat-ana " modernized into " Brit-on " means " One of the Barats or Brits." The earlier form of the name is better preserved in the name Dun-Barton or " Fort of the Bartons (or Britons)." We have already seen that it was spelt " Pryd-ain " by the Cymric Welsh and Pretan-(oi) by the Greeks. But the earlier form was simply " Bārat," in series with the " Prwt " or " Prāt " of the Newton Stone.

Similarly, " Brit-ain" for the " Land of the Brit," presumes a like original " Barat-ana " (or Brihat-ana), having for its affix the same Hitto-Sumerian *ana*. And this geographic use is in series with the Indo-Aryan names, Rajput-ana for " Land of the Rajputs," Gond-wana for " Land of the Gonds," etc. ; the Cappadocian Cataonia or " Land of the Catti," and the old Persian Susi-ana for Land of "Susi," and Airy-ana or Aīr-ān, the older form of Ir-ān or " Land of the Aryas or Aryans" for Persia. The Anglo-Saxon vagaries in spelling the name " Britain " well illustrate the dialectic variations in spelling proper names before the introduction of printing, and before the influence of the journalistic press has only relatively recently fixed the spelling of words rigidly in one stereotyped form—an important historical fact which

---

[1] This Sumerian *ana* is thus disclosed to be the Hitto-Sumerian source also of the Latin *una* " one," Greek *oin*-os, Gothic *einn*, *ains*, Swede *en* " one " ; Sanskrit *anu* " an atom " (i.e., the *one* separate particle) ; each by each and *ani* " a pin "—and the written Sumerian sign for this word " one " had the form of a pin.

requires always to be borne in mind when dealing with the ancient variations in spelling the same name : —

The Anglo-Saxons spelt the name " Britain " in their documents never as " Britain," but Bryten, Bryton, Breoton, Breoten, Breten, Broten, Brittan, Britten, Britton and Brytten.[1]

His further title of " Gy-āolownie " or " Gi-oln " requires a separate chapter to itself, as it discloses the identity of the Phœnician author of these inscriptions, Prwt or Prat, with the traditional " Part-olon king of the Scots " of the fourth century B.C., of the Ancient British Chronicles and the legends of the Irish Scots.

[1] B.A.S., 52.

# VIII

PHŒNICIAN BARAT OR " BRIT " AUTHOR OF NEWTON STONE INSCRIPTIONS DISCLOSED AS HISTORICAL ORIGINAL OF " PART-OLON, KING OF THE SCOTS," AND TRADITIONAL FIRST CIVILIZER OF IRELAND ABOUT 400 B.C.

*Disclosing Hitto-Phœnician Origin of clan title "Uallana" or " Vellaun(us) " or " Wallon " of Briton King Cassi-vallaun of Cad-wallon and of " Uchlani " title of the ruling Cassi Britons.*

> " The Scots arrived in Ireland from Spain. The first that came was *Parth-olomus* [Part-olon]; NENNIUS *History of the Britons*, 13.[1]
> " The clan of *Geleoin*, son of *Erc*-ol [*Ikr* ?] took possession of the islands of Orc [Orkney] . . . that is the son of *Partai* . . . went and took possession of the North of the Island of *Breatan*."—Books of Lecan and Ballymote.[2]

THE patronymic title of " *Prāt* " or " *Prwt* " used by this Phœnician Barat author of the Newton Stone inscriptions, taken in conjunction with his clan-title of " *Gy-aolownie* " or " *Gi-oln* "—now seen to be the " Geleoin " clan-title of the Irish-Scot histories above cited, and a name which drops in Briton, Gaelic, and Welsh its initial *Gi*, becoming " *olon* " or " *Wallon* "—leads us to the discovery of the historical identity of that king, with far-reaching effects upon the pre-history of the Britons and the hitherto unknown sources of their British Civilization. And it at the same time rehabilitates and establishes still further the historicity of

---

[1] In the Irish-Scot originals of Nennius' (Ninian's) Latin history the original form of the name is " Part-olon."

[2] In S.C.P., 23. The text gives Geleoin pp. 33, etc., often transcribed " Gleoin."

the Early British Chronicles and the traditional history books of the Irish-Scots, as cited in the heading, and in more detail below.

The juxtaposition of these two titles of the Phœnician Barat calling himself *Ikr* or *Icar*, namely *Prāt* or *Prwt* and "*Gi-oln*," coupled with the fact that the second inscription was in the Ogam, the especial sacred script of the Irish-Scots, suggested to me that the author was the actual historical original of "*Part-olon*, king of the Scots" and "son of *Erc*-ol *Parthai*," who, according to the Ancient British and Irish histories, arrived from the Mediterranean by way of Spain about 400 B.C. in the Orkneys, and who first colonized and civilized Ireland. Further examination fully confirmed and established this identity.

But before examining this evidence, his clan-title of "Gy-aolownie," or as it is written in the Ogam "Gioln," first requires some notice.

This name "Gy-āolownie" or "Gi-oln" is clearly the clan-name "*Geleoin*" or "*Gleoin*" of the Irish-Scot histories, to which belonged the first traditional King of the Scots in Ireland, Part-olon, and the clan which colonized North Britain in the prehistoric period, as cited in the heading, and also repeatedly referred to in the Irish traditional books. In the following further reference from these books we seem to have a memory of Part-olon's temporary location in Spain in the name "*Icathir*-si," which appears to be the "*Agadir*" name of the ancient Phœnician city-port of Gades, the modern Cadiz, outside the Pillars of Hercules; and also a memory of his remoter port of Tarsus, the ancient *Tarz* or *Tarsi* port of Cilicia, in the "*Traicia*" of this record:

"In the same year came [to Erin] . . . from the land of *Traicia* [*Tarsi* ?] the clan *Geleoin* . . . *Icathir*-si [Agadirs] was their name, that is . . . son of Part-olain."[1]

That title also is seen to be obviously the original of the second half of the title of "Katye-*Uchlani*," applied by Ptolemy, the Greek geographer of Early Britain topography,

[1] *Book of Lecan* fol. 286, and S.C.P., 30, and 323. See M.D., 315, for detailed note.

to the ruling tribe of Britons who occupied the home-province of the paramount king of the Britons in Cæsar's day, namely Cassi-*Uallaunus*, or Cassi-*vellaunus*, which extended from the Thames to the Wash and Humber (see later). And it is also seen to occur in its shortened form by dropping the initial *G* in the name of that king himself, as Cassi-*Uallaun*, the Cad-*Wallon* of the Cymri. This identity is seen in the equation :—

| Newton Stone | Irish-Scot Books | Ptolemy | Roman | Cymric |
|---|---|---|---|---|
| $Gy$-$\bar{A}olownie$ or $Gi$-$Oln$ | $=Geleoin$ $Gleoin$ | $=Uchlani$ | $=Uallaun(i)$ | $=Wallon$ |

The origin and meaning of that clan title now prove to be Hittite. The word *Ilannu* is defined in Babylonian as "The Hittite,"[1] whilst *Allānu* is "an oak"; and "*Khilaani*" or "*Xilaani*" is defined as "a *Khatti* (or Hittite) word for a corridor and porticoed windowed building or palace"; and it was especially used for Hitt-ite buildings in Cilicia;[2] and was imitated by the Babylonians.[3] This *Khilaani* is obviously cognate with the Akkadian *Khullanu* or *Xullanu* "wooden";[4] which thus discloses the Hitt-ite or Akkadian origin of the Greek word for "wood" *Xulon* or *Xylon*, and also of the English "*Yule*," which significantly is spelt in Gothic, *Juile* or *Jol*, and in Early English and Anglo-Saxon *Guili* or *Geola*, which also illustrate the dropping out of the initial *G* in the later word. It thus presumably designated originally the wooden character of these corridors and porticoed palaces of the Hittites, and latterly was applied to the builders themselves. The Phœnician branch of the Hittites were famous for their superior wood-craft as well as their masonry buildings. Thus Solomon says to the Phœnician king of Tyre, " Thou knowest that there is not among us [Israelites] any that can skill to hew timber like unto the Sidonians [Phœnicians]."[5]

[1] C.P.N. 31 ; also name of Kassis; *ib*. 85.  [2] M.D. 315.
[3] Thus, in the sixth campaign of Sennacherib the latter says (l. 82) that he erected a building "like a palace of the Khatti-land, which is called in the tongue of the Muru (or " Amorite " section of Hittites), *Khilaani* (or *Xilaani*)."
[4] M.D., 315. See S.E.D. under "Yule."  [5] 1 Kings 5, 6.

It thus appears that the Khilaani timber palaces of the Hittites with their porticoed windows and corridors were of the Gothic type, which is essentially a wooden style of architecture, especially as we shall find that the Hittite or Khatti or Guti were the primitive Goths. The Gothic style of architecture is nowadays supposed to have arisen no earlier than in the twelfth century of the Christian era ; but I long ago showed that it was used by the Indo-Scythians or Indo-Goths or *Getæ* (*i.e.*, Catti), in the second century A.D., in their sculptured representations of temples on the north-west frontier of India.[1] And this identity of the Hittites with the Goths now also explains the occurrence of the Gothoid arch in several ancient buildings of the Hittites in their old capital at Boghaz Koi in Cappadocia, dating back to at least about 1500 B.C.

As a clan-title, this " wooden palace " builder's title is found in Herodotus as Gelonus, the son of Hercules the Phœnician,[2] and Gelon, a contemporary King of Syracuse, a Phœnician settlement. It was probably used to distinguish culturally the manorial palace-dwelling Hittite overlords as " The Hall-dwelling aristocracy " from the lowly aborigines who lived mostly in caves or underground abodes, such as " Picts' houses." This wooden-palace origin for it appears probable also from the tribal title of " *Geloni*," mentioned by Herodotus, for a colony of fur-trading merchants in the Don Valley of Scythia or Goth-land (see Map), whose city was built entirely of wood, with " lofty " walls and temples,[3] and, like the Phœnicians and Early Britons, they were worshippers of the Corn Spirit Dionysos (see later) and they came from " the trading ports " of Greece,[4] suggesting Phœnician ancestry, as the Phœnicians were the chief traders in the ports of Ancient Greece.

In the form of *Khiluni* we actually find it used as a personal name amongst the Kassis of Babylonia, with the variant of

---

[1] See official reports of my deputation to collect " Greco-Buddhist " sculptures from Swat Valley for Imperial Museum, Calcutta in 1895. And L. A. Waddell " Greco-Buddhist sculptures from Swat Valley " in *Trans. Internat. Oriental Congress*, Paris, 1897. Sec. 1, 245, etc., when the photographs of these early Gothic arches were demonstrated by me.

[2] Herodotus, 4, 10, 3.   [3] *Ib.* 4, 108, 109.   [4] *Ib.* 4, 109.

# GIOLN TITLE AND BRITON "WALLON" 71

"Gilian."[1] This clan-title was also used by the Britons of Brittany in its ancient form of "Gualen,"[2] as well as by the Cymri for one of their chief seaports (in Carmarthen) Cet-gueli, the modern Kid-welly, which, the British Chronicles tell us, was an ancient port of the Scots or *Ceti* (*i.e.* Catti).[3] And dropping its initial *G* (like the *gueli* in Cet-gueli becoming *welly*) to form " Uallaun " it was the royal clan-title of the paramount Briton king of the Catti and Cassi of Britain, Cassi-uallaun or Cad-wallon, and also the ruling Briton clan-title throughout a great part of Britain.[4] One of the latter inscriptions, with a variant of " Katye-uchlani," is of especial interest here. It records the early Scottish clan-title of " Cat-uallauna " upon a monument of the second or third century A.D., near the south end of the Roman Wall at South Shields on Tyne.[5] This fine artistic monument of a Briton lady (see Fig. 19, p. 73), as its inscription tells us, was erected significantly by a Syrian "*Barat*" from the ancient Phœnician city of Palmyra, on the old trade-route from Tyre and Beirut to Mesopotamia, a city possessing a famous temple to the Phœnician Sun-god Bel, with a colonnade nearly a mile long. Its dedicator calls himself thereon " Barates," and records that he married a lady of the " Cat-uallauna " clan, whose death he mourns with the single pathetic word " Alas ! " Incidentally this monument is of great historical importance in showing

[1] C.P.N., 77 and 80.
[2] " Kad-Gualen " occurs in the ancient Breton chartulary of the Abbey of Beaufort (R. Maclagan *Our Ancestors*, 332).
[3] N.A.B., 14 ; Giles' ed. 389.
[4] *Uellaunius* occurs in an inscription at Caerleon, the ancient Briton capital at Monmouth (*Corpus Inscrip. Latin.* Berlin, 7, No. 126) *Cat-Uallauna* as clan-title of a Briton lady in inscription of about the second century at South Shields (*Ephemeris Epigraphica* 4, p. 212, No. 718a). Similarly, " *Ceti-loin* " as royal clan-title in an inscription of about fourth century at Yarrow in Selkirkshire. *Catuuelauni* occurs as name of tribe on monument of about third century at Castlesteads, Cumberland. C.B., 3, 456. *Uelauni* was a clan of Alpine people (*Corpus Inscript. Latin.* 5, No. 7817, 45) and *Uelaunis*, a man's name or title in Ancient Spain (*ib.* 3, No. 1589, 1590), where " Cat-*alonia*" is the name of an old province of the Phœnicians there.
[5] For details of this monument see Northumberland Archæolog. Socy.'s *Ephemeris* in previous note. I have personally examined this fine sculpture more than once in company with my old friend Dr. Jas. Drummond, formerly resident there, and to whom I am indebted for fine photos of the monument and its inscriptions by Miss Flagg.

that a Barat merchant from Syria-Phœnicia had come to Britain in the second or third century A.D., and had intermarried there with a Barat or Briton kinswoman of the Cat-uallauna or "Cath-luan" royal clan.

This Cat-uallauna clan also existed in the Selkirk district of Scotland about the fifth century A.D. At Yarrow stands a funereal monolith with a rustic Latin inscription of about the fifth century A.D., dedicated to the memory of a chieftain of the "*Ceti-loin*" clan—a monument which I have personally examined and taken a squeeze-impression of its inscription.[1]

The local tradition also of this "Gy-aolownie" or "Gi-oln" clan-title seems significantly to have survived in the neighbourhood of the Newton Stone in "*Clyan's* Dam," the name of an embankment near the Don to the South of the Mount Bennachie (see map, p. 19) and in the adjoining "Cluny," or anciently *Clony* or *Kluen*,[2] castle in the neighbourhood. And in the latter usage it seems noteworthy that the epithet is parallel to the use of "Khilaani" to denote a Hittite palace.[3]

[The dropping out of the initial guttural G is a not uncommon dialectic change; thus it is seen in this actual word as "Cet-*gu*eli" becoming the modern "Kid-*w*elly"; similarly "Gwalia" becomes "Wales"; "Gwite" or "Guith" (the other name for the Isle of Wight even in Alfred's day) becomes "Wight"; and "William" is the remains of an earlier "Gulielm" or "Guillame"; and Catye-uchlani became "Cat-wallaun," or "Cad-wallon." Thus "*Prāt-gioln*" of our Newton Stone inscription, presumably with the meaning of "Prat-the-Lord,"[4] became dialectically "*Part-olon.*" And be the meaning of "gioln" what it may, the fact nevertheless is clearly established that "*Prat-gioln*" is the source of the later form of "*Part-olon.*"]

---

[1] The first lines read *Hic memoriæ Ceti-loin*, followed by what Mr. Craig Brown reads as *ennig fii princep et nudi Dumno gen*, etc. A cast of this monument is in the museum at Hawick.

[2] This name has been supposed to be derived from the Welsh *glan*," a brink or side," but, apart from the anomaly of a Welsh name in this locality, its use here as "Clyan's Dam" presumes a human sense.

[3] Similarly "Cluny" is found in France for the famous galleried monastic palace of that name.

[4] In Irish-Scottish *glonn* = "champion, hero," in the Book of Lecan; see C.A.N., 341.

FIG. 19.—Briton Lady of *Cat-uallaun* clan, wife of *Barates*,
a Syrio-Phœnician.
(From sculpture of about 2nd century A.D. in South Shields.)

[1] Reproduced by permission of publishers of *Handbook to Roman Wall*.

Thus the Phœnician Barat author of our Newton Stone inscription is revealed as the historical original of the traditional Part-olon, the first "king of the Scots," who arrived from the Mediterranean *via* Spain about 400 B.C. and introduced civilization into Ireland, and whose clan colonized and civilized North Britain, as cited in the heading.

The detailed account of King Part-olon's arrival in Ireland, as preserved in the traditional histories of the Irish-Scots,— the historicity of which is thus established—now becomes of great historical interest and importance ; and especially the record of his relations with the North of Britain and Don Valley. At the outset it is to be noted that in the Latin versions of the Ancient British Chronicles by the Romish monks Nennius (or Ninian) and Geoffrey, the name " Part-olon," as it occurs in the Irish-Scot vernacular histories, is latinized into " Partholomus " in order to adapt it to the New Testament apostolic name of Bartholomus or Bartholomew.

The account of Part-olon's arrival in Ireland is thus recorded by Nennius in his history of the Britons written about 800 A.D.[1] :—

" Long after this (the arrival of the Picts) the *Scotti* arrived in Erinn from the coast of Spain. The first that came was Partholomus, with a thousand followers, men and women. But, a plague coming suddenly upon them, they all perished in one week."

The statement here that he arrived from Spain is of great significance, as further evidence of his being an Aryan Phœnician, coming, like Brut, by way presumably of the famous Phœnician seaport of Gades (the modern Cadiz) or " House of the *Gads* (or Phœnicians) "—*Gad* being, as we shall see, an especial variant of " Catti " used by the Phœnicians, and coined upon the tribal title of *Khat* or *Xat*, i.e. " Scot," ; and he is called in the Chronicles a " Scot." He is also reported by Geoffrey to have come from Spain ; see later.

The traditional place of his landing in Ireland is stated in the Ogam " Book of Ballymote "[2] to have been Scene in the Bay of Kenmare in Kerry county, and that place and

[1] N.A.B., 13.
[2] Dates to about the tenth century A.D. in its present recension.

## PART-OLON IN SCOTLAND & IRELAND 75

district is significantly the chief seat of the Ogam-inscribed monuments in the British Isles.[1] The old saga says :—

"They landed from their safe barks,
In the clear blue port of the fair land,
In the bay of bright shields of Scene."[2]

The devastating " plague " above referred to was possibly the hostile attack of the aboriginal race in Erin called Fomori, who, the Irish Chronicles tell us, attacked Part-olon and his party, but were defeated by him in a great battle ;[3] though Geoffrey's Chronicles, on the other hand, state that his descendants continued to live in and colonize ultimately the whole of Erin ; and the Irish Chronicles refer to these descendants of his sons there in later times.

But his inscription in Aberdeenshire now shows that he himself eventually left Kerry for the North of Scotland— possibly through a spirit of adventure for fresh worlds to conquer—leaving, according to tradition, two sons settled in Kerry.[4]

Some details of Part-olon's voyage from Spain *via* Ireland to the North of Scotland are preserved in Geoffrey's traditional Chronicles, but these appear to confuse his emigration northwards to Aberdeen with his settlement on the Irish coast of Kerry. Geoffrey records that Part-olon arrived in Ireland during the reign of the Briton king named Gurgiunt, who, about 407 B.C., succeeded his father King Belinus, the twenty-second in direct succession from Brutus (see Appendix I), and who ruled nominally the whole of Britain from Cornwall to Caithness,[5] with his chief capitals as Osc (or Caerleon) on the Usk, and Tri-novantum (latterly London) on the Thames. He also inherited from his father the province of " Dacia " (which, from the context, was obviously in Denmark, and not the Dacia of the

---

[1] Of the 193 Ogam-inscribed monuments in Ireland 92 are in Kerry ; and in the district of Scene in that county are 46 (B.O.I., 378).
[2] Book of Ballymote, trans. by Dr. Connellan, f. 12 ; and compare K.H.I.J., 67. "Scene" is spelt in ancient texts "Sgene," obviously cognate to "Scone," the crowning place of the ancient Scot kings near Perth.
[3] R.H.L., 589.
[4] Irish Chronicles call these sons Slainge and Rudraige (Roderick) K.H.J., 62.         [5] G.C., 3, 5.

Danube Valley) and he was returning thence through the Orkneys with his fleet when he met Part-olon there with his fleet.

Geoffrey records: "At that time Gurgiunt was passing through the Orkney islands, he found thirty ships full of men and women. And upon his enquiry of them the reason of their coming thither, their Duke named *Partholoim* approached him in a respectful and submissive manner, and desired pardon and peace, telling him that *he had been driven out of Spain*, and was sailing round those seas in quest of a habitation. He also desired *some small part of Britain* to dwell in, that they might put an end to their tedious wanderings ; for it was now a year and a half since he and his company had been out at sea. When Gurgiunt Brabtruc understood that they had come from Spain, *and were called Bar-clenses*, he granted their petition, and *sent men with them to Ireland* . . . and assigned it to them. There they grew up and increased in number, and have possessed that island to this very day."[1]

This Orkney location for Part-olon and his fleet whilst on their voyage from " Spain " appears to be a reference to his sea-passage from his colony in Kerry to the Garrioch Vale of the Don of Aberdeen, the site of his monument in question. That portion of the narrative which describes him as returning from the Orkneys to Kerry is presumably a confusion, introduced by later Irish copyists and translators of these ancient chronicles before Geoffrey's time, having substituted " Ciarraighe "[2] or Kerry of " Ireland " (where Part-olon had, according to the tradition, we have seen, established an Irish colony) for "Garrioch," the district of our Newton monument in the north-east of Scotland and not very far distant by sea from the Orkneys. Geoffrey expressly states that Part-olon " desired some small part of *Britain* " —not Ireland, though Ireland is mentioned later on, presumably to adapt it to the Irish-Scot tradition. And the relatively short stay of Part-olon in Kerry and his sudden disappearance from there, ascribed conveniently to " plague," would be thus accounted for, as well as his permanent colonization of the south of Ireland by the two sons left there.

Indeed, I find that positive, more or less contemporary,

[1] *G.C.* 3, 12.
[2] This is the Irish form of the name "Kerry," B.O.I., 16.

# CATTI IN ORKNEY & SHETLAND

inscriptional evidence for the presence of the early Catti or Khatti with their Cassi Sun-Cross, in the region of the Orkneys, actually exists to confirm the historicity of this tradition of the visit of the early Catti to " the Orkney Islands."

[At Lunasting on the mainland of Shetland (" or Land of the *Shets*," which name, as we shall find, is a softened variant of " *Khat*," or " *Xat*," or " Hitt-ite," and the " *Ceti* " of Early Scot monuments) is a pre-Christian Cross monument bearing an Ogam inscription and on its top a large engraved Sun-Cross of the " *Kassi* " type (see later). This inscription also has proved such a puzzle to Celtic experts, who have variously deemed it to be " Celtic," " Gaelic," " Welsh," etc., that the Celtic scholar, Dr. A. Macbain, petulantly declares that : " it is neither Welsh nor any other language ! "[1] It reads however, I find, without difficulty in a dialect of the Gothic of the Eddas (see text in foot-note [2]) ; and with strict literalness in translating the Gothic words reads as follows :—

" (This) Cross at *Xattui*-Cuh (city) of the *Xatt* (or *Khatt*).[3] (This) Cross (is erected by) *Xahht* Manann (son of) Hacc Ffeff (who) rests aneath,[4] weening in hope[5] nigh."[6]

---

[1] W. F. Skene, *Highlands of Scotland*, 1902, 398.

[2] It is published by B.O.I., 365, pl. 49 ; and compare Southesk P.S.A.S., 1884, 201*f*., whose transliteration of the Ogam differs but little from mine, and in particular he renders the critical names in question " *Xattui*-cuh," " *Aatts* " and " *Aahhtt* " respectively, transliterating the same sign X, when loosely written as *Aa* in the two latter instances. On the other hand, Dr. W. Bannerman (P.S.A.S. 1908, 343*f*.) reads the inscription in reverse direction or upside down ! My transliteration of this Lunasting inscription into Roman letters is as follows—the inherent short *a* of the consonants being expressed in small type and the other letters in capitals :

+XaTTUI CUH XaTTS :   ±H XaHHTT MaNaNN : HaCC FFEFF : NEDT. ON Na.

[3] The final *s* in the text XaTTS is the genitive not only in Gothic but in Hitto-Sumerian and Kassi, and it thus corresponds to possessive affix 's of the English language, now disclosed to be derived from the Hitto-Sumerian, through the British Gothic. On the *Cuh* affix, see subsequent text.

[4] The *Nedt* of the text is the literal equivalent of the English " neath," the Gothic Eddic *Nedr*, the Scandinavian *Nad*, " rest," neath, beneath ; (compare V.D. 448, 450) and is, I find, derived from the Sumerian and Kassi *Nad* " lie down, resting place." Compare B.B.W. II, 203—which is thus disclosed to be the remote Hitto-Sumerian source of the Scottish " nod " and English " neath " and " nether."

[5] The *On* of the text is the Eddic *On* for *Von*, *Won* or *Vān*, the English " ween " and " fain " and " yearn " and is usually translated by Scandinavians as meaning " hope " (*cp*. V.D., 472, 684,–5). It appears to be derived from the Sumerian *Inu* " to plan, heart, secret " (*cp*. B.B.W. ii. 14, and P.S.L. 192.).

[6] The final *Na* of the text seems the Eddic *Na* or " nigh." (*cp*. V.D., 447.)

The term *Cuh* for "town" or "city," for this old town of the Khatti or Xatti in Shetland, where this "Cassi" Cross monument is recorded as having been erected, is of especial Hitt-ite significance. It is now disclosed as being obviously the equivalent of the common modern name "*Koi*" for a "town" throughout the old "Land of the Hittites" in Asia Minor. Thus, the old chief capital of the Hitt-ites in Cappadocia is still called Boghaz *Koi* or "Boghaz town." It also seems to me to be the Hitt-ite origin of the common modern term for town or village in Indo-Persia, namely the nasalized "*Ga*(*n*)*w*." It also seems to be the Hitt-ite origin presumably of the affix *Cu, Go, Gow* of place-names in several of the older centres of civilization in Scotland, such as "Glas-*cu*"—the old spelling of "Glasgow"—and thus giving the meaning of "Town of the Gaels (?)"; "Cads-*cu*" or "Town of the *Cads* (or Phœnicians)," the old documentary spelling of Cadzow, the original name for Hamilton (residence of the premier Duke in Scotland) on the Clyde, with its old pre-Christian Cross (see Fig. in Chapter XIX.); "Lar-*go*" on the Fife coast, with its cave-deposits of prehistoric men, "standing stones" and pre-Christian Cross monuments; "Linlith-*gow*," an ancient residence of the kings in Scotland; and so on.

Further evidence for the presence of early *Khatti* in the Orkney region is forthcoming from the district-names on the adjoining mainland. Thus "*Caithness*," the ancient "*Kata*-ness" or "Nose (of the Land) of the *Caiths* or *Kata*," a people who are now disclosed to be the Catti or Khatti (or Hittites). And the contiguous "Sutherland" was, up till the Norse period of about the ninth century A.D., called "*Catuv*" or "*Cat*-land"[1] or "Land of the *Cats*," that is, the "Catti" or Hitt-ites. And the Duke of Sutherland is still called locally "Diuc *Cat*" or "Duke of the Cats" (*i.e.*, Catti).]

Moreover, the tribal title given to Part-olon by Geoffrey above noted, as "of the *Bar-clenses*" confirms still further his identity with the Phœnician author of our Newton Stone inscription. This prefix "*Bar*" is obviously the early contracted form of "Barat," which was written by the Sumer-Phœnicians simply as "*Ba-ra*"; and "*clenses*" is obviously a latinized form of our Phœnician's *Gyāolownic*" or "*Gioln*"—the "Uchlani" title of the Cassi tribe of Catti, which, we have already seen, represents apparently the Hittite

[1] *cp.* Mackay's commentary on Ptolemy's *Geography of Scotland* in P.S.A.S. 1908, 80.

title of "*Khilāni*," and a term which was especially current in Cilicia,[1] whence, our author tells us in his inscription, he came. And we thus see why the Briton Catti king, with lineage directly continuous from the first Brit-on king "Brut" (see Appendix I), and living in the more highly civilized part of Britain in the south, with only nominal rule north of the Forth (according to the Chronicles), should have befriended his fellow-clansman Part-olon in extending Hitto-Phœnician civilization and colonization in this remoter part of Britain, when he learned that he was of the "Bar-clenses," for this was the same Catti or Hitt-ite clan to which that Early Briton king himself belonged.

The further title given to Part-olon of "Son of *Sera* or *Sru*" in the Irish chronicles[2] is a striking confirmation of his Hitto-Phœnician ancestry. This ancestral name "Sera or Sru" obviously preserves the patronymic king Barat's front title of "*Sar*," which was the favourite form of the ancestral Barat's name selected by the founder of the First Phœnician Dynasty in Mesopotamia, who regularly called himself "Son (or descendant) of *Sar*."[3] It thus attests the remarkable authenticity of the tradition of the Irish-Scots, whilst further confirming the Aryan Hitto-Phœnician ancestry of Part-olon, who is now revealed on the solid basis of concrete history as the first civilizer, not only of Ireland, but of the north of Scotland, about four hundred years before the dawn of the Christian era.

The migration of Part-olon from Cilicia to the British Isles about 390 B.C., according to the British Chronicle historical tradition (see Appendix I), was probably owing to the massacring invasion and annexation of Cilicia and Asia Minor by the Spartan Greeks in 399 B.C. These Spartan invaders were significantly opposed by the Phœnician fleet in 394 B.C., but not finally defeated by the Phœnicians at

[1] M.D., 315.
[2] Book of Leinster (Book of Dun) 15*a*, 234, etc. "Pàrtolon mac Sdairn meic *Seura* meic *Sru* (see CAN 229). For reading Sera see R.H.L., 580*f*. Goialdus in *Topographia Hibernica* (Dict. 302, Rolls ed. 5, p. 140) calls him "*Sere* filius de stirpe Japhet filii Noē (Noah)."
[3] Detailed proofs in my *Aryan Origin of the Phœnicians*.

sea till 387 B.C. (see Appendix I). And the escape of Part-olon about 390 B.C. (and Part-olon is recorded to " have been driven out " of his country), occurring in this interval of the occupation of Cilicia by the Spartan enemies of the Phœnicians is significant, and is in keeping with the record in the British Chronicle, which is thus confirmed by the positive facts of known contemporary history of Part-olon's homeland in Eastern Asia Minor at that period.

# IX

## LOCAL SURVIVAL OF PART-OLON'S NAME IN THE DISTRICT OF HIS MONUMENT

*Disclosing Phœnician origin of names Barthol, Bartle and Bartholomew, and " Brude " title of Kings of the Picts.*

THE local survival of the name of this Brito-Phœnician Part-olon in several parts of the district of his monument at Newton confirms still further the decipherment of his name on his monument, as well as the ancient, though now forgotten, importance of his name in the history of Civilization in Northern Scotland.

Whilst there is *Wartle* and *Wart-hill* a few miles to the east of Part-olon's monument (*w, p* and *b* being dialectically interchangeable, as we have seen), and *Bourtie* is the name of the parish a few miles down in the Don Valley below the Stone, on the way to the sea, what seems more significant is the ancient hamlet bearing the name of " *Bartle* " or "*Barthol* Chapel" which stands about nine miles to the north-east of the site of the Stone (see map, p. 19) in the old parish of Tarves.

Bartle or Barthol Chapel occupies the site and preserves the name of an ancient Roman Catholic chapel dedicated to St. Bartholomew, which in pre-Reformation days was latterly transferred to the jurisdiction of the great monastic abbey of Arbroath in the adjoining county of Forfar. In the register of the Arbroath monastery are references to this chapel of Bartholomew, also called the " capella de Fuchull " (or Firchil), dating back to between A.D. 1189 and 1199, referring to its transfer to the monks of Arbroath.[1]

[1] For these historical details regarding Barthol Chapel I am indebted to the kindness of the Rev. A. R. Sutter, minister of Barthol Chapel parish. The present parish of that name was constituted in 1874 at the opening of a memorial church at Barthol by Lord Aberdeen, whose residence is at

It appears to have been regarded at the Vatican as of some historical importance, if the report is to be trusted, which says :— " Tradition has it that a certain nobleman heard at the Vatican prayers offered up for the restoration, amongst a list of others, of St. Bartholomew's chapel in Tarves, (now Barthol Chapel Parish)."[1]

"Bartle Fair," one of the oldest in the district, is held annually at Barthol Chapel, on the last Wednesday of August, that is a date corresponding to St. Bartholomew's Day, the 24th August in the Romish calendar. It is an old-time fair, where tubs, spoons, fir-lights (torches), sheep, etc., were sold; now it is chiefly confined to horses.[2]

The change of the old traditional name "Part-olon" by the monks into "Barthol" and "St. Bartholomew" is easily explicable from the known facts in the early history of the Christian Church, where the Romish priests in proselytizing the people were in the habit of incorporating the pre-Christian heroes of the latter into their lists of Christian saints. That change of the name, indeed, had already been made by Nennius[3] and Geoffrey[4] in their later translations of the British Chronicles, wherein they call Part-olon of the Irish Chronicles "Partoloim," "Partholomus," and "Bartholomæus."

With reference to this alteration of the name to "Bartholomew," it is interesting to note that the apostle Bartholomew or properly "Bartholomaios," as his name is written in the Greek text of the New Testament, bears an Aryan and not a Hebrew name,[5] which contains the element Barat or "Brit-on," conjoined also with the Aryan affix *oloma* which is a recognized

---

Haddon House, not far distant. The Arbroath Register records that between 1199 and 1207 Matthew, Bishop of Aberdeen, confirmed the grant which had been made to the monks of Arbroath, of the kirk of Tarves "with the capella de Fuchull"—which is shown to be identical with Barthol Chapel. And other records go on till 1247.

[1] From Mr. Sutter's notes.   [2] *Ib.*
[3] Sect. 13.   [4] Ch. iii., 12.
[5] Although his name is, as noted by S.B. Gould, " not Hebrew," it is usually assumed to be so, and is conjectured by Hebrew scholars to mean the Hebrew *Bar* = son and *Talmai* of "Talmai," and analogous to Peter's title of " Bar-jonah"; although the latter is never used by itself. As to the theory that Bartholomew is identical with Nathaniel, the *Encyl. Biblica* (489) says " It is a mere conjecture."

## ST. BARTHOLOMEW AN ARYAN PHŒNICIAN

variant of "olon." He appears to have been a Gentile; and according to St. Jerome was the only one of the twelve apostles who was of noble birth, and author of a "Gospel of Bartholomew," latterly deemed "heretical,"[1] possibly because of the inclusion of some Aryan Sun-worship. He is specially mentioned in connection with Philip, who also, like Bartholomew and Andrew, bore a Gentile and non-Hebrew name; and, according to the Roman Martyrology, was a native of Persia, and the traditional apostle for the shores of the Black Sea, Armenia, Phrygia and *Lyconia*[2]—that is, as we have seen, in the Barat regions, on the border of Cilicia. It thus seems probable that his proper name was also "Part-olon" or "Part-olowonie." And, curiously, the traditional place of St. Bartholomew's martyrdom was "*Albana*," which is usually identified with Albana, on the shore of the Caspian, north of the Caucasus, the modern Derbend.[3] Can it, however, be possible that the old Roman monks, in naming their chapel at Barthol in the Garrioch "St. Bartholomew's," were influenced by this Albana tradition, in the belief that it might be "Alban," the ancient name for Britain, to which part of the reputed bodily relics of St. Bartholomew had come? The miraculous distribution of the bodily relics of St. Bartholomew followed to some extent the sea-route followed by Part-olon. From Asia Minor the relics were believed to have sailed miraculously, by themselves, along the Ægean, and reached, amongst other places, Sicily, (Lipari), Spain (Toledo), and an arm reached Canterbury in Alban-Britannia. At Canterbury,[4] St. Bartholomew's arm, which performed many miracles, appears to have been one of the main attractions for the pilgrims to that shrine, and gave its name to "St. Bartholomew's Hospital" in the High Street at Canterbury, "erected" [or rebuilt (?)] by Thomas Becket, about A.D. 1150, as an hostel for the poor Christian pilgrims of Britain in this forgotten era

---

[1] *Encyclop. Biblica*, 489.
[2] B.L.S., ix, 253.    [3] *Ib.*, 258*f*.
[4] Canterbury, deriving its present name from the **Anglo-Saxon** title of *Cantivara-byrig* or "Burg of the Men of Cant or 'Kent '," was called by the Britons "Durwhern," which bears some resemblance to the "Tarves" of the Barthol Chapel.

of St. Bartholomew worship.[1] The Aryan Saint also gave his name to "Bartholomew Fair" (in Smithfield, London), which was the principal fair in England in the Middle Ages (from 1133 onwards) for cloth, pewter, leather and cattle and for miracle-plays; and St. Bartholomew's Priory on this site, and later St. Bartholomew's Hospital, was given the rights of sanctuary by Edward II. Perhaps the reason for Barthol Chapel, as well as St. Bartholomew's Day and Fair in the rest of Britain, falling into oblivion in the Roman Church, was the ignominy attaching to papacy through the infamous massacre on that day of the Huguenot Protestants in Paris in 1572.

Another medieval local "Bartholomew" of repute is found in the vicinity of the Newton Stone at Leslie on the Gadie River to the east of Mt. Bennachie (see map, p. 19). The founder of the Leslie family and Earl of Garrioch is called "Bart-olf" in a Charter of the twelfth century, and is reputed to have been a Saxon or Hungarian notable who came over with the suite of the family of Queen Margaret, sister of Edgar Atheling and spouse of Malcolm Canmore;[2] or he may have been one of the many Anglo-Saxon refugees who were driven to Scotland by the Norman Conquest of England. It seems possible that this Bartolf or Bartholomew, as he is also called, and who became the Earl of Garrioch who founded the house of Leslie, or "*Lesselyn*" (as this name was spelt in the old Charters) may originally have borne this latter name as his real surname—"Lassalle" and "La Salle" being Germano-French names—and that he may have adopted, with his "Garrioch" title, the old traditional name of Part-olon or Bartholomew, still clinging to that locality. The fact that the old Barthol Chapel was outside Garrioch proper, and was not finally transferred to the Arbroath

[1] It was the custom formerly in Brittany (or "Little Britain") for cataleptic patients to spend the night before St. Bartholomew's day dancing in the parish church—an infallible cure for fits. The custom is said not to be altogether extinguished in Brittany at the present day. (B.L.S., 260.) This custom of dancing with reference to fits suggests to me that "St. Vitus' Dance" possibly derives its name from the pagan Saint Burt or "Brit" or "Prwt," in which the *r* has dropped out, as in "Biddy" for "Bridget," especially as there is no reference to dancing or fits in connection with the youthful martyr St. Vitus in Gould's life of the latter.

[2] W.A.H., 36.

diocese until 1189-1199, presumes that it was in existence before Bartolf's time.

The "*Brude*" title, also, of so many of the ancient historical kings of the Picts in Scotland—whose chief stronghold in the north of Scotland at the dawn of literary Scottish history in the sixth century A.D. was Aberdeenshire to Inverness—now appears to be clearly derived from this "*Prwt*" or "*Prāt*," with variant "*Brut*," title of this early Phœnician "Part-olon, King of the Scots" of our monument.

When modern native Scottish history opens in the pages of Adamnan, the disciple and biographer of the Irish-Scot missionary prince Columba (*b.* A.D. 521, *d.* A.D. 597)[1] we learn that Columba, in his mission for the conversion of the pagan Picts of Scotland, visited, in A.D. 556, the king of the Picts named "Brude." This king whose name is also significantly spelt "*Bruide*" and "*Brides*," and latinized into "*Brudeus*" (parallel with "*Brutus*") resided in his fortress at Inverness, now called Craig Phadraig, on the Moray Firth—to which leads the old trunk road from Aberdeen which passes the site of the Newton Stone. Receiving Columba in a friendly manner, he invited him to a trial of skill against his Druid high priest; and on Columba defeating the Druid by his superior "magic," King Brude embraced Christianity and was with many of his subjects baptized by Columba—an event which, it should be noted, happened forty years before the arrival of St. Augustine in Britain to convert the English to Christianity. He also granted Columba permission to open a missionary station and build a monastery at Deer, about twenty miles to the north-east of this stone; and he also *confirmed Columba in his possession of the Island of Iona.* This latter incident indicates that King Brude or "Bruide" was king of the whole of Scotland and the Isles; and he held the Prince of Orkney hostage.

Significantly also, this kingly title of "Brude" or "Bruide," also spelt "Bridei, Bride, Brete and Breth,"[2] was used by the great majority of this King Brude's predecessors in the King-Lists of the Picts, as preserved in the Colbertine

[1] A.L.R., 149*f*.   [2] See S.C.P., 436.

MS. Codex.[1] This list, which is substantially identical with the versions of the same in the Irish Books of Ballymote and Lecan, extends from the first eponymous king of the Picts in Scotland, called " Cruithne," to *Bred*, the last king of the Picts, about A.D. 834.

This name " Cruithne " for the first king of the Picts in Scotland is held by Celtic scholars to be the Pictish form of spelling "*Pruithne*" or "Briton," on their theory that the Picts and Celts or Gaels substituted $Q$ for $P$ in their spelling of names, and also substituted $B$ for $P$ in such names—though it may be observed that Celtic scholars do not explain why the Picts and Gaels who had $Q$ in their alphabet do not use it in spelling this name, but employ a $C$ instead. If " Cruithne," however, really represents " *Pruithne*," as believed, then the first king of the Picts in Scotland bore a name substantially identical with " *Prwt*," the erector of the Newton Stone monument, and thus presumably was identical with him.

This " Cruithne " (or " Pruithne ") is stated to be the " son of Cinge," and this is expanded by the Irish Book versions above cited into " Cinge, son of Luchtai, son of Parthi or *Parthalan*."[2] This last statement is interesting and important as connecting Cruithne traditionally with Part-olon—a name which we have seen was only a family title, his personal name being Itar. But this making him to be the third descendant from Partolan is presumably a gloss by later Irish scribes to suit the Irish tradition that Partolan settled in Ireland and died there, and that it was his descendants of the third generation who migrated to Scotland.

" Cruithne " (or " Pruithne ") is followed in the Pictish king-list by the names of " seven sons " who are each supposed to have reigned consecutively after their father. But, as the Irish versions state, these names are those of the seven divisions or provinces of medieval Scotland, beginning

---

[1] The " Colbertine MS." is a fourteenth-century Latin copy made at York of an earlier old Gaelic or Irish original written in the tenth century A.D., and is now in the " Imperial " Library, Paris (No. 4126). It contains the well-known " Pictish Chronicle," of which the best published edition with translation is by W. F. Skene (S.C.P.), where a facsimile of the most important part of the MS. is given.
[2] S.C.P., 23 and 24.

## "BRUDE" TITLE OF KINGS OF PICTS

with "Fib" or Fife, and including "Fortrenn" or Perth, and "Got" or "Caith" in the Irish versions, which is Caithness.[1] The Irish versions further state that all the seven divisions of North Alban were under the paramount rule of "Onbeccan, son of Caith."[2] This prominence given to Caith (which, we shall see, is the tribal title "Catti") and his son indicates that the succession in Scotland passed from son to son, from the first king Fruithne (as Celtic scholars explain "Cruithne") who appears to be the Prwt (or Part-olon) of the Newton Stone, and that other four kings named with Onbeccan, after the seven provinces, were probably names in the contemporary branch dynasty in Ireland. The succession also in the case at least of the last two of these four kings, namely Gest and Wur-Gest or Ur-Gest, was clearly from son to son, as we shall see that the prefix *Ur* means "son of." This fact is of great significance, as showing that *these early kings of the Picts succeeded in the paternal line and not in the maternal line, and were therefore presumably Aryan and not themselves Picts, which latter* were in their matrilinear succession, which, we shall see, was a vestige of the primitive Matriarchist promiscuity of the Picts.

After these preliminary kings there now follows *an unbroken line of twenty-nine kings of the Picts, each bearing the title of* "Brude" *or* "Bruide"; and they are stated to have ruled jointly over both Hibernia and [North] Alban.[3] This remarkable list of "Brude" or "Bruide" kings is as follows, and it will be noted that some of the names are essentially Aryan[4]—the version in the Irish list, when differing in spelling from the Colbertine MS., is added within brackets:—

1. Brude Bont
2. Brude *or* Bruide-Pant (B.-Pont)
3. Brude-Ur-pant (-Ur-pont)
4. Brude-Leo
5. Brude-Ur-Leo[5] (Uleo)
6. Brude-Gant
7. Brude-Ur-gant
8. Brude-Guith[6] (Gnith)
9. Brude-Ur-Guith (-Ur-Gnith)
10. Brude *or* Bruide-Fecir (-Feth)

[1] S.C.P. xxii; 4 and 24.  [2] Colbertine MS. ed.S.C.P., 23.  [3] *Ib.*, 4 and 24.
[4] Thus Leo, and Gant = Knut or Canut (?), Guith = Goth, and so on.
[5] The Colbertine MS. reads here "Ur-leo;" see A.C.N., 137.
[6] *Ib.* "Guith" and "Urguith," 137, and Skene's eye copy facsimile also may be so read.

11. Brude-Ur-Fecir (-Ur-Feichir)
12. Brude-Cal
13. Brude-Ur-cal
14. Brude-Cuit[1] (-Cint)
15. Brude-Ur-Cuit (-Ur-Cint)
16. Brude-Fet
17. Brude-Ur-Fet
18. Brude-Ru
19. Brude or Bruide-Uru[2] (Ero)
20. Brude-Gart
21. Brude-Ur-gart
22. Brude-Cinid (Cind)
23. Brude-Ur-cinid (Ur-Cind)
24. Brude-Uip
25. Brude-Ur-Uip
26. Brude-Grid
27. Brude-Ur-Grid
28. Brude-Mūnd (Muin)
29. Brude-Ur-mūnd (Ur-Muin)

In scanning this king-list it is seen that "Brude" or "Bruide" is clearly used as a title, prefixed to the proper personal name of each king. Indeed, the Irish text says, "And *Bruide* was the name of each man of them, *and of the divisions of the other men* of the tribe (Cruithne)"[3]—and this latter statement is important, as presumably meaning that the "other Cruithne men" also bore this title of "Bruide" or "Briton."

It is also noteworthy that all of the names after the first are in pairs, in which the second is formed by first surname repeated with the prefix *Ur*. This *Ur* presumably represents the Celtic *Ua* "a descendant or son"[4]; and, what is of great importance is that this practice is precisely paralleled in the Sanskrit and Pali king-lists of the Aryan Barat kings, which often prefix *Upa* or "son of"[5] to the name of a king bearing the same name as his father. This fact now appears to disclose the Aryan source of the Cymric prefix *Ap* or *Up* in personal names, such as "Ap-John" or "Up-John," with the meaning of "Son of John." And it also proves that at least half (if not the whole) of these "Brude" kings were, like the first on the list, succeeded by their sons, i.e., by patrilinear succession.

Similarly, amongst the historical kings of the Picts, succeeding Columba's patron Brude (or "Bruide" or "Bridesh"),

---
[1] A.C.N., 37, and Skene's eye copy also may be so read.
[2] *Ib.* 137.
[3] See Skene's translation *op. cit.* 26. The Irish text of the Books of Ballymote and Lecan is: "Bruide adberthea fri gach fir dib, randa na fear aile; ro gabsadar l. ar c ut est illeabraibh na Cruithneach."
[4] *Cp.* C.A.N., 360.
[5] *Upa* in Sanskrit and Pali= "below", "under," and when prefixed to personal names, as it often is, means "son" *cp.* M.S.D., 194.

who is surnamed " son of Malkom (or " Melchon " or " Melchq ")," of 556 A.D.,[1] are the following bearers of this title " *Brude* " :—

Brude or " Breidei,"[2] son of Fathe or Wid, 640 A.D.
Brude or " Bredei," son of Bili or " Bile ", 674-693 A.D., contemporary with and mentioned by Adamnan.
Brude or " Bredei," son of Derelei, 699 A.D.
Brude or Bredi or Brete, son of Wirguist or Tenegus, 761 A.D.
Bred or Brude, son of Ferat or Fotel, the last King of the Picts, 842 A.D.[3]

Now, it is significant to find that, although these kings, entitled " Brude," Bruide " or " Bridei," were kings of the Picts —a race which, we shall see, were *non*-Aryan and *pre*-Briton aborigines—they themselves appear to have been not Picts in race but " Bart-ons" or Brit-on Scots, i.e. Aryans. The second of these later Brudes, or " Bredei-the-son-of-*Bili* (or *Bile*)," was the son of the Scot king " Bili " or " Bile " (that is a namesake of the Phœnician Sun-god *Bil* or *Bel* of our inscription) who is called " King of Strath-Clyde " and whose *dun* or fort was Dun-Barton or The Fort of the Bartons (i.e., Barat-ons) or Britons on the Clyde. His son Brude or Bredei is called " King of Fortrenn " or Perth, indicating his residence there.[4] He had, besides, a kinsman who was also king and called " King Brude," who latterly assisted in the defence of Dun-Barton against the Anglo-Saxon invaders.[5]

This presumes that the people whom Partolon-the-Scot ruled from the Don Valley in the fourth century B.C. were also Picts ; and that these later kings, bearing the title of Brudes or " *Bruides*," and claiming descent from " *Pruithne*," were of

---

[1] He was born 504 A.D. and died 583. Another king " Bruidhi son of Maelchon was slain in battle at Coicin (Kincardine) in 752 A.D., according to " The Annals of Tighernas," and in the same year " Taudar son of Bile " and king of Alclyde (or Dunbarton) died (S.C.P., 76). This king Bile (named after the Sun-god Bil) of Dunbarton died 722 and was *succeeded by his son*.

[2] For these variant spellings of the name Brude or Bruide in the Colb. MS. and Irish books see S.C.P. 3 and 28, etc. ; also " Register of the Priory of St. Andrew's." Fol. 46-49 in A.C.N. 145, etc.

[3] See foregoing also A.C.N. 139-147. This last king of the Picts was succeded in 843 by Kinade son of Alpin or Kenneth MacAlpin, whose son was Constantine.

[4] S.C.P., cxix.     [5] A.L.R. 149, etc.

his kindred, if not remote lineal descendants ; and that the confederacy between the Picts and the Scots, of which we hear so much in the history text-books, was a confederacy in which the Scots were the rulers and leaders in battle, and the Picts the subjects whom they had civilized, more or less. This relationship appears to have continued down to the ninth century A.D. when the Scot " kings of the Picts " were still using a dialectic form of the old ruling Aryan *Catti* title of " *Barat*," like the Aryan-Phœnician Khatti-Kassi king of our Newton Stone inscription, " Prat-(gya-) olowonie " or " Part-olon, King of the Scots," who, I find, also presumably bore the alternative title of " Cath-laun," as the first traditional king of the Picts (see Appendix II). And, as a fact, the Don Valley was an especial abode of the Picts in prehistoric times. The remains of their subterranean dwellings are especially numerous there.[1]

This now brings us face to face with the much-vexed and hitherto unsolved question " Who were the Picts ? " This question, however, can be better tackled after we have examined through our new lights the traces of the prehistoric aborigines whom Part-olon found in occupation of Ireland, which was also a Land of the Picts.

[1] Writing on " Picts' earth houses " J. L. Burton (Hist. of Scotland, i, 98) says " They exist in many places in Scotland, but chiefly they concentrate themselves near Glenkindy and Kildrumony on the upper reaches of the *River Don in Aberdeenshire. There they may be found so thickly strewn as to form subterranean villages or even towns.* The fields are honeycombed with them." And *cp.* J. Stuart on " Subterranean Habitations in Aberdeenshire." Archæologia Scotica, 1822, ii, 53–8.

# X

PART-OLON'S INVASION OF IRELAND ABOUT 400 B.C. DISCOVERS FIRST PEOPLING OF IRELAND AND ALBION IN STONE AGE BY MATRIARCHST *VAN* OR *FEN* "DWARFS"

*Disclosing Van or " Fein" Origin of Irish Aborigines and of their Serpent-Worship of St. Brigid and of the Matrilinear Customs of the Irish and Picts.*

> " Two score days before the Flood,
> Came *Ceasair* into Erin . . .
> Ceasair, daughter of Bheata
> The first woman *Ban* [*Van*?] who came
> To the Island of *Ban-bha* [Erin] before the Flood : "
> KEATING'S *Hist. of Ireland*, 48–50.[1]

IN searching the Irish-Scot traditional records for references to Part-olon and his Phœnician invasion of Ireland, the relative historicity of a considerable part of the Irish tradition for the remoter pre-historic period, extending back to the Stone Age, becomes presumably apparent. Although the old tradition, as found in the Books of Ballymote, Lecan, Leinster, etc., is manifestly overlaid thickly with later legend and myth by the medieval Irish bards who compiled these books from older sources, and expanded them with many anachronisms and trivial conjectural details, introduced by uninformed later bards to explain fancied affinities on an etymological basis ; nevertheless, we seem to find in these books a residual outline of consistent tradition, which appears to preserve some genuine memory of the remote prehistoric period. This enables us, in the new light of our discoveries in regard to Part-olon, to recover the outline of a seemingly genuine tradition for the prehistory of Erin and Alban, and for the first peopling of Erin in the hitherto dark prehistoric

[1] Ed. Joyce.

period of the later Stone Age, in the nomadic Hunting Stage of the early world before the institution of agriculture, marriage, and the settled life.[1]

Part-olon's invasion of Ireland (which, we have seen, occurred about 400 B.C.) is referred to in the Irish-Scot books as "*the second*" of the great traditional waves of immigration which flowed into that land.[2] The first of these traditional waves of immigration into Old Erin, in so-called pre-diluvian times, is of especial interest and historical importance, as it seems to preserve a genuine memory of the first peopling of Ireland in the prehistoric Stone Age.

This first traditional migration of people into Erin is significantly stated in the Irish-Scot records, as cited in the heading, to have been led by a woman, Ceasair or Cesair. This tradition of a woman leader appears to me to afford the clue to the matrilinear custom (or parentage and succession through the mother and not through the father), which "Mother-right," according to the Irish and Pict Chronicles, prevailed in early Erin (see later). This custom is admittedly a vestige of the primitive Matriarchy, or rule by Mothers, which was, according to leading authorities, the earliest stage of the Family in primitive society, in the hunting stage of the Stone Age, when promiscuity prevailed in the primeval hordes before the institution of Fatherhood and Marriage (see Fig. 20 for archaic Hittite rock-sculpture of a matriarch).

This tradition, therefore, that the first immigrants to Ireland were led by a woman is in agreement with what leading scientific anthropologists have elicited in regard to primitive society, and is, therefore, probably a genuine tradition. It is also in keeping with the first occupation of Erin having occurred in the Neolithic or Late Stone Age period (a period usually stated to extend from about 10000 B.C. to about 1500 B.C. or later), as is established by the archæological evidence in Ireland. It is also in agreement with the physical type of the early aborigines of

---

[1] This chapter was written before the appearance of Prof. Macalister's work on Ancient Ireland, and is in no way modified by the latter.

[2] *Book of Invasions* by Friar Michael O'Clery, 1627, based on Book of Ballymote fol. 12, and Book of Leinster, etc.; B.O.I., 14, etc.; and K.H.I.J. 63.

# BAN, FEIN OR VAN MATRIARCHS IN IRELAND 93

Hibernia, as elicited by excavations, and of the bulk of the present-day population, who are mostly of the dark, smaller-statured, long narrow-headed "Iberian" or "Mediterranean" type (see Chapter XII.), as opposed to the element of the tall fair Aryans, the Irish "Scots" of Bede and other early writers, now presumably located mostly in Ulster.

FIG. 20.—A prehistoric Matriarch of the Vans (?) of the Stone Age.
From a Hittite rock-sculpture near Smyrna.
(After Martin.[1])
Note the primitive type with low forehead and eyebrow ridges.

The name of this first Matriarch of Erin, "*Ceasair*," appears to be cognate with "*Kvasir*" of the Gothic Eddas, who was the "wise man" of the sacred magic jar or cauldron, and a hostage given by the *Wans, Vans* or "*Fens*" (presumably the "Fene" or "Fein" title of the early Irish) to the Goths.[2] While the Matriarch of the Vans and priestess

---
[1] This rock-cut bust was carved at the entrance to a sacred grotto, presumably of the Mother-cult, near the alpine village of Buja, to east of Smyrna, and near Karabel, with its Hittite sculpturings. Its drawing by A. Martin is given by Perrot (P.A.P. 68).
[2] A.Y.E. 160 etc.; and V.D. 361.

of the cauldron, was herself the " wise-woman " or wizardess and priestess of the Serpent and other demonist totemistic cults in primitive times—cults which survived into the modern world as witchcraft.

This Matriarch Ceasair, or Cesara, is reported to have landed with her horde at Dunn-m Barc or " The fort of the Barks or [Skin-] Boats," now Duna-mark in Bantry Bay on the south-west coast of Erin—the bay adjoining Part-olon's traditional landing place at Scene in Kenmare Bay. This name " Bantry Bay," means " Bay of the Shore of the *Bans*,[1] and is in series with " Fin-tragh Bay " or Bay of the Shore of the *Fins* further north, in which " Ban " or " Fin " appears to be an ethnic title of this matriarchist horde. The next neighbouring town on the east is *Ban*-don or " Town of the Bans," with a river of that name, which attests the great antiquity of that title ; and to its north is *Ban*-teer, and further east along the south coast is *Bann*-ow River, and the *Bann* River in Wexford, which, we shall see, is associated with a stand made by the tribe of this matriarch against later invaders, and the Boinne or Boyne River on the east coast, admittedly named after the River-goddess " Boann," with the old Irish epic town of *Finn*-abair (or *Fenn*-or),[2] and vast prehistoric dolmen tumuli at New Grange with intertwined Serpent symbols,[3] all presumably belong to this same series of the Ban, Fen or Van horde, or its descendants.

Indeed, we find in Ptolemy's map of Ireland, drawn before 140 A.D., that the tribe inhabitating the south-west of Ireland, from Kerry, where Cesair landed, and extending through Cork to Waterford were still called by Ptolemy " *Ioueoni-oi*"[4] (i.e. " *Weoni* " or " *Veoni*," the Greeks having no W or V) which we shall see is a dialectic variant of " Wan," " Van " or " Ban." And the chief seat of Cesair's descendants at the epoch of Part-olon's invasion of Erin, and where he defeated these aborigines, was called " The plain of *Itha*,"

---

[1] *Trag* or *Tracht*= " shore or strand," compare C.A.N., 359.
[2] See J. Dunn *Tain bo Cualange* (from Book of Leinster) 1914, 377.
[3] C.N.G., several specimens.
[4] P.G. lib. secundus, C. ii, p. 29 ; and map I (p.2) in Europa tabula. This map with a Greek verse is reproduced in British Museum *Early Maps* No. 3 postcard series.

which was thus presumably so named after "The plain of *Ida*," which in the Gothic Eddas was the chief seat of the Van or Fen Matriarch and her Serpent-worshipping dark-complexioned dwarfs.

The name "*Ban*" or "*Bean*," by which this Irish Matriarch as well as her country is called,[1] literally means in Irish "*Fian*," "female" or "woman," and is thus probably cognate with the matriarchist tribal title of Van or Wan and Fene; and its cognate is applied to the traditional aboriginal dwarf people of both Ireland and Alban, who were popularly associated in legends and myth with the Picts.[2] It also seems to be the source of the later popular term, "Fene" or "Fein" for those claiming to be aboriginal Irish. Those primitive Fenes, Fins or Bans appear, I think, to be clearly the primordial, aboriginal, dark dwarf race "*Van*" or "*Fen*" in the Gothic Edda Epics, who were the chief enemies of the Goths, in the solar cult of the latter. And, significantly, this primitive dark race of Van of "The plain of Ida" is called in the Eddas (which I have found to be truly historical records of the rise of the Aryans) "The Blue Legs,"[3] implying that they painted their skins with blue pigment, which suggests that they were the primitive ancestors of the "Picts," as they now are seen to be.

This same "Van" or "Ban" people, moreover, were, as we shall see clearly, at least in the later Stone Age, the early aborigines of Alban or Britain. Their name survives widely in the many prehistoric earth-work defensive ramparts and ditches over the country, still known as "Wans' Ditch" or "Wans' Dyke"[4] used synonymously with Picts' Dyke."

---

[1] In addition to the *Ban and Fin* local names noted, it will be seen in the text cited in heading that the whole of Ireland was called "Ban-bha" or Ban the Good (?)."

[2] M.F.P. *passim*.

[3] "Blain legiom" in Volu-spa Edda, E.C. 1. 20, and *cf*. Ed. N., p.2, verse 9, and Ed. V.P., i, 1941, 38.

[4] P.E.C. 3, p. xiii., notes that those Wans' Dykes which have been excavated were "Roman" or "post-Roman" in the cultural objects found. This, however, merely implies that these prehistoric Wans' Dykes which are in best preservation occupied such good strategic positions that they were utilized by the Romans and in post-Roman times, just as we shall find the Romans utilized old pre-Roman Briton roads, such as "Watling Street," by repairing and appropriating them.

This ancient ethnic name of "Wan" or "Ban" also survives broadcast in many places in Britain especially in the neighbourhood of these old Wan's Ditches and subterranean "Picts' Houses," and the so-called, though erroneously so, "Early Briton settlements."

Instances of the survival of such ancient "Van" and "Ban" names in Britain are cited below. In examining these series of the ethnic name "Van" in different dialects we shall see the dialectic equivalency of the labials B, P, F and V, and the interchange of the latter with W, the OU or IOU of the Greeks, which are all dialectic variations in spelling the same name, well recognized by philologists.

[Instances of the survival of these "Van" and "Ban" ethnic names in Britain are seen in the following :—Wan-stead near Houndsditch east of London, Wands-worth, Fins-bury, Finchley, Banbury, with its legend of " an old woman," Wantage, Wainfleet on the Wash, Wensley, Winslow, Win-chester, the *Venta* or *Vends* of the Romans, Win-chelsea, Windsor, Ventnor, Wendover, Windermere with Wans' Fell Pike, numerous Ban-tons, Bangor or "Circle of the Bans" on the Welsh coast, with so-called "Druid" circles and its namesake on Belfast Loch, and Banchory in Aberdeenshire with the same meaning and prehistoric "circles" and an early seat of the Picts.[2] And there are several Roman station names at important pre-Roman towns and villages bearing the fore-name of "*Vindo*" and "*Venta*" in series with *Pent*-land as an ancient title for Mid-Scotland, surviving in the "Pent-land" Hills of Lothian, and in the "Pent-land" Frith for the sea-channel on the extreme north of Britain, which "Vent" and "Pent," we shall see, is in series with "Vindia" as an ancient title of a Western Van region in Asia Minor. (see Map).

In Wales the famous "*Van* Lake" was until lately a place of popular pilgrimage for the Welsh, and significantly it was sacred to a fairy Lady of the Lake,[3] presumably a deified Van matriarch-priestess ; and South Wales, in which it was situated, was called Vened-ocia or Vent-uria[4] (the Gwynned of the Welsh), and the ancient Briton capital there, Caerleon, was called by the Romans "Venta Silurum" ; and Gwent, *i.e.*,

---

[1] See also M.I.S., 295.
[2] The first Christian missionary to the Picts, St. Fernan, a disciple of Paladius, died here in 431 A.D.
[3] R.H.L., 422.
[4] S.C.P., 153, as late as the twelfth century A.D.

"*Went*," was a title for the whole of Wales.[1] And the "Guenedota" or "Uenedota" of Ptolemy appears to be Cumbria.

In North Britain also, in Roman times, were many stations at pre-Roman towns bearing the prefix Vinda or Vindo, of which two were at the Tyne end of Hadrian's Wall, which is sometimes called locally "The Picts' Dyke," namely at Vindo-bala in the line of the wall, and Vindo-mora to its south and not far from the earth-works called "Early Briton settlements" in Northumbria. In Ptolemy's map, which from its practical accuracy remained the old navigating map up till about the fifteenth century, are several important Ban, Vin or Fin towns and peoples which have since lost that title. Thus inland from the Solway, a chief town of the Selgovæ (who, we have seen, were the "Siliks" or "Cilician Britons") was named "Bantorigon" (with the prefix Kar, i.e. Caer="fort"). In the Frith of Clyde, or "Clota" of Ptolemy's map, Vindogara appears to have been the ancient name of Ayr or Ardrossan ; and Vanduara was the name of Paisley, where the old local name for the Cart River on which it stands was Wendur (or Gwyndwr).[2] Banatia was the chief town inland between the Clyde and Fife, and there are more than one Vinnovion. In modern times, besides the survival of several Ban-tons, Findon or Findhorn, several bays called Fintry, Loch Fin or Fyne, are the Pent-land Hills in the Lothians, centring at Pennicuick, and on the extreme north the "Pent-land Frith."]

These latter facts suggest that the whole of North Britain, from at least the Lothians to Caithness, if not the whole of Britain, had formerly been known as "The Land of the Pents, Venets, Bans, Fins or Vans." Indeed, as we shall see later, the old name for Ancient Britain as "*Al-Ban*" means probably "The Rocky Isle of the *Van* or *Ban*."

The "Finn-men" pygmies also, in their skin-boats, of Orkney and Shetland tradition and legend, who were the *Peti* (or "Picts") dwarfs whom Harold Fair-hair is said to have exterminated in Shetland, and who, according to local tradition, were the ancestors of the small dark element in the Shetland population,[3] were obviously, I think, of this same prehistoric dwarf matriarchist race of Van or Fen, of whom Cesair in the later Stone Age led a horde from Alban into Bantry Bay and first peopled Ireland.

[1] R.H.L. 499, where "Nether Gwent" is used for South Wales, and presupposes an "Upper Gwent" for North Wales.
[2] M.I.S. 197, 326.   [3] M.I.S., 140.

Similarly, stretching across the continent of Europe eastwards, I find traces of the prehistoric presence and presumable routes of migration for the east, of this primitive dark dwarf race of Vans or Fens by the tracks left by their old ethnic title in place, district and ethnic names, which have persisted many millenniums after the primeval sway of these primitive Van hordes had been swept away by countless later waves of new invading tribes of different race and higher culture who dominated these primitive people, but yet retained many of the old Van place-names containing that ethnic title.

An early and presumably the original chief centre of dispersion of the main horde of dwarf Vans in the Stone Age was, I find from a mass of evidence which cannot be detailed here,[1] the shores of the inland sea or great Lake of Van in Armenia, on the west flank of Ararat at an elevation of 5,200 feet above the sea (see map and Fig. 21).

FIG. 21.—Van or "Biana," ancient capital of Matriarch Semiramis and "The Children of *Khaldis*" on flanks of Ararat.
(After Miss Bishop).
(This represents the modern city founded on that of the Hittites and Greco-Romans).

Lake Van, which is about twice as large as the Lake of Geneva, was traditionally the common head-water source of both the Tigris and Euphrates Rivers of Mesopotomia, until separated by a prehistoric volcanic upheaval, and the local geological and topographical conformation of those regions

[1] Details in my *Aryan Origins*.

is in keeping with this tradition. The large town of Van and its lake thus stands on the old land-bridge connecting the three continents of Europe, Africa and Asia; for Asia Minor is west of the Caucasus, and in its flora and fauna, and also geologically, is part of Europe rather than Asia proper. Situated on the great immemorial trade-route running east and west between Europe and Asia, it was traversed by Xerxes and his famous Ten Thousand, and an actual inscription by that Persian emperor on his hasty return from the Grecian campaign and Hellespont in 480 B.C. is engraved on the citadel rock there, showing the directness of the route to Europe. And significantly the founding of the town of Van is ascribed by Armenian tradition to Semiramis, that is, the great legendary Queen-matriarch of prehistoric times. And this part of Eastern Asia Minor was a centre of the Matriarchist cult of the Mother-goddess and her "*Galli*" priestesses down to the Greco-Roman occupation.

These matriarchist aborigines of Van, disclosed to be presumably of the primitive stock of the pre-Aryan Fein, are called "*Biani*" in the cuneiform inscriptions of their Hittite rulers about the ninth century B.C. They are also called therein "The Children of *Khaldis*,"[1] or "Children of the River"—which title, we shall find, is apparently the source of the names "Chaldee," "Galatia" and "Kelt," and anthropologists find that primitive men distributed themselves along the river-banks, and were literally "Children of the River." These Van or Biani were clearly, I find, the "*Pani*" aborigines of the Indian Vedic hymns and epics who opposed the Early Aryans in establishing their higher solar religion before the departure of the eastern branch of the Aryans to India. They were possibly also, I think, the remote prehistoric originals of the "Fan" barbarians, as the Chinese still term generally the barbarous tribes on the western frontiers of the Celestial Empire, as far at least as Asia Minor.

In physical appearance the primitive Vans, as the "*Pani*" of the Vedas and epics, are described as "dark or

[1] S.I.V., 1882, 454, etc.

black-complexioned " and " demons of darkness " who lived with their cattle in caves. They were presumably of the smallish-statured, dark, long-headed " Dravidian " tribes of Indo-Persia, akin to the Iberian type, and represented by the present-day nomadic Yuruk and Gipsy tribes of Van and the adjoining region of Armenia[1], as opposed to the modern " Armenians " in that region, who are one of the intruding round-headed Semitic races which swept into Asia Minor in later times, making it a medley of diverse races.

The westward line of migration, in the Stone Age period, of these primitive hordes from this early centre at Lake Van, when scarcity of food and pressure of over-population set them " hunger-marching," appears to be indicated, I think, by a more or less continuous chain of their ethnic name left along the trail of their movements from Lake Van westward, through Asia Minor to the Dardanelles and Bosphorus, and across Europe to Alban or Britain, (see map). This line of " Van " and " Khaldis " or " Galatia " names extends along the Upper Euphrates to the Halys Valley of Cappadocia, to Galatia and along the " *Vindia* " hills to Phrygia and the old " Phrygian Hellespont " and Bosphorus, and across those straits along the Danube to Vienna and Austrian Galicia to Fin-land and the southern shores of the Baltic and westwards to Iberia and Iberian Galicia and Gaul, and thence to the British Isles.

Remains of an interesting survival of the warrens of these primitive cave-dwelling Vans are found still tenanted at the present day, on this westward route at *Venasa* (modern Hassa) to the west of the crossing of the Halys River (Turkish, Kizil Irmak) and south west of Cæsarea (or Kaisarie), in the south west of Cappadocia, on the ancient trade route to the sea through the Cilician Gates of the Taurus.[2] Here in the great plain, studded with cliffs of soft dry volcanic rock, an area of " about fifty miles each way " is honeycombed with countless caves and subterranean branching burrows, resembling generally the " Picts' houses " and the so-called,

---

[1] See on these tribes Prof. F. v. Luschan, *Early Inhabitants of Western Asia* in JRAI, 1911, 228, 241.
[2] M.H.A., 167, etc.

but wrongly so, " Early Briton settlements " found in Britain. These cave-dwellings and burrows in the Venasa district are still occupied to the present day by swarms of a nomadic people commonly known to Europeans as " The Troglodytes (or ' Cave-dwellers ') of Cappadocia." These people live of choice in these old burrows, like conies. They are reported by travellers to be in appearance a race distinct from other modern races in Asia Minor, but have not yet been examined by anthropologists. From the name of their district " Venasa " and their cave-dwelling habits, they are presumably an isolated detachment of the primitive Van horde, which has become hemmed in and stranded by the passing tides of alien invaders which have swept over that land in later ages, from East and West. A recent visitor to these cave-dwellers, Mr. Childs,[1] gives graphic descriptions of these people and their warrens, from which the following account of one of the burrows is extracted :—

It, too, was honeycombed with passages and cells, of which some had been exposed by weathering as in the cliff. While I looked at this primitive dwelling, something moved in a hole close to the ground, and the head of a chubby brown-faced child appeared. It came out as much at home and unconscious of its surroundings as a slum-child in an alley ; but on seeing me drew back out of sight with the startled manner and instant movement of a wild animal."[2]

After such a picture of the subterranean lairs of the primitive Van in " The Land of the Hittites," we can better understand how the highly-civilized ruling Aryan race, the Hitto-Phœnicians, living in fine timber-built houses above ground, should distinguish themselves from the lowly aboriginal cave-dwellers by the epithet " Mansion-dwellers "—Khilani or " Gyaolowonie."

The chain of Van names left by the various swarms of these Van hordes of hunters in their progress westwards from the Van Lake region of Asia Minor into Europe and up the Danube valley by Vienna and its " Vanii regnum " or " Kingdom of the Vans," and Wend-land of Germany to

---

[1] W. J. Childs *Across Asia Minor on Foot* 1917, 217, etc.
[2] *Ib.* 227.

Fin-land, and westwards to Vannes, the port of the Veneti in Brittany bordering Alban, seems evidenced by the following amongst other such names, ancient[1] and modern, surviving even in regions where the dark Van dwarfish type is no longer prominent, or has been swept away (see map).

Vanand was the Greco-Roman name for the district between Van and the Upper Halys at Sivas.[2] Vanota was at the crossing of the Halys near Cæsareia on the border of Galatia, where St. Gregory wrote his twentieth epistle and noted that the name "Vanota" was not Greek, but native Galatian.[3] In Galatia, Vindia on the old Hittite royal road to Ephesus and the Bosphorus,[4] and Fanji.[5] In Phrygia, Oinia or Vinia,[6] and Panasios, and to the south Oionandos or Vinandos in Cilicia, Bindeos in Pisidia, and Pinara in Lycia.[7] On the Hellespont, Banes with its lake on inner end (modern Bari),[8] and Pionia in Troad on flank of Mount Ida on Samnos River.[9] On the Bosphorus, Pandicia or Pantichion, the first stage on ancient road from Rum (or Constantinople) to Asia Minor; and all in the traditional area of the Matriarchic Mother-cult and "Amazons."

Across Europe from the Hellespont and Bosphorus, up the Danube valley, the undoubted Van names in various dialectic forms are especially abundant. Wien or Vienna, the Vindo-bona of the Romans with its "*Vanii* Regnum" or "Kingdom of the Vans" still preserves the name of its original settlers. To its south is Veni-bazar in Albania, and in Roman times the Vennones and Pannonii tribes of the Vindelici race, which included the Briganti (i.e. Phrygian Vans), peopled the Upper Alpine Danube to the Rhine.[10] North of Vienna along the Upper Danube was located the old Wend tribe, extending across Austrian Galicia and Bohemia to Eastern Germany, with several "Vend" place-names, to the Baltic opposite *Fin*-land. And, regarding the latter name, it now appears possible that the modern stigma attaching to the name "Fin" may be owing to an old tradition based on the forgotten memory of the lowly origin and status of the race formerly bearing that name.[11] The whole southern

---

[1] The old Greco-Roman records for Asia Minor, derived from Ramsay's Historical Geography (R.H.G.), are mostly those of ancient Byzantine bishoprics and important mission stations.
[2] R.H.G. 290, who finds that that district extended from Kars to Sebasteia (Sivas).
[3] *Ib.* 288.   [4] *Ib.* 142.   [5] *Ib.* 226 and 405.   [6] *Ib.* 144.
[7] *Ib.* 386.   [8] *Ib.* 159, etc.   [9] *Ib.* 155.   [10] S. 206: 4, 6, 8.
[11] There are now two racial types in Fin-land, the tall, fair, long-headed Aryan type, and the short, darker, round-headed Slav or "Alpine [Swiss]" type, neither of whom are of the dark, long-headed type of the Van dwarfs who were of the Dravidian or "Iberian" type.

## ARRIVAL OF PREHISTORIC VANS IN BRITAIN 103

coast of the Baltic from Sarmatia westwards to Denmark was occupied by the Venedæ and Vindili tribes (with a sound bearing the name Venedicus).[1] In Iberia also the Viana port on the Linia river and another Viana in the Eastern Pyrenees may possibly preserve this ethnic name. Similarly may the Vienne and Ventia on the Rhone, Vanesia in Aquitania, retain that name; and clearly so Vannes, the capital of the Veneti of Brittany in Gaul, who gave Cæsar so much trouble and who were tributaries or allies of the Britons. Their capital is significantly the site of vast prehistoric dolmens and menhirs, a class of funereal monuments which was prevalent amongst the later Vans or Feins and their descendants in the British Isles under Briton rule.

Into Alban, latterly called "Britain," these nomad hunting hordes of primitive Matriarchist "dwarfs" from Van probably began to penetrate before the end of the Old Stone Age, as the receding glaciers withdrew northwards from the south of what is now called England and uncovered new land. They appear to have been the small-statured prehistoric race whose long-headed skulls (see Fig. 22) are found in the ancient river-bed deposits and caves, associated with weapons and primitive "culture" of the Old Stone Age, and also in some of the long funereal "barrows" of the New Stone or Neolithic Age, which latter is generally held to have commenced in North-western Europe about 10000 B.C.

The first hordes of these Van "dwarfs" probably crossed from Gaul by the old land-bridge which still connected Alban with the continent. They appear to be presumably the oldest inhabitants of Alban (excluding the few stray earlier forms of taller and broader-browed man of whom traces have been found in the south of England in the older Stone Age period) and so may perhaps be practically regarded as the aborigines of Alban. Indeed, the name " Alban " seems to me possibly coined from their ethnic name Van, Bian or Ban, with the prefix *Al*, as *Ail* in Celtic means " Rock," cognate with Chaldee *al, ili, ala* " high mount "[2] and English "hill"; so that "Al-Ban" might thus mean "The Rock (Isle) of the Ban or Van."[3] It is this rocky

[1] See Ptolemy's map and D.A.A., pl. 5.
[2] A.D. 41.
[3] An eponymic traditional source for "Albion" is referred to later.

aspect of North Britain, at least, which impressed Scott in his well-known lines :

> " O Caledonia ! stern and wild,
> Land of the mountain and the flood." [1]

And "Alban" for long remained a popular title for Scotland, after "England" had replaced "Alban" or "Albion" for South Britain.

Many millenniums must have elapsed after their arrival in Alban, before the small herds of such primitive dwarf nomads filtered through the river-valleys of Alban and into the enlarging northern land left by the retiring glacial climate and rising beaches. And many more millenniums must have elapsed before such a rude land-people, under pressure from behind by succeeding waves of fresh herds from the continent, would venture to migrate to Ireland across the sea, which would however be narrower at that period. When ultimately hard pressed and hemmed in by enemy clans against a narrow sea-board, it is conceivable that a small horde of these Matriarchists, seeking escape from annihilation, may have ventured out to sea in their small skin-boats for refuge in outlying islands, and eventually reached Erin. And such were probably the circumstances, I think, under which the Matriarch Cesair and her herd reached Bantry Bay in Erin in the later Neolithic Age,[2] where, safe from hostile pressure, they naturally would name that island "The Good *Ban* Land," (Ban-bha).

The first of these Ban or Van or Fene Matriarchs in Ireland, Cesair, presumably brought with her to Ban-try Bay or "The Bay of the Shore of the Bans," the two especially sacred fetishes of the Van Matriarchist Serpent-cult, the Magic Oracle Bowl or Witches' Cauldron (*Coirean Dagdha* or "Churn of Fire "[3] of the Irish Celts), and Fal's Fiery Stone

---

[1] Scott, *Lay of the Last Minstrel,* vi, 2.
[2] From the traditional landing place being on the south-west corner of Erin, it is possible that she and her herd started from Vannes on the western coast of Brittany or Lands End ; but more probably from Wales.
[3] " Dagda " is usually rendered " the good hero," from Celtic *dag.* " good" but it seems to me more probably to be derived from *daig* " fire, flame."

(Lia Fail of the Irish Celts).[1] These fetishes figure freely in the later Irish legends and myths, although they do not appear to be expressly mentioned until a later period, after Part-olon's invasion, when they are in the hands of a later branch of the same Serpent-cult people called "The tribe of the goddess Danu" (Tuatha de Danaan), who, significantly also are stated to have migrated to Ireland from Alban.

This tradition of the existence of these two Matriarchist Van fetishes amongst the prehistoric Feins in Ireland is of great importance for the origin of the prehistoric Serpent-cult in Ireland, and it affords additional proof of the identity of the prehistoric Fein Matriarchist immigrants into Ireland with the prehistoric Matriarchist Van or Fen dwarfs of the Van district of Asia Minor, as described in the Gothic Eddas. These Gothic epics—which, after detailed analysis, I find to be truly historical Aryan records of the establishment of the First Civilization in the World—make frequent reference to the use of the Magic Oracle Bowl or Witches' Cauldron for divination as a special utensil of the Serpent-worshipping Matriarchists in Van and Asia Minor and Chaldea. This magic bowl was especially associated with Kvasir, the namesake of Cesair, as already noted. And Fal's Fiery Stone was the materialized thunderbolt of the Dragon-serpent of Lightning, and the invincible magical weapon of *Baldr*, the son-consort and champion of the Van Matriarch in the Eddas; and his exploits therein as the champion of the Matriarch correspond generally with those of his namesake *Fal* in the Irish legends. This identity of the Irish *Fal* with the Van leader Baldr of the Eddas is further seen in the frequent title of the champion of the Irish Feins as "*Balor* of the Evil Eye." So intimately was Fal identified with the early Ireland of the Feins that Erin was called "Fal's Isle" (Inis Fail); and "Fal's Hill" was the title of the sacred hill at the ancient capital, Tara.

[1] In the later Irish legends Fal's Stone, essentially a missile, is made to be a fetish oracle, which cries out on the Coronation Day of the Celtic kings, and hence is supposed to be the Coronation Stone carried by the Scots from Ireland to Scone and afterwards taken to Westminster, as "The Coronation Stone." See Skene "*The Coronation Stone*."

This early introduction of the Serpent-cult and its fetishes into Ireland in the Stone Age by these Matriarchist Vans now explains for the first time the real origin of the numerous traces of Serpent-cult in Ireland and Alban in prehistoric and early historic times—the many prehistoric sculptured stones carved with effigies of Serpents, the interlacing Serpent-coils as a decorative design on prehistoric stone monuments and on monuments of the Early Christian period, and the numerous references to Serpents and Dragons in Ireland and Alban in the early legends. It also explains the tradition that " St. Patrick-the-Cat " (or Khatti or Scot) banished Snakes from Ireland by the Cross, or in other words banished the old Matriarchist Serpent-worship by introducing there the Religion of the Cross in 433 A.D.

The later title also of " Brigid " (or " Bridget ") for the female patron saint of the Irish and the Picts, which is usually supposed to have arisen with a more or less mythical Christian nun in Ireland, who is supposed to be buried in the same tomb as St. Patrick, is now seen to be obviously the transformed and chastened aboriginal old matriarch wizardess who in the Gothic Eddas is called Frigg, or Frigg-Ida, the " Mother of the Wolf of Fen " of the pre-Gothic or pre-Aryan aborigines of Van. Brigid is still given precedence as a " wise one " or wizardess over St. Patrick in the eleventh century " Prophecy of St. Berchan " :—

"Erin shall not be without a wise one
After Bhrigde and St. Patrick." [1]

Her alternative title also as " St. Bride " is confirmatory of this origin, as " Bride " was a usual title for Mother Frigg and her wizardess sisterhood priestesses in the Eddas. These sister wizardesses are often collectively called in the Eddas " The Nine Mothers " or " The Nine Maidens " ; and are described in the Welsh and other Celtic legends as " The Nine Witches of Gloster," feeding with their breath the Fire in the Cauldron of Hell.[2] This now accounts for the many

[1] S.C.P., 89.  [2] R.H.L., 372.

prehistoric monoliths and series of nine standing stones, called "Maiden" Stones or "The Nine Maidens," still standing in many parts of Ireland and Britain. These Maiden Stones symbolized the old Van Matriarchs, who are called "The Nine Mothers" in the Eddas, and who were afterwards idealized into Virgin Mothers and accorded divine honours by their Van votaries. And their idol-stones are often decorated with effigies of the Serpent.

This now appears to explain the prehistoric Van origin of the "Maiden Stones" of the pre-Aryan period, so numerous throughout the land; as, for instance, "The Maiden Stone" standing at the foot of Mt. Bennachie to the west of the Newton Stone, and also "The Serpent Stone" monolith with large sculptured Serpent, which stood not far from the site of the Newton Stone, and now placed alongside the latter. It also accounts for the first time for the frequency of the name "Bride" in early Christian Celtic Church names in Scottish Pict-land as well as Ireland, as "Kil-Bride" or "Church of Bride." It now becomes apparent that on the introduction of Christianity into Britain the old pagan Matriarchist goddess "Brigid" or "Bride" of the aborigines was for proselytizing purposes admitted into the Roman Catholic Church and canonized as a Christian saint, and appropriate legends regarding her invented.

The descendants of the Irish Matriarch Cesair and her horde appear to have been called *Fomor*, or *Umor*.[1] This seems evidenced by the tradition that Cesair's was the first migration of people into Ireland and that the second was that of Part-olon, and that the latter was opposed by the ferocious tribe of "demons" called Fomor.

The tribal name "Fomor" has been attempted to be explained by conjectural Celtic etymologies variously as "Giants" and conflictingly as "Dwarfs under the Sea."[2] "Fomor," I find, however, is obviously a dialectic variant of the name of a chief of a clan of the dwarf tribes of the Vans,

[1] Also written *Ughmor*. K.H.I., 68., etc.; and see R.H.L., 583.
[2] The Fomors have been conflictingly called both "giants" and "dwarfs under the sea" by different Celtic scholars seeking conjecturally for a meaning of the name by means of modern Aryan-Celtic speech, but these meanings are admittedly mere guesses. See R.H.L., 591.

called in the Gothic Eddas "Baombur";[1] and it is noteworthy that these dwarf tribes were of the race of "The Blue [painted] Legs,"[2] that is, presumably, the primitive, painted Picts. It is probably a variant also of the name "Vimur" which occurs in the Eddas as the name of the river—the Upper Euphrates, the modern "Murad"—which separated the Van territory from that of the Goths, and the ford at which was the scene of battles between the Goths and the Vans,[3] presumably the seat of Baombar and his tribe.

These Fomors, who opposed Part-olon on his landing in Ireland, are reported to have been ferocious "demons," and significantly they were led by an ogre *and his Mother*.[4] This is clearly a memory of the Mother-Son joint rulership of Matriarchy, wherein the favourite son-paramour, who in the Eddas is called Baldr, was the champion of the Matriarch and her tribe for offensive and defensive purposes. This Fomor son-leader was called "The Footless,"[5] which is a designation of the Serpent, and there are references to the Fomors and their allies having Serpents and Dragons as their defenders.[6] Significantly also he is frequently called in the later records of the Fomors by the name of "*Balor* of the Evil Eye," which equates with the title Baldr, the son-champion of the earlier Van Matriarch, and the "Fal of the Fiery Stone" weapon.

That these Fomors of the primitive horde of dark, dwarfish "Khaldis" or Bans, Vans or Fens, under the Matriarch Cesair, who first peopled Erin in the Stone Age, were and continued to be the real aborigines of Ireland, and were the ancestors of the later "Fenes," seems evidenced by the fact that they appear and reappear in all the accounts of the invasions subsequent to Part-olon's invasion, as the resisters of the various intruding invaders. Their leader also

[1] *Volo-spa Edda* Codex Regius, p. i, l. 24.
[2] See previous references on p. 95.
[3] Ed.N. 313. "Farma-Tyr" or "*Farma* of the Arrow," a title of Wodan as the opponent of the Goths, may also be a dialectic variant of the same name "Fomor."
[4] K.H.I., 68, etc.
[5] "The Footless"—*Cichol Gri cen Chos* in text cited by R.H.L., 583.
[6] R.H.L., 641.

continued to bear the old Van champion's title of "Balor of the Evil Eye," in the legendary accounts of the later invasions. Thus he is made to oppose even so late an invasion as the fifth, by "The Tribe of the goddess Danu" with the Serpent-cult fetishes, which show them to be a later horde of the same common stock. This affinity indeed is evident, apart from the Serpent fetishes, by the name of their champion being "*Lug*," that is, "*Loki*," one of the Vans and the arch-enemy of the Goths in the Eddas and also called "The Wolf of Fen," (i.e., Van); and his fatal weapon in Ireland as "Lug" was significantly, as in the Eddas, a "Sling Stone."[1]

The old Matriarchist Serpentine-cult of Van appears to have persisted in Ireland, even when it was called "Scotia," as the popular cult of the Feins down to the epoch of St. Patrick in 433 A.D., notwithstanding the contemporary existence of Sun-worship amongst the ruling race of Scots, with their legendary solar heroes, Diarmait and Conn-the-Fighter-of a-Hundred. The chief idol of Ireland which St. Patrick demolished by his Cross is described as "The Head [idol] of the Mound";[2] and it is identified as the idol of Fal of the Fiery Stone,[3] that is, the son-champion of the serpent-worshipping Matriarchist Fomors, "Balor of the Evil Eye."

These "Fomor" or Ban, Wan, Van, Fen or Fein aborigines of Ireland, dark, dwarfish "Iberians" who seem to have arrived in Erin from Albion in the late Stone Age, some time before 2000 B.C., now appear to have been presumably of the same race as the dwarfish aborigines of Albion, who were called by the Romans "Picts" or "The [Blue] Painted," and who, we know, were, like the Feins, of primitive Matri-linear and Matriarchist social constitution. And we have seen that the "Fomor" were presumably the prehistoric dwarfish "Baombur" aborigines of Van, who were described by the Aryan Gothic Eddas as of the race of "The Blue (Painted) Legs."

[1] R.H.L., 397.
[2] Cenn Cruaich in *Tri-partite Life of St. Patrick*, and see R.H.L., 200.
[3] R.H.L., 208.

This now confronts us with the further great and hitherto unsolved problems: " Who were the Picts? " and " What was the relationship of the Picts to the aborigines of Alban, Albion or Britain? "—questions, the answers to which form an essential preliminary to the discovery of the date of the introduction of civilization into Britain, and of the racial agency by which that civilization was effected.

FIG. 21A.—Sun-Eagle triumphs over Serpent of Death.
From the reverse of a pre-Christian Cross at Mortlach (of St. Moloch), Banff, with " Resurrecting Spirals " on face. See later.
(After Stuart 1. pl. 14).
Note the serpent is of the British adder type.

## XI

### WHO WERE THE PICTS?

*Disclosing their Non-Aryan Racial Nature and Affinity with Matriarchist Van, Wan or Fian " Dwarfs," and as Aborigines of Britain in Stone Age.*

> " The Picts, a mysterious race whose origin no man knows."—Prof. R. S. RAIT, *Hist. of Scotland*, 1915, 11.
>
> " No craft they knew
> With woven brick or jointed beam to pile
> The sunward porch ; but in the dark earth burrowed
> And housed, like tiny ants in sunless caves." *Prometheus Bound.*[1]

The mysterious Picts, whose origin and affinities have hitherto baffled all enquiries, nevertheless require their racial relationship to the aborigines of Britain and to the Aryans to be elicited, if possible, as an essential preliminary to discovering the agency by which Civilization was first introduced into Britain and the date of that epoch-making event.

The " Picts " are not mentioned under that name by Cæsar, Tacitus, Ptolemy or other early Roman or Greek writer on Ancient Britain. This is presumably because, as we shall find, that that was not their proper name, but a nickname.

The " Picts " first appear in history under that name at the latter end of the third century A.D. as the chief inhabitants of Caledonia.[2] They reappear in 360 A.D. as warlike barbarian

---

[1] Æschylus, *Prometheus Bound* ll. 456–459, translated by J. S. Blackie I 95.

[2] The name first appears in 296 A.D. in the oration of Eumenius to the Roman emperor Constantius Chlorus, which says : " the Caledonians and other Picts "—" Non dico Caledonum aliorumque Pictorum silvas at paludes, etc." (Latin panegyrics. Inc. Constantino Augusto, c.7.).

marauders in association with the Irish-Scots,[1] breaking through the Antonine Wall between the Forth and Clyde, and raiding the Roman province to the south, whence they were driven back by Theodosius in 369. On the departure of the Roman legions in 411, their renewed depredations in South Britain became so incessant and menacing that the king of the South Britons, Vortigern, eventually invoked in 449 the aid of his kinsmen the Jutes from Denmark to expel them, with the well-known result that the Anglo-Jute mercenaries turned fiercely on their hosts and carved out by their swords petty kingdoms in South Britain for themselves. Thenceforward the Picts and Scots aided the Britons in defending against their common foe, the Anglo-Saxons, what remained of independent Briton in the western half of South Britain—Strath-Clyde or the Cambries[2] from the Severn to the Clyde, with Wales and Cornwall, and Caledonia north of Northumbria.

In North Britain, from the sixth century to the eighth A.D., the Picts are disclosed in the contemporary histories of Columba and Bede, supplemented by the Pictish Chronicles, as occupying the whole of North Britain north of the Antonine Wall between the Clyde and Forth, except the south extremity of Argyle, which was occupied by Irish-Scots from Ulster. Besides this there are numerous references to " The Southern Picts "[3] south of the wall and especially in the Galloway province of the Briton kingdom of Strath-Clyde, bordering the Solway, where St. Ninian in the fourth century converted " The Southern Picts," and built in 397 his first Christian church at Whitherne.[4]

[1] The Scots as " Scoti " first appear under that name in history (apart from the Early British Chronicles) in 360 in the contemporary Roman history of the Roman military officer Ammianus Marcellinus (Bk. 20, i 1), and they are associated with the Picts in raiding the Roman province (see also Gildas c. 19). From the accounts of Claudian, the Briton monk Gildas (about 546) and Bede, these Scoti were Irish-Scots who raided and returned to Ireland with their booty. See S.C.P. cvii.
[2] " Cambries " is used by the contemporary historian Gildas the Younger as the title for the Briton kingdom of Strath-Clyde. See P.A.B. 1857, 49, etc. It included Cambria (Wales), Cumbria (Cumberland), Westmorland and Lancashire, and Strath-Clyde from Solway to Clyde.
[3] Thus Bede, B.H.E. 3, 4.
[4] So numerous were the Picts in Galloway, the people of which were called " Gall-Gaedhel " (S.C.P. cxciii) that in 741 the Irish-Scot king of Dalriada

In South Britain no historical references are found to "Picts" as forming an element of the early population, though the subterranean dwellings called "Picts' Houses" are widely distributed, and are associated in Devon and Cornwall with the "Pixies;" and some place-names contain the element "Pict" (see later). And Cæsar's statement about the general prevalence in Britain of polyandry of a promiscuous kind[1] amongst the natives in the interior, and of the "*interiores*" as being clad in skins[2] probably referred to the Picts, as Cæsar describes the Britons whom he met as being richly garbed.

In Ireland also, Picts are not mentioned under that Latin nickname, but they are generally identified with the "Cruithne," though this title, as we have seen, is used ambiguously, and does not properly belong to the Picts at all. That the Picts were of the same kindred as the aboriginal Irish Feins, is evident from the numerous records that the Picts in Scotland were in the habit of obtaining wives from Ireland[3] and that their matrilinear succession and use of the Irish "Celtic" were derived from the same.[4]

Then, in the middle of the ninth century A.D., with the final conquest of the "Northern Picts" in 850 by the Scot king Kenneth, son of Alpin, from Galloway, and his establishment as "King of the Scots" and his introduction of the name "Scot-land[5] for North Briton," *the "Picts" completely disappeared from history as suddenly as they first appeared.* No historical trace of that race is to be found thereafter, notwithstanding that there is no evidence whatever of any exodus or any wholesale massacre of these people.[6]

As a result presumably of this complete disappearance of

established himself there as "King of the Picts" (*ib.* clxxxvii); and St. Mungo or Kentigern of Glasgow (601 A.D.), the bishop of Strath-Clyde cleansed from idolatry "*the home of the Picts* which is now called Galwietha [i.e. Galloway] and its adjacent parts" (Kentigern's Life by Jocelyn of Furness.)
[1] D.B.G. v, 14, 4–5.   [2] *Ib* v. 14, 2.
[3] S.C.P., 123, 160, 298 etc.   [4] *Ib.* xcviii v. 98.   [5] *Ib.* 200, 299.
[6] In one chronicle (Scala chronica) it is stated that in 850, at a conference at Scone, the Irish-Scots by stratagem " slew the king and the chief nobles " of the Picts (S.C.P. cxci), but there is no reference or suggestion anywhere to any massacre of the people themselves.

this people, the name "Pict" has tended to become mythical; and the Picts are described in medieval and later folklore as malicious fairy dwarf folk, pigmies, pixies, fauns and elves; and significantly they are associated with the Irish fairies, the Fians, or Bans.

We are thus confronted by the questions: "Where did the Picts come from so suddenly?" and "Whither did they disappear just as suddenly?" Their sudden mysterious appearance and disappearance under the circumstances above noted suggested to me that both events were probably owing to a mere change in their tribal name as aborigines. And so it seems to prove.

"Pict" is an epithet, presumably a contemptuous nickname, applied to these people by outsiders, and never seems to have been used by these people themselves. It thus appears to be analogous to the terms "Greek" and "German" applied by the Romans to those two nations who never called themselves by these names. The term "Pict" appears to have been consciously used by the Romans (who are found to be the first users of it) in the sense of "painted" (*pictus*) with reference to the custom of these people to stain their skin blue with woad dye. In Scottish these people are called *Peht*,[1] in Anglo-Saxon *Pihta*, *Pehta* or *Peohta*,[2] and in Norse *Pett*;[3] and the Welsh bard Taliessin calls them *Peith*. These Norse and other forms, it will be noticed, contain no *c*, and are perhaps cognate with our English "petty," Welsh *pitiw*, and French *petit*, "small," to designate these people as dwarfish. And significantly it is seen from the map on p. 19 that the numerous Pictish villages in the neighbourhood of the Newton Stone and in the Don Valley, as similarly many towns over Britain generally, bear the prefix "*Pit*" or "*Pet*," presumably in the sense of Pict or the Anglo-Saxon "Pihta" or Scottish "Peht," to distinguish these native villages from the settlements of the Aryan rulers in the neighbourhood called "Cattie," "Cot-town," "Seati-ton," "Bourtie," &c. (See map).

[1] J.S.D., 389, where also Pechty, Peaght and Pegh.
[2] B.A.S., 182. "Peohta" is form used by King Alfred in his translation of Bede's "Picti."
[3] See below.

## ORIGIN OF NAME "PICT"

The remoter origin of the Nordic name *Pett* or *Peht* or *Pihta*, which was presumably latinized by the Romans into "Pict," seems to me to be probably found in the *Vit* or *Vet* or *Vitr*[1] title in the Gothic Eddas for a chief of a clan of the primitive "Blue Leg" dwarfs of Van and Vindia, who is mentioned alongside Baōmburr (who was obviously, as we have seen, the eponym of the Irish aboriginal Fomors) *V*, *B* and *P*, being freely interchangeable dialectically.

[This "Vit" means literally "witted" or "wise,"[2] and is also used in a personal sense as "witch" or "wizard," with the variant of "*Vitt*," "*Vitki*," literally "witch," and meaning "witch-craft and charms";[3] and in a contemptuous general sense as Vetta and Vætt "a wight" and secondarily as "naught" or "nothing" or "nobody"[4] and thus "petty"; and as *Vetti* and "*Pit*-(lor)", it is a Norse nickname.[5] It thus appears probable that "Pett" or "Pihta" or "Pict" are later dialectic forms of the epithet Vit, Vet, or Vetta or Vitki applied contemptuously by the Early Goths to a section of the dwarf "Blue Leg" ancestors of the Picts, and designated them as "The petty Witch Wights," that is, the Witch-ridden devotees of the cult of the Matriarch witch or wise woman.]

This early association of the Picts with "petty" and witches would now seem to explain why in modern folklore these dwarfish people are associated and identified with Fauns, Fians, Pixies and *wicked* Fairies—indeed the modern word "wicked" is derived from "Witch" and thus seen to have its origin in the Gothic *Vitki*, "the wicked witch" title of the Van ancestors of the Picts, a people who all along appear to have been devotees of the cult of the Serpent and its Matriarchist witches and their magic cauldron.

Indeed, this "Vit" epithet for the Picts, or "Pihtas," of the Anglo-Saxons, appears to find some confirmation from Cæsar's journal. While Cæsar nowhere calls any of the people of Britain "Pict," he, even when referring to the natives of Britain staining their skin for war, does not use the word *pictus* or "painted;" but uses *inficiunt* (i.e., infect or

---

[1] *Vit-r* (in which the final *r* is merely the Gothic nominative case-ending, in Volu-spa Edda (Codex Regius, p. 1, l. 25); and "*Vetr* of Vind's vale" in Vaf-thrudnis Mal Edda (Cod. reg. p. 15, ll. 20 and 22).
[2] V.D., 713.   [3] *Ib.* 713, 714.   [4] *Ib.* 720.   [5] *Ib.* 701, 477.

"tattoo"?). Yet curiously he is made to call the blue dye used for this purpose "*Vitro*," a word which is interpreted as "Woad" by classic scholars solely in translating this passage, though elsewhere in Latin it invariably means "glass."[1] This suggests that there is some corruption in the copies of Cæsar's manuscript here; and that "Vitro" of the text may perhaps have been intended by Cæsar for the Gothic "*Vitr*" title for the "Blue-legged" dwarfs or the "Picts."

Another early form of this nickname of "Pict" for the aborigines of Alban appears to me to be found in the title of "*Ictis*,"[2] applied by the early Ionian navigator Pytheas to the tin-port of Britain, a name identified also by some with the Isle of Wight. This tradition is confirmed by the name given to the Channel in the Pict Chronicles in describing the arrival in Alban of the Britons under Brutus, where the English Channel is called "The Sea of *Icht*."[3] This presumes that South Britain was possibly then named after its aborigines of those days, the Vichts, Ichts or Picts; just as at the other extremity we have the "Pentland Firth," which was earlier known to the Norse as the "Pett-land Fiord"[4] or "Firth of the *Petts* (or *Picts*)," from its bounding "The Land of the Picts." Indeed, the Danish writer of the twelfth century, Saxo Grammaticus, calls Scotland "Petia" or "Land of the Picts." This would now explain the statement of the Roman historian that a nation of the Picts in Britain was called "The *Vect*-uriones."[5]

The proper name for the "Picts," as used presumably by themselves in early times, was, I think, from a review of all the new available evidence, the title "*Khal-dis*" or *Khal-tis*,

[1] Moreover, the scientific name of the Woad plant is "*Isatis* tinctoria." and not *Vitrum*.
[2] "*Iktis*" is the form of the name preserved by Diodorus Siculus (*Bibl. Hist.* v., 22); and it has been identified with the "Vectis" of Pliny, who, however, places it between South Britain and Ireland, whilst he confounds "Ictis" as "Mictis" apparently with Thule. For discussion on Ictis v. Vectis and "Mictis," see H.A.B., 499, etc. The initial *V* often tends to be lost or become merged with its following vowel in Greek, see later, so that "Ictis" may represent an earlier *Vectis*.
[3] S.C.D. 57. [4] See Edda V.P., 2, 682.
[5] Ammianus Marcellinus, 27, viii., 5.

## PICTS AS CHALDEES OR CALED-ONS

*i.e.*, " The Children of the River (*Khal* or Gully)."¹ This title of " Khaldis " is applied to the aborigines of Van in Asia Minor in the numerous sacred monuments erected by their Aryan overlords there in the ninth century B.C. and later. And concurrently with this title they also called themselves (from their old home-centre " Van," " Wan " or " Fen " Fian or Fein), Biani or " Ban," like their branch which first peopled Erin.

Now, this riverine title " *Khal-dis* " appears to be not only the source of the ethnic name " *Caled*-on " but also the source of the numerous ancient river-names in Britain called variously Clyde or Clotia, Clwyd, Cald, Caldy, Calder and Chelt ; and such names as the Chilt-ern Hills and Chelten-ham near the old prehistoric dwellings at Gloster, as well as the title of Columba's mission to the Pictish aborigines—" Culdee." This application of the name " *Caled*-on " to the Picts is confirmed, as we have seen, by the Roman reference to the Picts as " Caledons " ; and it is emphasized by the further Roman record that " The Picts are divided into two nations, the Di-*Caled*-ones and the Vect-uriones,"² in which " Vect " appears to be cognate with " Pict." " Caled " (or Caled-on ) thus seems to have been the early title used by the Picts for themselves ;³ and, as we shall see in the next chapter, it is cognate through its original " Khal-dis " or " Khal-tis " with " Chaldee," " Galati " and " Kelts " or " Celts."

Identified in this way with the cave-dwelling, dwarfish, dark Vans or Wans and gipsy " *Chals* " of Van and Galatia in Asia Minor, whose prehistoric line of migration westwards overland to Western Europe and Britain has already been traced, the Picts also, who were also cave-dwellers, appear to have left traces of their " Pict " or " Pit " title in some places *en route*, as well as in Britain and Ireland, in addition to their Van name.

[1] On this name, see before, also next chapter.
[2] A.M.H., 27, viii, 5.
[3] Tacitus speaks of " the red hair and large limbs of the inhabitants of Caledonia " (*Agricola II*) ; but he is speaking not of aboriginal Caledons, but of the ruling race in Caledonia who were opposing Agricola, and who, we have seen, were Britons and Scots properly so-called.

[In Iberia (and the Picts, we shall see, were of the Iberian physical type) the *Vett*-ones inhabited in the Roman period the valley of the great Guadalquivir.[1] *Pictavia* was the ancient name for Piccardy,[2] a division of Gaul stretching from Iberia northwards to Brittany, and it was inhabited by the *Pict*-ones; and its chief capital still bears the Pictish name of Poitiers which significantly is in the province of " *Vienne*," obviously a variant of Van or " Bian."

In Britain, south of the Tweed, the old place-names bearing the prefix " Pit " and " Pet " have not survived so freely as those of " Wan " and " Venta." The ancient village of " Pitchley " in Northampton in the Wan's Dyke area was still called in Domesday Book " *Picts*-lei " and " *Pihtes*-lea,"[3] that is, the " lea of the Picts "; and it contains, as we shall see, prehistoric human remains, presumably of the Pictish period. In Surrey are the villages of Pett, Petworth, the " *Peti*-orde " of Domesday —and Pettaugh. Glastonbury in Somerset, with its prehistoric lake-dwellings, was called " Ynys *Vitr*-ain " or " Isle of *Vitr*-land," thus preserving the Gothic form of the Pictish eponym. " *Pet*-uaria " was the chief town between York and the Wash, in Ptolemy's day; it was in the *Fens* presumably of the lake-dwelling Vans or Fens, and to its north is a " Picton " in the valley of the Tees.

In Scotland, which was called " *Pictavia* " in medieval Latin histories and the Pict Chronicles, the prefix " *Pit* " and " *Pet* " is common in old village names, and presumably preserves the title of the aboriginal Picts for these villages of the natives, to distinguish them from the settlements of the ruling Aryan race in the adjoining villages called " Catti " and " Barat." For numerous series of these ancient village *Pit* names in sharp contrast with the " Catti " and " Barat " villages studding the Don Valley of Old Pictland around the Newton Stone, see Map, p. 19. One of these "Pit" names, it is noteworthy, is " Pit-blain," that is " The *Blue* Pit or Pict," in which the word for " blue " is the identical British Gothic word " blain," used in the Eddas for " The Blue Leg " tribe of dwarfs. And the " *Pent*-land " Hills to the south of the Forth preserve the same " Pict " title as the " Pentland " Firth does to the north, and in Shetland, in addition to the saga references to Picts, there are several places named *Petti*.[4]

[1] The ancient Baetis river of Baetica. S. 3, i, 6.
[2] " Piccard-ach " was an ancient name for the Southern Picts in Scotland, S.C.P. 74–76.
[3] A. W. Brown, *Archæolog. Jour.* 3–13, cited W.P.A., 180.
[4] Petti-dale and Pett-water on border of Tingwall parish, and Petti-garth Fell, and at Fetlar is " The Finn's Dyke " (Finni-girt Dyke).

[In Ireland, in an Irish epic tale of the first century A.D., Picts are located in Western Ulster.[1] But in the earlier period of the Irish legends the Picts are clearly, I think, the same primitive people who are called " The tribe of *Fidga*,"[2] of the plain of " Fidga," a locality not yet located. These " Fidga " are repeatedly mentioned as opposing the Sun-worshippers (i.e. the Aryan overlords), and *derived their origin from Britain (Albion)* ; *they used poison weapons, and were defended by two double-headed Serpents*,[3] showing that they were, like the Picts and Vans, devotees of the Serpent-cult. This Irish form of their name is in series with the Welsh name for the Picts, namely " Fficht ;" and they appear to have been of the same primitive race as the Van or Fen (or early Fein).]

This racial position for the Picts as the primitive pre-Aryan aborigines of Britain and Ireland in the Stone Age, thus confirms and substantiates, but from totally different sources, the theory of their non-Aryan nature advanced by Rhys. This philologist believed that the Picts were the non-Aryan aborigines of Britain, merely because of a few non-Aryan words occurring in ancient inscriptions in Scotland, which he surmised might be Pictish,[4] though this surmise was not generally accepted.[5] Nor did he find traces of such Pictish words in England or Wales, besides " The Sea of *Icht*," although he believed he found one solitary word in Ireland.[6]

In physical type, the Picts, according to general tradition, were dark " Iberian," small-statured and even pygmy,[7] more or less naked, with their skins " tinged with Caledonian or Pictish woad."[8] They have been allied to the semi-Iberian Basques,[9] whose language was radically non-Aryan, on

---

[1] *Tain bo Cualnge*, J. Dunn, 1914, xvii, 375.
[2] Tuath Fidga.
[3] Book of Leinster, 15a, and R.H.L. 631 and 641.
[4] *Rhind Lects.* 1889 ; P.S.A.S. 1892, 305, etc. ; *Welsh People*, 1902, 13, etc. '
[5] H.A.B., 409g., etc.
[6] This was inferred by him on the theory that the " Cruthni " designated Picts (*Welsh People* 1902, 13). But on the other hand he holds the opposite view that " Cruthni " was a Celtic spelling of " Priten " or " Briton, " which name, he thinks, means " Cloth clad," to distinguish the *Aryan* Britons or " Pritens " from the non-Aryan aborigines or Picts, which mutually destroys his argument.
[7] MacRitchie M.F.P., etc. He cites a fifteenth-century account of early pygmy Picts in Orkney, *Monthly Rev.*, Jan. 1901, 141.
[8] Wharton, on Milton.      [9] R.R.E., 375.

account of the latter occupying the old Pictavia region on the border of Iberia. Their primitive habits and living in caves and underground burrows or " Pict-dwellings," like the Vans or Khaldis,[1] as well as their immemorial occupation of the land, have doubtless accounted for their being in modern folklore identified with malignant fauns, Fians and Pixies, which latter name seems to preserve " Pict."

The early prehistoric Picts thus appear to have been the primitive aborigines of Albion in the late Old Stone Age and early Neolithic Age whose long-headed, narrow and low-browed skulls (see Fig. 22, p. 135) are mostly found in the lower strata of the ancient river-beds, and hence termed by Huxley " *The River-bed* " type. The peculiar, though unsuspected, literal appropriateness of this title will be obvious when we recall that these people seem to have actually called themselves " The Children of the River " (*Khal-dis* or " Caleds ") presumably through their finding their primitive livelihood along the river-banks and river-beds.

This river-bed race of primitive dwarfish men was shown by Huxley to have been widely distributed in remote prehistoric times over the British Isles, from Cornwall to Caithness, and over Ireland, and also over the European continent from Basque and Iberia eastwards.

[He especially records it from the Trent Valley of Derbyshire, in the Ledbury and Muskham skulls,[2] in Anglesea, the Thames Valley. In Ireland it is seen in the river-bed skulls of the Nore and Blackwater in Queen's County and Armagh.[3] He also observed this type of skull in the more ancient prehistoric sites on the European continent from Gaul and Germany and Switzerland to the Basque country (Picardy) and Iberia.[4] And he significantly added that he suspected that it would be found in the inhabitants of Southern Hindustan—which it has been in the dark aborigines of Central and Southern India,

---

[1] We have seen that the old and existing cave-dwellings and subterranean burrows of the Vindia region west of Van are of the same general characteristic prehistoric subterranean Picts' Houses and " Weems " or cave-dwellers in Early Albion. Thus the name " Pitten-weem " for a seaport on the Forth coast, with a series of caves with prehistoric human remains, and meaning " Caves of the Pitts or Picts " is especially obvious as an early settlement of cave-dwelling Picts.
[2] L.H.C., 120, etc. ; 123, etc.
[3] *Ib*. 123, 125, etc.  [4] *Ib*. 136.

the Dravids or Doms—just as he had already found it in the dark aborigines of Australia,[1] one of the lowest of the most primitive savage races of the present day. And his inferences have been fully justified.]

This widespread prevalence of the river-bed type of men in the Stone Age is confirmed and considerably extended backwards by Sir Arthur Keith in his classic "Antiquity of Man," recording mostly fresh discoveries and observations of his own. He establishes the fact that this type of river-bed skull existed over Britain as far back in the Old Stone Age as about 25,000 years ago, in the Langwith Cave in Derbyshire;[2] and at a somewhat later period in the Oban Cave in Scotland with Azilian (or Mentone) culture of the Old Stone Age, and at Aberavon, east of Swansea, and in Kent's Cavern at Torquay. In the Neolithic age of about eight thousand years ago it is found in the Tilbury man of the Thames Valley, who resembled the race of equal age found at Vend-rest (a name suggestive of the "Vend" title of the Picts), about sixty miles east of Paris. It is also found in the same Neolithic Period in the great megalithic tomb at Coldrum in the Medway Valley of the Kent Downs, near the famous Kit's Coty cromlech, where these long-headed people were still of relatively small stature—the men averaging 5 feet 4 inches and the women 5 feet, that is about 3 inches below the modern British average, though the brain had now reached practically the modern standard with a skull width of 77.9 per cent. of the length.[3] And significantly the large Neolithic village of *pit-dwellings*, with rude pottery and finely-worked flint implements in the neighbourhood at "*Ight*-ham," seems to preserve in the latter name "*Ight*-ham" or "Hamlet of the *Ight*," the later shortened title of the Picts, in series with the southern dialectic form of Pliny's "*Vectis*" for the Isle of "Wight," and "*Ictis*," the old Irish name for the English Channel, and the Eddic *Veig*, *Vige*, *Vit* and *Vikti* forms of the eponym for "Pict."[4] This modern name thus appears to preserve the old designation of that

[1] L.H.C., 130.
[2] K.A.M., 22.
[3] K.A.M., 89, etc.
[4] See before.

ancient Neolithic village of pit-dwellers as " Hamlet of the Picts."[1]

At Pitchley also, in Northamptonshire, an ancient village with a church building of the twelfth century, which is called in Domesday Book " *Pihtes-lea* and " *Picts-lei* "—names clearly designating it as " The Lea of the *Picts* "—the skulls unearthed from the numerous old stone-cists of a prehistoric cemetery under the church, and under the early Saxon graves, with no trace of metals and presumably of late Neolithic Age, appear to be of this river-bed type. One of the typical skulls is described as " having the peculiar lengthy form, the prominent cheek-bones and *the remarkable narrowness of the forehead* which characterize the ' Celtic ' races "[2] (see Fig. 22, p. 135).

In Ireland this river-bed type of Stone Age skull is also found as above noted. And we have seen that the Matriarch Cesair and her Ban or Van or Fen horde of the Fomor clan entered Ireland in the Neolithic Age presumably from Britain and were of the same Van or Vind race to which the Picts belonged. We have also seen that these primitive aborigines of Ireland were called " The tribe of *Fidga*," that is a dialectic form of " Pict," in series with the Welsh " Ffichti." This suggests that the river-bed aborigines of Ireland also were presumably the Picts. It seems, too, a dialectic form of the same name which is given as " *Gewictis* " for the aborigines of Ireland in the account of the invasion of Ireland by the Iber-Scots[3] or Scots from Iberia, especially as it was usual to spell the analogous Wight, or Vectis, with an initial G.

The Mother-Right, or Matri-linear form of succession through the mother and not through the father, which was prevalent amongst the later historical Picts down to the ninth century, when they suddenly disappear from history, is now explicable

---

[1] Another skeleton, found in a " circumscribed " cist of Neolithic age at Maidstone, is described by B. Poste as having the skull " very narrow in the front part and also in the forehead," but stature about five feet seven. —*Jour. Archæol. Assoc.*, iv, 65, cited W.P.A., 182.

[2] A.W. Brown in *Archæol. Jour.* iii, 113, cited W.P.A., 180–1.

[3] This chronicle states that a Scot from Spain (Iberna), named Iber-Scot, on landing " in yat cuntre, yat now is callit Irland, and fund it vakande, bot of a certanne of *Gewictis*, ye quhilk he distroyt, and inhabyt yat land, and callit it eftir his modir Scota, Scotia." S.C.P., 380.

## PICTS AS ABORIGINES OF IRELAND

by the Matriarchist Van origin of this race. The Pictish Chronicles, both of the Irish-Scots and the Picts of Scotland, make repeated and pointed reference to this custom and it is borne out by the lists of the Pictish kings. These show that the Pictish king was not succeeded by his own son, but by his brother, the next son of his mother, or by his sister's son; and many of the kings appear to be named after their mother, or specified as the son of their mother. The Picts in Scotland, probably to excuse themselves in the eyes of the Scots and Britons who were of the Aryan patrilinear society, state in their Chronicles that this custom was imposed on them by "the women of Ireland," with whom they appear to have kept up some kindred intermarriage. But it is significant that these aboriginal women of Ireland are not stated to be the "wives" of the men they consort with, but it is said "each woman was with her *brother*,"[1] which is suggestive of the primitive Matriarchist promiscuity before the institution of Marriage. These aboriginal women, called "Ban," (i.e. Van or "Biani") are stated to have imposed the matrilinear contract by oath:—

> "They imposed oaths on them
> By the stars, by the earth,
> That from the nobility of the Mother
> Should always be the right of reigning."[2]

It was probably Part-olon's attempts to abolish this Matriarchist promiscuity and mother-right by the introduction of the Aryan custom of marriage with patrilinear succession, which is referred to in the Pictish Chronicles as one of the great offences of "Cruithne" (*i.e.* Pruthne or Part-olon), that he "took their women from them."[3] Another vestige of this ancient matriarchy in Ireland appears in the custom in the first century B.C. by which a married woman retained her private fortune independent of her husband.[4]

It was this Pictish promiscuity presumably, regarding which

---

[1] Books of Ballymote and Lecan, S.C.P., 39.
[2] *Ib.* S.C.P. 40.
[3] *Book of Lecan*, S.C.P., 47.
[4] *Cf.* Dunn *Tain bo Cual.* (xviii).

Cæsar makes his remarkable statement that " the inland non-agricultural people " who were clad in skins and stained their skins blue (*i.e.*, obviously the Picts) : " by tens or twelves together have wives in common, and the offspring is credited to him who first had the mother as a virgin."[1] This is believed by some writers to be a misunderstanding by Cæsar. And in view of the briefness of his visit, confined to only a few months' strenuous campaigning in the south-east corner of England, in a foreign country, and dependent on interpreters, it seems probable that it is one of his several mistaken statements,[2] and that the Pictish custom in question was not polyandry, but matriarchy.

The Serpent-worship of the Picts also, which was so universal, as seen everywhere on the prehistoric monuments in Pictlands, and figuring freely also on the early Christian monuments and "Celtic" crosses of the Picts, is now explained by the matriarchist Van or Fen origin of this race. We have seen the prominence of the Serpent-cult Witch's Bowl or Cauldron amongst the Feins of prehistoric Ireland, and the Serpent guardians there of the Tribe of the "Fidga," *i.e.*, the Picts, the Serpent-cult enmity against the Sun-worshipping heroes Diarmait and Conn of the Irish-Scots, and the widespread carving of the Serpent and its coiled symbols on the prehistoric stone monuments in Ireland, and how St Patrick the Scot in the fifth century A.D. traditionally banished the Serpent-cult from Ireland and demolished the chief Matriarchist idol. In Britain, the Serpent and its interlacing coils are freely sculptured on many of the prehistoric monuments and early Christian crosses. In Scotland, the last refuge of the Picts, where their early monuments have most largely escaped destruction, this symbolism is especially widespread and occurs on many of the several hundreds of prehistoric monuments and early Christian crosses figured by Dr. Stuart in his classic *Sculptured Stones of Scotland*, and it is well exemplified in the great prehistoric " Serpent Stone," which now stands alongside the Newton Stone.

---

[1] D.B.G., v, 5. *Cf.* H.A.B., 414, etc.
[2] *E.g.*, His statement that the Pine and Beech do not grow in Britain, D.B.G., v., 5.

## PICTS ARRIVE IN ALBION IN STONE AGE

In Cornwall, the prehistoric whorls of pierced stone, called " Pixies' grindstones," and presumably amulets, are also called " *Snake* stones."[1] This Serpent-cult character of the Picts would explain the prevalence of human sacrifice amongst the Druid priests of the aborigines who were of this lunar matriarchist cult, and also the historical notices of the existence of cannibalism amongst the barbarian tribes of Caledonia as late as the time of St. Jerome (fourth century A.D.),[2] as well as the traditional immolation of a victim by St. Columba in founding his first church at Iona for the " Culdees " or Picts.

It thus transpires by the new evidence that the " Picts " were the primitive small-statured prehistoric aborigines of Albion or Britain with the " River-bed " type of skulls. They were presumably a branch of the primitive small-statured, narrow-browed and long-headed dark race of matriarchist Serpent-worshipping cave-dwellers of the Van Lake region, the Van, Biani, Fen, or Khal-dis or primitive " Chaldees," Caleds or Caledons, who, in early prehistoric times in the Old Stone Age, sent off from this central hive swarm after swarm of " hunger-marchers " under matriarchs, westwards across Asia Minor to Europe, as far as Iberia and the Biscay region, after the retreating ice. The hordes, which ultimately reached Albion overland, formed there the " aborigines " of Albion. They appear to have entered Southern Albion by the old land-bridge at Kent, after the latter end of the last glacial period, when the reindeer, mammoth and woolly rhinoceros still roamed over what is now called England. And then, long ages afterwards, in the late Stone Age, presumably before 2000 B.C., they gave off a branch to Erin under a Van, Ban or Fian matriarch, forming the aborigines of Ireland.

Having thus elicited the apparent solution to the long oustanding problem of " Who are the Picts "—the primitive non-Aryan race over which the Aryan Part-olon and his successors, the " Brude," " Bret," or Briton- kings ruled in Scotland,—and found that they were the aborigines of Albion, we are now in our search for the first advent of the

[1] *Cf.* L.H.C., 49.   [2] *Ib.* 30.

Aryans into Britain before Part-olon's epoch, still faced by an equally enigmatic and hitherto unsolved problem. This is the vexed question "Who were the Celts?" For the "Celts" have been supposed by philologists to be Aryans in race, and to be the first Aryan civilizers of Britain, whilst anthropologists find that they are not racially Aryan at all.

## XII

### Who were the " Celts " properly so-called ?

*Disclosing identity of Early British " Celts " or Kelts and " Culdees " with the " Khaldis " of Van and the Picts.*

> " The so-called *Celtic Question*, than which no greater stumbling block in the way of clear thinking exists . . . there is practically to-day a complete unanimity of opinion among physical anthropologists that the term *Celt*, if used at all, belongs to the brachycephalic [round-headed] darkish population of the Alpine [Swiss] highlands . . . totally lacking in the British Isles."—W. Z. RIPLEY, *Races of Europe*, 124, 126, 305.

RIGHTLY to elicit the real racial agency by which uncivilized Ancient Britain became Aryanized in Language, High Culture and Civilized Institutions in the pre-Roman period, it is still necessary for us to re-examine and strive to solve the vexed question of " The Celts " ; for the existing confusion in the use of this term forms one of the greatest obstacles to clear thinking on the subject, as cited in the heading. And this gross confusion has been a chief cause of the delay hitherto in solving the Origin of the Britons and the Aryan Question in Britain.

At the outset we are confronted by the paradox that, while philologists and popular writers generally in this country assume that the " Celts " were Aryans in race as well as in language, and were the parents of the Brythons or Britons, and the Scots and Irish—notwithstanding that the " Early Britons " are also called non-Aryan pre-Celtic aborigines— on the other hand, scientific anthropologists and classic historians have proved that the " Celts " of history were the *non-Aryan, round-headed,* darkish, small-statured race of south Germany and Switzerland, and that "*Celts* "*properly so-called are* "*totally lacking in the British Isles.*"[1] Thus, to speak, as is so commonly done, of " Celtic ancestry," the " Celtic temperament " and " Celtic fire " amongst any section of the natives of these islands, is, according to anthropologists, merely imaginary!

The term " Celt " or " Kelt " is entirely unknown as the designation of any race or racial element or language in the British Isles, until arbitrarily introduced there a few generations ago. Nor does the name even exist in the so-called " Celtic " languages, the Gaelic, Welsh and Irish. It is, on the contrary, the classic Greek and Latin title of a totally different race of a totally different physical type from that of the British Isles, and that word was only introduced there by unscientific philologists and ethnologists some decades ago.

The " Celts " or " Kelts " first appear in history, under that name, in the pages of Herodotus (480–408 B.C.). He calls them " *Kelt*-oi " and locates them on the continent of Western Europe.

He says: " For the Ister [Danube], beginning from the *Kelt-oi* . . . divides Europe in its course ; but the *Kelt-oi* [of Gaul?] are beyond the pillars of Hercules, and border on the territories of the Kunēsi-oi or Kunet-oi [supposed to be Finnistere] who live the furthest to the west of all the peoples of Europe."[2]

Strabo, writing a few decades after Cæsar's epoch, gives further details regarding the ancient Greek information on the Celts, whom he calls " *Kelt-āi* " :

He says : " The ancient Greeks . . . afterwards becoming acquainted with those natives towards the west, styled them ' *Kelt-āi* ' [Kelts] and ' *Iberi-ēn* ' [Iberians], sometimes compounding the names into ' Kelti-Iberien ' or ' Kelto-Scythian ' —thus ignorantly uniting various distinct nations."[3]

[1] But see later.
[2] *Herodotus* ii, 33 ; iv, 49 ; also Xenophon (d. 359 B.C.) *Hellenica*, vii, 1, 20.
[3] S. i, 2, 27.

Strabo habitually uses the term "*Keltica*" or "Land of the Kelts" for Gaul, which corresponded generally to modern France including Switzerland, and defines it thus :—

"Keltica" is bounded on the [south-] west by the mountains of the Pyrenees, which extend to either sea, both the Mediterranean and the ocean; on the east by the Rhine; on the north by the ocean from the north[west]ern extremity of the Pyrenees to the mouth of the Rhine; on the south by the sea of Marseilles and by the Alps from Liguria [Genoa] to the sources of the Rhine."[1]

He excludes Iberia or Spain–Portugal from Keltica, noting, "The Pyrenees chain . . . divides Keltica from Iberia": but he adds "Ephorus extends the size of Keltica too far, including within it what we now designate as 'Iberia' as far as Gades [Cadiz].[2] He includes Liguria [Genoa and Piedmont on the Italian side of the Alps] whose people he says were named by the Greeks "Kelto-Ligues," or Kelto-Ligurian.[3] It is also noteworthy that he calls the inhabitants of "Keltica" or Gaul not only "Kelt-āi" but also them and their land repeatedly "*Galatic*,"[4] (*i.e.*, a variant of Galatia and Kelt) and he includes the Belgae as Kelts.[5]

But Strabo, like Cæsar and all other Greco-Roman writers without exception, expressly excludes Britain from *Keltica* or "The Land of the Celts." Thus he writes : " its (Britain's) longest side lies parallel to Keltica [Gaul]."[6] And he emphasizes the difference between the physical appearance of the inhabitants of Britain and the Kelts or Celts of Gaul, describing the latter, the *Celts, as a short-statured race with light-yellow hair.*[7]

Cæsar also, in the well-known opening paragraph in his Commentaries, whilst affirming the identity of the *Celtæ* or "Celts" with the *Galli* or "Gauls," restricts the title "Celt" to Mid-Gaul west of the Seine, that is to Old Brittany, with Armorica, the Loire Valley, and Switzerland. He says :

" All Gaul (*Gallia*) is divided into three parts, one of which the Belgæ inhabit, the Aquitani another, *those who, in their own language, are called 'Celts'* (*Celtæ*), *in ours 'Gauls'* (*Galli*), *the third*."[8]

[1] S. iv, 1, 1 ; and compare ii, 1, 17, etc.
[2] *Ib*. iii, 1, 3 and iv. 4, 6.  [3] *Ib*. iv, 4, 3.  [4] *Ib*. iii, 1, 3 ; iv, 4, 2.
[5] *Ib*. iv, 4, 1.  [6] *Ib*. iv, 5, 1.  [7] *Ib*. iv, 5, 2.
[8] D.B.G. i, 1.

And neither Cæsar, nor Tacitus, nor any other of the Greek or Roman historians or writers ever refer to the Celts or Kelts as inhabitants of Britain or of Hibernia.

In British history and literature the first mention of Celts appears to be in 1607 in an incidental reference to the Celts *not* in Britain but in France;[1] and again, in 1656, in Blount's Glossography which defines " Celt, one born in Gaul,"[2] and again, in 1782, contrasting the British with the Celts in Gaul in the sentence : " the obstinate war between the insular Britons and the continental Celts."[3] But all of these references are unequivocally to the Celts in France, *and not in Britain.*

The manner in which the notion of a " Celtic " ancestry for the British, Scots and Irish was insidiously introduced into British literature now becomes evident, and affords a striking example of the inception and growth of a false theory. The credit for the first introduction of this notion into Britain—a notion which by frequent repetitions and accretions grew to be " the greatest stumbling-block to clear thinking " on the Celtic Question—now appears to be due to a Mr. Jones. In 1706 he published an English translation of Abbé Pezron's book issued in 1703 on " Antiquité de la Nation et de la Langue des Celtes," under the title of " Antiquities of Nations, more particularly of the Celtæ or Gauls, taken to be originally the same people as our Ancient Britains,"[4] in which he gave currency to that theory of M. Pezron. The seed thus thrown into receptive British soil seems to have taken root and grown into a sturdy tree, which now is popularly believed to be indigenous. Thus, in 1757, Tindal, in translating Rapin's History of England, says in his introduction (p. 7) " *Great Britain was peopled by the Celtæ or Gauls.*" And, in 1773, the theory that the Celts were ancestors of the Gaels had become current in Skye, for Mr. McQueen, in a discussion there with Samuel Johnson, says : " As they [*the Scythians*] *were the ancestors of the*

---

[1] Topsell, *Fourfold Beast*, 251.
[2] For these and subsequent references to early English occurrence of the name " Celt," see Dr. Murray's *Oxford English Dictionary*, " Celt."
[3] Warton, *Hist. Kiddington*, 67.
[4] Murray, *English Dict., re* " Celt."

*Celts* [in sense of British] the same religion might be in Asia Minor *and Skye.*"[1] And, by 1831, the seedling Celtic tree had become established in Britain as a mighty monarch of the forest which sheltered the Aryan theory of the Celts under its branches with the Celts as full-blooded Aryans in race. In that year Dr. Prichard, the ethnologist and philologist, in his "Eastern Origin of the Celtic Nations," describes the supposititious "British Celts" as Aryans in race, and ascribes to them the introduction of the various Aryan dialects current, before the Anglo-Saxon period, in the British Isles. And, in 1851, Sir Daniel Wilson, the antiquary, calls the British Isles "*the insular home of the Keltai.*"[2] The transformation of the people of the British Isles into "Celt" was then complete.

The older philologists were thus mainly responsible for this arbitrary extension of the name "Celtic" in a racial sense to the earlier inhabitants of the British Isles. The confusion arose through the popular misconception that because a people spoke a dialect of the same group of languages they were necessarily of the same race. The confusion began with the observation by the French philologists that the language of the Celts in Brittany or Mid-Gaul, or "Celtic" speech, as it was naturally called by them, was essentially similar in structure to that of the Brythonic or Cymri speech of the Welsh and the Breton of Brittany in Gaul. This Brythonic language was then presumed to be a branch of the Celtic of Gaul, and the term "Celtic" applied to it, and then extended in a racial sense to the Welsh people who spoke it. Similarly, the Gaelic or Gadhelic[3] speech of the Irish and the Scottish Highlanders was also found to have affinity with the Gallic and Welsh "Celtic," and all the people speaking those languages were also dubbed "Celts." The linguistic affinities on which this racial kinship was assumed, were tabulated in two groups by Dr. Latham in 1841,[4] based on the classification by Prichard and C. Meyer ; and this still

[1] Boswell, *Life of Johnson*, III. Hebrides Tour, Sept. 18th.
[2] W.P.G., 472.
[3] Irish *Gaedhlig*, Scottish Gaelic *Gaidhlig*, from Irish-Scot *Gaodhal* and Welsh *Gwyddel*, a Gael or inhabitant of Ireland and Northern Scotland.
[4] R. G. Latham, M.D., *English Language*, 1841.

remains the recognized classification of the " Celtic " dialects, of which the Gaelic is considered to be the more primitive and older.

### CELTIC GROUP OF LANGUAGES.

I. *Gallic or Cymric.*
1. Cymric or Welsh
2. Cornish (now extinct)
3. Armorican or Breton
   [" Celtic " proper]

' II. *Gaelic or Erse.*
1. Fenic or Erse or Irish
2. Gaelic or Highland Scottish
3. Manx

Still further had the Celtic theory grown apace. This so-called " Celtic Race " was also called " *Aryan* " in race, when it was observed that their language was akin to the languages which had latterly been classed as " *Aryan.*" This essentially racial title of " Aryan " had been introduced into English and other European languages by the discovery, in 1794, by the erudite Sir William Jones, the Chief Justice of Calcutta, that the Sanskrit language of the ancient Hindoos, who called themselves " *Arya,*" was radically and stucturally of the same type as the Old Persian, Greek, Latin, Celtic, English, and German (or " Teutonic ") languages of Europe,[1] and that the culture and mythology of the ancient Hindoos were essentially analogous to that of Ancient Greece and Rome and of the Goths. The physical appearance also of the purer Hindoos, claiming to be the descendants of the highly civilized ancient Aryas, resembled generally that of the North European peoples of Britain and Scandinavia. It was then assumed that the ancient " Aryas " who civilized India and Persia or Iran, and gave them their " Aryan " speech were presumably of the same common racial stock as the ancestors of the civilizers of Greece and Rome and Northern Europe, who had in prehistoric time civilized Europe and imposed on it their " Aryan " speech. This Indo-European stock of people was thus called " The *Aryan* Race " ; and the name " Aryan " was extended also to their several languages and dialects, which were classed as " Aryan " or " Indo-European," or by usurping German writers " Indo-Germanic." Thus

---

[1] This fact was fully established by F. Bopp, of Berlin, in 1820, in his *Analytical Comparison of Sanskrit, Greek, Latin and Germanic Languages,* and by subsequent writers.

the so-called " Celtic " languages were called a branch of Aryan Speech and the " Celts " themselves called " Aryans " in race ; and to these " Celts " the philologists and ethnologists arbitrarily assigned the credit for first introducing the Aryan language and Aryan culture into Alban or Britain and Ireland.

Disillusionment, however, came in the year 1864, when scientific anthropologists, following Anders Retzius, the Swede, had begun to apply exact measurement to the skulls and physical types of the various so-called branches of the Aryan race, as it had been found that the shape of the skull or head-form afforded the best of all criterions of race. In that year M.Paul Broca, who had begun four years earlier a systematic measurement of the head-forms of the people of France,[1] published his famous monograph on the head-forms of the Celts of Brittany[2]—the descendants of the original " Celts " of Cæsar and the classic writers. He found that so far from these " Celts " being of the Aryan physical type, namely tall, fair, and *long*-headed, they were, on the contrary, a short, darkish-complexioned, and *round*-headed race. The next year, 1865, appeared the celebrated collection of measurements of the ethnic types in the British Isles by Davis and Thurnam in their " Crania Britannica,"[3] on which they had been engaged since 1860, and Dr. Beddoe's papers.[4] This disclosed conclusively that the " Celtic "-speaking people of the British Isles, and more particularly the Welsh, were also short and dark-complexioned, but with *long*-heads or medium long-heads and thus were of a markedly different racial type to the " Celts " of Gaul ; whilst their skull-form and complexion excluded the greater portion of them from the Aryan racial type and affiliated them to the Iberians.

---

[1] P. Broca, " Sur l'ethnologie de la France " in *Mémoir. Soc. d'anthropol.* Paris. 1860. I, 1–56.

[2] Broca, " Sur les Celtes " in *Bullet. Soc. d'Anthropol.* 1864, 457 f. ; and " La Race Celtique Ancienne et Moderne Auvergnes et Amoricains, etc.," *Revue d'Anthrop.*, 1864, 11, 577 f.

[3] J. B. Davis and J. Thurnam, 1865.

[4] J. Beddoe, " On the head-forms of the West of England," in *Mem. Anthrop. Soc.*, London, 1864, ii, 37 f, and 348 f.

Those startling discoveries by scientific methods excited great commotion amongst the ethnologists and philologists, as it disproved their accepted theory that the "Celts" of Gaul were of the same kindred as the "Celts" of the British Isles, and that both were Aryans; whereas it was now disclosed on the contrary that they were of different races and that neither were of the Aryan Race, although both spoke an Aryan language in different dialects.

These scientific results were fully confirmed by further measurements, which were also extended over the greater part of Europe. As these measurements disentagle the British "Celts" from the continental, and also sharply differentiate the Aryan type from both, it is necessary to glance at their leading results which are here displayed in the accompanying Table ;[1] and illustrated in Fig. 22. This

RACIAL TYPES IN EUROPE.

| Race | Head and Cephalic Index[2] | Brow | Face | Hair | Eyes (iris) | Nose | Skin | Stature | Synonym |
|---|---|---|---|---|---|---|---|---|---|
| I. ARYAN or NORDIC | Long 75-79 | Broad | Medium or Longish | Light, sometimes Reddish | Blue or Lig Grey | Narrow aquiline | Fair | Tall | Scandinavian Caucasian Teuton properly No. II) |
| II. ALPINE or CELTIC | Round 80-88+ | Broad | Broad or Round | Flaxen, Chestnut to Darkish | Hazel | Broadish heavy | Fair to Brown | Medium Stocky | Germanic[4] (or Teutonic) Sarmatian Slav, Hun |
| III. IBERIAN or Mediterranean and River-bed | Long 72-78 | Narrow | Long | Dark Brown to Black | Dark | Broadish | Brown to Dark | Medium Slender | Pelasgian, Ligurian |

[1] This Table is based generally on that of Dr. Ripley (R.R.E., 121); but I have used Dr. Deniker's "Nordic" for No. I, with "*Aryan*" as its synonym, as Aryans are admittedly "Nordic," and I have rejected the ambiguous and misleading "Teutonic" which is ordinarily synonymous with "Germanic," which is a totally different type, namely No. II.

[2] "Cephalic Index" is the ratio of the extreme length of the head to its extreme breadth expressed in percentage. Under 80 the head is "Long," and 80 and upwards it is "Round" or "Broad" ("Germanic."). It is the surest criterion of race along with colour. The writer, of fair complexion, has a cephalic index of 76.1.

[3] See note 1.

[4] On general prevalence of "Alpine" type of head in Germany see Ripley, (*R.R.E.* map opp. p. 53); also Prof. Parsons, cited later.

shows three main racial types in the population of modern Europe, all three of which we shall find represented in Britain, namely : (I) The *Aryan*[1] or *Nordic* (or Northern), tall, fair, broad-browed, long or longish heads, (II) *Alpine* or " *Celtic* " (continental) or *Germanic*, short-statured, fair or darkish, broad-browed, round or broad heads; and (III) *Iberian* or " *Mediterranean*," shortish-statured, dark, narrow-browed, long-faced, long-heads, and including the prehistoric " river-bed " type of the Picts. The best of the distinguishing criterions of race is the Head Index in second column of table, in conjunction with colour.

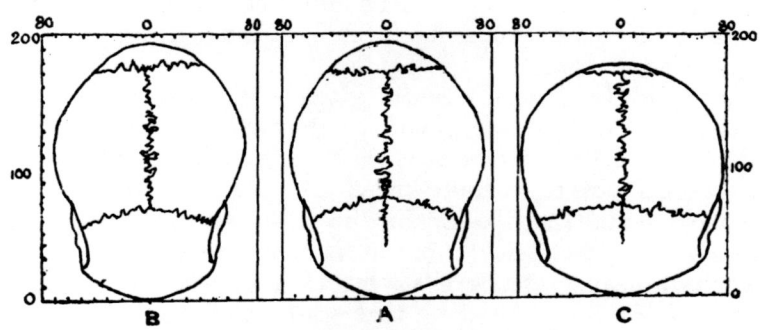

FIG. 22.—Three main Racial Head-Types in Europe.
(The head is viewed from above.)

A. Aryan or Nordic.
C. Alpine, or " Celtic," or Germanic (Teutonic)
B. Iberian or Mediterranean and " River-bed " type.

The first of these racial types of Europe, the *Nordic* or " Northern," which is the Aryan type, is now mostly restricted to north-western Europe. It included most of the classic Greeks and Romans, as evidenced by their sculptures and paintings and skeletal remains. It comprises a considerable element in the present-day population in the British Isles, the Scandinavians or Norsemen (including Swedes and many Danes), and a small proportion of the people of France and of the Rhine Valley, where, however, the skulls of the older burials show that the civilizers of Germany, like the Jutes and Anglo-Saxons, were of this type. And I shall

[1] See note 1 on p. 134.

show that the Early Britons and "Scots," properly so-called, as well as the Goths, belonged to this Aryan type, which was also the type of the eastern or Indo-Persian branch of the Aryans—the Barat-Khattiya,—and the Khatti or Hittites and Phœnicians.

The second, the "Celtic" or so-called "Alpine" [Swiss], extending from Brittany to Switzerland, also comprises the major type in the Rhine Valley, the Slav or Serb people of Mid-Europe, including the Prussians, Poles and a large proportion of the Russians, and an appreciable element amongst the people on the East Coast of Britain derived from the "Bronze Age" Hun invaders of prehistoric Alban in the later Stone Age who were essentially of this round-headed type.[1]

The third type is of especial interest in regard to the "British Celtic" question, and the dark racial element by which the "Celtic" language is chiefly spoken in the British Isles. This type is generally known as "*Iberian*," from one of its old seats, Iberia or Spain, and it was given the wider synonym of "Pelasgic"; but it is now generally called "Mediterranean," after Sergi's nomenclature, as it is found in modern Europe, mainly along that sea-basin from Spain to Greece and its Archipelago to Asia Minor. It is essentially of the same type as the prehistoric Stone Age inhabitants of the British Isles, the "river-bed" type of Huxley, and is also substantially the same type which is found in many of the long "barrows" or long grave mounds alongside the Aryan type there.[2] And it still forms the substratum of the modern

[1] This important fact of the persistence of *round*-heads in the modern population of Great Britain, which is not referred to by Ripley, has been noted by many anthropologists, especially by Sir Arthur Keith in regard to both England and Scotland. Regarding the latter, Sir A. Keith has recently stated that, while the West Coast of Scotland, as in the Glasgow district, contains only about 2 per cent. of round-heads in its population which is mainly long-headed like the rest of the British Isles, Edinburgh, on the East Coast, contains about 25 per cent. of round-heads in its population.

[2] Dr. Thurnam's well-known axiom still holds good : "long barrow, long skull ; round barrow, round head." From the South Coast and the Severn Valley—Glastonbury, Gloucester and Wilts—and northward over Britain, in the long barrows associated with the Aryan type (implying intermarriage) are found the remains of small-statured people with often *long*-headed and often narrow-browed skulls along with their polished stone-weapons and no bronze. See D.E.M., 318 f. On broad-browed, long-heads in long barrows, see later.

head-form in the British Isles. It thus appears that the titles "Hibernia" for Ireland, and "Hebrides" for the Western Isles, are probably survivals of the "*Iberia*" title for the primitive stock, which first peopled the British Isles in the Stone Age. Indeed, the Irish Gaels or Gaedhels or "Fene" claim origin from "the sons of Milead or Miledh,"[1] which is said to be Milesia in Spain,[2] *i.e.*, Iberia; and, in describing the later colonization of Erin, they say that a leading chief of the later Gaedhel Miledh immigrants was called "*Eber*" which appears to preserve this "Iberia" title:

"They spread themselves through Erin, to her coasts . . .
*Eber* (the Gaedhel) took the South of Erenn (Erin)."[3]

In consequence of these discoveries by anthropologists that the "Celts" belonged to the non-Aryan round-headed race, and the resulting paradox that the so-called "British and Irish Celts" were not Celts, and that there were no "Celts" in Britain,[4] the leading anthropologists, recognizing the logic of facts, gave up the use of the misleading terms "Celt" and "Celtic" in a racial sense in regard to the British Isles, and restricted these terms to the round-headed Celts of Gaul, according to the designation of these people in the classics. And even the term "Aryan" tended to drop out of use in a racial sense, when no historical trace of the Early Aryans in Europe could be discovered, and when it was found by M. de Quatrefages[5] and others that the physical type not only of the Prussians but also the prevailing type of the Germans—who had posed as being the leading "Aryan" civilizers of Europe—was Slavic and thus Non-Aryan. They now recognized more clearly than before the fact that mere language is by itself no criterion of Race, and that kinship in language does not necessarily imply kinship in race, as so many conquered races are observed to have adop*t*ed, or to have imposed on them the language of their overlords of a totally different race. As Huxley observed, no one could call a Negro of America either English or Aryan

[1] *Book of Lecain*, detailed references in Skene, *op. cit.*, 47.
[2] *Ib.* 319.   [3] *Ib.* 50, 51.   [4] But, see below.   [5] *La race prussienne*, 1871.

in race, merely because he spoke the Aryan English speech. And, as has been well said : " There is no such thing as ' a French race,' but rather many races speaking French ; no Italian race, but rather many races speaking Italian ; no Germanic race, but rather many races speaking German ; "[1] and we may add *there is no such thing as* " *The English race,*" but rather many races and mixed races living in the same political unity under the same laws and speaking the English Language.

The philologists, on the other hand, for whom the Celtic Theory seems to have possessed a fatal fascination, still clung, and do cling, to the title " Celtic " for the language spoken in the British Isles by the Gaels of Scotland and Ireland and by the Cymri of Wales. And the " die-hard " Celtists still give it a racial sense, and speak of the British " Celtic " speakers as " The Black Celts,"[2] and of the " Celtic temperament," and of the kilt as " the garb of Old Gaul," and of the " Celtic origin " of the Aryan Language in Britain. They thus keep alive the old mental confusion and mislead the public and popular writers. Thus we have the latest writer on history, Mr. Wells, misled into writing the jargon that : the *Keltic* invasion of Britain was by " tall and fair " people, and " Nordic Kelts," and that " it is even doubtful if the north of England is more Aryan than *pre-Keltic in blood.*"[3] ( !) With such conflicting uses of the term " Celtic " in circulation, even some anthropologists occasionally lapse into references to " the Celts of the British Isles," and to Celts as " a branch of the Aryan Race."

Who then are the race in Britain called " Celts " by our latter day writers ?

No traditional or historical reference or record whatever exists of the migration of any people called " Celts " into Early Britain.[4]

---

[1] A. Hovelacque, *Science of Language*, 1877, 243.
[2] Compare *Encyclop. Britannica*, 11th ed., 1910, 5, 611.
[3] H. G. Wells, *Outlines of History*, 1920, 83.
[4] Cæsar mentions that some Belgians had migrated to the south coast of Britain during and shortly before his day. These have been arbitrarily called " Celts " by some latter-day writers ; but Cæsar expressly excludes the Belgæ from the Celtæ (D.B.G.i,1.).

## THE "BRITISH CELTS" WERE PICTS

Anthropologists from their exact measurements of the people in Britain, tell us that "*the darkest population forms the nucleus of each of the Celtic Language areas* which now remain."[1] And this dark "Celtic-" speaking element is especially found in "the Grampian Hills in Scotland, the wild and mountainous Wales (and Cornwall) and the hills of Connemara and Kerry and Western Ireland."[2] And their average stature is relatively short, culminating in Britain, in South Wales, the Severn Valley and Cornwall.[3] It will thus be noticed that this "Celtic" area corresponds generally in Scotland with the area in which the later "Picts" suddenly disappeared, and in whose place have suddenly appeared the people called "Celts." In Ireland also the "Celtic" area generally corresponds with that part of the country specially associated with the Bans, Vans or Early Feins, who, we have found, were Picts. Cornwall, with its old tin-port of Ictis (or Victis?), was a chief "Celtic" centre on the old "Sea of Icht (or of the *Picts*.)"[4] And the Picts appear to have called themselves "*Khaldis*" or "*Khaltis*."

This new line of evidence leads us to the conclusion that the early "Celts" or "Kelts" were presumably the early Picts calling themselves "*Khaldis*" or "*Khaltis*," a primitive people who, I find from a mass of evidence, were the early "Chaldees" or Galat(i) and "Gal(li)" of Van and Eastern Asia Minor and Mesopotamia in the Stone Age.[5] Their western hordes would seem to have retained their title of "Khaltis" or "Galati" or "Gal," when in the Old Stone Age they penetrated westward into Gaul on the Atlantic and formed there the primitive Kelts or Celtæ of Gaul and of Pictavia on the border of Iberia, and the Gauls and Gaul are actually called "*Galatæ*" and "*Galat*" by Strabo.[6] And at a later period when the round-headed Sarmatian Alpines invaded Gaul from the Rhine and Switzerland and drove out the Picts, they seem to have retained the old aboriginal name for that land and its people:—"Gaul" and

---

[1] R.R.E., 321. [2] *Ib.*, 319. [3] *Ib.*, 327-9 and map.
[4] On this "*Icht*" as "Pict," see later.
[5] Details in *Aryan Origins*.
[6] S. i, 3, 21, etc.; iv, 2, 1, etc.

"Khaltis," "Kelt" or "Celt." Yet, although in Britain the name "Kelt" or "Celt" does not appear in the fragmentary surviving history of Ancient Britain under that exact spelling, it, nevertheless, is represented in its dialectic variant of "*Caled*" in "Caled-on"; and in "Culdees," the title of the Pictish mission of Columba. It may possibly survive also in "Gadhel," the common Gaelic spelling of "Gael," by transposition of the letters in spelling—a recognized dialectic change called paronomasia—of an earlier "Galdhi," representing "Khaldi" or "Kaldi." And its shortened form "Gal" possibly survives in "Gael," and in "Gwalia" for Wales. So, after all, perhaps the British "Celts" are more entitled to use the "Celt" title than the round-headed "Celts" of Gaul, who, according to classic historians and anthropologists, are the only true "Celts."

This identity of the ancestors of the "British Celts" or "Kelts" with the "Khaldis" or "Caleds" or Picts is in keeping with the physical traits and head-form of the latter. The people of the "Celtic-" speaking areas are preponderatingly of the dark, long, narrow-headed, narrow-faced, smaller-statured Iberian type of the Khaldis or Picts; and this is also the prevailing type of the substratum of the people throughout the British Isles.[1]

The modern "British Celts," however, as well as the bulk of their kindred still forming the main substratum in the population of the British Isles generally, have become a somewhat heterogeneous race, through more or less intermixture with the other two races of later invaders and civilizers. Thus their original dark aboriginal Pictish or

---

[1] Thus Dr. Beddoe describes the "Celtic area" race in Scotland: "The head and face are long, and rather narrow, the skull base rather narrow, the brow and occiput prominent." Hair mostly "dark brown" to "brownish black" and even "coal-black" (*B.R.B.*, 245). Hector Maclean records, "the head is high, long and often narrow, the face frequently long . . . . the lips are usually full, often thick, and more or less projecting" (*A.R* iv, 129). Ripley, on the commonest type in the British Isles generally, says: "The prevailing type is that of a long, *narrow* cranium, accompanied by an oval, rather than a broad or round, face" (*R.R.E.*, 303). And Wilson, on the British "Celts," notes "the remarkable *narrowness of forehead* which characterizes the Celtic Race [in the British Isles]." (*W.P.A.*, 181). And he says: "We begin to discover that *the Northern and Southern Picts were no other than the aboriginal Celtæ*" (*Ib.* 15); although he confounds the issues by supposing that the dark Picts were Aryans.

## "BRITISH CELTS" ARE NON-ARYAN PICTS

Iberian stock has been mixed more or less on the East Coast and Midlands with the non-Aryan round-headed and broad-browed, fair "Alpine" or Slav or "Hun" invaders from the time of the beaker-using men of the Late Stone Age, about 2000 B.C. onwards;[1] and later over all the British Isles, they have been mixed more or less with their Aryan rulers and civilizers, the tall, long-headed, broad-browed, fair "Northern" invaders, the Britons and Scots, properly so-called, with their later kindred Anglo-Saxons, Norse and Normans. As a result of this partial intermixing during many centuries (which is discussed in a later chapter on the mixing of the races) there have arisen several intermediate composite types. Many of the "British Celts" thus now possess a considerable strain of Aryan blood, manifesting itself in physical traits and especially in a lighter colour of the hair and eyes, whilst fondly idealizing their Celtic ancestry into a sentimental cult. But the major portion of the population, not only in the modern "Celtic" areas, but all over the British Isles generally retains appreciably a preponderating Pictish type.

Thus, in regard to the civilization of the British Isles, we find that the modern theory that it was the "British Celts" who first introduced the Aryan language and civilization into Britain is merely a survival of an unfounded assumption by later philologists, which assumption rested on the further unfounded assumption that the "British Celts" were originally Aryans in Race.

We are now in a position to take up, on much clearer ground than has hitherto been possible for previous enquirers, the great and hitherto unsolved question as to how and when the Aryan language and civilization were first introduced into Britain, and by what racial agency.

[1] These round-head "beaker" men, as found in Aberdeen stone cists, were of small stature, averaging 5 feet 4 inches, with broad, short faces and widish noses and muscular build, *1.B.B.* 69. But in the South, on the East Coast of England, they averaged 5 feet 8-9 inches, with cranial index of 80 to 84, with broad brows and roundish faces. A. Keith, *J.R.A.I.*, 1915.

## XIII

### Coming of the " Britons " or Aryan Brito-Phœnicians under King Brutus-the-Trojan to Albion about 1103, B.C.

> " The Britains almost severed from the World." VIRGIL, *Bucolics*, i, 67.
> " At length he (Brutus-the-Trojan) came to this island named after him ' Britannia,' dwelt there and filled it with his descendants." NENNIUS, 10.

THE historicity of the traditional Ancient British Chronicles which has thus been established in regard to the coming of the Brito-Phœnician king of the Scots, Part-olon, about 400 B.C., to the land of the Picts, by means of his own Newton Stone inscriptions and associated evidence, presumes that the earlier portion of these Chronicles, dealing with the somewhat earlier period, also contains genuine historical tradition.

Now this earlier portion of the Chronicles records circumstantially the first arrival of the Britons by sea, in Albion under " King Brut-the-Trojan " about the year 1103 B.C., and his colonization and first civilization of the land, and his bestowal thereon of his " Trojan " (Aryan) language and his own patronymic name " Brit," in the form of " Brit-ain " or " The Land of the Brits or Brit-ons." This tradition, we shall now find, is fully confirmed and established by a mass of new historical facts and associated evidence.

These Ancient British Chronicles are nowadays known only through the Latin translations[1] made by early British monks,

---

[1] English versions of these by J. Giles and others. Geoffrey's version was first translated into modern English by A. Thompson, Oxford, 1718; and reproduced mostly by Giles.

# COMING OF ARYAN BRITONS 1103 B.C. 143

Gildas Albanius (fifth century A.D.)[1] Nennius (about 822 A.D.)[2] and Bishop Geoffrey of Monmouth (about 1140 A.D.),[3] and the Welsh and Irish-Scot fragmentary versions of the same.[4] These Ancient Chronicles are stated by their various editors to have been translated or compiled from earlier versions—"in the (ancient) British tongue" says Geoffrey—which, being presumably on parchment, have now perished.

The ancient tradition was thus handed down in writing from generation to generation by the Britons, who, we shall find, were familiar with writing long before their arrival in Britain. And, as usual, it would be modernized from time to time into the vernacular of the period by later transcribers, just as modern writers modernize Chaucer and the early versions of the Arthur Legend. This tradition was universally regarded as genuine history down till about a century ago.[5] The Brut or "Brutus" tradition was current in early Welsh bardic literature and formed a class styled "The Bruts," including Layamon's. And Geoffrey's version was a mine from which our great poets and dramatists have drawn materials and inspiration for many of their romances on British life in the pre-Roman period, such as Shakespeare's *King Lear* and *Cymbeline*.

The arbitrary rejection of these traditional Ancient British Chronicles as a source of pre-Roman British History by

[1] The title "*Gildas*" is said to have been borne by two monks, and both princes, sons of King *Gawolon* or Caw, King of Strathclyde, with capital at Dunbarton. "Gil-das" or "Gilli-tasc" means "Prince of the Church." (*P.A.B.* 69). The elder, surnamed Albanus, called his history of Early Britain "Cambreis" or "History of the Cambrias," a title for Britain. Only fragments of it remain. He died at Glastonbury in 512. The younger, surnamed Badonius or "of Bath," wrote a scurrilous and non-trustworthy history commencing only with the Anglo-Saxon period (*Ib.* 69, etc.).

[2] On his date and personality, see *P.A.B.* 43, etc. Several MSS. are dated 976 A.D. For antiquity of the Nennius tradition before age of Nennius, see H. Zimmer, *Nennius Vindicatus*, Berlin, 1893; and Mommsen, *Mon. German. Hist. Chronica Minora*, 3, 14, etc.

[3] He became bishop of St. Asaph in 1152.

[4] The Irish "Nennius" is ascribed to a British bishop of Ireland named Marcus and dates to 822, see *P.A.B.* 49, etc.

[5] See *G.O.C.* xi, etc.; *S.C.P.* clxix, 57, 118, 378, etc. The wide prevalence of the version by Nennius is evident from there being no less than 33 copies of the old MSS. of about the tenth century still existing.

modern writers since about a century ago[1] is based upon a kind of objection and mere dogmatic assertion which, if applied to early Greek and Roman History and to the Old Testament tradition, would equally entail their total rejection also.

The common allegation that there was no higher civilization in Britain before the Roman occupation, and that the Britons were "painted savages roaming wild in the woods" is not supported by any evidence whatever, and certainly not by Cæsar himself, nor by any other authoritative Roman historian. In his remarks upon the people of Britain, based upon his own observations during his few months' campaign in Kent and South Herts, and on what he was told by interpreters, Cæsar describes the people generally as civilized. He states that they were settled agriculturalists, lived under kings, of whom there were no less than four in Kent alone; that "the Kentish men [the only men he passed amongst] were *civilized* people . . . and their customs are much the same with those of the Gauls"[2]—that is to say, a people highly civilized and richly and luxuriously clothed. He also says that Britain "is well peopled and has plenty of buildings much of the fashion of the Gauls, they have infinite store of cattle, *make use of gold money*, and iron rings which pass by weight, the midland countries produce some tin, and those nearer the sea iron."[3] And many Early British coins have been discovered in France and Belgium[4] attesting pre-Roman Briton international trade. It was only the uncivilized people of the interior—whom he calls the "*interiores*," and who were, as we have seen, the non-Briton Pictish aborigines—in regard to whom he says that they stain their skins blue and "they seldom trouble themselves with agriculture, living on milk and flesh, and are clad with skins."[5]

---

[1] So universal is this capricious attitude of modern writers, the one following the other often presumably without having examined the texts, that even the editor of the commonest English edition of these Chronicles, Mr. Giles, loses no opportunity in preface and footnotes to disparage his text.
[2] *D.B.G.* v, 5.  [3] *Ib.* v, 5.
[4] E.C.B. 38, 51, 95-7.  [5] D.B.G., v, 5.

Cæsar also records the high military efficiency of the Briton troops: "the legionary soldiers were not a fit match for such an enemy," and "the enemy's horse and war-chariots . . . inspired terror into the (Roman) cavalry."[1]

And here it is significant to note that the dreaded war-chariots of the Briton cavalry (which were peculiar to the Britons and unfamiliar to the Romans), and of which Cassivellaunus, the "Catti," alone retained 4,000 after he disbanded his army[2] *were of the same type as those of the Hittites or Catti*, as described and sculptured by Ramses II. (c. 1295 B.C.) at the Battle of Kadesh, a port of the Hitto-Phœnicians[3] (see Fig. 23).

FIG. 23.—Hitto-Phœnician War-Chariot as source of Briton War-Chariots.
(From reliefs of Abydos, after Rosellini, 103.)

This unexpected formidable opposition by the civilized Britons, despite the secessions from Cassivelaunus, contrived by the invidious diplomacy of Cæsar, explains why the latter so promptly abandoned his second intended conquest of Britain and retired speedily to Gaul within a few weeks, without

[1] E.C.B. v, 6.   [2] D.B.G. 4.33.2.
[3] The popular notion that the Briton War Chariots were armed with scythes has no historical or archæological foundation. Neither Cæsar nor Tacitus mentions such an appendage; nor is such figured on Briton Chariots on coins, and no such scythes exist on War-Chariots which have been found interred with Briton chiefs in their graves, à la Tut-ankh-amen.

making any serious attempt at subjugating Britain. And the later Roman occupation of Britain by overwhelming forces, beginning with Claudius in 43 A.D., may perhaps be more justly paralleled to the present political occupation of the Rhine Valley by the allied forces after their " civilized " enemy was hopelessly crippled by superior force, than the mere military occupation of an " uncivilized " country.

The objectors to the pre-Roman Civilization in Britain—whose objection merely rests on their credulous acceptance of the dogmatic teaching of some generations of uninformed teachers obsessed with exaggerated notions of Roman influence on Briton—also shut their eyes not only to the inconvenient testimony of the pre-Roman coins of Early Britain, but also to the testimony of the early scientific navigating explorer Pytheas,[1] who, about 350 B.C., or *about three centuries before Cæsar*, circumnavigated Britain and first mapped it out scientifically with latitudes. He was a native of *Phocea*, north of Smyrna in Asia Minor, and a place-name which is obviously a contraction for " *Phœnicia*," as the adjoining sea-port on the headland on the Ægean was called " Phœnice." A colony of his countrymen were settled at Marseilles, engaged in the export tin trade from Cornwall, from which the tin was transported overland through Gaul by pack-animals from a Brittany port to save the dangerous sea-passage by the Bay of Biscay and the Pillars of Hercules. Sailing from Marseilles, presumably to exploit the tin-producing country of Britain, which he calls " Pretanic,"—in series with Aristotle's reference to it, in 340 B.C., as " *Britannic* "[2]—he visited first the Old Phœnician tin export-port of Ictis or St. Michael's Mount in Penzance Bay (see Fig. 24), then, sailing round the west coast, surveying and landing at several places, he eventually reached Shetland (his Thule). He found the people every-

[1] Pytheas is cited as a standard scientific authority by ancient geographers and astronomers from Hipparchus down to Strabo. His original work is lost and only known through extracts by the ancient writers. These were collected by Fuhr, 1835; and are summarized by *H.A.B.*, 217-230.
[2] Aristotle, *De Mundo*, sec. 3, " Beyond the Pillars of Hercules is the ocean which flows round the earth. In it are two very large islands called Britannic ; these are Albion and Ierne."

## BRITON CIVILIZATION IN 500 B.C.     147

where settled, peaceful agriculturalists, and even in Shetland they were agricultural and made wine from "corn and honey."[1] And over a century before Pytheas, the Phœnician admiral Himlico, from Carthage, voyaged, about 500 B.C., round part of Britain to report on the tin-producing region there. He states that the Phœnicians of Gades and Carthage were in the habit of sailing the British seas, and refers to "the hardy folk" of Britain.[2]

The further excuse for rejecting these Early British chronicles, that there are no contemporary inscriptions to support their ancient tradition, is one which, if accepted, would sweep away not only the early traditional history of Greece and Rome, which is accepted although resting on mere literary tradition, but also nearly all the Old Testament History, and much of the history of the Early Christian Church. There is absolutely no inscriptional evidence whatsoever, nor any ancient classic Greek or Roman reference, for the existence of Abraham or any of the Jewish patriarchs or prophets of the Old Testament, nor for Moses, Saul, David, Solomon, nor any of the Jewish kings, with the mere exception of two, or at most three, of the later kings.[3] All of these are accepted and implicitly believed to be historical by our theologians merely on the strength of their having been believed by our Christian ancestors, because they were believed by the Jews themselves. The only difference between the accepted Jewish tradition and the rejected British tradition is that the former is actively taught as true by incessant repetition in church and Sunday schools to everyone from childhood upwards; whereas the equally well authenticated Early British traditional history is actively disparaged and stigmatized by modern writers, the one mechanically repeating the other, as mere fabricated

---

[1] S. iv, 5, 5.
[2] Festus Avienus in *Ora Maritima*, 110, etc.
[3] The only ancient Israelite kings of which there appears to be any epigraphic or contemporary record are "Jehu, son of Khumri" (which latter name is supposed to be "Omri" of the Old Testament), who is mentioned in the tribute-lists of the Assyrian King Shalmaneser II. in 842 B.C.; and "Hezekiah of Judah" who is mentioned in the tribute-lists of the Assyrian Sennacherib in 701 B.C. (C.I.W.A. I, pl. 38 and III, pl. 5, No. 6.)

fables or forgeries, despite the above-cited facts to the contrary. But there is inscriptional evidence, as we shall see.

Nor is the alleged objection that there is no classic Greek or Roman reference to the name of King Brutus,[1] even were it true, which it is not, sufficient grounds for rejecting the circumstantial British tradition regarding him. There is no classic reference to the Aryan ancestors of the historical Greeks nor to the names of the other descendants of Æneas, that, Homer states, revisited and re-occupied Troy in the dark period following its sack and destruction by the Achaians. Nor is there any classic Greek or Roman reference to any of the Jewish patriarchs, prophets and kings or even to the Hebrews themselves. But I find, as detailed in Appendix IV, that Homer does appear to mention King Brutus as "Peirithoos" repeatedly, both in his Iliad and Odyssey, as one of the most famous of immortal heroes and associated with Hercules of the Phœnicians. Moreover, the Homeric hero who was the confederate of Peirithoos, namely, Coronos Caineus, appears to be Brutus' colleague in the conquest of Albion, the Phœnician prince "Corineus" of the British Chronicles.

Even for the traditional birth-place of Brutus-the-Trojan being located in the Tiber province of Latium, some evidence also is now forthcoming which connects Latium directly with both Troy and Ancient Britain. The Roman tradition of Æneas the Trojan—and the traditional great grandfather of Brutus—preserved by Virgil relates that Æneas, in his flight from Troy after the great war, carried with him, on his ship, his "household guardian 'gods' (*penates*)" from Troy to Latium in Italy.[2] Now in Latium were unearthed two prehistoric shrines (see Fig. 24 for one of them) which might possibly be the actual ones brought by Æneas there. They are of the same hut-like form as the sacred buildings figured

---

[1] Thus the translator of the common English version, Mr. J. A. Giles, warns his readers (p. 92) saying, " It is unnecessary to remind the classical reader that the historians of Greece and Italy make no mention of Brutus and his adventures."

[2] *Æneid* i, 382. The flight of Æneas to the Tiber appears to have been considered an historical event by the Romans. Julius and others of the Cæsars claimed descent from his son *Iulus*, as well as did the legendary Romulus.

## TROJAN SUN SYMBOLS IN BRITAIN 149

on Hitto-Sumerian seals of the Sun-cult along with Crosses and Swastikas,[1] and *the surface of this Latium shrine, Fig. 24, is also covered by Crosses and Swastikas of exactly the same pattern which occurs on the solar amulets of Troy* (see Fig. 46)[2] *and on the rock-sculptures and ancient solar monuments and coins in the British Isles* (see Fig. 47 and later Figs:.).[3] And the prehistoric inscriptions in Britain, now deciphered for the first time in Chapter XVIII are of the Trojan type and invoke God and his archangel by the same names as the Trojan.

FIG. 24.—" Trojan " solar shrine at Brutus' birth-province (Latium) with identical Hittite symbols as in Ancient Britain.
(After Chantre).[4]

This establishes the fact that the same solar religion with identical symbols as the Trojan was introduced into Latium, the birth-province of Brutus, as was introduced by Brutus and his Trojan Britons into Early Britain.

The now rehabilitated Early British Chronicles are found to be fairly trustworthy sources for the Coming of the Britons and the Early History of pre-Roman Britain. In their present form they no doubt contain, as similar traditional records do, many trivial details introduced by later generations of transcribers and translators, which may have been

---
[1] W.S.C., 484–494.
[2] On this Cross on Trojan amulets, see S.I. 1820, where Cross is of the same many-lined design as on shrine, but rounded for wear and pierced for threading.
[3] On such Briton crosses, see Fig. 47, and in Wales: W.L.W., 88 and 90; Scotland: S.S.S., ii, 101; Ireland: C.N.G., Fig. 84; Swastikas of this form: S.S.S. i, 124, 274 and ii, 67, &c.
[4] C.M.C., p. 90.

marginal notes on the older texts suggesting incidents based on conjectural etymologies of the proper names. The genuineness of the texts is also suggested by the frank record of the vicious traits of several of the kings as well as the virtues of others; and the circumstantial accounts of court intrigues, assassinations and the tyrannical feudal abuse of the sovereignty, reflect a very life-like picture of human happenings. Indeed, it appears probable that the earlier textual tradition was, like the earlier tradition of the Indo-Aryan or Eastern branch of the Barats, little more than a bare consecutive list of the kings from the founder of the first dynasty with the chief events in the life of the founder and of one or two others of the more important later kings. And many of the expanded details may be the additions of later copyists and bards embodying their personal opinions or conjectures, just as Tennyson admits having taken great licence with the old Arthur legend in his *Idyls of the King*. But it appears unlikely that there was any deliberate falsification, or that the main outlines of the tradition were materially altered.

Of the existing versions of these Chronicles those of Nennius and Geoffrey of Monmouth are obviously the most authentic and fullest, and they are in general agreement. Nennius tells us that his was a compilation by himself from the ancient British texts and the annals of the Romans and other authorities whom he specifies; whereas Geoffrey states expressly that his was a translation into Latin of " an ancient book in the British tongue." The following extracts and summary of the life and voyage to Britain of " King Brut-the-Trojan " are from Geoffrey's text, and refer only to Nennius when he differs therefrom or supplies additional details.

We shall now let the Old British Chronicles speak for themselves: in recording the arrival in Albion of the Britons under King Brutus about 1103 B.C., and his civilization and Aryanization of this land:[1] (for reference to chief place-names see Map.)

[1] The translation by A. Thompson as revised by Giles (G.E.C.) is generally followed. There is a later translation by S. Evans, 1904.

# CHRONICLE OF BRUTUS, FIRST BRITON KING 151

### Birth and Early Life of Brutus-the-Trojan.

" After the Trojan war, *Æneas*, fleeing with *Ascanius* from their destroyed city, sailed to Italy. There he was honourably received by King *Latinus*,[1] which raised against him the envy of Turnus, King of the Rutuli, who thereon made war against him. Engaging in battle, Æneas got the victory, and killing Turnus, obtained the kingdom of Italy (Latium) ; and with it Lavinia, the daughter of Latinus.[2] After his death Ascanius, succeeding to the kingdom, built Alba on the Tiber, and begat a son named Sylvius, who . . . took to wife a niece of Lavinia . . . and had a son called Brutus.

" At length, after fifteen years were expired, the youth accompanied his father in hunting, and killed him accidentally by the shot of an arrow. . . . Upon his father's death he was expelled from Italy, his kinsmen being enraged at him for so heinous a deed."

### Brutus in Greece.

" Thus banished, he went into Greece, where he found the posterity of Helenus, son of Priamus, kept in slavery by Pandrasus, King of the Greeks. For, after the destruction of Troy, Pyrrhus, son of Achilles, had brought hither in chains Helenus and many others ; and to revenge on them the death of his father had commanded that they be held in captivity. Brutus, finding they were, by descent, his old countrymen, took up his abode among them, and began to distinguish himself by his conduct and bravery in war, so as to gain the affection of kings and commanders ; and above all the young men of the country. . . . His fame spreading over all countries, the Trojans from all parts began to flock to him, desiring, under his command, to be freed from subjection to the Greeks. . . . There was then in Greece a noble youth named Assaracus, a favourer of their cause, for he was descended on his mother's side from the Trojans. . . . Brutus having reviewed the number of his men and seen how Assaracus's castles lay open to him, complied with their request." [It is then related that Brutus fought a battle with the army of Pandrasus at the river *Akalon*, and eventually routed the enemy and captured the

---

[1] King Latinus of Mid-Italy is stated in Nennius' version to be " the son of Faunus [?Van], the son of Picus [Pict ?], the son of Saturn " (*Nennius*, sect. 10).

[2] Virgil gives this version of the adventures of Æneas—the arrival of that exile on the coast of Latium in Italy, King Latinus' entertainment of him and promise of his only daughter and heiress of his crown, the rage of her admirer Turnus and his invasion of Latium, and his defeat and death at the hands of Æneas.—Virgil, books 7-12.

king and extracted from the latter his consent for the Trojans to depart from Greece, provided with the ships and provisions necessary for this purpose and " gold and silver," as well as the hand of his beautiful daughter Ignoge for Brutus.] . . . " He (Pandrasus) accordingly delivered to the Trojans three hundred and twenty-four ships, laden with all kinds of provisions and gold and silver, and married his daughter to Brutus."

*Cruise of Brutus and His Fleet from Greece to Gades.*

" The Trojans, now released from his (Pandrasus') power, set sail. . . . The winds continued fair for two days and a night together, when at length they arrived at a certain island called *Leogecia* [Leugas, the modern Leucas, about 35 miles south of the mouth of the Acheron River of Epirus; see Map], which had been formerly wasted by pirates and was then uninhabited. . . . In it was a desolate city in which they found a temple of Diana and in it a statue of that goddess, which gave answers to those that came to consult her. . . . Then they advised their leader to go to the city, and after offering sacrifices, to enquire of the deity of the place what country was allotted to them for their place of settlement. . . . So that Brutus, attended by Gerion the augur and twelve of the oldest men, set forward to the temple. Arrived at the place, and presenting themselves before the shrine with garlands about their brows, as the ancient rites required, they made three fires to the three deities Jupiter, Mercury and Diana, and offered sacrifices to each of them. Brutus himself, holding before the altar of the goddess a consecrated vessel filled with wine and the blood of a white hart, prayed :—

> ' Goddess of Woods, tremendous in the chase
> To the mountain boars and all the savage race!
> Wide o'er the ethereal walks extend thy sway,
> And o'er the infernal mansions void of day!
> Look upon us on earth! unfold our fate,
> And say what region is our destined seat?
> Where shall we next thy lasting temples raise?
> And choirs of virgins celebrate thy praise?'[1]

" After repeating this prayer, he took four[2] turns round the altar, poured the wine into the fire and then laid himself down upon the hart's skin, which he had spread before the altar,

[1] This graceful and fairly literal poetical translation is by Pope from the Latin verse of the historian Gildas the Elder. See P.A.B., 53.
[2] Four, we shall see, is the mystic Hitto-Sumerian and Phœnician number for " Mother Earth."

# VOYAGE OF BRUTUS TO ALBION

where he fell fast asleep. In the night, in his deep sleep, the goddess seemed to appear before him and thus responded :—

> ' Brutus ! there lies beyond the Gallic bounds
> An island which the western sea surrounds,
> By giants once possessed ; now few remain
> To bar thy entrance, or obstruct thy reign.
> To reach that happy shore thy sails employ ;
> There Fate decrees to raise a second Troy,
> And found an empire in thy royal line
> Which Time shall ne'er destroy, nor bounds confine.'[1]

" Awakened by the vision . . . he called to his companions and related the vision, at which they greatly rejoiced and were urgent to return to their ships and hasten westwards in pursuit of what the goddess had promised.

" Without delay they set sail again and after a course of thirty days came to Africa. From thence they came to the *Philenian Altars* [volcanic sunken rocks east of Carthage ; see map][2] and to a place called *Salinæ* [port Selinus in S.W. corner of Sicily], and sailed between *Ruscicada* [Ras Sidi (ali-el-mekki) Cape at what was later Carthage Bay],[3] and the mountains of *Azara* [the Auza Mts. in Algeria], where they underwent great dangers from pirates, whom they nevertheless vanquished and captured their rich booty.

---

[1] Pope's translation.
[2] These " Altars " are clearly the dangerous sunken rocks off the Mediterranean Coast of Africa, east of Italy mentioned by Virgil in his account of the voyage of Æneas to the Tiber, where that hero saw :—

> " Three hapless barks
> Caught by the southern blast *on rocks unseen*—
> A ghastly ridge emerging 'mid the waves,
> By Tuscan seamen ' *Altars* ' called—are hurled."
> —Virgil, *Æneid*, i, 129-131.

South of Etna near Malta or Pantellaria, are some sunken volcanic rocks, which still abound in hot springs *with jets of steam* (see *Géographie Universelle* i, 571) ; and this last-named feature would suggest " Altars." But the title " Philenian " clearly associates the locality with the African coast of Libya where there was a port of " Philænon " on the shore of Cyrene. There were also two heroic " Carthaginian " brothers called " Philæni " who submitted to be buried (or drowned ?) alive for the sake of their country, who presumably derived their name from this Libyan port. The title of " Altar " suggests that they were of the same volcanic formation as those of Pantellaria.

[3] The rocky cape forming the northern headland of the Bay of Carthage is now called " *Ras Sidi*," wherein the term *Ras* appears to be the Akkadian *Resu* or " Head," so that *Ras* or *Resu* may have been used in remote times for " head-land " by Akkadian mariners such as the Phœnicians were. And significantly *Ras* is the name for headlands on the coast of Levantine Phœnicia.

"From thence, passing the river *Malua* [Wady *Mulaye*, west of Oran, forming the east frontier of Morocco] they arrived at *Mauretania* [Morocco], where, for want of provisions, they had to go ashore. . . . When they had well stored their ships, they steered to the Pillars of Hercules . . . and came to the Tyrrhenian Sea [Gulf of tne Tyrian-Phœnician city of Gades or Cadiz]. Upon its shores they found four several clans descended from the banished Trojans who had accompanied [the Trojan Phœnician] *Antenor*[1] in his flight. The name of their commander was Duke *Corineus*, a modest man in council, but of great courage and boldness, who could overthrow even gigantic opponents. When they learned from whom he was descended they joined company with him and those under his government, who from the name of their leader were afterwards called the ' Cornish ' people.

### *Voyage from Gades to Albion*

" From thence they came to *Aquitaine*, and, entering the mouth of the Loire, cast anchor. *Goffarius Pictus*, who was king of Aquitaine at that time, hearing of the arrival of a foreign people with a great fleet upon his coasts, sent messengers to demand whether they brought peace or war. The messengers met Corineus, who was come ashore with two hundred men to hunt in the woods. They demanded who gave him permission to enter their king's forests and kill his game. Corineus answered there was no occasion for asking leave, upon which one of them, named Imbertus, rushing forward with full-drawn bow, shot at him. Corineus, avoiding the arrow, ran up to him and with his bow in hand broke his head, and the rest escaped with the news to Goffarius. The Pictavian raised an army to revenge the death of his messenger." [Here follows an account of the battle between the Picts and the legion of Brutus and Corineus, in which the latter performs herculean prodigies of slaughter single-handed with his battle-axe, and the Picts are put to flight. Brutus pursued them through Aquitaine " to the place where the city of Tours now stands, which he afterwards built,"[2] and called it after " a Trojan named *Turonus*, the nephew of Brutus," who was slain and buried there. Brutus " enriched his men with the spoils of the slain."]

" Brutus, afflicted to observe the number of his forces daily lessened, while that of the enemy increased . . . at last determined to return to his ships while the greater part of his followers was yet safe and hitherto victorious, and to go in

[1] See details later.
[2] Nennius also credits Brutus with building " Turnis, the city of the " Turones " or Tours in Gaul. (*Nennius*, sect. 10).

# ARRIVAL OF BRUTUS IN BRITAIN 1103 B.C.

quest of the island the goddess had told him of. So, with the consent of his company, he repaired the fleet and, loading it with the riches and spoils he had taken, set sail with a fair wind to the promised land, and arrived on the coast of *Totnes*.[1]

## Arrival in Albion and Colonization of the Country as "Brit-ain" about 1103 B.C.

"The island was then called *Albion*,[2] and was inhabited by a few 'giants.' Notwithstanding this, the pleasant places, plenty of rivers abounding in fish, and its pleasing woods made Brutus and his company desirous to fix their habitation in it. They therefore passed through all the provinces, forced the 'giants' to fly into the caves of the mountains, and divided the country among them according to the directions of their commander.

"After this they began to till the ground and build houses, so that in a little time the country looked like a place long inhabited. At last Brutus called the island after his own name '*Brit-ain*,' and his companions '*Brit-ons*' . . . from whence afterwards the language of his nation, which at first bore the name of Trojan [Doric] or rough Greek, was called '*British*.'

"But Corineus, in imitation of his leader, called that part of the island which was given to him as duke, '*Corinea*'[3] and his people '*Corinene*' [Cornish men] after his own name; for though he had his choice of provinces before all the rest, yet he preferred this country [Corn-wall], which is now called, in Latin, '*Cornubia*.' For it was a diversion to him to encounter the said 'giants,' which were in greater numbers there than in all the other provinces. Among the rest was one detestable monster named Goëmagot. . . . On a certain day, when Brutus was holding a solemn festival to the gods in the port where they first landed, this 'giant,' with a score of his companions, came in upon the Britons, making great slaughter. The Britons at last killed everyone but Goëmagot, who was spared to wrestle with Corineus.[4] . . . Corineus, snatching him on his shoulders, ran with him to the shore and from the top of a high cliff hurled down the savage monster into the sea.

[1] On Totnes landing, see later.
[2] "Albion" is the form used about 340 B.C. by Aristotle in *De Mundo*, 3.
[3] "*Kernaw*" is an old name for Cornwall in Gilbert's *Parochial Hist. of Cornwall*, about 1580.
[4] This refers only to the "giants" of Totnes with its old tin and copper mines. The other "giants of the provinces" are referred to in a previous paragraph.

". . . The place where he fell is called Lam Goëmagot, that is, ' Goëmagot's Leap ' unto this day.[1]

### Founding in Britain of New Troy " Tri-Novantum " or " London " about 1100 B.C.

" Brutus, having thus at last set eyes upon his kingdom, formed the design of building a city, and with this view travelled through the land to find a convenient site. And coming to the river Thames, he walked along the shore and at last pitched upon a place fit for his purpose. Here he built a city which he called ' *New Troy*,' under which name it continued for a long time after, till at last, by corruption, it came to be called ' *Tri-Novantum*.' But afterwards, when *Lud*, the brother of Cassibellaun, who made war against Julius Cæsar, obtained the government of the kingdom, he surrounded it with stately walls and towers and ordered it to be called after his own name, ' *Kaer-Lud*,' that is, the ' City of Lud ' [or ' Lud-Dun,' corrupted into ' Lon-don '].[2]

### Making Laws for Government

" After Brutus had finished building the city, he made choice of the citizens that were to inhabit it, and prescribed them laws for their peaceable government. . . . At the same time also, the sons of *Hector*, after the expulsion of the posterity of *Antenor*, reigned in Troy ; as in Italy did *Sylvius Æneas*, the son of Æneas, the uncle of Brutus, and the third king of the Latins.

### Death of King Brutus about 1080 B.C. and Division of Britain

" During these events Brutus had by his wife Ignoge three famous sons, named *Locrin, Albanact* and *Kamber*. These, after their father's death, which happened in the twenty-fourth year after his arrival, buried him in the city which he had built ; and then, having divided the kingdom of Britain [excepting Cornwall] among them, retired each to his government. Locrin, the eldest, possessed the central part of the island, called afterwards from his name ' *Lœgria*,' Kamber had that part which lies beyond the river Severn, now called Wales, but which was for long named ' *Kambria*,' and hence the people

---

[1] This rock is said by Gilbert (*op. cit.*) and Camden (*Britannia*, 1586) to be, according to local tradition, the " Haw " at Plymouth and the " giant " is there known as " Gogmagog."

[2] See Appendix V for details.

still call themselves in their British tongue ' *Kambri*.' Albanact, the younger brother, possessed the country he called ' *Albania*,' now Scotland.

" After they had a long time reigned in peace together, *Humber*, king of the Huns, arrived in Albania, and having killed Albanact in battle, forced his people to flee to Locrin for protection. Locrin, on hearing this news, joined his brother Kamber and went with the whole strength of the kingdom to meet the king of the Huns . . . and put him to rout. . .

" Locrin married Corineus' daughter named Guendolœna . . . and had a son named Maddan, who was put under the care of his grandfather Corineus to be educated." [The Chronicles record the succeeding reigns down to the Roman period. In the reign of Ebraucus or York (who founded York and Dun Barton) occurred the annexation of Germany by Britons.]

*Civilization of Germany by Britons about* 950 B.C.

" The sons [of King Ebraucus, fourth in descent from Brutus[1]], under the conduct of their brother Assaracus, departed in a fleet to Germany, and having, with the assistance of [the descendants of] Sylvius Alba, subdued the barbarian[2] people there, obtained that kingdom."[3]

Several points raised by this traditional British Chronicle regarding the voyage to and conquest of Alban or Britain by King Brutus-the-Trojan—who, we have found, was the great Homeric hero Peirithoos (see Appendix IV)—now call for examination.

The sea-route reported to have been followed by him in his voyage from the Acheron (or Akalon) River in Epirus to Britain is clearly and unequivocally evident by the complete identification, which I have made,[4] of all the places, without any exception, mentioned in the narrative. These places follow one another in strict geographical order (see map). It is seen that the course taken was at first due south until the Libyan coast of Africa was sighted at Philœnon in Cyrene. And as the sunken rocks called " Altars " were

---

[1] See Appendix I, List of Briton Kings.
[2] G.C. ii. 3.    [3] G.C., ii, 8 and see later.
[4] On these place-names the latest writer, Mr. J. A. Giles, writes (*op. cit.*, 101) : " It is probably impossible to discover whether these names describe existing places, or *are purely inventions of the author*. (*Sic !*) "

also sighted by Æneas on fleeing from Troy to the Tiber, according to Virgil's tradition, this suggests that the Trojan (and Phœnician[1]) sailors, in voyaging westwards along the Mediterranean, were in the habit of sailing due south until the coast of Africa was sighted, and then coasting along that sea-board, guided by its well-known rocky headlands as landmarks.

The time taken for the first stage of the voyage, from the mouth of the Acheron or the city up that river to Leogecia, the ancient Leugas and modern Leucas, (which is south of Corfu), that is, a distance of about 35 miles, is stated to have been " two days and a night." This seems quite probable in view of the difficulties in starting off such a large fleet of small boats and the necessity for them keeping together. The second stage from Leogecia to the coast of Africa at Philænon, which is in a direct line due south only about five hundred miles, is stated to have taken " thirty days." This long period may have been due to contrary winds, or the " thirty days " may perhaps refer to the whole time under sail from the re-embarking at Leogecia till the next landing in Mauretania (see Map).

The " Vision " of Brutus at the temple of Diana may or may not have really happened. It is only said to have occurred in a dream. The mere offering of worship to the popular goddess of the Chase and of Destiny, with a cup of wine and few drops of hart's blood poured upon the altar fire, was a very probable occurrence, especially as Brutus was bent on a " chase," and was begged by his men to make the offering as we are told. Similar and more bloody sacrifices were often made by Alexander-the-Great—coming from the land of the same Parthini tribe in Epirus—at popular native shrines. And it was the usual practice amongst sailors to worship the local divinity on starting on voyages, and we have seen that the goddess called " Diana " by Geoffrey was a form of the Phœnician tutelary Britannia.

The account of this " Vision " occurs in a fragmentary portion of the lost earlier version of the Chronicles by Prince

---

[1] One of Æneas' ships was manned by Orontes, presumably named after the river of the Hitto-Phœnician port Kadesh.

Gildas the Elder of Dunbarton. He was a famous Briton poet, and either he or still earlier redactors of these Chronicles may have introduced it as a bardic embellishment to signalize worthily so important an historical event as the first coming of the Britons to Britain. Such prophetic visions, not to mention their familiar frequency in the Jewish Old Testament, are not unknown in the case of such historical personages as Alexander the Macedonian and even Cæsar, to signalize some particular achievement or foretell a fate. So this vision in no wise detracts from the historicity of the British tradition.

Besides, it now becomes clear that Brutus was no Columbus in the discovery of Albion or Britain. Nor did he require any such adventitious aid as a supernatural vision to inform him of the existence of Albion and its attractiveness for annexation. Albion was already, at that period, well known to the Phœnicians, we shall find, as a rich tin-producing country, and Cornwall was already occupied by a small colony of the rival relatives of Brutus, before he arrived there. It thus appears that Brutus doubtless deliberately set sail with his fleet from the River Acheron for the express purpose of annexing and occupying Albion.

The colony of four clans of fellow-Trojans found by Brutus " on the shores of the Tyrrhenian Sea," outside the Pillars of Hercules, is of immense historical and ethnological importance in establishing the affinity of the Trojan descendants of Dardanus with the Phœnicians, and the kinship of Brutus with the Phœnicians. The settlement of these Trojans on this " Tyrrhenian Sea " was, of course, Gades, which was traditionally visited by Hercules[1] and contained one of his most famous Phœnician temples.[2] It was founded traditionally as a colony by the Phœnicians of *Tyre*,[3] which thus accounts for the name of its gulf as the " Tyrrh-enian Sea "— a title also applied to the Gulf of Tuscany where there was similar Phœnician or Punic colony at " Punicum " bordering Latium, in a province ruled by the Phœnician " Tyrrh-eni "

---

[1] Herodotus, 4, 8.  [2] S. 3, 5, 3, etc.
[3] Vellenis Paterculus ed. Elzevir Leyden (1639), 1, 2 ; and Strabo, 3, 5, 5.

or Tyrians. This Phœnician settlement at "Gad-es," or "The House of the *Gads* or Phœnicians," was presumably founded mainly as a "half-way house" to the tin-mines of Cornwall and its off-lying isles of the Cassiterides, now submerged by the sinking of the land. Herodotus records that the chief source of the supply of tin, which was essential for the manufacture of bronze, for the ancient world came from the Cornwall Cassiterides. He says:

"The Cassiterides from which our tin comes. . . . It is nevertheless certain that both our tin and our amber are brought from these extremely remote regions (the Cassiterides and North Sea) . . . in the western extremities of Europe."[1]

This tin-trade and its distribution were entirely in the hands of the Phœnicians.[2] And it now seems that the "Tin-land beyond the Upper Sea" (or Mediterranean) of the Amorites subject to Sargon I. about 2800 B.C., was the Cassiterides of Cornwall, see App. VI.

The "Trojan" traders whom Brutus found settled at Gades were under the leadership of Duke *Corineus*, bearing this significantly Greco-Phœnician name,[3] and a former associate-in-arms of Brutus. The four clans of these Trojans of Gades are stated in our text to have been the descendants of "banished Trojans who had accompanied *Antenor*." This Trojan hero, it will be remembered, is described by Homer as a leading prince of Troy, who rode in the same chariot with King Priam as ambassador at the parley with the Achaian Greek invaders.[4] He was spared by the latter in their massacre of the Trojans on account of his honourable conduct in indignantly rejecting the proposal of a party of Trojans to murder the Achaian ambassadors, Ulysses and Menelaus, and was thus allowed, with the remnants of his family, to escape along with Æneas and his son Ascanius He sailed to Italy with attendants called Veneti, like Æneas, but chose Illyria at the head of the Adriatic, and there founded Padua[5] adjoining "Venice," which latter name seems to preserve his ethnic title of "Phœnice" or

---

[1] Herodotus, 3, 115.　　[2] S. 3, 5, 11.
[3] A Greco-Phœnician tombstone at Carthage is erected to "*Karneios*."— See P. Delattre, *La Nécropole Punique* (excavations of 1895-6). Paris, 1897, 143.
[4] *Iliad*, 3, 263 and 213.　　[5] Virgil, *Æneid*, 255-292

# PHŒNICIAN KINSMEN OF BRUTUS

"Phœnician." And he was so celebrated that he received a statue as a demi-god from the Phœnicians at Tyre.[1]

Antenor's descendants and their relationships to Brutus are displayed in the following genealogical Table[2] :—

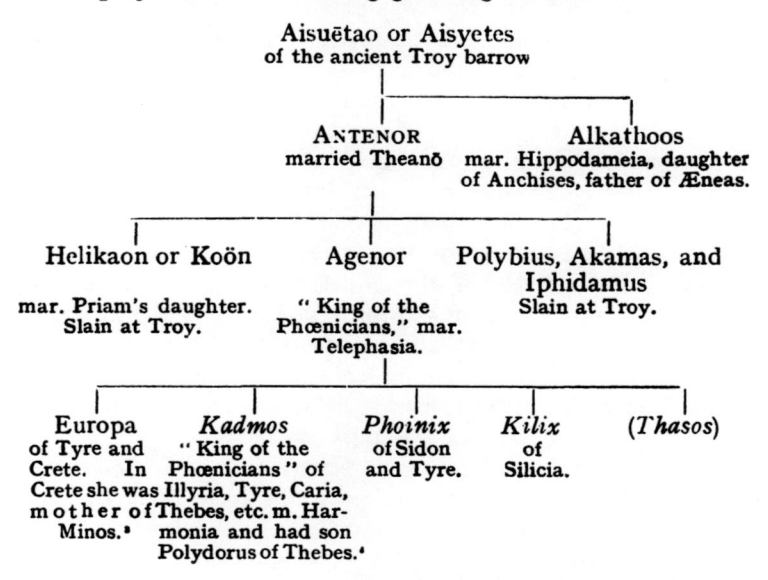

```
                    Aisuētao or Aisyetes
                    of the ancient Troy barrow
                           |
            _____
            |                          |
         ANTENOR                    Alkathoos
       married Theanō          mar. Hippodameia, daughter
                               of Anchises, father of Æneas.
            |
   _____
   |              |                         |
Helikaon or Koön  Agenor        Polybius, Akamas, and
                                       Iphidamus
mar. Priam's daughter.  "King of the       Slain at Troy.
Slain at Troy.          Phœnicians," mar.
                        Telephasia.
                             |
   _____
   |         |            |           |            |
Europa    Kadmos       Phoinix      Kilix      (Thasos)
of Tyre and  "King of the   of Sidon      of
Crete. In  Phœnicians" of  and Tyre.   Silicia.
Crete she was Illyria, Tyre, Caria,
mother of Thebes, etc. m. Har-
Minos.[3]    monia and had son
             Polydorus of Thebes.[4]
```

The four clans, therefore, at Gades, of the descendants of the banished Trojans who accompanied the exiled Antenor, were presumably the descendants of the four sons of his son "King Agenor-the-Phœnician," who was so famous a sailor that he was called "Son of Poseidon or Neptune." These sons are seen in the Table to be Kadmos or "Cadmus," Phoinix, Kilix and Thasos, the first two of which are usually called by ancient classic writers, "Phœnicians," as well as their father. And incidentally it is seen that the famous King Minos of Crete was also a Phœnician. It seems possible that Duke Corineus, through his Homeric title of "Koronus *Kaineus*" was a descendant of Antenor's eldest son *Koōn* (see

---

[1] See fragments of Dius and Menander preserved by Josephus, *Contr. Ap* 1, 17 and 18; also Arrian, *Emp. Alexander*, 2, 24.
[2] I have compiled this Table from the references in Homer's *Iliad*, Herodotus, Strabo, Pausanias, etc.
[3] Herodotus, i, 2 and 173; 4, 45.   [4] Hesiod, *Theogony*, 935.

Table), who was slain by Agamemnon. The Table also shows the inter-relationship by marriage between Antenor-the-Trojan and King Priam and Æneas, the great grandfather of Brutus. Their ancestor Aisuetao of the " ancient barrow " (or funeral mound) at Troy[1] was presumably a descendant of Dardanus, the founder of the royal dynasty of Troy,[2] and thus kinsman of Æneas and Brutus.

The place of landing of Brutus in Alban is stated to have been Totnes, in the sound of the Dart in Devon; and it is in keeping with the fateful fitness of things that the first harbour selected by the great admiral Brutus and his early Phœnician Britons for their first British fleet in Alban's waters should have latterly been the favourite resort of the British " sea-dog " Sir Walter Raleigh, and be the location of the " Britannia " training ship for our navy of the modern empire of Britain. There still exists at Totnes, on the fore-shore street, the traditional stone called " Brutus Stone " (which I have seen) with the local tradition that upon it Brutus first set foot when landing in Alban.

This tradition of his landing at Totnes and not in Cornwall seems confirmed by the record in Nennius' version of the Old Chronicles, which states that there were already some relatives of Brutus in possession of Alban, and presumably at the tin-mines in Cornwall, before the arrival of Brutus. He states :—

" Brutus subdivided the island of Britain whose [previous] inhabitants were the descendants of the Romans [properly Trojans from Alba on the Tiber] from *Silvius Posthumus*. He was called ' Posthumus ' because he was born after the death of Æneas, his father : his mother was Lavinia. . . . He was called ' Silvius ' . . . from whom the kings of *Alba* were called ' Silvan.' *He was [half-] brother* to Brutus . . . . but Posthumus, his brother, reigned among the Latins."[3] And he had, according to Geoffrey,[4] a son called Sylvius *Alba*.

This tradition of the prior rule in Alban, presumably by deputy, of the Alban Silvius, the " half-brother," or rather half-uncle, of Brutus, is also preserved in the early Scottish

[1] *Iliad* 2, 793.
[2] Details in *Aryan Origin of Phœnicians*.
[3] N.A.B. sects. 10 and 11.   [4] G.C. chap. 8.

Chronicle of the Alban Duan of 1070 A.D., which was composed presumably for the coronation of the Scottish king Malcolm III., whose queen was the famous Margaret, and who was crowned in that year and to whom it was addressed. This poem, however, represents the intruder under the title of " Alban " as the son of Ascanius or " Isicon " instead of the grandson of Æneas by his Latin wife, which latter tradition appears to be correct. It is also noteworthy that the form of the name in this Scottish poem for Brutus as ' *Briutus* " approximates more closely the Homeric " Peiri-'*hoos* " and the Latin " *Pirithous*." The poem says :—

" What was the first known invasion
Which grabbed the land of Alban ?

*Alban* grabbed it with many of his seed,
He, the elder son of *Isicon* [Ascanius] :
Brother was he of *Briutus*, yet scarce a brother,
He named *Alba* of Boats.

But banish'd was this big brother
By Briutus across the ' Sea of *Icht*,'
Briutus grabbed Albain for his ain
As far as wooded Fotudain [Tweed ?]."[1]

The precise relationship of Brutus to his " big brother, yet scarce a brother," Silvius *Alba*, the " Alban " of this Scottish poem, whom he evicted from Alban, is seen in this genealogical Table, which I have compiled from the Chronicles of Geoffrey and Nennius :—

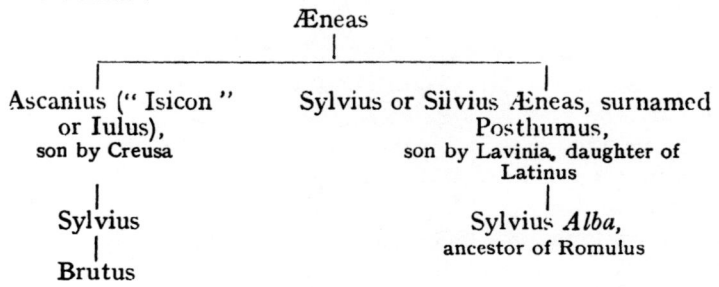

```
                         Æneas
                           |
          _____
          |                              |
Ascanius (" Isicon "          Sylvius or Silvius Æneas, surnamed
   or Iulus),                        Posthumus,
 son by Creusa                 son by Lavinia, daughter of
                                      Latinus
          |                              |
       Sylvius                      Sylvius Alba,
          |                      ancestor of Romulus
        Brutus
```

[1] See S.C.P., 57, for text and for a freer translation than mine. "Fotudain" equates with the *Otadini* tribe of Ptolemy who occupied the S.E. of Scotland between the Tweed and Forth, South of the "*Gad*-eni" tribe.

It is thus seen that "Alban" or "Albanus" who occupied part of the south of Alban before the arrival of Brutus, and presumably about 1130 B.C., the supposed date of founding of the Phœnician settlement at Gades, was the son of a half-brother of the grandfather of Brutus.

The "Sea of *Icht*," across which Briutus banished his senior relative Sylvius Alba, or his agents, derived its name (in series with the Isle of Wight), as we have seen, from the same Pictish source as "*Ictis*,", the title used by classic Greek writers for the tin-port of St. Michael's Mount in the Bay of *Penzance*—which latter name also is now disclosed to be based presumably on one of the many place-names of "Phœnice" bestowed on their settlements by the Phœnicians, especially as a former name of Penzance, as we shall see later, was "Burriton," a dialectic form of Baraton or "Briton."

St. Michael's Mount or Ictis is physically like the type of the strategic islets so frequently selected by the seafaring Phœnicians for their ports, such as Tyre, Gades, etc. It is an islet contiguous to the mainland and admirably adapted for defence on the landside, yet open to the sea (see Fig. 25). Its towering, graceful, spiry crest stands up, an unmistakable landmark seen far out at sea:—

> "Here the Phœnician, as remote he sail'd
> Along the unknown coast, exulting hail'd,
> And when he saw thy rocky point a-spire,
> Thought on his native shore of Aradus or Tyre."
> —*Bowles.*

It was also called "Fort of the Sun (Din-Sol)" presumably from its Phœnician Sun-temple, of which see later.

The neighbouring mainland off St. Michael's Mount, and extending to Land's End and along the West Coast of Cornwall to Carnbræ, is still honeycombed with the old tin and copper workings of the Phœnicians, amongst the mounds of which I have several times rambled, and which are still locally ascribed to the Phœnicians.

It would thus appear from the use of the name "Sea of *Icht*," that it was from the tin-mines and tin-port of Ictis in

Cornwall that Brutus banished his big " brother " Sylvius Alba, or his agents, across the Sea of Icht—that is, back in the direction of his own kingdom on the Tiber.

FIG. 25.—Phœnician Tin Port in Cornwall, *Ictis* or St. Michæl's Mount in Bay of Penzance.
(After Borlase 395.)

This prior occupation of Cornwall by kinsmen of Brutus would now seem to explain why Brutus landed at Totnes instead of Cornwall, which was already in the possession of his rival exploiters. It also explains why Duke Corineus, the commander of the four Phœnician clans at Gades, who were mainly dependent on the tin-mining industry in Cornwall, from which they were presumably ousted or forestalled by their rival kinsmen from the Tiber, so readily joined Brutus in his expedition to annex Alban, and doubtless so on the express stipulation that he would receive Cornwall with its monopoly of the tin trade. It also would explain why Brutus handed over the duchy of Cornwall to Corineus to conquer without going there himself, whilst he personally moved on to the Thames Valley and settled there.

The date for this invasion of Alban by Brutus and his associated Phœnicians is fixed directly by totalling up the reported years of reign in Britain of Brutus and his continuous line of descendants and successors down to Cassivellaunus and his successors in the Roman period, as the traditional length of the reign of each king is recorded (see details in Appendix I.) There is nothing improbable or at all surprising in a ruling race of Phœnician ancestry having preserved a complete written list of their kings with the length of reigns of each on parchment records, the originals of which have now perished; for the Phœnicians are admitted by the ancient Greek classic writers to have introduced the art of writing into Europe; and writing was a practical necessity for these early industrial sea-traders in the keeping of their accounts—a class of documents which form the majority of the ancient records recovered by excavations on early oriental civilized sites.

These regnal years in the Early British Chronicles, when totalled up, give the epoch of Brutus' arrival in Alban or Britain at about 1103 B.C. (see Appendix I.). This date is corroborated by the usually-accepted date for the Fall of Troy at "about 1200 B.C."[1]; for, as Brutus was of the third generation from Æneas, and was already a mature hero of many exploits at the epoch of his arrival, this would place his invasion somewhere about 1100 B.C. Geoffrey's Chronicle also states that, after Brutus had finished the building of his new city on the Thames, " the sons of Hector (son of Priam), after the expulsion of the posterity of Antenor, reigned in Troy," which would yield a corresponding date. It is also highly suggestive of such a date for Brutus' arrival, as well as for the independence and veracity of these British Chronicles, that their compilers, in bringing Æneas past the bay which was latterly occupied by Carthage, should, unlike Virgil, who brings Æneas to Carthage, nevertheless make no mention of Carthage. This was obviously owing to the fact that Carthage was not founded traditionally until about

---

[1] The epoch of this great Trojan War is estimated by the archæological remains unearthed at the excavations of the site of ancient Troy, or Novo-Ilium, at the modern Hissarlich (or Ancient Fortress) being found to belong to the Mycenian period of culture, which extends from about 1500 to 1200 B.C.—the last being the terminal date for the destruction of this Troy according to Dörpfeld, *Troja and Ilion*, 1902; and compare S.L., 292.

## PREVIOUS TROJANS IN BRITAIN

850 B.C., that is, about two and a half centuries subsequent to the passage of Brutus and his fleet.

The date for the prior arrival of Sylvius Alba's party may probably be placed, from the relative age of that Tiberian king (as seen in above Table), at a few decades before the arrival of Brutus, about 1103 B.C., though we shall find from the evidence of the Stone Circles and the prehistoric cup-markings that Sumerian Barat-Phœnician merchants had formed isolated mining and trading settlements in Albion before 2800 B.C.

It was, perhaps, a memory of this invasion of the Land of the Picts in Albion by Brutus and his kinsman Duke Corineus, the descendant of the canonized Phœnician King Antenor, whose son was King *Agenor* (see Table, p. 161), which is referred to in a fifteenth-century Chronicle of the Scots, containing a rather confused account of the history of the Picts, when it states :—

" Ye Pechtis [war] chasyt out of yir awin landis callit Sichia [?Icht] be ane prynce of Egipt callit Agenore [the Phœnician]."[1]

This migration of King Brutus and his Trojan and Phœnician refugees from Asia Minor and Phœnicia to establish a new homeland colony in Albion, which event the British Chronicle historical tradition places at 1103 B.C. (see Appendix I) was probably associated with, and enforced by, not merely the loss of Troy, but also by the massacring invasion of Hittite Asia Minor, Cilicia and the Syria-Phœnician coast of the Mediterranean by the Assyrian King Tiglath Pileser I. about 1107 B.C. to 1105 B.C.[2]

[1] *Chronicle of the Scots* of 1482 A.D.   S.C.P. 381.
[2] This mighty Assyrian emperor, and conqueror also of Babylonia, records in his still extant inscriptions that he subdued and destroyed the chief cities in " the broad Land of Kumanī (of the Mitanni or Medes), the Land of Khatti (or Hitt-ites), and on the Upper Sea of the West (Mediterranean)" —*Annals of Kings of Assyria*. Brit. Museum 1902, pp. 82, &c. And he mentions especially his conquest of Arvad (Aradus) the old city of the Amorites and at that time, the chief city-port of the Phœnicians in the Levant, and his sailing in a Phœnician ship on " The Sea of the West " (The Mediterranean).

## XIV

ARYANIZING CIVILIZATION OF PICTS AND CELTS OF BRITAIN BY BRUTUS AND HIS BRITO-PHŒNICIAN GOTHS ABOUT 1100 B.C.

*Disclosing Phœnician Origin of Celtic, Cymric, Gothic and English Languages, and Founding of London and Bronze Age.*

> "Brutus called the island, after his own name, 'Britain,' and his companions 'Britons.'"—*Ancient British Chronicles.*[1]
> "The tribes subject to the *Cedi* [*Ceti* or *Getæ* Goth Phœnicians] are skin-clad."—*Rig Veda Hymns.*[2]

THE introduction of civilization and the Aryan language by King Brutus or Briutus and his Phœnician associates into Albion, or as he now called it "Brit-ain" or "Land of the Barats or Brits," is described in circumstantial detail in the Ancient British Chronicles, which is confirmed by more or less contemporary and other evidence.

The name of the aborigines, unfortunately, is not preserved in the existing versions; but we have seen that these aborigines, whose extant skeletal and other remains date back to the Old Stone Age, were clearly the Picts or "British Celts." And a memory of them seems to be preserved in the Scottish version of the Brutus legend, which places the newly-arrived Brutus, as we have seen, on "The Sea of Icht (or of the Picts)," when he "banishes" from the island his "big brother," his kinsman the Tiberian Sylvius Alba and his people, who had preceded Brutus in the possession of the tin-mines and in the domination of the island. And significantly the traditional place where Brutus landed is still reputed the especial haunt of the earth-dwelling dwarfish "Pixies," who, we have seen, are a memory of the earth-burrowing Picts.

[1] G.C. 1, 16; and N.A.B., 7.   [2] R.V., 8, 5, 8.

## PRIOR "GIANT" PHŒNICIANS IN BRITAIN 169

The "giants," who are described in the Chronicles as opposing the invasion by Brutus and Corineus and their Briton followers, were obviously not the aborigines, but, as we shall find from other evidence, an earlier trading branch of the Aryan-Phœnicians—the Muru or Amuru or "Amorite" giants and erectors of the Stone Circles and "giants' tombs"—who had been exploiting the tin and copper mines for many centuries and even a millennium or more before the arrival of Sylvius and his trading agents. But they had not systematically colonized the land or civilized the aborigines.[1]

The systematic civilization of Britain thus begins practically with Brutus. He occupied the country as far north as the Tweed, the Chronicles inform us, and he at once began the work of welding the various Pictish tribes into one nation under their Aryan rulers, through the bonds of a common Aryan language and the civilizing Aryan laws.

Brutus signalized his annexation of Alban by giving the latter a new name. He was, as we have seen, an Aryan of the Barat tribe, of which the Phœnicians were the chief representatives; and he had just come from Epirus where, on its Macedonian border, was a colony of that tribe with a town called "Phœnice," bearing that tribal title as "Parthini" or "The Parths," in series with Brutus' own personal name of "Peirithoos." We have also seen, and shall further see, that the Phœnicians were in the habit of applying this tribal title to their new colonies. We are now told in the Chronicle that "Brutus called the island [of Alban] after his own name '*Brit-ain*' and his companions '*Brit-ons.*'" The original form of this name "Brit-ain" was, as we have seen, "Barat-ana" or "Land of the Barats,"[2] a form which

---

[1] The references to Brutus' associate Corineus as carrying the defeated "giant" leader, and running with him on his shoulders, shows that the "giant" was no larger than himself.

[2] The usually conjectured derivation of "Britain" (despite the circumstantial traditional account of its origin in the Chronicles which is in keeping with the facts of the application of this name in Phœnician lands elsewhere) is that evolved by Sir J. Rhys. He derives the name "Britain," from the Welsh *Brith* and *Braith*, "spotted, parti-coloured"—a reference to the painting or tattooing of the body." (R.C.B., 211). But, evidently not quite satisfied with this, he thinks it is derived from the Welsh *Brethyn*, "cloth," and adds: "It would appear that the word *Brython* and its congeners meant 'clothed,' or 'cloth-clad' people. (*Ib.*, 212.)

is preserved in a relatively pure form in " Dun-Barton " or
" Fort of the Bartons "—the " Dun Breatan " of the Gaelic
Celts. In the Welsh Triads also, where Brutus is called
" *Prydain*, son of Aedd the Great," it is stated that he named
the island after himself " Isle of Prydain " (Inis Prydain).
And we shall see that Brutus and his Barats and their
descendants covered the country with place, river and
mountain names transplanted from their ancestral homeland
in Asia Minor and Syria-Phœnicia. And similarly, Brutus'
associate, the Phœnician Duke Corineus, who was probably
related to Corunna in Spain with its legends of Hercules
and the Phœnicians,[1] is traditionally recorded to have given
his name to Cornwall.

The Higher Aryan Civilization which Brutus now introduced and propagated throughout a great part of Britain,
began with the establishment of Agriculture, which we have
found was originated by the Aryans and made by them the
basis of their civilization. The Chronicles tell us that
Brutus and his Britons set at once " to till the ground and
build houses."

The building of houses, we have seen, was such a speciality
of the Hitto-Phœnicians that it gave them, from their timber-
houses, the title of " Khilani," " Gelouni " or " Gi-oln,"
which was borne also by the Phœnician Barat Part-olon.
The perishability of timber-houses would account for the
fact that there seem to be few extant remains of ancient
Briton buildings of this early period, except stone foundations,
which may possibly be as early, and some of the " Cliff
castles " (the marvellously well selected strategic sites and
defensive military details of which excited the admiration
of General Pitt-Rivers, the great archæologist) and some of

[1] " Corunna," on the Iberian coast near Finisterre, is intimately connected
with the Phœnicians and their demi-god Hercules. At the mouth of the
bay stands a remarkable beacon to which a vast antiquity is assigned.
Local tradition ascribes it to Hercules and others to the Phœnicians.
Laborde discovered an inscription near the base which stated that it was
constructed by Caius Severus Lupus and dedicated to Mars. But this was
probably reconstruction. Now Corunna is the Tor Breogan of Irish
bardic writers who state that Breogan was the son of *Bratha* [*i.e.*, " Barat "
or " Brath "], a leading chief of the Iberian *Scots*, who erected this tower
here after his own name, and that from the top of the town his son *Ith*
saw the shores of Erin on a clear day. See B.O.I., 27.

the numerous towers of stone masonry ("Broch"), suggesting the truly cyclopean masonry of the Hitto-Phœnicians. So late as the fourth century, A.D., Bede writes that a house was built "after the manner of the Scots, *not* of stones but of haṛd oak thatched with reeds." This was the above-mentioned Hittite timber house presumably.[1] The masonry foundations of such wooden houses were found at Troy.[2] Indeed, it seems probable that the artistic, timbered style of old mansions and cottages, especially in the south of Britain, is a survival of the famous timbered Hittite houses of these ancient Britons. The building of fine houses by the Phœnicians in Britain must of itself have been a great uplifting factor in the civilization of the land which hitherto had known only subterranean burrows, as the aborigines would doubtless imitate, more or less, the above-ground houses of their overlords. The pile huts of the few lake-dwellings may thus possibly be derived from the Hitto-Phœnician timber-house examples. The common Briton affix for towns of *-bury, -boro, -burg* (as well as "Broch") and Sanskrit *pura*, are now seen to be derived from the Hittite or Catti *Buru* "a Hittite town, citadel or fort."[3]

In surveying his newly-acquired land of Britain, we are told that Brutus " formed a design of building a city, and with this view travelled through the land to find out a convenient situation, and came to the Thames." As long before Brutus' day the land had been in the possession of the Phœnician Morites, who also traded in Amber in the North Sea, the topography of South Britain and its sea-coast was probably more or less known to Brutus and his kinsmen followers. The Chronicle account says he travelled " through the land " to the Thames from Totnes. It may be that Brutus, after his signal defeat of a leading party of the " giant " Morites at Totnes, as he had such a small land force for an enemy's country, yet possessing a considerable fleet, coasted along the south coast eastwards along the Channel from Totnes, marching inland to reconnoitre at

---

[1] Diodorus Siculus writes that "the cottages of the Britons were of wood thatched with straw." (*Geog.* 4,197).
[2] In the 5th City, in Early Bronze Age. S.I. 573 and 710.
[3] Cp. M.D. 186.

times when the open down permitted, with his fleet in the offing, somewhat as Alexander the Great, in his annexating survey of South Persia on his return from India, marched along the northern shore of the Persian Gulf with his fleet under admiral Nearchus in the offing for strategical reasons.[1]

Certain it is, I find, that the majority of *the chief river-names from Totnes to the Thames, including the latter river-name itself, are clearly transplanted namesakes from the rivers of Epirus, whence Brutus sailed, and rivers of Troy and Phœnicia.* These Phœnician, Epirus and Trojan names were, presumably, bestowed thereon by Brutus or his early descendants; just as a similar series of such names has been applied to the Cornwall coast to the west of Totnes, and just as modern British colonists transplant the cherished names of their old homeland to their new colonies.

Thus " Penzance " or " Pensans," we have seen, is presumably a corruption of " Phœnic-ana " or " Place of the Phœnicians," and it was also formerly called " Burrit-on "[2] *i.e.,* " Place of the Barats." The eastern promontory of the Bay of Penzance is " *Cudder* Point," that is, apparently, " Point of *Gadir*," an old name for the Phœnician port of Gades.[3] " *Maraz*-ion " or " *Maras*-ion,"[4] also the name for the ancient Phœnician tin-port in this bay at St. Michael's Mount and the Ictis of the Greeks, adjoining the rich Godolcon tin mines, about three miles inland, with prehistoric stone-circles in the neighbourhood, *is clearly named after the ancient inland capital of the Syrio-Phœnicians in Upper Cilicia,* namely, " *Marash* " (see Map) with its famous Hittite-inscribed monuments and Ogamoid writing

---

[1] " *Brute*-port " was the old name for Brid-port in Dorset at the end of the old " Roman " road, with many barrows and famous for its daggers. C.B., 1,65.

[2] L.H.P., 80.

[3] " Gadeira," is used by Strabo for " Gades " (825: 17, 3, 2), and " Agadir " on Phœnician coins of Gades (see before). *Ir* is Sumerian for " City," so *Gad-ir* = " City of the *Gad* or Phœnicians."

[4] This name is also variously spelt in documents of the thirteenth century onwards as " *Marghas*-bigan " (in Duke Richard's charter), " *Marhas*-deythyou *alias* Forum *Jovis* " (Leland, about 1550, in History, 6, 119–120), in which the second part of the name is supposed to be the equivalent of " Jove." Camden later gives the name as " Marision," but trying to equate it to " Jove," and his own idea of a market there on Thursday, arbitrarily spells it " Markes-jeu " (1, 17). On the borough mace of Elizabeth's reign it is spelt " Margasiewe," and in Commonwealth documents " Margazion." Charles II. reverts to " Marhazion," and in 1726 the name occurs as " Marazion," which still persists. See C.B., 4 and 17, and L.H.P., 70 and 133, etc.

## BRUTUS GIVES PHŒNICIAN PLACE-NAMES 173

already mentioned. That Cilician city was called by the Greco-Byzantines "*Marasion*,"[1] thus disclosing the Hitto-Phœnician original and source of the Marazion or Marasion in Cornwall. Again, the river which divided Corineus' province from that of Brutus is named *Tamar*, which name is presumably derived from the "*Tamyras*" or "*Damour*," the name of a chief river between Sidon and Beirut in Phœnicia. Near the Hoe at Plymouth also, the traditional site where Corineus pitched down the "giant" chief, we have "*Catti*-water" and the old place-name of "*Catte*-down," which presumably represents either the "Down of the *Catte*" or an older "Catte Dun" or "Fort of the *Catti*," wherein "Catti," with its variant "Cad," was, as we have seen, a favourite title of the ruling Barat Phœnicians. And of similar Barat significance seem the names of the old "Cliff Castles" of the Britons in Cornwall, called "*Caddon*" and "Castle *Gotha*," near Phœbe's Point at St. Austell.

Similarly, from Totnes to the Thames the coast is studded with such Asia Minor and Hellenic names. The promontory outside the bay of Totnes was called by the Romans, who preserved and latinized most of the old pre-Roman Briton names, "*Hellenis*" (the modern Berry Head), thus preserving an old Briton name of "Hellenis," which is presumably a souvenir of the "Helloi" or Helleni tribe of the Hellenes in Epirus, whence Brutus sailed with his bride. The next large river on the way to the Thames is the modern *Exe*, called by the Romans under its old Briton name of "*Isca*," also written "*Sca*"[2] which presumably preserves the old sacred name of the river of Troy,[3] the *Sca*-mander or Xanthus. That the front name "*Sca*" was a separate and superadded name, and possibly a contraction of "Ascanios," seems evident from the modern river being called merely "Mendere." For the Sca-mander (or Sca-mandros of Homer) was presumably also called "*Asc*-anios."[4] This title therefore of "Isca," for the Exe,

---

[1] See R.H.G., 279; M.H.A., 263. It is called "Marasin" by later Byzantine ecclesiastic writers.
[2] Its fort is called, in the 12th Itinerary of Antoninus, "*Sca* Diumnunnorium" as well as "*Isca* Dumunnorium." See C.B.G., cxxvi.
[3] Homer calls it "divine" (*dios*), *Iliad*, 12, 21.
[4] Strabo cites Euphorion (681 : 14, 5, 29) as saying : "near the waters of the Mysian *Ascanios*." Mysia is the province in which Troy and the Troad are situated ; and Apollodorus speaks of "a village of Mysia called Ascania near a lake of the same name, out of which issues the river *Ascanios*" (Strabo *ibid*.) ; and the Sca-mander issues from a lake-cavern on Mt. Ida (see M.H.A., 69). This specification of "Mysia" excludes the Bithynian Ascanios and its lake as well as the S.E. Phrygian Ascanios and its lake on the Meander. It is also significant that the chief town of the Parth-ini tribe in Macedonia, already referred to in connection with Brutus, was called "*Usc*-ana," and the river on the border of Epirus was the *Axius* (S. 328 &c.). And there was a *Scæa* Wall and *Scæa* Gates at Troy (S. 590).

appears to disclose the Trojan source of the name of the numerous favourite residential rivers in Britain called Esk, Usk, Exe, etc. Thus the river at the site of the Briton King Arthur's capital of Caerleon in Monmouth was also called "*Isca*" by the Romans, the modern "Usk." And just as there are several Isca, Esk, Usk or Exe rivers in Britain bearing this favourite name, so there were others in the Troad and Thrace.[1] Near Exeter, the *Isca* of the Romans is "*Cad*-bury" or "Burg of the *Cads* (*i.e.* Phœnicians)," with prehistoric "camp" mounds.

Further east, the next large river, the *Axe*, of Ax-minster, and famous for its textile products, has the same Exe or Esk or Isca name and has in the neighbourhood "*Catti*-stock" with ancient "Picts' dwellings" to attest its antiquity. Further east, we come to the "Avon" (of Salisbury Plain, Stonehenge, etc.) which bears obviously the same name as the "*Aban*" river of Damascus (mentioned in the Old Testament),[2] a Syrian city which was in the occupation of the Hitt-ites in the fourteenth century B.C.,[3] and in which the "*Ab*" of its name also means "Water," as does "Avon" in the Briton language. Passing Hants, where "*Barton*-stacey" and "*Barton*-mere," both with prehistoric remains, and preserving in their names the earlier form of the "Barat" title like Dun-Barton, we come to the Ancient Briton island-port of *Sels-ey* or "Isle of the Sels," which, we have already seen on the evidence of the Phœnician inscription on its early Briton coins, means "Isle of the Cilicians." Beyond this, near Beachy Head, is the *Ouse*, which is clearly named after the "*Aous*" river of Epirus, which separates the latter from Macedonia. And the "*Thames*," the "Tamesis" of the Romans, is clearly named after the "Thyamis," the greatest river of Epirus, the Phœnician origin of which name seems evident by its chief tributary being named "Cadmus," the name of the famous colonizing and civilizing sea-king of the Phœnicians, with its chief city port "Ilium," a title of Troy, and the port of the next river to the north is named "Phœnice."

Arrived at the Thames, thus evidently named by Brutus after the chief river of Epirus in Greece, whence he had just come, bringing his princess bride, we are told that he "walked along the shore and at last pitched upon a place

---

[1] A Scæus river in Troad and Thrace (S. 590) and Axus or Oaxes in Crete. The name *Sca, Axi* and *Usc* seems cognate with Sumerian *Agia* or *Egā*, "Flood (of Euphrates &c," *cp.* Br. 11593) and akin to Sanskrit *Ux* "to sprinkle," Irish-Scot and Gælic *Uisg*, "river," (and root of "Whisky") and Latin *Aqua*.
[2] 2 Kings, 5, 12.  [3] A.L., 139 and 143.

## BRUTUS FOUNDS LONDON ABOUT 1100 B.C.

very fit for his purpose. Here he built a city which he called ' New Troy ' . . . till by corruption of the original word it came to be called ' *Tri-Novantum* ' . . . but afterwards ' Kaer-Lud ' that is, ' The City of Lud ' "— that is, " Lud-dun " or " London."[1] The new evidence confirming this account of the founding of London by Brutus about 1100 B.C.—that is, over *three and a half centuries before the traditional founding of Rome*—and clearly identifying the Early Briton Londoners with the " Tri-Novantes " of Cæsar, is detailed in Appendix V. This, therefore, corroborates the tradition of the Trojan founding of London preserved by Milton :

" O City, founded by Dardanian hands,
Whose towering front the circling realms commands ! "

Thereafter Brutus, we are told, " prescribed Laws for the peaceable government " of citizens—just as, later, the famous Law-codes of two of his descendants in the fifth and 4th cents. B.C. were translated by King Alfred into Anglo-Saxon for the benefit of the English.[2] This prescription of Laws by an Aryan-Phœnician implies *Writing* in the Aryan Phœnician Language and Script, and also Education in reading that official writing and Aryan language. In writing, the Phœnicians are admitted by the universal Greek tradition to have been the teachers of Europe. And we have seen the form of the Aryan Phœnician writing and language of about 400 B.C. on the Newton Stone.

This now brings us to the hitherto unsolved and much-disputed question of the agency by which the Aryan language was first introduced into the British Isles and the date of that great event.

The introduction of the Aryan language into Britain has latterly been universally credited by modern writers to the " Celts," merely on a series of assumptions by Celtic philologists which, we have seen, are unfounded, namely,

[1] " Kaer," the Cymric for " Fortified city," is now seen to be derived from Sumerian *Gar*, " hold, establish, of men, place " (Br. 11953, &c.), cognate with Indo-Persian *Garh*, " fort," Sanskrit *Grih*, " house," Eddic Gothic *Goera* " to build " (V.D. 224) and *Gard* or " Garth."
[2] G.C., 2, 17 and 3, 5 ; and *cp*. pp. 387-8.

that the Celts were Aryan in race, and a branch of the round-headed Celts of Gaul and conjectured to have entered Britain from Gaul for the first time about "the seventh or sixth century B.C.,"[1] although there is no tradition of such a migration, nor is the word "Celt" even known in the "British Celtic" languages.

The real introducers of the Aryan language into the British Isles are now disclosed to be the Aryan Phœnician Britons under King Brutus.[2] As the conquering and civilizing race they imposed their own Aryan speech, as the official language, upon the aborigines of Britain. And they gave their own Aryan names, in the manner we have already seen, to most of the places, mountains and rivers, forming the hitherto so-called "Celtic" place- and river-names.

The Aryan language, thus introduced and spoken by these ruling Early Britons under King Brutus about 1103 B.C., was clearly neither "Celtic" nor the supposititious "Gaulish Brythonic of the Welsh of the fourth century B.C.," which are disclosed to be relatively modern provincial dialects of this original Briton Speech. What, then, was this Early Briton Speech, as it is given no place whatsoever in any of the schemes of classification of the languages of Britain by our modern philologists? It is called, in Geoffrey's translation of the Early Chronicles, as we have seen, "*Trojan* or rough Greek which [thereafter] was called *British.*" The actual words for these terms, as they occurred in the "very ancient book [MS.] in the British tongue" translated by Geoffrey into Latin are unfortunately lost. The term "Greek" (or Græcum) could not have been employed in any very ancient text, as it is merely a term introduced by the later Roman writers about the middle of the first century B.C. for the country, people and language[3] of the Attica peninsula, and whose people latterly called themselves "Hellenes" and their country "Hellas," and

---

[1] Rhys, *Rept. Brit. Ass.*, 1900, 893. In R.C.B., 1904 (p. 2) the supposed date is conjecturally extended to be "probably more than a millennium B.C."

[2] The slight aryanizing influence of the Phœnician Morite merchants previous to Brutus is here disregarded.

[3] T.W.P. 93—4.

## BRITISH LANGUAGE, TROJAN OR DORIC 177

it is a term entirely unknown to Homer as well as the early classic " Hellenic " writers, although it is customary nowadays to call the latter " Greek." Geoffrey thus presumably, or a previous transcriber, employed in his translation this term " Greek " merely to render the old British textual name intelligible to his modern readers, at a time when Latin and Greek were the languages of the learned throughout Europe, and to convey to his readers the fact that this " ancient British tongue " belonged to the same family as the ancient Hellenic or so-called " Greek " language, which was a leading branch of the Aryan Speech of civilized Europe.

The term " Trojan," on the other hand, as applied to this Early Briton language in Geoffrey's translation, probably preserves, more or less, the general form of the name occurring in his old British text, in the sense of " Doric."

[" Trojan " or " Troian " is the latinized word for the Hellenic *Trōes*, a native of Troia (or Troy), as the people and their city are called by Homer. Now, the most ancient branch of the Aryans in Greece, who are incidentally referred to by Homer as the " *Dōriees*," the " Dorians " of the Latinist writers, were, I find, the original inhabitants of Troy,[1] which would explain why the Dorians had their revenge on their distant kinsmen, the Achaians, who destroyed Troy (as described in the Iliad) by driving the latter out of Greece[2] in the eleventh century B.C.; and secondly, the Homeric " Trōes " for Trojan is presumably a dialectic form of " Dōriees " or " The Dorians "—for the interchange of the dentals $T$ and $D$ is common throughout the whole family of Aryan languages, and is especially common even at the present day in Greece and amongst the Greek-speaking people of Asia Minor, so that the modern guide-books to Greece and Asia Minor warn travellers[3] that the initial $D$ of written or printed names is usually pronounced, in the colloquial, $Th$ or $T$. And the transposing of the $o$ and $r$ in spelling is not infrequent.]

The " *Doric* " language of the ancient Hellenes was distinguished from the later refined and polished " Attic " of the classic " Greeks " by its rough simplicity and the free use of broad vowel sounds. This " Doric " character

---
[1] Details in my *Aryan Origins*.
[2] South Greece or Peloponnesus is called " The *Dorian* Island " by Pindar, *N.*, 3, 5; and by Sophocles, *C.C.*, 6, 95, etc.
[3] See M.H.A. [71].

of the Early Briton language is well seen in Part-olon's spelling on the Newton Stone of several of the proper names, especially in his spelling of "*Gyaolowonie*" for his ethnic title, which is written "Gioln" in his Ogam version for the information of the Pictish Celts, who spelt that name in their Chronicles of the ninth century A.D. also "Galan" or "Gulan." It thus seems probable that the word used in Geoffrey's old British manuscript text was "Dōros," which he latinized into "Trojan," and that his description of the original language spoken by the Trojans under Brutus as "Trojan or *rough* Greek" was the original rough Doric language current amongst the Trojans about 1107 B.C. And significantly this term "Doric" still survives to the present day as an appellation of the dialect of the Scots, with its distinctively broad vowel sounds.

Contemporary specimens of this ancient Trojan Doric, that is, the Early "British" Doric language and writing, fortunately still exist from the fourteenth to the twelfth centuries B.C. They were unearthed in considerable numbers by Schliemann in his excavations at Hissarlik, the site of the ancient Troy. The language in which this Trojan Doric is written shows that Homeric Greek, which in its archaisms differs so widely from the classic Greek of later times, was related to it[1] and presumably derived from it; while the script in which this Trojan language is written bears a close resemblance to the early alphabetic letters found in Cyprus at Kitium or Citium and other sites of the Phœnicians and Khatti in that island. This ancient Trojan Doric script so closely resembled in many respects the script on Part-olon's Newton Stone, that it supplied me with some indications for the decipherment of that inscription. And I find that this Trojan script and language was clearly akin to the language and writing of the later Aryan Phœnicians, and to the Runes of the Goths, and to the legends stamped on the pre-Roman British coins of the Catti, and was the parent of the language and writing of the present day in Britain—the so-called "English" language and script.

Its affinity to the Runes of the Goths is especially

[1] Prof. Sayce, S.I., 691, etc.

## ENGLISH BASED ON BRITISH GOTHIC

obvious and historically significant. We have seen that the inscription of Part-olon-the-Scot, and its more or less contemporary inscription at Lunasting, exhibit the radical and grammatical structure of the *Gothic*—the language of a people who are disclosed, as we have seen, to be Khatti, Catti, Guti or Gad or Hitt-ites, primitive Goths. In view of this fact, and the fact that the great epics of the Goths, the *Eddas*—which, I find, are truly historical and not mythical in their personages[1]—are found by the best authorities to have been mostly composed in Britain, and in a Gothic dialect which was presumably the Early British language as current in Britain about the beginning of the Christian era, I find that this Gothic of the Eddas, the tongue of our Briton ancestors, based on the old Trojan Doric, was the real basis of the " English " language and *not the Anglo-Saxon*, although the latter is a kindred dialect. Thus this early British Doric seems best described as " *Early British Gothic,*" and such I venture to call it. The essentially Gothic character of the " English " language is evident also from the greatest of English classics, the English translation of the Bible, wherein it will be seen that the early translators, Wycliffe (1389 A.D.) and Tyndale (1526), on which our modern version is based, largely followed the wordings used by old Bishop Ulfilas the Goth in his Gothic translation of 350 A.D., although his Visi-Gothic dialect had diverged considerably from the Gothic of the British Eddas.

" Anglo-Saxon," on the other hand, has no early writings extant to attest what the language of these Germanic invaders was at the period before and when they entered Britain in 449 A.D. The early Saxon language was markedly different from the so-called " Anglo-Saxon " of Britain, which latter first appears in the poems of Cædmon about 650 A.D., that is, over two centuries after the Anglo-Saxon invaders had mixed with and adopted the Laws of the Britons who spoke British Gothic.[2] Cædmon, although now called " the first Anglo-Saxon or English poet," appears to

---

[1] Thor, 1st king of 1st Aryan dynasty was only latterly deified.
[2] But his poems are only known in the vernacular in a MS. dating no earlier than 1000 A.D., except his *Hymn* cited by King Alfred about a century earlier.

have been a native of Ruthwell in Dumfries in Scotland, from the signed Runic inscription of "Cadmon" on the beautiful votive stone Cross there, containing extracts from the "Dream of the Rood," a poem which is usually ascribed to him. And although he specially wrote for his Anglo-Saxon masters, he wrote in an idiom so different from the standard Anglo-Saxon of the South, and so similar to the British Gothic of the Eddas, and used idioms and sentences so similar to those of the Gothic Eddas that his language has to be distinguished as "Northumbrian." Beowulf's reputed poem also, which is only known from a paraphrase by a "Northumbrian" bard of the eighth century, relates exploits amongst the Danes and Geats (or Goths) and the Goths of Sweden and the Catte-gat (or "Gate of the Catti" or Goths) which presumes Gothic influence in his so-called "Anglo-Saxon." And Cynewulf of the eighth century betrays his Gothic influence by signing his MS. in *Runic (i.e., Gothic) writing—of which significantly absolutely no trace has ever been found on any ancient monument in Germany*, although Runic inscriptions from at least about the fourth and fifth centuries onwards (that is before the "Anglo-Saxon" invasion, the Angles not arriving in Britain till the middle of the sixth century) are common in the North of England and in Scotland, as well as in Scandinavia and Denmark, all Gothic lands. Indeed the name "Cædmon" which is spelt "Kadmon" or "Cadmon" on the Ruthwell Cross, and occurring in the latter form as the name of a witness to a Bucks charter of 948 A.D.,[1] is seen to mean obviously "Man of the *Cad* or *Kad*," that is, as we have seen, an ordinary title of the Hitto-Phœnicians, and in series with the Briton "Cad-wallon," &c. And Dumfries is on the border of the "*Gad*-eni" tribe area of Ptolemy.

It is thus evident that the so-called "Celtic" and "Brythonic Celtic" languages in the British Isles are merely provincial dialects derived from the Aryan Trojan Doric, introduced by King Brutus-the-Trojan about 1103 B.C.; and that the standard official and developed Aryan language

[1] Birch *Cart.Saxon.* 2.39, cited by Gaskin *Cædmon* 1902, 10; and *cp.* Hewison *Runic Roods* 1914.61.

of Britain was the British Gothic, which is the basis of the modern " English " language ; and that the Trojan Doric script introduced by Brutus, and cognate with Part-olon's Phœnician script and archaic Greek and Roman, is the parent of our modern alphabetic writing.

The Laws which Brutus prescribed, and the law-codes of his descendants of the 5th and 4th cents. B.C. (Molmut and Martin), translated by King Alfred for the Anglo-Saxons, were doubtless founded on the famous law-codes of the Sumerians and Hittites, which are admittedly the basis of the Mosaic and Greek and Roman Law. It will surprise most readers, not lawyers, taught by the history books to regard the Early Britons as " barbarians," to find that the great English Law-authority on " The Rise and Progress of the English Commonwealth," Sir F. Palgrave, shows that the Britons were superior in their civilization, as in their religion, to *the Anglo-Saxons who adopted the Briton Law generally for their code in England.*

Palgrave writes : " The historical order prevailing in this code (of the Britons[1]) shows that it was formed with considerable care, and the customs it comprehends bear the impress of great antiquity.... The character of the British legislation is enhanced by comparison with the laws which were put in practice amongst the other nations of the Middle Ages. The indignant pride of the Britons, who despised their implacable enemies, the Anglo-Saxons, as a race of rude barbarians, whose touch was impurity, will not be considered as any decisive test of superior civilization. But the Triads, and the laws of Hoel Dda (founded on Molmut's), excel the Anglo-Saxon and other Teutonic customals in the same manner that the elegies of Llywarch Hên, and the odes of Taliesin soar above the ballads of the Edda. *Law had become a science amongst the Britons ;* and its volumes exhibit the jurisprudence of a rude nation shaped and modelled by thinking men, and which had derived both stability and equity from the labours of its expounders."[2]

The Art introduced by Brutus into Albion was presumably the advanced art of the Trojans and Phœnicians, as sung by Homer and unearthed by Schliemann and others ; though

---

[1] Briton code of Molmut revised by Howel the Good (Hywel Dda), King of Cymri, 906–48 A.D.
[2] F. Palgrave, *Rise and Progress of English Commonwealth*, I. 37.

in the rough laborious life of bringing a new country into civilization and cultivation it doubtless suffered deterioration in Britain. This art, hitherto called "Early Celtic," is represented by numerous specimens, unearthed from tombs, etc., of bronze, gold and jet jewellery, decorated bronze shields and weapons and ornamented monuments, in which the æsthetic use of the solar spiral ornament of Troy, the Ægean and Levant, and the solar " key-pattern " swastika (still surviving largely in modern decorative art) and Sun-Crosses of the Hitto-Phœnicians is noteworthy (see Figures later). The identity of some of the Early Briton art motives with those of the naturalistic " New Egyptian art " introduced into Egypt from Syria-Phœnicia in the period of Akhen-aten will be seen later on. The naturalistic drawing on the Early Briton coins especially, we shall find, much excels that of the Anglo-Saxon and medieval period in England.

As an instance of Early Briton art may be cited an inlaid dagger-handle unearthed from a tomb near Stonehenge, which is thus described by an expert : " It could not be surpassed, if indeed equalled, by the most able workman of modern times."[1]

Works of public utility, such as the construction of arterial roads for commerce, etc., are referred to in the Chronicle records of descendants of Brutus.[2] The so-called " Roman roads " bearing the old Briton names of *Stane* Street, *Watling*[3] Street, *Erming* Street, etc., are studded with Ancient Briton town sites, as we shall see, and thus presumably were roads mentioned in the British Chronicles which were engineered by the Ancient Britons in the pre-Roman period and merely repaired by the Romans, to whom they are now altogether credited by those latter-day writers who have erroneously believed that the Britons were savages.

[1] Hoare, *Ancient Wilts*, 1, 202, pl. 27, 2, and E.B.I, 232.
[2] G.C., 3, 5, etc.
[3] " Watl-ing " is a variant of the Eddic Gothic " OAdl-ing " or " Œdl-ing " royal clan, with later variants of Æthel-ing, etc., in which *ing* is the Gothic tribal affix. Other variants of this Early Briton name, in the time of Edward the Confessor, Harold and Canute are spelt in charters " Wædel," " Wadel," " Ædel," " Adel," " Udal," cp. W. G. Searle, *Onomasticon Anglo-Saxonicum* 473, 534, 582. The name is Sumer *Etil* " Lord " (Br. 1506).

The Bronze Age was clearly introduced into Britain by the earlier Phœnician Mor-ite or Amor-ite exploiters of the Jin mines many centuries before the arrival of Brutus, and probably before 2800 B.C.[1] On account of the preciousness of Bronze, however, it would appear that the Early Phœnician miners themselves used bronze sparingly and prohibited its use by the natives, and, as it will be seen later, they employed stone tools in working the ores for export to their bronze factories in the East. Brutus appears to have popularized the use of bronze, as indicated by its more frequent occurrence as tools. Metal axes would presumably be required by these Aryans to clear the forests for settlement and agriculture.[2] And he probably introduced iron and steel into Britain, as both of these metals are referred to by Homer as used by Trojan heroes, and the use of iron is also referred to by his contemporary, Hesiod.

The Religion which the Phœnicians disembarked and transplanted in Britain, as they did in their other colonies, was the exalted monotheistic religion with the idea of One God of the Universe, symbolized by his chief visible luminary the Sun, as we shall see in a later chapter on Phœnician " Bel " worship in Early Britain, as attested by its early monuments other than the Newton Stone. The uplifting effect of this lofty religion upon the aborigines must have been enormous, sunk as the latter were in the degrading matriarchal cults of serpent demons of Death and Darkness, demanding human and other bloody sacrifices.

The Phœnician " Sun-worship " was latterly, as we have seen, associated with the idealized Aryan Barat tutelary angel, Britannia. It was, perhaps, this divinity who is referred to as " Diana " in the Chronicles as inspiring Brutus to the conquest of Britain. That latter name was possibly substituted by the later editors to adapt it to the well-known analogous tutelary of the later classic writers. In this regard it is significant, in connection with the traditional

---

[1] Sir J. Evans divided the Bronze Age in Britain into 1st Stage, 1400–1150 B.C. (flat daggers) ; 2nd Stage, 1150–900 B.C. (stout daggers), and 3rd Stage, 900–400 B.C.
[2] Bronze sickles were found in Aberdeen, Perth and Sutherland shires. E.B.I., 199–200—where finds in the South of England are also noted.

founding of London by Brutus, to find that on the site of St. Paul's Cathedral there is a tradition of a once-famous temple to Diana. The old buildings in its neighbourhood are called, in the church records, " *Cameræ Dianæ* " or " Rooms of Diana," and in the reign of Edward I. numerous ox-heads were dug up in the churchyard which were ascribed to the sacrifices to Diana performed there.[1]

The maintenance of the higher religion was an essential part of the Aryan State system, and the kings were for long the high priests and priest-kings. Cæsar mentions that students from Gaul and other parts of the continent flocked to the colleges in Early Britain for religious instruction.[2] And the fact that the ruling Aryan Briton kings and their " Britons " properly so-called (as distinguished from the aborigines) adhered to the higher ancestral religion of the Sun-cult, and not the blood-thirsty Druidism of their subjects, is evidenced by the Early Briton coins and the numerous stone monuments of the pre-Christian period in Britain, which are purely Solar in their symbolism. So purely solar was the higher religion in Ancient Britain that Pliny reports that the ancient Persians—the most famed of the later Eastern Sun-Fire worshippers—seemed to have derived their rites from Britain.[3]

The character of these Early Britons is reflected to some extent in their Chronicles. The Phœnician admiral Himilco of Carthage who visited Britain about the sixth century B.C. to explore " the outer parts of Europe "[4] records that the Britons were " a powerful race, proud-spirited, effectively skilful in art, and constantly busy with the cares of trade."[5]

Their patriotism and independence is strikingly reflected in the magnificent oration of the Briton chief Galgacus as recorded by Tacitus,[6] and displays high proficiency in literary composition and rhetoric. The character of King Caractacus was highly extolled by the Romans. The high

[1] C.B., 2, 81.  [2] D.B.G., 6, 8 ; 6, 13 (11) and f.  [3] *Nat. Hist.*, 30.
[4] Pliny states that he sailed *via* Gades (*Nat. Hist.*, 2, 67, 109).
[5] " Multa vis hic gentis est. Superbus animus, efficax sollertia. Negotiandi cura jugis omnibus." Fragment preserved by Festus Avienus, *Ora Maritima*, v, 98–100.
[6] *Agricola*, 30.

BRITON CULTURE & CIVILIZATION    185

Briton sense of honour and self-respect with contempt for slanderers seems crystallized in the old motto of the Keiths (i.e. Khatti), the Earl marischals of Scotland :

> "Thay say, Qwhat say They ?
> Thay haif sayd.   Let thame say ! "

As regards refinement and education, it is noteworthy that the young Briton wife, Claudia Rufina, of a high Roman official, whose praises Martial sang in the first century A.D., held her own in the brilliant society at Rome :

> " Claudia !  Rose from the blue-eyed Britons !
> Capturer of hearts !  How is it thou'rt such a Latin person ?
> Such graceful form ?  It makes believe thou'rt Roman !
> Thou'rt fit to be Italian or Athenian maid."[1]

She was traditionally the Claudia who was the friend of St. Paul.[2] And not to mention the old tradition of the Chronicle and numerous other independent records that the famous Christian empress and canonized saint, Helena, the mother of Constantine the Great, was a British princess, the daughter of King Col of York, we have the beautiful monument to the dignified Briton lady of the Cat-uallaun ruling clan in North Britain, erected at S. Shields, by her sorrowing husband, Barates the Syrio-Phœnician. (See Fig. 19.)

The intellectual, social and religious culture introduced by Brutus into Britain about the end of the twelfth century B.C. must thus have been of the advanced standard of the Phœnicians of that period.  This must have exercised still further an inspiring and uplifting effect upon the lower mentality of the Pictish aborigines, and have tended to alter their habits of life and character somewhat in the direction of those of their civilizing Aryan overlords.

The colonizing activities of the adventurous Briton descendants of Brutus soon manifested themselves again, after they had penetrated the greater part of Britain, in

---

[1] " Claudia cæruleis cum sit Rufina Britannis," etc.   Martial, *Epigram.* 11, 53.   Her husband was Aulus Pudens.
[2] 2 Timothy, iv, 21.   Her identity was upheld by Matthew, Archbishop of Canterbury ;  and J. Bale.   See C.B.G., I, xciii.

founding a new colony on the Rhine. That remarkable record in the Chronicle states that about 970 B.C. a colony of the sons of King Ebraucus, the fourth in linear descent from Brutus, sailed from Britain with a fleet and, conquering Germany, settled there. This now appears to disclose the hitherto unobserved *British Origin of the " Anglo-Saxons " and the " Anglo-Saxon " language*—the term " Anglo-Saxon," which is now so common in popular usage, was unknown to the Danish and Germanic invading Jutes, Angles and Saxons of the fifth century A.D. themselves, and appears to have been first coined only in 1783 in Bailey's *Dictionary* as a term for the language of the Saxon Chronicle and of Alfred and that period. " Anglo-Saxon " as a racial or ethnic term is even more recent.

This Briton invasion and colonization of Germany by King Brutus' descendants, about 970 B.C., now accounts for the first time for the Aryanization in speech of the various non-Aryan Slavonic or Sarmatian tribes of Germany, and also supplies the date for this great epoch-making event in the history of continental Europe. It also explains the origin and existence of the " Continental *Britanni* " mentioned by Pliny as living on the banks of the Somme,[1] the *Cat-alauni* tribe on the Marne ; and the various Catti or Gothic tribes in the Rhine Valley described by Tacitus,[2] namely the *Catti* or *Chatti*, the most heroic of the tribes in Germany,[3] the *Chauci* (? Saxons), *Qadi* of Moravia, the *Goth-ones*, and *Goth-ini* with their iron-mines on the Vistula and Oder, the *Sit*-ones, and the *Cimbri* in Jut-land, where we find, a short time later, " Goths " and " Goth-land " ; while the *Angli* (Angles, the " *Yngl*-ing Goths " of the Eddas) occupied in the first century A.D. the neck of Schleswig-Holstein of Denmark or Jut-land adjoining the Cimbri (or Cymri).

An early Briton occupation of Denmark (the home of the

---

[1] Pliny, *N. Hist.*, 4, 106.     [2] *Germania*, C., 29-44.
[3] The " Catti " or " Chatti " are not mentioned by Cæsar, as they were outside the frontier of the Roman empire and influence. Some writers have sought to identify them with the " Suevi " of Cæsar's Commentaries, but Tacitus sharply differentiates the " Catti " from the " Suevi." This Early Briton migration of Catti or Goths to the Rhine Valley would account for the remains of long-headed skulls of Aryan type in the early prehistoric graves there.

# ANGLES AND SAXONS A BRANCH OF BRITONS 187

Angles) is also recorded in the British Chronicles anterior to the 5th century, B.C.[1]

It is thus seen that the Anglo-Saxons were a branch of the British Barat-Phœnicians or Britons, and that the " Anglo-Saxon " language is derived from the Briton " Doric " or Dorian (or Troian) Gothic, or the British Gothic introduced into Britain by Brutus and his Barat Phœnician Catti or Goths about 1100 B.C.; and, to some extent, still earlier, by the Amorite Catti Phœnicians from about 2800 B.C.

[1] GC. 3. 11.

FIG. 25A. Prehistoric Catti Sun Crosses and Sun Spirals graved on Sepulchral Stones at Tara, capital of ancient Scotia or Erin.
After Coffey (C.N.G. Figs. 34, 36.)
Described in Chaprs. XIX and XX.

## XV

### Phœnician Penetration of Britain Attested by "Barat" Patronym in Old Place and Ethnic Names

*Disclosing also Phœnician Source of "Mor," "Cumber," "Cymr" and "Somer" Names*

> "The principal nations of the *Bārats* are the Kurus [Syrians] and the able *Panch* [*Phœnic*-ians]."—*Ancient Indian Epics.*[1]

THE ancient Aryan Barat tradition that "the whole world" was conquered by "the able *Panch*," or Phœnicians, has already been cited in the heading of page 1. And the ancient Aryan custom of taking their forefather *Barat's* name as a personal and tribal title (cited in the heading of chap. VII) has already been cited and further instanced by King Brutus or Peirithoos, properly "Barat," and King Part-olon of the Newton Stone monument, both calling themselves and their new colonies after the name of their most famous forefather, King Barat,[2] the *Khatti* or *Catti* or "Hitt-ite" or Goth; the most celebrated ancestral king of the Hitto-Sumerians or Phœnicians; and some scores of Part-olon's descendants in North Britain also took that cherished old ancestral name.

Now, I find throughout Britain evidence of the Phœnician Barat rule and Civilization of these islands, in long pre-Roman times, exists widespread all over the country, in the ancient ethnic and dynastic "Barat" and "Catti" titles in the old place and river names of Britain, from farthest south to farthest north.; and in the "Somer" and Mor, Amorite names.

---

[1] *Vishnu Purana*, 2, 3 and other *Puranas*. V.P., 2, 132, etc.

[2] In Sanskrit *Barat* is not spelt with a final expressed *a*; and in the Hindi vernacular it is pronounced "*Bārat*."

Ancient racial, place and river names are found to be amongst the most imperishable of human things. This persistence of ancient place-names has been fully recognized by the leading archæologists as a " *safe* " means of recovering ancient history. Thus Sir F. Petrie remarks with reference to the ancient place-names in Palestine and Phœnicia as found in the Amarna cuneiform letters of about 1400 B.C. :—

" When we see the names Akka, Askaluna, Biruta, Gazri, Lakish, Qidesu, Tsiduna, Tsur, Urashalim [that is the modern " Akka " or Acre, Ascalon, Beirut, Gezer, Lachish, Kadesh, Sidon, Sour, (the " Tyre " of Europeans) and " Jerusalem "], *all lasting with no change—or only a small variation in the vowels—down to the present day . . . it needs no further proof that ancient names may be safely sought for in the modern map.*"[1]

By the survey of these persistent ancient names surviving in the modern maps, we thus discover the early locations and distribution of the Barat Phœnician in their colonizing penetration of Early Britain. These names originally designated, presumably, isolated settlements and ports of the Barats, which were simply called " Barat town " in contrast to the aboriginal village in the neighbourhood. (See next chapter for the place-affixes to the tribal name Barat or Brit.)

We shall now survey briefly, in the light of our discoveries, the occurrence in the maps of this dynastic clan-title of Barat or " Brit-on " bestowed by these Brito-Phœnicians upon many of the early sites selected by them for colonization on the coast and in the interior of Britain, when they began to penetrate the land and form permanent settlements therein. As most of these " Barat " place-names presumably designated early settlements of the ruling clan, as attested by the very ancient remains at most of them, they afford, along with those of the " Catti " series of the tribal title, some clue to the routes and avenues by which this civilizing penetration was effected, and also a clue to some of the chief early centres from which the Aryan Civilization was diffused over the land. Most of these early " Barat " centres have now

[1] Sir W. F Petrie, *Syria and Egypt* 15.

become relatively insignificant, through being swamped by the swarms of later new towns founded on new lines of traffic to suit new industries, iron, coal and other manufactures, but some of them still retain their ancient importance under their old name, as *Burton*-on-Trent, *Barton*-on-Humber, Dun-*barton*, *Part*-ick and *Perth*, whilst others, such as *Barden* (Norwich) have changed their names, or, as " Bristol," (formerly Caer *Brito*) are now scarcely recognizable.

We also discover that the "*Cymry*" (pronounced *Cumri*) or *Cumbers* of Wales, Cumberland, and the North Cumbræ of Strath-Clyde appear to derive their name from the alternative tribal epithet of the Phœnicians, namely, "*Sumer*." This latter was a term occasionally used by the early ruling race in Babylonia, the " Sumerians " of modern Assyriologists, and who, I find, were Phœnicians.

This identity of the Cymry or Cumbers with the " Sumers," suggested by my discovery in various ancient mining centres in Britain and especially in the land of the Cymry or Cumbers of several scribings in the old " Sumerian " script of Babylonia (see later), is confirmed by finding that " Sumerian " is the basis of the British or " English " language, of which we shall find many further instances incidentally, as we proceed. It is also confirmed by the Welsh Cymry traditional account of the arrival of King Brut or " Prydain " (as his name is dialectically spelt in Welsh) in Britain, as found in the Welsh Triads, which confirm from an altogether independent source the tradition preserved in the Chronicles of Nennius and Geoffrey.

The First Triad[1] says : " Three names have been given to the Isle of Britain from the beginning . . . ' Clās Merddin [literally, The Digging of the *Mers* or *Mor*-ites ?] and afterwards Fel Ynys. When it was put under government by *Prydain*, son of Aedd-the-Great, it was called ' Inis *Prydain*,' and there was no tribute paid to any but to *the race of the Cymry*, because they first possessed [or invaded] it."

The Sixth Triad, supplementing this one, says : " First *Hu Gadarn*, originally conducted *the nation of the Cymry* into the Isle of Britain. They came from the Summer Country, which is called *Deffro-Bani*, and it was over the hazy sea[2]

[1] Welsh Triads (Trioedd Ynys Prydain) in *Myvyrian Archæology of Wales*, vols. 2 and 3.
[2] " Hazy or Misty Sea " is a recognized poetic name for the Mediterranean used by Homer (*Iliad*, 23, 743).

# BARAT PHŒNICIAN NAMES IN BRITAIN 191

that they came to the Isle of Britain and to *Llydaw* [Lud-dun ?][1] where they continued."[2]

The different dialectic and phonetic spelling of the same names, Prut, Prydain, Briton and Britain we have already seen; and especially the widely-varied ways in which the Anglo-Saxons spelt " Britain " and " Briton," which accounts for a number of the present variations in spelling the " Barat " element in the place-names in question.

Starting from Brutus' or Barat's capital of " New Troy or London," we find Barat or Brit-on names of early Briton settlements radiating throughout the various home counties and the South of England and the Midlands. And significantly they often possess early Bronze Age and " ancient village " remains, and are largely found on the pre-Roman arterial roads, many of which, having been repaired and used by the Romans, are now called " Roman " roads. Proceeding westwards and to the south we find the following[3] :—

In Kent : *Bred*-hurst, near Kits' Coty dolmen and the " Roman " Watling Street.
*Bord*-en, on Watling Street, near Milton.
*Britten*-den, adjoining Newenden, at ancient mouth of the Rother (1, 322)[4]

---

[1] " Llydaw " is usually conjectured to mean " Sea-coast " and thought by Celtic scholars to be Armorica in Brittany (Lobineau, *Histoire de Bretagne*, 5, 6); but it now appears to be probably Lud-dun or " London."
[2] Here the Welsh Triads record that " Prydain," *i.e.*, the Cymric spelling of Brutus or Barat as " Brit-on," gave his name to Britain and that he was of the race of the *Cymry*. The Sixth Triad, in supplementing this information, gives Prydain's personal name as " *Hu-Gad-arn*," *i.e.*, " Hu-the-*Gad* or Phœnician," and the affix *Arn* is obviously " Aryan," and cognate with the Cymric *Aran*, " high," the Cornish *Arhu*, " to command," and the Irish-Scot *Aire*, " a chief or prince," literally, " exalted one," which also, as seen later, is the literal meaning of " Aryan " in the Indo-Persian languages. The land from which he came, " *Deffro-Bani*," seems to be perhaps the Welsh contracted corruption of the compound name " Epirus-Pandosia," *i.e.*, the very place in Greece whence, we have seen, Brutus or Peirithoos sailed to Britain—the prefixed *D* may have been a mistake of an earlier copyist, though *D* is sometimes introduced in Welsh spelling, thus " Gwy*d*ion " is the Welsh spelling of " Gawain " of the British Arthur legend. We now see why the elder Gildas called the whole of Britain " *Cambre* " or " The Land of the Cambers, Cumbers, or Cymry," *i.e.*, Sumers.
[3] The numbers enclosed within brackets refer to the pages in Camden's *Britannia*, 2nd ed. Gough.
[4] See previous note.

| | |
|---|---|
| Sussex : | *Burton*, between Midhurst and Chichester (or Regnum of Romans), with prehistoric barrows,[1] and near the Roman Stane Street (1, 288).<br>"*Brighton*," the "Brighthelm-ton" of the Anglo-Saxons suggests a possible "Briton," as the old priory and market-house is called "*Barth*-olomew" and the adjoining parish is "*Kymere*" (*i.e.*, Cymyr) (see Camden 1, 290, 291.) It has old Stone and Bronze Age remains[2] and Briton coins.[3] |
| Surrey : | *Burton*, near Roman Stane Street from Chichester. |
| Hants : | *Barton* Cliff on Chichester Bay, with *Somer*-ford adjoining.<br>*Burton* Stacey, on Roman Icknield Street.<br>*Briten*-den, former name of Silchester, the ancient "Vindonia" of Romans and capital of the Segonti tribe, with adjoining river called "*Lod-don*" (1, 171 ; 322).<br>*Barton*, with prehistoric remains.[4]<br>*Buriton*, with prehistoric earthworks,[5] and adjoining *Bord*-ean with Bordean Cross.<br>*Broughton*, with prehistoric urn burials.[6]<br>*Barton* and *Barton* Point, in Wight, opposite Gos-port and Portsmouth (1, 210).<br>*Brad*-ing, on the Brading Downs in Wight, ancient town with Roman remains. |
| Wilts : | *Bradon* Forest, with 2 *Partons* and 2 *Somer*-fords on its north and south.<br>*Burton*, south of "Wans' Dyke," near Devizes, with *Cummer*-ford on the Roman road to the north.<br>*Brit*-ford on Avon, S. of Salisbury, with prehistoric "camps" and Stone Age remains,[7] in *Cad*-worth Hundred.<br>*Bratton*, near Eddington on Salisbury Plain, with prehistoric earthworks and barrows.[8]<br>*Broden*-Slack, with prehistoric earthworks.[9]<br>*Port*-on, on Roman road to Silchester from Sarum or Salisbury, S.E. of "Cad-bury Camp" and Cor-Gawr or "Stone-henge" ("Hanging Stones"), with numerous graves of Early Briton kings and nobles and their families of the Bronze Age. |

[1] W.P.E., 168.  [2] *Ib.*, 64 and 106.  [3] E.C.B., 206.  [4] W.P.E., 62.  [5] *Ib.* 235.
[6] *Ib.*, 162.  [7] *Ib.*, 64.  [8] *Ib.*, 169, 170, 250.  [9] *Ib.*, 250.

## BARAT NAMES IN BRITAIN

| | |
|---|---|
| Dorset : | *Brit*-port or *Brute*-port, the old name of Bridport, at end of Roman Road (" Fosse Way,") and formerly an appanage of the Crown with many barrows (1.65). |
| | *Bride*-head, with many prehistoric barrows.[1] |
| | *Burton* and *Burton* Cliff, to east of Bridport. |
| | *Portis*-ham, east of latter. |
| | *Brad*-ford, at Dorchester, on Roman road. |
| | *Burton*, west of above. |
| Devon : | *Barton*, Eddon-, on north of Dartmoor. |
| | *Brad*-ford, on Dartmoor, with cromlech. |
| | *Brid*-ford, at Moreton Hampstead. |
| | *Broad*-bury, near Okehampton, with barrows.[2] |
| Cornwall : | *Bartine*, in St. Just parish, with Stone Circles (1, 19) and well sacred to Euny (Oannes?).[3] |
| | *Pridden*, near St. Buryan, with menhir.[4] |
| | *Braddock*, with prehistoric interments.[5] |
| | *Burrit*-on, a former name of Penzance.[6] |

Northwards also we find these early Barat or Brit-on names radiating through the home-counties and Midlands, as, for instance :—

| | |
|---|---|
| Essex : | *Prittle*-well, near Southend, with prehistoric earthworks.[7] |
| | *Berden*, near Clavery (2, 142). |
| | *Bart*-low Hills (2, 140). |
| Suffolk : | *Breten*-ham on the *Breton* tributary of the Stour, and the Com-Bretonium of Antoninus (2, 154). |
| | *Barton* (2, 161). |
| | *Barton* Mere, near Bury St. Edmunds, with Bronze Age prehistoric village.[8] |
| Herts : | *Pirton*, in Cashio Hundred, on Icknield Way. |
| | *Brydens* Hill, north of Elstre. |
| | *Barton* Green, with Stone Age remains.[9] |
| | *Burden* Bury on Verulam R. north of St. Albans, on Watling Street. |
| Bucks : | *Brit*-well, near Farnham. |
| | *Braden*-ham. |
| | *Barton*, with " London Stone " to the S.W. of Buckingham. |
| | *Bourton*, near latter. |

[1] W.P.E., 158.  [2] *Ib.*, 157.  [3] L.S., 219.  [4] W.P.E., 198.
[5] *Ib.*, 154 and 228.  [6] L.H.P., 78.  [7] W.P.E., 202.  [8] *Ib.*, 279 and H.A.B., 151.
[9] W.P.E., 62.

## 194 PHŒNICIAN ORIGIN OF BRITONS & SCOTS

| | |
|---|---|
| Oxfords : | *Barton*, east of Oxford. |
| | *Bartholomews* (St.), adjoining Oxford. |
| | *Burton*, near Hampton. |
| | *Brad*-well, near latter. |
| Bedfords : | *Barton*, with *Barton* Hills, near Hitchin, on Icknield Way. |
| | *Pirton*, ditto. |
| Northamptons : | *Barton* Latimer, north of Pytchley ("Pict's-lea.") |
| Cambridges : | *Barton*, near Cambridge, on road from Oxford. |
| | *Bart*-low (2, 140). |
| Norfolk : | *Barden* River, tributary of Yare, at Norwich, Venta Icenorum of Romans (2, 176), possibly presuming that the ancient city name was Barden, as there is no other place-name here of "Barden." |
| | *Bretten*-ham, with Briton coins.[1] |
| Lincolns : | *Barton* on Humber (2, 338), and to its south is *Glan*-ford, suggestive of Part-olon and Cadwallon's title of "Gioln." |
| | *Barton*, near Lincoln. |
| | *Berewita*, near Spalding Croyland (2, 345). |
| Yorks : | *Barton*, four towns of this name (3, 248; 279; 281; 415.) |
| | *Brad*-ford, seat of cloth manufacture. |
| | *Brid*-ling-ton, with several early "British camps." |
| | *Broughton*, in Craven, with early remains (3, 283).[2] |
| Northumberland : | *Birt*-ley, with numerous "British villages."[3] |
| Nottingham : | *Burton* (2, 400). |
| Leicester : | *Bredon*, with old priory (2, 306). |
| | *Breedon* Hill, with prehistoric earthworks.[4] |
| Stafford : | *Barton* (2, 504). |
| | *Berth*, near Whitmore, with prehistoric earthworks.[5] |
| | *Burton*-on-Trent (2, 497). |
| Northampton : | *Barton* Seagrave (2, 281). |
| | *Burton* (2, 268). |

The Severn Valley was another early avenue of Briton civilization, and its Welsh bank remained largely free from Roman domination and influence, with its ancient capital of the later Briton kings, down to the Cymric Arthur, at Caerleon or Isca on the Usk ; and on the west the peninsula

[1] E.C.B., 120.  [2] W.P.E., 251.  [3] *Ib.*, 241.  [4] *Ib.*, 238.  [5] *Ib.*, 247.

## BARAT NAMES IN SEVERN VALLEY 195

of Gower, the ancient *Guhir*[1], associated with the King Arthur legend, wherein that name " Guhir " is obviously the transplanted " Kur " or " Syria," the homeland of the Syrio-Phœnicians, as we have seen. On the south is Somerset or " The Seat of the Somers, Sumers or Cymyrs " ; and the western promontory at the Severn mouth is " Hercules Point," the " Herakles Akron " of Ptolemy (or modern " Hart-land Point "), indicating the former presence of the Hercules-worshipping Phœnician navigating colonists there. The Upper Severn rises in Mont-Gomery, which name is now seen to mean " The Mount of the Cymry, Somers, or " *Gomers* "—the latter being also the Hebrew form of the ethnic name " Sumer." In the Severn Valley we have the following series of Barat names :—

Somerset :  *Parret* River at *Somer-ton*, which was " anciently the chief town of the whole country which takes its name from it,"[2] with " Avalon Isle," associated with the King Arthur legends.
*Puriton*, at old mouth of Parret River.
*Barton*, near Axbridge and Cheddar.
*Bruton* or *Briweton*, with old abbey (1, 99) and prehistoric earthworks.[3]
*Burton* Pynsent, near Taunton, seat of Chatham family (1, 96), with prehistoric earthworks[4].
*Bratton*, near Wincanton and east of Cadbury, with ancient " camps " (1, 120, 149).
*Priddy*, on Mendip Hills, with numerous prehistoric barrows.[5]
*Burthe*, with Bronze Age remains.[6]

Gloster :  *Brito* (" Bristol "). The ancient name for Bristol was " Caer *Brito*,"[7] and altered to " Brightston " by the Saxons.
*Bred*-on Hill, with *Kemer*-ton " Camp " and Roman remains.[8]
*Bourton*-on-the-Water, with prehistoric barrows,[9] and on Roman road.
*Bird*-lip and " camps," with Stone Age remains and earthworks at Bird-lip, Cooper's and Crickley Hills.[10]

[1] " Guhir " of Nennius, also spelt " Guyr." See C.B.G., 3, 123.
[2] C.B., 1, 79.  [3] W.P.E., 245.  [4] *Ib*., 245.  [5] *Ib*., 167.  [6] *Ib*., 106.
[7] Nennius, cited by C.B., 1, 86.  [8] W.P.E., 234.  [9] *Ib*., 160 and 387.
[10] *Ib*., 233.

| | |
|---|---|
| Worcester : | *Bart*-on, near Upton on Severn.<br>*Pirt*-on, to N.W. of above.<br>*Bred*-on, on Severn at mouth of Avon, with old monastery mentioned by Bede.[1]<br>*Brad*-on Hills, on Avon, with *Kemmer*-ton and *Comber*-ton, adjoining.<br>*Bredi*-cott at Worcester. |
| Hereford : | *Broad*-ward, with Bronze Age remains.[2] |
| Monmouth : | *Byrdhin* River at Caerleon, or Isca, on the Usk (3, 115). |
| Glamorgan : | *Briton* Ferry, at mouth of Neath, leading to Gower (3, 132).<br>*Porteynon*, in Gower. |
| Montgomery : | *Brythen* Hills, on Upper Severn, N.E. of Montgomery town. |

In Western Wales, in the coastal counties and Anglesea, are the following :—

| | |
|---|---|
| Cardigan : | *Borth*, on Dovey estuary (3, 150), near cairn of Taliesin, the great Welsh bard (sixth century, A.D.). |
| Carnarvon : | *Bard*-sey Point and *Bard*-sey, with traditional abbot, St. Cad-van, of Cad-van's Stone (3, 172).<br>*Brith* Rivil, on shore, connected with Vortigern. |
| Anglesea : | *Bwrdd* Arthur, a high hill with ruins of ancient buildings, near Trevaur, with cromlechs (3, 201). |

In Cumbria and Isle of Man are the following :—

| | |
|---|---|
| Mona : | *Braddon*, with its Runic-inscribed monuments. |
| Cheshire : | *Barton* (3, 53). |
| Lancashire : | *Barton*, near Eccles.<br>*Burton*, near coast, north of Lancaster, presumably on the coast of Morecambe Bay, an old road to lead mines, about 1100 B.C.<br>*Forton*, north of Garstang, on Wyre.<br>*Bard*-sey, at north entrance to Morecambe Bay, with Stone Circle.[3] |

[1] B.H.A., 2, 471 ; 488.  [2] W.P.E., 105.  [3] W.P.E., 201.

| | |
|---|---|
| Westmorland : | *Barton* in Ambleside, with prehistoric remains. |
| | *Barton-on*-Street, on old Roman road, near Haringham (3, 329). |
| | *Burton* (3, 412). |
| | *Burton* in Kendal, with ancient remains (3, 405). |
| | *Brathay* River with *Broughton*, near Ambleside, with Bronze Age remains.¹ |
| Cumberland : | *Broughton*, on Derwent, near *Camer*-ton. |

The Clyde Valley was another great artery through which Early Briton Civilization flowed into the remoter limbs of North Britain, with *Dun-Barton* or " Fort of the Bartons or Britons "² as a distributing centre. At the time of Ptolemy the upper estuary of the Clyde was occupied by the " Gad-enoi," that is, " The people of the *Gad* or Phœnicians "; and we shall see later the numerous " Gad " and " Catti " names in this area.

Below Dun-Barton are the " *Cumbræ* Isles " with the beautiful island of *Arran* or " Land of the *Arya* or Aryans," with its highest mountain peak Goat-Fell or " Mount of the Goats or Goths " and stone-circles. Arran was one of the seven sacred burial places of the Irish-Scots, as recorded in the Ogam Chronicle of Kerry ; and it was called by the Norsemen, in the ninth century A.D., " *Kumrey-ar* " or " (Abode) of the Cumbers, *i.e.*, Sumers."³

Above Dun-Barton we have *Part-ick*, or " The Wick (or town) of the Parts," at the highest navigable point of the river (until deepened a few miles further to Glasgow in modern times) at the mouth of the Kelvin rivulet ; thence along the latter valley across the narrow waist of Scotland to the Forth on the East Coast girdled by the " Picts ' Wall," or " Grim's Dyke," an earthen rampart, presumably originally erected by the Britons as a defence against the Northern Picts and Huns, and afterwards utilized and strengthened by Antoninus, after whom it is now generally

---

¹ W.P.E., 106.
² The aboriginal Celtic name for " Dun-Barton " was and is " Al-Clutha " or " Rock of the Clyde "—" Clutha " being " Clyde," the " Clothi " of the Romans.
³ " Kumra " is Eddic for Cumber-land.

called by modern writers. This strategical and natural line is followed also by the modern engineers of the inter-ocean canal and railways. Midway at the watershed between the Kelvin and Forth Valleys stands "*Cumber*-nauld" or "*Cum'er*-naud" or "Hold of the *Cumbers* or *Cum'ers*" or Sumers, near a chief Roman fort on the Wall on the south, with its Camelot of the Arthur legend locally represented at Camelon on the Carron tributary of the Forth, where were the ruins of an ancient building known as "Arthur's O'on,"[1] which place is believed by some writers[2] to be the historical Camlan, the site of the final battle between the historical Cymric King Arthur and Modred wherein both perished.

The Forth frith is significantly commanded by the island of Inch *Keith* or "Isle of the *Keiths* or Ca ti," opposite which rises "Arthur's Seat" dominating Edinburgh, the "Dun Eden or Edin" of the Scots;[3] and at its base flows the river Esk—the Trojan-Phœnician origin of which name we have seen—and the place-names "*Pinkie*" and "*Penicuik*" on that river, with the intervening *Borth*-wick on or near the Roman Watling Street, also suggest the name "Punic" or "Phœnician."

Thence, coasting northwards, we pass the Wemyss Caves with prehistoric solar cult gravings (Figs. 60, 68) and St. Andrews to *Perth*, the ancient *Berth*[4] or "City of the Berths or Perths," which latter dialectic form of Barat is seen to be in series with "Part-olon"; and there is another *Bertha*, with Roman and ancient Briton remains, a few miles distant, at the confluence of the Almond and Tay.[5] Significantly also there is a "*Comrie*" to the west of Perth, and the great plain at Perth and the adjoining Scone (the old seat of crowning of the Scottish kings) is named "*Gowrie*," and also with Stone circles in series with the Arthurian "Gower" on the Severn.

---

[1] The ruins of "Arthur's O'on" (or Oven), so called as long ago as 1293, were demolished long ago by the Carron Iron Foundry to make a dam for their works. The site appears to be visible from Arthur's Seat.
[2] S.C.P., 14, 161, and *Celtic Scotland*; and M.E.C., 73. This Camlan is placed in Cornwall by Geoffrey (*Hist. Brit.*, 11, 2.)
[3] S.C.P., xxii and cxlii.    [4] C.B., 4 134.    [5] *Ib.*, 4, 140.

# BARAT NAMES IN DON VALLEY & IRELAND 199

The Don Valley, to the north of Perth, the site of Partolon's inscribed monument, contains in the neighbourhood of that monument, besides a considerable number of villages called "Catti" (see Map, p. 19) as distinguished from Pictish villages with the prefix of "Pit," also some of the Barat series, namely, "*Bourtie*," "*Barth*-ol" and "*Ports*-town."

In Ireland the vestiges of the early Briton place-names are not wanting. I have not yet searched specially for them, but may instance *Brittas* Bay in Wicklow, with the town of Red Cross; another *Brittas*, the ancient seat of the O'Dunns, and Bally *Brittas*, both in Queen's County,[1] *Brutain*, with the adjoining Newton *Breda*, in Down,[2] and *Burton* in Cork.[3] And Ireland of the Irish-Scots has also its "Holy Isles," with very ancient remains, including a magnificent "prehistoric" fort of cyclopean masonry in the *Hitt-ite* style, in Galway Bay, and also significantly named "*Aran*" or "*Arran*," which like the name "*Erin*" and "*Ir*-land," in series with the "Airy-ana" or "Ir-an" or "Land of the Aryans" of the ancient Sun-worshipping Aryans in the Orient.

[1] *Ib.*, 4, 311 and 312.  [2] *Ib.*, 4, 425.  [3] *Ib.*, 4, 278.

# XVI

## "Catti," "Keith," "Gad" and "Cassi" Titles in Old Ethnic and Place-Names evidencing Phœnician Penetration of Britain and its Isles

*Confirming Hitto-Phœnician Origin of the " Catti " and " Cassi " Coins of Pre-Roman Britain*

> " His [the *Khaitiya's*[1]] sources of subsistence are Arms and the Protection of the Earth. The Guardianship of the Earth is his special province. . . . By intimidating the bad and cherishing the good, the (Khattiya) ruler who maintains the discipline of the different tribes secures whatever region he desires."—*Vishnu Purana Epic.*[2]

THE Phœnician Barats' rule and civilization of Britain and its Isles in the pre-Roman period is also attested, I find, by the widespread prevalence of the Phœnician Barats' tribal title of Khatti, Catti, Gad and Kassi, in the old place and river names from south to north—from Cudder Point of Penz-ance with its old Phœnician tin and copper mines, a name now seen to preserve the *Punic* or *Panch* title of the Phœnic-ians, to *Caith*-ness and *Shet*-land or Land of the *Caiths*, Khats or Catti, *Xats*, Shets, Ceti or Scots. The essentially ruling character of the Catti (or Khattiya) race is evidenced by the citation from the Indian epic in the heading, and explains the " Catti " title of the ruling Britons in the pre-Roman period on their coins, as well as the title of their ruling race in their home province, in the south of England, as the " *Caty*-euchlani " of Ptolemy.

---

[1] See p. 8 for the old Indian Pali form of this tribal name as *Khattiyo*, which is spelt *Kshatriya* in the later Sanskrit.
[2] V.P., 3, 8 ; and 3, 87.

## CASSI PHŒNICIAN NAMES IN CORNWALL

Penzance and Cornwall with its Cassi-terides tin islands seem to have been especially associated with the " Cassi " clan title of the Hitto-Phœnician Barats. We have seen that an ancient name for Penzance was " Burrit-on," presumably a form of " Place of the Barats or Brits." And it was clearly the tin-mines of Cornwall and its outlying islands, the *Cassi*-terides[1], which first attracted the Phœnician Barats to Britain in the Bronze Age of the Old World for a supply of tin, the sparsely distributed and most essential constituent for the manufacture of bronze, of which latter, as well as tin, the Phœnicians were the chief manufacturers and distributors ; and their chief source of supply appear to have been the Cornish mines in Britain. Some of these mines were presumably worked by the Phœnicians about 2800 B.C. or earlier, as we have seen. From all accounts, it was the " Cassi-terides " mines which were the first worked by them ; and that name, as well as the old-world name for " tin " of " *Cassi*-teros " of Homer and the classic Greeks, or the Sanskrit *Kastīra*,[2] appear to preserve the " Cassi " title of that leading clan of the sea-going Phœnicians, as the chief distributors of this invaluable metal of the Old World.

[This origin of that name seems confirmed by the fact that in Attic Greek the name for both tin and the Cassi-terides tin-islands is spelt as " Ka*tt*i-teros " and Ka*tt*i-terides," thus using the same equivalency which was used in Britain for the " Cassi " and " Catti " tribes and coins. And in the Indian Sanskrit tradition " *Kastīra* " is tin, and the place-name " Kàstīra," or " Place of Kastīra or Tin," was located in the " Land of the *Bāhīkas*," a despised outcast tribe who also gave their name to " a sheet of water," and who now seem to be the *Peahts* or Picts of the Sea of " *Victis* " or " Icht " in Cornwall. Moreover,

---

[1] These islands, which lay to the west or south-west of Land's End, are now submerged with the general sinking of the south coast of Britain.
[2] Tin was called by the Greeks " *Cassi-teros*," by the ancient Indo-Aryans " *Kas-tīra*," by the Arabs " *Kaz-dir*," and by the Assyrians and Sumerians, according to Prof. Sayce over forty years ago (S.I., 479) " *Kizasadir*," " *Kasduru* or *Kazduru* "—though these latter terms are not found in the recent Assyrian and Sumerian lexicons. The term " Stannum," now applied to tin, was originally used, as by Pliny, for an alloy of silver and lead, not tin itself ; and the latter (tin) was called by him " White Lead " (Plumbum album), in contradistinction to lead, which was called " Black Lead " (Plumbum nigrum)—Pliny. *Nat. Hist.*, 34, 16 ; 33, 9.

"*Coss*-ini" is the title given by a Greek writer[1] to the people of the tin-producing country of South-Western Britain.][2]

It thus appears probable that the first batch of Phœnicians who worked these Cassiterides mines belonged to the "Cassi" clan to which our Brito-Phœnician Part-olon belonged. But it seems not improbable that Brutus and his Phœnician kinsmen also bore this clan title, which their later descendants, the Briton kings of the late pre-Roman period, stamped upon their "Cassi" coins and gave them their "Cassi" title, as recorded by Cæsar. The sea-going Cassi clan had chains of colonies stretching along the Mediterranean, (see map); and Strabo states that the Phœnicians under Cadmus occupied the Cadmus district of Epirus[3] with the New Troy on the Thyamis river (whence Brutus came); and the coastal tribe adjoining the Acheron river (whence Brutus sailed, was called "*Cass*-opæi" with a port called "*Cassi*-ope (or Cassi-opo); and similarly opposite the mouth of the river of Phœnice in North Epirus was another port named "*Cassi*-ope" also of the same tribe.[4] And this name "*Cassi*-ope" appears to mean "Fort of the *Cassi* tribe."[5]

Just as we have seen that Brutus and his Phœnician Barat colonists and their descendants bestowed their own ancestral eponymic royal title of Barat or "Brit-on" on many of their early settlements throughout their new home-land in Britain, so also they bestowed, I find, their more general tribal title of *Khatti* or "Catti" (or "Hitt"-ite or "Goth"), as well as their special Phœnician modification

---

[1] Artemidorus, cited by Stephanos de urbibus: C.B., 1, 1.
[2] These people were called Ostimii by Pytheas (the Ostiæi of Strabo, 2, 4, 3 and 195: 4, 4, 1.) and said to "dwell on a promontory which projects considerably into the ocean," and it adjoined "Uxisama" (*i.e.*, Ushant (Strabo, 1, 4, 5), which thus indicates Cornwall.
[3] S., 320; 7, 7, 1.    [4] *Ib.*, 323: 7, 7, 5.
[5] This affix "*ope*" is also found in Epirus in "Can-ope" on the Acheron river, and in Sin-ope, the chief port of Cappadocia on the Euxine; and in "Parthen-ope" the old name for Naples (S. 654: 14, 2, 10). This latter word "*Parthen*," *i.e.*, "Barat-ana" or "Brit-ain" is clearly in ethnic series with "Cassi" and means "Place of the Parthen or Barats." This "Ope" is obviously derived from the Akkadian *Uppu*, "a ring or fence," cognate with *Apapu* "surround, enclosure," and *appa-rum*, a "rampart." (M.D., 78, 79, 80), and is presumably the source of the Latin *Oppidum*, "a town," and English "hoop."

## CATTI OR HITT-ITE NAMES IN BRITAIN

of that title as "*Gad*" or "*Cad*" upon many others of their new colonies, rivers and hills in Britain.

The dialectic differences in the spelling of these place-names, as seen in the forms in which they are now fixed in their modern spelling—such as the occasional alteration of the vowel *a* into *e*, *i*, *o* or *u* and the *t* into a *d* and the initial *K* softening sometimes into *C*, *G* and *S* and occasionally *J*—are obviously due partly to local dialectic provincialisms, and partly to individual vagaries in the early phonetic spellings of the same name, as were widely current before the forms were rigidly fixed by printing and the press.

[It is interesting to notice that the not infrequent use of *i* for the *a* vowel in the original "*Khat*" is in series with the Hebrew and Semitic Chaldic corrupt spelling of this name as "*Khit*" or *Hit* or *Hitt* ("*Hitt*-ite"), and this *i* dialectic form is seen to be especially common in Kent and Sussex, *e.g.*, in "Kit's Coty." Moreover, the initial *K* is sometimes dropped out in the later spellings, as in the Hebrew and Semitic Chaldic spelling of this name—just as in the Welsh Keltic dropping of the *G* in "Gwalia" to form "Wales," and of the *G* in "Gwith" to form "Wight"—so that an original "Khatt-on" becomes "*Hatt*-on," and we actually have "Hith" or "Hithe," a seaport of Kent, which thus literally corresponds to the Hebrew "*Heth*" and "*Hitt*" for "*Khatti*." These dialectic variations in the spelling are thus somewhat like the mosaic of architectural styles in an ancient cathedral which has been added to or restored from time to time, so as to display the earlier and more primitive style, side by side, with the styles of the later periods. Probably some of these dialectic variants are due to later immigrations speaking slightly different provincial dialects of the primitive Sumerian Khatti or Gothic. Indeed this practice of dropping out the initial C (=Kh) is well seen on the Briton coins stamped "*Att*" or "*Atti*" for "Catti" (see Fig. 3, p. 6).]

The early settlements of the Hitto-Phœnician Catti or Khatti, as indicated by the incidence of that tribal name, are especially numerous in the South of Britain, which was the first part to be colonized and civilized. The names of the early settlements often merely designate the place simply as "The Settlement of the Catts or Chats," such as "*Catt*-on," "*Cade*-by," "*Chat*-ham" or "*Cater*-ham" or "Home of the *Catti*," in contradistinction to the settlements of the Picts or Wans (or Vans) often in the neighbourhood—as the Catti appear to have often settled in the vicinity of old Pictish villages—bearing such names as "*Pitten*-den," "*Pit*-ney," "*Pitten*-ham," "*Pitch*-ley" or "*Wan*-stead," "*Wans*-den," etc., or "The Den or Dene or Lea of the *Picts* or *Wans*." Those "Catti" names bearing distinctive Aryan affixes such as "field," "well," "mill," "hurst," "combe," "bury," "cot" etc., were presumably of somewhat later date, to distinguish these newer settlements from the earlier ones bearing merely the tribal name. The affix "*ing*" is the Gothic (*i.e.*, Early Briton) tribal affix.

The great number of these early Barat or Brit-on settlements containing the Aryan tribal "Catti" prefix in their names appears to imply that in that early period *the Catti ruling race lived apart by themselves in their own settlements*, and did not mix or inter-marry with the aboriginal Picts, and hence they used the prefix "*Cad*" or "*Catti*" to racially distinguish their early towns from the settlements of the non-Aryan aborigines. This would also explain the Chronicle record that Brutus, after building his new capital, "made choice of the citizens who were to inhabit it."

These "Catti" series of early place, river and hill names in Britain, imposed by Brutus and his Phœnician Barats and their descendants, often designate sites upon the old so-called "Roman" roads, and where are found prehistoric remains, funereal barrows with their cultural objects of the "Late Stone" and Bronze Ages. They thus disclose for the first time, along with the "Barat" and "Cassi" series, the hitherto unknown racial character and name of the authors of these "prehistoric" barrows and Bronze Age weapons and implements, namely, Aryan Barat or "Catti" Hitto-Phœnicians or Early Britons.

From "New Troy" or London these "Catti" names, in their various dialectic forms, radiate south and westwards as follows :—

Kent :          *Cat*-heim or *Cat*-hem (or "Home of the Catti," from Gothic *heim*, "home"), the ancient Briton name for Dover.[1]

[1] *Cf.* T.W.P., 148.

## CATTI NAMES IN SOUTH BRITAIN 205

Kent (*cont.*): *Chat*-ham, with many prehistoric remains of Stone and Bronze Ages[1] on Watl-ing Street (1, 339).[2]
*Keith*-Coty, modern " *Kit's* Coty," south of Chatham, with prehistoric remains and Briton coins[3] and traditionally associated with the Briton king *Cati*-gern (1, 331). And compare the " Ketti " menhir in Gower Cærmarthen.
*Chid*-ing, with sacred stone near Tonbridge (1, 332).
*Chitt*-en-den, with Briton coins.[4]
*Cud*-ham or *Chud*-ham.
*Sid*-cup.
*Sid*-ley.
*Sitt*-ing-bourne, with Bronze Age remains[5] and Briton coins, on Watling Street.[6]
*Had*-low, near Tonbridge.
*Hith* and *Hith*-haven, modern Hythe (or " Place of the Hitts or Heth, *i.e.*, Hittites "), one of the Cinque Ports, with Bronze Age remains,[7] on ancient mouth of Rother (1, 321),[8] and terminus of " Stoney Street " branch of Watling Street, and possibly the port at which Cæsar landed.

Surrey: *Cater*-ham, ancient *Keter*-ham.
*Cattes*-hull, modern *Cates*-hill, on Wye, near Godalming, former village of early Saxon kings (1, 242).
*Gatton*, on Mole, tributary of Thames, with Roman coins (1, 242, 252).
*God*-elming, modern " Godalming," with early Briton coins,[8] and Saxon remains, on Stane Street (1, 248).
*God*-stone (1, 252).
*Chidd*-ing-fold, near Roman Stane Street.
*Shotter*-mill, ditto.

Sussex: *Cats* Street, near Heathfield.
*Cats*-field, near Bexhill.

---

[1] At Chatham and adjoining Otterham and Hoo, Stone Age remains, and Bronze Age at Hoo and Rochester. W.P.E., 63 and 105.
[2] The numbers enclosed within brackets refer to Camden's *Britannia*, 2nd ed. Gough.
[3] E.C.B., 122, 197, 354. [4] *Ib.*, 95, 422. [5] W.P.E., 105. [6] E.C.B., 190.
[7] *Ib.*, 105. Remains at neighbouring Haynes Hill.
[8] The ancient port is now left dry by raising of the beach.
[9] E.C.B., 50, 64, 83.

| | |
|---|---|
| Sussex (*cont.*) | *Cotten*-den Street, near Ticehurst, on ancient highway.<br>*Chid*-ham, near Chichester, off Roman Stane Street.<br>*Chit*-hurst, near Midhurst.<br>*Chitt*-ing-ton, north of Lewes.<br>*Chitt*-ing-ly, near Hurstmonceux.<br>*Gotham* and *Sedles*-combe.<br>*Sid*-les-ham, on Selsey harbour, with Briton coins,[1] and *Sommer*-by adjoining. |
| Hants : | *Cad*-land, near Hythe on Southampton Water (1, 189).<br>*Chater*-ton, in Portsmouth (1, 199).<br>*Chute* Forest, on Icknield Roman Way (1, 205).<br>*Hithe*, modern Hythe on Southampton Water.<br>*Guith*, the " Quiktesis " of Ptolemy, modern Wight (1, 174).<br>*Gat*-comb, with Bronze Age remains, in Wight.[2]<br>*Gads* Hill, with ancient " camps " and earthworks, in Wight (1, 174 and 178). |
| Wilts : | *Cad*-worth and *Cawdon* Hundred, on Salisbury Plain, south of Stonehenge.<br>*Cad*-ley, with adjoining *Chute*, on Icknield Way.<br>*Chad*-ham (1, 158–9).<br>*Chadden*-ton, south of Purton.<br>*Cuite*-ridge, west of Bratton (Eddington).<br>*Chitt*-erne St. Mary, with two Early Briton settlements.[3]<br>*Chid*-bury Hill or *Sid*-bury, with prehistoric earthworks and many barrows (1, 158).<br>*Chute* and *Chute* Causeway, on Roman Road to Circencester.<br>*Cod*-ford, St. Peters and Parish, on Salisbury Plain, with prehistoric earthworks and " castle "[4] (1, 149).<br>*Sid*-bury, north of Tidworth, with Stone Age remains.[5] |
| Dorset : | *Cathers*-ton, at Lyme Regis.<br>*Catt*-stoke, on Frome, with prehistoric earthworks (1, 68).<br>*Chet*-nole, north of same.<br>*Chett*-le, with " prehistoric village " and barrows.[6]<br>*Chidi*-ock, near Brid-port. (1, 74).<br>*Hod* Hill, with early iron bars as currency.[7] |

[1] E.C.B., Selsey, 66, 90.  [2] W.P.E., 105, at Arre-ton Downs.
[3] *Ib.*, 280.  [4] *Ib.*, 250.  [5] *Ib.*, 251.  [6] *Ib.*, 157, and 277.  [7] H.A.B., 251.

## CATTI NAMES IN DEVON & CORNWALL

Devon :
*Catte*-down Cave (preserving an old place- or hill-name " *Catte*-down "), near Plymouth, with Stone Age remains.[1]
*Cad*-bury or *Cad*-bery, south-west of Tiverton, with prehistoric and Roman remains (154)[2].
*Cad*-bury at Ottery (1, 35) and on N. Dartmoor.
*Chett*-le, with prehistoric barrows.[3]
*Chid*-ley, on Teign (1, 35).
*Chud*-leigh, on Teign (1, 53).
*Cud*-lip, on Tavy, on Dartmoor, above the copper mines.
*Gid*-leigh, on Dartmoor, near Cromlech at Brad-ford.
*Chittle*-hampton at S. Moulton, on Taw (1, 32).
*Sid*-mouth, with prehistoric barrows.[4] (1, 57, 59).
*Sid*-bury, with prehistoric settlements.[5]

Cornwall :
*Cadd*-on Point, with prehistoric cliff-castle and earthworks.[6]
*Cudder* Point, in Penzance Bay, south of St. Michael's Mount.
*Cad*-son-bury, with prehistoric earthworks, near Callington.[7]
*Gotha* Castle, near Phœbe's Point, St. Anstell, with earthworks.[8]
*God*-olcan, modern *God*-olphan, near Land's End, famous for its tin mines; and the lordship of same has arms with two-headed spread eagle (1, 4) of Hitto-Sumerians.
*Sith*-ney parish, including Helston (1, 16).
*Ouethi*-ock, near *Prideaux*, with prehistoric earthworks.[9]

Northwards from " New Troy " or London these old " Catti " names radiate through the adjoining counties to the Midlands and are prolonged into Northumbria. The later old home-kingdom of the paramount Briton king, Cassivellaunus, or Caswallon or Cadwallon, the " Land of the *Caty*-euchlani " of Ptolemy, is rich in the Cat, Cass, and Gad Hitto-Phœnician ethnic titles for place and river names, just, as we have seen, it was in regard to the Barat series. This central Briton kingdom extended from the north bank

[1] H.A.B., 60.  [2] *Ib.*, 229.  [3] W.P.E., 157.  [4] *Ib.*, 157.  [5] *Ib.*, 230.
[6] *Ib.*, 226.  [7] *Ib.*, 226.  [8] *Ib.*, 226.  [9] *Ib.*, 227.

of the Thames, from the western border of New Troy or London, northwards to the Wash and Humber ; and thus included the modern counties of Middlesex (West), Herts, Bucks, Oxford, Bedford, Northampton, Huntingdon, Cambridge, Nottingham, Rutland, Leicester and Lincoln. (For details see Appendix III.)

Similarly, from Somerset in the Severn Valley, we find, a series of the early " Catti " names radiates through Cambria or Wales to some extent, but more freely through Cumbria to Dun Barton (or " Fort of the Britons") with its Cumbræ Isles. The very free distribution of this Catti and Barat title in Somerset or " Seat of the Somers " and in Gloster, with its relative absence in Wales and mainly confined there to the Severn coast, suggests that Somerset and Gloster, with the northern bank of the Severn estuary, from Caerleon or Isca on the Usk to Gower, formed the real *Cymry* Land ; and that the title Cymri or Cambria for Wales and the Welsh people was presumably a later designation, after the non-Aryan Welsh Silures and cognate Pictish tribes had obtained their Aryan " Cymry " speech from their Aryan Catti Barat rulers and civilizing colonists of Somerset and Gloster in the Severn Valley. (The detailed distribution of the " Catti " names in this area is given in Appendix III.)

Similarly also, from Dun-Barton and the Frith of Clyde, at the top of which Ptolemy significantly located the " *Gadeni* " tribe (*i.e.*, the *Gad* or Phœnicians) we have Catti or Gad names in Arran (or " Land of the Arri or Arya-ns "), the " *Kumr* Isle " of the Norse[1]—with its prehistoric Stone Circles and barrows on the flanks of *Goat* Fell, the ancient Kil-Michael and *Cata*-col with the legend of an ancient Gothic sea-king slain by the aboriginal chief Fion-gal, the Fein.[2] And in the adjoining Bute is Kil-*Chattan* or " Church of *Chattan*," with its prehistoric standing stones, facing the *Cumbræ* Isles. In Glasgow an ancient boundary

---

[1] Arran (called by the Norse *Kumr ey*-ar or " Isle of the Kumr or Cymri " and Sudr-eyiar or " Southern Isle ") is anciently spelt Aran, Arane, Aren, as well as Arran—see J. McArthur, *Antiq. of Arran*.
[2] *New Statistical Account of Scotland*, "Arran."

# CATTI AND CASSI PLACE NAMES IN BRITAIN 209

in the records for "Redding the Marches" was "*Cayttis'* dyke."[1] This series of Catti or Gad names also stretches, I find, in series with the Barat names across the narrow waist of Scotland to the Forth to *Hadd*-ing-ton and Perth, and onwards north along the East Coast to the Don Valley of our Newton Stone and to *Caith*-ness or anciently *Cat*-ness (or Nose of the *Caiths* or *Cats*) and to Shet-land (or Land of the *Shets* or *Ceti*), where, as we have seen, I find actual inscriptional Ogam evidence for the use of *Xattui* or *Khattui* as the "prehistoric" name of the old capital of "Shet-land," also spelt "*Zet*-land" and "*Het*-land."[2] (For details of this series of Khatti names see Appendix III.)

The "*Cassi*" series of titles for place-names, on the other hand, is necessarily much more limited, as the Cassi or Kassi were a dynastic clan of the Barat Catti ruling tribe who followed the religious reform of their ancestral priest-king *Kasi* in adhering to the purer monotheistic Sun-worship of the founder of the First Dynasty of Aryan kings.[3] We have already seen that the first Phœnicians who worked the tin mines in the Cassi-terides of Cornwall, as well as Brutus himself, were probably of the Cassi clan of the Catti or Hitt-ites, as Part-olon also was.

Besides the occurrence of this eponymic title in "Cassi-terides"—a name which seems repeated in several of the inland place-names here appended[4]—I find the following ancient place-names have presumably this "Cassi" element in divers dialectic forms :—

| | |
|---|---|
| Herts : | *Cassio*-bury, seat of modern Earls of Essex near Verulam, the capital of Cassi-vellaunus, with many Briton coins in district.[5] |
| | "*Cashio* Hundred," extending through Herts from south to north, and including Cassio-bury. |
| Bedford : | *Keysoe*, near old camp and Cadbury Lion and *Perten* Hall. |

[1] Glasgow Herald, 24th April, 1923.
[2] Gazetteer Scot. 2,715.
[3] Details in *Aryan Origin of the Phœnicians*.
[4] It occurs in Cornwall, Wilts, etc., as seen in the list, in places not associated with the tradition of any Roman *castra* or camp.
[5] E.B.C. Verulam, 119, 251, 253, 257, etc., and St. Albans, 234, etc.

| | |
|---|---|
| Lincoln : | *Caus*-enn or Gausennæ of Romans (2, 353). |
| Leicester : | *Coss*-ing-ton, on R. Soar, off Foss Road. |
| Bucks : | *Ches*-ham, on the Chess, with ancient earthworks and circle[1] and Briton coins.[2] |
| | *Chis*-beach, north of Hambleden. |
| Middlesex : | *Chis*-wick on Thames. It was presumably part of the staked ford held by Cassivellaunus (as described in Appendix V). |
| Kent : | *Gos*-hall, near Ash, with Briton coins.[3] |
| Sussex : | *Ciss*-bury and Cissbury Hill, near Worthing, with Stone and Bronze Age remains.[4] (1, 270, 289). |
| Hants : | *Cos*-ham, at neck of Portsmouth Island. |
| | *Gos*-port, adjoining Portsmouth (1, 200). |
| Wilts : | *Cos*-ham, ancient royal village of Saxons (1, 130). |
| | *Casterly* " Camp," north of Great Bedwyn, on Salisbury Plain, with ancient earthworks.[5] |
| Devon : | *Caws*-and Beacon, with early stone cist.[6] |
| Cornwall : | (*Cassiter* Street in Bodmin). |
| | *Chysoyster*, with prehistoric village.[7] |
| | *Gudzh* promontory, in Helston Bay. |
| Monmouth : | *Cas*, on Severn. |
| Cheshire : | *Goostrey*, with barrows.[8] |
| Cumberland : | *Gos*-forth on Irth River, with pre-Christian Cross, etc. |
| | *Kes*-wick, with Stone Circle and old copper mines (3, 422, 435), under *Sca*-Fell. |
| Northumberland : | *Gos*-forth, or *Ges*-forth, near Roman Vindobala (Rutchester) (3, 513). |
| | *Gosse*-ford, near Wallsend (3, 495). |
| | *Caistron*, near Hepple, with prehistoric earthworks.[9] |
| Haddington : | *Gos*-ford House, opposite Inch Keith |
| Caithness : | *Keiss*, on east coast, between Wick and John o'Groats, with early stone Cists and Cairns containing prehistoric " Chief's Cist " and cairn, with tall, long-headed chief, as opposed to skeletons of the short-statured aborigines, with underground " Pict dwellings " in neighbourhood.[10] |

[1] W.P.E., 225. [2] E.B.C. 218. [3] E.C.B., 207. [4] W.P.E., 106; 248.
[5] *Ib.*, 250. [6] *Ib.*, 196. [7] *Ib.*, 275. [8] *Ib.*,154. [9] *Ib.*, 241
[10] See L.H.C., 15, etc.

## CATTI & CASSI NAMES ON BRITON COINS

In Ireland, also, there is a considerable series of these old "Catti" and "Cassi" place-names in old sites, which will now be obvious to the reader.

We now see more clearly than before why the pre-Roman Briton kings, inheriting such a celebrated "Catti" and "Cassi" ancestry—an eastern branch of the latter royal clan having given to Babylonia its famous "Cassi" or "Kassite" Dynasty for a period of over six centuries, from about 1800 B.C. to 1170 B.C., as well as our King Part-olon, the "Kazzi" or "Qass" of the Newton Stone monument in Scotland—should have proudly stamped these treasured ancestral titles on their coins in Early Britain.

Of these pre-Roman Briton coins, in gold, electrum, tin or or bronze, bearing, as we shall see later, solar symbols of the Sun, Sun-Cross, Sun-Horse and the Sun-Eagle or "Phœnix"—as the Aryan-Cassi-Phœnicians were pre eminently Sun-worshippers—we have already seen examples of some of those stamped with the titles "Catti" and "Cas(si)" (see Figs. 3 and 11, pp. 6 and 48).

The name "Catti" on these coins is conjectured by the chief authority on Early British coins to be the personal name of several otherwise unknown Briton "princes," who, he supposes, bore the same name;[1] whilst, on the contrary, an earlier writer, the Rev. Beale Poste, supposed that it was not a personal name, but the title of an ancient British "province, state or community."[2] My new historical evidence now discloses that the latter view was more in keeping with the freshly elicited facts. That title "Catti" is now seen to designate the dynastic tribe of ruling Briton kings; and to be the literal equivalent of "Khatti" or "Hitt-ite," which was the racial title of the Phœnician Barat Aryans who worked the tin mines in Cornwall, and whose descendants or kinsmen established themselves in the interior in South Britain as Catti kings, and afterwards extended their civilizing and Aryanizing rule throughout the British Isles.

The "Cassi" or "Cas" stamped coins (see Fig. 11, p. 48) are the same general type as the "Catti," with the same

[1] Sir J. Evans, E.C.B., 141    [2] P.B.C., 283.

solar symbols, though strangely all reference to these "Cassi" coins is omitted by Evans in his monograph. Coins of this Catti-Cassi type, actually bearing the legends "Catti" or "Cas," are unfortunately very rare, as, being usually of gold, such coins have presumably been melted up by the finders to make jewellery, in order to escape the penalties incident to treasure trove, as remarked by Beale and others. But other later coins of this same type bearing kings' names and other legends (*e.g.*, "Tascio," see later) are fairly numerous. They are found from Cornwall through Devon and Somerset and far up the Severn Valley to near Wroxeter. They are also found from Kent to Northumberland, and a few even in Scotland. They are most common, however, in the old home-kingdom of the later paramount Briton kings, who were at the time of Cæsar represented by Cassi-vellaunus, namely, the Land of the Caty-euchlani or "Catuellani," from the Thames to the Humber. Thus these early Briton coins are found in those regions where we have discovered the widespread evidence of ancient Catti rule surviving in the many ancient and pre-Roman Briton place-names, with prehistoric remains there. The absence of kings' names upon the earlier Catti or Cas Briton coins seems to be explained by the fact that the early Briton kings were, like the early Phœnicians, members of a commonwealth of confederated Aryan city-states which presumably used the coins in common.

The current notion also that the Early Britons derived their coinage by imitating a stater of Philip II. of Macedonia (360–336 B.C.)[1] can no longer be maintained. Indeed, one of the chief advocates of this old theory was latterly forced to confess, on further observation, that the Macedonian stater could not be the *sole* "prototype" from which the Early Briton kings modelled their coinage.[2] But more than this, it must now be evident to the unbiased observer that the Early British coins, with their symbolism, exhibit nothing whatever Macedonian in their type. The horseman and

---

[1] A theory re-advocated by Evans (E.C.B., 24, etc.), and adopted by Rhys (R.C.B., XV, etc.), and by Rice Holmes (H.A.B., 248, etc.).
[2] E.C.B., *Supplement*, 424.

## MACEDONIAN THEORY OF CATTI & CASSI COINS 213

chariot, which is sometimes figured on the Early Briton coins, and often as a winged or Pegasus horse, is by no means Macedonian in origin. It appears on coins and in glyptic art long anterior to the Macedonian period; and we have seen that Brutus came from the Macedonian frontier, within which was a colony of Parth-eni; so that the Britons doubtless derived that symbol independently from the same remote Barat source from which the Macedonians derived its unwinged form. And there is no trace on the Macedonian coins of the many solar Phœnician symbols which are stamped on the coins of the Britons, as we shall see later.

In support of this Macedonian theory of Briton coinage, it is noteworthy that a type of coin was arbitrarily selected by its advocates, which is admittedly *not Briton but " Gaulish."* It is a type found commonly in Gaul, and when found in Britain it is more especially associated with the Gaulish tribe of Atrebates in Berkshire and other places inhabited by that tribe, who are usually identified with the " Belgæ " immigrants, who, Cæsar says, had recently before his arrival settled in the South of Britain. So obviously " Greek " or Macedonian was this Gaulish type of coin that the fact was already noted in Gough's Camden[1] and by Poste.[2] But the confusion of argument in rearing upon this Gaulish type the Macedonian theory of British coinage is obvious by the statements that " this [Gaulish] type is beyond all doubt the earliest of the British series,[3] and derived through Gaul,"[4] yet on the same page this conclusion seems contradicted by admitting that " the British coins are in all probability *earlier* than the Gaulish "[5]—which latter are placed at 150–100 B.C., as opposed to the earliest British, which he assigns to " a date somewhere between 150 and 200 B.C.[6]

The Ear of Corn, the symbolic Aryan-Phœnician meaning of which we shall see later, so frequently figured on the Catti-Cassi coins of the Early Britons (see Fig. 3 and later), and of Cunobeline,[7] and on Phœnician and Phœnicianoid coins

---

[1] In the text " Greek " is specified (1, cxiv); but the Index (p. 433) says " Macedonian."   [2] P.B.C., 7.
[3] E.C.B., 25.   [4] *Ib.*, 26.   [5] *Ib.*, 26.   [6] *Ib.*, 26.
[7] See A.A.C., Pl. xxiii. Figs., 1, 2, 3 and 4.

of Spain,[1] and in the coins of Phœnicia and Cilicia,[2] and absent in the Macedonian stater, is figured both as a solitary ear of corn and as crossed ears to form the sign of the Sun-Cross, as we shall see later. For the Barat Catti and Cássi, although seamen, were also essentially Aryan agriculturalists; and, as we have seen, their kinsmen, the Cassis of Babylonia, ploughed and sowed as a religious rite under the Sign of the Cross (see Fig. 12, p. 49). Now, the solitary ear of corn on the Briton coins is exactly paralleled in design in the early coin of Metapontum in the Taranto Gulf of Southern Italy, of about 600–480 B.C., which was presumably a port of the Phœnicians.[3] And we find it in the Phœnician coins of Cilicia, and in the early Trojan amulets associated with Hitto-Sumerian inscriptions (see later Figures).

[This sea-port of Metapontum was traditionally founded by Nestor *on his return from the Trojan War*;[4] and it stands only about 200 miles due west, across the mouth of the Adriatic from Epirus, whence Brutus came with his bride. Nestor, significantly, moreover, was a friend and associate of Peirithoos (*i.e.*, Brutus), and assisted the latter along with Coronus Caineus (*i.e.*, Corineus) in rescuing Peirithoos' bride from the Kentaurs of Epirus. Metapontum, or Metabum, was a famous ship-building port, as well as noted for its agriculture and " golden corn,"[5] on the borders of the *Bruttii* land of S. Italy,[6] and appears to have been actually within the Land of the Bruttii,[7] who, we have seen, were Barat Phœnicians. These facts, therefore, whilst disclosing an early and presumably Phœnician source for the Ear of Corn device on the Early Briton coins—the Corn being part of the Phœnician solar symbolism, as we shall see—suggests that Nestor (name in series with that of the Trojan-Phœnician king Antenor and his son Agenor) was himself a Phœnician, and that his city-port

---

[1] A.A.C., Pl. iii, Figs. 1, 2, 5, and Pl. iv, Fig. 8; Pl. vi, Figs. 3, 6, 9.
[2] Even in the Greco-Roman period. See H.C.P., cxx, 43, 113; and H.C.C., 16, 164.
[3] See Fig. 5, Plate V in G.A.C. This coin bears on its obverse the same Ear of Corn design in " incused " form, which feature is assumed to imply that the coin was " restruck on a coin of Corinth " (G.A.C., 204 and 459). But it appears to me more probable that this " incusion " is a survival of the " *punch*-marking," which was the rule in the earliest coins, struck a century or so before this period, and that the coin was entirely independent of Corinth. *Cf.* S, 222 : 5, 2, 5; and 264. Nestor was the son of Neleus, king of Pylos in S.W. Greece, south of Epirus, and accompanied Hercules in his voyage for the Golden Fleece.
[4] S., 264 : 6, 1, 15.  [5] *Ib.*, 264.  [6] *Ib.*, 253 : 6, 1, 3.  [7] *Ib.*, 254 : 6, 1, 4.

## CATTI & CASSI PERSONAL NAMES IN BRITAIN 215

Metapontum with its ship-building trade was a colony of the Phœnicians; and that this coin with the Ear of Corn, as in the Briton coins, was Phœnician in origin as well as Phœnician in symbolic solar meaning, as seen later.]

Vestiges also of the name of the Catti, Khatti or Gad tribal title of the Aryan-Phœnician civilizers of Britain clearly survive in several personal surnames of the present day, whose bearers presumably inherit that Aryan-Phœnician title by patrilinear descent.[1] Thus, for example, the following surnames are more or less clearly of this origin and varying only in different phonetic forms of spelling the same name :— Keith, Scott (from Xatti), Gait, Gates, Cotes, Coats, Coutts, Cotton, Cotteril, Cheatle, Cuthell, Cautley, Caddell, Cawdor, Guthrie, Chadwick, Cadman and Caedmon, Gadd, Gadsby, Geddes, Kidd, Kitson, Judd, Siddons, Seton, etc., and the lowland Scottish clan of Chattan. And amongst the Cassi series—the Kazzi or Qass of the Newton Stone—are Case, Casey, Cassels, Cash, Goss, Gosse, and the still-persisting French term for the Scot of "Ecossais." And similarly with the surnames derived from Barat or Prat, Gioln or 'Alaun, Sumer and Mur, Mor or Muru—*e.g.*, Barret, Burt, Boyden, etc., Gillan, Cluny, Allan, etc., Summers, Cameron (of Moray-Firth), etc., Marr, Murray, Martin, etc.

[1] Surnames are generally stated to have been first introduced into Britain by the Normans, *i.e.* by a branch of the Nordic Gothic Aryans. Yet there are many classic instances of family surnames in ancient history, patrician and other. It is in any case probable that, when the fashion of surnames was made obligatory in Britain, those families who were so entitled adopted the name of their tribe, clan or subclan, which indeed we find as a fact many of them did. Such modern surnames thus seem to supply a presumption of some racial significance through the father's side, despite the intermixture through more or less intermarriage with other racial elements.

FIG. 25B. Catti coin inscribed *Ccetio* from Gaul.
(After Poste.)

# XVII

## Prehistoric Stone Circles in Britain, Disclosed as Solar Observatories Erected by Morite Brito-Phœnicians and their Date

### Disclosing also Method of "Sighting" the Circles

> "The hoary rocks of giant size
> That o'er the land in Circles rise,
> Of which tradition may not tell,
> Fit circles for the wizard's spell."—
> Malcolm, "Autumn Blast."
> "These lonely Columns stand sublime,
> Flinging their shadows from on high,
> Like dials which the wizard Time
> Had raised to count his ages by."—
> Moore.

The great "prehistoric" Stone Circles of gigantic unhewn boulders, dolmens (or "table-stones") and monoliths, sometimes called "*Catt* Stanes," still standing in weird majesty over many parts of the British Isles, also now appear to attest their Phœnician origin. The mysterious race who erected these cyclopean monuments, wholly forgotten and unknown, now appears from the new evidence to have been the earlier wave of immigrant mining merchant Phœnician Barats, or "*Catti*" Phœnicians of the *Muru, Mer* or *Martu* clan—the "Amorite Giants" of the Old Testament tradition; and from whom it would seem that Albion obtained its earliest name (according to the First Welsh Triad) of "Clās *Myrd*-in (or Merddin)" or "Diggings of the *Myrd*."[1] (On Morites in Britain probably about 2800 B.C., see Appendix VII., pp 413-5.)

[1] This Early Phœnician title of *Muru, Mer, Marutu* or *Martu*, meaning "Of the Western Sea (or Sea of the Setting Sun)", which now seems obviously the Phœnician source of the names "*Mauret*-ania" or "*Mor*-occo" with its teeming megaliths, and of "*Mor*-bihan" (or "Little *Mor*") in Brittany, with its Sun-cult megaliths, is also found in several of the old mining and trading centres of the earlier Phœnicians in

## STONE CIRCLES & MORITE PHŒNICIANS

It was long ago observed that the distribution of these prehistoric megaliths or "great stones," over a great part of the world followed mainly the coast lines, thus presuming that *their erectors were a seafaring people*, though of unknown prehistoric identity and race.[1] Moreover, as these monuments are most numerous in the East, it is generally agreed that this cult in Britain, Brittany, Scandinavia, Spain and the Mediterranean basin was derived from the East. Latterly, owing to the great antiquity of Egyptian civilization, and to a few of these monuments (of which some are funereal) being found on the borders of Egypt, it has been conjectured by some that this cult arose in, and was spread from, Egypt. But as there is no evidence or presumption that the Ancient Egyptians were ever great mariners, it is significant that *the agents, whom Prof. Elliot Smith is forced to call in to distribute the monuments over the world, are the Phœnicians*. Prof. Smith supplies a great deal of striking evidence to prove that the chief agents in spreading these megalith monuments (as well as other ancient Eastern and characteristically Phœnician culture) "along the coastlines of Africa, Europe and Asia and also in course of time in Oceania and America" were the Phœnicians;[2] although as an ardent Egyptologist he still credits the origin of the cult of these rude stone prehistoric monuments to the Egyptians, notwithstanding the relative absence of such unhewn monuments in Egypt itself.

This Phœnician agency for the "distribution" of these megalith monuments is further attested by an altogether different class of evidence, even more specifically Phœnician than the seafaring character of their erectors. It has been observed by Mr. W. J. Perry that "the distribution of megalithic monuments in different parts of the world would

Britain, associated with Stone Circles and megaliths and mostly on the coast, *e.g.*, *Mori*-dunum, port of Romans in Devon, and several *More*-dun, *Mor*-ton and Martin, Cær *Marthen*, West *Mor*-land, rich in circles and old mines, *More*-cambe Bay, *Morav* and its Frith and seat of Murray clan, &c.

[1] Pitt-Rivers, J.E.S., 1869, 59, etc.; J.(R.)A.I., 1874-5, 389, etc. And Ferguson, F.R.M. map, p. 532; and T. E. Peet, *Rough Stone Mons.*, 1912, 147, etc.

[2] S.E.C., 3, etc., based partly on Mrs. Z. Nuttal's great work on *Fundamental Principles of Old and New World Civilizations*, Harvard. 1901.

suggest that *their builders were engaged in exploiting the mineral wealth of the various countries.*"[1] He proves conclusively by a mass of concrete facts that *these megaliths all the world over are located in the immediate neighbourhood of ancient mine workings for tin, copper, lead and gold or in the area of the pearl and amber trade.* His details, geographic and geological, regarding the correlation of these monuments to mines in England and Wales, are especially decisive of the fact that their builders were miners for metals and especially tin, and not agricultural colonists; for many of the monuments with remains of prehistoric villages and mines are located on barren mountain tracts, where only the old mine workings could have attracted these people to settle on such spots[2] (see Sketch Map). And he concludes, in illustration of what was happening at the other mines with their megaliths, that " the men who washed the gold of Dartmoor were also extracting the tin and taking it back to the Eastern Mediterranean in order to make bronze."[3]

Strange to say, notwithstanding the clear indications that this seafaring people who erected these megalith monuments in Britain came from the Eastern Mediterranean, and were solely engaged in mining operations, expressly for tin, were Phœnicians, yet Mr. Perry, in this article, does not even suggest the obvious inference that they were Phœnicians, nor even once mentions that name. There was, however, no other ancient seagoing trading people of the Early Bronze Age who explored the outer seas, came from the Eastern Mediterranean, had a monopoly of the bronze trade of the Ancient World, and who worked in prehistoric times the tin-mines and gravels in Cornwall and Devon.

[1] P.M.M. (A.) 1915, 60, No. 1. Regarding India, for instance, in the Hyderabad State, the Inspector of Mines, Major Munn, found that *Stone Circles and dolmens were invariably situated close to mines* of gold, copper and iron. *Manchester Memoirs*, 1921, 64, No. 5.
[2] Where no metalliferous strata are found on the sites of megaliths, as at Stonehenge, etc., in Wilts and in Devon, there are found old flint-factories for the tools needed by the miners to extract the ores in Cornwall, etc. P.M.M. (B.) 11–18. Surface tin, now exhausted, formerly occurred more widely in the drift and gravels, as tin and gold are in the same geological formations, so that it may have occurred on surface near Stonehenge, etc. Cæsar says that the tin supply came from the *Midlands*, (*D.B.C.*, 5, 5) where no trace of tin now exists.
[3] P.M.M. (B.), p. 7.

## DISTRIBUTION OF STONE CIRCLES IN ENGLAND

Moreover, actual articles of special Phœnician character or association, apart from bronze, have been found at some of these megalithic monuments and in the sepulchral barrows near those sacred sites. At the Stonehenge Circle and some others have been found shells of the Tyrian purple mollusc, oriental cowries and jewellery including blue-glazed and glass

Sketch Map showing Distribution of Stone Circles and Megaliths in England and Wales.
(After W. J. Perry.[1])

beads such as were a speciality of the Phœnicians. The blue-glazed beads of an amber necklace exhumed from an Early Bronze tomb near Stonehenge and others found in that circle itself and at other prehistoric sites, are of the identical kind which were common in Ancient Egypt within the

[1] By permission of Manchester Lit. and Phil. Socy.

restricted period of between about 1450 B.C. to 1250 B.C.[1] But *the obvious Phœnician origin of these blue beads at Stonehenge and other parts of Britain* has not been remarked. The Phœnicians were the great manufacturers of fine necklaces in the ancient world, as recorded by Homer, and specialists in glass and glazes, as attested by the remains of their great glass factories at their port of Cition and elsewhere.

Now, the blue-glazed beads in question *first appear in Egypt at the beginning of the Phœnician Renaissance in that country*, usually called " The Syrian Period " of Egyptian Civilization—Egyptologists suppressing its proper title of " Phœnician " in the modern vogue of depreciating Phœnician influences. This " Syrian " fashion, which transformed and exalted Egyptian art and handicraft, was introduced about 1450 B.C. with the seizure and annexation of Phœnicia, and the carrying off captive to Egypt hundreds of the artists and skilled craftsmen of Tyre, Sidon, etc., as well as their chief art treasures as plunder. Writing of that great event, Sir F. Petrie tells us that the " Syrians " [*i.e.*, Phœnicians] " had a civilization equal or superior to that of Egypt, in taste and skill . . . luxury far beyond that of the Egyptians, and technical work which could teach them rather than be taught."[2] And great numbers of their artists and skilled workmen were carried off, and continued to be sent as tribute, to Egypt.[3] Significantly, these blue-glazed beads first appear in Egypt at the beginning of this Phœnician period, *and they suddenly cease when the Phœnicians regained more or less their independence from Egypt about* 1250 B.C. The inference is thus obvious that the blue beads found at Stonehenge Circle and elsewhere in Britain are Phœnician in origin, and were carried there by Phœnicians of about that period. And here also it is to be noted that the finest of the art treasures recently unearthed at Luxor from the tomb of Tut-ankh-amen, along with those of his predecessor Akenaten the Sun-worshipper and his Hitto-Mitanian (or Mede) ancestors, which belong to *this same period*, and are admittedly of a naturalistic type foreign to previous Egyptian art, are also now disclosed as Aryan Phœnician.

[1] H.R. Hall, *J. Egypt. Archæology*, 1. 18-19.   [2] P.H.E. 2, 146.   [3] *Ib.*, 147.

# PHŒNICIAN BEADS & ART IN ANCIENT BRITAIN 221

Significantly many of the motives of this "Syrian," properly Phœnician, art are reproduced on the monuments and coins of the Early Britons. Thus, for example, the finely carved chair of "Syrian" workmanship found in the tomb of the "Syrian" high priest who was the grandfather of Akhen-aten (see Fig. 26) contains a sacred scene unknown in Egyptian art, but which, we shall find later (chapter XX), is common not only on Phœnician sacred seals and coins, but *also on the prehistoric monuments and coins of the Ancient Britons.*

FIG. 26.—Phœnician Chair of 15th century, B.C., with Solar scene as on Early Briton Monuments and Coins.
From tomb of Syrian high-priest in Egypt.
(After A. Weigall.[1])
Note the Goat is worshipping Cross, as in Phœnician and Briton versions, pp. 334-5.

Still further fresh evidence for the Phœnician origin of the megalithic monuments in the British Isles and Western Europe has recently been elicited by the explorations of M. Siret in the ancient tumuli near megaliths of the Late Stone Age in Southern Spain and Portugal, the Iberian "half-way house" of the Phœnicians on their sea route to

---

[1] *Life of Akhnaton*, p. 48. It was found in tomb of the Syrian high priest Yuaa, maternal grandfather of Akhen-aten, and his mummy discloses him to be of a fine Aryan type (*Ib.*, pp. 24, 28).

their tin-mines in Britain. This discloses the existence there in the Late Stone Age of colonies of Eastern sea-traders, presumably from " Syria " and in contact with Egypt and N. Europe, who searched for metallic ores and bartered manufactures like the Phœnicians. Their culture was in several ways like that of the builders of the Stone Circles in Britain.

[M. Siret found[1] that these prehistoric Stone Age settlers in S. Spain were civilized sea-going traders from " Syria," seeking ores, and they traded in and manufactured [as did the Phœnicians] oriental painted vases in red, black and green pigments—the latter two colours derived from copper, also statuettes in alabaster of non-Egyptian type, supposed to be " Babylonian," alabaster and marble cups and perfume flasks of Egyptian type, burials with arched domes and corridor entrances of Egypto-Mycenian type, amber from the Baltic and jet from Britain, and a shell from the Red Sea ; and they introduced already manufactured the highest grade flint implements of the Late Stone Age period, and axes of a green stone which is found in veins of tin ore. They exported to the East all the tin and copper ore they obtained ; and although thus engaged in the bronze trade, they appear to have left no traces in Spain of that precious metal in their graves. This is explained on the supposition that they kept the natives in the dark in regard to the value of bronze ; and that they preceded the later bronze-using people of the Bronze Age proper.]

Against the probability of Phœnicians being the erectors of the prehistoric megaliths in Britain and Western Europe it was argued by Fergusson, who attempted to prove that both Stonehenge and Avebury were post-Roman, that no dolmens had been reported from Phœnicia in his day.[2] Since then, although Syria-Phœnicia is as yet little explored, " a circle of rough upright stones " is reported to stand a few miles to the north of Tyre itself ;[3] and several " Stone Circles " have been reported by Conder[4], Oliphant and others in South Syria as well as in Hittite Palestine,[5] and especially

[1] *L'Anthropologie*, 1921.
[2] F.R.M., 409.
[3] Stanley, cited by A.P.H., 105.
[4] C.S.S., 42 ; *Heth* [= *Hittite*] *and Moab*, chaps. 7 and 8 ; *Thirty Years Work in Holy Land* (Pal. Expl. F.) 142 and 176, 187, pp. 394, 410, etc
[5] See distribution map and figures, H. Vincent, *Canaan*, Paris. 1914,

# CIRCLES IN AMORITE PHŒNICIA-PALESTINE 223

to the east of the Jordan ; and Macalister has unearthed at Gaza, etc., rows of megaliths in the "cup-marked rocks in their neighbourhood." But, we have seen, that the later restricted Roman province of "Phœnicia" itself formed only a part of the Eastern Phœnician empire, while in the Persian Gulf area which the earlier Phœnicians occupied before coming to the Levant, Stone Circles like Stonehenge, dolmens and other megaliths are reported along with "Catti" names (see Map).

[Between the Persian Gulf and the Red Sea, in the district of Kasin, are reported three huge rude Stone Circles, which are described as being "*like Stonehenge*" and, like it, composed of gigantic trilithons about 15 ft. high ;[1] and several huge Stone Circles in the neighbourhood of Mt. Sinai, some of them measuring 100 ft. in diameter.[2] On the old caravan route from the Cilician coast *via* "Jonah's Pillar" to Persia (or Iran of the ancient Sun-worshippers), several megaliths are incidentally reported by travellers. Near Tabriz, to east of Lake Van, are "several circles" of gigantic stones ascribed to the giants "Caous" (?Cassi) of the Kainan dynasty.[3] In Parthia, at Deh Ayeh, near Darabgerd, is a large circle.[4] On the N.W. frontier of India, on the route from Persia near Peshawar, is a large circle of unhewn megaliths about 11 ft. high, and resembling the great Keswick Circle in Cumberland.[5] And amongst the many megaliths along the Mediterranean coast of Africa, so frequented by the Phœnicians, are several Stone Circles in Tripoli and the Gaet-uli hills with trilithons, like Stonehenge.[6]]

The probability that the Phœnicians were the erectors of the megalithic tombs, often in the neighbourhood of the Circles, in Britain is also indicated, amongst other things, by the substantial identity proved by Sir A. Keith to exist between the tomb of the Late Stone Age Briton with that of the "Giant's tomb" in Sardinia.[7] This latter island also abounds in Stone Circles,[8] and its earliest civilizers and

---

[1] S. Palgrave, *Central and East Arabia*, 1, 251, and others cited by F.R.M., 444, etc.
[2] Palmer, *Desert of the Exodus*.
[3] Chardin, *Voy. en Perse*, 1, 267. These stones are described as "hewn."
[4] W. Ouseley, *Trav. in Persia*, 2, 124. (with figure).
[5] A. Phayre, J.A.S. Bengal. 1870, Pt. I, No. 1. It is about 50 feet in diameter, like many British circles.
[6] Barth, *Trav. in Cent. Africa*, 1, 58 and 74.
[7] K.A.M., 19.   [8] P.C.S., 56, etc.

colonists were Phœnicians, whose remains and inscriptions from its southern Port Hercules northwards, are abundant, as we have seen.

The approximate date for the initial erection of these rude Stone Circles and other early megaliths in Britain appears to have been many centuries and even a millennium or more before the arrival of Brutus about 1100 B.C., or about 2800 B.C. or earlier. This is evident from the geographic and geological correlation of these monuments to the prehistoric tin and copper mine workings, flint-factories and neolithic villages. These relationships make it clear that these monuments were erected by the earlier branch of the sea-trading Phœnicians, who were exclusively engaged in mining for the bronze trade in the East, and using that metal in Britain sparingly themselves, and not engaged to any considerable extent, if at all, as agricultural colonists, such as were Brutus and his later Brito-Phœnicians, who used bronze more freely, as attested by their tombs, bronze sickles, etc. Whilst the numerous " Barat," " Catti " and " Cassi " place-names on so many of their sites and the " Catt-Stanes " testify that their erectors were " Catti " or " Cassi " Barats or Brito-Phœnicians, as were the Amorites.

The physical type of the builders of these Stone Circles and megaliths is obviously that represented by the skeletons of tallish Nordic type found (with some others of the smaller river-bed and mixed Iberian or Pictish type) in the long barrow burial mounds, chambered cairns and stone cists of the Late Stone and Early Bronze Ages in the neighbourhood of these circles. And it was presumably early pioneer stragglers of this same Nordic race at the end of the Old Stone Age who are represented by the " Red Man " of Paviland Cave, in the Gower peninsula of Wales, of the mammoth age,[1] and the " Keiss Chief " in the stone cist at

[1] This early man of the tall, long-headed and broad-browed type found at Crô-Magnon in Bordeaux was unearthed at the " Goat's Hole " cave at Paviland, and first described by Dean Buckland in 1824 (*Reliquiæ Diluv.*); and later by Boyd Dawkins (*Arch. Jour.*, 1897, 338, etc.) and others. He is named " Red Man " on account of the rusty staining of his bones (by a red oxide of iron) regarded as a religious rite. Beside him, in addition to his rude stone weapons, were a necklace and rings of ivory and the paw-bone of a wolf as a religious charm.

Keiss (Kassi?) in Caithness. Both of these are interred with rude stone weapons, and are of the superior and artistic Crô-Magnon type of early men, which seems to have been the proto-Nordic or proto-Aryan. Indeed, the associate of the Keiss chief had a cranium described by Huxley[1] as " remarkably well formed and spacious " and of the modern Nordic type. These early Nordic people, who were buried near the Circles, were generally found in their tombs laid on their *right* side, and *their face usually facing eastwards to the rising Sun*, thus evidencing their solar religion and belief in a resurrection.

The purpose of the great Stone Circles now appears, somewhat more clearly than before, from the new observations now recorded, to have been primarily for solar observatories; whilst the smaller Circles seem mainly sepulchral, and sometimes contain dolmens and interments of the Bronze Age.[2]

Popularly called " Druid Circles," the larger ones, on the contrary, are now generally believed by archæologists to be of solar purpose. This opinion was formed by observing that they are generally erected on open high ground commanding wide views of sunrise and sunset, and that the orientation of many of the Circles, as indicated by the outlying stones and avenues (which are preserved in several instances and which existed formerly in many others where now removed[3]) is often to the North-East (as at Stonehenge), *i.e.*, in the direction of sunrise about the midsummer solstice or longest day

---

[1] L.H.C., 88. This Keiss chief is described by Laing (*ib.* 15) as " a tall man of very massive proportions," lying extended, *with his face to the East.* Huxley found his cranial index was 76, with projecting eyebrow ridges which gave the forehead a " receding " aspect and the forehead " low and narrow," but, as shown in his Fig. (No. 11), it is wider than the Iberian type. The other tall type of man at Keiss (cist 7) is described by Laing as " nearly 6 feet in height, whilst those previously found did not exceed 5 feet or 5 feet 4 inches (*ib.* 14). Huxley found his cranial index to be 78, " the forehead, well arched though not high, rises almost vertically from the brow." Nose is good, jaws massive and chin projecting (*ib.* 85, etc.)

[2] These have been called by Mr. A. L. Lewis " Burial Circles " and " Barrow Circles " (Man, 1914, 163 f.), and their stones are not usually pillars, but short stumpy boulders.

[3] Thus at Shap in Westmorland, visited by me, Camden describes " a double row of immense granites extending about a mile " (C. B. Gough, 3, 414) of which only a few blocks now remain.

in the year. So it was supposed that they were intended for observing and fixing officially this date in the calendar year, for economic as well as sacred purposes, as this date was one of the chief festivals in the Sun religion.[1] On the other hand, a few archæologists are still of opinion that all the Stone Circles are essentially sepulchral,[2] although no traces of any ancient burial are found in the larger Circles.

The conflicting results obtained by different modern writers in attempting to estimate the exact orientation of these Circles, and the manner in which they were used by their erectors as solar observatories, is, owing to ignorance of the exact point from which the erectors made their observations, and also to different individual opinions as to what was the true centre of the circle, as most of the Circles are not perfectly circular. Hitherto the point of observation for taking the sight-line of the sunrise has been assumed to be the "centre" of the Circle.[3] It is supposed that the observer stood at this centre, and looked along the axis to the N.E. indicated by the outlying stones or avenue, and that, when the rising sun was seen along this line, it fixed the required solstice date.

But I found by personal examination of many of those great Circles which are still more or less complete, such as at Stonehenge, Keswick, Penrith, etc., that *the point of observation was not at the Centre of the Circle but at the opposite or S.W. border, where I found a marked Observation Stone in the same relative position* as in all the greater Circles containing the S.W. Stone which I examined, and which has hitherto escaped the notice of previous observers.

This "Observation Stone" I first found at the fine Keswick Circle, which is locally called "Castle *Rigg*," or "Castle of

---

[1] A. L. Lewis, *Arch. Jour.*, 49, 136, etc., J. R. A. I., 1900, etc. Sir N. Lockyer and others. Lockyer supplied some confirmatory solar observations in regard to Stonehenge and other Circles with outlying stones and avenues to N.E. (L.S., 62, etc., 153, 265, etc.); but he impaired his results by taking arbitrary lines and by introducing extravagant astronomical theories, supposing these Circles' use to be for observing the rising of stars; and he, moreover, believed that the early Circles were intended for the observations of May Day of an agricultural and not a solar year.

[2] Sir A. Evans, *Archæol. Rev.*, 1889, 31, 3, etc. R. Holmes, R.A.B., 476, 479, etc.

[3] L.S., 58, 176, etc.; and similarly other writers.

## SCRIPT ON KESWICK OBSERVATION STONE

the Rig," a title of the Gothic kings, and cognate with the Latin *Rex, Regis*, and the Sanskrit *Raja* of the Indo-Aryans, and the " Ricon " of the Briton coins (see later). In searching for possible markings on the stones of this Circle in August, 1919—no markings having been previously reported —I enlisted the kind co-operation of my friend Dr. Islay Muirhead, in a minute scrutiny of each individual stone, and we started off in opposite directions. Shortly afterwards a shout from my friend that he had noticed some artificial marks on a stone on the western border brought me to the spot, where I recognized that the undoubted markings on this stone (see Fig. 27) resembled generally the Sumerian linear script with which I had become familiar. The marks read literally in Sumerian word-signs " Seeing the Low Sun " which was presumably " Seeing the Sun on the Horizon,"[1] and it was written in characters of before 2500 B.C.

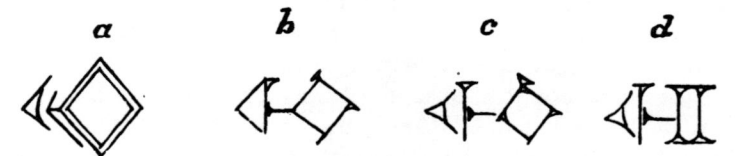

*a*      *b*      *c*      *d*

FIG. 27.—Sighting "Sumerian" Marks on Observation Stone in Keswick Stone Circle.

*a.* Sign on Stone of Keswick Circle, viewed from north.
*b.* Sumerian word-Sign in Script of 3100 B.C.[2]
*c.*      do.           do.      2400 B.C.[3]
*d.*      do.           do.      1000 B.C.

The position of this marked or inscribed stone in the Keswick Circle is in the S.W. section of the Circle. It is the stone marked No. 26 in the annexed survey-plan of the Keswick Circle by Dr. W. D. Anderson.[4] The stone is an undressed boulder, like the other stones of the Circle, but is broad and flattish and, unlike most of the other stones of the

---

[1] See Fig. 27 *b-d*. Br. 9403.    [2] cp. B.B.W. 414.
[3] *Ib.* 414, and T.R.C. 243.
[4] C.A.S., XV (New Series) 1914-15, 99. The Keswick Circle, like many others of the larger Circles, has a radius of about fifty feet. In the Plan the unshaded stones are supposed by Dr. Anderson to indicate sunrise, and the shaded to have been probably used for star observations."

Circle, it could never have been a *standing* pillar-stone. It is what I call, in view of the evidence to be seen presently, "The Observation Table-Stone," and it bears the inscribed signs on its flattish top. It appears to be in its original site, but swung round or fallen somewhat forward to the S.E., presumably through undermining (possibly in search for buried treasure, as has happened with similar stones elsewhere). Or it may have been deliberately swung slightly out of its original position and tilted to its present position by the later erectors of the inner quadrangle or so-called "temple" (see Plan), which is clearly a late structure and presumably Druidical, erected after the site was abandoned by the "Sun-worshippers" (probably after their conversion to Christianity) and analogous to the quasi-Druidical building which, we shall see, was erected within the Stonehenge Circle. For this marked stone of the Keswick Circle is now orientated towards the northern border of the inner "temple," and in a line which has no solar or astronomical significance whatsoever. The engraved signs, despite the weathering of ages, are distinct though somewhat shallow, the lines being about a quarter of an inch deep and about a third of an inch wide.[1] And these signs on this stone in Cumber-land or the "Land of the Cymrs or Cumbers" (or Sumers) may be read as the Sumerian word-sign for "Seeing the Sunrise."[2]

The manner in which the Sunrise was observed by the early astronomers who erected this Keswick Stone Circle in "prehistoric" times is now clearly disclosed by the location, orientation and inscription on this Observation Stone, bearing these markings. A reference to the plan on p. 229 will show that these engraved marks on this stone (No. 26), forming an Observation Table-Stone, namely, the "diamond" and

---

[1] The "diamond" portion of the sign is not a true rectangle (and this also is the case in the Sumerian script) but has a width of $4\frac{1}{16}$ inches from N. to S. and $3\frac{1}{2}$ inches from E. to W., with sides about 3 inches in length.

[2] The marking on this Keswick stone is substantially identical with the Sumerian compound word-sign, which is a picture-sign for Eye (or *Si*, thus disclosing Sumerian origin of our English word "see" (and the Sun, in which the Sun is for lapidary purposes represented as a "diamond" shape. This compound sign is given the value of "Rising Sun" (B.B.W., 2, 215); and thus meaning literally "Seeing the Rising Sun."

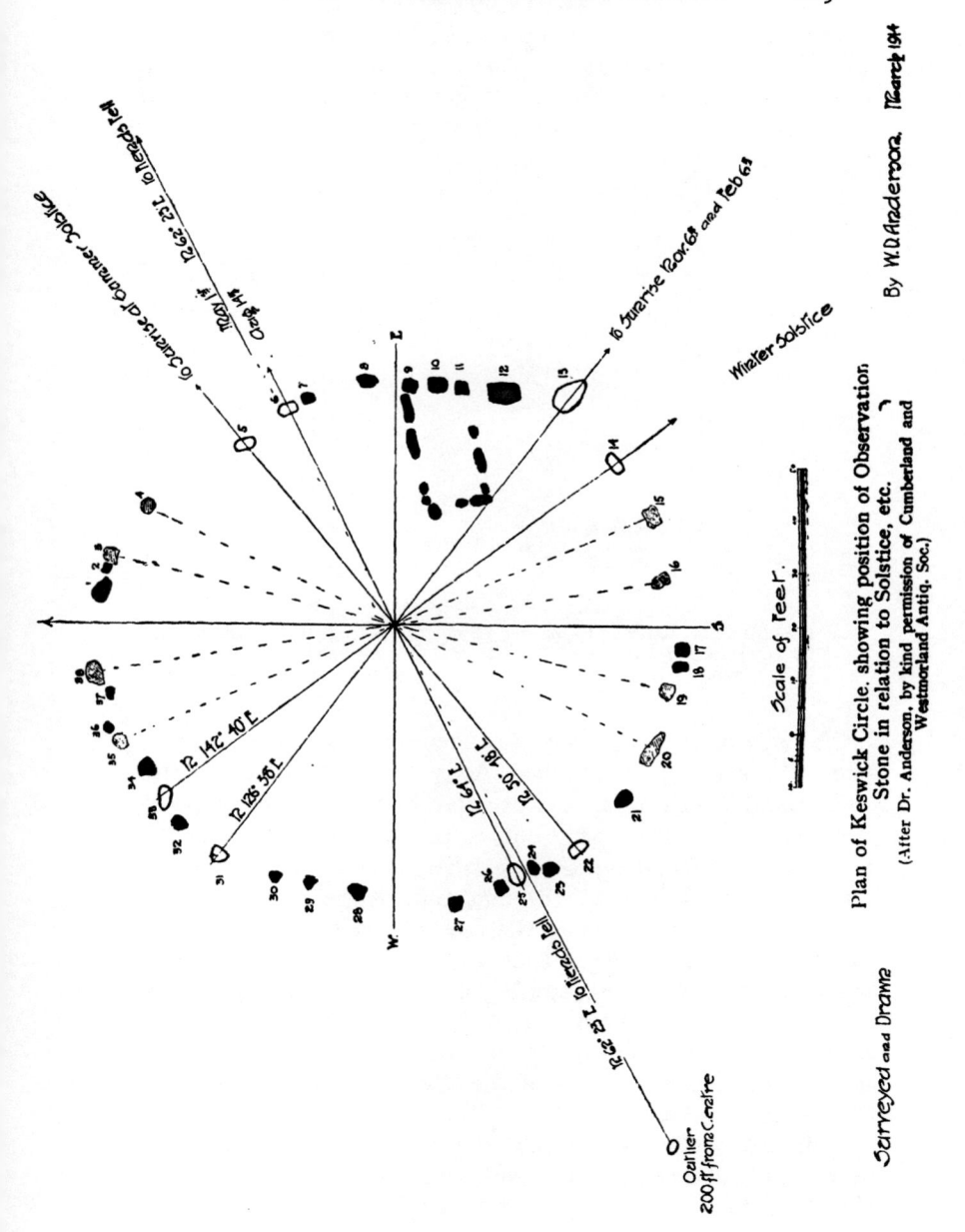

# PLAN OF KESWICK STONE CIRCLE

arrow-head-like signs, were used like the back-sight of a rifle (see Fig. 28), aimed at the point of the Sunrise, so as to obtain an exact sight-line in " Shooting the Sun " as with a sextant.

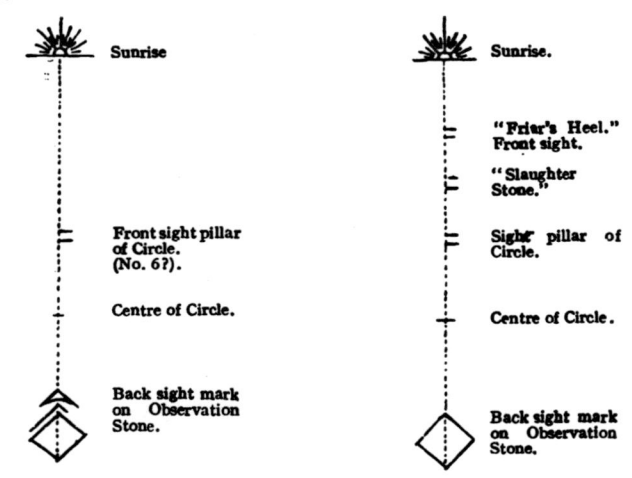

```
         Sunrise                              Sunrise.

                                              "Friar's Heel."
                                              Front sight.
                                              " Slaughter
                                              Stone."

         Front sight pillar                   Sight pillar of
         of Circle.                           Circle.
         (No. 6?).

         Centre of Circle.                    Centre of Circle.


         Back sight mark                      Back sight mark
         on Observation                       on Observation
         Stone.                               Stone.
```

FIG. 28.—Mode of Sighting Sunrise by Observation Stone in Keswick Circle.

FIG. 29. — Sighting Sunrise by Observation Stone in Stonehenge Circle.

The eye of the observer, stationed at this Table-Stone in the S.W. of the Circle, looked along the middle line of the " diamond " (the apex and angular sides of which, supplemented by the arrow-head angles, correspond to the angular notch on the back-sight of a rifle) and gained thereby a sight-line which passed through the centre of the Circle, and beyond this passed in the axis of the circle out to the horizon along the edge of the corresponding standing pillar-stone on the N.E. (presumably stone No. 6 on plan, which acted like the front-sight of a rifle). When the Sunrise point coincided exactly with this sight-line, it yielded the required date in the Solar calendar of the Phœnician erectors of this Stone Circle observatory.

This observation stone and its marking may now help to settle the existing confusion of opinion as to the position of the "centre" of this particular Circle. For this Keswick

Circle is not a true circle, but is somewhat pear-shaped; and Dr. Anderson's " centre " differs considerably in position from the centre as estimated by previous observers.[1]

[Moreover, his alignment of the midsummer solstice sunrise in the plan appears to have been drawn, not from the actual visible sunlight point on the hilly skyline to the east of the Keswick Circle, but from the theoretical sunrise point on the invisible lower horizon beyond the hills, which is considerably to the north of the actual sunrise on the hilly skyline.[2] All these differences, if corrected, may tend to bring the solstice sight-line towards the stone with the Sumerian markings No. 26. In view of all these differences of personal equation in the various estimations of the centre of the circle and in the summer solstice line, it is desirable that further fresh observations of this line and the actual centre be made with special reference to this stone No. 26 bearing the markings.]

Following up the discovery of the Observation Stone at Keswick, I searched several other of the larger Circles for corresponding stones in the S.W. sector for such markings; and I found similar flattish stones in the same relative position in all of the larger relatively complete Circles containing that sector which I have been able to examine.

At Stonehenge, which I visited later in that year (1919) I went by my compass straight to the corresponding S.W. stone in the Stonehenge "older" Circle; and, although hitherto unremarked by previous writers, I found that it was a Table-Stone, and that *this Stonehenge Table-Stone bore the same old diamond-shaped sign engraved upon the middle of its flat top as at Keswick.*

This Stonehenge Observation Table-Stone with its Sumerian markings is unfortunately very much worn by the weather and more especially by the feet of visitors, who use it as a stepping stone, its top being flat and only about two feet above the ground level, and the stone of a somewhat

---

[1] C. W. Dymond in his plan in C.A.S., 1879–1880, obtains a centre to the west of Dr. Anderson's, in the middle line of the N. and S. entrances; and Prof. J. Morrow (*Proc. Durham Univ. Philosoph. Socy.*, 1908–1909) selected a centre to the south of this, and about 18 inches N.W. of Dr. Anderson's centre (see Anderson *loc. cit.*, 102). There is also an earlier plan with different orientation by J. Otley in 1849 (see L.S., 35).

[2] See Anderson, *loc. cit.*, 104–106.

friable boulder sandstone formation (the so-called "Sarsen" stone). On my arrival I found people standing upon it, and this friction by the feet of visitors during the centuries has worn down the signs very shallow and almost worn them away in places. Yet the engraved marking is nevertheless still quite unmistakable in its main features. The "diamond" is of almost identical size with that of the Keswick Circle, and is somewhat more rectangular in shape

This Observation Stone at Stonehenge lies probably in its original spot and prone position; and is not a "fallen" stone or fragment, as supposed. Its location with reference to the great horse-shoe crescent of colossal lintelled "trilithons," the so-called temple, a structure which now forms the most conspicuous feature of the modern Stonehenge, discloses the important fact that this "trilithon" temple is of relatively late origin, and erected by a different people from those who erected and used the Stone Circle, and belonging to a *non*-Sun-worshipping cult. This is evidenced by the fact that the "trilithon" temple *completely blocks the view from the Observation Stone* to the centre of the Circle and from thence out along the axis of the outlying index pillars and great avenue to the N.E. to the point of Midsummer Sunrise; and also by the fact that the users of this "trilithon" temple and its "altar" stone must in their ritual have habitually turned their backs on the Rising Sun. This trilithon temple was thus presumably erected by later Druids, like the later "temple" within the Keswick Circle. The Druids were anti-solar, and worshippers of the Moon-cult of the vindictive aboriginal Mother goddess and addicted to bloody and human sacrifices, which were antagonistic and abhorrent to the "Sun-worshippers." It thus appears probable that this "trilithon" temple at Stonehenge was erected by later Celtic Druids within the old Circle of the Sun-worshipping Aryan Britons, after the latter had abandoned it, presumably on their conversion to Christianity; and that it probably dates to no earlier than about the sixth century A.D., when we are told by Geoffrey that the Druid magician Merlin erected buildings of gigantic stones at

## OBSERVATION TABLE-STONE AT STONEHENGE 233

Stonehenge.[1] And the tooled or worked condition of the stones supports this late date.[2]

The orientation of the original old Stonehenge Circle of the Sumerian "Sun-worshippers" for the Midsummer solstice observation is abundantly attested by the great earthen embanked "avenue" extending from the Circle for about five hundred yards to the N.E. in the axis of the Circle, and in the exact line of the summer solstice sunrise; and also by the two great monolith pillars of undressed Sarsen stone, obviously for sight-lines placed in the middle line of this "avenue," namely the so-called "Friar's Heel," about 250 feet from the Circle, and a similar one nearer the Circle, now fallen and fantastically called "The Slaughter Stone" on the notion that it was originally laid flat and used by the Druids to immolate their victims there.[3]

The function of this Observation Stone at Stonehenge was clearly identically the same as that of the corresponding Observation Stone at Keswick. It also acted in the same way as the back-sight of a rifle in aligning the Sunrise or "Shooting the Sun." Before being blocked out by the erection of the trilithon horse-shoe temple, it commanded a straight view to the N.E., through the centre of the old Circle and out beyond the edge of the N.E. pillar of the Circle, along the northern edges of the two outstanding index or indicator monolith pillars (the "Slaughter Stone" and "Friar's Heel") and right along the middle of the great "avenue" beyond these to the point of Midsummer solstice sunrise. This fact is graphically shown in the annexed diagram (Fig. 29), wherein the real use of the outstanding indicator monolith pillars is now disclosed for the first time. It is seen to be the northern perpendicular edges of these pillars which provided the sight-line, and *not the top of the middle peak* of the "Friar's Heel" pillar, as surmised by

---

[1] G.C., 8, 10–11; and C.B., 1, 134.
[2] Sir A. Evans on archæological grounds dates the massive part of Stonehenge with its trilithons no earlier than "the end of the fourth and beginning of third century B.C." (*Arch. Rev.*, 1889, 322, etc.); whilst Fergusson ascribed it to the Roman period or later.
[3] It is not impossible, however, that it may have been so used by the Druids after it had fallen and the circle was abandoned by the Sun-worshippers.

Sir N. Lockyer and others. This "Friar's Heel" peak, indeed, while soaring to the south of the middle line of the "avenue" and far above its plane, could not possibly give the point of Sunrise *on the horizon*, as by the time the Sun had risen to the top of the Friar's Heel pillar the actual sunrise had long passed, and that at a point considerably to the north of the Friar's Heel peak.

Similar observation stones I also found in several other of the larger Circles containing the S.W. sector, and bearing the diamond marking obviously for the back-sighting in the observation.[1] It is thus evident that the primary purpose of these great prehistoric Stone Circles erected by the Brito-Phœnicians was for solar observatory determination of the summer solstice; though the existence of outlying indicator stones and avenues in other directions in some Circles suggests that they were used secondarily sometimes for fixing other solar calendar dates. These great observatories thus attest the remarkable scientific knowledge of solar physics possessed by their erectors, and their habit of "shooting the sun," as well as their great engineering skill in moving and erecting such colossal stones.

These Stone Circles have been supposed to have been used also as Sun temples. This has been inferred from the existence of special entrances at the cardinal points, and also from the elaborate avenues attached to some of them, and supposed to have been used for ritualistic processions; and it is also suggested by the apparent later use of some of them by the Druids as temples. They were undoubtedly considered sacred, as seen in the frequency of ancient burials in their neighbourhood. This is especially evident at Stonehenge where the great numbers of tombs of the Bronze Age in the neighbourhood of that monument, and the remarkable riches in gold and other jewellery interred along with the bodies implies that it had been a sacred burial place for the royalty and nobility of a considerable part of Ancient

---

[1] Thus "Long Meg" Circle, near Penrith in Cumberland (where the Observation Stone is a roundish boulder "table" with mark on the top nearly breast high), and the Circles at Oddendale and Reagill in Westmorland near Shap.

Britain for many centuries. And even the round-headed Huns of the East Coast had been attracted to it, as evidenced by some round barrows with round-headed skulls.

They also appear to have been used at times as Law-Courts. Homer, in describing the famous shield of Achilles, which was probably made by the Phœnicians, like most of the famous works of art in the Iliad, states that elders of the early Aryans were represented thereon as meeting in solemn conclave within the Stone Circle.[1] And in Scotland the Stone Circle was also used at times as a Law-Court.[2] This supplies the reason, I think, why these Circles are sometimes called "*Hare-Stanes*," as at Insch near the Newton Stone, and elsewhere.[3] This term "Hare" seems to me to be the "Harri" or "Heria" title of the ruling Goths in the Eddas, which I show is the equivalent of the Hittite title of "Harri" or "Arri" or "Arya-n." It is thus in series with the title of the Circles at Keswick, etc., as "Castle *Rig*"—"Rig" being the title of the Gothic kings and princes. And the name "Kes-wick" (with its ancient copper mines) means "Abode of the *Kes*" i.e., the Cassi clan of the Hittites.

We thus see that the great prehistoric Stone Circles in Ancient Britain were raised by the early Mor-ite scientific Brito-Phœnicians as solar observatories, to fix the solsticial and other dates for the festivals of their Sun-cult; and that their descendant Britons continued to regard them as sacred places down to the latter end of the Bronze Age and the beginning of the Christian era; and this sacred tradition survived until a few centuries ago.

[1] "The elders were seated on the smooth stones in the sacred circle," *Il.*, 18, 504.
[2] In the Aberdeen Chartulary of 1349 is a notice of a court held at the Standing Stones in the Don Valley, "apud stantes lapides de Rane en le Garuiach," when William de St. Michael was summoned to answer for his forcible retention of ecclesiastic property (Regist. Episcop. Aberdon, 1, 79); and again, in the Chartulary of Moray a regality court was held by Alexander Stewart, Lord of Radenoch and son of Robert II. at the Standing Stones of Raitts, stating "apud le standard stanes de la Rath de Kinguey." And when the Bishop of Murray attended this Court to protest against certain infringements of his rights, it is stated that he stood *outside* the circle :—": extra circum." *Regist. Episcop. Morav.*, p. 184.
[3] And Kirkurd, Peebles; Feith Hill, Inver Keithney, Banff. *Trans. Hawick Archæol. Socy.*, 1908, p. 26.

# XVIII

PREHISTORIC "CUP-MARKINGS" ON CIRCLES, ROCKS, &C., IN BRITAIN, & CIRCLES ON ANCIENT BRITON COINS & MONUMENTS AS INVOCATIONS TO SUN-GOD IN SUMERIAN CIPHER SCRIPT BY EARLY HITTO-PHŒNICIANS

*Disclosing Decipherment and Translations by Identical Cup-marks on Hitto-Sumerian Seals and Trojan Amulets with explanatory Sumerian Script; and Hitto-Sumerian origin of god-names " Jahveh" or " Jove," Indra, " Indri"-Thor of the Goths, St. " Andrew," Earth-goddess " Maia" or May, " Three Fates " & English names of Numerals*

> " Time, which antiquates antiquities, and hath an art to make dust of all things, hath yet spared these minor monuments."—Sir THOMAS BROWNE.

BEFORE proceeding to examine the mass of new evidence for the former widespread prevalence of " Sun-worship " amongst the Ancient Catti Barats or Britons who erected the prehistoric Stone Circles in Britain, and amongst their descendants down to the Christian period, it is desirable here to see what light, if any, our newly-found Hitto-Sumerian origin of the Britons may throw upon the prehistoric " Cup-markings " which are sometimes found carved upon stones in these circles, in funereal barrows, upon some standing stones, dolmens and stone-cist coffins, and on rocks near Ancient Briton settlements, over a great part of the British Isles (see Fig. 30), and in Scandinavia and other parts of Europe and the Levant, associated with megalith culture, and whose origin, carvers and meaning of the Cup-markings have now been completely forgotten.

# CUP MARKINGS IN BRITAIN & TROY

These Cup-markings have long been the subject of many varied surmises, admittedly or patently improbable;[1] and especially so the latest theory that they are merely "decorations."[2]

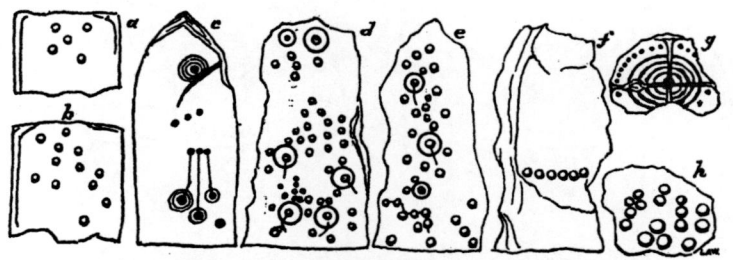

FIG. 30.—Prehistoric "Cup-markings" on Monuments in British Isles.

a. Stone in chambered barrow at Clava, Inverness-shire. S.A.S., Pl. 10, 4.
b. Another stone in same. S.A.S., Pl. 10, 3.
c. Stone in underground "house" at Ruthven, Forfarshire. S.A.S., Pl. 25, 3.
d. Standing stone at Ballymenach, Argyle-shire. S.A.S., Pl. 18, 2.
e. Another stone at same. S.A.S., Pl. 17, 3.
f. "Caiy" stone, 11 ft. high, near "British camp" and sea, Coniston, near Edinburgh. S.A.S., Pl. 17, 1.
g. Jedburgh stone. S.A.S., Pl. 16, 1.
h. Laws, Forfarshire. S.A.S., Pl. 12, 5.

As I observed that many of the ancient Briton pre-Roman coins also were studded with circles, single and concentric, in groups or clusters (see Figs. in next Chapter), which generally resembled the prehistoric "cup-markings"; and that some of the ancient Greco-Phœnician coins of Cilicia and Syrio-Phœnicia contained analogous groups of circles associated with the same divinities as in the Briton coins, and that *many of the "whorls" of terra-cotta dug up from the ruins of Ancient Troy by Schliemann, and which I had found were amulets, also contained numerous depressed cup-marks like the British, in definite groups and associated with the solar Swastika or Sun Crosses, and containing Sumerian writing hitherto unobserved and explanatory of the "cups" and connecting the British cup-markings with the Trojans and so confirming the British Chronicle tradition,* I therefore

---

[1] Review of theories in S.A.S., 92, etc.    [2] Windle, W.P.E., 123-4.

turned to the sacred seals of the Hitto-Sumerians, to find if they might supply a clue to the origin and meaning of the Trojan and British " Cup-marks."

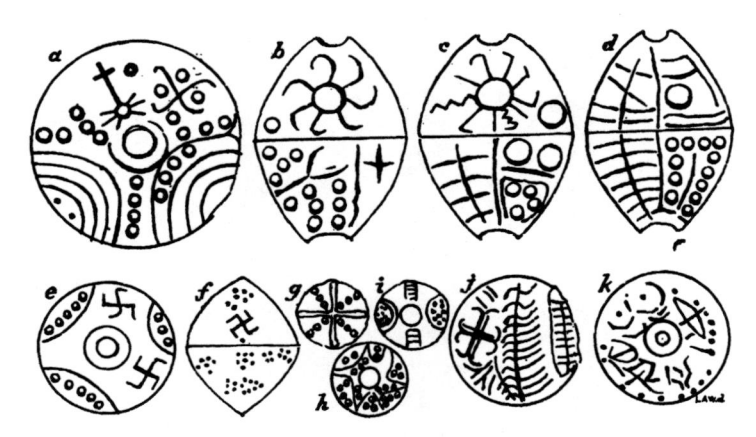

FIG. 31.—" Cup-markings " on Amulet Whorls from Troy, with explanatory Sumerian writing.
(From Schliemann.)[1]

Note definite groups of " cups " and dots with Crosses and Swastikas and in *a* True Cross springing from Rayed Sun. The large central hole is for string attachment of amulet. Interpretation on p 252.

I then found that the ancient sacred seals and amulets of the Hitto-Sumerians, from the fourth millennium B.C. onwards, figured similar groups of circles, some of them " ringed," and associated with Sun and Swastika (see Fig. 32). And from their repeated recurrence attached to the figures of a particular god or gods, it seemed clear that they were used to designate that particular god or gods (see Fig. 33). Further examination confirmed this. It thus became evident that these circles, arranged singly and in groups of specific numbers, formed a recognized method

[1] *a.* Terra-cotta amulet. S.I., No. 1954. Note True Cross springing from Sun.
*b.* Panel of a globe amulet, No. 1993. Note reversed Swastika for resurrecting or returning Sun.
*c.* Another panel of same.   *d.* Another panel of same.
*e.* No. 1988.   *f.* No. 1999.   Panel of a globe amulet.
*g.* Terra-cotta seal No. 493.   *h.* Amulet in 1929.
*i.* Amulet 1953.   *j.* 1984.   *k.* 510.

## CUP MARKINGS IN HITTO-SUMERIAN 239

of designating particular gods, or aspects of the One

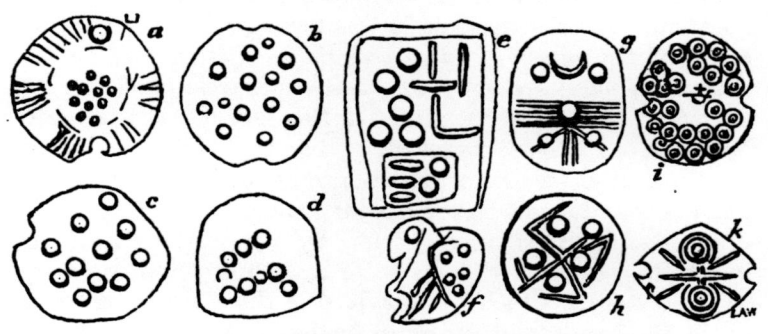

FIG. 32.—"Cup-marks" on archaic Hitto-Sumerian Seals and Amulets.
(After Delaporte.)

a. D.C.O. (L.) 4 pl. 1 from Tello, with concave "cup-marks."[1]  b. Ib. pl. 16 from Susa, marks convex.  c. Ib. pl. 23 from Susa.  d. Ib. pl. 23.  e. Ib. pl. 32.  f. pl. 20, with concave marks. All from Susa.  g. Ib. pl. 54.  h. Ib. pl. 57 from Gaza.  i. Ib. pl. 58, Gaza.  k. Ib. pl. 58, Gaza.

Universal God and his angels amongst the Hitto-Sumerians.

FIG. 33.—Circles as Diagnostic Cipher Marks of Sumerian and Chaldee deities in the "Trial of Adam the son of God *Ia* (*Iahveh* or Jove or *Indara*)."
From Sumerian Seal of about 3000 B.C., after W.S.C. 300b. For description see p. 252. Note all the personages wear horn head-dress, like the Goths and Ancient Britons. Also note long beard and clean shaven lips.

In order to understand the meaning and origin of the religious values attached by the Sumerians to the circles and their numbers, it is necessary to refer to the system of

[1] Dr. Delaporte reports it is pierced by two holes, and on reverse is a buckle for attachment. This implies its use as a "button-amulet," like those found in Troy and Britain, also with similar lined Cross (see Chapter XX).

numeration invented and used by the Sumerians, which is admittedly the basis of our own modern system of numerical notation. All the more so is this necessary, as I find that *many of the names of our numerals in English, and in the Aryan languages generally, are also derived from the Sumerian names for these numbers*, although this fact has not hitherto been noticed. This, therefore, affords still further evidence for the Sumerian origin of the Aryans, and of the Britons and Scots and Anglo-Saxons in particular.

Simple numerals were written by the Early Sumerians by strokes, such as / for 1, // for 2, /// for 3 and so on up to 9[1]—a system which has survived in the Roman numerals up to IIII, and on the dials of modern clocks and watches. But when engraved on stones, these lower numeral strokes were at first formed by the easier process of drilling, by the jewelled drill worked by a bowstring fiddle, thus forming circular holes, ◯, the so-called "cups." The numeral One was called by the Sumerians *Ana, Un* or *As*, which is now seen to be the Sumerian origin of our English "One" (Scot *Ane*, Anglo-Sax. *An*, Old English *Oon*, Gothic *Ein* and *Ains*, Scand. *Een*, Greek *Oinos*, Lat. *Unus*, French *Un*); whilst *As* is now disclosed to be the Sumerian origin of our English "Ace" (Old English *As*, Greek *Eis*, Latin *As*, "unity"). And it is of great significance that this word *As*, which the Sumerians also used for "God" as "Unity," is the usual title *As* or *Asa*, for the Father-god, in the Gothic epics, the Eddas, which, as we have seen, are now believed to have been largely composed in Ancient Britain.

Similarly, the numeral "Two" was called by Sumerians *Tab* or *Dab*, which is now disclosed as the Sumerian origin of our English word "Two" (Scot and Anglo-Sax. *Twa*, Gothic *Tva* or *Tvei*, Scand. *Tva, Tu*, Greek and Latin *Duo*, Sanskrit *Dva*—B and V or W being often interchangeable dialectically, as we have seen. The Sumerian reading for "Three" is uncertain; but the numeral "Four" reads *Gar*[2] and *Ga-dur*,[3] which thus equate with the Indo-

---

[1] Nine was also written by the Sumerians as "ten minus one," as it still survived in the Roman.
[2] Br., 11943.   [3] Br., 10015, and see below.

# SUMERIAN ORIGIN OF ARYAN NUMERALS 241

Persian *Car*, Latin *Quatuor*, Fr. *Quatre*, Sanskrit *Catur*, Gaelic *Ceithor* and our English *Quart* and *Quarter*). Six is *As* and in Akkad *Sissu*; Seven is *Sissina* (or "Six" plus "One") and *Sibi* in Akkad; and Eight is *Ussu*, which equates with the Breton *Eich*, *Eiz*[1] and fairly with the Sanskrit *Asta* and Scot and Gaelic *Acht*. And the Sumerian names of other numerals may also prove, on re-examination, to be more or less identical with the Aryan.

The occult values attached to certain numbers by the Sumerians, through ideas associated with particular numbers, was the origin of the mystical use of numbers in the ancient religions of the East and Greece referred to by Herodotus and other writers, as current amongst the adepts in the mysteries of the Magians, Pythagoras, Eleusis, and later amongst the Gnostics, and surviving in some measure in religion to the present day. Thus "One" as "Unity" and "First," was secondarily defined by the Sumerians as "complete" and "perfect," and thus also represented "God, heaven and earth." When formed by a circle or "cup-mark," it especially represented the Sun and Sun-god, who are also represented by a circle with a central dot in Egyptian hieroglyphs. Different sizes of circles, and concentric circles, and semicircles or curved wedges had different numerical and mystical values attached to them as shown in the accompanying Figure[2]; and all of these forms and groups of

○  = 1 or 10 (*A*, *Ana*, *U*, *Un*, *Buru*), Earth, Heaven, God Sun, Sun-god.[3]

D, ᗷ, ⊂⊃ = 1 (*Ana*, *As*), One, God, sixty (as a cycle).

○  = 3,600 (*Sár*), great cycle,[4] perfection, totality.

◎  = 36,000 (*Saru*), all-in-all (well of totality,[5] Infinity ?).

FIG. 34.—Circle Numerical Notation in Early Sumerian with values.

[1] G.D.B., 197.
[2] This is based on researches of Thureau-Dangin. T.R.C., pp. 78, etc.
[3] Br., 8631, etc.; as Earth, Br., 8689; as "That One," Br., 8765.
[4] = 60 × 60.
[5] *Cp.* B.B.W., p. 192, 364. *Sara* in Sanskrit also = a pool and sea, and well.

circles are found in the prehistoric "cup-marks" in the British Isles.

This early method of numerical notation by circles was especially used by the Sumerians in their religion to designate God, and different aspects of the godhead and Heaven, Earth and Death, and in the later polytheistic phase to distinguish a few different divinities, as we have seen in the sacred seal in Fig. 33. Thus, whilst the single circle, or numeral for one, was, like the sign of the rayed Sun itself, used to designate "God" (as First Cause), the Sun and Sun-god and latterly gods in general and Heaven, the higher numbers in definite groups of small circles designated different members of the godhead, &c., as recorded in the bilingual Sumero-Akkadian glossaries.

With the aid of these circle marks we are able to *identify the Hitto-Sumerian god-names on the seals and tablets with the names of the leading Aryan gods of classic Greece and Rome, of the Indian Vedas, of the Gothic Eddas, and of the Ancient Britons, as inscribed on their pre-Roman coins and monuments,* and not infrequently accompanied in the latter by the same groups of circle marks. In this table, for convenience of printing, an ordinary O type is used to represent the perfect circle of the originals.

O = 1 or 10 (*A, Ana, Aṡ, U, Un*, etc.).
God[1] as Monad, *Ana*, "The One,"[2] Lord, Father-god *I-a* (or *Bel*), or *In-duru*,[3] Sun-god *Maṡ* or *Mashtu* ("Hor-*Mazd*").[4] Earth, Heaven and Sun.

OO = 2 or 20 (*Tab, Tap, Dab, Man, Min*[5] *Niṡ*).
or O   Sun-god as "Companion of God," also called
O   *Buzur*,[6] *Ra*[7] or *Zal*[8] (= "Sol"), also *Nas*-atya in Hittite and Sanskrit. Is dual—or 2-faced—the visible Day Sun and Night or "returning" Sun,

[1] Br., 8688.   [2] Br. 8654.   [3] See later.   [4] See later.
[5] *Min* was possibly used in Britain as synonym, in view of the nursery counting out rhyme, "Eeny, *Meeny*, Mainy Mo," etc.
[6] Br. 9944. *Buz* is described as the "*Gid*" or Serpent *Cad*-uceus holder, which accounts for the 2 serpents figured on rod of Sun-god and below the Sun on some Sumerian seals and on Egyptian figures of the Sun and on rod of Mercury.
[7] B.B.W., No. 337. 6, 8, 56 ; and Langdon, J.R.A.S., 1921, 573.
[8] Br., 7777.

# CIRCLE OR CUP-MARK SUMER SCRIPT

and origin of Dioscorides. Frequent on Briton monuments and coins.[1]

OOO = 3 or 30 (*Eš, Usu*)
    Moon, Moon-god *Sin*. Also(?) Death (*Bat* or *Matu*)[2] and Earth (*Matu*), *Sib*[3] or *Batu*[4] or " Fate " =
    The Three Sybils or Fates.

OOOO = 4 or 40 (*Gar*[5] *Gadur*,[6] *Nin, Madur*).[7]
or OO    Mother Goddess *Ga-a*[8](=Gaia) or *Ma-a*[9](=Maia,
OO    Maya or May) and numerically = " Four " (quarters), " Totality " and " Multitude."[10]

OOO = 5 or 50 (*Ia, Ninnu, Taš-ia*).
OO    Archangel messenger *Taš-ia*,[11] *Taš* or *Tesu(b)*, " man-god of *Induru*,"[12] " Son of the Sun," " Son of *Ia* " (Mero-*Dach* or " *Mar-duk*," " *Illil*,"[13] *Adar* "). Also his temple.[14]

OOO = 6 or 60 (*Aš*, Akkad *Siššu*).
OOO    Sea-storm god or spirit, *Mer, Muru* or *Marutu* (Akkad *Ramman*,[15] *Adad* and Sanskrit *Maruta*).

OOOO = 7 or 70 (*Siššu, Imin*, Akkad *Siba*).
OOO    " Field of *Taš* "[16] Capital city. (=?*Himin* or " Heaven " of Goths and " 7th Heaven "?).[17]

OOOO = 8 or 80 (*Ussa*).
OOOO    " Field of *T š* '[18] [8 was number of Dionysos].[19]

OOOOO = 9 or 90 (*Ilim*).
OOOO    " He-Goat."[20] God *Elim*[21] (Bel, " En-Sakh " or " En-Lil " or *Dara* ?) [9 was number of Prometheus].[22]

---

[1] Is judge and chief heavenly witness seeing all things; and chief oracle and oath god.

[2] Signs, Br., 9971, read *Ma-tu* preferably to *Ba-tu*, thus equating with Akkad *Matu, Mutu*, " die, death," and Aryan Pali *Mato*, Indo-Persian *Mat*, " Death." This is confirmed by its Akkad synonym *Mutitu* = " Condition of Death " (*cp.* M.D., 619); and a defaced Sumerian word for " Death " in glossary is spelt *Ma*..(P.S.L., 110), presumably " *Matu*."

[3] Br. 8194; M.D., 1065.    [4] Br., 9993 and 8197.

[5] Br., 10014 and 11943.    [6] Br., 10015.

[7] *Ibid.*, 10015, wrongly read " Ea," cp. Br., 5414 and 11319.

[8] *Ib.*, 10015 and 5412.    [9] *Ib.*, 5414.    [10] Br., 10024.

[11] Br., 10038, for signs, and Br., 11253, etc., for values.

[12] Br., 10038.    [13] Br., 10037.    [14] T.C.R., 517.

[15] Br., 12198.    [16] Br., 10050.

[17] On *Im* = " Heaven," *cp.* Br., 2241. Pleiades are not in the list.

[18] Br., 10053.    [19] W. Westcott, *Numbers and Occult Power*, 83.

[20] Br., 8884. M.D., 271; also " Gazelle " and " Chamois " (S.H.L., 283 and 533).

[21] Br., 8883.    [22] Westcott, 85.

| | |
|---|---|
| O | =3600 (Sar, Di). "Perfect, complete, Goodness." God Ana ("The One").[1] Sun-god Śur (Aśur or Bil).[2] Highest Judge (Di)[3] Heaven, Paradise.[4] |
| ⊙ | =36,000 (Śaru, Infinity). |
| OO | (Ia) God, Ia or Induru (Indara.)[5] |

We thus find that the Father-god of the Sumerians (and of the Hitto-Phœnicians), whose earliest-known name, as recorded on the Udug trophy Bowl of the fourth millennium B.C., is " Zagg " (or Za-ga-ga, which, with the soft g gives us the original of " Zeus," the Dyaus and Sakka of the Vedas and Pali, and the " Father Sig " or Ygg of the Gothic Eddas) is recorded by the single-circle sign as having the equivalent of Ia or Bel, thus giving us the Aryan original of " Iah " (or " Jehovah ") of the Hebrews, and the " Father Ju (or Ju-piter) " or Jove of the Romans.

This title of Ia (or " Jove ") for the Father-god (Bel), as represented by the single circle, is defined as meaning " God of the House of the Waters," which is seen to disclose the Sumerian source of the conception of Jove as " Jupiter Pluvius " of the Romans. This special aspect and function of the Father-god was obviously conditioned by the popular need of the Early Aryans in their settled agricultural life for timely rain and irrigation, with water for their flocks and herds, as well as their seafaring life. We therefore find him often represented in the sacred seals of the Sumerians and Hittites, from about 4000 B.C. onwards, as holding the vase or vases of " Life-giving Waters," which are seen issuing from his vase, and which he as " The Living God " bestows upon his votaries (see Fig. 35).[6]

This beautiful conception of the bountiful Father-god by our Early Aryan ancestors, and authors of the cup-mark inscriptions, at so very remote a period, which is preserved in their sacred seals as well as in the contemporary inscribed tablets, renders it desirable here to draw attention to the vast treasure-house of authentic early history of our ancestors which is conserved in these sacred seals of the Sumerians,

[1] Br. 8213.  [2] Br., 8209 and 8212 and on Bil, see later.
[3] Br., 8201.  [4] Br., 8219.  [5] Br. 8272.  [6] See f.n. 2, p. 246.

## ARYAN FATHER-GOD IN SACRED SEALS

Hittites, Phœnicians, and Kassi and other Babylonians, in order to understand aright the cup-mark inscriptions and symbols on the " prehistoric " Briton monuments and Briton coins and the deity who is therein invoked  Many thousands of the actual original seals of the Early Aryan kings, high-priests, nobles and officials, and many of them inscribed, have fortunately been preserved to us down through the ages. They form a vast picture-gallery of authentic facts, vividly portraying, not only the religious beliefs and ideals of our Aryan ancestors, and their conception of God and the Future

FIG. 35.—Father-god *Ia* (*Iahvh* or " Jove ") or Indara bestowing the " Life-giving Waters."

From Sumerian seal of King Gudea, about 2450 B.C.
(After Delaporte.[1]  Enlarged 1¼ diameters.)
Note the horned Gothic head-dress and costumes of that period, with long beard and clean-shaven lips. The Sun, as angel, with his double-headed Serpent Caduceus, introduces the votaries. The flower-bud on top of vase is the Sumerian word-sign for " Life."

Life, but also preserve the contemporary portraits of early Aryan kings, queens, priests and people, the details of their dress and the high æsthetic feeling and civilization of those early periods. And the very highly naturalistic art and technique displayed in the drawing is all the more remarkable when it is remembered that the drawing is on such a minute scale and delicately engraved on hard jewel stones.

These seals and their contemporary tablet-records disclose the important fact that the Aryan Father-god (Bel) was already imagined in human form, and on the model of a

[1] D.C.O.(L).I.  By permission of Librairie Hachette; and *cp*. W.S.C., 368*a* and 650.

S

beneficent earthly king so early as about 4000 B.C. He is of fine Aryan type (see Figs. 33, 35, etc.), with Gothic horned chaplet, richly robed, and usually enthroned beside the Sun. This was evidently also the conception of the Universal God by our Aryan ancestors, even when the more idealistic of them refrained from making his graven image, and figured him merely by the simple circle of " Unity " and " Perfection," as engraved on many Hitto-Sumerian seals and on the cup-mark inscriptions in prehistoric Britain.

Although calling him " *I-a* " (or Jove), that same word-sign was also read by the Sumerians as *In-duru*, the " *Indara* " of the Hittites, the *Indra* of the Vedas, the "*Indri*-the-divine " title of Thor in the Gothic Eddas. And this name of Indara, we shall find later, is the source of the name and of the supernatural miraculous part of the Church legend of St. *Andrew*, the patron saint of the later Goths, Scyths and Scots.

The dual circles or " cups " for the Sun, connote the ancient idea that the Sun apparently moved round the earth and returned East for sunrise under the earth or ocean somehow so as to form two phases, as the " Day " Sun and the " Night " (or submarine " returning ") Sun—a notion also believed by the writers of the Hebrew Old Testament.

These dual circles for the Sun, denoting his day and night phases, seen in Fig. 33, are again seen in the seal of about 2400 B.C. in Fig. 36, which represents the owner of the votive seal being introduced by the archangel $Ta^sia$[1] to the Resurrecting Sun-god (two-headed as before) emerging on the East (or left hand) from the waters of the Deep (and behind him the swimming " Fish-god " of the Deep), wherein the Sun-god's name is written *Ra* or *Zal*, inscribed immediately underneath the two circles.[2] These names for him now disclose the Sumerian source of the Egyptian *Ra*

[1] See later.
[2] The other name in panel to left, immediately under the head of the " Fish-god " of the Deep, reads *A-a*, and is defined as " God of the Water Vase of the *Uku* (? Achaia) people " (Br. 10692), and appears to represent the Sun-god's father Ia, the Creator, resurrecting from the Deep, or his " House of the Waters "—the Spirit of God moving upon the face of the Waters. " Indra loves the Waters " (R.V. 10. 111. 10). " Indra lets loose the Waters for the benefit of mankind." (R.V. 1. 57. 6 etc., 4. 19. 8 etc.).

## RESURRECTING SUN AS TWO "CUPS" 247

and Sanskrit *Ra-vi* (or "Rover") name for that luminary and its presiding "deity." Whilst *Zal* discloses the Sumerian source of the Gothic, Latin and Old English "*Sol.*"

FIG. 36.—Two-headed Resurrecting Sun-god designated by Two Circles.
From Hitto-Sumer seal of about 2400 B.C.
(After Delaporte.[1] Enlarged 2 diameters.)

This dual phase of the Sun's apparent progress westwards and back again eastwards was familiar to the Ancient Britons and Scots, as seen in the numerous prehistoric rock and other sculptures, and in Early Briton coins, where the Night or "returning" Sun is figured as a second disc, joined by bars to the Day Sun (as the so-called "Spectacles" of Scottish archæologists, Figs. in next chapter), or as a double Spiral, with the Night Sun figured as a Spiral in the reversed or "returning" direction (see Figs. 38 &c.). It is also similarly figured in Hittite seals and on Phœnician sacred vases from the Levant, Crete and the Ægean, both as the conjoined double disc (see Fig. 37 &c.), and as the double Spiral with the second reversed or "returning"; and this latter is sometimes shown *in both the Hittite and Ancient Briton and Scot representations*, as entering the Gates of Night (see Figs. 37 and 38), wherein the gates have the same latticed pattern, and it is also to be noted that, *in these Irish Scot prehistoric sculptures, the Sun is represented by two cup-marks, as in the Hitto-Sumerian.* This again evidences

[1] D.C.O.(L.) No. 251, pl. 76.

the Hittite origin of the Britons and Scots, and their common symbolism.

FIG. 37.—" Returning " or " Resurrecting " Sun entering the Gates of Night on Hittite seals.
(After Ward.)[1]
Note in top Seal the Night Sun as Reversed Spiral, and the Winged Sun with its "Celtic" Cross, above a pillar of 7 fruits (=? 7 days of week or 7 circles of Heaven).

The triad of circles, representing both 3 and 30, designates the Moon, presumably from its three phases of waxing, waning and dark, and also its lunar month of 30 days; and they also appear to be defined as "Death" (*Bat, i.e.,* "Fate.") And the triad means "Fate," named *Sib* (literally "the speaker" or sooth-*sayer*),[2] thus disclosing the Sumerian origin of our word "Sibyl" and of "The Three Fates" and the "Three Witches" in *Macbeth*—a vestige of the matriarchist cult.[3] And the "Seer of the Fates" is called *Bat*, thus showing the Sumerian source of our English words "Fate" and "*Fat*-al." It also means "Earth." As "Death," see Fig. 40.

The four-fold circles designate "Totality" (from the four quarters?), also the Mother Goddess, "*Ma-a*," thus disclosing the Sumerian source of the Earth Mother's name

---

[1] W.S.C., 863, 1100.
[2] Another definition of *Sib* or *Zib* is "One who cuts or measures off Fate" (B.B.W., 191), which thus literally equates with the functions of the Three Fate Sisters of the classic Greeks, and discloses their Sumerian origin.
[3] Hecate, the queen of Hell, was 3-faced.

# RESURRECTING SUN TWO CUPS IN IRELAND

as *Maia* of the Greeks, *Mahi* and *Maya* of the Vedas and Indian epics, and the " goddess Queen May " of the Britons, and the source of our English " Ma " for " Mother," whilst she was also called " *Ma-dur*," now disclosed as the Sumerian source of our English " Mother." Her name also reads " *Ga-a*," the Sumerian source of her alternative Greek title of " *Gaia*."

FIG. 38.—" Returning " or " Resurrecting " Sun, in prehistoric Irish Scot rock graving *two cup-marks*; as with Reversed Spiral entering the Gates of Night.

(After Coffey.)[1]

Note the dual cup-marks in both, and that it is the Returning Spiral on extreme right (or West) which enters the latticed Gates in *a*, while in *b*, the 7 wedges in the opening in the Gates=Heaven, the direction of Resurrecting Sun. Compare with Briton Coins in FIG. 44, showing Sun-Horse leaping over the Gates of Night.

The pentad group of circles designated the archangel of God, *Tāś-ia, Taśup* of the Hittites and *Da up Mikal* of the later Phœnicians (who, we shall find, is the Archangel Michael of the Gentiles). His name Taśia, we shall find also, occurs freely in the Aryan titles of archangels in the Gothic Eddas (*Thiazi*), in the Vedas (*Daxa*, etc.), on Greco-Phœnician coins (as *Tkz, Dzs*, etc.), feminized by the later polytheistic Greeks into *Tyche,* and on the coins and monuments of the Ancient Britons (as *Tasc, Tascio*, etc.), *and also usually associated in the Briton coins with the pentad group of circle marks*, as we shall see later on.

He is represented sometimes by the pentad of circles (see Fig. 39), but usually in human form (as we shall see), and sometimes winged (see Fig. 40, etc., and numerous specimens

[1] C.N.G., Fig. 24, from tumulus at Tara.

on Phœnician Coins, and on Early Briton monuments and coins, figured in next chapters).

FIG. 39.—Pentad Circles designate " Tašia " (Archangel) on Seal of 3rd millennium B.C.
(After Delaporte.[1])
See description later. Note Cross above vase, horned head-dress, and Goat and Bull behind god.

FIG; 40.—Archangel Tašia (winged) invoked by Mother (4 circles) for Dead (3 circles).
From Hittite seal amulet of about 2000 B.C. (after Lajard.)[2]
Note dead man (? husband) carries Cross above a handled Cross, and tied to wrist an amulet (picturing this seal?). The Warrior-Angel has 8-rayed Sun and endless chain of Sun's revolutions at his side.

That his name was spelt "*Tās*" by the Phœnicians and Sumerians is evident, amongst other proofs cited later, by the Early Phœnician seal here figured (Fig. 41). This spells his name "*Ta-āš*," in which the Sumerian word-sign of the right hand=*Ta*, and the six circles have their ordinary Sumerian phonetic value of *Aš*. He is here accompanied

[1] D.C.O.(L.), pl. 125, 1.
[2] Lajard, *Culte de Mithra*, 354, and W.S.C., 873.

# TĀS RESURRECTING SUN-ANGEL IN "CUPS" 251

as is very usual, by the Sun-bird (Phœnix), Sun-fish, and, Goat (which latter we shall find is a rebus for "Goth")—his votaries.

FIG. 41.—Phœnician Seal reading "Tāś" (Archangel).
From grave in Cyprus of about 3rd millennium B.C.
(After A. Cesnola.)[1]

The seven-circle or heptad group designated, as we have seen, "Heaven" (*Imin*), and occurs frequently in the Sumerian and Hitto-Phœnician seals and amulets (see Fig. 42), as well as in the cup-marked inscriptions in Britain.

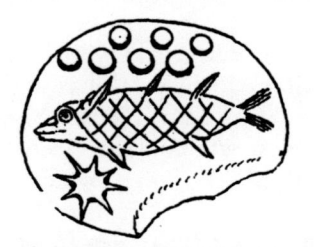

FIG. 42.—Heptad Circles for "Heaven" (Imin)
on Babylonian amulet.
(After Delaporte.)[2]
Note the 8-rayed Sun is swimming eastwards with the Sun-fish (of 7 fins)[3]
to Heaven (7 circles) above.

The nonad circle group designates the title of the Father-god Bil or Indara as the "He-Goat" (*Iilim*), the totem or mascot of the Khatti or Getae Goths—the sacred Goat of the Cymri. And the He-Goat is a frequent associate of Thor or Indri-the-divine in the Gothic Eddas.

[1] *Cyprus*, pl. 33, 24, and W.S.C., 1189.
[2] D.C.O. (L), pl. 91, 1, No. 617, on a sapphire.    [3] *Cp.* S.H.L. 482.

It will also be seen, in scanning the circle key-list in the table, that the first or single circle, or cup-mark, title for God, *Ia* or Jove, or " The One God," has the value *A* (*i.e.*, the Greek *Alpha*) : whilst the last title for Him is the large double *O* (*i.e.*, the Greek *O-mega*—a name now seen to be also derived from the Sumerian *Makh*, " Great," and surviving in the Scottish "Muckle" and our English " Much" and " Magnitude," etc.). It thus appears that the Early Sumerians and our own "pagan" Ancient Briton ancestors called the Father-God *Ia* or Jove by the very same title as God is called in the Apocalypse, namely "*Alpha* and *O-mega*, the First and the Last." Thus, while finding the essentially Gentile origin of that title, we also gain its original inner meaning.

Having thus recovered the keys to the religious and occult values of the circles or "cup-marks" in Sumerian, we are now able, through these keys, to identify for the first time with precision the respective images of God and his angels, or minor divinities, figured on the sacred seals of the Hitto-Sumerians, as in Fig. 33, p. 239. In that seal, of which ten other specimens of the same scene are figured on other seals by Ward,[1] it will be noticed that all of the personages wear the horned head-dress, like the Goths and Ancient Britons. The Father-God in human form is seated on a throne under the 8-rayed Sun, below which is a crescent ;[2] and facing him below is the hieroglyph of a head, which in Sumerian is the word-sign for his title of " Creator."[3] Next to him, as " Witness," stands the official designated by two circles, the Sun-god (see key-list)—the " all-seeing " Day and Night Sun. He is two-faced, facing both ways, Janus-like (as in Hittite and in some Briton monuments and coins) and bears the Caduceus rod (called *Gid* or " Serpent rod " in Sumerian, thus disclosing the Sumerian origin of the name " Caduceus ") which is topped by the double Sun-circle with two subject Serpents of Death and Darkness attached—disclosing the Sumerian origin of the two Serpents attached to the Sun's

---

[1] W.S.C., 291–300.   [2] The crescent is absent in No. 295.
[3] Br., 9112–4. That he is Ia or **Indara** is evidenced by his being figured in many seals of this scene with the spouting waters, as in Fig. 35.

# KEY TO SUMER CUP-MARK SCRIPT

disc in Egyptian. The prisoner as a "Bird-man"—by his lower parts of the tail and feet of a chicken, and the young puppy which he holds—is designated by these Sumerian hieroglyphs as "The Son *Adamu* (or Adam),"[1] who gives his name to this famous Chaldean epic scene. His accuser, marked by 3 circles, is the Moon-god of Darkness and Death (see key-list) ; and the outer official is marked by a circle with a dot to its left top, which is the Sumerian word-sign for "A Spirit of Heaven."[2]

Our key-list to this Circle script of the Sumerians thus discloses that the scene engraved on this sacred Sumerian seal is the famous trial scene in the Chaldean epic of "How Adam broke the Wing of the Stormy South Wind"—an epic of which several copies have been unearthed in Babylonia in cuneiform tablets.[3] This epic relates that "Adam, the Son of God Ia" was overturned with his boat in the sea by the stormy South Wind, and that he retaliated by "breaking the wing" of the stormy South Wind, and was arraigned before his Father-God for trial for this audacity. It is, I find, a poetic version of the epoch-making invention of sails for sea-craft by the early Hittite historical king who is called in the still extant cuneiform documents of the third millennium B.C. "Adam(u) the Son of God," and a version of the same story is preserved in our Gothic Eddas.

This key-list will now, moreover, be found to apply equally well to the many other Hitto-Babylonian seals[4] containing diagnostic circle-marks for divinities, as well as those in which the circles represent the divinities without figured representations. It also explains for the first time the cup-markings on the numerous "whorls" unearthed at Troy, the old capital of the Hittites, and now discovered to be amulets ; and it explains the corresponding circles on the ancient Briton coins (as figured later), and the cup-markings of prehistoric Britain.

The Trojan cup-marks on the amulets (see Fig. 31), now

[1] Br., 9075.   [2] *Ner.*, Akkad "*Anu-Naki*," Br., 10149.
[3] H. Winckler, *Die Thon-tafeln v. El Amarna*, 166, *a* and *b*, and E. T. Harper, *Beit.z. Assyr.*, 2,418 *f.* ; and partly translated with text in L. King, *First Steps in Assyrian*, 215, etc.
[4] Figured in W.S.C.

deciphered by means of the hitherto unnoticed Sumerian writing of about 3000 B.C. associated with them,[1] confirm and establish the Sumerian origin of these cup-markings, and extend our knowledge of their meaning and use. They are found in Troy solely with the Sun-cult, and associated with the same solar symbols and Crosses as are the circles on the coins and monuments of the Ancient Britons (see Figs. later)—who, by their own tradition, came from Troy.

The Sumerian writing on the Trojan amulets is in the archaic script which is found on the earliest sacred Sumerian seals and tablets of about 4000–3000 B.C. And it discovers unequivocally that *these cup-marks with their associated True Crosses and Swastikas are prayers to the One God for resurrection from the dead, " like the Sun " in its supposed resurrection from the nether regions of Death and Darkness.* This now explains why in Babylonia sacred seals, in series with these, were found attached to the wrists of skeletons in tombs,[2] and why the seals from Cyprus, which frequently contain these circles, single and in groups, were found almost exclusively in *Phœnician* tombs of the Copper-Bronze Age ;[3] and why, in Britain, the cup-markings are mainly found on sepulchral dolmens and on stones in funereal barrows.

The cups on these Trojan amulets (see Fig. 31, p. 238), and reduced sometimes to dots on the smaller ones, it will be noticed, are arranged sometimes single (1 =God, The One), but usually in groups of 2( =The Sun), 3 (=Earth or Death), 5(=Archangel *Taś* or " *Teshub Mikal*, who, we shall see, is the Archangel " Michael ") ; whilst 7(Heaven) and 4(Mother, quarters or " multitude ") are also not infrequent. The Crosses figured are in the form of the True Cross in elongated form (which is seen in *a* in the Figure to spring from the rayed Sun) or equal-rayed of St. George's Cross shape (*d* and *g*) or as Swastikas (straight-footed *c, e, f,* etc., or curved-footed *a, b*). And it is significant that *these early*

---

[1] In attempts hitherto at deciphering the writing on Trojan seals and whorls, it has been assumed that the script is a form of Cyprus writing (Sayce, S.I., 691, etc.), with more or less doubtful alphabet. But the script on the whorls here figured (*a–d, j, k*) is unequivocally Sumerian, as attested by the references to the signs in the Standard Sumerian of Brünow and Thureau-Dangin.

[2] W.S.C., 4.  [3] W.S.C., 346.

## TROJAN RESURRECTION BY CROSS

*Trojan Sumerians prayed to God and to his angel-son Taś or Taśia, to resurrect them through the " Wood " Cross of which they figure the effigy on their amulets.* And we know, from the old Sumerian psalms, that the Sumerians credited the Son of the Father-god—(" The Son *Taś* or *Dach* " or " Mar-Duk ") with resurrecting them from the dead, as in the following line :—

"The merciful one, who loves to raise the dead to life— Mar- Duk "[1] [Son *Taś*.]

Let us now read the contracted inscriptions on these Trojan amulets by the aid of the standard Sumerian script and its therein associated cup-mark cipher script, and hear the prayers offered by these pious Early Sumerians, and ancestors of the Britons of Troy, to God, whom they beg to resurrect them through his " Wood " Cross like the resurrecting Sun. In these contracted prayers, in which the intervening verbs and connecting phrases have to be supplied, the old idea of the moving and returning, or subterranean " resurrecting " Sun is repeated.

$a_1$ " O One and Only God (1 cup), as the returning Sun (Swastika with two feet reversed) passes through the quarters (4 cups), through the Earth or Death (3 cups), through the multitude (4 cups) of the Waters (curved line word-sign for " water "), through the multitude of the Waters (repeated word-signs with doubled dot), and resurrects above as the Risen Sun (2 cups above the Waters on East or left hand), over the Earth (3 cups), so resurrect me by this Sign of thy Cross of the Sun (Cross springing from rayed Sun)."

*b.* " O God (1 cup), as the returning Sun (Swastika with reversed feet) passes through the quarters (4 cups) cutting through (Sumerian Y-shaped word-sign for ' cut through ') to Heaven (7 cups), so resurrect me, O *Ia* (Jove or *Induru*, by word-sign of elongated /)[2] by this sign of thy Cross (Cross sign)."

*c.* ' O perfect God (1 large cup), as the returning Sun (Swastika with reversed feet), the good and perfect Sun (2 large cups) passes from (Sumer word-sign for ' from ')[3] the caverns of the Earth (word-sign)[4], so resurrect me, O *Ia*, Lord of the Waters (word-sign)."[5]

[1] S.H.L., 99.   [2] Br., 10068.   [3] Br., 28.   [4] Br., 9583-4.
[5] Br., 2625.

d. " By thy *Wood-bar* (*i.e.*, Wood Cross by its Sumerian word-sign)[1] O God (large cup), through the Waters (by Sumer word-sign) of the quarters (4 small cups), through Earth or Death (3 cups), O Only God (linear sign) and thy Archangel *Taś* (5 cups), resurrect me to Life (Sumer word-sign for Tree of Life)."[2]

e. " As the revolving Sun (Swastika Cross) passes through the Earth (3 cups), as the revolving Sun (Swastika) passes through the caverns of the Earth (word-sign), so pass me."

f. " O Archangel Taś (5 dots) of the Sun (2 dots), Lord (1 dot) of the returning Sun (reversed Swastika), as Taś (5 dots) passes through the quarters (4 dots) to Heaven (7 dots), so pass this man (word-sign,)[3] O Lord (1 dot) *Taś* (5 dots)."

g, h and i. In similar strain.[4]

j. " O Infinite God (large circle with dot), the Harvester (word-sign)[5] of Life (word-sign), cut through, cut, cut (word-signs) by thy Sun Cross (Cross and 2 dots[6]) the Earth or Death (3 strokes) for my resurrection."

k. " O Lord (1 dot) from (word-sign) Mother Earth (4 dots), this Seer (or Physician) man from the temple (word-sign)[7] of the Sun (2 dots), pass through the Waters (word-signs), resurrect like the Sun (2 dots) by this Cross (sign of Cross)."

This discovery that these Trojan cup-marked " whorls " of the Sumerian Trojan ancestors of the Britons of about 3000 B.C. are solar amulets, inscribed with prayers or Litanies for the Dead, couched in exalted literary form, and invoking *Ia* or Jove for resurrection through the Sign of the Cross, whilst of far-reaching religious importance in itself, now explains why sacred seals containing such " cup-markings " were buried with the deceased in Phœnician tombs, and why the Cup-markings are chiefly found associated with tombs in prehistoric Britain.

Even still more striking and historically important is the

---

[1] Br., 5701-2.  [2] Br., 2322.  [3] Br., 6399, and T.R.C., 289.
[4] The ladder-like sign is Sumerian word-sign for *Tuś* as " Marduk," Br., 10515.
[5] Br., 4411, etc., and B.B.W.1., p. 43, and T.R.C., 61. It might also read " Creator " (Br., 4304, and B.B.W. 170, p. 163).
[6] Two dots are shown on the side of the Cross in the side view, S.I., 1984.
[7] By word-signs, Br., 4666, 6399, 7710.

# PRAYER FOR RESURRECTION BY CROSS

archaic *Morite tablet of about* 4000 B.C., in mixed Circle and linear Sumerian script, like the Trojan amulets, in Fig. 43.

FIG. 43.—Muru or "Amorite" archaic tablet of about 4000 B.C. in Circle and Linear Sumerian Script. From Smyrna.
(E. A. Hoffman[1].)
Note the initial word-sign for "tomb" is the picture of the ancient barrow of the Indo-Aryans with its finial, called "thupa" or "tope."

It is said to have been found at the old Hittite sea-port of Smyrna on the Ægean to the south of Troy, with prehistoric Hittite rock-gravings and sculptures in its neighbourhood. It contains a beautiful and pathetic prayer for the resurrecting from the dead into paradise of a princess and Sun-priestess of the Bel-Fire cult, named Nina, and *who is significantly called therein an " Ari," i.e., " Arya-n " and " Muru,"* i.e., *" Mor " or " Amorite."* It invokes the archangel Taś for the aid of the resuscitating " Underground Sun " and the " Wood "-Cross, and reads *literally* as follows :—

" Tomb of the good girl.
    Master ! Hasten unto the Underground Sun (this) vessel
        of (thy) assembly !
    O Tus-a (Mar-Dach), Taś, all perfect Taś !

" O Caduceus (-holder) of the Sun take up O Lord, all perfect
        One,
    The princess Nina (by) the Wood Mace (Cross) uplifted (in
        thy) hand !

[1] See Appendix VI for details.

> O Taś hasten (thine) ear !
> The sick one of Bil's Fire-torch, O all perfect One, O Taś,
> The *Ari* [Aryan] the *Muru* [Amorite] (take up) !
>
> " Horse(-man) hasten, the faithful one lift up !
> Cut, O Shining One, O Taś, the earth from her amidst the mound !
> All perfect One Taś !
> Caduceus(-holder) of the Sun, All perfect One !
> In the house of Tax-the-angel (let her) abide."

And it is significant that a large proportion of the words of this Morite tablet of about 4000 B.C. are radically identical with those of modern English, thus the second and third words, " good girl," occur literally in the Sumerian as " *kud gal* " (for further details see Appendix VI., pp. 411-2).

Turning now to the prehistoric Cup-markings in the British Isles, in the attempt to unlock their long-lost meaning and racial authorship by these keys to the circle-script of the Sumerians, confirmed by the associated ordinary Sumerian script on the Trojan amulets, we find that the localities in which these cup-marks occur are precisely those which we have found associated with the early invading Hitto-Sumerians, Barats or Brito-Phœnicians. They are found engraved upon some of the stones of the Stone Circles, but mainly on funereal dolmens and stones of barrow graves usually in their neighbourhood and on rocks near Ancient Briton settlements.[1] The original and simpler form of the grouping of the cup-marks is best seen in the stones unearthed from funereal barrows and stone cist coffins of chieftains, which preserve the original group numbers of the cups more clearly than the exposed standing stones and rocks, which often have had many straggling groups of cups added by later generations, which tend to confuse the recognition of the group number of the cups. And here, it is to be noted that we are dealing solely with the true " cups " and cups with the single or double ring, and not with the many-ringed or multi-concentric circles (confined to the British Isles and

[1] For list of chief sites of cup-marks in British Isles and Scandinavia, see S.A.S., 14, etc. ; and W.P.E., 123-7, 195. Many others have since been found.

Sweden), known as "Rings," which are clearly later than the cups, and carved with metal tools, and which appear to be conventional forms of the solar spiral, now seen to be a symbol of the dual Sun, as the circling " Day " and returning " Night " Sun, as we shall see in the next chapter.

These Early Briton cup-markings, as seen in their simpler and original forms (see Fig. 30, p. 237), are arranged generally in the same groupings as in the Hitto-Sumerian seals and Trojan amulets. *They are found to be substantially identical with the Sumerian cup-marked solar amulets of Early Troy, and thus to be Litanies for the resurrection of the Dead by the Sun Cross, and couched in almost identical words, and thus confirming the Trojan origin for the Britons as preserved in the tradition of the Early British Chronicles.*

Reading the prehistoric British cup-markings by these new keys, we find that the specimens illustrated in the Fig. pray in the same contracted Hitto-Sumerian and Trojan form, and are addressed to the same " Solar " God and his archangel Taś, as follows :—

a. " O Archangel *Taś* (5 cups) of the Sun Cross (the cups are arranged in form of Cross),[1] save me ! "

b. " O Archangel *Taś* of the Sun Cross (5 cups cross-wise), as the Setting Sun (2 cups) passes through the under-world region of Death (3 cups) and resurrects as the Rising Sun (2 cups), so resurrect me ! "

c. " O Thrice Infinite God *Ia* (*Jove* or *Indra*, 3 large circled cups), from Death (3 cups), from the Darkness of Death (3 cups with falling lines)[2] unto the Infinite (2 circled cups) O Infinite *Ia* (large double circled cup), deliver me, O God (1 cup) ! "

d. " O Infinite *Ia* (large circled cup), by thy Archangel *Taś* (5 cups) pass me through Death (3 cups), the double Death (6 cups), as the Sun (2 cups) passes to Thee, *Ia* (large circled cup)." [The other 3 large circled cups and their associated small cups on the lower left-hand border have evidently been added at a later period ; but they repeat the same theme. The solitary cup in

---

[1] This cross, formed also with circles, is figured upon the body of the Archangel Taś on Phœnician coins; see Figs. later on.
[2] The falling lines of these cup-marks resemble those of the Sumerian word-sign for Darkness; see D.R.C., 262 ; B.B.W., 380. And the Akkad name for that sign is *Erebu*, disclosing source of Greek *Erebos*, " Darkness."

the bottom left-hand corner would be the concluding " O God ! " (1 cup)[1]]

e. This is essentially the same as *d*, with 2 later additions—the large circles with associated small cups—and as end word of the lowermost " Heaven (7 cups) of the Sun (2 cups)."

f. This single line of 6 cups may be an invocation or votive offering by a sailor prince to the Sea-Storm-wind Spirit *Mer* or *Muru* for his safety or rescue at sea ; or his personal name *Mer* or *Muru*, which was a personal clan name of the sea-going Hittites of " The Western Land of the Setting Sun " or the coastland of Syria-Cilicia—the " Mor-ites " or " Amor-ites " of the Hebrew Old Testament.

The belief in a future life of bliss associated with the Sun, entertained by our " pagan " Briton ancestors, in whose tombs such cup-markings are found, is evidenced further in the next chapter.

The date and authorship of these cup-markings in Britain are seen to be presumably the same as for the erection of the Stone Circles. That is to say, the Cup-markings were evidently engraved by the earliest wave of pioneer mine-exploiting Phœnician Barat merchants of the Late Stone and Early Bronze Age from about 2800 B.C. (or earlier) onwards,[2] and many centuries before the arrival of Brutus and his Trojan Phœnician Barats in the later Bronze Age.

It will thus be seen that my new evidence for the Hitto-Phœnician origin and solar character of the cup-markings

---

[1] By its ordinary phonetic value it = *As*.

[2] Phœnicia and Asia Minor have not yet been explored for cup-marks, but similar cup-marks to those of Ancient Britain have been found in Palestine, which was invariably called by its Babylonian suzerains " The Land of the *Hittites*." Dr. Macalister found at Gezer and neighbourhood numerous cup-markings on rocks, monoliths, dolmens and tombs of neolithic age (Bliss and Macalister, *Excavs. at Gezer*, Figs. 65, 66 and p. 194, etc.), and others were found at Megiddo by Schumacher. Those figured by Macalister, especially of former figure, are in large and small cups, and in groups of 1 and 2 chiefly, also 5, 4 and 3. (See also H. Vincent, *Canaan d. l'Exploration Recent.* Paris, 1914, 92, etc., 128, etc., 253.)

In the Phœnician Grave Seals from Cyprus, the Circles are mostly simple or ringed, and in groups of 2 (The Sun), but other groups also occur (see C.C. plate 12–14). And it is noteworthy that perforations (which appear to be deeper " cups " on the Standing Stones in Cyprus are also found in the Menan Tol in Cornwall and in a number in Gloucester (W.P.E. 194).

## BRITISH CUP-MARK SCRIPT DECIPHERED 261

in Britain and Scandinavia, etc., establishes, from altogether new and independent data, the truth of the conjecture for a Phœnician origin of these cup-marks formerly hazarded by Prof. Nilsson of Sweden, a conjecture which was rejected by contemporary and later writers for want of any concrete or presumptive evidence in its support.

Thus we find that the prehistoric Cup-markings in Britain on many of the Stone Circles and standing stones, dolmens and other tombs of the Late Stone and Early Bronze Age, and on the rocks in their neighbourhood are of the same Sun-cult as the Stone Circles, and presumably made by the erectors of the latter. The Cup-marks form a cryptic Hitto-Sumerian religious script used as invocations, prayers and charms. These British Cup-markings, as well as the Circles and associated pre-Christian Crosses on Ancient Briton coins, are discovered to be identical with those found on the solar amulets of the Trojans, accompanied by explanatory archaic Sumerian, now observed and deciphered for the first time. The god-names, moreover, in these prehistoric British Cup-markings, and in the ancient Sumerian, as well as the numeral names, as used by the Sumerians and Hitto-Phœnicians, are the identical chief god-names and numeral names, as used by the ancient Aryans, the classic Greeks, Indo-Aryans, Goths and Ancient Britons and in English.

*We have thus gained still further positive and conclusive proof of the Aryan Origin of the Sumerians and of the Hitto-Phœnician Origin of the Britons and Scots; and further solid evidence connecting the Early Britons with the Trojans, as recorded in the Early British Chronicles.*

FIG. 43A.—Tascio or *Dias* horseman and horse of the Sun on Briton coins of 1st cent. B.C., with Cross and Circle marks.
(After Poste.)
This is the Horse invoked in last stanza of Amorite tablet, pp. 257-8. Note the 5 circles of Tascio, and *cp.* figs. on pp. xv., 285, etc.

# XIX

## "Sun-Worship" & Bel-Fire Rites in Early Britain Derived from the Phœnicians

*Disclosing Phœnician Origin of Solar Emblems on pre-Christian Monuments in Britain, on pre-Roman Briton Coins, and of "Deazil" or Sun-wise direction for Luck, etc., and John-the-Baptist as Aryan Sun-Fire Priest.*

> "The Days were ever divine as to the First Aryans."—EMERSON.[1]
>
> "We must lay his head to the East! My father [Cymbeline] hath a reason for it."—Prince Guiderius in SHAKESPEARE'S *Cymbeline.*
>
> "O Sun-God, thou liftest up thy head to the world, Thou settest thy ear to (the prayers) of mankind, Thou plantest the foot of mankind."
>
> "In the right hand of the king, the shepherd[2] of his country, May the (symbol of the) Sun-God be carried."—Sumerian Psalms.[3]
>
> "The able *Panch* [Phœnic-ians], the *Chedi* [Ceti or Catti] are all highly blest, and know the Eternal Religion—the Eternal Truths of Religion and Righteousness."—Mahā-Barata.[4]

THE " Sun-worship " which we have just seen reflected in the prehistoric Stone Circles and Cup-marked script in Britain, that are now disclosed to be Phœnician in origin, leads us to discover still further evidence of the Phœnician origin of the " Sun-worship " in Ancient Britain, which was formerly widespread over the land.

This former Sun-cult is attested by the turning of the face of the dead to the East in the Stone and Bronze Age tombs—the memory of which also in the Iron Age is

---

[1] *Society and Solitude,* 7, 137.  [2] *Siba,* disclosing Sumerian origin of English word " Shepherd."
[3] S.H.L., 490–491.  [4] M.B., *Karma Parva,* 45, 14–15, *cp.* M.B.P., 1, 157.

preserved by Shakespeare in his Cymbeline above cited. It is also attested by its very numerous sculptures and inscriptions on pre-Christian monuments in Britain, besides those of the Cup-marked inscriptions, and of caves and the Newton and other widely diffused sculptured stones; by the profusion of its symbols and stamped legends on the pre-Roman coins of Ancient Britain, by the vestiges of Bel and Beltain rites which still survive in these islands, from St. Michael's Mount in Cornwall to Shetland, and in the " Deazil " or Sun-wise direction in masonic and cryptic rites, and in the " lucky way " of passing wine at table, and in other ways now detailed.

The Early Phœnicians were, as leading Aryans, an intensely religious people. They made religion the foundation of their state and gloried in their knowledge of the Higher Religion, as recorded in their Vedic hymns and in their own epic cited in the heading. And similarly, even in regard to the later Phœnicians, it is noted:—

" In every city the temple was the chief centre of attraction, where the piety of the citizens adorned every temple with abundant and costly offerings."[1]

These Early Phœnicians—contrary to the now current notions of popular writers who have confused the real Phœnicians with the mixed Semitic and polytheistic people remaining in the later province of " Phœnicia " after it had been mostly abandoned by the Phœnicians, properly so-called—were *monotheists*, or worshippers of the One God of the Universe, whom they usually symbolized by his chief visible luminary, the Sun, as we have already seen established by a mass of concrete evidence.

This important fact, now so generally overlooked by modern writers, was well expressed by the late Prof. G. Rawlinson in his great work on the " History of the Phœnicians." He says[2]:—

" Originally, when they first occupied their settlements upon the Mediterranean, or before they moved from their primitive seats upon the shores of the Persian Gulf, *the Phœnicians were Monotheists*. . . . It may be presumed that at this early

[1] R.H.P., 320.   [2] *Ib.*, 321–2.

stage of the religion there was no idolatry; when One God alone is acknowledged and recognized, the feeling is naturally that expressed in the Egyptian hymn of praise: ' He is not graven in marble ; He is not beheld ; His abode is not known ; there is no building that can contain Him ; unknown is his name in heaven ; He doth not manifest his forms ; vain are all representations.' "[1]

It was this pure and lofty Monotheism of the Early Phœnicians, expressed in their so-called " Sun-worship " or " *Bel*-worship," which they are now found to have cherished down the ages in the Mediterranean. From it the early Phœnician merchant princes derived their happy inspiration ; they carried it with them as they ploughed the unknown seas ; they invoked it in their hours of danger, and transplanted it at their various colonies and ports of call ; and they carried it to Early Britain and disembarked and planted it along with their virile civilization, upon her soil about 2800 B.C. or earlier.

The early Aryans appear at first to have worshipped the Sun's orb itself as the visible God. In thus selecting the Sun, it is characteristic of the scientific mind of these early Aryans that in searching for a symbol for God they fixed upon that same visible and most glorious manifestation of his presence that latter-day scientists credit with having emitted the first vital spark to this planet, and with being the proximate source and supporter of all Life in this world.

But at an early period, some millenniums before the birth of Abraham, the Aryans imagined the idea of the One Universal God, as " The Father-God " behind the Sun, and thereby gave us our modern idea of God. This is evident in the early Sumerian hymns, and in the prehistoric Cup-marked prayers in Britain ; and it is also thus expressed in one of the oldest Aryan hymns of the Vedas, in a stanza which is still repeated every morning by every Brahman in India, who chants it as a morning prayer at sunrise:

" The Sun's uprising orb floods the air with brightness :
The Sun's Enlivening Lord[2] sends forth all men to labour."[3]

[1] *Records of the Past*, 4 : 109–113.
[2] *Savitri*, " The Enlivening or Vivifying God." *Cp.* M.V.M., 34.
[3] R.V., 1, 124, 1.

As "Father-God" and creator and director of the Sun and the Universe he was usually called, as we have seen, by the Hitto-Sumerians *Induru* or "*Indara*," the *Indra* of the Eastern Aryans and " Indri " of the Goths, and to him most of the Sumerian and Vedic hymns, and the Early Briton votive monuments are addressed.

[Thus as Induru (or " Indara ") he is regularly called by the Sumerians " the Creator ; " and so in the Vedas Indra is invoked as " Creator of the Sun " (3, 49, 4), " who made the Sun to shine (8, 3, 6) and raised it high in heaven " (1, 7, 3). He is " Man's sustainer, the bountiful and protector," (8, 85, 20), " the most fatherly of fathers " (10, 48, 1), " aye, our forefather's Friend of old, swift to listen to their prayers " (6, 21, 8). " There is no comforter but Thee, O Indra, lover of mankind " (1, 85, 19). Yet so specially was his bounty associated with the Sun that he still is hailed : " Indra is the Sun " (10, 89, 2).]

It was presumably the re-importation of this Aryan idea of The One Father-God symbolized by the Sun, from Syria-Phœnicia into Egypt, which occurred in or shortly before the reign of the semi-Syrian Pharaoh Akhen-aten, the father-in-law of Tut-ankh-amen, and whom we have heard stigmatized so much lately as " the heretic king " (*sic*), merely because he introduced into Egypt a purer and more refined form of Sun-worship over that contaminated with the animal worship of the ram-headed god Ammon, which predominated there in his day. The Living God behind the Sun, called by him " The Living *Aten*," is usually supposed, materialistically, to designate the radiant energy of the Sun in sustaining Life by his beams. But He is referred to as the universal creator, a god of Love and " *Father* of the king," and he has " hands," and in his pictorial representation each of the Sun's beams ends in a helping hand stretched forth to man. The famous sublime hymn to this " God of the Sun," by Aken-aten and recorded in Egyptian writing over three centuries before David, is generally regarded as the non-Jewish source from which the Hebrews derived the 104th Psalm.[1] Now this priest-king Akhen-aten was the grandson, son and husband respectively of " Syrian " or Mitani

---

[1] Prof. Breasted ; and *cp.* A. Weigall, *Life and Times of Akhnaton* 134, etc.

princesses—the "Mitani" being a branch of the Hittites—and his "propagation" of Aten-worship began when he was only 16 years old, two years after his marriage to a "Syrian" princess, and the Aten symbol was previously used by his mother, also a Syrian, when she was regent of Egypt. All the circumstances lead Sir F. Petrie and other authorities to believe that this "Aten" Sun-worship, *as well as Akhenaten's new art*, which adorns Tut-ankh-amen's tomb, was derived from "Syria,"[1] *i.e.*, Syria-Phœnicia; and that "new" art is seen to be patently Phœnician.

The later representation of God in human form by the Sumerians and some of the later Aryans was presumably led down to by their long habit of invoking him as "Father" and "King," and thus conjuring up a mental picture of a father and king in human form. Such "graven images" we have seen in the Sumerian seals (Fig. 33, etc.); and amongst some of the later Phœnicians (see Fig. 1, p. 2), and on Phœnician coins, (Fig. 64, etc.), Babylonian seals, in Medo-Persian and later Mithra cult (see Fig. 10, p. 46), and among the classic Greeks and Romans. But the purer "Sun-worshippers" appear to have religiously abstained from making graven images of God, as in the Ancient Briton coins and pre-Christian monuments, as in our Newton Stone; nor is there any reference to such images in the Gothic Eddas. Thus the purer Sumerians sing in their psalms:

"Of Induru [Ia or "Jove"], can anyone comprehend thy Form?
Of the Sun-god, can anyone comprehend thy Form?"[2]

On the other hand, the Phœnicians frequently made statues of Hercules, who, Herodotus tells us, was merely a canonized human Phœnician hero, and thus analogous to St. George. They carved the image of their marine eponymic tutelary Barati or Britannia on their coins (see Fig. 5, p. 9), and elsewhere, as a protecting angel and not God. They also carved grotesque little images of misshapen "pygmies," which, Herodotus states, they carried on the

[1] P.H.E., 2, 210-214.
[2] S. Langdon, *Sumerian Psalms*, 77, where the name is spelt *Ea*.

prow of their ships[1]—these were evidently "gollywog" mascots, carried perhaps to humour their native crews, who were probably in part Pictish pygmies. But these are not figured on the representations of Phœnician ships.

" Bel," or properly " Bil," is the title used for this " Sun " god in the Newton Stone Phœnician inscription, in both its versions—in the Ogam the short vowel is not expressed—and this form B-L (i.e., Bil or Bel) occurs in late Phœnician inscriptions elsewhere,[2] as the title of their Father God. And it is the title surviving in Britain in connection with the " Bel Fire " rite at midsummer solstice.

This name Bil or " Bel " is now disclosed to be derived from the Sumerian (i.e., Early Aryan) word for " Fire, Flame or Blaze," namely Bil, for which the written word-sign is a picture of a Fire-producing instrument with tinder sticks.[3] It is defined with the title of " God," as " God BIL of the Sun, Darkness and Wisdom " ;[4] and the Sumerian word-sign for the " Sun " itself is defined in the glosses as meaning " God Bēl," i.e., the old Father God of the Sun-temple at Nippur, the oldest Sun-temple in Babylonia, and the Bel who in the oldest Sumerian hymns " settled the places of the Sun and Moon."[5]

As this word " Bil," however, is a purely Sumerian (i.e., Aryan) word, when the Semites of the Chaldees in Babylonia borrowed from the Sumerians the idea of this Father-God, and having no name of their own resembling it with the meaning of " Fire " or " Flame," they appear to have equated that name to their Semitic word " Bal " or " Baal " meaning " Lord, Master or Owner," which they also spelt " Bel " and " Bilu " ;[6] but which possesses no suggestion of Fire, Flame or the Sun, like the original Sumerian or Aryan word. Yet this Semitic Bēl, thus derived from the solar Aryan Sumerian Father-God Bil, is often invested with Fire, as the paramount god of their Babylonian

[1] Herod., 3, 37. H. describes these " pygmies," which he calls Pataikoi, as deformed like Vulcan the smith. They are believed to resemble the misshapen dwarf figurines of " Ptah, the Smith," common in Egypt.
[2] B.P.G., 20.
[3] Br., 4566, and cp. P.S.L., 58; B.B.W., 2 pp. 99-100. It is also spelt by an analogous sign which is pictured by a Fire-Torch (cp. B.B.W., 2, 101).
[4] Br., 4588.    [5] S.H.L., 103.    [6] M.D., 156-158.

pantheon. And it was clearly through this Semitic form of Bil that the Israelites admittedly appropriated his attributes for their later tribal God " Jehovah,"[1] who is so often described as encompassed by Fire, and as appearing in Fire to the Hebrew prophets, and as a Pillar of Fire leading the Israelites in the desert ; and as " a consuming Fire."[2]

Now it is of great British and Scandinavian significance that this word *Bil* or " Blaze " or " Flame " gives us still another of those radical words that have occurred incidentally and disclose the Sumerian origin of a series of words in the English and kindred modern Aryan languages. It discloses the Sumerian origin of the Old English " *Bale* " for Blaze, Flame and Fire, the Scottish *Bail*, and the corresponding words in the Norse, Swedish, etc., as seen in this equation :—

*Sumerian Origin of " Bil " or " Bel " Blaze and Flame Words in English and N. European Aryan Languages.*

| Sumer | Gothic Eddic[3] | Norse and Swede | Anglo-Saxon | Scot[4] | Old English | English |
|---|---|---|---|---|---|---|
| Bil | = Baela | = Bal, Blis | = Bael | = Bail | = Bele | = Bl-aze[5] |
|  | B l | Belyse |  | Bele |  | Fl-ash |
| =" Blaze |  | Blus |  |  |  | Fl-ame |
| " Flame  =,, | =,, | =,, | =,, | Blase |
| " Fire " | & pyre. | ,, |

We now see the significance of the name " St. Blaze " for the taper-carrying saint introduced into Early Christianity as patron of the intermediate solar festival of Candlemas Day; and probably also of the name " Bleezes " or " Blazes " for the old house on the hillock at the foot of Bennachie,

---

[1] Thus one of the latest Semitic authorities writes :

" Jahweh [Jehovah] assumes the attributes of the Baals." (J.R.B., 74). And " The Baals of the Canaanites [*i.e.*, pre-Israelite people of Phœnicia Palestine] we know were *personifications of the Sun* " (*Ib*. 75).

[2] Exodus, 3, 2 ; 19, 18 ; Isaiah, 6, 4 ; Ezek., 1, 4 ; Deut., 4, 24.
[3] V.D., 54, 91. [4] J.S.D., 23.
[5] This and the corresponding Scandinavian forms seem to be a bilingual Sumerian compound *Bil-izi—Izi*, being another dialectic name for the word with the same meaning " Fire," and appears cognate with Sanskrit *Vilas*= " Flash " and the Greek *Phalos* " bright."

# BEL FIRE RITES IN BRITAIN

commanding a view of the Newton Stone site, and possibly the site of an altar blazing with perpetual fire to Bel, to whom that stone was dedicated.

The " Bel-Fire " or " Bel-tane " rites and games which still survive in many parts of the British Isles are generally recognized to be vestiges of a former widely prevalent worship of " Bel " in these islands, extending from St. Michael's Mount in Cornwall to Shetland, which is now seen to have been introduced by the Phœnicians, and to be a survival of the great solar festival celebrations at the Summer solstice. The name " Bel-tane " or " Bel-tine " means literally " Bel's Fire."[1]

The rite of Bel-Fire now surviving in the British Isles is mostly a mere game performed by boys and young people on Midsummer eve in the remoter parts of the country. On a moor, a *circle* is cut on the turf sufficient to hold the company and a bonfire is lit inside, and torches are waved round the head (presumably in sunwise direction, see later) while dancing round the fire ; after which the individuals leap through the flames or glowing embers.[2] As a serious religious ceremony it was not infrequently practised until about a generation ago by farmers in various parts of the country and in Ireland, who on the eve of the Summer solstice passed themselves, and drove their cattle through

---

[1] " Bel-tane " or " Bel-tine " is defined by old Scottish, Irish and Gaelic writers as " Fire of the god *Bil* or *Bial* or *Bel*." Thus the Irish king Cormac at the beginning of the tenth century A.D. describes " *Bil*-tene " as Lucky Fire, and defines *Bil* or *Bial* as " an idol god." (Cormac's *Glossary*, ed. Stokes, 19, 38) ; and Keating states " Bel-tainni is the same as *Beiltcine*, that is, *teine Bheil* or Bel's Fire." Its second element *Tan* in Breton and *Tane, Tine* or *Tene*, means " Fire ' in Scottish and Irish Scottish with variant *Teind* or *Tynd*, " a spark of Fire " (J.S.D., 38, 564) and Eddic Gothic *Tandr*, " to light or kindle Fire," thus showing Gothic origin of English " *Tinder*." This *Tan* or *Tene* seems to be derived from the Akkadian *Tenū* for the Crossed Fire-producing sticks (M.D. 1176) with meaning also " to grind [firewood]," *ib*. The Breton form of the name for Bel-Fire of *Tan-Heol* is the same *Tan* (Fire) transposed + *Heol*, " the Sun " or *Bil*.

[2] Such a game was practised in the writer's boyhood in the West of Scotland. And Mr. S. Laing, the archæologist, who was born in 1810, writes with reference to these Bel-Fires lighted on the highest hills of Orkney and Shetland. " As a boy, I have rushed with my playmates through the smoke of these bonfires without a suspicion that we were repeating the homage paid to Baal." (*Human Origins*, 1897, 161.)

the flames,[1] to bring good luck for the rest of the year.[1] This clearly shows that it was essentially a simple rite of ceremonial Purification by Fire and presumably a rite of initiation into the Solar Religion by " Baptism with Fire," with the addition of Protection by the Sun as Fire. The fire employed to ignite the bonfire was doubtless the sacred Fire produced by friction of two pieces of tinder sticks or " fire-drill," as this method of producing sacred fire was employed so late as 1830 in Scotland, and was formerly common in the Hebrides,[3] where old customs linger longest.

This appears to be the same rite which is repeatedly referred to in the Old Testament of the Hebrews as practised by the pre-Israelite inhabitants of Canaan (*i.e.*, Phœnicia-Palestine), in which children were passed through fire in consecration to " Moloch "—spelt *Melek* in the old Hebrew —a name which is evidently intended for the " Meleq-art "[4] title of Hercules in the later Semitic Phœnician inscriptions, as the " Baal of Tyre," and other Phœnician cities; and thus connecting it with the Phœnicians :—

" And they built up the high places of Baal, to cause their sons and daughters to pass through the fire to Moloch [Melek]."[5]

But it seems that the Semites of Canaan who adopted the externals of the Sun-cult of their Aryan overlords, had in their inveterate addiction to bloody matriarchist sacrifices, human and other—practices also formerly current amongst the Hebrews[6]—sometimes actually burned their children to death in sacrifice, in their perverted form of worshipping Bil or Bel.[7] Now this sacrificial perversion of the simple and innocuous Bel-fire rite appears also to have been prevalent in Britain to some extent amongst the aboriginal

---

[1] Cormac in the tenth century describes two fires for the cattle to pass between.
[2] *Cp.* H.F.F., 44, etc.
[3] Carmichael, *Carmen Gaddica*, 2, 340; and Martin, *Descript. West. Islands*, ed. 1884, 113.
[4] This name, spelt *M-l-q-r-t*, is usually considered to represent Melek-qart or " King of the City."
[5] Jeremiah, 32, 35, and *cp.* 2 Kings, 23, 10.
[6] W. R. Smith, *Relig. of Semites*, 1889; H. L. Strack, *The Jew and Human Sacrifice*, Lond., 1909, for sacrifices of first-born, etc.
[7] 2 Kings, 17, 31; 21, 6. Ezekiel, 16, 21; 20, 26, etc.

Chaldees, who were also, as we have seen, addicted to human sacrifice in their Lunar cult of matriarchy with its malignant demons, under their Druid priests. Thus they changed the date of this Bel-Fire festival from the Midsummer solstice to their own May Day festival of their Mother-goddess on the First of May, which began their lunar Vegetation Year. Thus we have the vestiges of this sacrificial so-called " Beltane " rite surviving in Britain on May Day with the ceremonial sacrifice of a boy victim by lot.

[This sacrificial May Day " Beltane " rite seems, from the numerous accounts of its wide prevalence up till a few decades ago, to have been the more common, as the Aryan element is so relatively small. After cutting a circle and lighting the bonfire and torches, a cake is made of oatmeal, eggs and milk and baked in the fire, and divided up into a portion for each boy, one of the cakes being daubed black with embers. The pieces are then put into a cap, and drawn blindfolded, and whoever draws the blackened piece is the " devoted " person or victim, who is to be sacrificed to obtain good luck for the year. This " devoted " victim is, of course, nowadays released or acquitted with a penalty, which is to leap three times through the flames.[1]]

It was possibly, I think, the eating of the body of the human victims thus sacrificed by the Druid Chaldees on May Day, as a sacrament, which forms the basis of the historical references by St. Jerome and others in the early centuries of our era to the prevalence of cannibalism amongst savage tribes in Britain.

The sacred fire for igniting the fire-offering to Bil or Bel, as the God of the Sun, was generated by the Early Aryans and Phœnicians by the laborious friction of two tinder sticks or fire drill, the oldest method of fire-production. *This generation of the sacred fire by friction of two tinder sticks was also the method employed in Britain down to the Middle Ages*, for preparing the " Perpetual Fire " in shrines, and for the special " Need-Fires " in cases of dire need from plague, pestilence, drought or invasion and also presumably for lighting these Bel-Fires. The repositories for these

---

[1] For details and refs. see H.F.F., 44, etc., 336.

sacred "Perpetual Fires," thus generated, still exist in Britain in some of our churches—in Cornwall, Dorset and York—in the so-called "Cresset-stones," some of which are placed in lamp niches furnished with flues, as pointed out by Dr. Baring Gould, who remarks that in the early centuries of our era, on the introduction of Christianity, "the Church was converted into the sacred depository of the Perpetual Fire."[1] And as showing conclusively that the "Need-Fires" lit in Bel-Fire fashion by the friction of the two tinder sticks were pagan, their lighting was expressly forbidden by the Church in the eighth century; and the Church "New-Fire" was transferred to Easter Day, to adapt it to the re-arranged Christian dates, and was obtained by striking flint and steel. *"But the people in their adversity went back to their old time-honoured way of preparing their sacred fire by wood-friction in the pagan (Bel) fashion."*[2] And it is significant to notice that St. Kentigern or St. Mungo (about 550 A.D.), the patron saint of Glasgow and bishop of Strath-Clyde down to the Severn, and whose many churches still bear his name in Wales and Cornwall, is recorded to have produced his sacred fire-offering by friction with two sticks. These medieval British doubtless derived their knowledge of generating this sacred fire from the ancestral descendants of the Phœnician Part-olon and Brutus and his predecessor Barats, just as the Phœnicians had generated their Perpetual Fire in the temple of Hercules at Gades (Cadiz), the penalty for extinguishing which was death.[3]

The truly solar character of the proper Bel-Fire festival of the Aryans to whom animal sacrifice was abhorrent, is seen not only from its date being at the Summer solstice, but also from the use at that festival of a wheel symbolizing the Sun, which they rolled about to signify the apparent movement of the Sun, and that the latter is then occupying its highest point in the zodiac and is about to descend; and, significantly, this Wheel is also rolled about at Yuletide, the old pagan Fire-Festival at the shortest day, *i.e.*, the Winter solstice.[4]

[1] *Strange Survivals*, 120.   [2] *Ib.*, 122.   [3] C.A.F., 7.
[4] Durandus on Feast of St. John, H.F.F., 346.

## BEL FIRE & JOHN-THE-BAPTIST'S DAY

In the Christian period, this pagan Bel-Fire festival of the Summer solstice was early adjusted to Christianity by the Roman Church, for proselytizing purposes, making St. John the Baptist—who, we shall see, is represented in art as carrying the Fire Cross, whose priestly father offered simple Fire-incense offerings in the temple,[1] and who " came to bear witness of *The Light* "[2]—the patron saint of the old pagan Bel-Fire festival and transferred the Bel-Fire festivities to the eve of St. John's Day, the 24th of June, when they are still, or were until lately, celebrated in many parts of England,[3] as well as in Brittany and Spain,[4] also former colonies of the Phœnicians.

This fact of the association of the Bel-Fire rites with John-the-Baptist suggests that the latter, who bears an Aryan Gentile and non-Hebrew name, was himself an Aryan Gentile and of the Fire-Cross cult ; and this seems supported by many other facts, presuming Gothic affinity, which require mention here. His initiatory rite of Baptism is wholly unknown in Judaism, whereas it is a part of the ancient ritual of the Sumerian and Aryan Vedic and Eddic Gothic Sun-cult, wherein Baptism is called by the Goths *Skiri* (or " The Scouring ") which is *radically identical with the name* " *Sakhar* " *applied to it by the Sumerians*.[5] And John-the-Baptist is called " *Skiri*-Jōn " by the Christian Goths of Iceland and Scandinavia ;[6] and " Purification (by Water) Day " was officially called in Scotland, down to the reign of James VI., " *Skiri*-Thuirsday."[7] Moreover, *the father of John-the-Baptist was a Fire-priest,*[8] and presumably a Gentile,

[1] Luke, 1, 9. [2] John, 1, 7. [3] Details in H.F.F., 346, etc. [4] *Ib.*, 348–9.
[5] *Sakhar* (Br. 5082, and *Sakar* (Br. 4339). The founder of the 1st Sumer dynasty about 3100 B.C., who uses the Swastika and figures himself as a Fire-priest, often records his presentation of a " Font-pan " or " Font of the Abyss " (*Abzu-banda*) to different temples which he erected (Thureau-Dangin *Les Inscript. Sumér*, 17, etc.) Sargon I. about 2800 B.C., as high-priest who uses the Swastika, describes himself as " water-libator " and devotee *Nu-iz-śir* (= " *Nazir* " ) of God—" the *Sakhar* (or Baptist) Lord " (C.I.W.A., 3, Vol. 4, No. 7. And John-the-Baptist was also a " Nazir " or consecrated devotee (Luke i. 15, and *cp*. Numbers vi, 2 f.).
[6] V.D., 550. [7] J.S.D., 486:
[8] He offered simple Fire-incense in the temple " in the course of *Abia* " (Luke i, 5.) *Ab,* the 5th month of the Syrio-Chaldean calendar, was devoted to the worship of Bel the Fire-god, and was called by the Sumerians " Month of *Bil* or *Gi-Bil* " (?Gabriel). Br. 4579, 4587 ; Meissner 3101, or " Month of making Bil-Fire " (Br. 4621).

and his name "Zacharias," which has no meaning in Hebrew, is apparently the Sumer title of *Sakhar* " Baptist," with the personal affix *aś* or " one," corresponding to the English " ist."

The presence of Gentile Sun-priests in the temple on Mt. Moriah at Jerusalem is explained by the fact that, besides the name " Moriah "—which is recognized as meaning " Mount of the *Morias* or Amorites "[1]—that temple, long before the occupation of Jerusalem by David and its rebuilding by Solomon, was a famous ancient *Sun*-temple of the Hittites or Morites. Ezekiel says, " Jerusalem, thy father was an Amorite, and thy mother an Hittite."[2] And Jerusalem, the " IRUSLM " of the Hebrews, was already " a holy city " under that non-Hebrew name, and called by its Hittite king about 1375 B.C. (*i.e.*, over three centuries before the time of David), in his still existing original official letters, " The city of the Land of *Urusalim, the city of the Temple of the Sun-god Nin-ib-u-śu* "[3]—wherein the latter part of the name (*Ib-u-śu*) appears now to disclose the title of the pre-Israelite inhabitants of Jerusalem, the " *Ibus* " of the Old Testament Hebrew, the " Jebus-ites " of our English translation.[4] This Hittite (or Jebusite) king of Jerusalem, who is regarded as a kinsman of the Aryan Kassi princes of Babylonia,[5] bore the Gentile name of *Erikhi* or Urukhi-ma,[6] and was obviously a Sun-Fire worshipper. In his official letters to Aken-Aten, to whom he was at the time tributary, he addressed that Sun-worshipping Pharaoh, who, it will be

[1] *Encycl. Biblica*, 3200.    [2] Ezekiel, 16, 3 and 45.
[3] Amarna Letters found in Aken-Aten's archives. AL(W) 183, Berlin No. 106, lines 15, 16. Text reads : " Al mat *U-ru-sa-lim-u* ki, al-Bid an *Nin-Ib-u-śu* mu."
[4] Similarly, in the other Amarna reference to this temple AL(W) No. 55 (Brit. Mus. 12) l. 31, the word read " Nin-ib " is followed by " *buz*." " Ib " and " Nin-ib " are defined as the Sun-god Uras (Br. 10480, etc.). " Ib " also means " enclosure," temple (Br. 10488 and M.D. 1146) and " seer or priest " (Br. 10482). *Ib-u-śu* thus would mean " Temple priest of Winged Sun." " *Ib-uś* " is also defined as *Ib* + " Thresher-of-Corn " (Br. 10491 and .4713) and the Jebusite king had his threshing floor on Mt. Moriah (2 Sam. xxiv, 16, etc.).
[5] Kassi princes were staying with him and he defended them : AL(W), 180 ll. 32, etc.
[6] The first element *Eri* or *Uru* is the Sumerian for " man or hero " (Br. 5858) and thus disclosed as Sumer source of Greek '*Eros*, Sanskrit and Latin *Vir*, Gothic *Ver*, Anglo-Saxon *Were* and English " hero."

remembered, called himself " Son of the Sun," as " My Sun, the great Bil Fire-Torch."[1]

The Israelitic occupation of the Sun-temple and its court on Mt. Moriah, from about 1012 B.C. onwards, was evidently only a joint one, shared with the Jebusites, Hittites and Amorites of Palestine and their descendants. Shortly before his death about 1015 B.C., King David, we are told, purchased from the Jebusite king of Jerusalem, Araunah (whose name is in series with that of Urukhi and "Uriah the Hittite"), a site on " the threshing place " of that king, " where the angel of the Lord was," in order to build there an altar.[2] That spot was thus outside the Jebusite temple itself, as sacrificial altars were in the open air. It is noteworthy that " the angel of the Lord " was already there before David obtained a part of the site ; for it is significant that *the " Sun-god " Nin-ib is otherwise styled " Taś," i.e., the Hitto-Sumerian Archangel of God and the " Tascia " of the Briton coins and monuments*, as we have seen. We thus have confirmation through the Old Testament tradition of the existence of this pre-Israelitic temple of the Aryan Archangel of God on Mt. Moriah, as recorded in the original contemporary letters of its pre-Israelitic king. And David's great fear of that angel[3] is explained by the latter being the Hittite tutelary of Jerusalem and Palestine which David had invaded.

The temple which Solomon began to build on Mt. Moriah about 1012 B.C., and which was built mainly through the agency of Phœnicians from Tyre, was presumably merely the rebuilding of the old Hittite Bil or Bel shrine, and continued to be shared by the Jebusites, of whom we are informed that " the children of Judah could not drive them out, but the Jebusites dwell with the children of Judah at Jerusalem unto this day "[4]—*i.e.*, until the date of compiling the Old Testament, about the 6th century B.C.

---

[1] AL (W) 181, (184, etc.). Berlin text, l. i, reads *Zal-ia gi-Bil ma* wherein *Zal*=Sol or Sun, and *ma*=Sumerian source of English " my."
[2] 2 Sam. xxiv, 16–24. The Revised Version translates the text literally as " all this did Araunah the king give unto the king."
[3] 1 Chron. xx, 15–30.
[4] Joshua xv, 63 ; Judges i, 21.

The Solomon temple had for its porch the characteristic Phœnician pillars of the Bel Sun-temple, it was consecrated by "Fire from Heaven,"[1] it contained images of the Sun,[2] and of Sun-horses,[3] and it and its court continued to be used, more or less, for Sun and Bel worship down to the period of its destruction about 580 B.C.

[Solomon worshipped "Baal"[4] as well as Iahvh—and "Baal" is used in the Old Testament occasionally as a title of Iahvh or Jehovah.[5] He set in the porch the two colossal pillars of the Phœnician Bel temples under their Phœnician names, and supposed to represent the Phœnician deity.[6] About this time "the Children of Israel served Baal;"[7] and fifty years later a successor, Ahab, "served Baal and worshipped him,"[8] so that there were only "seven thousand in Israel, all the knees of which have not bowed unto Baal."[9] Twenty years later Ahaz, with his high-priest Urijah, placed an altar of Baal of Phœnician pattern in the temple and erected "Baal altars in every corner of Jerusalem."[10] Two centuries later, Manasseh placed Baal altars and vessels for Baal worship inside the temple;[11] and Bel and Sun-worship still were practised in the temple and its courts about the time of its destruction by Nebuchadnezzar, about 580 B.C., as recorded by Ezekiel.]

The Sun-worship in the temple, as described by Ezekiel, is especially significant. He refers to a non-Judaist image at "the door of the gate of the inner court where was the seat of the image which provoketh to jealousy,"[12] and he calls it by the name used by the later Phœnicians for their image of Melqart and Resef (Taśia).[13] He further says: "In the *inner court* of the Lord's house, at the door of the temple of the Lord, between the porch and the altar, were about five and twenty *men with their backs to the temple of the Lord and their faces towards the East, and they worshipped*

---

[1] 2 Chron. vii, 1.   [2] 2 Chron. xiv, 5 ; xxxiv, 4 and 7, Revised Version.
[3] 2 Kings xxiii, 11.   [4] 1 Kings xi, 5.   [5] Hosea, ii, 16 ; Jer. xxxi, xxxii.
[6] 1 Kings vii, 21. These two pillars are described by Herodotus, ii, 44. They bore the Phœnician names of "Buz-Iakin" (Boaz-Jachia). *Cp. Encycl. Biblica*, 4933.
[7] Judges ii, 11–13.   [8] 1 Kings, xvi, 31.   [9] *Ib.* xix, 18.
[10] 2 Chron. xxviii, 24 ;  2 Kings xvi.
[11] 2 Chron. xxxiii, 3 ;  2 Kings xxi, 3 ;  xxiii, 4.
[12] Ezek. viii, 3, etc.
[13] C.I.S.T., 88, 2, 3, 7 ; and 91, 1. This "Salmu," properly Sumerian "Salam," is especially applied to Sun-god. M.D., 879.

the Sun towards the East."[1] And here it is important to note that the sacred place of the Sun-worshippers was in the court inside the porch, on the flat top of the sacred mount of their ancestors, and outside the Jewish sanctuary containing the tabernacle and ark, which for them was defiled by its bloodshed meat offerings.

Similarly, in the new temple, rebuilt by the Sun-worshipping Cyrus the Medo-Persian, as " The house of God of Heaven," and begun about 535 B.C.[2]—for which services he was affiliated to Iahvh as " The Messiah " or " The Lord's anointed "[3]—Bel worship appears also to have been practised, more or less.[4] And significantly in Herod's new temple, which was still in course of building when Christ began His ministry,[5] there was an outer court inside the walls of the " temple " enclosure, called " The Gentiles' Court,"[6] thus recognizing the right of access for Gentiles (Fire-worshippers?) to a part of the summit of the sacred mount of their Aryan ancestors. This Outer Court was presumably the part of the " Temple " in which the father of John-the-Baptist performed his " course of Abia," and the part frequented by Christ.

The word " Temple " in our English translation of the Bible is used in different senses, and for different words. It is used for the Hebrew words for " Palace," " The House," " House of God or of Iahvh," which variously designated the smallish building in the centre of the great court, enshrining the ark in a dark chamber, surrounded by cells for offices, the storage of vessels, furniture and treasures. *It was not a place of worship, in the sense of a meeting-house of worshippers.* " The small size of the Temple proper is accounted for by the fact that *the worshippers remained outside, the priests only went within.*"[7] The altars were in the court in the open air. " *In this great or outer court the*

---

[1] Ezek. viii, 16.     [2] Ezra, i, 2, etc. ; vi, 4, etc.
[3] Isaiah xlv, 1, and *cp.* xliv, 28.
[4] Ezra ix, 1, etc., about 450 B.C. Hosea ii, 16, etc., xiv, 3 ; and later books Amos to Malachi. Antiochus I. about 250 B.C. set up an altar to Jupiter (1 Maccab. i, 23, etc., and Josephus *Ant.* xii, 7, 6).
[5] John ii, 20. It was not completed till 62–64 A.D. *Encycl. Biblica*, 4948.
[6] *Enc. Bib.*, 4945.
[7] *Cambridge Companion to Bible*, 153.

*prophets generally addressed the people, as also did our Lord on many occasions ; and even this court is termed ' The House of the Lord,' and is ' The Temple ' in the New Testament."*[1] It must certainly have been this outer court of " the temple " which Christ called " My Father's House," from whence he drove out " the sheep and the oxen, and he poured out the changer's money, and overthrew their tables " ;[2] for neither religiously nor physically could these have been within the temple-house proper. It was " in the presence of all his people *in the courts* of the Lord's house " that David paid his vows[3] : " For a day *in thy courts* is better than a thousand."[4] And it is to be noted that the gateway on the N. side—*i.e.*, where the non-Judaist Phœnician " image of jealousy " was formerly located—was called " *The Gate of Sparks*," and it had an upper chamber.[5] This was possibly where the father of John-the-Baptist performed his Fire-offering course in " The month of Making Bel-Fire " ; and the simple burning of incense is repeatedly referred to in the O.T. as the usual form of Baal worship.

The Cross-sceptre or staff traditionally carried by John-the-Baptist was also an especial emblem of the " Sun-god " Nin-ib of Jerusalem. As " Son of God " that " Sun-god " is given in the Sumerian the synonym of " God of the Cross $+$,"[6] wherein that Cross in the form of St. George's Red Cross is defined as " Wood-Sceptre," also " Fire " and " Fire-god " under the name of *Bar* or *Maś*[7] (*i.e.*, the English " Bar " and " Mace "). There were thus very real, although forgotten, historical reasons for the crusaders seeing visions of St. George's Red Cross upon the battlements of Jerusalem beckoning them on to rescue this old ancestral Aryan shrine from the Saracens. Indeed, it now appears as if the numerous

---
[1] S. Lee, *Hebrew Lexicon*, 636, *cp.* Jer. xxvi, 2 and 2 Kings xi, 13.
[2] John ii, 14–15. The word used in the Greek text here, translated " temple," is *'ieron, i.e.*, " holy or sacred thing," and is seldom used for a temple building (*cp.* Liddell & Scott, 727) ; whereas in verses 19–20 the word for " temple " is *naos*, the classic word for a temple " building."
[3] Psalms cxvi, 19.    [4] *Ib.* lxxxiv, 10.
[5] *Encl. Bibl.*, 4946, the word is *Nisus*.    [6] Br., 11096.
[7] *Bar*=Gi-Bil or " Great Fire-god " (Meissner, 998) ; also *Baru,* a priest (Meissner, 994), thus defining the Sumerian priest as " the carrier of the *Bar* or Wood-Cross."

# JOHN-THE-BAPTIST AN ARYAN FIRE-PRIEST 279

commands by Christ to his hearers and disciples, each to "take up his Cross and follow Me,"[1] were references to the visible, Fiery Red Cross sceptre-symbol of the Sun-cult of the One Father-God of the Hittite temple of Jerusalem, the symbol carried by John-the-Baptist who baptized Christ, and *not* an anticipation of the Crucifix.[2] And Christ baptized "with *Fire*."[3]

This now suggests that not only the Cross-carrying John-the-Baptist and his father, the Fire-priest Zacharias, but also Christ of Galilee of the Gentiles, were Gentiles of the Aryan religion of the One and Only Father-God with his symbol of the Sun Cross, and its associated rite of Baptism, and whose ancient Aryan shrine was at Jerusalem. This appears to explain the anti-Judaist teaching of Christ and John the Baptist, and why Christ and the father of John, as well as his earlier priestly namesake, were slain by the Jewish priests.[4] It also seems to explain the visit of "the wise men from the East" to Jerusalem, at the Nativity of Our Lord. The persons generally called "wise men from the East" were, we find, as corrected in the Revised Version of the New Testament, "*Magi*,"[5] a term solely used for the priests of the Sun and Fire-cult; and this name is obviously derived from the Sumerian *Maś*, as "bearer of the Maś or + Cross." Moreover, the related words translated in our English version "from the East" occur in the original Greek text as "from *Anatolia*"[6]—Anatolia being the middle part of Asia Minor, including Cappadocia, the old homeland of the Hittites and their Sun-cult, and the traditional home of St. George and his Red Cross.

[1] Matt. xvi, 24, etc. The word used here for cross is *stauros*, usually employed in classic Greek for a stave, or wooden bolt, cognate with Gothic *stafr* or staff, sanskrit *stavara*, "firm." It seems cognate with the Akkad word for this + sign *Śadadu*, defined as "The Wood of Winged God, the Light Red Cross" (Br. 1800)..
[2] The same Greek word *stauros* is used for the Crucifix in the New Testament.
[3] Matt. iii, 11.
[4] Matt. xxiii, 25; 2 Chron. xxiv, 20; G.L.S., Novr. 148 on Zacharias and *cp. Enc. Bibl.*, 5373 for refs.
[5] Matt. ii, 1.
[6] '*Apo anatolōn*. Yet *anatolē*, literally "Rising up," especially of Sun, is used sometimes poetically for "East."

It is also noteworthy that the traditional place to which the infant Christ was carried in the Flight to Egypt was the great Temple of the Sun at Heliopolis, or " The House of the Phœnix "—the resurrecting Sun-bird of the Phœnicians and the Ancient Egyptians, to the north of Cairo.[1] And there, to the present day, is " The Virgin's Tree " and " The Virgin's Well," where, by the tradition of the Copts, one of the oldest sects of the Early Christians, the Virgin and Child with Joseph rested in Egypt.[2] This, again, appears to connect Christ with the Aryan Sun-cult.

Racially, also, we are informed that the Virgin Mary was " the cousin of Elisabeth,[3] the mother of John-the-Baptist," and that Elisabeth was " of the daughters of Aaron."[4] Now " Aaron," latterly used as a generic term for the priesthood in Jerusalem, is shown by leading biblical authorities to have been " a name extremely probably absent altogether from the earliest document of the Hexateuch in its original form, and apparently introduced by the editor"[5] scribes later. This raises the possibility that the name *AHRN*, as " Aaron " is spelt in the old Hebrew, is really derived from the name of " Araunah," the Jebusite king and evidently priest-king of the Sun-temple at Jerusalem; for the Hittite kings were usually priest-kings, and the title *Ibus* or " Jebus-ite," we have seen, implied priesthood. That name, commonly rendered " Araunah," is spelt in the old Hebrew variously as ARUNH, AURNH, ARNIH, and *ARNN*. The statement, therefore, that Elisabeth was " of the daughters of Aaron," might mean that she was a descendant of Araunah, the Hittite or Jebusite priest-king of Jerusalem, and that her cousin Mary, the mother of Christ, was also in the royal line of descent from the pre-Israëlitic Aryan king of Jerusalem. Such a descent would account for the repeated references to the

---

[1] Herodotus ii, 73.
[2] Baedeker's *Lower Egypt*, 333 ; Lunn, *Mediterranean*, 1896, 251. The ancient sycamore is about 250 years old, and replaced a former old sacred tree, and was railed in by the late Empress Eugénie at the opening of the Suez Canal. The Phœnix Sun-bird was supposed to appear every morning to the faithful on the top of the sacred Persea tree there (B.G.E. ii, 97, 371).
[3] Luke i, 36.  [4] Luke i, 5.  [5] *Enc. Bibl.* 2.

## MICHAEL'S MOUNT OR CASTLE OF THE SUN

Jewish fears that Christ claimed a temporal kingship as " King of the Jews " (? Jebus) in Jerusalem.[1]

The location of the holy family in Nazareth of " Galilee of the Gentiles " is also suggestive of Gentile and Hittite relationship. Nazareth is near and almost overlooked by the mount, the scene of " The Sermon on the Mount," which is still called, from its double peak, " The Horns of the Hittites." Gentilic Galilee was the scene of most of Christ's preaching. Here he selected his disciples, most of whom, besides Bartholomew, we shall find bear Aryan Gentile names, as did John-the-Baptist, and his father Zacharias, the Bel-Fire priest.

Resuming now our survey of the Bel-Fire rites in ancient Britain, we find that one of the earliest or earliest of all centres in Britain for these ancient Bel-Fire rites was at the ancient Phœnician tin-port itself in Cornwall, or " *Belerium*," as the Romans called it. That tin-port, St. Michael's Mount, rising as a spiry islet, and natural temple, off Marasion with its Stone Circle, and connected with that town at low tide, was formerly called " Din-Sol " or " Castle of the Sun."[2] Its old sacred character is also reflected in its Roman title of " Forum Jovis " or " Market of Jove," as Bel we have seen was *Ia* or " Jahveh," and he was usually called " Jove " (or Jupiter) by the Romans in their eastern provinces and elsewhere, where the Bel cult was prevalent ; and the thunderbolts which they put in the hands of Jove were of crackling tin, possibly with reference to that Phœnician metal. The Fire festivals surviving, or till recently surviving here and in Cornwall generally, are held on the eve of St. John the Baptist's Day, and are significantly

---

[1] The references to Jewish rites of circumcision, etc., in regard to Christ are not necessarily historical but possibly additions of later Jewish convert copyists for proselytizing purposes. They do not appear in Mark, the earliest and most authentic of the gospels. The Davidic genealogy also, which differs widely in its two versions in Matthew and Luke, refers only to Joseph, who is represented as not being the father of Our Lord.

[2] It is called " Din Sol " in the Book of Landaff (C.B., 1, 4 ; and L.H.P., 91). *Din* is Cornish for the Cymric and Scottish *Dun*, " a fort or town " (as in " Dun-Barton "), and is the Gothic Eddic *Tun*, " an enclosure or dwelling," and thus the Gothic source of the English " Town," from Sumer *Du* (*Du-na*) " dwelling, mound " (Br. 9579, 9591). *Sol* is the Cornish and Gothic Eddic for " Sun " (also in Latin), which is now disclosed to be derived from the Sumerian *Zal*, " The Sun."

associated especially with the tin mines worked by the ancient Phœnicians.

["The boundary of each tin mine in Cornwall is marked by a long pole with a bush on the top of it. These on St. John's Day are crowned with flowers. It is usual at Penzance to light fires on this occasion and dance and sing around them.[1]
"Still to this age the hills around Mount's Bay are lighted at Midsummer eve with the bonfire, and still the descendants of the old Dunmonii wave the torch around their heads after the old, old rite."[2] And similarly in Devon, etc., etc.[3]]

The Stone Circles, which we have seen to be early Phœnician, also appear to have been especial sites of these Bel-Fire rites, and for the production of the sacred Fire.[4] And we have seen that these rites were latterly held within a circle cut on the turf, which suggests that the Stone Circles were thus used as Sun temples. And we have found that the "Cup-mark" inscriptions on circles and their neighbourhood are prayers of the Sun-cult.

Altogether, the Phœnician origin and introduction of the Bel-Fire rites into Britain, as part of the old "Sun-worship," thus appears to be clearly established.

The Sun-wise direction of walking around a sacred or venerated person or object in the direction of the hands of a clock or watch, in the direction of the Sun's apparent movement in northern latitudes, from east to west, is admittedly part of the "Sun-worship" ritual. It is inculcated in the old Aryan Vedic hymns and epics for respect and good luck and is called "The Right Way" or "Right-handed Way" (pra-)*Daxina*, the "*Deasil*" or "Right-hand Way"[5] of the Scots, who call the opposite direction "Withersins" or "Contrary to the Sun," which is considered unlucky. This sun-wise direction is that in which the votaries are usually figured walking on the old Sumerian sacred seals in approaching the enthroned "Sun-god"; and it is the direction in which all Indo-Aryan votaries approached and passed

---

[1] H.F.F., 347.   [2] L.H.P., 15.   [3] H.F.F., 44, etc., 347, etc.
[4] For Circles at Stennis, Merry Maidens, etc., L.S., 191, etc.; and D. MacRitchie, *Testimony of Tradition*.
[5] Or Dessil, in Gaelic Deesoil, Deisheal, J.S.D., 150. The root of these words is *Da*, "the right hand" in Sumerian.

Buddha, and in which Buddhists and Hindus still pass their sacred monuments, as opposed to the disrespectful and unlucky way of the devil-worshippers in the contrary direction. This Sun-wise direction and its solar meaning as " The Right Way " were commonly practised and well-recognized formerly in England, as evidenced by Spenser in his *Faery Queen*, when he makes the false Duessa in her enmity to the Red Cross Knight and Fairy Queen emphasize her curse by walking round in the opposite direction :—

" That say'd, her round about she from her turn'd,
*She turn'd her contrary to the Sunne,*
Thrice she her turn'd contrary, and return'd,
All contrary: *for she the Right did shunne."*

It is still practised in Britain in masonic ritual and by superstitious country folk in walking round sacred stones and sacred walls supposed to possess lucky or curative magical virtues. It is the " lucky way " of passing wine at table. And it is the direction adopted by the Sumerians and all Aryans and Aryanized people for their writing, as opposed to the Semitic or Lunar style, in the reversed or retrograde left-handed direction.

This Sun-wise or " Right Way " was the direction in which the Fire was carried and the circumambulation made in the Bel-Fire ceremonies.

[Thus, in recording the practice of this " Dessil " in the Hebrides, Martin states " there was an antient custom to make a fiery circle about the houses, corn, cattle, etc., belonging to each particular family. A man carried fire in his *right* hand, and went round, and it was called Dessil from the right hand, which is called Dess." And he adds that Dessil is " proceeding sun-ways from East to West."[1]]

Solar symbols in Ancient Britain are also especially profuse and widespread on the pre-Roman Briton coins, pre-Christian monuments and caves, although they have not hitherto been recognized as of solar import. On Early Briton coins the very numerous circles (often arranged in

[1] H.F.F., 175.

groups like cup-marks) sometimes concentric and rayed, along with wheels and crosses, spirals, single-horse sometimes with horseman, hawk or eagle, goose, winged disc, etc. (see Fig. 44), now disclosed to be purely solar symbols, have not hitherto been recognized as such, but are described by numismatists merely as " ring ornaments, annules, pellets or rosettes of pellets " and the rayed discs as " stars," and regarded apparently as being merely decorative devices, and without symbolic meaning.[1] And the horse and horseman type, although invariably represented single, and not in competition nor with chariots, are fancied to be horse and chariot racing in Olympian games borrowed from Macedonian coinage, notwithstanding that the latter is devoid of the Briton associated solar symbols.

The *circle* symbol for the Sun's disc was early used by the Sumerians, as we have seen, in their cup-mark script, and it is one of the common ways of representing the Sun in the Sumerian and Hitto-Phœnician seals. In these seals the Sun is also represented by the dual and concentric circle, rayed circle, petalled and rosetted circles, spirals and swastikas, *precisely as we find it figured in all these conventional ways in the Early British coins.*[2]

The equivalence and interchange of these various conventional ways of representing the Sun are well seen in the series of Briton coins here figured (Fig. 44).

It will be noticed that the Sun above the Sun-horse is figured as a simple disc or the dual Sun-disc (corresponding to " cups ") in *b*, rayed in *a*, rosetted as circles around a central one in *c*, as a wheel with 2 concentric circles and spirals in *d*, as circled disc with reversed or returning swastika feet and concentric circle with spirals in *e*, and as Sun-hawk with the dual Sun-disc in *f*. In *g* and *i* the upper Sun symbol is 8-petalled, rayed, and the horse tied to one of the Sun-discs and in *i* the horse is reversed with the "returning" Sun ; whilst in *h* the single Sun-disc is borne by the Sun Eagle or Hawk with head duplicated to picture the "returning " Sun. In *c*, moreover, is seen the legend *Aesv*,

---

[1] E.B.C., 46 and 58, etc., *passim ;* and numismatic works generally.
[2] See Sumerian and Hitto-Phœnician originals in D.C.O. ; W.S.C., etc.

## SUN SYMBOLS ON EARLY BRITON COINS

spelt in other mintages *Asvp*, etc.[1] which significantly is the Vedic Sanskrit name for the Sun-horse, now found to be derived from the Sumerian word for "horse."[2] No more

FIG. 44.—Sun Symbols: Discs, Horse, Hawk, etc., on Early Briton Coins.
(After Evans)[3]

Note varied forms of Sun's Disc above horse, as circle, rayed, wheel, spiral, swastika, winged Disc. Also Cross in *a*, Horse tied to Sun in *g* and *i* and the legend *Aesv*, the Vedic name for Sun-Horse. And in *a* the Sun-horse leaps over the Gate of Sunset, as in Hittite Seals, see Fig. 37.

complete evidence, therefore, could be forthcoming for the solar character and Hitto-Sumerian origin of these emblems

[1] *Asvp, Eciv, Eisw*, see E.B.C., 385–6, 389, 410, and C.B.G., 1, lxxxix.
[2] Sumerian *Ansu* (or *AS?*), "a horse," Akkad *Sisŭ*, Br., 4986, and Pinches *Signatures*, 5, col. 3, where it means "ass."
[3] E.B.C., Plates: *a*, Pl. 411; *b*, 5, 14; *c*, 15, 8; *d*, 14, 3; *e*, 14, 1; *f*, 14, 6; *g*, E., 2; *h-i*, E., 4.

on the Ancient Briton coins. The interchangeability of the Sun's vehicle seen in the British coins, etc., as Horse (*Asvin*), Deer (or Goat), Goose, and Hawk or Falcon is voiced in the Vedas, and often in dual form :—

> " O *Asvin* (Horse) like a pair of Deer
> Fly hither like Geese unto the mead we offer . . .
> With the fleetness of the Falcon."—R.V. 5, 78, 2-4.

The Deer, Goat and Goose, symbols associated with the Sun by Hitto-Sumerians and Phœnicians, and on Briton coins, etc., are seen in next chapter.

This solar character of these devices on the Early Briton coins is still further seen in the specimens in Fig. 67. p. 349. The Sun is borne on the shoulders of the Eagle or Hawk, which in the third transfixes with its claws the Serpent of the Waters or Death. In the second the winged horse is tied to the Sun and is passing over the 3 "cup-marks" of "Earth" (or Death). And on its obverse is the legend *Tascia*, the name of the Hitto-Sumerian archangel of the Sun, as we found in the cup-mark inscriptions in Britain and in the Hitto-Sumerian seals and amulets from Troy; and in the name of the Sun-temple in Jerusalem. It is a very common name on the Briton coins, as we shall see. *This name "Tascia" thus connects the Briton coins and Cup-marks directly with the Hitto-Sumerian seals and the amulets of Troy.*

The Sun-Horse, figured so freely on the Briton coins, does not appear on Early Sumerian or Hittite seals, where its place is taken by the Sun-Hawk or Eagle. But it appears later and on Phœnician coins[1] and on the Greco-Phœnician coins of Cilicia from about 500 B.C. (see Figs. later), and on archaic seals from Hittite Cappadocia.[2] This horse is presumably the basis of Thor's horse (or Odinn's) of the Goths and Ancient Britons—on which Father Thor himself as Jupiter Tonans, The Thunderer, with his bolts, latterly rode, and he is so figured riding on early Briton monuments.

[1] For the galloping horse on Phœnician coins of Carthage and Sicily, sometimes with Angel and Ear of Barley, see Duruy, *Hist. Romaine*, 1, 142, etc., and P.A.P., 1, 374.
[2] C.M.C., Figs. 141, 148.

The traditional worship of "Odinn's horses" still persists in some parts of England—for example in Sussex, where I observed bunches of corn tied up to the gables of several old timbered cottages and steadings, and was told that it was to feed "Odinn's horses" as a propitiation against lightning bolts. Offerings of grain to Indra's Sun-horses are repeatedly mentioned in the Vedic hymns; and the horses are invoked also in prayers as the vehicle for Indra's visitations :—

> " They who for Indra, picture his horses in their mind,
> And harness them to their prayers,
> Attain by such (pious) deeds an (acceptable) offering."—
> —R.V., I, 20, 2.

The Sun-horse of the Ancient Britons is also the source of the modern superstition regarding the good luck of finding a horse-shoe pointing towards you—on the notion that it might have been dropped by Odinn's horse.

The *Spirals* also, which are found on British coins (as in Fig. 44, etc.), on Bronze Age work and on prehistoric monuments and rocks in Britain, and usually in series of twos, are already found in Sumerian, Hittite and Phœnician Seals, and as a decorative device on vases, etc., in old Phœnician settlements in Cyprus and Crete and along the Mediterranean. Yet the meaning of this spiral does not appear to have been hitherto elicited. It is now seen by our new evidence to represent the dual phases of the Sun of the Sumerians. The right-handed or westward moving spiral represented the Day Sun, and the left-handed or eastward moving spiral represented the "returning" Sun at Night—as we have already seen illustrated through the Sumerian cup-marks with standard Sumerian script and on the amulets of Troy. The concentric "Rings," which have usually a radial "gutter," and are often arranged in twos and sometimes threes, now appear to be merely an easy way, by means of the "gutter," of giving the effect of a spiral.

And so widespread was "Sun-worship" formerly in Ancient Britain, and so famous in antiquity were the

Ancient Britons as " Sun-worshippers," that Pliny remarks that the Ancient Persians, who are generally regarded as the pre-eminent Sun-worshippers of the Old World, actually seemed to have derived their rites from Britain.[1]

These further facts in regard to the source and prevalence of " Sun-worship " and Bel-Fire rites in the religion of the One God in Early Britain furnish additional proof that these elements of the Higher Civilization and Religion and their names were introduced into the British Isles by the Aryan Barat Catti, or Brito-Phœnicians.

FIG. 44A. St. John-the-Baptist with his Cross-sceptre or Sun-mace.
(After Murillo.)

[1] Nat. Hist., 30.

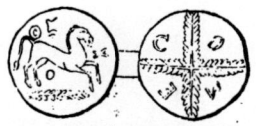

FIG. 44B.—Ancient Briton coin with Corn Sun-Cross, Andrew's **X** Cross, Sun-horse, etc.
(After Poste.)

## XX

## SUN CROSS OF HITTO-PHŒNICIANS IS ORIGIN OF PRE-CHRISTIAN CROSS ON BRITON COINS AND MONUMENTS AND OF THE " CELTIC " AND " TRUE " CROSS IN CHRISTIANITY

*Disclosing Catti, " Hitt-ite " or Gothic Origin of " Celtic " or Runic Cross, Fiery Cross, Red Cross of St. George, Swastika and " Spectacles," Crosses on Early Briton Coins, etc. ; introduction of True Cross into Christianity by the Goths ; and ancient " Brito-Gothic " Hymns to the Sun.*

> " Through storm and fire and gloom.
> I see it stand,
> Firm, broad and tall,
> The Celtic Cross that marks our Fatherland,
> Amid them all !
> Druids and Danes and Saxons vainly rage
> Around its base,
> It standeth shock on shock, and age on age,
> Star of our scatter'd race ! "[1]

STILL further striking new evidence of the Phœnician origin of the Britons and Scots, properly so-called, and of their Civilization and pre-Christian Religion of the Cross, and of its effect upon the British form of Christianity is now discovered through the Sun Cross on the Phœnician monument at Newton, and on so many of the other pre-Christian monuments in Britain, and on the Early Briton pre-Roman Catti Coins, and in the Runic or so-called " Celtic " Cross, the Fiery Cross, the Red Cross of St. George,

[1] T. Darcy McGee in *Lyra Celtica*, ed. E. A. Sharpe. 366.

the crosses of the Union Jack and associated Crosses on the Scandinavian ensigns.

The name "Cross" is now discovered to be derived from the Sumerian (*i.e.* Early Phœnician) word *Garza*, which is defined as "Sceptre or Staff of the Sun-God," and also "Sceptre of the King."[1] And its word-sign is pictured by the two-barred Cross, or battle-axe (*Khat* the root of *Khat-ti* or Hittite, see Fig. 46 *b*) springing from the rayed Sun (Fig. 46 *g̃*). In its simpler form it is the Cross of the Trojan amulets (Fig. 31 *a*, p. 238, and Fig. 46 *h* & *i*); and it survives to the present day in practically its original form in the "Mound" symbol of sovereignty (Fig. 47 *H*) borne in the hand of kings in the modern Aryanized world.

The Sun Cross, engraved by our Phœnician Cassi, king of the Scots, on his votive pillar at Newton to the Sun-god Bil, and engraved on many other pre-Christian monuments (see Fig. 47), and stamped upon many Early Briton coins (Fig. 3, etc.), now supplies us for the first time with the key to the manner in which the True Cross or "Fiery Cross" emblem of Universal Victory of the Sun-God Bil, which is figured so freely upon Hittite and Sumerian sacred seals from the fourth millennium B.C. onwards, was substituted in Christianity by the Goths for the Crucifix of Christ—which Crucifix was of quite a different shape from the True Cross or Sun Cross, now used in modern Christianity.

The earliest form of the True Cross or Sun Cross was, I find, the shape +,[2] wherein the arms are of equal length —the so-called "Greek Cross" and "Red Cross of St. George," and "The Short Cross" of numismatists. It occurs in this form as the symbol for the Sun and its God in the sacred seals of the Hitto-Sumerians from the fifth

---

[1] Br. 5644 and 5647.
[2] This is given as the first sign in the Ogam inscription on the Newton Stone, as transcribed by Mr. Brash (B.O.I., 361) ; and a personal examination of the stone supports the view that it was not merely a vertical stroke but bore a horizontal "stem" line, though the latter is now somewhat scaled off. In any case the long single-stroke Ogam sign is represented as + in the Ogam alphabet; and see Fig. 46*a*.

## ORIGIN OF CROSS AS DIVINE SYMBOL

millennium B.C. downwards;[1] and it thus becomes evident why it is called " The *Red* Cross of St. George of Cappadocia," as it was " The *Fire* Cross" of the Hittites, whose chief centre was Cappadocia. It was very freely used also, as we have seen (Fig. 12, p. 49 and Fig. 46), by the Aryan " Cassi " Dynasty of Babylonia from about 1800 to 1100 B.C., decorated by borderlines as their emblem for the Sun and its God. It was ordinarily called " The Wooden *Bar* or *Maś*," that is, literally, in English, " The Bar or Mace (in sense of a sceptre)," and thus discloses, incidentally the Sumerian origin of those two English words; and it is figured as a sceptre in the hand of the Sun God in early Sumerian sacred seals. It was also called *Pir* with meaning of " Fire,"[2] thus disclosing the Sumerian origin of our English words " *Fire* " and " *Pyre*," Gothic, Scandinavian, Anglo-Saxon, and Old English *Fyr* " Fire " and the Greek " *Pyr*."

This form of the True Cross, which occurs on so many pre-Christian monuments in Britain,[3] is called by modern ecclesiastic writers " The Greek Cross," merely because it was adopted by the Greek Christian Church about the fifth century A.D. as the form of the Christian emblem for their converts in the old Gothic region of Byzantium, who had been using this Gothic Cross as their sacred emblem from time immemorial. And it is noteworthy that the Greek Church, as well as the crusaders later, continued to use this cross in its old original Catti or Gothic sense, as a simple symbol of Divine Victory *and not as a crucifix*, never representing any body thereon; but, on the contrary, they usually colour it red, its original colour, as the red or fiery Cross of Fire.

The origin of this earliest form of the True Cross, I find, was the crossing of the twin tinder sticks used for producing by their friction the sacred fire, symbolizing the Sun's Fire. And this same process, which is still used for fire-production by primitive tribes in India, America, etc., at the present

---

[1] See illustrations in W.S.C., W.S.M. and H.H.S.   [2] Br. 1724.
[3] See numerous examples figured in S.S.S. for Scotland and W.L.W. for Wales. There is no corresponding work for England.

day (see Fig. 45), was in use in Early Britain down to the Middle Ages in the hands of St. Kentigern and others, as we have seen, for generating the sacred fire. The Vedic hymns of the ancient Indo-Aryans contain numerous references and directions for the production of the Sacred Fire in this way ; and significantly *it is the Barats who are chiefly referred to as producing the Sacred Fire with twin fire-sticks, and especially their " Able Panch " or Phœnician clan of priest-kings,*

> [Thus : " The *Bārats*—Srava the divine (and) Vāta the divine—
> Have dextrously rubbed to Life effectual Fire :
> O God of Fire, look forth with brimming riches,
> Bear us each day our daily bread ! "][1]

and it is these twin fire-sticks which, we have seen, were mystically used to form the sacred Ogam script of the Irish Scots and of the Newton Stone (Fig. 7, p. 30).

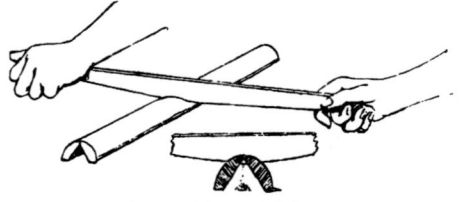

FIG. 45.—Twin Fire-sticks crossed in Fire-production, as used in modern India.
(After Hough).[2]
Note the sticks are bamboo. The lower section shows how the heat of the sawing ignites the falling sawdust as tinder.

The Cross was thus freely used as the symbol of Divine Victory of the Sun on the earliest Sumerian (or Early Aryan) sacred seals from about 4000 B.C., and continued so to be used by the Hittites, Phœnicians, Kassis, Trojans, Goths and Ancient Britons, and worn as an amulet down through the ages into the Christian period. It was figured both in its simple form, and also decorated and ornamented in various

[1] R.V., 3, 23, 2.
[2] W. Hough, *Methods of Fire-making.* Rept. U.S. Nat. Museum, Boston, 1890–95.

## FORMS OF CROSS, HITTO-SUMER & BRITON 293

ways like a jewel, as seen in the accompanying Figs. 46 and 47. The former Fig. gives the forms of the Cross as found on Sumerian, Hittite, Phœnician, Kassi and Trojan seals, inscriptions, vases and amulets; whilst *Fig. 47 shows the identical Hitto-Sumerian and Phœnician conventional variations in the form of the Cross as found on the prehistoric and pre-Christian monuments and pre-Roman coins of Ancient Britain.*

This simple equilateral form of the Sun Cross of Divine Victory, was sometimes ornamented by the Catti (or Hittites) and Sumerians by doubling its borders, so as to superimpose one or more crosses inside each other, as in the " Cassi " Cross (see Figs. 12, 46), and by decorating it with jewels or fruits (Fig. 46) and by broadening its free ends to form what is now called " The Maltese " Cross, which is found on the ancient Sumerian sacred seals and as amulets on the necklaces of the priest-kings in Babylonia, etc. (Fig. 46, *e, E*).[1] And it is a variety of this amulet or necklace form, with a handle at the top, or pierced with a hole above for stringing on a necklace or rosary, which has hitherto been called " The Phœnician " or " Egyptian " or *Crux ansata*, or " Key of Life-*to-come* " (Fig. *z, S*) ; whilst the other forms of crosses of the St. George type, though found on the same old Phœnician sites, have been arbitrarily deemed non-Phœnician. But this so-called " Phœnician " or " Egyptian " Cross is not uncommonly figured on Hittite sacred seals as a symbol of the Sun-god,[2] the reason being that the Phœnicians, as we have so repeatedly seen, were also Khatti, Catti, " Hatti " or " *Hitt*-ites " themselves.

Another common form of this simple Sun Cross is the *Swastika*, which we have, carved, in the centre of the Phœnician votive pillar to Bel at Newton. This is formed from the simple " St. George's Cross " by adding to its free ends a bent foot, pointing in the direction of the Sun's apparent movement across the heavens, *i.e.*, towards the right hand and thus forming the " *Swastika* " or what I call

---

[1] Bonomi, *Nineveh*, 333, etc. See W.S.C. for numerous other examples.
[2] Fig. 40, p. 250. W.S.C., 808-9, etc., etc.

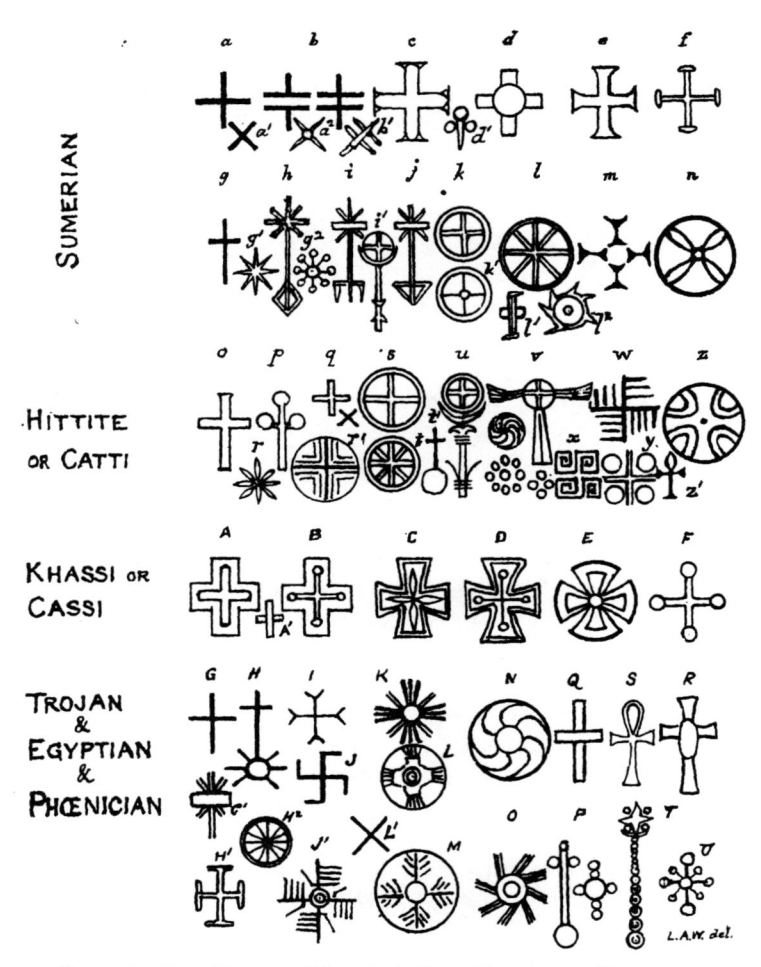

FIG. 46.—Sun Crosses, Hitto-Sumerian, Phœnician, Kassi and Trojan, plain, rayed, and decorated on seals, amulets, etc., 4000–1000 B.C.

NOTE.—Compare with Ancient Briton forms in Fig. 47; and note, *re* "Celtic" Cross, numbers $i^1$, *k* to *n* and $r^1$ to *v* and *z*. Detailed references in footnote ¹ on p. 296.

# ANCIENT BRITON FORMS OF THE CROSS

FIG. 47.—Ancient Briton Sun Crosses derived from Hitto-Sumerian, Phœnician and Trojan sources on prehistoric and pre-Christian Monuments and pre-Roman Coins in Britain.

Note, in comparing with remote originals in Fig 46 especially the pronged Cross for adoration (J), Cuneiform (Crosses C and L), "Cassi" Crosses (P-R), Swastikas, key and curved (T and K²) Grain and Fruit Crosses (H²-J¹); and "Ankh" or Handled Crosses (V¹). Detailed reference in footnote [1] on p. 297.

## 296 PHŒNICIAN ORIGIN OF BRITONS & SCOTS

[1] References to Hitto-Sumerian Crosses in Fig. 46. Abbreviations: C=C.M.C.; Co=C.S.H.; D=D.C.O.; H=H.H.S.; S=S.I.; W=W.S.C.; WM=W.S.M.

- *a*   Sumer sign for Sun-god *Bil* (Br., 1802, 1778) or Fire-god with word-value *Bar*, also *Pir* or " Fire " (Br., 1724) and defined as " flame, fire, wood, twin " (Br., 1810, 1756, 1811, and B.B.W., pp. 41–3), *i.e.*, Twin fire-sticks. On seals W, 14, 539, etc., D(L), Pl. 41, 5 and 8 ; D(B) 24, 68, etc.
- $a^1$   Oriented or **X** Cross, W, 368, 488, etc. ; D(L), Pl. 13, 18 ; 24, 15, 58, 26, etc. : Co, 223–6, etc. $a^2$ Other form of same W, 488.
- *b*   Sumer sign for " Sceptre " also= " Shining and Sun-god of Street " (Br., 5573, 5617 and B.B.W., p. 131, No. 48). On seals W, 215, 1205. $b^1$ Same oriented W, 490, and a three-barred W, 273. *c–d*, Fruit Crosses (*Gurin*), Br., 5903–5 ; W, 455, etc. $d^1$, W, 24.
- *e*   W, 700, 755, 1071, etc. ; 538.
- *f*   W, 532, etc., 1293, and Saltire (**X**), W, 559.
- *g*   W, 41a, etc.   $g^1$ Rayed Cross, very common, W, 37a, etc.
- $g^2$   W, 23, 24, 542, 620, etc.   *h* W, 139b, 223, 244, etc.
- *i*   W, 126, 270, 282–3, etc.   $i^1$ " Celtic," W, 454a, etc.
- *j*   W, 274, 319, 339, etc.   *k* Common, W, 226, 324, etc.
- *k*   W, 324, 850, 946, etc.   *l* W, 36, etc.
- $l^1$ and $l^2$, Swastikas, W, 1307, Circular-saw type, 494, 496, 592, etc. 215, etc. ; often 8-toothed.
- *m*   Cuneiform sign for god Bil (Br., 1478, 1497) quadrupled as Cross and defined " God and Heaven " (C.I.W.A., 2, Pl. 48, 30); *cp.* W, 54. On Mycena gold buttons, S.M., Nos. 405, 407, 412.
- *n*   W, 869, 1282, H, 45.   W, 329, 340, 448, Co. 39.
- *o*   In Hittite inscripts. *e.g.* Marash Lion, also H.C., pl. A. 11a, etc. ; W, 829, and H, 44, Pl. 2.
- *p*   In Hittite inscripts frequent. H.C., Pl. A, ll. 4 and 6 ; W, 24, etc.
- *q*   W, 913. H.C., 27. H, 35, 44. Co., 190, for **X** see $a^1$.
- *r*   W, frequent Co, 152, 158.   $r^1$ D, Pl. 128, and oriented, Pl. 14, 5–7, 98, 9b; H, 127–131, 216 ; Co., 57, 75 ; 354, 358.
- *s*   W, 850, etc. WM, 237, 798 ; Co., 20, etc., etc. H, 215.
- *t*   W, 839, etc. C, 158, from Boghaz Koi, Co., 11, 17, etc.
- $t^1$   Co., 95, 106.   *u* W, 946, etc.   *v* W, 831, etc. Curved Swastika, W, 798, 928 ; Rosette, W, 542, 796, 868, etc., S.I. 309 ; WM, 179, 192, etc. ; H, 54, 108, 218 ; Co, 276–280, etc. ; Pellet Cross, W, 768.   *w* Multiple limbed Swastika, H, 130. SL, 1915.
- *x*   Key Swastika on priest's dress, see Fig. 62 and G.L.H., Pl. 56–7 ; and on bronze stag, C, Pl. 24, 12.
- *y*   D(L)pl. 59. 1 ; 106, 1a, W. 832.
- *z*   C, Pl. 6, 1, 2, 4, etc. ; H, Fig. 10 and Nos. 131, 216.
- $z^1$   Handled Cross (*Ankh*) common on Hittite seals, W, 808, etc.
- *A*   Fig. 12 ; and W, 46, 543, etc., 1220.   $A^1$ W, 539 ; in Hittite D(B), 297; and oriented CS, 12, 6.   *B* W, 525–6, etc., 537, etc.
- *C*   *Ib.*, 535, etc. ; on Hittite pottery, C, Pl. 11.   *D*, W, 41, 514, etc.
- *E*   W, 1280–81 and p. 394, as amulet on neck of priest kings.
- *F*   *Ib.*, 532.   *G* SI, 1871, 1976.   CC. 121, pl. 12, 10. 11: W. 1197–8.
- $G^1$   S.I. 1452, 1946, 1993, *cp.* Egypt. hieroglyph for " East " or Orient.   *H* Fig. 31, p. 238 S I., 1954.   $H^1$ *Ib.*, 1432.
- $H^2$   *Ib.*, 1824, 1829, etc.   *I* *Ib.*, 1250, 1879.
- *J*   Very common, S.I., 1840, etc.   $J^1$ *Ib.*, 1915.
- *K*   *Ib.*, 1977.   *L* *Ib.*, 1914.   $L^1$ *Ib* 1858, 1864, 1871–6, etc.
- *M*   *Ib.* 1901, 1920.   *N* Curved Swastika *Ib.* 230, 1833, 1991, etc.
- *O*   *Ib.* 1837 ; in Hittite seals, W 215, 194, etc., WM, 130, and *cp.* Briton Ogam, Fig. 5.B.   *P* C.C. pl. 121.

## ANCIENT BRITON FORMS OF THE CROSS

Q   G.H., Figs. 78 and 169 and pp. 37, 67. Crossed wood coloured red with sense of " fitted " and " devouring flame."
R   Red-painted Cross of 2 bars wood, *ib.* Fig. 67 and p. 61. Its later form resembles " brazier " sign *Akh* for " Fire," *cp.* G.H., 42.
S   Handled Cross or *Ankh* as " Key of Life."
T   W, 832.   *U* D(L), 97, 10, and *cp.* P.A.P., 2, 240.

* References to Ancient Briton Crosses of Hitto-Sumerian and Trojan type in Fig. 47. Abbreviations : B= B.C. ; C= C.N.G. ; E= E.C.B. ; S= S.S.S. ; W= W.L.W.

A   Common, especially in Ogam inscripts. B.O.I. and S.I., 29, etc. ; and W, 3, 4, etc. ; E, Pl. A, 6, B, 2, 14, etc. Oriented × common, see Fig. 54, p. 317.
B   S.I., 138 ; C, 34 ; Oriented, S.I., 129, 57-8, etc. ; W, 83, 84 ; E, Pl. B, 11, 15, C 13, etc.   *C* S.I., 2, 9, 74, 120 ; 124 ; W, 39, 52, 66 ; with " Lock of Horus," S, 2, 71, Illust. Pl. 26, 35 ; W, 79.   *D* S., 2, 52, 74 ; W, 22, 52.   *E*, S, 2, 35, etc., 62, 84, 93 ; W, 13, 22 ; S, 2, 74, 82, 114 ; W, 22, 29, 61, etc.   *F* W, 101, long 89.
G   Common S, 2, beaded W, 38.   *H* "The Mound," E, Pl., 1, 1, 2, 7, etc., C, 88, and *cp.* Sumer-Hittite, Fig. 46, *h*, *l*¹, stemmed Carsi, W, 48.   *I* S, 2 Illust. 31, 33 ; wheeled, W, 80, 81.
J   S, 2 Illust. 31, 32 ; W, 21, barbed, 48.
K   S, 2,105 ; W, 95.   *K*¹ S, 2, 124.   *L* S, 2, 53, Illust. 26(4) ; W, 83, modified, S, 22.
M   S, 2, 73-4, 77, 122 ; W, 53, 4 ; 58-9.   *N* E, 3, 5 and F, 6.
O   W, 73 ; E, Pl. 3, 5, etc.   *P* S, 2, 29, 35 ; W, 58, 74.
P¹  W, 88b, Oriented, W, 37 (2) ; 90, S, 2, 101 ; C, Fig. 84 ; and as grain crop E, Pl. B, 11, C, 9, etc.
Q   S, 1, 42 ; 2, 113 ; W, 61 (6), long, 18, 57b.   *R* see Fig. 12A and S, 2, Illust. 27 (29) ; W, 14 (2).   *S* Common on coins, E, Pl. A, 1, 2, etc. and on monumts., S and W, 38 (2), 97 (1).   *T* Key pattern Swastika, S common, Vol. I, 35, 52, 72, etc. Vol. II, 72, 74, etc. ; W, 38 (3), 62, 84, modified, 57, etc. ; B, 396 (4).   *T*¹ W, 25, 39, etc., E, 3, 9, 12, etc.
U   S, 2, 72.   *V* S, 2, 74.   *V*¹ S, 2, 15, 103 ; W, 58, 79, 83.
V¹  S, 74, etc., W, 23, 61, etc.
W   Frequent S. ; C, 88, W, 61, etc., E, Pl. A, 6, B, 2 ; C, 4 ; 1, 1, etc.
X   C, 36, Newton Stone and common.
Y   E, Pl. B, 11, 15, D, 11, 13, etc.   *Z* E, Pl. B, 10, D, 7, E, 1, etc., etc.
A¹  E, Pl. B, 11, 8, 11, etc. ; W, 14, 37, 39, 90.   *B*¹ W, 61 and *cp.* 14, etc.   *C*¹ W, 73.   *D*¹ Fig. 25A, p. 187.
E¹  S, 60, from Foulis Western near Crieff, Perthshire, with Key Swastikas on limbs of Hittite type, and curved Swastikas on each boss.
F¹  S, 129, No. 11 Cross from Drainie Elgin and not infrequent S, 35, 45, 49, 57, etc.   *G*¹ S, 2, 121, Illust. 27 (29) ; W, 29, 80.
H¹  S, 35, from Farr in Sutherland with key Swastikas on limbs and curved on centre boss, and many others in S.
H²  S, 27, etc.; W, 83.
H³  Grain Cross, E, 5, 8, etc., and Stukeley, Pl. 2, 5, etc.
I¹  Common " Celtic ", W, 57, 61, etc.
J¹  S, 27, from Shandwick in Ross. Each boss bears curved Swastika, and many others in S.   *J*² E, 3, 5.   *J*³ E, 1, 6.
K¹  Boss of *J*¹ with Swastika ¼ actual size, *cp.* Hittite and Trojan. V.N.   *K*² S, 123, and *cp.* 118 ; W, 70, 90, etc., Fig. 49.
L¹  E, 3, 6.   *N*¹ E, 1, 6.

the "Revolving Cross." This discloses for the first time the real origin and meaning of the Swastika Cross and its feet,[1] and its talismanic usage for good luck. This Swastika form of the Sun Cross occurs on early Hittite and Sumerian seals and sculptures and is very frequent in the ruins of Troy (see Fig. *J j*)—where it is very frequent on whorls, used especially as amulets for the dead, with the feet reversed as the Resurrecting Cross. It is found widely in India of the Barats and in most places to which the Phœnicians penetrated. Thus it is found with other solar Phœnician symbolism in Peru amidst the massive ruins of the dead Inca civilization which the Phœnicians had established there, and of which vestiges survive in the solar cult of the modern Indians there. What is of immediate importance is that it occurs on the Brito-Phœnician Part-olon's monument to the Sun-god at Newton, and on many other pre-Christian monuments in Britain (see Figs. 5 A and 47) and on early Briton coins (Figs. later).

The simple equal-limbed cross was also sometimes figured inside the circle of the Sun's disc (Fig. *i, k*, etc.), and sometimes intermediate rays were added between the arms to form a halo of glory (Fig. *h-l*, etc.). *This now discloses the Catti or " Hittite " origin of the " Wheeled " Crosses of pre-Christian Britain* known as the " Runic Cross," or more commonly called " *The Celtic Cross.*" This name of " Celtic " has been lately given to it because it was largely adopted by Columba and Kentigern in their missions to the Picts and " Celts " of Scotland, Wales and Cornwall, and is supposed to have been invented by " Celts." On the contrary, it is now seen to have been imported by the Catti Phœnician Barats or Britons as part of their Sun-cult ; and the scenes sculptured on these ancient " wheeled," as well as free-limbed, prehistoric Crosses in Britain are non-Christian, and essentially identical, I find, with those graven on the ancient Hittite and Sumerian seals and other monuments of the Sun-cult from about 4000 to 1000 B.C., and were erected on pedestals for adoration as high crosses (Fig. 46, *i, n, u, z*).

[1] See the current theories summarized by D'Alviella *Migration of Symbols*, 1894, 32, etc. And compare my *Buddhism of Tibet*, 1895, 30, 287, 389.

## CRUCIFIX OF CHRIST NOT TRUE CROSS

This equal-limbed Cross, when used as a sacred sceptre in the hands of the Sun-god or his priest-king (or in the hands of Barati, see Fig. 16, p. 57), or when erected for adoration, was elongated by the addition of a stem or pedestal—this is seen in the most archaic Sumerian seals of the fifth millennium B.C., and also found in the ruins of ancient Troy, where sometimes this elongated Cross is pictured springing from the rayed Sun (see Fig. 46, *H*). This now discloses the origin of the common form of the True Cross in Christianity now current in Western Europe and usually called " The *Roman* or Latin Cross " and adopted for the Crucifix of Christ, which, however, we shall see was of quite a different shape.

Now arises the question of the relationship of these long antecedent pre-Christian sacred Aryan Sun-Crosses to the " True " Cross in Christianity, where it is now used as the Crucifix. When we examine the history of the Cross and Crucifix in Christianity, what do we find?

*The Crucifix of Christ was of quite a different shape from the True Cross*, which, indeed, never appears to have been used as a crucifix in ancient times. The historical Crucifix of Christ is figured and described in Early Christianity as of the shape of a **T**,[1] the so-called " St. Anthony's Cross " ; and it occurs extremely rarely in Early Christianity,[2] because *the crucifix was not a recognized Christian symbol of the Early Christians*. Thus no mention whatever is made of it, or of any cross, by St. Clement of Alexandria (*d.* 211 A.D.) in specifying the emblems which Christians should wear.[3] The reason for this omission is generally admitted by our ecclesiastical writers to be that the Early Christians were ashamed of the Crucifix on account of it being a malefactor's

---

[1] F.C.A., 23, 25. The " Cross " of the Jews mentioned in Ezekiel 9, 4–6, is called " the T Cross," and this is the form of the Cross used by Jews as a charm against snake-bite, and by others against erysipelas or " St. Anthony's Fire."

[2] For Christ's Crucifix as T-shaped cross, see second-century jewel figured by Farrar (F.C.A., 48) ; and on third-century tomb of Irene in Callixtine cemetery (F.C.A., 25). It is also thus figured on Early Christian tombs in Britain, ed. S.S.S., 1 pl. 28, in upper register of face of Nigg Cross, Ross-shire (along with old solar symbols) and in S.S.S., 2, Pl. 52, at Kirkapoll, Argyle.

[3] Clement *Pedagogus*, 3, 11, 59 and F.C.A., 7.

emblem—" the accursed tree " of the Hebrews, and the *infelix lignum* or " unhappy wood " of the Romans.[1]

Not even in the time of Constantine (*d.* 337 A.D.), the great propagator of Christianity (and born in York, it is traditionally reported, of a British mother), was the True Cross known in that faith—Constantine's sacred emblem for Christ and Christianity was merely a monogram of the first two Greek letters of Christ's name, XP, which had no transverse arms, nor any suggestion of a rectangular cross. Yet, on the other hand significantly, Constantine *before his profession of Christianity in* 312 A.D. *issued coins (some of them supposedly minted at London) stamped with the Cross, as the pagan emblem of the Sun*, and associated with a figure of the rayed Sun-god, and eight-rayed Sun, and the pagan title " To the Comrade of the Invincible Sun " (*Soli Invicto Comiti*).[2] On one of the coins bearing this legend the Sun-god is represented standing and crowning Constantine.[3] And it was obviously as a Sun-worshipper that Constantine erected at Constantinople the famous colossal image of the Sun-god brought from Troy.[4] The Cross which he stamped on his early coins was the pagan Hitto-Sumerian form of Sun-Cross *e* in Fig. 46, that is to say, the " Greek " Cross.[5] That pagan title of " Comrade of the Invincible Sun " was also used by the Roman emperor of the East, Licinius, presumably before Constantine ;[6] and he was in especially close relations with the Eastern Goths, who used this Cross from time immemorial, and from whom he presumably adopted it. Yet when Constantine became a Christian, on giving up Sun-worship, *he also gave up using the Cross*, and used instead as his exclusive symbol of Christianity a device which had not the form of the Cross at all, as the latter was the exclusive symbol of Sun-worship.

*The True Cross does not seem to have been certainly found*

---

[1] F.C.A., 20.
[2] F. W. Madden, N.C., 1877, 246-8, etc., 292.
[3] *Ib.*, 253.
[4] " Ilium in Phrygia," *ib.* 249. This appears to be Troy or Ilium. Old Phrygia formerly extended up to the Hellespont.
[5] Figures of these coins by Madden *loc. cit.*, Plate II, 1 and 2.
[6] *Ib.*, 247.

in Christianity as a Christian emblem before 451 A.D. ;[1] and then significantly it appears on the tomb of Galla Placidia, the widow of the Gothic Christian emperor Atawulf, brother-in-law and successor of Alaric, the famous and magnanimous Gothic Christian emperor. This tomb with its Cross of the Hittite form (see Fig. 46, o) and a similar one on the tomb of her son (d. 455 A.D.), is at Ravenna in the Northern Adriatic, a home of Early Byzantine or Gothic art in Italy and the capital of the Roman empire of the Goths. From this time onwards the True Cross comes more and more into general use as the symbol of Christ and Christianity; *but not yet as a substitute for the Crucifix.* It is now found in use—both in the elongated form, as on this Ravenna tomb, and with the equal arms, as found in the pre-Christian monuments and coins of Early Britain—as the sceptre and symbol of Divine victory, as it was in the Sun-cult; but no body is ever figured impaled or otherwise upon it.

The obvious reason and motive for this importation into Christianity in the fifth century A.D. of the old Aryan Sun-Cross symbol of Victory of the One God of the Universe of the Khatti, *Getæ* or Goths now becomes evident. The " Western " (properly " Eastern " Goths) were early converted to Christianity, about 340 A.D., by their priest-prince,

---

[1] This is the statement of Farrar (F.C.A., 26). But he mentions a Cross, presumably a " Greek " one, reputed on a tomb of a Christian in 370 A.D., of which no particulars are given nor evidence for the date, citing as his authority Boldetti; also a " Greek " Cross on the tomb of Ruffini, who was especially associated with the " Arian " Goths and who died about 410 A.D. Sir F. Petrie, in an elaborate review of Early Christian Crosses (*Ancient Egypt*, 1916, 104) cites a Cross on a coin of the Roman emperor Gratian in 380 A.D.; but Gratian was not a Christian. The Romans were addicted to putting symbols on their coins which were current amongst their subjects and the Cross was a common Gothic symbol. Professor Petrie gives several slightly earlier dates, though some of these require revision; *e.g.*, Galla Placidia on p. 104 is stated to have died 420, whereas the usually accepted date is 450 (H. Bradley, *Goths*, 105) or 451; but all of the earlier dates fall subsequent to the period of conversion of the Visi-Goths by Ulfilas. The ornate crosses of the Arian Goths at Ravenna about 510 A.D. (Petrie *loc. cit.* 107), decorated with smaller wheeled Crosses, and the limbs ending in discs, as well as most of the other forms figured by Petrie, disclose their clear line of descent from the Hitto-Sumerian and Kassi types (see Fig. 46, *d*, etc., *B-F*, etc.). The Cross used by the Early Christian Egyptians as a symbol and *not* a crucifix, with loop at its top (see Fig. 47, *c*) and which is called " The Lock of *Horus*," *i.e.*, The Sun-god, also thereby asssociates this Cross with the Sun; and it occurs on early British monuments (Fig. 47 C).

Bishop Ulfilas, whose translation for his kinsmen of the New Testament Gospels into Gothic remains one of the earliest versions of the gospels in any language. The Goths naturally transferred to their new form of religion, Christianity, which had so much in common with their old ancestral monotheistic faith, the most sacred symbol of that ancestral faith, The True Cross, which we have seen was freely figured as such, not only by the Sumerian Babylonian and Hittite or Catti Sun-worshippers, but also by their kinsmen, the Catti Goths of Britain on their coins of the pre-Christian period.

*But the True Cross of Victory thus introduced by the Goths into Christianity as a symbol of Christ was not used as a substitute for the Crucifix* until many centuries later. It was, for several centuries, used merely as the simple Cross, as the Solar symbol of Victory by itself, without any body fixed on it; and even when, in the eighth century, Christ was figured on it, even then it was *not the Crucified Christ.* " Not until the eighth century is Christ represented on the Cross to the public eye; but even then it is a Christ free, with eyes open, with arms unbound; living, not dead; majestic, not abject; with no mortal agony on His divine eternal features."[1] It thus was not used as a crucifix, but still as the Sun-Cross of Victory, placed behind Him as a halo of glory, as in the fashion of the old Sumer-Babylonian and Medo-Persian Sun-worshippers in representing the Sun-god in human form. For the Christian artists had not yet dared to associate this pure and glorious symbol of the Living Sun-god with blood or Death.[2]

*Not until the tenth century was Christ represented to the public eye on The True Cross as a Crucifix*, and impaled thereon, blood-splashed, in agony and death,[3] in the form

---

[1] F.C.A., 401.
[2] But see next footnote; and on "reverent dread" of representing Christ on the Cross in the seventh century see F.A.C., 400.
[3] F.C.A., 402. But as early as 586 A.D. a Syrian monk in Mesopotamia in an illustrated convent manual of the Gospels, now in the Florence Library, painted the Dead Christ on the Cross as a crucifix, though it remained unique and not known to the public. The belief held by some that a crucifix in form of the Latin Cross, carved on a cornelian and another on ivory date as early as the fifth century (Garrucci, *Diss. Arch.*, 27) is not accepted by Farrar as authentic.

now familiar. From this very late date the True Cross then began, for the first time, to be called, or rather mis-called, in modern Christianity, " The Crucifix," and to be represented as such in Christian art. And the glorious ancient Aryan " pagan " tradition of the True Cross as the symbol of Divine Victory and Devil-banishing was then transferred to this new form of " Crucifix," now that it had been given the form of the sacred old Aryan Sun Cross.

This transference to Christ's Crucifix of the form and glorious tradition of the ancient Aryan Sun-Cross of the Hittites or Goths is thus one of the great positive contributions made by the Goths to Christianity. Amongst their other great contributions to Christianity is " Gothic " architecture—the noblest of all forms of religious styles of building—and ancient semi-pointed arches of quasi-Gothic type are still seen in the ruins of Hittite or Catti buildings dating back to at least the second millennium B.C. The Gothic translation of the New Testament, also by prince Ulfilas, one of the earliest of the extant versions of the Christian Scripture, is a chief basis of our " English " translation of the Gospels. It was the Goths also, in the purity of their ancestral Monotheist idea of God, who successfully resisted the introduction of the Mother-Son cult by the Romish and Alexandrine Church into their Christianity in Nestorian Asia Minor and Byzantium, and thence also in Gothic Britain and North-western Europe.

It was this same steadfast Gothic Monotheism, inherited from the Aryan Gothic originators of the idea of The One God, through our own " pagan " ancestral Gothic Early Britons and their descendants, which has clearly kept British and Scandinavian Christianity free from the taint of the aboriginal Chaldee Mother-Son cult and the host of polytheist saints which disfigures most of the continental forms of Christianity. It is also this ancestral Gothic Monotheism which now explains for the first time the origin of the " *Arianism* " of the Goths—the lofty and refined philosophical Gothic conception of Monotheism, which our modern ecclesiastic and ethical writers are totally at a loss to account for amongst such a " rude untutored barbarous " pagan people, as they have hitherto supposed the Goths to be, notwithstanding the noble pictures left by contemporary Roman writers of the admirable character and personality of Alaric and other historical Gothic kings. But this "Arianism" of the Goths is now seen to be the natural and logical outcome of the purity of the Gothic idea of Monotheism, as inherited from their ancestral "pagan" cult of the Father-god and his Sun-Cross of the Aryans.

This Sun-Fire Cross also now discloses the Gothic or Phœnician *Catti* origin of "The Fiery Cross," familiar to readers of Scott's semi-historical romances, as carried by the Scottish clans through the glens in summoning the clans to a holy war. It is now seen to be a vestige of the ancient sacred Red Fire Cross of the Catti or *Xatti* or "Scot" Sun-worshippers.

The "Red Cross of St. George" of Cappadocia and England also is seen to be the original form of the Cappadocian Hittite or Gothic Fiery Red Cross of the Sun, carried erect as the sceptre or standard of divine Universal Victory. The ecclesiastical attempts at explaining the origin of St. George with his Red Cross and his transference from Cappadocia as patron saint to England, in common with Asia Minor, *Syria-Phœnicia*, Russia, Portugal and Aragon, form one of the paradoxes of Church history. It affords another illustration of the manner in which the Early Christian Fathers, for proselytizing purposes, introduced into the bosom of the Catholic Church "pagan" deities in the guise of Christian saints.

All the ecclesiastic legends of St. George locate him in Cappadocia; but the personality of the Christian saint of that name is so shadowy as to be transparently non-historical. There are two supposed Christian St. Georges, one a disreputable bishop of that name of Cappadocia and Alexandria, who was martyred by a mob about 362 A.D.; while a third, more or less mythical, is known only by two medieval references and said to have been martyred about 255 A.D.[1] The great Gibbon, who does not recognize either of the latter, dismisses the former, saying: "The infamous George

[1] B.L.S., April, 308.

of Cappadocia has been transformed into the renowned St. George of England, the patron of arms, of chivalry and of the garter."[1] And a recent authority, in his account of this saint, concludes that the traditional "Acts" of St. George "*are simply an adaptation of a heathen myth of a solar god to a Christian saint.*"[2] But neither Gibbon nor anyone else hitherto appears to have found any evidence for the origin of St. George and his Red Cross with the Dragon legend, nor as to how St. George and his Red Cross came to be connected with England.

The name "George" is usually derived from the Greek *Geōrgos*, "a husbandman," from *Geōrgia*, "fields." The latter is now seen to be obviously derived from the Sumerian *Kur* or *Kuur-ki*, "Land," which was the title applied by the Sumerians to Cappadocia-Cilicia, as "*The Land*" of the Hittites or Goths. This *Kur* is the source of "*Suria*," the name recorded by Herodotus for *Cappadocia*,[3] the inhabitants of which he calls "*Suri-oi*," *i.e.*, the "White Syrians," or Hittites, of Strabo, the people who, we have seen, were the founders of Agriculture. "George" or "Georgos" thus appears originally to have designated a Hittite of *Kur-ki* or Cappadocia—K, G, and S being dialectically interchangeable. "*Guur*" or "*Geur*" is also the ideograph value of a word-sign for The Father-god Bel, which has the meaning of "The Father Protector";[4] and in the Sumerain seals it is Father Bel or Geur who slays the Dragon (see Fig. 55), though in the later Babylonian legend this achievement is credited to his son, the so-called "Younger Bel" (Mar-duk or Taśia). Thus Bel as *Geur*, the Dragon-slayer and protector of the Hittite Cappadocia, is the original of St. George.

In the early Sumerian, Hittite and Babylonian seals and sculptures, the figure of the Sun-god Bel slaying the winged Dragon is very frequent,[5] and we have seen that the Sun Cross was a recognized Devil-banishing weapon and talis-

[1] G.D.F., 2. c, 23. [2] B.L.S., April, 301.
[3] Herodotus 1, 6, and 72, etc. [4] Br. 1140-1, 1146. Meissner 647.
[5] See W.S.C., Figs. 127-135b, etc. The rayed Sun is usually figured near the god, or over the dragon, and in 129 and 132 the god appears to wield a Cross. The scene of Bel overcoming the Winged Dragon is ever more common in Assyrian sacred seals, *e.g.*, W.S.C., Figs. 563-646.

man. In Egypt, also, long before the Christian era, there are numerous effigies of the Sun-god Horus (*i.e.*, the Sumerian *Śur*, Sanskrit "*Sura*," Hindi "*Suraj*," Persian "*Horu*," The Sun,")[1] as a warrior and sometimes on horseback slaying the Dragon represented locally as a crocodile, and the Horus Sun-cult is usually stated to have been introduced into Egypt by Menes, who, I find, was a Hitto-Phœnician. Moreover, the pre-Christian spring festival of the pagan Sun-god as "Mithra" *was celebrated on St. George's Day, April 23rd*, under which the Sun-god bore the title of "Commander of the Fields,"[2] and "George" is cognate with the Greek *Georgia*, "Fields," and *Geòrgos*, "a Husbandmān," and the Hitto-Aryans were, as we have seen, the founders of husbandry, and worshippers of Bel or Geur.

This Hitto-Sumerian origin for "St. George of Cappadocia" and his Red Cross and Dragon legend now explains his introduction into England by the Catti (or "*Hitt-ites*"), and how he became the patron saint there, and how he is figured freely on pre-Christian monuments with solar symbols in Britain. He and his Dragon-legend were clearly introduced and naturalized there by our Hittite or Catti Barat or "Briton" ancestors from Cappadocia and Cilicia long before the dawn of the Christian era.

These new-found facts and clues now disclose that not only St. George's Red Cross, but also the other associated Crosses in the Union Jack, namely, the Crosses of St. Andrew and St. Patrick, are also forms of the same Sun Cross.

Our *Heraldic* Crosses also are not only derived from the Hitto-Phœnicians, but even their actual Hittite names still persist attached to some of them, besides their generic name of "Cross." The "George" Cross we have already seen, and the "Cross saltire," or Andrew's Cross **X**, has its origin and meaning discovered in the next chapter. One of the other crosses or "bearings" in British Heraldry is called "*Gyron*" (Fig. 48 *a*), for which no obvious meaning has hitherto been found. Now this Gyron is seen to be practi-

---

[1] Detailed proofs of this identity in my *Aryan Origins*.
[2] Von Gutschmid, *Ber. der Such Ges.*, 1861 (13), 194, etc.; and H. Hulst, *St. George of Cappadocia*, 1909, 3.

# VARIANT SWASTIKA SUN CROSSES

cally identical with the Cross painted on ancient Hittite pottery from Cappadocia (see Fig. 48 b); and of a type bearing the Hitto-Sumerian name of *Gurin* or " The Manifold or Fructifying or Harvest Cross."[1]

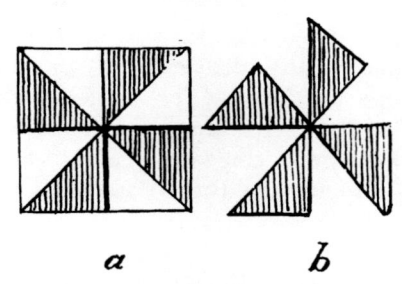

FIG. 48.—" *Gyron* " Cross of British Heraldry is the " *Gurin* " Cross of the Hittites.
(b after Chantre.[2] Its truncated tops are apparently due to foreshortening on the curved surface of the pottery.)

It seems to be a form of the Hittite Swastika with multiple feet as in Fig. 46 w and J[1]; which is also found on Early Briton monuments (Fig. 47 U and H[2]); and it appears to have been a solar luck-compelling talisman for fruit crops. It bears the synonym of *Buru* or " Fruit," *i.e.*, " Berry,"[3] and thus discloses the Hitto-Sumer origin of our English word " Berry."

The Swastika or " Revolving Cross " is now seen to have been figured in a great variety of ways. And significantly we find that *all the varied Hitto-Phœnician and Trojan forms of the Swastika are reproduced on the monuments and coins of the Ancient Britons.* It is figured as a rod with two feet passing through the Sun's disc (Fig. 46 $l^1$), as a disc with angular teeth like a circular saw ($l^2$), a disc with tangent rays ($O$), disc with curved radii in direction of rotation ($v^1$ and $N$), key-pattern ($x$), all of which forms are found in Early Britain (Fig. 47). The "*Spiral* ornament" itself is also now seen to be merely a form of the revolving Swastika.

The direction of movement of the revolving Sun, especially

---

[1] Br., 5903, 5907; also called *Girin* and *Gurun*. P.S.L., 168. See Fig. 46 c, d, W for simpler forms. On " Harvest " cp. L.S.G. 275.
[2] C.M.C., Pl. 113, from Cæsarea, near the Halys R.   [3] Br., 5905.

of the returning or "resurrecting" Sun, is also indicated on Hittite seals, not by feet but by fishes swimming towards the East, *i.e.*, the left (see Figs. 42 and 49). A striking instance of the identity in motive of the Hittite and Briton representations of these solar symbols is seen in Fig. 49. The details of the Catti or Hittite seal of about 2000 B.C. are seen to be substantially identical with those on the old pre-Christian Cross at Cadzow (or Cads-cu, the "Koi" or town of the Cad or Phœnicians), the modern Hamilton, an old town of the Briton kingdom of Strath-Clyde, in the province of the Gad-eni—the Brito-Phœnician Gad or Cad or Catti.

FIG. 49.—Identity of Catti or Hittite Solar Monuments with those of Early Britain.
*a, b,* Cadzow pre-Christian Cross (after Stuart[1]).
*c,* Hittite seal of about 2000 B.C. (after Ward[2]).

In the Hittite seal (*c*) the revolving 8-rayed Sun with effluent rays is connected by bands to the setting Sun which has entered the Gates of Night or Death, figured as barred doors. A short-tailed animal (Goat) is on each side, the left-hand one followed by the Wolf of Death (see later); and the direction of the Resurrecting Sun is indicated by two fishes swimming eastwards (to the left). The 5 circles (or "cups")=Taśia, the director of the Resurrecting Sun; the 4 circles=Death, repeated as 4 larger concentric circles. The Briton monument (*a*) reproduces essentially the same scene. The central spiral on the Cross turning towards the left is the equivalent of the revolving Sun returning to the East. Above it and the curved lines, representing the

[1] S.S.S.T., 118. I have verified details on spot.   [2] W.S.C., 991.

## "SPECTACLES" A FORM OF SWASTIKA

Waters of the Deep as on the Trojan amulets (Fig. 31), the fish is swimming to the East, whilst the dead fish on its back = the dead person. Below are two animals, one the horned Goat, and the other apparently the Wolf of Death. Surmounting all is Taśia with his horned head-dress overcoming the Lion adversaries (see later). In the reverse (*b*), is the two-footed Swastika surmounted by Taśia the Archangel. This Early Briton Cross is thus a solar invocation to Tasia for " Resurrection from Death, like the Sun."

Another form of the Swastika Sun Cross, differing somewhat in shape from the usual type as carved on the Phœnician pillar at Newton and elsewhere, is found on the pre-Christian Ogam monument at Logie in the neighbourhood of the Newton pillar (Fig. 5B, p. 20), and formed part of a Stone Circle.[1] This symbol is also found frequently on prehistoric stones in Scotland, and occurs also in the neighbourhood at Insch, Bourtie, and lower down the Don at Inverurie and Dyce with its Stone Circle,[2] though not hitherto recognized as a Swastika or as associated with Sun-worship, and merely called by writers on antiquities " The Spectacles with broken Sceptre or Zig-zags," and of unknown meaning and symbolism.

This emblem, the so-called " Spectacles," carved on the lower portion of the Logie Stone, is now seen to be a decorated Swastika, in which the duplicated disc of the Sun (the so-called " lenses " of the Spectacles) replaces two of the limbs of the ordinary Swastika Cross, to represent the morning and evening Sun and the Sun-wise direction of movement from east to west (or left to right), as we have already found in the " Cup-mark " inscriptions and Sumerian seals. This direction of movement is graphically indicated by an arrow-head (the so-called " broken sceptre " of Scottish archæologists) pointing in that direction, while the perpendicular stem is slanted to emphasize the movement and thus giving a $\Sigma$-shape. The Hitto-Phœnician origin of this

---

[1] One of the remaining four, all of which are carved with symbols which are now found to be solar, S.S.S., I, 4, and Pl. 3, Figs. 1 and 2 and Pl. 4, 1, and II, page xlviii.
[2] S.S.S., and others on Pl. 14–16.

Y

design is evident from the Phœnician[1] coin from Gaza here figured (Fig. 50) in which darts are also used to show the

FIG. 50.—Swastika on Phœnician (or Philistine) Coin from Gaza disclosing origin of the Scottish Spectacle darts.
(After Wilson and Ward.)
Note the darts show direction of the rotation.

direction of revolution as in the Scottish Swastika; and in Hittite seals the return revolution of the Sun is also indicated pictorially by darts (see Fig. 37, p. 248) as well as by the direction of swimming sea-fish, back to the rising Sun (see Fig. 49).[2] The double solar discs, connected by horizontal bands, as in the Scottish "Spectacles," are also carved in Hittite seals (see Fig. 59A, etc.);[3] and a Swastika with a central Sun disc is given on an ancient Sumerian seal;[4] and also occurs on prehistoric Scottish monuments.

The retrograde movement of the victorious Sun through the Realms of Death is also figured on Briton monuments by darts placed at the ends of a rod-Swastika which transfixes the Serpent of Death (as in Fig. 51). Many specimens of this have survived; one of which forms "The Serpent Stone" now standing alongside the Newton Stone, and it is surmounted by the Double Sun-Disc or "Spectacles,"[5] and depicts the Victory of the Resurrecting Sun. *Thus the proofs for the Catti or Hitto-Sumerian solar origin of the prehistoric "Spectacles" Swastikas in the Don Valley and elsewhere in Britain are absolute and complete.*

On the coins of the Ancient Catti Britons the Sun Cross is figured very freely, in addition to the circle of the Sun

[1] It is called a "Philistine" coin, but I find the Philistines were a branch of the Phœnicians.
[2] W.S.C,, 993.
[3] *Ib.*, 993. It is absolutely identical with prehistoric monuments in Scotland, S.S.S., Pl. 47. For Briton example, see Fig. 68B, p. 350.
[4] *Ib.*, 1307.     [5] S.S.S., i. 37. The Serpent is the British adder.

# SACRED CROSS IN PRE-CHRISTIAN BRITAIN 311

itself noted in the previous chapter. It is figured in the form of the "short Cross" or "St. George's Cross" (see Figs. 3, 44, 47 $A$, $W$, etc.) ; also by pellets giving that form (Fig. 47 $G$,[1] $N$,[1] etc.) ; and as ornamental or decorated crosses and frequently by ears of corn of the " Tascio " Corn Spirit series, both perpendicularly as in the ordinary True Cross of short form (Fig. 47), and oriented or "saltire" in the style of St. Andrew's Cross, and associated with other emblems of the Sun-cult. And the " Rood screens" and " Rood lofts" in our Gothic cathedrals still attest the former prominence of the Cross or " Rood " in early and medieval Christianity in Britain, with its leading Gothic racial elements.

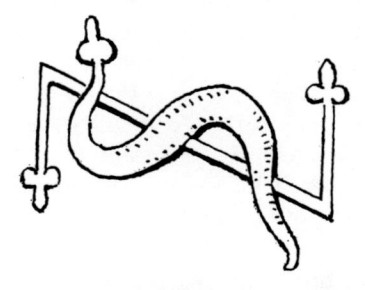

FIG. 51.—Swastika of Resurrecting Sun transfixing the Serpent of Death on Ancient Briton monument at Meigle, Forfarshire.
(After Stuart.)[1]

The True Cross, thus venerated as the emblem of Universal Victory of the One God symbolized in the Sun, was worn on the person, as we have seen, on a necklace, for adoration or as an amulet or charm. The manner of holding the portable handled or pierced form of Cross for adoration or abjuration is seen in Fig. 52 from a Hittite seal,[2] wherein additional rays of fiery light (or limbs of a St. Andrew's Cross) are added. As the Cross was made of wood, the ancient specimens have all now perished ; but the frequent references in the Gothic Eddas to " The Wood " (which was made of the red Rowan Ash or " Quicken " Tree of Life), and its ash used for banishing devils and conquering enemies

---
[1] S.S.S. ii. Ill. Pl. 25, 17.
[2] Lajard in *Mém. Acad. des Inscrip. et Belles Lettres*, 17 361, from a Hittite cylinder in Bibliothèque Nat., Paris.

indicates its wide prevalence in Ancient Britain and Scandinavia. And the modern popular superstition "to touch Wood " in order to avert ill-luck is clearly a survival of this ancient " Sun-worship " of the wooden Cross. The meaning of this superstition is now seen to be, to touch the devil-banishing Wood Cross of Victory of the Sun-cult, which every Aryanized Briton carried on their person as a luck-compelling talisman against the devils and Druidical curses of the aboriginal Serpent-Dragon cult.

But neither the Cross on the pre-Christian Briton Cross monuments or carried on their persons and still carried on our national British standards, nor the Sun itself, of which the Cross was the symbol, were the objects of worship among these Early Aryans, so-called " Sun and Fire-worshippers," but the Supreme God behind the Cross and the Sun, as we shall see further in the next chapter.

In illustration of the Early Aryan hymns which our ancestral Sumero-Phœnician Britons offered up in adoration to the " God of the Sun " at their Cross monuments, and presumably also at their solar Stone Circles in early " pagan " Britain, let us hear what the orthodox Sumerian hymns to the Father God of the Sun sing over a thousand years before the birth of Abraham :—

SUMERIAN (" CYMRIAN ") PSALMS TO THE SUN-GOD.
" O Sun-God in the horizon of heaven thou dawnest !
  The pure bolts of heaven thou openest !
  The door of heaven thou openest !
  Thou liftest up thy head to the world,
  Thou coverest the earth with the bright firmament of heaven
  Thou settest thy ear to the prayers of mankind ;
  Thou plantest the foot of mankind. . . ."[1]
              *        *        *        *
" O Sun-God, judge of the world art thou !
  Lord of the living creation, the pitying one who (directed) the world !
  On this day purify and illumine, the king, the Son of God,
  Let all that is wrought of evil within his body be removed !
  Like the cup of the *Zoganes* cleanse him !
  Like a cup of clarified oil make him bright !

[1] Sumerian Hymns in C.I.W.A., 4, 20, 2, translated by Prof. Sayce (S.H.L., 491).

# SUMERIAN & GOTHIC HYMNS TO SUN

Like the copper of a polished tablet make him bright!
Undo his illness. . . .
Direct the law of the multitudes of mankind!
Thou art eternal Righteousness in heaven!
Justice in heaven, a bond on earth art thou!
Thou knowest right, thou knowest wickedness!
Righteousness has lifted up its foot,
Wickedness has been cut by Thee as with a knife."[1]

" O Sun God, who knowest (all things)! Thine own counsellor art thou!
Thy hands bring back to thee the spirits of all men.
Wickedness and evil dealing thou destroyest.
Justice and Righteousness thou bringest to pass. . . .
May all men be with Thee! "[2]

It will thus be seen that these pious ancestral early Aryan Sumerians under the bright beams of the Sun caught those still brighter beams of the Sun of Righteousness.

And the same " Sun-worship " is reflected in the Eddas of the Northern Goths, as, for instance, in the *Solar Liod* or " Lay of the Sun," an artless swan-song of a dying old Gothic chieftain, on his last view of the Sun at sunset :—

" I saw the Sun! the shining Day-Star!
Drop down to his home i' the west!
Then Hell-gates heard I the other way
Thudding open heavily.

I saw the Sun set dropping to Hell's stoves,
Much was I then heel'd out o' home.
More glorious He look'd o'er the many paths
Than ever He had looked afore.

I saw the Sun! and so thought I,
I was seeing the Glory of God.
To Him, I bow'd low for the hindmost time
From my old home i' this earth."[3]

It will now be understood from these Sumerian, Vedic, Barat and other hymns of the Gentile Barat Khatti or

---

[1] Sumerian Hymns in C.I.W.A., 4, 28, 1 (S.H.L., 499 f.).
[2] *Ib.*, 5, 50, 51 (S.H.L., 156).
[3] For text see Ed. V.P., 1, 205, where is given a rather " free " translation. There are other stanzas which seem to be later additions of the Christian period.

Goths of the Cross-cult, how the Goths and Britons, already endowed with such an exalted religion, so readily embraced the religion of "Christ of Galilee of the Gentiles" and also transferred to it their sacred Cross—which they also called "Cross" or *Garza*—as it possessed so much in common with the old "pagan" religion of their own Gentile Gothic ancestors, the Getæ, Gads, Guti, Catti, Khatti or "Hitt-ites."

We thus discover by a large series of facts that the Sun cult was widely prevalent in pre-Roman Britain under its Catti kings, and that it was introduced there about 2800 B.C. or earlier, by the sea-faring, tin-exploiting and colonizing Catti or Hitto-Phœnician Barats or Britons from Cilicia-Syria-Phœnicia, who were the Aryan ancestors of the present-day Britons.

FIG. 52.—St. Andrew, patron saint of Goths and Scots, with his Cross.
(After W. Kandler.)

# XXI

## St. Andrew as Patron Saint with His "Cross" Incorporates Hitto-Sumerian Father-god Indara, Indra or Gothic "Indri"-Thor & His "Hammer" Introduced into Early Britain by Gothic Phœnicians

*Disclosing pre-Christian Worship of Andrew in Early Britain & Hittite Origin of Crosses on Union Jack & Scandinavian Ensigns, Unicorn & Cymric Goat as Sacred Goat of Indara, " Goat " as rebus for " Goth " ; and St. Andrew as an Aryan Phœnician.*

> " O Lord *Indara*,[1] thou sturdy director of men,
> Thou makest the multitude to dwell in peace ! "—*Sumerian Psalms.*[2]
> " The Waters collected in the Deep,
> The pure mouth of *Indara* has made resplendent."—*Sumerian Psalms.*[3]
> " *Indra*, leader of heavenly hosts and human races !
> Indra encompassed the Dragon—
> O Light-winner, day's Creator ! "— *Rig. Veda*, 3, 34, 2-4.
> " Slaying the Dragon, Indra let loose the pent-up *Waters*."[4]
> " Indra, hurler of the *Four-angled Rain-producing Bolt*."—*Rig Veda*.[5]

STILL further evidence for the Hitto-Phœnician origin of the Britons, Scots and Anglo-Saxons is found in the legend of St. Andrew with his X Cross as the patron saint of the Scyths, Gothic Russia, Burgundy of the Visi-Goths from the Rhine to the Baltic, Goth-land and Scotland. We shall now find that the Apostle bearing the Aryan Gentile and non-Hebrew name of " Andrew " was presumably an Aryan Phœnician, and that the priestly legend attached to

---

[1] " Indara " (=" Induru ") is here used instead of its synonym Ea as given in this translation.
[2] Langdon, Sumerian Psalms, 109.
[3] S.H.L., 487. (See note 1.)    [4] R.V., 4, 19, 8.    [5] 4, 22, 2.

315

him incorporates part of the old legend of his namesake *Induru*, a common Sumerian title of the Father-god Bel, who is the Hittite god *Indara*, "*Indri* or *Eindri*-the-Divine," a title of Thor of the Goths;[1] and *Indra* the Father-

FIG. 53.—Indara's **X** " Cross " on Hitto-Sumerian, Trojan and Phœnician Seals.

*a* W.S.C., 368 f., 1165, 1201 ; W.S.M., 190, 192 ; D.C.(L.), 1, Pl. 13,
 15 and 19 (over 4 goats), Pl. 24, 15 ; Pl. 58, 26, 30, etc.
 Phœnician from Cyprus C.C. 117, 118, 252, etc.   Trojan S.I.,
 1864, 1871, etc.         *b* W.S.C., 1165
*c*  W.S.C. (Phœnic), 1171, 1194–5, 1199–2000, etc.; C.C., Pl. 12 and 6,
 15, 16, 18, etc.       *d* W., 951 ; D.C.(L.), 1, Pl. 18, 20, etc.
*e*  W., 488, 952, 1169, 1203 ; C.C., 237.
*f*  D.C.(L.), 1, Pl. 24, 17, with two Goats, Pl. 321b ; 54, 7, 61, 1b.
*g*  D.C.(L.), 2, 106, 1a.      *h* W, 559.       *i* D.C.(L.), 1, 17, 1.
 S.I., 2000.      *k* W, 490.      *l* W., 973, 1007.  C.C., 252.
*m*  D.C.(L.), 16, 2.      *n* D.C.(L.), 1, 14, 5–7, 11, 16 ; *Ib*., 2, 98, 9b.
*o*  S.I., 1910.       *p* C.C., Fig. 118.

[1] *Indri-di* or *Eindri-di*, *cp*. V.D., 123, where, however, it is sought to derive the name from *reid*, " to ride," although the name is never spelt with " reid."   *Di* as Gothic affix appears to=" God," with plural Diar (*cp*. V.D., 100), and cognate with *Ty*, " god," in series with the *ty* in Fimbul-ty, " Angan-ty " and " Hlori-di."   This latter title of Thor now appears to be *Hlèr*, " the Sea-god " (V.D., 274) and cognate with *Hlyr*, " tears " [? Rain] (V.D., 270) and for *Hlori* as a recognized spelling of Hleri, see V.D. 270.

## ANDREW'S CROSS IS HITTO-PHŒNICIAN

god of the Eastern branch of the Aryan Barats. And we shall find that the worship of Andrew with his **X** Cross was widespread in Early Britain and in Ireland or Ancient Scotia in "prehistoric times," long before the dawn of the Christian era. And he is the *INARA* stamped with Cross, etc., on Ancient Briton coins (see Fig. 74, p. 384).

The **X** "Cross," now commonly called "St. Andrew's," or in heraldry "Cross Saltire" (or "Leaping Cross"), is figured freely, I find, on Hitto-Sumerian, Trojan and

FIG. 54.—"Andrew's" Cross on pre-Christian monuments in Britain and Ireland and on Early Briton coins.[1]

Phœnician sacred seals as a symbol of Indara, from the earliest period downwards, both simply and in several conventional forms, see Fig. 53. And significantly *these*

[1] *a* common.   *b* E.C.B., *B*, 15, F, 6, 8 and 1, 1–4, 7, 8, etc.; C.N.G., Fig. 27.   S.S.S., 83, W., 88ᵈ, common in key-pattern.   *c* E.C.B., A, 1–6, etc.   *d* E.C.B., B, 14 and common in "Celtic" crosses.   *e* E.C.B., F, 8; 7, 8, 128, etc.   *f* common, E.C.B., 3, 4, etc., and cup-marks; and without central. E, 86; S.S.S., 1, 24.   *g* E.C.B., A, 1, etc. S.S.S., 1, 24.   *h* frequent; W., 43.   *i*, W.L.W., 43.   *k* Fig. 47 F¹ and S.S.S., 1, 57, 58, 129, 138.   *l* E.C.B., C, 13.   *l¹* E.C.B., 16, 9, and with circle centre, B, 11.   *m* E.C.B., 14, 9.   *n* S.S.S., 2 101; W., 37, 2, 902. G.N.G., Fig. 84.   *o, p* E.C.B., 5, 4.

various conventional Hitto-Sumerian and Trojan and Phœnician forms of Indara's **X** "Cross" are also found in more or less identical form on prehistoric monuments and pre-Christian coins in Ancient Britain as the "St. Andrew's Cross," see Fig. 54, which compare with previous Fig.

This so-called "Cross of St. Andrew," although resembling the True Cross of equal arms in a tilted (or "saltire") position, does not appear to have been a true Cross symbol at all, but was the battle-axe or "hammer" symbol of Indara or Thor. In Sumerian, its name and function is defined as "Protecting Father or Bel,"[1] with the word-value of "*Pap*" (thus giving us the Sumerian source of our English word *Papa* for "Father" as protector). It is also called *Geur* (or "George") or *Tuur* (or "Thor"), and defined as "The Hostile,"[2] presumably from its picturing a weapon in the hostile attitude for defence or protection, and it is generally supposed, and with reason, to picture a battle-axe.[3]

It is especially associated with Father Indara or Bel,[4] as seen in the ancient Hittite seal here figured (Fig. 55), representing Indara slaying the Dragon of Darkness and Death—a chief exploit of Indara or Indra (see texts cited in the heading)—wherein Indara, the king of Heaven and the Sun, is seen to wear the "St. Andrew's Cross" as a badge on his crown; whilst the axe which he wields is of the Hittite and non-Babylonian pattern. Describing this famous exploit, the Vedic hymns which describe Indara's bolt as "*Four*-angled" (see text cited in heading) also tell us :—

"With thy Spiky Weapon, thy deadly bolt,
O Indra, Thou smotest the Dragon in the face."[5]

We thus see how very faithfully the Indo-Aryan Vedic tradition has preserved the old Aryan Hitto-Sumerian

---

[1] Br., 1141, 1146; M., 648.   [2] Br., 1143, and for *Tuur* Br., 1140 and 10511.   [3] Oppert, *Exped. to Mesopot.*, 58 and B.B.W., 2, p. 28.
[4] The identity of Bel with *I-a* or *In-duru* or *Indara* is very frequently seen in Sumerian seals by Bel being figured with the attributes and symbols of Ia or Induru. Thus in the Trial of Adam (Fig. 33), Bel is represented in his usual form, whereas in the majority of specimens of that scene he is represented as in Fig. 57, with the Spouting Waters of Ia or Indara, as also in Fig. 35.
[5] R.V., 1, 52, 13.

## INDARA OR ANDREW SLAYING DRAGON 319

tradition as figured on this seal of about four thousand years ago ; and how it has preserved it more faithfully even than the Babylonian tradition, which latterly transferred the credit of slaying the Dragon to Indara's son Taś or " Mero-*Dach*," though even on that occasion he has to be hailed by his father's title of " *Ia* "[1] or " *Indara* " himself !

The Sumerian name for this X " Cross " deadly weapon of Indara has also the synonym of *Gūr*, " hostile, to destroy," which word-sign is also pictured by a blade containing an inscribed dagger with a wedge handle, and defined as " hew to pieces " and " strike dead "[2]—which word *Gūr* thus gives us the Sumerian origin presumably of the Old English *Gar*, a spear,[3] and " Gore," to pierce to death. This proves

FIG. 55.—Indara (or "Andrew") slaying the Dragon. From Hittite seal of about 2000 B.C.
(After Ward.)[4]
ote the X on the crown, and the fire-altar below the Dragon, which the latter was presumably destroying.

conclusively that the X " Cross " was a death-dealing bolt or weapon as described in the Vedic hymns ; and the modern device of the skull and cross-bones seems to preserve a memory of the original meaning of the X " Cross " as the deadly axe or " hammer " of Indara or Thor. And its

[1] *Cp.* King, *Seven Tablets of Creation*, Tab. 7, p. 116, etc.
[2] Br., 932 ; B.B.W., 45 and P.S.L., 164.
[3] Thus " Brennes . . . lette glide his *gar* " (*i.e.*, " Brian let fly his spear "), Layamon's *Brut.*, 5079. In Eddic Gothic *Geir*=" spear," Anglo-Sax. *Gar*.
[4] W.S.C., 584. Seal is in *Biblioth. Nationale*, Paris, 411. His Axe is of Hittite shape, as opposed to the Babylonian and Assyrian Scimitar.

Sumerian name of *Gūr*, also spelt *Geur*, is thus presumably the Sumerian origin of the title of "St. *George*" as the slayer of the Dragon—" St. George " being none other than Indara or Thor himself under that protective title, and thus identical with Andrew.

This battle-axe protective character of this **X** " Cross " of Indara (or Andrew) is also well seen in the Hitto-Sumerian seals, in which it is placed protectively above the sacred Goats of Indara returning to the door of Indara's shrine or "Inn,"[1] see Fig. 57n, p. 334, wherein we shall discover that the " Goat " is a rebus representation of " Goth," the chosen people of Indara or Ia, Iahveh, or Jove, who himself is described in the Sumerian hymns as a Goat,[2] the animal especially sacred to Indra,[3] and to Thor in the Eddas. In that Figure this cross-bolt is pictured, not only in the simple **X** form, but also with the double cross-bars, like the Sumerian picture-sign for the battle-axe (see Fig. 46, *b* and *b*[1], and Fig. 59) ; and representing it, tilted over or oriented, as when carried over the shoulder or in action. *Now this Sumerian form of Indara's (or Andrew's) bolt is figured on many ancient Briton monuments and pre-Christian Crosses and Early Briton coins in this identical form of " Thor's Hammer "* (see Fig. 47, *B* and *F*[2] and Fig. 54) ; and thus disclosing the Sumerian source of the " Hammer of Thor " or " Indri " (or Indara) as figured by the British and Scandinavian Goths.

The peculiar appropriateness of this Sumerian battle-axe sign of Indara for the patron saint of the Scots is that it is, as we have seen, the Sumerian word-sign for *Khat* or *Xat*, the basis of the clan title of *Catti* or *Xatti* (or " *Hitt*-ite "), which, we have seen, is the original source of "Ceti" or " Scot "[4] As a fact, it occurs not infrequently on pre-

---

[1] In Sumerian the name "*In*," for the hospitable house of Indara, discloses the source of our English " Inn."

[2] *Indara*, the Creator-Antelope (*Dara*) . . . The He-Goat who giveth the Earth (S.H.L., 280 and 283) and see Figs. 59, etc. On *Elim* for He-Goat see before.

[3] " The dappled Goat goeth straightway bleating To the place dear to Indra." R.V., 1, 162, 2.

[4] See previous notes. " Khatti " defined the Catti tribe as " The Sceptre-wielders " or ruling race.

# INDARA OR ANDREW AS ST. GEORGE 321

Christian monuments in Scotland, oriented in the key-pattern ornament in Fig. 47$F^1$, p. 295, not only at St. Andrews itself but elsewhere in Scotland, and also in Wales and in Ireland, the ancient " Scotia " (see footnotes to Fig. 47). Moreover, the Swastika Sun-Cross is likewise oriented in Scotland in the St. Andrew's Cross tilt in its key-pattern style.[1] This shows that this tilting of this Catti or " Xati " Sumerian was deliberately done in Scotland, and thus presumably implies that *the Scots in Scotland up till the beginning of our Christian era preserved the memory that this Sumerian sign " Xat " represented their own ruling clan-name of Catti, " Xati," " Ceti " or " Scot."*

FIG. 56.—Indara's **X** Bolt or " Thor's Hammer " on Ancient Briton monument.
(After Stuart.)[2]
(See Figs. 47, *B* and $F^1$ for other Briton examples of this Sumerian bolt.)

In transforming the Hittite Sun-god " Indara " or " Indra " into the Christian saint " Andrew," we find the analogous process resorted to as in the case of St. George, with the added facility that " Andrew," or " Andreas," was already the name of one of the Apostles. But the name " Andrew " is admittedly not a Hebrew or Semitic but an Aryan name, and now seen to be a religious Aryan name based on that of the Father-god Indara or Indra. Indeed, it is believed by biblical authorities that Andrew the Apostle,

[1] S.S.S., I, Pl. 62, 63, etc.
[2] S.S.S., I, 138. From Strathmartine, Forfarshire.

who was the first disciple of Christ of " Galilee of the Gentiles " and the introducer of his brother Peter to Christ, was an Aryan in race.[1] He was significantly a disciple of John-the-Baptist (of the pre-Christian Cross, cult), before he followed Christ, he introduced Greeks to Christ and was associated with Philip, an Aryan Greek,[2] who, we have seen, was the companion of the Aryan apostle Bartholomew. With such an Aryan extraction and name he was naturally represented as the Apostle to Asia Minor (of the Hittites) and to the Scythians,[3] who were Aryanized under Gothic or "*Getæ*" rulers; and their name "Scyth," the *Skuth-es* of the Greeks is cognate with " Scot."

Indeed, Andrew the Apostle appears to have been racially an Aryan Phœnician. He, like his brother Simon Peter—both elements of whose name are admittedly Aryan Gentile and non-Hebrew [4]—was a fisherman with nets. This occupation presupposes a non-Hebrew race, as there is no specific bible reference to any Hebrews being sailors or fishermen with nets. The fish-supply of Jerusalem came from the Phœnicians of Tyre.[5] And the name of the village in which Andrew and his brother Peter and Philip dwelt on the north shore of the Sea of Galilee, was specifically Phœnician and non-Hebrew. It was called " Beth-Saidān "[6] or " Beth-Saida." " Beth " is the late Phœnician form of spelling the Sumerian *Bid*, " a *Bid*-ing place " or " Abode,"—thus disclosing the Sumerian origin of the English word " bide." And " Saidān " or " Saidā," which has no meaning in Hebrew, is obviously " of Sidon." The Phœnician seaport of Sidon was latterly, and is now, called " Saida ; " and is within fifty miles from Beth-saida, with which it was connected by a Roman road through Dan or Cæsarea Philippi, on the frontier of Phœnicia, with an ancient Hittite fortress with a temple of Bel, now significantly called ". St. George."[7] And the two-horned mountain rising above Bethsaida and the adjoining Capernaum, and the scene of " The Sermon on the Mount," is called " The Horns of the

---

[1] B.L.S., Novr., 594.   [2] John, 12, 22.   [3] Eusebius, *H.E.*, 3,5.
[4] *Encycl. Bibl.*, 4534 and 4559.   [5] Nehemiah, 3, 3 ; 13, 16.
[6] In Greek text Matt. 11, 21; Mark, 6, 45 ; 8, 22.
[7] El Khidr—by Arabs.

## ST. ANDREW AS AN ARYAN PHŒNICIAN

Khatti or Hatti," *i.e.*, the Hittites, and we have seen that the Phœnician sailors of Sidon and Tyre were Hittites. It thus appears probable that Andrew, Peter, Bartholomew and Philip were not only Aryan in race, as their names imply, but that they were part of a colony of Sidonian Phœnicians, settled on the shores of the sea of "Galilee of the Gentiles."

And it is noteworthy that Christ, whose first disciples were Aryan Gentiles, and who himself dwelt and preached chiefly in " Galilee of the Gentiles," visited " the coasts of Tyre and Sidon "[1] worked there a miracle on a Syrio-Phœnician woman,[2] had followers from Tyre and Sidon,[3] and he specially connects Bethsaida with Tyre and Sidon.[4]

The miraculous part of the legend grafted on to Andrew the Apostle by the Early Christian Church, in making him the Apostle to the Scyths, Goths and Scots, who were traditional worshippers of Andrew's namesake, Indara, is now seen clearly to incorporate a considerable part of the myth of his namesake, the God Indara of the Goths and Scyths. Whilst the general Romish and Greek Church legends make Andrew travel as a missionary in Scythia,[5] Cappadocia of the central Hittites, Galatia, Bithynia, Pontus (including Troy) in Asia Minor, in Byzantium and Thrace of the Goths, Macedonia, Achaia, and Epirus[6] (whence Brutus sailed to Britain), the Syrian Church history relates that Andrew [like " Indara, who maketh the multitude to dwell in peace "[7]] *freed the people from a cannibal Dragon who devoured the populace* ; and the means which he used to destroy this monster and its cannibal crew was " *to spout water over the city and submerge it.*"[8]

Now this function of being a " Spouter of Water " for the welfare of mankind, was a leading function of God Indara amongst the Aryans, who were essentially agriculturists and dependent on irrigation for crops. His name is usually spelt in Sumerian, as we have seen, as " House of the Waters " ("*In-Duru,*" or "Inn of the *Duru,*" *i.e.*, Greek

[1] Matt. 15, 21 ; Luke 7, 24.   [2] Mark 7. 3. 6.   [3] Mark 3. 8; Luke 6, 17.
[4] Matt. 11, 21-22. Tyre and Sidon had early Christian congregations (Acts 21. 3-7), and the bishops of the Christian synod of Tyre (335 A.D.) were *Arians* (R.H.P. 544).   [5] Eusebius, *H.E.*, 3,5 ; and B.L.S., Novr., 594.
[6] B.L.S., Novr., 594.   [7] See extract in heading.   [8] B.S.L., Novr., 595.

'*Udor* and Cymric *Dwr,* " Water ").[1] And Indara is very freely represented in the Hitto-Sumerian seals from the earliest period as " Spouting Water " for the good of mankind and to the discomfiture of the Dragon, who blocked the water-supply (see Figs. 35 and 57).

FIG. 57.—Indara spouting Water for benefit of mankind and their cattle and crops.
From Hitto-Sumerian Seal (enlarged 2 diameters).
(After Ward.)[2]
Note.—This is same scene as in Fig. 33, but Bel has here his vase of spouting waters.

This Water-spouting of Indara is also freely celebrated *in the Indian Vedic hymns wherein Indra is actually described as " garlanded " with the Euphrates River, precisely as figured in the above Sumerian seal,* and as described in the Sumerian psalms, thus establishing again the remarkable literal identity of the Indo-Aryan Vedic tradition with the Sumerian.

" I, Indra, have bestowed the Earth upon the Aryans,
And Rain upon the man who brings oblations.
I guided forth the loudly roaring Waters."—*R.V.* 4, 26, 2.

" O Indra ! slaying the Dragon in thy strength,
Thou lettest loose the Floods."—*R.V.,* 1, 80, 11 ; 4, 17, 1 ; 19, 8.

" Indra, wearing like a woollen garland the great Parusnī [Euphrates] River,[3]
Let thy bounty swell high like rivers unto this singer."—*R.V.,* 4, 22, 2.

[1] Indo-Pers. *Darya, Derya* " Sea."   [2] W.S.C., 283–5.
[3] The Euphrates was called by the Sumerians *Buru-su* or *Puru-su,* and in Akkad. *Paru-sinnu,* which latter appears to be the source of its Vedic name of " *Parusnī.*"

## ST. ANDREW AS AN ARYAN PHŒNICIAN

" The Waters of Purusu [Euphrates], the waters of the Deep . . .
The pure mouth of Induru purifies."—*Sumer Psalm.*[1]

And a similar function is ascribed to Jehovah in the Psalms of David.[2]

It would, moreover, now appear that in fixing the place of St. Andrew's alleged martyrdom in *Achaia* in Greece, and under a proconsul called *Ægeas*, the early Church had merely incorporated still further that part of the Hitto-Sumerian or Gothic myth of God Indara, wherein he bore the title of "*Aix* or *Aigos*," The He-Goat (or " Goth "),[3] whilst his chosen people, the Sumers and Goths, were historically known as " Ægeans " or " Achaians " and their land as " Achaia."[4] For there seems to be no real historical evidence whatsoever for the martyrdom of St. Andrew the Apostle ; and the Syrian history which is presumably the most authentic, makes no mention of his martyrdom.

And even the extraordinary and hitherto inexplicable folk-lore tradition attaching to St. Andrew's Day, for maidens desirous of husbands to pray to that saint on the evening of his festival (30th November), as described by Luther, and current amongst the Anglo-Saxons,[5] is now explained by Indra's traditional bestowal of wives :

" Indra gives us the wives we ask."—*Rig Veda*, 4, 17, 16.

In order to account for St. Andrew as the patron saint of the Scots (whom some writers, from the radical similarity of the name, have imagined to be " Scyths "), as the historical tradition prevents the Apostle Andrew from having proceeded further west in Europe than Greece, a Scottish story was fabricated[6] that some of the bones of St. Andrew were

---

[1] *Cf.* S.H.L. 477, wherein the " E-a " synonym of *In-duru* is given.
[2] " Thou visitest the Earth and waterest it ; thou greatly enrichest it with the River of God." *Psalm* 65, 9.
[3] See later.    [4] Details in my *Aryan Origin of the Phœnicians.*
[5] Luther (*Colloquia Mensalia*, 1, 232) states that in his country the maidens, on the evening of St. Andrew's day, strip and pray to that saint for a husband. And the same custom prevailed amongst the Anglo-Saxons. H.F.F., 8.
[6] B.L.S., Novr., 454. The legend found first in the Aberdeen Breviary is termed by Baring-Gould " the fable."

stolen from his shrine in Greece by a Greek monk in the eighth century A.D. and brought by him to St. Andrews in Fife, although no mention of such a transfer or of that monk is found in the Romish calendars on the dispersion of the relics of that saint or later ; and the tale is otherwise self-contradictory.[1] Presumably, therefore, there was an early Phœnician Barat " pagan " shrine to Indara or Indri Thor or Andreas at St. Andrews—which is near the mouth of the Perth river—at the foundation of the priory there at the conversion of the local Picts and Scots to Christianity in the eighth century A.D.[2]

This existence of a pagan shrine of Indara at St. Andrews in the pre-Christian period is confirmed by the unearthing there of a considerable number of pieces of ancient sculpture and fragments of crosses bearing no Christian symbols, but which, from their appearance, are believed to have been pagan and had " *been broken up and thrown aside as rubbish,*"[3] or buried as casing for graves, or built into the foundations of the twelfth century cathedral.[4] Amongst these fragments of crosses, which are of the Hitto-Sumerian pattern, are many ornamented with the double-barred Indara's or Thor's Hammer in key pattern.[5] And one slab of elaborate sculpture bears, as its chief figure, what is obviously intended for *Indara killing the Lion* by tearing asunder its jaws,[6] in defence of a sheep and deer or

---

[1] *Ib.*, 454. The Greek monk is called Regulus and is said to have brought the relics in the eighth century from Patras in Greece, the reputed place of St. Andrew's martyrdom and burial. But the Romish calendars state that all the relics of St. Andrew were removed from Patras by Constantine to Constantinople in 337 A.D. *Ib.*, 598.

[2] Several other towns in Britain appear to bear this Andreas or Gothic Eindri-de name, such as Anderida, the old name for Pevensey in the Roman period, the port where William the Norman landed in the Channel ; Andreas in the Isle of Man with Runic monuments ; Ender-by in Lincoln. And *Indre* was the old name and present provincial name of Tours, which the British Chronicles relate was founded by Brutus. An analogous name seems St. Cyrus, an ancient port and ecclesiastic settlement between St. Andrews and the Don River. " Cyrus," we have seen, is a form of " George " or *Gur*, a synonym of Indara ; and the only two saints called " Cyrus " are one in Egypt, and the other in *Carthage*, who has no distinct historical Christian basis (*cp.* B.L.S., July, 321) and thus probably also Phœnician.

[3] S.S.S., 2, p. 5.   [4] *Ib*, p. 4.
[5] S.S.S., 1, Pl. 62 and 63, and 2, Pl. 9, 10, 11 and 18.
[6] S.S.S., 1, 61.

## ST. ANDREW'S CROSS IS INDARA'S HAMMER

antelopes—which is a famous exploit of Indara (as cited below) ; and this scene is very frequently figured on Hitto-Sumerian seals and sculptures. This same scene is also significantly pictured on a fragment at Drainie in Moray,[1] where is the same double-headed Hammer of Indara or Thor on the Cross in Fig. 47F', and on several others in the same locality. And it is also noteworthy that one of the first Christian churches erected at St. Andrews was dedicated to St. Michael the Archangel,[2] that is, as we have seen, and will see further, the archangel of Indara or Andrew.

This exploit of Indara in killing the devouring Lion as well as the Dragon demon to "make the multitude to dwell in peace," now appears to explain another folk-custom on St. Andrew's Day *in England*, which has hitherto been inexplicable. In Cornwall it is, or was till lately, a custom on St. Andrew's Day for a party of youths, making a fearsome noise blowing a horn and beating tin pans, to pass through the town for "*driving out any evil spirits which haunt the place*," and later the church bells take part in it.[3] In Kent a rabble assembles on that day for hunting and killing squirrels ; and a similar squirrel-hunting wake takes place in Derbyshire[4] ; and the squirrel in Gothic tradition is synonymous with "demoniac."[5] This custom of expelling evil spirits on St. Andrew's Day, whilst evidencing the former worship of that saint in England, presumably celebrates the expulsion by Indara of the Lion and Dragon demons.

Altogether, in view of the many foregoing facts and associated evidence, it is abundantly clear that St. Andrew, as patron saint of the Scots, Scyths and Goths, was the Hitto-Phœnician god Indara or Indri-Thor of our Catti or Xatti ancestors, transformed into a Christian saint by the Early Christian Church for proselytizing purposes. And that in picturing St. Andrew as impaled on an X Crucifix, he is represented as hoisted upon his own invincible "hammer."

St. Patrick's Cross also appears to have had its origin in the same "pagan" fiery Sun Cross as that of "St. George."

---

[1] S.S.S. 130.   [2] S.C.P., 185.   [3] H.F.F., 8.
[4] *Ib.*, 8 and 562 ; but in Derbyshire at an earlier date in Novr.
[5] *Cp.* V.D., 483.

St. Patrick, as we have seen, was a Catti or Scot of "The Fort of the Britons" or Dun-Barton, who went to Ireland, or "Scotia" as it was then called, on his mission to convert the Irish Scots and Picts of Erin in 433 A.D. He appears to have incorporated the Sun and Fire cult of his ancestral Catti into his Christianity. This is evident from his famous "Rune of the Deer" in consecrating Tara in Ireland—wherein the name "Deer," the Sumerian *Dara,* now seen to be the source of our English word "Deer," is the basis of one of the Hitto-Sumerian modes of spelling the god-name of In-Dara, who, we shall see, is symbolized by the Deer or Goat. And the Sun is also called "The Deer" in the Gothic Eddas, and thus explains the very frequent occurrence of the Deer carved as a solar symbol on pre-Christian Crosses and other monuments in Britain, as well as on Early Sumerian and Hittite sacred seals, and sculptures, as figured and described below.

In his "Rune of the Deer" St. Patrick invokes the Sun and Fire in banishing the Devil and his Serpent Powers of Darkness:—

"At Tara to-day, in this fateful hour
I place all Heaven with its Power,
And *The Sun* with its Brightness,
And the Snow with its Whiteness,
*And Fire with all the Strength it hath.*
    \*    \*    \*    \*    \*
All these I place
By God's almighty help and grace
Between myself and The Powers of Darkness!"[1]

And there are repeated references to St. Patrick using his Cross to demolish Serpent and other idols and to work miracles with it, as did the Hitto-Sumerians. And he did so at a period before the True Cross had become identified with the Crucifix.

Thus, we discover that the *Crosses of the British Union Jack, as well as the Crosses of the kindred Scandinavian ensigns are the superimposed "pagan" red Sun Crosses and Sun-god's Hammer of our Hitto-Phœnician ancestors,* which those "pagan" forefathers had piously carried aloft as their own

[1] Ed. E. Sharpe in *Lyra Celtica,* 17.

## UNICORN OF ANDREW IS INDARA'S

*standards to victory through countless ages*, and which have been unflinchingly treasured as their standards by their descendants in England, Scotland and Ireland, even after their conversion to Christianity, and who ultimately united them into one monogram at the reunion of the kindred elements in the British Isles into one nation—two of the Crosses in 1606, and " St. Patrick's " added in 1801.

ROYAL ARMS OF SCOTLAND
FIG. 58. Unicorn as sole supporter of old Royal Arms of Scotland and associated with St. Andrew and his " Cross."
Note the Unicorn is bearded like a Goat, and wears a crown like Hittite, Fig. 4.

The Unicorn, also, which is the especial ancient heraldic animal of the Scots, the sole supporter of the royal arms of

Scotland, the surmount of the ancient town or market crosses of Edinburgh, Jedburgh, etc., the supporter or shield of the chief families bearing the family surname of " Scott,"[1] and joined to the Lion (or, properly, Leopards) of England by James I. (VI. of Scotland) on the Union, is now disclosed to be the sacred Goat or Antelope of Indara, the *Uz* or *Sigga*, Goat, or *Dara* or Deer-Antelope of the Hitto-Sumerians, imported into Early Britain with Indara worship by the Barat Phœnician Catti or Early Goths in the " prehistoric " period. It is already seen figured in the early Hittite rock-sculpture (Fig. 4, p. 7) as ",One-horned," standing by the side of the first Aryan Gothic king. This " one " horn, however, is merely the apparent result of this royal totem Goat wearing over its horns the long Phrygian cap of the Early Goths, like the king himself and his officials, but this latterly gave rise to the legend that the totem Goat had only one horn.

The Goat was the especially sacred animal of Indara, as recorded in the Sumerian and Vedic texts, some of which are cited in the heading ; and Indara himself was, as therein cited, called by the Sumerians " The He-Goat ";[2] and Thor and his Goths are also called " He-Goats " in the Gothic Eddas, wherein Thor is called " *Sig*-Father," the identical name by which Bel also is called,[3] *i.e.*, by the Sumerian Goat name.

The title *Sig* or " the horned," the root of *Sigga* " Goat,"[4] appears to have given its name to the peaked Hittite or " Phrygian " cap *Sag* (seen in that figure) as well as to its wearers, and thus explains the horned head-dress of the Hitto-Sumerians, Early Britons and Goths. It had the synonym of *Gud*[5] which seems to be the source of both " Goat " and " Goth." *Gud* or *Gut* appear to be applied

[1] *E.g.*, Scotts of Buccleugh line.
[2] *Indara*, the Creator-Antelope (*Dara*) . . . The He-Goat who giveth the Earth. (S.H.L., 280 and 283. On *Elim* for He-Goat see before.)
[3] Br., 3374. *Sig* is also title of the Mountain Goat (Br. 3376, and *cp.* under *Armu* M.D., 102) ; and is the source of *Caga* " goat " in Sanskrit.
[4] Br., 3388 (horn), 10899 (goat). Its Akkad equivalent, *sapparu*, seems source of Latin *capra*.
[5] Br., 3504, also " horn " (3515).

to the Goat itself.¹ Hence the ruling Hittite titles of " Sag " and " Gud " and " Gut " would explain why the Goths or Guti were called by the Greco-Romans both *Getæ* and *Sakai* or *Sacæ*—the latter being obviously the source of " *Sax*-on," and of the royal Indo-Aryan clan of *Sakya* to which Buddha belonged, and the latter Hittite tribe of " *Sagaś*," who recovered Palestine from Akenaten,² and whose name is defined as " people named *Kas-sa*,"³ *i.c.*, obviously the Kaśi or Kassi. Similarly, the *Uz* Goat name, which appears to have become *Uku* when applied to the people,⁴ seems to be the source of the name " *Achai*-oi " or *Achai*-ans for the leading tribe of early Aryans in Greece, as well as the Greek *aix* and Sanskrit *aja* for " goat. "

The Goat appears thus to me to have been selected for this totem position by the Early Aryans or Sumerians or Goths, partly on account of its name resembling rebus-wise the tribal name of " Goth," partly because of the Early Aryans having been presumably Goat-herds in the mountains before their adoption of the settled life and their invention of Agriculture and Husbandry, and partly because the bearded and semi-human appearance of the Goat's head offered a strikingly *masculine yet inoffensive* effigy for their institution of the Fatherhood stage of Society, in opposition and in contrast to the primeval promiscuous Matriarchy of the Chaldee aborigines of the Mother-Son cult, with its malignant and devouring demonist totems of the Serpent, Bull-Calf, Vulture or Raven, and Wolf of Van or Fen (the Wolf exchanging also with the ravening Lion), and demanding bloody and even human sacrifices. And the fusion of these four totems is the origin of the Dragon.

Thus we find that the antagonism of the Goat (or " Unicorn ") to the Lion (or Wolf or Dragon) is figured freely on Sumerian and Hitto-Phœnician seals from the earliest

¹ *Gud*=" sharp-pointed " (Br., 4708) or " horned animal " (P.S.L., 159); and *Gut*, " horned animal," also *Gut*, " warrior class " (Br, 3677 and 5732, P.S.L., 169). The horned head sign *Al* with Sumer equivalent of *Gud*=*Alu*, " stag " (M.D., 39) and *Al* has Sumer equivalent of *Guti* (Br., 942–3, and M.D., 939) and cognate with *Elim* or *Ilim*, " He-Goat."
² AL (W), 67, l. 21 ; 88, l. 13 and 18, etc. They are also called *Habiri* in Sumerian and *Hafr* is the ordinary title for the Goth soldiers of Thor in Eddas, and is defined as " He-Goat " (V.D., 231). ³ Br.,4730. ⁴ Br.,5915.

period, and *also on Early Briton monuments and coins* (see Figs. 59, 60), and that Indara himself is sometimes represented as a Goat or Deer (*Dara*) as the slayer or tamer of the demonist Lion, as is recorded also in the Vedic hymn which says : " Indra for the Goat [Goths] did to death the Lion."[1] Yet so little is our modern heraldry aware of the facts of origin, meaning and function of the " Unicorn," that it now represents that invincible Aryan totem of the Sun Cross—and of *Ia* or Jove and Thor and of Heaven, and of our ancestral Aryan originators of the World's Civilization—in the form of a one-horned horse, but significantly *bearded like a Goat*, and bound in chains and set alongside of its vanquished foe of Civilization, which is supposed to have been its victor—the ravening Lion totem of the demonist Chaldee aborigines ! Whereas in the old Hittite seals, it is the Lion which wears the collar and chain (see Fig. 59 L.), whilst the Unicorn or Goat is the victor through Indara and his archangel.

The Goat, " the swift-footed one of the mountains of sunrise," is represented by the Sumerians as the Sun itself and a form of the Sun-god, though less frequently so than is the winged Sun or Sun-Hawk or Phœnix—the horse only appearing in the very latest period. In the Vedic hymns also, the Sun is sometimes called " the Goat," with the epithet of " The One Step," presumably from its ability to traverse the heavens to the supplicant in " one step " :—

"The Ruddy Sun . . . the One-Step Goat,
By his strength, he possessed Heaven and Earth."[2]

This " One Step Goat " in the Vedas is in especial conflict and contact with the Dragon of the Deep, just as we have seen was the Resurrecting Sun, the vanquisher of the Serpent-Dragon of the Deep and Death.

In this capacity and in its struggle with the Lion or Wolf of Death, and as the rebus for " Goth," the Goat is freely represented on Hitto-Sumerian seals and on Phœnician and Greco-Phœnician coins, in association with the Sun Cross and the protecting Archangel *Tas* ; see Fig. 59 and also

[1] R.V., 7, 18, 17.   [2] Atharva Veda, 13, 1, 6.

later. And significantly *it is similarly figured on Early Briton prehistoric monuments, pre-Christian Crosses, and Ancient Briton coins, and also in association with the Sun Cross*, and often the protecting Archangel *Taś* or *Tasc*, see Fig. 60, and further examples later.

This picture of a " Goat " (in Old English *Goot* and *Gote*, Eddic Gothic *Geit*, Anglo-S. *Gat* and Scots *Gait*) in these scenes appears clearly to be used as a rebus picture-sign for " Goth " (properly *Got* or *Goti*[1]) or *Getæ*, Sumerian *Guti*, *Kud* or *Khat*; just as the battle-axe picture-sign was used for their tribal title of " *Khat-ti* " or " *Hitt-ite*." The hieroglyphic practice of using rebus pictures for proper names continued popular in Greco-Phœnician and Greek coins in Asia Minor down to the Roman period.[2] This now explains also the references to the sacred Goat and Indra in the Vedic hymns. *e.g.*, " The lively Goat goeth straightway bleating to the place dear to Indra."[3]

We now discover that the Sumerians and Hitto-Phœnicians or Early Goths called themselves, or their leading clans, by the names of " Goat," or by names which were more or less identical in sound with their name for Goat, and so made it easy for the picture of the Goat to represent rebuswise their title of " Goth."[4]

This sacred character of the Goat as the totem animal of the Sumerians and Goths, and the source of the legend of the Unicorn, in its victory over the Lion, and as the hallowed animal of Indara or Andrew, now explains the fact of the Goat being still the mascot of the Welsh Cymri, and also the frequency of St. Andrew's Cross in the pre-Christian and early Christian monuments in Wales,[5] and in parts of England. And the figures of the Goat in association with

---

[1] The later historical Goths of Europe and Eddic Goths spelt their name *Got* and *Goti*, the *th* ending is a corruption introduced by the Romans.
[2] These devices are called by numismatists " speaking badges " or " *types parlants*." Examples are Bull (*tauros*) at Tauro-menium, Fox (*Alōpēv*) at Alopeconnesus, Seal (*phōkē*) at Phocæa, Bee (*melitta*) at Melitæa, Goat (*aix*), supposed to be confined to cities called Aegae, Rose (*rodon*) at Rhodes, etc. ; *cp*. M.C.T., 17, etc., 188.
[3] R.N. 1, 162, 2.
[4] Further details in my *Aryan Origin of the Phœnicians*.
[5] See references in above notes.

FIG. 59.—Goats (and Deer) as "Goths" of Indara protected by
Cross and Archangel Tas (Tashub Mikal) against Lion
and Wolves on Hitto-Sumerian, Phœnician and
Kassi Seals.

(After Ward, etc.)

Compare with Briton examples in Fig. on opposite page. Detailed references on p. 336.

FIG. 60.—Ancient Briton Goats (and Deer) as "Goths" of
Indara protected by Cross and Archangel Tascia (or Michael)
against Lion and Wolves.

From ancient monuments, caves, pre-Christian Crosses and Briton Coins. Compare with Hitto-Phœnician examples in Fig. on opposite page. Detailed references on pp. 336 and 337.

# 336 PHŒNICIAN ORIGIN OF BRITONS & SCOTS

St. Andrew's Cross and other solar symbols on the Early Briton coins, and especially in the tin coins of Cornwall (and sometimes with the name *Inara* and "*Ando*,")[1] and in forms identical with those existing on Hitto-Phœnician

[1] " Andy " is a recognized contraction for " Andrew," see, *e.g.*, Carnegie's autobiography.

REFERENCES TO FIG. 59, P. 334.

- *a* W.S.C., 23, archaic Hittite seal (of about 3000 B.C.[3]). Goats defended from Wolves by Cross, and below are day and " night " linked Sun's disc, the original of " spectacles " on British monuments.
- *b* *Ib.*, 69. Goat worshipping Cross, with rayed Cross below.
- *c* *Ib.*, 526, 539. Another of same.   *d Ib.*, 494, with Crosses, revolving rayed Sun of Swastikoid form.
- *e* *Ib.*, 996. Archaic Hittite seal. Wolves attacking Goat which is saved by revolving Sun in " spectacles " form.
- *f* C.S.H., 308 (Hittite). Goat at decorated Cross defended against Wolf.
- *g* W.S.C., 525. Kassi seal of Tax (Tas or Tashub) saving Goat under the Cross from the Wolf, with rayed and lozenge Sun ornament in base.
- *h* C.C., Figs. 295-298. Tax or Tashub-Mikal saving Deer from Lion; from Phœnician coins of Azubal from Phœnician ruins at Kitium in Cyprus, inscribed " King Bel."   *i* W.S.C., 597. Another of same from Hitto-Sumer seal.
- *k* C.S.H., 302. Another Hitto-Phœnician form of same under Cross-like tree or " Fruit-Cross."
- *l* W.S.C., 949. Hittite seal of Tashub-Mikal winged, and clothed in lion's-skin as Hercules, defending Goats under " Celtic Cross ; " and behind is vanquished lion chained, with collar and rope. Note also " Ionic " capital already in this Hittite seal of about 1400 B.C. Analogous Hittite seals in W.S.C., 946-7, 955, 987, etc.
- *m* *Ib.*, 1195. Goat worshipping St. Andrew's Cross and Sun discs from seal in Phœnician grave in Cyprus.   *n Ib.*, 488. Goat protected by St. Andrew's Crosses.   *p Ib.*, 490. Another with a 2-transverse-barred Cross.
- *q* A.E., 1917, 29 (after M. Bénédite) Tax taming the Lions, on ivory handle of dagger of about 4000 B.C., supposed to be from Asia Minor.
- *r* W.S.C., 1023. Tax and assistant vanquishing the Lion, at the winged " Celtic " Cross of the Sun, on Hittite sacred seal.

REFERENCES TO FIG. 60, P. 335.

- *a* E.C.B., H. 9. Archaic tin Brito-Phœnician coin (in Hunter Museum, Glasgow) showing Goat under three Sun discs, engraved in precisely the same technical style as archaic Hittite Cross Seal, Fig. 59, *a*, and in the Sumero-Phœnician *m* and *p*. Six other varieties in E.C.B., Pl. H.
- *b* S.S.S., 2. Illust. Pl. 31, 10-11. Prehistoric rock-graving from Jonathan's Cave, East Wemyss, Fife. Compare Hitto-Sumerian, Fig. 59, *a-d*. The Goat or Deer is going for protection to Cross, which is studded with knobs like the Hitto-Sumerian " Fruit " Crosses. Other analogous Goat and Deer Stone Crosses, S.S.S., 1, 59, 69, 89, 91, 93, 100 ; 2, 101, 106.

## GOTHS AS INDARA'S GOATS IN BRITAIN 337

sacred seals and Phœnician coins, affords still further conclusive evidence of the former widespread prevalence of the cult of Indara or " Andrew " in Early Britain, and of the Barat Catti Phœnician origin of the Britons and Scots.

 *c* *Ib.*, Nos. 24-27. Another of same from same cave. The Goat or Deer kneels in adoration, or for protection (as in Hitto-Sumerian, Fig. 59, *b*, *c*) below tablet containing vestiges of an inscription with trace of an **X** Cross, and below the double Sun-disc or " spectacles."
 *d* S.A.S., Pl. 35, 1. Another graving from same cave showing Deer or Goat protected by Sun disc and " Fruit " Cross and " Spectacles " (latter omitted here through want of space). *Cp.* Hitto-Phœnician, Fig. 59, *d* and *m*.
 *e* S.S.S., 2, 52. Reverse of Cross from Kirkapoll, Tiree of Early Christian period, which significantly figures the Crucifix, on its face, in the primitive original **T** form, and not as the True Cross, like the monument itself. Identical scene of Wolves attacking Goat or Deer in Hittite seal, Fig. 59, *e*, and analogous to Phœnician coins *h* of Fig. 59, *e* and *f*. The man with club stepping down to rescue his deer is Hercules-Tascio as in Phœnician coin *h*, and in Fig. 59, *e*, *f*, where he is *seated* above the Cross and holding the Cross-sceptre as club, see also *g*. On opposite face his place is taken by winged St. Michael spearing the Serpent-Dragon (see also top of *g*), common on pre-Christian Crosses.
 *f* S.S.S., 1, 127. Ancient Cross from Meigle, Perthshire ; showing Goat or Deer protected by the Cross from the Wolf. *Cp.* Hittite type in Fig. 59, *f*.
 *g* S.S.S., 1, 83. Another Tascio-Michael Goat and Cross scene from Glamis in Forfar. The Wolves hold up their head as in Hittite type, Fig. 59, *a* and *e*. Again, on top is Hercules-Tascio with his club and holding an object like a ploughshare. And on left is his winged form as Michael the Archangel. *Cp.* Hittite types in Fig. 59, *g*, *h*, *k*, *l* and *m*.
 *h* E.C.B., 12, 7. Coin of Cunobeline. Tascio (Michael) winged reining up his horse to rescue his Goats.  *i* E.C.B., A., 1 and 2. Archaic form of same showing pellet Crosses, **X** Cross and Rosette Sun. The **X** or St. Andrew's Cross is clearer in A, 6. *Cp.* Hittite, Fig. 59, *l*, and for **X** Cross *m*.
 *k* E.C.B., 16, 2. Wolf fleeing from **X** or St. Andrew's Cross (decorated as Grain or Fruit Cross) and from Sun discs. Other wolves fleeing from Sun or Sun horse in E.C.B., Pl. E, 6 and 7 ; F, 15 ; 4, 12 ; 11, 13, 14. *Cp.* Hitto-Phœnician, Fig. 59, *m*, *n*, *p*, for Goats protected by the **X** or Andrew's Cross.
 *l* S.S.S., 1, 74 and author's photos of pre-Christian Cross at Meigle, Perthshire. Tascio taming the Lions. *Cp.* Hittite, Fig. 59, *q*. In this Briton mon. the lions are duplicated on each side of Tascio, who is robed generally similar to Hittite.
 *m* S.S.S., 1, 82. Another of same from pre-Christian Cross at Aldbar, Forfar. *Cp.* Hittite seal, Fig. 59, *r*, top register, above winged " Celtic " Cross.

FIG. 60A.—Ancient Briton " Tascio " coin inscribed *DIAS*.
(After Poste, and *cp*. Figs. A, B, p. xv.)

## XXII

CORN SPIRIT "TAS-MIKAL" OR "TASH-UB" OF HITTO-SUMERS IS "TASCIO" OF EARLY BRITON COINS AND PREHISTORIC INSCRIPTIONS, "TY" GOTHIC GOD OF TUES-DAY, AND "MICHAEL-THE-ARCHANGEL," INTRODUCED BY PHŒNICIANS

*Disclosing his identity with Phœnician Archangel " Tazs," " Taks," " Dashap-Mikal," and " Thiazi," " Mikli " of Goths, " Daxa " of Vedas, and widespread worship in Early Britain; Phœnician Origin of Dionysos and " Michaelmas" Harvest Festival and of those names.*

" O Son Taś,[1] Lord of the World!
Mighty hero supreme, who subjugates hostility . . .
Gladdener of Corn, Creator of Wheat and Barley!
Renewer of the Herb . . .
Director of the Spirits [Angels] of Heaven.
Thou madest the tablets of Destiny."
—*Sumer Litany.*[2]
" Bearer of the Spear of the hero."—
" The Great Messenger, the pure one of Ia."—*Ib.*[3]
" O Dashap-Mikal bless us! "—
*Phœnician Inscriptions.*[4]

WE have already found that the tutelary *Taś* or *Diaś* of the Sumerians or Early Phœnicians, also called " Son *Taś* or *Dach* " (" Mero-Dach "), " The first-born Son of God *Ia* " (Jahveh, Jove or Indara), was the archangel messenger

[1] " Mero-dach " is the corrupt Hebrew form of this Sumer name, the " Mar-duk " of Assyrians, which was adopted in this translation. But we have already seen that the Sumerian reads *Mar-u* or *Mar-uta* (=" Son " +" Sun or Light "), wherein the second word occasionally has the value of *Dag*. The older forms of his name, however, we have seen were *Taś, Tax* or *Dasi*, so for uniformity *Taś* is used here and throughout this chapter.   [2] S.H.L., 537.   [3] *Ib.*, 480., 517.   [4] C.I.S. references p. 341.

## HITTITE ANGEL TASHUB ON BRITON COINS

of Ia, and that he was freely invoked and figured upon sacred seals and amulets by the Sumerians, Hittites, Trojans and Phœnicians, just as we discovered that he was invoked in the prehistoric cup-mark inscriptions in Britain. And we have found that he was the chief divinity figured along with the Cross defending the Goats or Deer, symbolizing the "Goths," in the Hitto-Sumerian Trojan and Phœnician seals and amulets and on Phœnician and Greco-Phœnician coins, just as we find him figured on the ancient monuments and coins of the Early Britons (see Figs. 60, etc.) in which latter he bears not infrequently the stamped name of "*Tasc*" or "*Tascio*" or "*Dias*,"[1] and is figured sometimes winged and frequently along with ears of corn and the Corn "Cross" of his father Indara or Andrew of the **X** type (see Fig. 61).

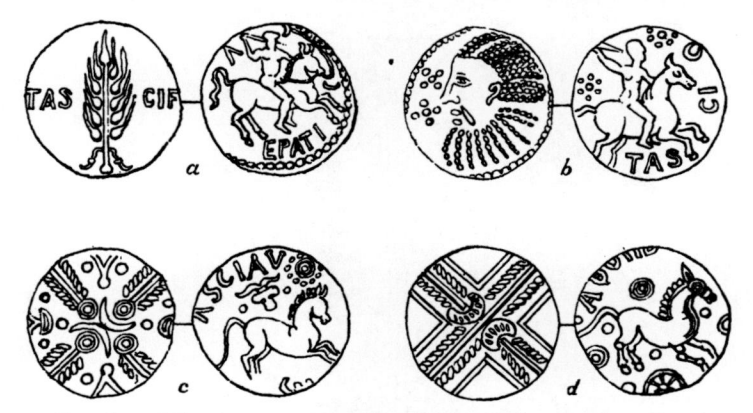

FIG. 61.—"Tascio" or "Tascif" of Early Briton Coins is Corn Spirit "Taś" or "Tash-ub" of Hitto-Sumerians.
(Coins after Evans).[2]

NOTE.—Corn "Crosses" of Indara or Andrew X type in *c* and *d*, and pellet or "cup" Crosses in *b*, with head and beard as in archaic Hittite rock sculpture of Tash-ub in Fig. 62.

We now find further that Taś is hailed as "The Gladdener of Corn, Creator of Wheat and Barley," as cited in the heading. This discovers his identity with the Corn Spirit of the Greeks, "Dionysos"—which name, indeed, of hitherto unknown origin and meaning, we now find was

[1] As *Dias*, see Figs. A and B, page xv. Sumer script in *A* read *Diaś* or Judgment of God.
[2] *a* E.C.B., Pl. 8, 12; *b*, *Ib*., 6, 3; *c Ib*., 5, 8; *d Ib*., 14, 9.

## 340 PHŒNICIAN ORIGIN OF BRITONS & SCOTS

apparently applied to Taś in Sumerian; thus discovering the Sumerian origin of Dionysos in both name, function and representations. This also explains for the first time why Corn and Barley are so frequently figured on the " Tascio " coins of the Ancient Britons, and along with Tascio on Phœnician coins, and why the popular Hittite divinity "*Tash-ub*" or "*Tash*-of-the-Plough" is figured holding stalks of Corn on the Hitto-Sumer seals, and as a gigantic warrior *clad in Gothic dress* holding Corn stalks and bunches

FIG. 62.—Tascio as "Tash-ub," the Hittite or Early Gothic Corn-Spirit. From archaic Hittite rock-sculpture at Ivriz in Taurus.
(After von Luschan and Wilson.)

NOTE.—He is dressed as a Goth, with snow-boots, and Goat-horns on his conical Trojan or Phrygian cap, and he carries stalks of Barley-corn and bunches of Grapes, and behind him is a Plough. The adoring high-priest has solar swastikas, in key pattern, embroidered on his dress.

of Grapes beside a Plough, in the archaic Hittite rock sculpture in the Cilician Gates of the Taurus at Ivriz, near Heraclea (Fig. 62), as Taś or Tascio is the defied *Hercules*.

Moreover, we find that Tascio is the Hitto-Phœnician original of St. Michael the Archangel in name, function and

## TASCIO IS PHŒNICIAN ST. MICHAEL

representation. The later Phœnicians, calling him " Dash-up "[1] occasionally add the title " Mikal " in invoking his blessing[2]; and this name also appears, I find, upon the Phœnician coins of Cilicia of the fifth century along with the figure of Taxi in Phœnician script as " *Miklu* " (see Fig. 66); and as " *Mekigal* " in the Sumerian name for the old Harvest festival corresponding to Michael-mas.

And we shall find that the Hitto-Sumerian cult of Michael the Archangel, introduced by the Phœnicians, was widespread over Ancient Britain in the Phœnician period, from the Phœnician tin-port of St. Michael's Mount in the south to the two " St. Michael's Wells " near our Phœnician inscriptions in the Don Valley in the north, and in the name of other early churches and wells dedicated to St. Michael still further north. Vestiges of this cult of St. Michael the Archangel, *as the Corn Spirit*, introduced into Britain by the Phœnicians, are now seen to survive to the present day in the name of " Michaelmas " for the Harvest Festival (September 29th) in Britain, in association with his sacred sacramental Sun-Goose[3] (see Fig. 66), the " Michaelmas Goose " of that festival :—

" September, when by Custom, right Divine,
Geese are ordain'd to bleed at Michael's shrine."[4]

and in the " St. Michael's Bannock or Cake " of the Michael-mas festival in the Western Isles of Scotland."[5]

The notion of investing God with an archangel appears to have arisen long after the Aryans had " created " the idea

---

[1] See below. The *D* and *R* are often identical in Phœnician.
[2] C.I.S., 90, 2; 91, 2; 935; 94, 5; and pp. 1, 94–99, 105, etc.
[3] The Goose was sacred taboo in Ancient Britain, D.B.G., 5, 12, 6.
[4] King's *Art of Cookery*, 63, H.F.F., 409.
[5] Martin, describing the *Protestant* inhabitants of Skye, writes, " They observe the festivals of Christmas [Yule], Easter, Good Friday and that of St. Michael. Upon the latter day they have a cavalcade in each parish, and several families bake the cake, called " St. Michael's Bannock.' *W. Islands of Scotland*, 213, and 100. Regarding St. Kilda, Macaulay writes, " It was, till of late, an universal custom among the islanders on Michaelmas Day to prepare in every family a loaf or cake of bread, enormously large. This cake belonged to the Archangel. Everyone in each family, whether strangers or domestics, *had his portion of this kind of showbread*, and had some *title to the friendship and protection of Michael* " (*Hist. of St. Kilda*, 82).

AA

of God in the image of man as "The Father-god," and after they had given him a host of angels to counteract the swarms of malignant demons with which primeval man and the Chaldean Mother-Son cult had infested the earth, air and "the waters under the earth." The process by which the archangel was invented and his functions arranged and developed now seems to become evident. The Father-god or "Bel" was early given by the Aryans the title of "*Zagg*" or "*Sagg*"[1] (or "Zeus"), as it exists on the earliest known historical document, Udug's trophy Stone-Bowl from the oldest Sun-temple in Mesopotamia at Nippur. This "*Zagg*" has the meaning, "The Shining Stone + Being, Maker or Creator," thus giving the sense of "Rock of Ages" to the God as the Creator.

This early Aryan name for God, about two millenniums before the birth of Abraham, with its sense of fixity, is soon afterwards found spelt by the Early Sumerians in their still-existing inscriptions as *Zax* or *Zakh*, in the form "The Enthroned *Zax* or *Zakh*" (*En-Zax*),[2] with the meaning "The Enthroned Breath or Wind."[3] This presumably was to denote God as The Breath of Life, and perhaps also his invisibility as a Spirit. This ancient Aryan idea of God as "The Breath of Life" is preserved in the reference in Genesis to the creation of man: "God *breathed* into his nostrils the Breath of Life and man became a living soul."[4] And in the Old Testament, God "flies on the wings of the Wind,"[5] and in the New Testament the working of God's Spirit is compared to the Wind.[6] Such slight alterations in the spelling of divine and other proper names in order to denote a different though correlated sense, were often made by the Sumerians, and are parallel to their spelling of "Induru" as "Indara," with a different shade of meaning.

This idea of the "enthronement" and fixity of The Father-god in human form in heaven, with its sense of vast remoteness and aloofness from the earth, was presumably

---

[1] Spelt alphabetically, *Za-ga-ga*, see before.
[2] Br., 5928. Hitherto disguised by Assyriologists reading *Zax* by its semitic synonym of *Lil*.
[3] Br., 5932.     [4] Genesis, 2, 7.     [5] Psalm xviii, 10, etc.
[6] John iii, 8.

# ORIGIN OF MICHAEL THE ARCHANGEL

the reason why the Sumerians, in their human craving for the more immediate presence of God on the earth, delegated his powers on earth to a deputy in the person of " The firstborn Son of Ia," the Archangel " Taś " or Taxi (Mero-Dach or Mar-Duk), who ultimately was made in Babylonia to overshadow his Father and was given most of the titles of the latter—not only " King of Heaven and Earth," " Lord of the Lands," " Creator," and " Holder of the Tablets of Fate," but even " Slayer of the Dragon of Darkness," which achievement thus became credited to him as St. Michael.[1] And the later Chaldean polytheists made him king of their motley pantheon, amongst whom the various departments of Nature were parcelled out, and they even also called him " Bel " or Father-god.

But amongst the purer Hitto-Sumerians and Phœnicians, adhering to monotheism and its " Sun-worship," Tas appears to have retained his original character of the archangel of The One God, although he is addressed as a " god," which also has the general sense of " divinity." Thus in many of the Sumerian psalms and litanies he is the mere agent on the earth of the Father-god who is enthroned in heaven. He is " The great Messenger, the pure one of *Ia*,"[2] " Companion of Heaven and *Ia*,"[3] " The Merciful One who loveth to give Life to the Dead,"[4] " Lord of Life and Protector of Habitations,"[5] and " Ever ready to hear the Prayers of mankind," he transmits these to his Father, The Enthroned Zax (Zeus) in heaven and carries out the orders of the latter. And we have such scenes pictured in Hittite seals, *e.g.*, Fig. 63, which shows a sick man on his bed attacked by the Dragon of Death, and he appeals to Taś, who in turn intercedes with his Father-god Indara.

Thus we read in the old Sumerian psalms and litanies such invocations and incidents as the following :—

" May thou, Son Taś, the Great Overseer of the Spirits of Heaven, exalt thy head !"[6]
" (To) the Corn-god I have offered ! . . ."

[1] Indra alone killed the Dragon without aid of " Maruta " (Marduk). R.V., 1, 165, 6.
[2] S.H.L., 517.   [3] *Ib.*, 501.   [4] *Ib.*, 501.
[5] Langdon, S.P., 277.   [6] S.H.L., 517.

"May the god of Herbs, the Assembler of God and man . . .
Deliver such and such a man, the son of his God,
And may he be saved!"[1]

FIG. 63. Archangel Taś interceding with God Indara for sick man attacked by Dragon of Death. From Hittite Seal of about 2,500 B.C.
(After Delaporte.)[2]
Note bed of sick man, and sacred Goat of Indara; and *cp*. Psalm xxxiv, 6–7.
The Circles (cups) above man=*Muru* or "Amorite"; and Sumer sign above dragon="Raven of Sin-Fire" (Br., 2227), *Lax* or *Lakh* "Fire"="*Luci*-fer," or *Loki*.

Then the archangel Taś, hearing this prayer, repairs to his Father in Heaven, "The Good Shepherd who rests not, who causeth mankind to abide in safety;"[3] and presents the prayer:

"The Son Taś has regarded him [the supplicant].
To his Father Ia, into the house he descends[4] and says:
'O my Father, the Evil Curse like a demon has fallen on the man!'
Ia to his son made answer . . .
'Go my son, Son Tas!
Take the man to the House of Pure Sprinkling,
And remove his ban, and expel his ban.'"[5]

Or Ia or Indara replies:—

"O Son Taś, substance of mine, Go, my Son!
Before the [Cross of the?] Sun-god take his [the afflicted's] hand,
Repeat the spell of the pure hymn!
Pour the (cleansing) Waters upon his head!"[6]

Or:—"Go, my Son Taś!
Let the Fire [-Cross?] of the Cedar tree,
The tree that destroys the wickedness of the incubus,

[1] S.H.L., 468. [2] D.C.O. (L) pl. 82. 406. [3] L.S.P., 245.
[4] Here "descends" is used, when Ia or Indara is supposed to reside in the Waters. [5] S.H.L., 472. [6] Ib., 516.

On whose core the name of Ia is recorded,
With the spell supreme . . . to foundation and roof let ascend
And to the sick man never may those seven demons
   approach ! "[1]

The Archangel's association with Corn and Agriculture as " The Corn Spirit," was in series with his Father's titles of " Lord of the Lands " and of Agriculture, in the Sumerian psalms.

Thus in these psalms " The Enthroned Zax " is hailed :—
" Lord of the Harvest Lands, Lord of the Grain Lands !
Husbandman who tends the fields art thou, O Zax the Enthroned !"[2]

" Tender of the plants of the Garden art thou !
Tender of the Grain Fields art thou ! "[3]

" Father Zax, the presents of the Ground are offered to thee in sacrifice !
O Lord of Sumer, figs to thy dwelling-place we bring !
To give Life to the Ground thou dost exist !
Father Zax, accept the sacred offerings ! "[4]

It is easy to see now, in the light of our discoveries, why the Early Aryans or Hitto-Sumerians, Khatti or Catti Goths were naturally led to institute a patron saint or Archangel of Agriculture and The Plough. They were, I find, the founders of the Agricultural Stage of the World's Civilization, and made Agriculture the basis of their Higher Civilization and the Settled Life—and it still remains the basis of the Higher Civilization to the present day. They also took from it their title of " *Arri* "—or " *Arya* " (Englished into " *Arya-n* ")—which, I find, is derived from the Sumerian *Ar*, " a Plough " (which thus discloses the Sumerian origin of the Old English " to *Ear* (*i.e.*, plough) the ground," Gothic *Arian*, Greek *Aroein*, Latin *Ar*-are). And they made ploughing and sowing sacred rites under the Sun Cross, as we have seen in the Cassi seal of about 1350 B.C. (see Fig. 12, p. 49) and the same scene is figured on seals of the fourth millennium B.C. In establishing Agriculture, the Aryans, as a small band of civilized pioneers,

[1] S.H.L., 470.  [2] L.S.P., 199, 201.  [3] *Ib.*, 277.  [4] *Ib.*, 279.

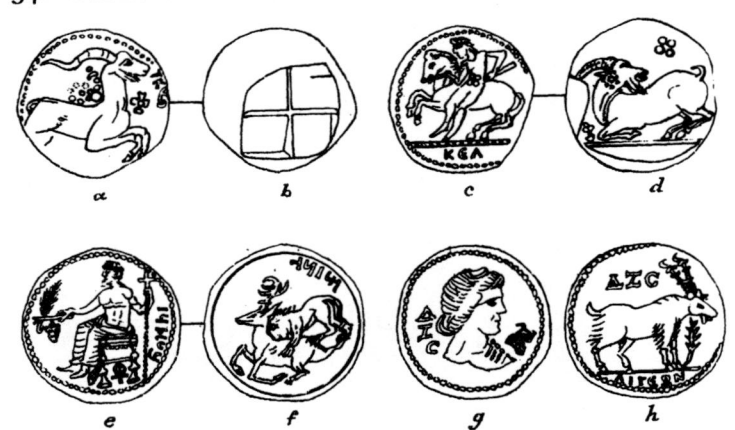

FIG. 64.—Archangel *Taš-Mikal* defending Goats (and Deer) as " Goths" with Cross and Sun emblems on Greco-Phœnician coins.

(From Cilician coins of 5th century B.C. onwards in British Museum.)
Note Goat springing to Cross (*a—b*) and Crosses (*a—e*), legends *TKS, TKZ*, and *DZC*, Goat and Cross under throne of Bel Tarz, who bears Cross standard ; and compare with opposite figures on Briton Coins.

- *a* One of the oldest Cilician coins of " Early Fifth Century, B.C.," supposed to be from Celenderis, sea-port (founded by Phœnicians), W. of Tarsus, see Hill H.C.C., Pl. 814. Goat is springing to the Cross, with Sun circle and Cross above it, formed by circles as in Briton coins, and bearing in front Phœnician legend reading, apparently, " TKS." *b* Reverse with stamped Cross.
- *c* Celenderis coin of about 450–400 B.C. (H.C.C., 9, 2) shows Hercules-Tascio descending from his Sun-horse to defend Goat (on reverse, *d*). Note Cross on his back, formed by circles, as in Briton coins and Hitto-Sumerian seals, and his club in right hand.
- *d* Reverse of *c*, with Goat kneeling before Cross, behind rock, and adoring or invoking Cross in sky ; representing Hercules-Tascio as messenger of Sun-god. Other analogous coins, H.C.C., 9, 1 and 3–9 ; 13–16 ; and 10, 1–5, etc.
- *e* Hercules as " Lord of Tarsus " on coins of Tarsus of period of Mazæus, 361–333 B.C. (H.C.C., 30, 6), bearing Phœnician legend, " Bal *TKZ*" or Lord *Takz* (see text). Hercules-Takz seated on throne above *a Goat's head and handled Cross, and bearing in left hand the Cross* ; as standard with fruited stalk ; and in right bestows grapes, reaping sickle and ear of Corn (= Dionysos).
- *f* Reverse of *e*. Stag (kin of Goat) attacked by Lion—which was killed by Hercules. Other variant coins of this type, H.C.C., 30, 1–5, 7, 8, and numerous Hitto-Sumerian and Cypro-Phœnician cylinders, etc. (see later).
- *g* Coin supposed to be from Aigea (modern Ayas), port to E. of Tarsus, of period of Macrinus, 217–218 A.D. (H.C.C., 4, 9). Showing bust of young Dionysos with bunch of grapes, and behind, his name. *DZC*, *i.e.*, equivalent of " *Tasc* " or " *Dias* " of Briton coins. Very numerous coins of this type with legend DZC (see text).
- *h* Another Aigea coin of same period (H.C.C., 4, 11), showing long-maned mountain Goat, standing before branch or stalk of corn, *and bearing on top of his horns two Fire-torches* (or sacred Fire of the Sun cult) and legend *DZC* (*i.e.*, " Tasc ") as before.

## TAS-MIKAL DEFENDING GOATS AS GOTHS

had to defend themselves and their fields by force of arms against the depredations and bitter religious hostility of a world of hungry savage nomadic hordes of Serpent- and

FIG. 65.—Archangel *Taš* defending Goats ("Goths") with Cross and Sun emblems on Early Briton coins.
(After Evans and Stukeley.)
Note Goats with Cross and Sun signs by circles, as in Greco-Phœnician on opposite page and legends *Tas, Tasciio*.

*a* Long-maned Goat coin (E.B.C.,G. 4) as in Cilician coin, Fig. 64 *h*, and in Hittite seals (Fig. 59, etc.) with Sun-circles. Obverse bears a Hercules head generally similar to *b* ; with a Sun circle rosette as in Cilician coin, Fig. 64 *a*, etc. It is essentially a copy of the latter archaic Cilician coin with springing goat and Sun-circles.
*b* Obverse of similar type of coin (E.B.C., 8, 2) with head of Hercules bearded in style of Hittite rock-sculpture (Fig. 62). Its legend is read "VER" by Evans, as place of mintage of Verulam (St. Albans), the capital of Cassi-vellaunus ; but it may read "HER" = "Hercules."
*c* Reverse of *b* (of similar type to *a* and Cilician Fig. 64 *a*), showing Cross and rayed Sun behind and above Goat, also circle pelleted Cross on body of Goat identical with that on body of Hercules on Cilician coins, Fig. 64 *c*.
*d* Winged Goat on obverse of coin stamped "*Tasc*" (E.B.C., 6, 1). The winged Goat is not infrequent in Hitto-Sumer seals and Cilician coins.
*e* E.B.C., 11, 5 Cunobelin coin = Winged Tascio or "Resef Mikel" or St. Michael bestowing wreath or fruited Sun. *Cp.* Cilician coin, Fig. 64 *e*.
*f* E.B.C., 10, 12 and 13. Goat nourished by Hercules as "Tasciio." For Goats fed by hand of Tax or Tascio in Hitto-Sumerian seals, see W.S.C., 380, 387, etc.
*g* E.B.C., 5, 10–12. "*Taš*" or "*Tasc*," with "Celtic" and St. Andrew's *Crosses* and spear, galloping to rescue Goats (Goths). On obverse, *Corn Cross* in form of *St. Andrew's Cross*, with Sun discs. For other Corn Crosses of Tax, the Corn Spirit, see former figures.
*h* S.C.B., Pl. 8, 2, etc.

Devil-worshipping aborigines. They achieved their success through the leadership of the great warrior Aryan king, the second king of the First Aryan Dynasty of the traditional lists, who was, I find, the inventor of the Plough and establisher of Agriculture.[1] Later, the Aryans gratefully apotheosized him and made him their patron saint and the prototype of the Archangel of their Sun-cult, and represented him armed as a warrior, and he is thus the human original of the Archangel Taxi or Taś, the "*Tash*-ub" or "Tash of the Plough" of the Hittites, the *Tascio* of the Briton coins and monuments, and St. Michael the Archangel of the Gentiles who, under his Father, fought against and overcame " the Dragon, the Old Serpent, and his angels," who warred against " the Sons of God "—a favourite title of the Aryans, appearing in early Sumerian inscriptions, and reflected in Genesis.

We now discover why the Archangel Taś or Taxi was invoked in the prehistoric " cup-mark " inscriptions of the Early Britons, and was so freely figured on the great majority of the very numerous mintages of coins of the Early Britons or Catti, many of which bear his name stamped thereon as "Tasc, Tascio, Tascia, Taxci, Tcvi," etc. (see Figs. 61, etc.), along with ears of Corn and Sun Crosses, both the erect True Cross and the **X** " Cross " or Hammer of his Father " Andrew " or Indara, and as Grain-Crosses, and as defending the Goats or Deer symbolizing the " Goths " or Catti Aryans, and *figured in the same conventional manner on the Briton coins as he is represented on the sacred seals of the Catti or Khatti Hitto-Sumerians and on the coins of the Phœnicians* (compare Figs. 64 and 65 for some of these identities).

We also now see why Taś, as the archangel of the Sun-cult and St. Michael, is figured on the Early Briton coins and prehistoric and pre-Christian monuments often with wings, and often accompanied by the Sun Hawk or Eagle, or the Sun Goose (Michaelmas Goose), or Phœnix of the Phœnicians, as well as with the Sun Horse often winged, and the Sun disc, *and all in more or less identical form with the conventional*

---

[1] Details in my *Iryan Origin of the Phœnicians.*

## PHŒNICIAN ST. MICHAEL ON BRITON COINS

*representations of "Taś"-Michael on the Hittite sacred seals and on the Phœnician coins of Cilicia*, in the "Land of the Khatti" or Hittites (see Figs. 66 and 67, etc).

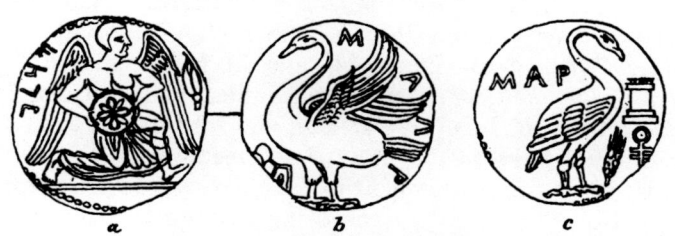

FIG. 66.—Taxi as "Michael" the Archangel bearing rayed "Celtic" Cross, with Corn, Sun Goose or Phœnix on Phœnician Coins of Cilicia of fifth century B.C.
(Coins after Hill.)[1]

NOTE in *a* the Phœnician legend *MKLU* or "Mikalu"; and in *c* Phœnix Sun-bird before Fire-altar, with bearded Corn and two-barred handled Cross.

FIG. 67.—Tascio or St. Michael the Archangel on Early Briton pre-Christian Coins.
(Coins after Evans.)[2]

Note in *a* the fruited Sun-disc, bearing 12 pairs of fruit, corresponding to the months of the year. In *b* "Tcvi" with head of Dionysos (*cp*. Fig. 64). *c* Winged Michael with club of Erakles and legend "ER." *d* "Tascia" Sun Hawk with two strokes="Sun." *e* Winged Sun Horse tied to Sun, over three "cup-marks" = Earth, or Death (vanquisher of).

[1] *a–b*, H.C.C., Pl. 16, 13; in *a MKLU* in Phœnician Script, in *b MAGR*, presumably for Magarsus, ancient seaport at mouth of Pyrenees in Cilicia.   *c Ib.*, Pl. 16, 12.

[2] *a* E.C.B., Pl. 3, 11.   *b–c*, *Ib.*, 3, 14.   *d Ib.*, Pl. 6, 7.   *f Ib.*, 8, 14.   Sun bearing Eagle transfixes the Serpent of the Deep and of Death.

In Egypt also—now seen to have been Aryanized by the Catti Phœnicians—" Michael " actually appears under earlier forms of the latter name as " *God of the Harvest* " and also " *of the Red Cross*." As " *Resef* " (*i.e.*, Rashap Mikal) he is a god of the Middle Period admittedly imported from " Syria " (*i.e.*, Syria-Phœnicia) and he is represented as a warrior *with the Goat's head* as a chaplet, and carrying the handled Cross of Life (see Fig. 69), and his relation to Food-Grain is indicated in his name *Resef*, meaning Food-Grain.[1] He also bears titles equivalent to " Archangel " in " Governor of the Gods " (the Egyptians being inveterate polytheists) and " Lord of the Two-fold Strength among the Company of the Gods."[2] And as " *Makhi-al* " (or Makhi-ar) he is the " Harvest God " and equivalent of Michael.

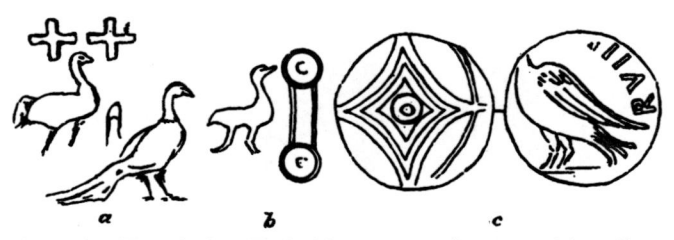

*a*      *b*      *c*

FIG. 68.—Phœnix Sun-Bird of Tascio with Crosses and Sun-discs, from Early Briton Cave gravings and Coins.

(After Simpson, Stuart and Evans.)[3]

Note lozenge-lined Cross of Hittite and Trojan pattern. *Cp.* Figs. 44 and 46.

The Ancient Egyptians called their Harvest god " *Makhi-al* " (or *Makhi-ar*),[4] and named that month after him, the " *Mekir* " of the Copts for that Harvest month, and also the god of the Harvest.[5] Now this is practically his identical name, as current amongst the Hittites about 2400 B.C., where we find it spelt " *Ma-khu-ur* ";[6] and he also had a month called after

---

[1] Resef in Egyptian=" Food." B.E.D., 433 and Resi=" Corn," 431.
[2] B.G.E., 2, 282.
[3] S.A.S., Pl. 342 and *cp*. S.S.S., 2, Illust. Pl. 33, 1.    *b* S.A.S., Pl. 35, 2. *c* E.C.B., 8, 1.
[4] *Cp.* B.Œ.D., 286a, *l* and *r* have the same letter-sign in Egypt.
[5] *Ib.*, 2862, and *cp.* B.G.E., 293. His harvest month was the sixth month of the Egyptian calendar.
[6] Sayce, Cappadocian Cuneiform Tablets from Kara Eyuk, *Babylonia*, 1910 (4), 2, 7.

him.[1] He was also known to the Egyptians as "The Harvest god *Makh*-unna,"[2] or "*Makh* of the Food-Stuff of Life," and also with an alternative spelling as "*Makh* of the Red Cross";[3] for significantly this Cross is painted red in the Egyptian tombs, and is described as "The Devouring Fire,"[4] *i.e.*, The Fiery Cross of the Sun.

This now explains the Egyptian references to this Red Cross as giving also the meaning "eat" (of food), an association which has hitherto puzzled Egyptologists,[5] but is now seen to be the association of St. Michael or Tash-ub (or Rasep-Mikal) with the Harvest, as Corn Spirit in the cult of the Cross.

In Ancient Mesopotamia the fuller and apparently original form of his "Michael" name is found as "*Me-ki-gal*" about 2400 B.C. It is applied to the great Harvest Festival and Harvest month called "The Barley Harvest Cutting" —*Se-kin-kud*, in which *Se*, the Akkadian *Zeru*, or "Seed grain" is disclosed as the source of our word "Seed" and "Ceres," and *Kud* or "cut" as the Sumerian source of our English word "cut."

So important was the Corn or Barley in the economy of the Sumerians that they latterly made that month of Mekigal or the Barley Harvest the first month of their Agricultural year and the month of their chief festivities, although still retaining the solar year in the background.[6] Now the meaning of this name of the Archangel *Me-ki-gal*, as defined in the Sumerian, is of immense importance for the history of religion. It is defined as "The Door of the Place of Calling in Prayer"[7] or "The Door of Heaven."[8] Thus the Aryan Archangel Michael is called as intercessor between Earth and Heaven, "The Door of Heaven," which thus accounts for the great popularity of his worship, and his title of "Saviour,"[9] and explains why the Phœnician votive

---

[1] Thureau-Dangin, *Rev. Assyriologique*, 1911, 8, 3, 2 *a*, 9 and *b* 13.
[2] *Cp.* hieroglyphs B.E.D., 319b.   [3] *Ib.*, 319b.
[4] G.H., pp. 37 and 67 and P.L. 6, Fig. 78.   [5] *Ib.*, 37 and 67.
[6] H.E.R., 3, 73, etc., and Langdon, *Archives of Drehem*, 1911, 15, etc.
[7] For the Sumerian written signs of the name, see Langdon (above) tablets Nos. 24, 37, 43, etc., etc.
[8] On "Door" word-sign, see B.B.W. No. 87, and on *Me* as "Heaven," see *ib.* 2, p. 239.
[9] See above.

inscriptions to Bel invoke "the blessings" of "Resef Mikel" or "Mikel of the Food-Corn."

The foregoing Egyptian abbreviated forms of the name "Michael" as *Makh* and *Makhu*, etc.,[1] are interesting as having parallels in the Sumerian, Syriac, Sanskrit and Gothic. Even the Hebrew form "Micha-el," which has been adopted as the English form of his name, has been generally regarded as having for its final syllable the Semitic *el* or "god," which thus gives the proper name as "Micha." In Syriac charms St. Michael, as the protector of the grain crops against damage, is invoked as "Miki, Mki-ki."[2] In the Gothic Eddas he is Miok, Moeg, Mag-na and Mikli, son of Thor.

[In the Vedas, "*Magha*-van" or "Winner of Bounty (Magha)," a title of the Sun-god Indra and of some of his devotees; and the Vedic month Māgha is the chief Harvest month and the month of great festival. He also seems to be the *Mash* divinity of the Amorites and Babylonians, who was a "Son of the Sun-god,"[3] and the bearer, as we have seen, of the "Mash" or "Mace" as the Red Cross.]

This identity of Taś or Taś-Mikal, under these slightly variant spellings, in Egypt, Vedic India, Phœnicia, Hitto-Sumer, and Ancient Britain is absolutely confirmed and established by the essential identity in the representations of this divinity along with the Cross and his Goat (or "Gothic" rebus). He is figured with the Cross and Goat, as we have seen on the Hitto-Sumer seals (Figs. 59) and on Phœnician coins (Figs. 64) and on ancient Briton coins (Figs. 65, etc.), and Early Briton monuments (Figs. 60, etc.). Similarly is he figured in Ancient Egypt (as Reśef or Resaph) with the Cross and Goat (Fig. 69) and in India as *Daxa* (or "the Dextrous Creator") with the Goat's head and field of Food-crops (Fig. 70).

His Goat relationship is celebrated in the Sumerian

---

[1] Other Egyptian spellings of his name are *Makhi*, a seasonal god (B.E.D., 275ᵇ) and *Mākhi*, god of Fire altar (*ib.*, 286ᵃ).

[2] H. Gollancz, *Syriac Charms*, lxxxii.

[3] See Clay, *Empire of Amorites*, 179. "Mash" is an interchangeable title of the reflex solar divinity whose name is usually conjecturally rendered "Ninib" and "Uras" (*ib.*, 179), whose Hittite shrine in Palestine was at "Uras-ilim" or Jerusalem, as we have seen.

# TAS, TAX OR DIAS IN VEDAS, EGYPT & BRITAIN 353

litanies, where he is hailed as "Divine leader, the He-Goat"[1] (Indara); and as the protector of "the Goat-man"[2] (*i.e.*, Goth).

FIG. 70.—Tascio or Taxi as "Daxa," Vedic Hindu Creator-god.
(After Wilkins.)[3]
Note his Goat's head, and standing in field of Food-Crops and giving his blessing.

FIG. 69.—Tascio in Egypt as "Rešef," or Corn-Spirit.
(After Renan.)[4]
Note his Goat's head chaplet and handled Cross-of-Life, and Spear.

The spelling of the name "Tascio" on Briton coins is also parallel in its variations to the variations in the Hitto-Sumerian and Sanskrit and in the Phœnician and Greco-Phœnician coins.

Thus in Briton coins the name is spelt Tas, Tasc, Tasci, Tascio, Tascia,[5] Taxci,[6] Tcvi, Tascif,[7] Tascf,[8] Tasciovan, Tasciovani, Tigiio,[9] Dias,[10] Deas, Deascio.[11] In Sumerian Taxi, Takhi or Diaś, also Ta-xu,[12] Taś, Tuk or Duk. In Hittite

[1] *Elim.*, C.I.W.A., 2, 55, 31f. and S.H.L., 284, 446; *cp.* M.D., 271.
[2] *Cp.* S.H.L., 447. *Sigga-ni*+" man," and *Sigga*="Goat."
[3] *Hindu Mythology*, 309.   [4] C.I.S., 1, 38.
[5] See Fig. 67.   [6] E.C.B., 5, 9.   [7] See Fig. 62.
[8] E.C.B., Pl. 10, 7.   [9] *Ib.*, 17, 3.
[10] Figs. *A* and *B*.
[11] Brit. Num. Jour., 1912. P. Curlyon-Britton, 1-7.
[12] Br., 4052, and significantly it is written by character for "Wing" or Hand+Bird, *i.e.*, "The Winged Michael." A variant *Tiś-xu* (hitherto read Tiś-pak) is "The Bird Messenger of God."

Tash-ub (or "Tash of Plough"), Teisbas or Dhuspuas in Van inscriptions, and Su-Tax or Su-Takh (or "Tax the Sower"); and he is the "Dagon" of the Philistines. In Indian Vedas Tvashtr (or "Taks") and Daxa or Daksha for solar Creative gods of food and animals, of whom the first fashions the bolt of Indra, creates the Horse, so frequently associated with Taś in the later period, has the food and wine of the gods, and bowl of wealth and confers blessings. On the Phœnician and Greco-Phœnician coins of Cilicia the name is spelt Dioc, Dzs, Dek and Theoys;[1] and in coins of Phœnicia Dioc, Dks, Thios, Tēs, Theas and Theac.[2]

And significantly the name "Tasc" still survives in the Scottish *Task* for "Angel or Spirit."[3] And he is presumably the "*Thiazi*" or *Ty* giant warrior assistant of Thor in the Gothic Eddas, the *Tuisco* of Saxons and Germans, who gave his name to Tues-day, the "Tys-day" of the Scots—for which the corresponding French name "*Mar*-di" seems to preserve his Sumerian synonym of "Maru" (or Mar-duk). The Greek title of "Dionysos" (or properly, *Dionusou* or *Diōnusos* of Homer) hitherto inexplicable, now seems to be possibly the Sumerian synonym for Taś as "*Ana-śu*" or "The Descending God,"[4] presumably to denote his angelic messenger function, with divine prefix *Di* (the Sumerian *Di*, "to shine") and hellenized into "Di-onysos."[5]

As the patron saint of Agriculture, Corn Spirit and Heavenly Husbandman or "Spirit of the Plough," Taś or Taxi, who, we have found, figured with the Plough in the Early Hittite rock-sculptures (Fig. 62, p. 340), bore in the Early Sumerian (or Phœnician) inscriptions the title of "Daśi *of the Spear of Ploughshare Produce*"[6]—wherein the word for "Spear" (*Gir*, the old English *Gar*) is poetic for "Plough"; and the word for "Fruit sprout produce" is pictured by a ploughshare, *Lam*,[7] which is presumably the Sumerian source of the name of the Scottish Early Harvest festival "Lam-mas." Thus, at this early period, the Aryan

[1] See Figs. 64, etc., and H.C.C., lxxxix, cxiv, etc.
[2] H.C.P., 214–6; 259, 261, etc.; 164, etc.; 53, etc.
[3] J.S.D., 549.   [4] Br., 10834.
[5] "Tasc-*onus*" was the name of a celebrated "Roman" potter of Samian ware.
[6] Da-śi lam-gir, hitherto rendered with signs transposed as "Nin-gir-su."
[7] Br., 309 and *cp*. B.B.W., 2, p. 8.

founders of Agriculture seem to have "beaten their swords into ploughshares"—the Spear of the Hittite warrior-god "*Tash*-of-the-Plough," Tash-ub or Dash-ub Mikal, which indeed seems represented in his hand as of plough shape in some of the Ancient Briton coins (see Fig. 65g).[1]

Now this discovers to us the long-forgotten meaning of a complex symbol found very often on prehistoric monuments in Britain and hitherto called merely descriptively "The Crescent and Sceptre." This symbol of unknown meaning significantly occurs in the neighbourhood of our Phœnician monument of Newton on three prehistoric sculptured stones, removed from a moor bordering the N.E. foot of Mt. Bennachie and the Gady, and now preserved in the adjoining village of Logie (see map, p. 19), whence they are called "The Logie Stones," one of which is figured at p. 20 (Fig. 5B), wherein this complex symbol occupies the middle of the stone above the "Spectacles" and below the circular Ogam inscription at the top.

This hitherto inexplicable prehistoric symbol of the "Crescent and Sceptre" is now discovered to represent the earth-piercing of Taś, the heavenly husbandman—piercing the earth by his spear-plough and heaving up the soil into ridges for cultivation; and the direction of the piercing it will be noticed is in the Sun-wise lucky direction, towards the west. The lower symbol, the so-called "Spectacles and Sceptre," we have already discovered is the solar swastika in the form of the conjoined Day and "Night" (or "resurrecting") Sun of the Sumerian theory, with the arrows indicating the direction of movement from the East to the West, and thence "returning" underneath to the Eastern sunrise. Another of these prehistoric monuments with the Earth-piercing and solar "Spectacles" is at the adjoining village of Bourtie (or village of Barat?).[2]

This identification of the "Crescent and Sceptre" with the Spear-plough of Taś is confirmed and established by the Ogam inscription carved on the top of the stone, around the margin of the Sun's disc; and it has hitherto remained undeciphered, because in the absence of clues there was no

[1] E.C.B., Pl. 5, 10 and 12.  [2] S.S.S., 1, Pl. 132, 3.

indication where the stroke letters began or ended, so as to make any recognizable sense to Ogam's scholars.[1] It reads. I find, in the sunwise direction, B(i)l Tachab Ho R(a), see Fig. 71.

Bü L · Ta Qa B · HO · Ra

FIG. 71.—Logie Stone Ogam Inscription, as now deciphered, disclosing invocation to Bil and his Archangel " Tachab " or " Taqab " (or " Tashub.")[2]

This gives the translation :

" To Bil (and) Tachab, Ho raised (this)."

Here it is noteworthy that this other Briton inscription to the Sun-god Bil has precisely the same ending formula of R(a) or "raised" as in the two of the Cassi-Phœnician Part-olon's adjoining monuments to the same god ; and it is presumably of or about the same date as the latter.

The name of the erector, Ho, is in series with the Cymric traditional name of " *Hu* Gadarn " (or *Hu* the *Gad* or Phœnician, the Noble or Chief?) for the first traditional Cymric king from the Ægean who arrived in Britain.[3] It is presumably the source of the modern " Hugh." Significantly " *Hu'a* " was the Cassi name of a royal ambassador of the Cassi emperor of Babylonia to the Egyptian Pharaoh, in the Amarna letters of about 1400 B.C. ;[4] and " *Hu Tishup* " also appears as an Aryan Cassi name,[5] and *Hu* is a common front-name in the personal names of the Cassis of Babylonia and Syria-Cilicia.[6] The erector " Ho " was thus presumably a Cassi Barat in race, like Part-olon ; and we

---

[1] See B.O.1., 358.
[2] The 5 strokes above the line may be read *CH* or *Q*—here *CH* appears to be the intended value.
[3] *Welsh Triads*, 6 and 7.
[4] Hu'a, ambassador of emperor Burna Buriash to Pharaoh Amen-hotep III., A.L.W., 9, 5.
[5] C.P.N., 82.   [6] *Ib.*, 80–82.

have seen that the Cassis in their Sun-worship figured Taś on their sacred seals with the Cross and Goats, and they ploughed and sowed under the sign of the Cross.

Other incidental evidence of the early establishment of Agriculture in the Don Valley by the Cassi-Phœnician Part-olon and his descendants is found in the fact that the Don Valley is one of the relatively few parts of Britain where Bronze sickles have been unearthed ;[1] and the place where the greatest hoard of these have been found bears the significant name of " *Arre*-ton,"[2] presumably " Town of the Aryans." As further local evidence for the Tascio-Michael cult are the two ancient sacred wells called " St. Michael's " in the parish of the Newton Stone.[3]

In respect of the above evidence for the Aryan Kassi cult of the Corn Spirit *Taxi* in the Don Valley, it is interesting to find that Ptolemy in his "Geography" calls the tribe inhabiting the Don Valley at the beginning of the Christian era " *Tezal*(oi) " and the town " Taixalon," a name which appears to contain this " Taxi " Corn cult title. These people probably inhabited, I think, the modern " *Dyce*," with its Stone Circle (see map, p. 19), now about four miles up the Don from Aberdeen city, but probably in those days nearer the sea. This " Dyce," with its local variants *Dauch* and *Tuach*, possibly preserves, I suggest, Ptolemy's ancient Briton name of " Taixalon,"[4] with which may be compared Texel Isle, off Friesland, in the home of the Anglo-Saxons. It is further remarkable that the shield of the city arms of Aberdeen should contain *the Cross and three sheaves of Corn*.

In view of all this evidence for the local prevalence in the Don Valley of the cult of the Corn Spirit Tascio St. Michael, it is interesting to find that the patron saint of the cathedral

---

[1] Evidence of ancient commerce between Aberdeen and the East is indicated by ancient Grecian coins having been found at Cairnbulg in 1824. These included a gold tetradrachm of Philip of Macedon, 3 Greek silver coins of the same period and a brass coin of the *Brutii* of Magna Grecia. N.S.S., 4, 292.
[2] Arreton Down near Newport in the Isle of Wight. E.B.I., 204, 222–4.
[3] S.S.S., 1, 1.
[4] Ptolemy's work is known to have been based upon the earlier work of Marinus of Tyre, from an ancient Phœnician Atlas, so that his names are presumably older than his own date. The affix *alon* = the *olon* or " Hittite " title of Part-olon.

at Aberdeen, now usually called "St. *Machar*" or St. *Macker*," was also known as *Tochanna*,[1] especially as we have seen that Michael's name was sometimes anciently spelt by the Hittites and Egyptians as " Makhūr, Makhiār, and Mekir." This St. Machar or Macker or " Tochanna " is a more or less legendary missionary personage, said to have been sent to the Picts of the Don Valley by Columba in the sixth century A.D. But in view of what we have seen of the quality of the other legend regarding St. Andrew from the same source,[2] and the fact that this St. Machar legend is also discredited in essentials,[3] it seems possible that this " Machar " was an old locally current name attached to the pagan cult of St. Michael or " Makhiar," and was erected into a Christian saint in proselytizing the local votaries of the Michael Corn cult there, just as Indara's shrine a little further south was converted into " St. Andrews," where significantly *the first Christian Church was dedicated to Michael*,[4] *i.e.*, "*The First-begotten Son of Indara or Andrew.*"

The introduction of the Gentile St. Michael[5] into Christianity dates probably to the very commencement of the latter. The angel who imparted healing virtues to the pool at the old Hittite city of Jerusalem at the time of Christ[6] is generally considered to have been Michael, as that was his special function in the numerous St. Michael Wells in later Christianity, and also, as we have seen, in the Sumerian litanies. St. John, in his Apocalypse, gives

---

[1] B.L.S., Novr., 315-6. He is also called variously Mocumma, Tochanna, and Dochonna; but " Machar " is the common form.
[2] The Aberdeen Breviary is the chief source of both the St. Andrew and St. Machar legends, *ib*.
[3] B.L.S., 316. [4] S.P.S., 185, etc.
[5] Michael, we have seen, was entirely a Gentile creation in origin and name. That name nowhere occurs as the name of an angel in the Old Testament except in Daniel (10, 21, and in 12, 1, where called " prince "); and then it is in Greek script, and *not Hebrew*. And the account of Daniel and the lions therein is seen to be a post-exilic borrowing from the famous Hitto-Sumerian and Babylonian representations of Indara or Taś taming the Lions, so frequently figured on Hitto-Sumerian seals (see Fig. 59), and on pre-Christian Briton monuments (Fig. 60). The name " *Dan* " is Sumerian for " supreme ruler " and *Bel* (Br., 6191); and the Akkad " *Dānu*," Judge," seems to be derived from it, as it is an especial title of the Sun-god as " The Judge " (M.D., 258). And *Dan* is a title of Thor in the Gothic Eddas.
[6] John, v, 4.

Michael the recognized titles of Archangel of Heaven and Vanquisher of " the Dragon, the old Serpent," just as in the Sumerian texts. St. Paul deprecates the worship of angels amongst the Christians in central Asia Minor of the Hittites.[1] The tomb of the non-Christian emperor Hadrian was consecrated to St. Michael.[2] Constantine rebuilt an old shrine to Michael on the Bosphorus, where cures had been effected by Michael, *at the site of an old temple which was traditionally built by the Argonauts,*[3] i.e., *the pioneer exploring sailors under Hercules of the Phœnicians.* And Constantine also built, or rebuilt, two other shrines to Michael on the Asiatic coast opposite Constantinople.[4] And many of the earliest Christian churches, from the beginning of the fifth century onwards, both in Asia and Europe, were dedicated to Michael and in some of these the Saint retained the attributes of Zeus. One of these fifth-century churches in Italy bears an inscription calling Michael " *The God of the Angels who has made the Resurrection,*"[5] i.e., *precisely his ancient title in the Sumerian litanies, Trojan amulets, and in the cup-mark inscriptions of prehistoric Britain.*

The Early Fathers of the Christian Church also credit Michael with the same functions ascribed to him in the Sumerian texts and pre-Christian monuments and coins in Britain.

[In the rubrics of the fifth century A.D. details are given for his festival, and *Food* and *Wine* offerings are prescribed. *A fast of forty days* in his honour are mentioned,[6] presumably for his conquest of the Dragon Satan. The orations in the seventh century of Theodosius, archbishop of Alexandria, make Michael declare :

" I am Michael, the governor of the denizens of Heaven and Earth, who brings the offerings of men to God, my king, who walks with those whose trust is in God."[7] " I hearken unto everyone who prayeth to God in my name."[8] His chief enemy

---
[1] Coloss., ii, 18.   [2] H.E.R., 8, 620.
[3] W.M. Ramsay, *Church in Roman Empire*, 477, etc., and H.E.R., 8, 621.
[4] H.E.R., 621.
[5] Site of temple of Jupiter, Clitum, in Umbria with inscription, " S.C.S. deus Angelorum qui fecit Resurrectionem." H.E.R., 8, 620.
[6] In *Life of St. Francis*, H.E.R., 8, 622.
[7] E. Budge, *St. Michael*, 40.   [8] *Ib.*, 100.

is the Devil; and he delivers from Hell (Amenti) when called upon in the hour of need.[1] And his healing through Water and sacred springs and wells is widespread. *And he had a devil-banishing Cross made of Wood.*[2]]

St. Patrick, the Scot of Dun-Barton in the fourth and fifth centuries, was traditionally a votary of Michael, who is credited with having commanded Patrick to cross the sea to convert " his brither Scots " in Scotia or Ireland,[3] where many of the oldest churches are dedicated to Michael. The vast number of early churches dedicated to St. Michael in Britain is indicated by there being no less than *forty-five in the Welsh or Cymric diocese of St. David's alone* ;[4] and they are also especially numerous in the old Phœnician settlements in Cornwall and Devon. And the " Healing Waters " of the Wells and springs of St. Michael—" the House of Pure Sprinkling " and " the pure healing waters of Taś(-Mikal) " of the Sumerian litanies—in the British Isles, the Continent and Asia Minor are innumerable.

In the Early English Church the pre-eminence of Michael is evidenced by the fact that the Michael Epistle and Collect in the English Prayer-book formerly *came before the Gospels as the first Lection.*[5] It was St Michael, and not St. George, slaying the Dragon, which first appears on English coins. And the mintage of the Michael-Dragon gold coins by Edward IV., called " Angels," was for centuries in popular demand for " touching " in the miraculous cure of " King's Evil ; " and its motto significantly was " By the *Cross* do Thou save me ! "—as on the Hitto-Sumerian seals, Trojan amulets and Early Briton monuments.

Indeed, so essentially " prehistoric " is the name and significance of " Saint Michael " that the most recent clerical authority on his cult says : " Given an ancient dedication to St. Michael and a site associated with a headland, hill-top or spring, on a road or track of early origin, it is reasonable to look for *a pre-Christian sanctuary*—a prehistoric centre of religious worship."[6]

[1] E. Budge, *St. Michael*, 46.   [2] *Ib.*, 89.
[3] *Genair Patraice*, 4 and Gloss., and H.E.R., 8, 622.
[4] H.E.R., 8, 622.   [5] H.E.R., 8, 623.
[6] Rev. T. Barns in H.E.R., 8, 621–2.

We thus further discover, and also for the first time, the remote origin and economic meaning of the racial title "*Ary*" or "*Ary-an*," and find that it is a Hitto-Sumerian word "*Arri*," originally designating the White Syrians or Hitt-ites or "Catti," or Early Goths, as the "Earers" or Ploughers, in their capacity of founders of the Agricultural Stage of the World as the basis of the Higher Civilization; and Agriculture still remains the economic basis of modern Civilization. We discover still further evidence for the Hitto-Sumerian Language being the parent of the radically Aryan words of the Aryan Family of Languages, and especially of the Briton or British Gothic which (and not Anglo-Saxon) is the basis of the "English" Language at the present day. We also discover that these Aryan "Earers" and so-called "Sun-worshippers" adopted as their patron-saint, under Indara (or Andrew) or St. George his Archangel son as "Corn Spirit" in their Sun-cult. And they formed him on the model of their historical Aryan Hittite king who had invented the Plough about 4300 B.C., Taś-Mikal (or Mekigal), who is now disclosed as the historical human basis of Michael the Archangel of Heaven, of the Gentiles, the "Tascio" of the pre-Roman Briton Catti coins, the *Taxi* or *Dasi* of these Sumers, "*Dag-on*" of the Philistines, the *Daxa* of the Indian Vedas, and the "Dionysos" and *Tychè* of the Greeks, by hellenized names coined from Sumerian originals. We further find that this solar cult of Michael the Archangel and Corn Spirit, associated with the solar symbol of the True Cross of Universal Victory by the Sun, and the late harvest festival of Michaelmas, was widely prevalent in Early pre-Roman Britain, where it was disembarked and transplanted at St. Michael's Mount with its associated Sun-Fire cult about 2800 B.C. or earlier by the tin-exploiting, colonizing Hitto-Phœnician Barats, the Ploughers of the Deep and builders of the great solar Stone Circles, and the pagan gravers of the contemporary cup-marked Sumerian votive inscriptions of the prehistoric period, who invoked the blessing of "Sancti Michaele," just as did King Alfred.[1]

[1] King Alfred's prayer at end of his translation of Boethius.

And these "Sun-worshipping" Hitto-Phœnician Catti Barats or Early "Brit-ons," whose long-lost history and origin are now recovered for us in great part in these pages by my new keys, are disclosed by a mass of incontestable attested facts and confirmatory evidence to be a leading branch of the originators and propagators of the World's Civilization and of the Higher Religion of the One God, with belief in Resurrection from the Dead and its devil-banishing symbol of the Cross, and to be the Aryan ancestors of the modern Brit-ons or Brit-ish (including the Scots), properly so-called, as opposed to the preponderating aboriginal and other non-Aryan racial elements in the population of the British Isles at the present day.

FIG. 72.—" Bird-men " on Briton monuments as Phœnician *Taš-Mikal* or " St. Michael."
From monuments at Inchbrayock and Kirriemuir, Forfarshire.
(After Stuart. S.S.S., 1, 43 ; 2. 2.)

# XXIII

## ARYAN PHŒNICIAN RACIAL ELEMENT IN THE MIXED RACE OF THE BRITISH ISLES AND ITS EFFECT ON PROGRESS OF BRITISH CIVILIZATION

> " Are we not brothers ? So man and man should be :
> *But clay and clay differs in Dignity,*
> Whose dust is both alike."—SHAKESPEARE, *Cymbeline.*
> " Indra hath helped his Aryan worshippers
> In frays that win the Light of Heaven.
> He gave to his Aryan men the godless, dusky race :
> Righteously blazing he burns the malicious away."–*Rig Veda*, 1, 130, 8.
> " Indra alone hath tamed the dusky races
> And subdued them for the Aryans.— R.V., 6, 183.
> " Yet, Indra, thou art for evermore
> The common Lord of all alike."—*Rig Veda*, 8, 547.
> " And to him who worships truly Indra gives
> Many and matchless gifts—He who slew the Dragon.
> He is to be found straightway by all Who struggle prayerfully for the Light."—*Rig Veda*, 2, 19, 4.

WE have found, by a mass of concrete attested facts and other cumulative confirmatory evidence, that Civilization properly so-called is synonymous with Aryanization ; and that it was first introduced into Britain in the Stone Age, about 2800 B.C., or earlier, by Hitto-Phœnician " Catti," or Early Gothic sea-merchants from the Levant engaged in the Tin, Bronze and Amber trade and industries, who were Aryans in Speech, Script and Race—tall, fair, broad-browed and long-headed. Of the leading clan of Aryans, they bore the patronymic of *Barat* or "*Brit*-on," and, settling on the island of Albion, conquering and civilizing the dusky aborigines therein, they gave their own patronymic to it, calling it "Barat-ana" or "Brit-ain" or "Land of the Barats or Brits."

There were several successive waves of immigration of this Aryan Catti-Barat civilizing stock from the coast of Asia Minor and Syria-Phœnicia by way of the Mediterranean into the British Isles ; and the different sections of that Aryan civilizing race called themselves variously Muru or Martu ("Amorite"), Cymr, Somer or Cumber, Barat or Briton, Goth or Gad, Catti, Ceti, Cassi, Xat or Scot, or Sax or Sax-on.

Their descendants continued to be the ruling race therein until modern times, excepting the Roman period, though even then several sections continued to maintain their independence in Wales, Cumbria, Scotland and Ireland. The later invaders, Jutes, Angles, Saxons, Norse, Danes and Normans were merely kindred North Sea colonists of the same Aryan racial Catti or Gothic stock ; while the minor immigrations of batches of Belgians and others from the Continent into South Britain, mentioned by Cæsar, do not appear to have been racially Aryan. And we have seen that the fair round-heads of Germanic type of the East Coast and Midlands were also racially non-Aryan.

The Phœnician Catti or Gothic Aryan strain, derived from the first civilizers of Britain, although more or less mixed with aboriginal blood in the course of centuries, has nevertheless still survived in tolerable purity, as evidenced by the typically Aryan physique of great numbers of their descendants. And it constitutes the leading Aryan element in the present-day population of these isles, the mass and substratum of which, although now Aryanized in speech and customs, still remain preponderatingly of the non-Aryan physical type of the "Iberian" aborigines, and are racially neither Briton nor British, nor Anglo-Saxon, English, nor Scot, properly so-called.

It is desirable now to examine the extent of the intermixture of these Aryan and non-Aryan races in the British Isles, and its apparent and probable effects on the progress of British Civilization.

The Early Aryan Gothic invaders and civilizers are seen to have been essentially a race of highly-civilized ruling aristocrats; and relatively few in numbers in proportion to the aboriginal population of the country. In physical type they were of the Aryan race, that is to say, tall-statured, fair-complexioned, with blue or greyish eyes, broad-browed and long-headed, as opposed to the small-statured, dark-complexioned, narrow-browed, and long-headed Pictish " Iberian " aborigines of the Stone Age, and the fringe of somewhat superior-cultured Stone Age race of medium-sized, fair-complexioned, broad-browed, but round-headed Slavonic or Germanic Huns, the beaker-using men of the "Round Barrows," who came from the Baltic and Germany, who settled along the East Coast and in the Midlands; and whose descendants still exist there to a considerable extent at the present day in relatively pure form.[1] It is presumably the bones of these Early Aryan Gothic invaders which are found in the Stone Cists (as at Keiss) and in the Dolmens, and also to some extent in the Long Barrow graves, though in the latter alongside are some skulls of the narrow-browed and small-statured aboriginal type, with cephalic indices so low as 73·73, suggesting some racial intermixture even at that early period.[2] But it seems probable that the bodies of the Aryans were largely cremated, as Fire was a heavenly vehicle in the Sun-cult, and there are references in the Gothic Eddas, as well as in Homer, in regard to the Trojans, to the committing the bodies of heroes to the funeral pyre.

Anterior to the arrival of Brutus about 1103 B.C. the Catti-Phœnician occupation of Albion appears to have been only very partial and sporadic with little intermixing with the aborigines. These early "prehistoric" exploiters of the Tin, Copper, Gold and Lead mines, and Jet and Amber

---

[1] This "Germanic" round-headed type is still marked along the East Coast. Thus, whereas Glasgow has only 2 per cent. of round-heads, Edinburgh has 25 per cent. (Sir A. Keith, in address to Universities Club from *Glasgow Herald*, Nov. 25, 1921).

[2] Prof. Parsons has recently shown that the Long Barrow race differs little in their skull form from the modern average inhabitants of London. —J.R.A.I., 1921, 55, etc. Most of the Long Barrow skulls figured by him have relatively broad brows; *cp*. Figs. on pp. 63 and 64 *ib*.

trades, appear to have been floating colonies of merchant seamen and adventurers, who at first occupied strategic islets or peninsular seaports offlying the chief native trade marts or mines, such as the Phœnicians usually selected for defensive purposes in most of their early colonies, on the model of Tyre, Sidon, Acre, Aradus, Carthage and Gades (or Cadiz). Of such a character are Ictis or St. Michael's Mount, Wight, Gower, the Aran isles off Galway, Dun Barton, Inch Keith, etc. Later they established themselves inland in the hinterland of their ports, as evidenced by their Stone Circles and other rude megalith monuments, which were chiefly, as we have seen, in the neighbourhood of their mines, or near their flint-factories for the manufacture of high-quality stone implements for their mines and miners, when Bronze was still too precious to spare. And these Early Phœnician pioneer exploiters of the mineral wealth of Albion do not appear to have attempted any systematic Aryanization or colonization of the country, or to have settled there with their wives and families to any considerable extent. What early civilization the aborigines of Albion then received was mainly through being employed in the mines and workshops of the Phœnicians.

Permanent settlement with systematic civilization and colonization with cultivation appears to have begun only with the arrival of Brutus and his Britons about 1103 B.C. They brought their wives and families with them. They were strictly monogamists, as was the Aryan custom. At first they appear to have lived apart from the aborigines in home towns and villages of their own by themselves, presumably from their exclusive racial instincts, or possibly in part for self-defence, being so few in numbers. This is evidenced by the great number of the earliest towns and ports bearing merely their own Aryan racial or tribal names. It is supported also by the British Chronicle tradition that Brutus "made choice of the citizens that were to inhabit" his first-founded city—London. The relationship and attitude of these highly-civilized Aryan invaders towards the primitive Stone Age aborigines of Alban or Britain must have been much of the same aloof kind as obtains at the present day in the contact between civilized Europeans and the primitive races in Africa, Asia and America. And the comparative fewness of these ruling Aryans to the mass of the indigenous population may perhaps be compared to the few handfuls of British civil servants who suffice nowadays to rule large dependencies of the British Empire.

Intermarriage of the Aryans with the non-Aryan uncivilized primitive people of a different colour and inferior mentality was naturally repugnant to the racial instinct. And even marriage with an aboriginal princess was viewed with disfavour. Thus we have Virgil lamenting in regard to the re-marriage of Æneas, the great-grandfather of the Aryan king Brutus, with a native princess in his Italian exile :

"An alien bride is the Trojan's bane once more."[1]

As time went on, however, and the Aryans multiplied, and in the meantime the aborigines had gradually been raised in the scale of civilization by passing through the mill of Aryanization in speech, customs and habits of life, a certain amount of intermarriage would doubtless begin to take place. Especially was this likely to happen under the usual policy of the Hitto-Phœnician statesmen, who early recognized that the stability of the state depended largely on its being based upon Nationality. Hence in their colonies, as seen in Asia Minor, Mesopotamia, the Levant, Ancient Greece, etc., they were in the habit in their citystates of welding together the diverse racial and tribal units of a region into one Nation, united by the bonds forged by a common Aryan Speech, and by living together under the same Aryan Laws, with equal rights of citizenship and a common patriotism. For the Hitto-Phœnicians were the founders of Free Institutions and Representative Government.[2]

With the growth of democracy such commingling of racial blood would tend to become still more common. And the opening up of freer communications with the interior by arterial roads and latterly, in modern times, by

---

[1] *Æneid*, 6, 94.    [2] Details *Aryan Origins*.

rail, and the gravitation of the rural population to the towns with the rise of cosmopolitan feeling has broken down the racial barrier to a great extent, and completed the fusion more or less of the diverse races. And all memory of the original sharp ancestral distinction between the superior and civilizing Aryan ruling race and the inferior non-Aryan indigenous race has now become more or less completely forgotten, even by the relatively pure Aryan element which has remained least affected by such intermarriages. And the outstanding differences in physique resulting from this intermixture exhibited amongst the mixed race of the present day, in respect to stature, complexion, colour of hair and eyes, and shape of head and face, are generally now regarded as merely curious, fortuitous or accidental personal peculiarities, although obviously more or less hereditary.

As a result of this more or less free intermixture of non-Aryan blood with the Aryan, operating through many centuries, there is now, perhaps, no such thing as an *absolutely pure-blooded* Aryan left in the British Isles. Yet in spite of the free mingling that has taken place, it must be evident even to the casual observer that there still exists at the present day, a considerable proportion of the population in the British Isles which is *relatively pure-blooded* Aryan in physical type, just as the round-headed Stone Age Germanic type has still survived in their original location along the East Coast in relatively pure form.[1]

Tending to conserve the Aryan type, by restraining free intermixture with other races, is the conscious or subconscious racial instinct which has been variously called " race pride," " race prejudice " or " race antipathy," as has been shown by Sir Arthur Keith and other anthropologists. These observers remark that this feeling still exists to the present day in the British Isles, and is exhibited as between the fair Lowland Scots and the dark or " Celtic " Highlanders, between fair Irish and the dark " Iberian " Hibernian " Celts," and between the fair Cymri and the dark Welsh and Devon and Cornish " Celts."

[1] See footnote, p. 365.

Another factor which tends to conserve the Aryan type appears to be the remarkable provision of Nature for securing " the survival of the fittest," by which she refuses to lose the painstaking progress made through long evolution towards a higher type by chance interference with her machinery, or by diluting her products. It has been found that the progeny of a marriage between two races of different physical types and head-form are not the mere mean or average between the two parent types, but belong to one or other of the separate parent (or grandparent) types as regards head and brain formation,[1] the different racial head-forms tending to refuse to mix, like oil and water. Thus the intermarriage of a long-head and a round-head usually results in one or other of the children being long-headed, and another round-headed, like one or other of their parents, and not an intermediate type of head. " The result was in many cases not a mixture, as if we mix red and white wine, but it was often a manifest reversion to the original types. In this way, good old types, once fixed by long inbreeding, do not necessarily get lost by intermarriage, but often return with astonishing energy."[2]

In this way the subsequent intermarriage of individuals of a relatively pure Aryan type would tend to enhance and fix the predominance of the Aryan blood strain introduced into Britain by the Britons, with all the superior intellectual endowments for progress which the Aryan type stands for.

There is no need in these days to argue against the idea advocated by Freeman and Green that the Britons were totally exterminated by the Anglo-Saxons. There is no historical evidence whatsoever to show or even suggest that the Anglo-Saxons—fierce pagans though they were, and the destroyers of Christianity amongst the Britons in the area they invaded—were such inhuman butchers as to massacre wholesale the men, women and children

---

[1] Mere colouration or pigmentation—the colour of the skin, hair and eyes—on the other hand, are immediately altered by inter-marriage in a more or less mechanical ratio, in accordance with the scale in Mendel's laws of heredity.

[2] Prof. F. v. Luschan, *The Early Inhabitants of Western Asia*, Jour. Royal Anthrop. Instit., 1911, 239.

in Britain or in South Britain, surpassing in brutality even the Turkish massacres of the Armenians. Not only is there no historical reference to any such atrocious massacre or even minor massacres;[1] but on the contrary we have, so late as 685 A.D., or over two centuries after the Anglo-Saxon invasion, a Briton king, Cadwalla, ruling over the Anglo-Saxons in the kingdom of Wessex,[2] the chief kingdom of the Anglo-Saxons in England. It is now recognized that the South-eastern Britons submitted to their defeat by the Anglo-Saxon forces, just as their Briton ancestors had submitted to their defeat by the Roman forces, and as the Anglo-Saxons themselves with their subject Britons latterly submitted to their final defeat by the Normans; whilst, on the other hand, the more independent Britons of the Western half of Britain continued to maintain their independence against the Anglo-Saxons more or less throughout the whole period of the Anglo-Saxon domination of the Eastern half of England. And the Britons in Scotland, north of Northumbria, although divided amongst themselves, successfully maintained their entire independence under their own Briton rulers, not only against the Anglo-Saxons, but against the conquerors of the latter, the Normans. And we have seen that the so-called " Anglo-Saxon " language of England is neither Angle nor Saxon, but rather Briton or British Gothic.

Similarly, in the Norman invasion, which put an end to Anglo-Saxon rule, there was no extermination of either the Britons or Anglo-Saxons. The Nor-mans or North-men were also a branch of the Aryan Barat Goths or Catti, who merely happened to be frenchified in dialect, by a short sojourn in Normandy; but they retained their ecclesiastic architecture of Gothic type, They also were soon absorbed by the Britons in both blood and speech, adding a few French idioms to the Briton stock of speech now known as " English." But as the English historian Palgrave truly says :—" Britons, Anglo-Saxons, Danes and Normans

---

[1] See N.P.E., 261, etc.; 281, etc.
[2] Ib., 278; and see G.C., 12, 2. He appears to be the " Cædwalla " of Ethelwerd's Chronicle, Giles *Old English Chronicles*, 14.

were all relations : however hostile, they were all kinsmen, shedding kindred blood."[1]

It is thus evident that the terms Briton, British, English, Scot, Cymri, Welsh or Irish in their present-day use have largely lost their *racial* sense and are now used mainly in their *national* sense. Thus a great proportion of those who proudly call themselves " English " have little or no Angle or Saxon blood in their veins, and are not strictly entitled to call themselves " English " at all. And similarly with Scot, Cymri and British properly so-called : a person born in Scotland even of remote native ancestry is not necessarily of the Scot race properly so-called ; but is more often than not of the non-Aryan physical type of the Pict or " Celt." Yet, although so composite in race, the British nation, through its insularity, is even less heterogeneous in composition than most of the many continental countries which have secured or clamour for self-determination on " racial " grounds, an idea derived from the spread of Western Aryan " Nationalism."

The aggregate Aryan racial element in the population of the British Isles appears to be considerably smaller than what has hitherto been assumed, owing to the original Aryan immigrant stock having been so relatively small in proportion to the main body of the aboriginal population, with their greater prolificness. Yet it is now widely distributed in its relatively pure individual strain, and not confined to one particular class in society. Although the Aryans originally formed the aristocracy of the British Isles, the Aryan type, as evidenced by the Aryan physique and confirmed by Aryan patronymics, appears to be found nowadays more frequent in the ranks of the middle-class society.[2] Certainly the existing aristocracy, which has been

---

[1] Sir F. Palgrave, *English Commonwealth*, 1, 35.
[2] As regards Colour, Prof. Parsons finds, on revising and supplementing Beddoe's statistics, that in the modern population of Britain " the upper classes [including the middle class] have an altogether lower index of nigrescence than the lower " (J.R.A.I., 1920, 182)—that is to say, the upper and middle classes are fairer than the lower. Regarding Red Hair, which so frequently accompanies a fair and freckled skin and blue or light eyes, he finds it " is more common in the upper [including middle] than in the lower classes " (*ib.*, 182).

so largely recruited in modern times from miscellaneous party politicians and successful capitalists, has not only no monopoly of the Aryan type, but is to an appreciable extent obviously of the non-Aryan type—which is, perhaps, also to be explained in part by the fact that the Aryan rulers were in the habit of often confirming aboriginal chiefs in their chieftainship subject to Aryan suzerainty. And not a few individuals of this relatively pure Aryan physique are also to be seen amongst what are called " the Lower Classes," and may possibly explain to some extent the fact that whatever the general quality of the " Lower Classes " may be, it has always furnished capable candidates for vacancies in the " Upper."

In regard to the general topographical distribution of this relatively pure Aryan type in Britain, comparisons on such a matter may seem somewhat of the proverbially invidious kind. But, as we have seen that the Anglo-Saxons and Britons are of the same racial stock, and that both the Cymri and Scots are Britons, it is merely a question as to the facts in regard to the relative survival and distribution of the Aryan physical type in the kingdom. This type is admittedly found by observation and statistics in greater proportion to the general population to the north of the Tweed than to the south. Even as regards mere relative tallness, which is one of the associated Aryan traits, Scotland heads the list as containing the highest average stature in Europe,[1] even when its Aryan average is much reduced by including the non-Aryan element which forms the main body of its population. The relatively high proportion of the Aryan type in Scotland is, perhaps, owing to that country having been apparently a refuge for a considerable proportion of the more independent Briton Catti in order to escape the Roman domination, as has been already referred to. It may also be that it is on account of Scotland being in this way endowed with an extra reserve of the relatively purer Aryan stock of the old Aryan ruling race, that the saying has arisen that the Scots appropriate a disproportionate share in the administrative positions all the world over, and that when

[1] D.R.M., 584.

they cross the Tweed to the southern part of the land of their Catti ancestors, they are sometimes petulantly stigmatized there as "interlopers," from the time of Johnson downwards.

In Ireland the Aryan type appears to be especially numerous in Ulster, though found all over Erin or the ancient "Scotia," where the great bulk of the population is of the Iberian "Celtic" type. It thus would seem that the unhappy Irish Question is largely a matter of race antagonism or race war between different racial elements with different inherited psychology and temperaments and holding different ideals and outlooks on Life, even when nurtured in and leavened by Aryan Civilization.

And similarly the modern industrial and political unrest among the masses, with bitter strife between Capital and Labour and between Thrift and Unthrift, and the growth of crude revolutionary notions against the established order of Civilization, with proposals not unfrequently antagonistic to the cherished Aryan tradition of Freedom, and destructive of the foundations of that Civilization which has raised the masses of the people from the misery of the Stone Age "herd" into the material and social blessings which they now enjoy, are obviously to a considerable extent the result of the deep-seated race antagonism still surviving amongst the conflictingly diverse racial elements comprised within the British nation. And the like explanation may be given of the corresponding industrial unrest in other Aryanized countries.

In view of the Early Aryans having been the originators of the Higher Civilization, which has raised mankind to a higher plane of life, and having been at the same time the chief agents in the Propagation and Progress of Civilization it would be interesting to ascertain in what proportion the Aryan physique is present in the modern leaders of our Nation—in the spheres of government, science, industry, capital and labour and in "socialism."

Returning to the question of the physical and mental results of the mixing of races, we find that, when the process continues to go on *for a prolonged period*, the ultimate effect is to produce a mixed or hybrid race, which is of quite a different type from either parent race. This is what is now taking place to a considerable extent in the British Isles. Thus Sir Arthur Keith says :—

"A marriage across a *racial* frontier gives rise to an offspring so different from both parent races that it cannot be naturally grouped with either the one or the other."[1]

This evolution of a mixed or hybrid race is well seen in the Basque race of the Biscay regions, a people who have been affiliated to the Picts, as we have seen, and among whom the process of mixing has been going on for a longer period than in Britain. The Basques occupy the country between the dark, long- and narrow-headed and long-faced Iberians of Spain—the primitive Pictish type—on the one side, and the fair, broad- or round-headed and round-faced " Celts " of Gaul on the other side. As the produce of the prolonged intermixing of these two adjoining races, we have got a mixed or intermediate form of head and face. In this mixed race, the head is somewhat broader than in the Iberian type, with broader brow, yet retaining the narrow lower part of the Iberian face. This results in a wedge-shaped face with broad brow and narrow chin.

It is a somewhat similar mixed race which is now arising in Britain. A wedge-shaped face identical to that of the Basque race, with expanded frontal lobes of the brain and roundish head, is resulting from the prolonged crossing between the indigenous Pictish or Iberian race with the round-headed *non-Aryan* Germanic or Hun stock of the East Coast and Midlands, which appears to have been numerically almost as strong as the original Aryan stock in Britain. On the other hand, the prolonged intermixture of the *Aryan* element with the Pictish which forms the mass of the population, tends to produce the same wedge-shaped face with broad brow, though the resultant cranial form, owing to both of these races being long-headed, is also long-headed. This apparently accounts for the growing tendency to an " elongation " of the somewhat roundish

[1] Sir A. Keith, *Nationality and Race*, 1919, 9.

face of the Aryan type which has been remarked by Sir Arthur Keith. And the relative stature of many of the individuals of the darker mixed race tends to become increased, and to give in the case of the admixture with the Alpine or " Germanic " type a tallish and relatively *round*-headed dark " Celtic " type in some cases.[1]

On the mental character and psychology and temperamental predispositions of this new mixed race, the effect of this fusion of the diverse racial blood, with broadening of the Pictish brain, is not inconsiderable. It should be expected to bridge over to some extent and minimize the latent racial antagonisms between the respective parent races. This interbreeding is supposed to unite as compensatory benefits certain desirable temperamental traits which are possessed by one or other of the parent races and are absent in the other. Thus the " Celtic " or Pictish race is usually credited with being passionate and the sole possessor of that emotional trait popularly called " Celtic fire," though also possessing fatalistic traits tending to retard progress, both of which are alleged to be more or less absent in the Aryan type.

The psychological and temperamental contrast between the " Celtic," or Keltic, and the Aryan races in Britain has been thus summarized by a leading anthropologist :—

" The *Kelt* is still a Kelt, mercurial, passionate, vehement, impulsive, more courteous than sincere, voluble or eloquent, fanciful if not imaginative, quick-witted and brilliant rather than profound, elated with success, but easily depressed, hence lacking in steadfastness."

The *Aryan* type, according to the same authority, still remains

---

[1] Dr. Beddoe describes the result reached by this mixing of types at the period of the Roman occupation as in the skulls of the Romano-British interments. " These skulls are intermediate in length and breadth between the long-barrow and the round-barrow forms ; they have the prominent occiput [back of head] of the former with some degree of the parietal dilatation [round- or broad-headedness] of the latter. . . . This character belongs to neither of the other types but seems to me a probable result of their partial fusion." (B.R.B., 18). For a much later period, comprising one or two centuries past, a large series of skulls from an old graveyard on the Celtic-speaking borderland at Glasgow has recently been analysed by Prof. T. H. Bryce and Dr. J. Young and discloses amongst other things the broader brow and head of this mixed racial type in Scotland. See *Trans. R.S. Edin.*, 1911.

" stolid and solid, outwardly abrupt, but warm-hearted and true, haughty and even overbearing through an innate sense of superiority, yet at heart sympathetic and always just, hence a ruler of men ; seemingly dull or slow, yet pre-eminent in the realms of philosophy and imagination (Newton and Shakespeare)."[1]

The advantages of race mixture are advocated by many recent psychologists. Galton and Havelock Ellis have brought forward a variety of evidence, tending to show that great Englishmen are born on the borderland between the old Briton and Saxon settlements, and were presumably the result of "race mixture." But this does not appear to be really a case of race mixture, as the Britons and Saxons are of the same race, whilst the Pictish and "Celtic" elements are widely diffused throughout the whole land.

It remains to be seen whether the higher outstanding Aryan capacity for ruling, and the Aryan genius for constructive progress in science, philosophy, and the Higher Civilization, and the high moral fibre of the Aryan, suffer any relaxation in the new mixed race ; and whether the grand old Aryan type is dethroned, swamped and becomes extinct. This is a problem for the Eugenists.

In the achievement and preservation and progress of the Higher Civilization there is to be noted the supreme prominence which the Aryan founders of Civilization placed upon the indispensableness of the Religion of the One and Only Universal Father-god as the corner stone in the fabric of the Higher Civilization, as seen evidenced everywhere in the profusion of their magnificent Aryan votive religious monuments and inscriptions from the earliest period, and in their sacred hymns, as cited in the heading and in previous chapters. This practical necessity for the Higher Aryan Religion, with its exalted ethics, in the preservation and progress of Civilization is altogether ignored by Socialists, Communists and Anarchists in modern times. Our newly-found fresh light on the Origin of Civilization and on the Aryan men and supermen of genius who founded it and discovered the true paths for its future progress, discloses

[1] K.M., 532.

more clearly even than before the necessity for the Higher Religion occupying a foremost place in Civilization ; and that the short-sighted godless attempts at " government " by the French and other revolutionists and the Bolsheviks were and are foredoomed to failure, if Civilization itself is not to be utterly destroyed.

Here, it is also to be noted that the racial titles of " Briton " and " British " apply also equally to several of our colonies, not excepting that former great colony of Britain across the Atlantic, the great Western republic, severed from its Motherland by the intolerable tyranny and feudal despotism rampant under George III. The United States is essentially British in its origin and original colonists, and still remains " British " in its fundamental constitution, civilization and language. Although now such a vastly composite nation, through the fusion of Briton, Norse and German, Latin and Slav, it is to be remembered that, besides being founded by British colonists and organized by the Englishman George Washington, the stream of emigration which flowed into the States down to the middle seventies of last century was almost entirely British and Scandinavian, with the predominating element British. The essential unity of the two kindred Aryanized nations, the British and the " American," was ably expressed by the great American statesman, the U.S. ambassador Mr. Page, when he said :

" Our standards of character and of honour and of duty are your standards ; and life and freedom have the same meaning with us that they have with you. These are the essential things, and in this we have always been one."

It therefore behoves these two of the greatest of the Aryanized kindred nations in the world to translate their union of Thought into union of Action, in working together for the preservation and progress of the Higher Civilization of the Aryans, for the welfare of the World, and as a bounden duty which they owe their immortal ancestors, from whom they have inherited the priceless boon of British Civilization, the virile Aryan Brito-Phœnicians.

We thus find that in the complex welter of mixed races

which has arisen in Britain through long centuries of more or less intermarriage of its Aryan civilizers with the aborigines and the East Coast Germanic race, there still exists here and in our colonies, a considerable element of the relatively pure Aryan racial stock representative of that originally introduced into Britain by the world-civilizing Aryan Phœnicians. And this Aryan stock, descended from the original Gothic civilizers of Britain, still appears to form the backbone of the social, economic, industrial and political anatomy of the State; and it seems to hold out the best promise for the progress, efficiency and happiness of the British Nation and British Commonwealth for the Future.

FIG. 73.—Early Bronze-Age Briton button-amulet Cross. From barrow grave at Rudstone, Yorks.
(After Greenwell. *Brit. Barrows* 54.)
It is of jet, with eyelet on under surface for attachment.

## XXIV

### Historical Effects of the Discoveries

WHILST it is impossible to enter here on a general discussion of the historic consequences of the discoveries set forth or referred to in the foregoing pages, one or two results may, I think, be appropriately mentioned in closing this brief monograph.

What I have to say falls conveniently under two headings, the bearing of the new facts and views, first on the History of Human Progress, and secondly, on special points in that history, the Origin and Racial Affinities of the Phœnicians, the Sources of the British People, the Relation of the Primitive Aryan Religion to the later cults and so forth.

As regards the former question, that of the History of Culture, it must, I think, be admitted that we had for long been approaching an *impasse*. Facts had been accumulating which were putting accepted theories somewhat out of focus. There was first the long-standing difficulty of the great outburst of literature and science all over the known world, and affecting such widely-separated centres as Greece, India and China from the eighth to the fourth centuries B.C. And there was the more recent incongruity connected with the independent and seemingly indigenous cults of the Mediterranean hind-lands, and more especially of Central and Northern Europe.

To those of us who take long and broad views it had, during recent decades, been becoming increasingly obvious that many of the peoples inhabiting these outlying lands, when they first appeared in history, displayed both scientific and literary cultural elements which could nowise be explained by the accepted doctrine of a general affiliation of all progress to Hellenism and Hebraism. For example, there are many things in Gothic and " Celtic " and British

Religions and Literature which, so far from being explicable by the current theories, are in violent opposition to both the scientific and artistic standards and traditions derived from the Hellenic and Jewish peoples of which the Roman conquerors of the world made themselves the missionaries.

If, however, we adopt the theory adumbrated by the above account of the Phœnician people and Civilization, that behind both Greek and Hebrew culture there was an earlier and more widespread Aryan influence, affecting during anterior millenniums, not merely the coast-dwellers of the Mediterranean, but more or less the whole known world, and conveyed over the three continents—and even to Peru—largely by the enterprise of the Aryan Phœnicians, we shall, I think, have a theory, founded largely on facts, which will explain much that has hitherto appeared anomalous in the history of Civilized Europe and Asia.

I should like, then, to suggest for the consideration of readers, whether we do not find in such a theory the answer to the two main problems left unsolved by the current doctrine. And further, and more particularly, whether we do not obtain from it an explanation of much that was indigenous, and opposed to Hellenism and Hebraism, in the Literature and Statesmanship and Religion of Central and North-Western Europe during the medieval and modern periods.

It had long appeared probable that Civilization is largely a matter of Race and that, in Europe and Indo-Persia, the chief agency in effecting it has been an Aryan strain, operating in a way hitherto not understood amongst widely separated peoples and races. To this theory, the supposed Jewish influence on Religion and the supernatural illumination of which it was supposed to be the vehicle, constituted a serious objection, which was very inadequately met by imagining a sifting and adapting of Jewish ideas by the practical genius of Rome and the subtle intelligence of the Greeks, all the more so as there was no historical evidence whatever of any such borrowing from the Hebrews, who are nowhere even mentioned by Greco-Roman writers.

The difficulty is now wholly removed by the new evidence

showing that nearly all the monotheistic ideas and literary motives which have hitherto been regarded as characteristically Jewish, were borrowed by the Israelites from the Hitto-Phœnicians or Goths, and were therefore essentially Aryan. Nevertheless, for the past two millenniums, it has been owing to the Jews, that we have had preserved and transmitted to us in the Western Christian World, embedded in several of the books of their Old Testament, in Job (whose author was the fourth traditional Aryan king), in most of the Psalms (one of which has been instanced in the text), Proverbs, Enoch (the third traditional Aryan priest-king), much of Isaiah and others, many of the priceless treasures of the first Aryan illumination amongst our Hitto-Phœnician or Gothic ancestors.

Besides supplying the missing links in the proof as to the Aryan Origin of Civilization, the new evidence shows the fuller inheritance by the British than by others of the "Hitt-ite" or Gothic Race-character, by the unique survival, in Britain, not only of the most authentic of all literary histories of the rise of the Aryans preserved in the Eddas, and of the primitive Gothic or "Hitt-ite" emblems, but also of the things for which these emblems stand, the Language, Culture and Mental aptitudes of the Early Aryans.

The new evidence, in pointing to the British and their constituent Gothic elements as the purest representatives of the Gothic or *Khatti* (Hitt-ite) culture and heredity, sheds light upon much that would otherwise be unintelligible in the history of Western Civilization. In the first place, the high Aryanization of Britain, and the relatively low Aryanization of Germany with its round-heads, may in part explain the desire of Cæsar to incorporate Britain, and his determination to exclude Germany, from incorporation in the Roman Empire. Then later, when reaction set in and it was obvious that Cæsar's larger designs could not be carried out, Britain's purer Aryanism enabled it to maintain an attitude of independence towards the debased semi-pagan power which established itself on the ruins of the Western Empire.

Indeed, British progress throughout the Middle Ages was,

owing largely to racial idiosyncracy, identified with resistance to outside influences. Deriving their Christian form of religion from Rome, the British have treated it in the main as a matter of ritualistic routine. To its dogma they have been respectfully indifferent. Its lofty ethics, when practically inconvenient they have ignored. This peculiar independence and self-assertiveness of the British was displayed not less conspicuously by poets than by statesmen and theologians. It was a true instinct which led Shakespeare to glorify the murderers of Cæsar, for in the absence of the decadent medieval empire, not merely British, but European art might have had a more felicitous, because more natural, development than it really enjoyed. In truth, the artistic went deeper than either the political or the religious revolt. It was a protest not so much against this or that effete doctrine, as against imperialism in principle, against finality in the realm of the ideal.

That the British have inherited the sea-faring aptitude and adventurous spirit of the Aryan Phœnicians appears obvious. Whether they in the same degree reflect, and have profited by, the ancestral monotheistic Religion, is not quite so plain. And yet, I think, there is something to be said in favour of an affirmative on this question, too.

It cannot be pretended that Sun-worship is a truly scientific religion—and the worship of that luminary itself appears to have been the earlier form of the Aryan Sun-cult, and continued amongst many of the Aryans, after the majority had made the Sun merely the symbol of the Universal Father God. The Sun, after all, is only a part, and a comparatively small part even, of the visible Universe; and no more than any other visible object can it be specially identified with the Incomprehensible Power behind all—whose glory Job declares that the heavens with all their contents " utter but a whisper "—which is the real object round which the specifically religious emotions group themselves. As, however, the public demand a non-scientific religion, a religion, that is to say, which represents mankind as the great object of the Creator's care, and which appeals rather to the senses and emotions than to the reason, the question arises whether Sun-worship does not present us with an idea which satisfies that popular demand with less departure from scientific requirements than those other miraculous and anthropomorphic types, which so many European nations have cultivated since the days of Phœnician ascendancy, and which finally took form in the ceremonies and superstitions of the Catholic Church. If the Power at the root of things is to be conceived of as having a kindly feeling for mankind, then the Sun is surely the visible manifestation of that feeling, and embodiment of that idea, seeing that it is the source of all Life in this world, and that by which alone Life is ceaselessly maintained. And it was the anthropomorphizing of the Sun as the Father-God by the Hitto-Sumerians, which, as we have seen, is the source of the modern conception of God.

Do we not thus find in the modern British Religion in most of its sects—in its tolerance, its good sense, its adaptability, its sense of reality, its power to incorporate and live on friendly terms with the various forms in which pious sentiment seeks expression, its opposition to the attempts to domineer over the mind and spirit of others, its minimization of theory, and exaltation of ritual and show, its aversion to the Mother-goddess cult and to every kind of asceticism, whether in doctrine or practice, its insisting that Religion shall submit to the same test as other institutions which profess to serve the nation, that of Usefulness—some features that harmonize well with the exalted and humane spirit of the Sun-worshippers, and that " hark back," if the expression be allowed, to that old indigenous positivistic view which the Aryan " Hitt-ite " Phœnicians brought with them from the East, and which was otherwise manifested in the literature of the British people, and notably in the person of its two greatest poets, Shakespeare and Milton ?

Yet other fruits of Britain's exceptional Aryan inheritance were her establishment of democratic institutions, centuries before they were adopted by other countries, and her world-wide colonial and commercial enterprise, reproducing the maritime adventures of the Phœnician Aryans, from whom, we have seen, the British people, properly so-called, are in part descended.

The higher Aryanization to which these and other peculiarly British characteristics bear witness is a chief guarantee that the sacrifices of the nations in the late war, in order to secure the ultimate triumph of Right over Might, will not have been made in vain. After all, human nature, like flowers, turns to the sunlight, and the final predominance of the superior heart and brain is assured.

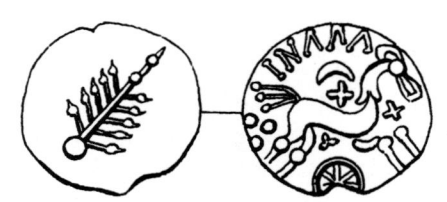

FIG. 74.—Ancient Briton " Catti " coin of 2nd cent. B.C. with Sun-Crosses, Sun-horse, etc., and legend *INARA* (Hitto-Phœnician Father-god *Indara* or " Andrew ").

(After Evans. E.C.B., 149, and see above, p. 317).

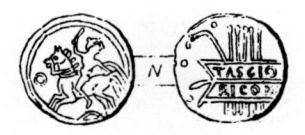

FIG. 75.—Tascio (Hercules) coin of *Ricon* ruling Briton clan.
(After Poste, and see E.C.B., 8, 6–8.)
Note the pentad "spears" as Tascio's sacred cup-mark number.

# APPENDICES

## I

CHRONOLOGICAL LIST OF EARLY BRITON KINGS, FROM BRUTUS-THE-TROJAN, ABOUT 1103 B.C., TO ROMAN PERIOD

*Compiled from Early British Chronicles of Geoffrey of Monmouth and Supplemented by Records of Dr. Powel, etc.*[1]

THE fact that these complete and systematic chronological lists of the Early Briton kings, from the advent of Brutus downwards without a break, have been fully preserved by the Britons, implies familiarity with the use of writing from the earliest period of Brutus. And we have seen that King Brutus-the-Trojan and his Brito-Phœnicians were fully equipped with the knowledge and use of writing.

These chronological king-lists record the names and lengths of reign of the several paramount kings of Early Britain in unbroken, continuous succession from Brutus down to the Roman period of well-known modern history.

Their authenticity is attested not only by their own inherent consistency and the natural length of each reign in relation to the events recorded in the Chronicles, and by their general agreement with the few stray references by Roman writers to some of the later kings, and with the royal names stamped upon Early Briton coins, but also by their being *confirmed by the royal names on several Early Briton coins*, which names are unknown to Roman and other history; and *these ancient coins had not yet been unearthed, and thus were unknown, at the period of Geoffrey* and other early editors of these Chronicle lists of the Early Briton kings. Thus we shall see that they supply the key to the "RVII" name stamped on some of the Briton coins, the identity of which name has not hitherto been recognized, but which is now disclosed as the "ARVI" title of Caractacus as recorded in the ancient Chronicles of Geoffrey and others, and in Roman contemporary literature and disclosing coins of Caractacus and other kings hitherto supposed to have no coinage. And they supply the date and position of *two famous Ancient Briton sovereigns whose Codes of Laws were translated by King Alfred for the benefit of the Anglo-Saxons*. These lists were also reputed sources of Tudor genealogy.[2]

The dates of reign are recorded, as is usual, with only few exceptions, in ancient dynastic lists, not in a special era, but merely in the line of consecutive years of the successive reigns. In order, therefore, to equate those regnal years to the Christian era (as there is no fixed or even approximate date known for the Homeric Fall of Troy to determine the initial date of Brutus), I have started from the datum point fixed by the tradition that Christ was born in the 22nd year of the reign of Cuno-belin[3] (No. 71 on list), a well-known Briton king whom both the Chronicles and his very

---
[1] Powel and Harding's dated lists are respectively detailed by Borlase, *op. cit.*, 404, etc., and are compared with others by Poste, *Britannic Researches*, 227, etc.
[2] Powel, cited by Borlase, *op. cit.*, 405, with reference to Henry VII.
[3] Tradition recorded by Powel, see Borlase, *op. cit.*, 406.

numerous coins place as the contemporary and protégé of the Roman emperor Augustus who reigned 27 B.C.–14 A.D., and thus included the epoch of the birth of Christ.[1] This datum point, moreover, agrees fairly well with another fixed date, Cæsar's second invasion of Britain in 54 B.C., in regard to which Geoffrey's Chronicle records that Cassibellan died " seven years " after that event,[2] that is, in 47 B.C., which the Chronicle chronology, as now equated, places at 45 B.C., that is a variation of only two years, and there is this variation in the estimated birth-date of Christ.

I have adopted the length of reigns recorded by Geoffrey as far as they go, as they are usually identical with those of Dr. Powel's lists, and for the remainder I have adopted Powel's regnal years in preference to those of Harding, as the latter presumably included as regnal years those years during which crown-princes acted as co-regents with their fathers, although the sum total of years between the accession of Brutus down to the period of Cassibellan in Powel and Harding respectively differs only by *two* years.[3]

It is noteworthy that all the lengths of reign are perfectly natural terms of years, and the lists contain no supernatural lengths of reign such as disfigure some ancient chronologies which nevertheless are generally accepted as " historical." It will also be seen that the Early Britons had already a highly-civilized king ruling in London before the Israelites had yet obtained a king.

ABBREVIATIONS : G = Geoffrey   r = reigned
                k = king        s = son
                m = married     w = wife
                P = Powel

| No. | Date of Accession B.C. (approximate). | Name. | Length of Reign in Years. | Events and Remarks. | Contemporary Historical Events B.C. |
|---|---|---|---|---|---|
| 1 | 1103 | Brutus, great grandson of Æneas, m. Ignoge, daughter of King Parnassus of Greece. | 24 (P. 15) | Conquers Britain and founds Tri-Novantum or London. | Assyrian massacring invasion of Hittite Asia Minor and Syria by Tiglath Pileser I. 1120. Saul 1st k. of Israel 1095. |
| 2 | 1079 | Locrinus, s. of 1. | 10 (P. 20) | Invasion of Huns on Humber repelled. | |
| 3 | 1069 | Guendolen regent, w. of 2, and daughter of Duke Corineus. | 15 | | |
| 4 | 1054 | Madan, s. of 2 and 3. | 40 | | David becomes k. of Jerusalem 1047; and Hiram Phœnician k. of Tyre. |
| 5 | 1014 | Mempricius, s. of 4. | 20 (omitted by P.) | | |
| 6 | 994 | Ebrauc, s. of 5. | 40 | Founded York and Dun-Barton and invaded Gaul. | Solomon builds temple 1012–991. (Sylvius Latinus r. in Alba Longa in Italy.) |
| 7 | 954 | Brutus II. or Grene shylde, s. of 6. | 12 | His brothers conquered and ruled Germany. | |
| 8 | 942 | Leyle or Leir, s. of 7. | 25 | Founded Carlisle. | (Sylvius Epitus r. in Alba Longa.) |
| 9 | 917 | Rudhebras or Hudibras, s. of 8. | 39 (P. 29) | Built Canterbury and Caer Guen or Winchester. | (Capys, s. of Epitus r. in Italy.) |

[1] The date for the birth of Christ introduced into the later versions of the British Chronicles by their earlier Christian editors was, of course, the traditional date for the beginning of the Christian era, and not the actual date of that event in 4 B.C. as estimated by modern historians.
[2] Geoffrey *op. cit.*, 4, 11.    [3] See Borlase. *op. cit.* 406.

# KING LIST OF ANCIENT BRITONS

| No. | Date of Accession B.C. (approximately). | Name. | Length of Reign in Years. | Events and Remarks. | Contemporary Historical Events B.C. |
|---|---|---|---|---|---|
| 10 | 878 | Bladud, s. of 9. | 20 | Built Bath with Fire - temple and public baths. | Syria-Phœnicia under Assyrians 877-633. |
| 11 | 858 | Leir II., s. of 10, with 3 daughters and no son. Regan m. Henuinus, duke of Cornwall. | 60 | Built Caer Leir or Leicester. Is Shakespeare's "King Lear." | Homer lived (*Herodot.* 2, 53). |
| 12 | 798 | Cordeilla, youngest daughter, m. Aganippus, k. of Gaul. | 5 | | |
| 13 | 793 | Cunedagus or Condage, s. of Henuinus and grands. of 11. | 33 | | |
| 14 | 760 | Riveal or Rivalo, s. of 13. | 46 | | Traditional founding of Rome about 750. Isaiah the prophet, 740. |
| 15 | 714 | Gurgustius, s. of 14. | 37 | | Fall of last king of Hittites at Car-Chemish by Assyrian Sargon II., 717. |
| 16 | 677 | Sisilius or Scicilius. | 49 | | Scythian invasion of Assyria frees Phœnicia, 635. |
| 17 | 628 | Jago, nephew of 15. | 28 | | Probable founding of Athens. |
| 18 | 600 | Kymar or Kynmarcus, s. of 16. | 54 | | Israelites carried into captivity by Nebuchadnezzar, 587. |
| 19 | 546 | Gor-bogudo or Gorbodus. | 63 (Harding 11) | At end of reign civil war and both sons killed. | Cyrus the Mede takes Asia Minor and Babylon, 546-538. |
| 20 | 483 | Cloten, duke of Cornwall, inherits. | 10 (Harding) | | Hanno, Phœnician admiral, circumnavigates N.W. Africa before 500 B.C. Phœnicia furnishes 300 ships to Xerxes' fleet in 480. (*Herodot.*, 7, 89 f.) |
| 21 | 473 | Dunwallo Molmutius or Moduncius, s. of 20. | 40 | Restored paramount rule and enacted Molmutian Laws and Law of Sanctuary. | Herodotus, about 450. |
| 22 | 433 | Belinus, s. of 21, with brother Brennus. | 26 (Harding 41) | Brennus rules jointly with Belinus, then with the latter for 5 years and conquers Gaul and afterwards sacks Rome and conquers Dacia in Gothland. | Media (including E. Cappadocia) revolted from Persia 414. |
| 23 | 407 | Gurgwin, Gorbonian or Gurgwintus Barbtrucus, s. of 22. | 19 | Meets Part-olon as kinsman and agrees to his occupying part of British Isles. | Spartan Greeks invade and annex Asia Minor and Cilicia, 399. Phœnician naval fight against Spartans, 394. PART-OLON arrives in Britain about 395 B.C.(?) |
| 24 | 388 | Guytelin or Guithelin Batrus. | 27 | | |

| No. | Date of Accession B.C. (approximate). | Name. | Length of Reign in Years. | Events and Remarks. | Contemporary Historical Events B.C. |
|---|---|---|---|---|---|
| 25 | 361 | Sisilius or Scicilius II., s. of 24, under regency of mother Martia. | 7 | Queen Martia is author of book on "Martian Law," translated by King Alfred. | Phœnician fleet defeats Spartans and regains Asia Minor and Cilicia for Persians, 387. |
| 26 | 354 | Kymar II., s. of 25. | 3 | | Philip of Macedon, 359. |
| 27 | 351 | Danus or Elanus, s. of 25. | 8 | | Pytheas, Ionian navigator, circumnavigates and surveys British Isles. |
| 28 | 343 | Morvyle or Morindus, s. of 27. | 3 | Invasion of Northumbria by Morini from Gaul. | |
| 29 | 335 | Gorbonian II., s. of 28. | 10 | | Alexander in Syria-Phœnicia-Cilicia, 332. |
| 30 | 325 | Arthegal or Argallo, s. of 28. | 1 | Deposed for tyranny. | |
| 31 | 324 | Eledure "the Pious," brother of latter. | 3 | | |
| 32 | 321 | Arthegal restored. | 10 | Buried at Leir in Leicester. | Syria-Phœnicia and Asia Minor under the Greeks, 323-265. |
| 33 | 311 | Eledure again. | 1 | | |
|  | 310 | Jugen or Vigein with Peredour, brothers of latter. | 11 (Hard. P. 8) | | Seleucus (Nikator), k. of Asia Minor and Syria-Phœnicia, 312. |
| 34 to | 299 295 to | Eledure again. Gorbonian III., s. of 29 and 32 successors reigning 185 years; details in Geoffrey, 3, 19 ; and length of each reign in Harding and Borlase. | 4 185 | | 1st Punic War against Carthage, 264-241. Hannibal, Phœnician general, invades Italy, 221. Romans wrest Spain from Carthage, 211. |
| 67 | 110 | Beli II. or "Belinus the Great" or 'Hely.' Had 3 sons, Lud, Cassibellan and Nennius. | 40 | Appears to be the "Cunobelin" or "King Belin" of the older Briton coins. | |
| 68 | 70 | Lud or Ludus, s. of 67. Had 2 sons, Androgeus and Tenuantius, under age when he died, hence succeeded by his brother. | 11 | Altered name of Tri-Novantum to Lud-dun or "London." | Roman period in Palestine begins. |
| 69 | 59 | Cassi-belan, s. of 67. | 15 (Hard. 33) | Is "Cassivellaunus" of Cæsar. | Cæsar's invasion, 55-54 B.C. |
| 70 | 44 | Tenuantis (or Theomantius), s. of 68, and in Cassibellan's reign, Duke of Cornwall. | 22 (Hard. 17) | Supposed "Imanuentis," k. of Tri-Novantes of Cæsar who was killed by Cassivellaunus, and whose son was Mandubratius. | Cleopatra dies and Egypt becomes a Roman province, 30 Roman Empire begins under Augustus, 27. |
| 71 | 22 | Kymbelin or Cunobelin, s. of 70. Had 2 sons, Guiderus and Arvi-ragus. | 29 (Hard. 10) | Christ born in "22nd year" of his reign. (P.). Is Shakespeare's "Cymbeline." | Christ born in 4 B.C. |

# KING LIST OF ANCIENT BRITONS

| No. | Date of Accession B.C. (approximate.) | Name. | Length of Reign in Years. | Events and Remarks. | Contemporary Historical Events B.C. |
|---|---|---|---|---|---|
| 72 | 7 A.D. | Guiderius, eldest s. of 71. | 28 | | |
| 73 | 35 A.D. | Arvi-ragus or Agrestes or Cateracus, Cara-docus or Caratacus, 2nd s. of 71. | 28 | The "Caratacus" or "Caractacus" of Romans, betrayed to Romans by queen of Brigantes in 51 A.D. | Claudius conquers Britain, 43-52 A.D. Last independent paramount Briton king, stated, in the Chronicles, to have married Genuissa, sister of Claudius, on conclusion of peace. |

The following identifications of kings in these Chronicle lists, not already specially noted in the foregoing text, call for remark.

Brennus (or Bryan), brother of King Belinus (No. 22 on list) is reported in the Chronicles to be the famous Brennus who led the Gauls in the sack of Rome, placed in 390 B.C. But this Briton tradition, along with the rest of the Chronicles, has been summarily thrust aside by modern writers, the one following the other without serious consideration, as being preposterous and an anachronism as well. Seeing, however, that Rome and Roman civilization and traditional history are of so much later origin than London and British civilization and traditional history, and that the Roman date of 390 B.C. for that event appears to rest merely upon a tradition, and that the British tradition appears to be circumstantial and authentic, and otherwise in agreement with the Roman account of that event, the evidence for the Roman date of 390 B.C., as opposed to the British date of "before 407 B.C." requires re-examination. The Roman tradition states that the Gauls were led by Brennus in that raid in retaliation for Roman opposition to the Senones, or Seine tribe of the Gauls, in their siege of Clusium in Etruscany of the Tyrrheni, in which country they wished to establish a colonial settlement. Now the British Chronicles relate with circumstantial detail that between 420 and 408 B.C. the Briton prince Brennus, who had married the heiress-daughter of the Gallic Duke of the Allobroges, had, upon the death of the latter and with the assistance of his brother King Belinus, conquered Gaul and "brought the whole kingdom of Gaul into subjection."[1] The Senones tribe of Gauls occupied the left bank of the middle Seine, below whom, as we have seen, were the coastal provinces of the Casse or *Cassi*; whilst significantly on the adjoining eastern bank were the *Catalauni* tribe of the Marne Valley. And the Chronicle account also states that Brennus led the Senones to Rome "in revenge on the Romans for *their breach of treaty*."[2] This raid appears to have been analogous to that later one by their kinsmen Goths under Alaric in the fifth century A.D., and, like it, was also for the breach by the Romans of their treaty.

Cassibellan (No. 69 on list), the "Cassivellaunus" of the Romans, although nowhere credited in the British Chronicles nor in Roman history with any son, is nevertheless given a son "Tascio-vanus" by modern numismatists,[3] on the mere assumption that three coins of Cunobelin (No. 71 on list) which bear the legend "Tascio-vani F." and "Tasc F"[4] designate him thereby as "Son of Tascio-vanus," in which the F is regarded as being a contraction for the Latin *filius*, "a son." The third coin, which is slightly defaced, bears the legend "Tasc. FI," with a final letter of which only

---
[1] Geoffrey, *op. cit.*, 3, 8. [2] *Ibid.*, 3, 9.
[3] Birch, *Numismat. Chronicle*, 7, 78 ; and J. Evans, *Anc. Brit. Coins*, 220, etc.
[4] Evans, *op. cit.*, Pl. 10, 7 ; Pl. 12, 1.

DD

the vertical stroke I remains,[1] and which they suppose was an L and read the word as "Fil," which would represent the Latin *Filius*. "a son." But this incomplete end-word has also been read "Fir";[2] and so uncertain is its reading as "Fil," that even the numismatists who use that reading admit that "we have to wait for better specimens of this type before the reading 'Tasc. Fil' can be regarded as absolutely and indisputably proved."[3] Yet they nevertheless systematically use it as if it were established, and everywhere call Cunobelin "the son of Tascio-vanus." But "Tascio-vani," as the word is really written, has, as we have seen, quite another and a divine significance.

This supposititious king "Tascio-vanus" is attempted to be supported by the fact that a final F occurring on a few of the later coins of the sons of Commius as "Com. F.," clearly designate them in Roman fashion as "The Son of Commius." But both Commius and his sons were *non*-Britons. They were Gallic chiefs and latinized protégés of Cæsar imported by the latter into South Britain and established there for the political purpose of breaking up the power and resistance of Cassivellaunus and the Britons. On the other hand Cunobelin was also doubtless romanized to a considerable extent, as he is referred to in the British Chronicles as having been "brought up by Augustus Cæsar,"[4] and the Roman influence on the designs of his later coins is obvious. But it by no means follows that the addition of F or Fi on three of his very numerous coins designates him as the son of a human king named "Tascio-vanus," wholly unknown to history.

Further, this "Tascio-vanus" is assumed to be the equivalent of "Tenuantis" (No. 70 on list), who, in the Chronicle, was the father of Cunobelin, and whose name is also variously spelt as Tenantius and Theomantius, as if "Ten" or "Theom" could ever become "Tascio." Then, altogether disregarding the Chronicle records, this Tascio-vanus is arbitrarily made to be not only the father of Cunobelin, but also the son of Cassibellan or Cassi-vellaunos, instead of the latter's brother King Lud (No. 68 on list), as is recorded in all versions of the Chronicles. In accordance with this forced identification all the numerous different mintages of coins inscribed Tascio, Tasc, Tas, Tasciov, Dias, etc. (28 in number) although not bearing Cunobelin's name are then thrust on to this supposititious "Tasciovanus," the supposed father of Cunobelin, and the supposed son of Cassivellaunus.

But the Chronicles, in their different versions, are quite clear upon the point that Cassibellan was the *uncle*, and not the father, of Cunobelin (see List, Nos. 69 to 71). Moreover, as a fact, the very numerous coins stamped Tascio, Tasc, Tas, Taxi and Tascia, which are widely distributed, are all of the Catti type, and nearly all of them contain the Corn or Ear of Barley which is sometimes arranged in the form of the Cross as the St. Andrew's Cross of the Corn Spirit, whom we have found to be Tascio, with numerous superadded small Crosses and also circles, symbolizing, as we have seen, the Sun. This Corn also appears in many or perhaps most of the "Tascio" coins of Cunobelin, and in several is figured the warrior Hercules, who, we have seen, is Tascio, and the winged Sun horse or horseman. And we have seen that Tascio was the Corn Spirit and archangel of the Barat Britons. No doubt the divine name "Tascio," like that of Bel, was piously taken by some kings and men of the Sun-cult as a personal name. And, as we have seen, it was a common practice with the early Hittite Barat Aryans, as the "discoverers" of the idea of God, to call themselves, as the chosen people, the "Sons of God." Thus, even should it be found that the doubtful letter on the solitary Cunobelin coin makes the reading "*Tasc. Fil*" or "*Son of Tasc*" or "*Tascio*," it will merely show that Cunobelin called himself

---

[1] Evans, Pl. 12, 4 and p. 331.
[2] Poste, *Coins of Cunobelin*, 214.
[3] Evans, *Coins*, 331.
[4] Geoffrey, 4, 11.

"Son of God," or "Son of the archangel *Tascio*"; and analogous to the Divine Cæsar title of the Roman emperors. The reason why no Briton coins bearing obvious kings' names prior to or of the period of Cassibellan presumably is that the Britons, like the Phœnicians in their early coins, (*e.g.*, of Syracuse and other earlier settlements) impressed on their earlier coins not the name of their sovereign but of their tutelary (or Bel).

This divine sense of the title " Tascio " on these Briton coins appears also clearly evidenced by its form as " *Tascio Ricon* " (Fig. 75) and " *Tasci Riconi* " on four different kinds of coins with the Sun horseman and wheel and Sun circles and a design which seems to be a Sheaf of Corn,[1] and which admittedly has no connection with Cunobelin. The *Ric* element in this name is clearly the Gothic Rig, or Rik or Reik, " a king " (from Rik, " mighty " or " rich ") and cognate with the latin Rex, Regis; and it thus suggests the great Ancient Briton city-port in Sussex called by the Romans " *Regnum*," the modern Chichester, and its people, " the *Regni*," a title applied broadly to the men of Sussex, and presuming a Briton form of *Ricon*. These coins, so far as I am aware, have not been actually found at Chichester; but coins are made to circulate and these coins are found in Essex, Hunts and Norfolk. Now it is significant that the great Ancient Briton arterial paved highway called " Stane Street " ran directly from Regnum or Chichester to the Wash, and connected these three counties. *This title of " Tascio Ricon " would mean " Tascio of the Regni (confederate state)."* It is thus obviously analogous to the numerous coins of Tarsus bearing the legend " Bal Tarz "[2] (with figures of the warrior Father-god) as " Bel of Tarsus."

Similarly, the Briton coin stamped " *Tascio Sego* " (see Fig. 43A, p. 261) equally unconnected with Cunobelin,[3] and bearing the Sun-horseman and wheel and Crosses and circles (of the Sun) is now seen to be obviously of the same tutelary kind. The *Segonti-aci* were a tribe of Britons mentioned by Cæsar, alongside the Cassi tribe, as submitting to him at his crossing of the Thames at Kew.[4] This tribe occupied North Hants, presumably up to the Thames, with their capital at Silchester (north of Winchester), where, significantly, in addition to numerous early Roman coins and other Roman inscriptions, was found a votive inscription in the foundations of an altar to the Phœnician god " Hercules of the Saegon ";[5] and Hercules, as we have seen, was the warrior type of Tascio. And this inscription discloses that he was still at the Roman period the recognized local tutelary of that Briton tribe. This coin legend thus obviously means " Tascio of the Segonti (confederate state)." Similarly, again, the coins stamped " *Tascia Ver*," " *Tasc Vir* " and " Tas V,"[6] obviously mean " Tascio of the Verulam (or St. Alban confederate states)."

In the light of this tutelary use of this prefixed title of " Tascio " it now becomes evident that the legends on several coins of Cunobelin, reading *Tasci-iovantis*,[7] *Tasci-iovanii*,[8] *Tasci-ovan*,[9] etc., are possibly contractions for " Tascio of the Tri-*Novantes* (or Londoners' confederate state) " and Cunobelin's capital was at " Tri-*Novantum*," or London, though minting also at Verulam. This now discloses the divine tutelary meaning of the title " Tasciiovanti " and " Tasciovani," the hitherto supposititious so-called " Tasciovanus, son of Cassivellaunus."

All this strikingly attests the widespread prevalence in Ancient Britain

---

[1] See Evans, *op. cit.*, Pl. 8, Nos. 6-9.
[2] Hill, *Greek Coins of Cilicia*, Pl. 28, etc.; and Ramsay, *Cities of St. Paul*, 128, etc.
[3] The coin is in the Hunterian Museum of Glasgow University, see for Fig. Evans, *op. cit.*, Pl. 8, 11. Several other Briton coins with the legend " Sego " are known.
[4] Cæsar, *De B. Gall.*, 5, 21.
[5] Camden, *Britannia*, Gough's second ed., 1, 204. The inscription reads " Deo Her[culi] Saegon[-tiacorum]," etc. See Gough for full text and translation.
[6] Evans, *op. cit.*, Pl. 7, Nos. 1, 7 and 11.
[7] *Ibid.*, Pl. 12, 3.   [8] *Ibid.*, Pl. 10, Nos. 12 and 13.   [9] *Ibid.*, Pl. 10, No. 10.

of the Sun-cult of the Hitto-Phœnician archangel Taxi or Tascio, with its Sun-Crosses and Corn emblems, which cult we have already found in the Don Valley of the Texali tribe, and in the neighbourhood of the Phœnician Barat Part-olon's votive Cross to Bel at Newton and elsewhere.

Androgeus, again, the eldest son of King Lud (No. 68 on list) and nephew of Cassibellan, and who, the Chronicle tells us, was duke of Kent,[1] is disclosed by the Chronicle to be obviously the *Andoc, Ando, And,*[2] *Antd, Anted,*[3] *Antedrigv,*[4] and *Avnt,*[5] stamped upon various Briton coins, and thus further establishing the historicity of the British Chronicles.

Guiderius (No. 72 on list), the eldest son of Cunobelin, is, I find, clearly the minter of the coins bearing the legend CAV-DVRO, *i.e.*, " Cau-duro."[6]

And lastly, the last independent Briton king " Arvi-ragus " of Geoffrey's Chronicle (No. 73 on list), and the " Cate-racus " or " Cara-dog " of the Welsh records, " Caratacus " (erroneously called " Caractacus " by the Romans), the famous younger son of Cunobelin, whose virtues and bravery are so highly extolled by Tacitus, is now disclosed by the Chronicles to be the author of the Briton coins stamped " RVII " and " RVI'S."[7] This name was suggested by Evans to represent a hypothetical king " Rufus or Rufinus."[8] But this RVI of the coins now clearly identifies their minter with " Arvi-ragus " or Caratacus of the Chronicles. The form *Rvii* appears to be the latinized genitive and *Rvi's* the corresponding Briton Gothic genitive of *is*, the source of our English *'s*, and thus giving us a bilingual form of that legend in Latin and British Gothic. *Indeed, the identity of the title " Arvi-ragus " with Caratacus was well known to and used by contemporary Roman writers.* Thus Juvenal (born about 55 A.D.), in reflecting the love and respect or fear of the Romans and his suzerainty over the kinglets of Britain, in regard to their once-captured Briton king, Caratacus, relates how a certain blind man, speaking of a turbot that was taken, said :—

" *Arviragus* shall from his *Britan* chariot fall,
Or thee his lord some *captive king* shall call."[9]

This title " Arvi-ragus " appears to be probably a latinized form of the earlier racial title of the " Arri " or Aryans, as the " Plough-men "—*Arvi* being the Latin for " ploughed " from the Latin and Greek *Aro* or *Aroō*, " to plough." And *ragus* is presumably a latinized dialectic spelling of the British Gothic *Rig* or *Reiks*, " a king " and cognate, as we have seen, with Latin Rex-Regis and " Raja."[10] This would give the title of " King of the Plough-men (or Arri)," and the prominence of agriculture in Britain is attested by such frequent representations of ears of Corn on the Briton coins.

This alternative title of " Arvi-ragus " for Caratacus clearly shows that the Briton kings, like the other Early Aryan and Phœnician kings, and like the well-known instances of Early Egyptian kings, were in the habit of using more than one title.

Now this dropping out of the initial letter of Caratacus' name of " Arvi " in his coins suggests that certain other Briton coins, previously ascribed to him by Camden and others, but latterly erected by Evans into coins of an otherwise unknown Briton king of the name " Epaticcus," do really belong to Caratacus after all. The coins inscribed C V EPATIC (see Fig. 61, p. 339) were read by Camden as " Cearatic " and identified by

---

[1] Geoffrey, 3, 20.   [2] Evans, *op. cit.*, Pl. 5, Nos. 5 and 6.
[3] *Ibid.*, Pl. 1, No. 8 ; and Pl. 15, Nos. 9–11.   [4] *Ibid.*, Pl. 1, No. 7.   [5] *Ibid.*, Pl. 17, No. 8.
[6] *Ibid.*, Pl. 15, 14.   [7] *Ibid.*, Pl. 7, Nos. 12 and 14 ; and Pl. 8, No. 1.
[8] *Ibid.*, 262 and 263.   The legend is there read " RVFI ? " and " RVFS," but no sign of an F is seen in any of the figures of these coins in the plates.
[9] Juvenal *Satires*, 4, 26 : Regem aliquem capies, aut de temone Britanno decidet Arviragus.
[10] There is, perhaps, a pun on this *Raja* or *Reiks* in Juvenal's above cited satire, as *Raja* in Latin is the flat turbot-like Ray fish.

## COINS OF CARATACUS

him as of Caratacus.[1] But Evans, by adding the two detached prefixed(?) letters C V to the end of the group EPATI equated them to the EPATI and EPAT[2] legends on other coins, which do not bear obvious or legible prefixed letters, and thus obtained a king's supposititious name, Epaticcus.

The objections raised by Evans against ascribing these coins to Caratacus, and objections which are still accepted, are firstly that the letter P is not used in its Greek value of R, but as the Roman letter P; and secondly, that in the series of coins with the head of Hercules, *taking the place of the " Tascio" legend*, and bearing the letters EPATI and EPAT, there is no preceding letter, and therefore the name cannot be read " Ceratic."

It seems rather remarkable to find that those numismatists who believe that the Ancient Britons copied their coinage from the Greeks should yet deny the possibility that the Britons knew or may have used to some extent " Greek " letters. Especially so is this the case with regard to the letter P which the Greeks admittedly borrowed from the later Phœnician letter P along with its value of R. On the contrary, Cæsar tells that the Druids who had their chief stronghold in Britain in his day, " *use the Greek letters.*"[3] And, as a fact, the Briton coins themselves testify the use of so-called " Greek " letters occasionally. Thus Cunobelin, the father of Caratacus, on two different mintages of coins, uses the Greek letter Λ for the Roman L in spelling his own name,[4] implying that Caratacus' father used some Greek letters in writing and that his people understood it, just as Ulfils, the Goth used some Greek letters in his writings for the Goths, though this particular " Greek " letter for L is essentially identical with the Runic Gothic sign for that letter. Again, Androgeus, the uncle of Cunobelin, in writing his name " Antedrig-v,"[5] uses the Greek Γ for the letter G therein. Moreover, in one at least of his coins, in spelling his name he uses the Greek letter Θ or *Th* for D;[6] and this substitution of that Greek letter for the Roman D frequently occurs in the coins with the legend " Addedomarios,"[7] the form of which name also is "Grecian."

In view of this positive evidence for the use of Greek letters occasionally on the Briton coins of the father of Caratacus and other predecessors, there is no improbability in Caratacus himself using them occasionally. There is thus no longer any valid objection to reading the P in the above series of coins with its Greek value of R, which gives us in the first case " Cueratic " (see Fig. 61, a);[8] and this fairly equates with the Roman " Caratacus " and the Welsh " Caradog." In the other two coins of this series with the contracted form of the name (b and c of same Fig.) the scroll behind the head of Hercules (or Tascio) which is seen in complete form in b of that Fig. represents, I venture to suggest, the Greek letter ʓ or Z, a letter which, we have seen, was used by Part-olon. This would give the reading of " Zerati " or " Zerat " as the contracted form of the king's name, and we have seen that " Zet-land " is a dialectic form of " Catti or Ceti-land " or Goth-land. But be this Z initial as it may, there is no doubt whatever that these coins belong to the self-same king whose name is spelt "Cueratic" in the first. Even without this initial letter it would still remain his coin, for we have seen his dropping of the initial letter in his " Arvi " title, and we have also seen the dropping of the cognate initial letter G of " Gioln " to form " olon," of " Gwalia " to form " Wales," and in " Guillaime " to form " William." It is thus evident that these three different coins belong to Caratacus, alias Arvi-ragus.

Thus the testimony of the Briton coins establishes clearly and positively the historicity of the traditional Ancient British Chronicles as authentic historical records.

---

[1] Camden, *Brit.*, ed. 1637, p. 98; omitted by Gough, as location of coin was temporarily lost.
[2] Evans, *Coins*, Pl. 8, Nos. 12–14. [3] *De Bel. Gallicc*, 6, 14.
[4] Evans, *Coins*, Pl. 10, Nos. 2 and 3. [5] See above. [6] Evans, *Coins*, Pl.15, 11.
[7] *Ibid.*, Pl. 14, 2, 5 and 9.
[8] The initial letters C and V are above the warrior horseman (Tascio).

II

PART-OLON'S IDENTITY WITH "CATH-LUAN," FIRST TRADITIONAL KING OF THE PICTS IN SCOTLAND

> "Cath-luan was *Arya* sovereign over all [the Cruithne in Erin], and he was the first king of them who acquired [North] Alban."—*Books of Ballymote and Lecan.*[1]

As I observed that certain versions of the Irish-Scot traditions—for example, that cited in the heading—represent King Cath-luan as taking the same position as the Catti king Part-olon, the first traditional "Briton" king of Ireland and North Britain, this suggested to me that "Cath-luan" was possibly a title of the Cassi king Part-olon, in which his tribal title of Catti is substituted for his "Part" or "Barat" title. And so it seems to prove.

The form of the name "*Cath-luan*," also spelt "*Cath-luain*," is obviously a dialectic contraction for Part-olon's title of "Kazzi (or *Catti*)-*gyaolowonie* (or *Gioln*)" in our inscription; and in series with "Cassi-vellaunus," the title of the paramount king of the Cassi or Catti Britons in the pre-Roman period, who was the "*Cad-wallon*" of the Welsh Cymri. This identity seems clearly evident from the latter name.

Still closer to "Cath-luan" is the dialectic form of the title of the early Scottish royal clan "*Cat-uallauna*," which is recorded on the monument of the Barat of Cassi-vellaunus' clan of Britons, called by Ptolemy, as we have seen, "*Catyeuchlani*," and by Dion Cassius, in recording their later invasion by Aulus Plautius, "*Catuellani*."[2]

"Cath-luan" is obviously the dialectic form of the title of the early Scottish royal clan "*Cat-uallauna*," which is recorded on the monument of the second or third century A.D. at South Shields by the Barat of Syria already referred to.

The literal equivalency of Cath-luan with the titles borne by the Catti Part-olon or "Prat-(gya)olowonie" in his Newton Stone inscription is fully established by the variants in the spelling of the name of his later namesake, the Briton king of 630 A.D. in the Saxon Chronicle additions to Nennius' *History of Britain*, wherein the self-same name is variously spelt in the same MS. as follows:—

> "Cat-guollaun," "Cat-guollaan," "Cat-lon" and "*Cath-lon*."[3]

Cath-luan is reported to have been (as we found Parth-olon was) the first king of the Cruithne or Pruithne (*i.e.*, as we have seen, Britons) in Northern Alban. And the traditional account of his origin is also in keeping with that of our Phœnician king Prwt-gyaolowonie (or "Giooln "). The Irish books state:—

> "The Cruithni came from the land of *Tracia*; that is, they are the children of *Gleoin*, son of Ercol. *Aganthirsi* was their name."

This "Tracia" is, perhaps, for an admittedly sea-going people, "Trazi" or "Tarz," the old names for Tarsus, rather than for Thrace, which was also in the Land of the Goths. Tarsus, the famous sea-port city, was in the

---

[1] *Books of Ballymote and Lecan*. See Skene, *op. cit.*, 31. The Irish-Scot word *Aire*, usually translated "king, sovereign, prince or chief," appears clearly to be the literal equivalent of the *Arya* ("Arya-n") title of the Indo-Persians, the "Arri" or "Harri" of the Hittites and the "Harri" or "Heria" title of the Gothic king in the Eddas, as we have seen.
[2] Dion Cassius, 51, 20.
[3] British Museum Harleian MS. 3859 of 977 A.D. See Skene, *op. cit.*, 14, 70 and 347.

# PART-OLON'S IDENTITY WITH CATH-LUAN 395

Hittite province of Cilicia, which latter Prwt-gioln records on his monument as his father-land. And the " Gleoin " title is clearly the " Gioln " or " Gyaolowonie " title inscribed on his Newton Stone.

The curious addition to this record that " Aganthirsi " was also the name of his clan suggests that the later bardic compiler of this tradition sought to identify these Gleoin people with the colony of the Geloni tribe of quasi-Greek merchants in Scythia, north of the Black Sea, described by Herodotus as living amongst a Scythian tribe adjoining the Agathirsi Scyths. If this word " Aganthirsi " really existed in the early traditional documents, it may have been intended for " Agadir," the name of the old Phœnician sea-port city of Cadiz in Iberia, whence Part-olon is reported to have come.

The " Geloni " people of the colony in Scythia, described by Herodotus, were probably a colony of Hitto-Phœnician " Khilaani " traders. Herodotus tells us[1] that they were originally resident in Greek trading ports, but were expelled thence, and were engaged in Scythia as fur-merchants. They were blue-eyed and red-haired[2] and worshipped Dionysus (as did the Phœnicians), and " had temples adorned after the Greek manner with images, altars and shrines of wood." What is especially significant is that " all their city is built of wood, its name is ' Gelonius,' . . . it is lofty and made entirely of wood." All this suggests that the buildings were of the style of the " Khilaani " palace and mansion of the Hitt-ites. Significantly also, these Geloni were related to the Phœnician sea-port of Gades (Cadiz) with its famous temple of the Phœnician Hercules, in Iberia, outside the Pillars of Hercules. Herodotus relates the legend that they were the descendants of this Phœnician hero, Hercules, who, on returning from Gades, drove the herds of Geryon into Scythia and left there two sons, Gelon and Agathyrsis, from whom those two tribes were descended.[3]

It is also remarkable that this presumably Phœnician colony of Geloni in Scythia was likewise settled amongst a primitive nomad people who, like the Picts, painted their skins blue, and whom Virgil calls " the painted Gelons."[4] But Herodotus is at pains to point out that this painted nomad tribe in whose land the Geloni traders had their colony were the aborigines and erroneously called " Geloni " by the Greeks. He says that their proper tribal name was " Bud-ini " and that they were a totally different and inferior race to the Geloni.

"They do not use the same language as the Geloni nor the same mode of living, and are the only people of those parts who eat vermin ; whereas the Geloni are tillers of the soil, feed upon corn, cultivate gardens, and are not at all like the Budini in form or complexion."

We thus seem to have here in this colony of Gelons in Scythia in the fifth century B.C. another parallel instance of what occurred in the Don Valley about the same period, of a colony of fair Phœnician Barat " Giolns " with a high civilization settled amongst a population of primitive nomads who painted their skins blue and were otherwise seemingly akin to the Picts of Scotland.

Further similarity between Cath-luan and Part-olon is seen in the tradition that the former first arrived in and possessed a part of Erin before proceeding to North Alban or Scotland.[5] His opponent in Ireland was " Herimon," or " Eremon," which might possibly be a scribal variant for the Umor or Fomor men who opposed Part-olon in Ireland. The tradition that Part-olon, as well as Cath-luan, held possession of the South Coast of Ireland probably indicates that Part-olon established and kept a colony there in addition to his kingdom in the North of Scotland.

[1] Herodotus, 4, 108.   [2] Turner's *Notes on Herodotus*, 4, 108.   [3] Herodotus, 4, 8–10.
[4] " Pictosque Gelonos," Virgil, *Georgics*, 2, 114–5.
[5] Skene, *op. cit.*, 125–6.  Cath-luan is traditionally reported to have landed or fought a great battle on the " Slaine " River, which is usually identified with the Slaney River of Wexford, that is, further East than Part-olon's traditional landing place.

In Scotland we are told that Cath-luan established his rule by force of arms :—

> "And [North] Alban was without a king all that time till the period of . . . *Cath-luan*, son of *Cait-mind*, who possessed the kingdom by force in Cruthen land, and in Erin, for sixty years, and after him Gud possessed it for fifty years."[1]

Though in another version it would appear that his occupation had been relatively peaceful :—

> "From thence (Erin) they conquered Alba . . .
> Without destroying the people,
> From Chath (Caith-ness) to Foirciu [Forth]."[2]

Like Part-olon, the "Gioln," who is recorded in the British Chronicles to have visited Orkney, we are told that "the clan Gleoin" of Cath-luan also visited Orkney and occupied it :—

> "The clan of *Gleoin*, son of *Erc-ol*, took possession of the islands of *Orcc* [Orkney] . . . and were dispersed again from the islands of Orcc."[3]

And it seems possible that this leader's name "Erc-ol" may be intended for the "Ikr" personal name of Part-olon, as recorded on his Newton Stone monument.

The ancestry of Cath-luan also is generally identical with that of Prwt-gioln. As seen in the extract in the heading, he was an "*Aire*," that is, *Arya* or Aryan. He was a Pruithne (Cruithne) and was "the son of *Cait-*mind,"[4] in which compound word *mind* means "the noble,"[5] and thus presumably describes him as "The son of the Noble *Catti* or Khatti or Hitt-ites." And his two sons bore the prefixed title of "*Catin*,"[6] which is obviously the equivalent of the "Cadeni" title of Ptolemy for the people of the Clyde Valley, and a title, as we have seen, of the Phœnicians.

All this evidence thus seems to establish the identity of the Catti Part-olon with Cath-luan, the first Aryan king of the Picts in Scotland.

---

[1] MS. Bodleian Laud., 610, in Skene, *op. cit.*, 27.
[2] *Books of Ballymote and Lecan.* Skene, *op. cit.*, 43.   [3] *Ibid.*, 23.
[4] Skene, *op. cit.*, 27.   [5] See Calder, *op. cit.*, 347.
[6] The two sons of Cath-luan were Catino-Lodhor and Catino-Lochan. Skene, *op. cit.*, 31.

# CATTI PLACE NAMES IN HOME COUNTIES

## III

"CATTI" PLACE AND ETHNIC NAMES EVIDENCING PHŒNICIAN PENETRATION AND CIVILIZATION IN THE HOME COUNTIES, MIDLANDS, NORTH OF ENGLAND & SCOTLAND

THE further details of the "Catti" series of Place, River and Ethnic Names referred to in Chapter XV are here recorded.

In the Home Counties, Midlands and the North of England we find the following series of old Catti names evidencing Phœnician penetration and civilization.

Middlesex : *Hatt*-on, on the *Gade* or Colne (?Gioln) River, which entered the Thames at Bushey and Kingston, with its Bronze Age remains.[1]

Herts : *Cats* Hill, on Lea River below *Had*-ham, on Roman Erming Street continuation of Stane Street.
*Cater*-lough, near *Camber*-low, with Bronze Age remains.[2]
*Cotter*-ed, S.E. of Baldock, with Bronze Age remains at adjoining Camberlow above.
*Cad*-well, near *Pirt*-on, with Stone Age remains, on Icknield Way (or Street) in *Cashio* Hundred.
*Codd*-ing-ton, near Luton, on Upper Verulam R.
*Coddi*-cot and " *Coddi*-cot Street," in *Cashio* Hundred.
*Gade* River, which joins Colne at *Cassio*-bury (seat of Earl of Essex) above *Scotch* Hill.
*Gad*-bridge, on Gade R., at Hemel Hempsted.
*Gaddes*-den, on Gade R., above latter, with Bronze Age remains.[3]
*Gates*-bury Mill, on Rib rivulet.
*Hat*-field on Lea, with Bronze Age remains[4] (2, 123, 133).
*Had*-ley Wood, near Enfield.
*Had*-ham, on Ash River, above Cat's Hill.
*Hoddes*-don, on Lea.

Bucks : *Cad*-mer End, near Ackham-stead.
*Cots*-low Hundred.
*Chad*-well Hill, near Risborough.
*Ched*-ing-ton, on *Sca*-brook, at Ivinghoe.
*Cudd*-ing-ton, on North Thames, with Briton coins.[5]
*Chit*-wood, near Barton, S.W. of Buckingham.
*Chots*-bury, west of Great Berkhamsted.
*Godd*-erd, adjoining Cadmer End.
*Godd*-ing-ton, near Chit-wood.
*Whadd*-on Chase, with Briton coins.[6]

Oxford : *Chad*-ling-ton Hundred, and Chad-ling-ton, on Thames, near Akeman Street, with prehistoric barrows and earthworks.[7]
*Gat*-hampton, at Goring on Thames.

[1] B. C. Windle, *Remains of Prehistoric Age in England*, 106.
[2] *Ibid.*, 105. [3] *Ibid.*, 105, at Westwick Row. [4] *Ibid.* 104.
[5] Evans, *op. cit.*, 299, 421. [6] *Ibid.*, 57, 61, 65, etc., 421. [7] Windle, *op. cit.*, 106, 243.

Oxford (contd.): *Cuddes*-den, with old bishop's palace (2, 30).
*God*-stow.
*Kidd*-ing-ton, near Akeman Street.
*Shut*-ford, near Henley, with prehistoric barrows.[1]

Berks: *Cats*-grove, near Reading (1, 232).
*Chudd*-le-worth and parish (1, 229).
*Chute* Causeway, on " Roman " road to Wansborough camp (1, 228).
*Yatten*-den, with Bronze Age remains[2].

Bedford: *Cadd*-ing-ton and parish, near Dunstable, adjoining Watling Street (2, 57) with Stone Age remains.[3]
*Cad*-bury Lane, near old " camp " and Keysoe.
*Cotton* End, S.E. of Bedford.
*Cutts*, east of Caddington.
*Good*-wick Green, near *Cad*-bury Lane.
*Shit*-ling-ton, near Pirton and Barton, near Icknield Way.

Northampton: *Cates*-by, on Avon (2, 267).
*Cotter*-stoke, with Roman remains (2, 286).
*Cot*-ton, east of Addington, with prehistoric " camp " earthworks.[4]
*Cott*-ing-ham, near Rockingham, on " Roman " Welland Way.
*Gad*-ing-ton or Geddington, ancient royal seat (2, 281).
*Gedd*-ing-ton, on Avon, with royal castle of Edward I. (2, 268).
*Goth*-am (2, 268).
*Ketter*-ing, adjoining Gadington and near Burton (2, 268).
*Hadd*-on, near Watling Street, north of Pytchley (see p. 204) and Burton Latimer.

Huntingdon: *Cat*-worth, on " Roman " road to Leicester (2,256).
*God*-manchester, on Erming Street, near Huntingdon, with Offord *Cluny* to S.W.
*Gidd*-ing or *Ged*-ing (2, 256).

Cambridge: *Cot*-ton, near Cottonham at Cambridge, on road to Oxford (2, 226).
*Chatt*-eris, near *Somers*-ham Ferry, with tradition of " Some British King," 2, 235, and remains of Early Iron Age.[5]
*Cott*-en-ham, at Cambridge (2, 226).
*Ged*-ney Hill (2, 241).
*Whittle*-sea, with Bronze Age remains.[6]

Lincoln: *Ketes*-by, near Ormsby (2, 383).
*Cade*-by, near latter (2, 383).
*Cats*-cove, near Gedney (2, 342).
*Ged*-ney and parish and hill, with Roman remains (2, 342).
*Cotes*, Great-, on Humber, near Grimsby, with *Somer*-Cotes on coast.
*Cot*-ham (2, 386).
*Cattle*-by, adjoining Burdon Pedwardine (2, 355).
*Cad*-ney, on old river mouth south of Barton on Humber.
*Codd*-ing-ton, at Newark, off the Fosse Way.
*Chater* River, tributary of Weland (2, 352).
*Gout*-by, near Wragley.
*Hatt*-on, near Wragley and Goutby.
*Hath*-er, near Burdon Pedwardine (2, 355).

[1] Windle, *op. cit.*, 106.　[2] *Ibid.*, 104.　[3] *Ibid.*, 61.　[4] *Ibid.*, 240.
[5] *Ibid.*, 61.　[6] *Ibid.*, 104.

# CATTI PLACE NAMES IN PROVINCES

**Lincoln** (*contd.*): Along the pre-Roman canal of "Cares-dyke" from Peterboro' to Lincoln there occur the following "Catti" names along its course (2, 351):—
*Cates*-bridge, on "Roman" road.
*Cat*-wick.
*Cats*-grove, near Shepey.
*Cat*-ley, near Walcot.
*Cat*-thorpe, near Stanfield.

**Yorks**: *Catte*-rick, on Swale, with prehistoric "dyke,"[1] on Watling Street.
*Catter*-dale, in Wensley-dale, with fine bronze sword and sheath with iron blade.[2]
*Caude*-well or *Cawde*-welle, with ancient ruins and "camp" (3, 337, 338).
*Cott*-ing-ham, on Hull River (3, 247).
*Gates*-hill, near Knaresborough, with prehistoric earthworks (3, 295).
*Goath*-land, with prehistoric barrows.[3]
*Geth*-ling of Bede[4], modern "Gilling" (3, 257).
*Sett*-le, with Stone and Bronze Age remains in Victoria Cave.[5]
*Hutt*-on, Craneswick, with prehistoric barrows.[6]
*Hot*-ham Cave, with Bronze Age remains.[7]
*Hat*-field, associated with a Caed-walla, king of the Britons (3, 272-3).

**Durham**: *Hett*-on, with prehistoric remains.[8]

**Northumberland**: *Cat*-leugh, with prehistoric earthworks.[9]
*Chatt*-on and *Chatton* Law, with prehistoric barrows, earthworks and circles.[10]
*Gates*-head.

**Nottingham**: *Cott*-on, on Trent.
*Goth*-am, near Barton, on Upper Trent.
*Ged*-ling, near Nottingham, on branch of Trent.

**Leicester**: *Cat*-thorpe, on Avon.
*Cottes*-batch, on Watling Street, at junction with Fosse Way.
*Cotes*, adjoining Barton, on River Soar.
*Cade*-by, with chalybeate spring, near Ashby-de-la-Zouch (2, 305).

**Stafford**: *Cats* Hill, near Watling Street, with tumulus (2, 503).

**Derby**: *Cats* Stone, great mono'ith, on Stanton Moor (2, 424).

**Warwick**: *Chads*-hurst, the *Ceds-le*-hurst of Domesday Book (2, 450).

**Rutland**: *Kett*-on, on *Chater* River, above Stamford.
*Cat*-mose Vale or "Plain of the Catti,"[11] (2, 325).
*Goad*-by (2, 319).

**Norfolk**: *God*-wick (2, 180; 201).
*Eaton*, with Bronze Age remains.[12]

**Suffolk**: *Sito*-magus, Roman fort, with Roman remains at Wulpitt (2, 165).
*Codd*-en-ham, with Briton coins.[13]
*Had*-leigh, adjoining above and near Breten-ham (2, 165).

---

[1] Windle, *op. cit.*, 254.   [2] A. W. Franks, *Archæologia*, I, 251.   [3] *Ibid.*, 172.
[4] Bede, *Hist. Ecclesiast.*, 3, 14.   [5] Windle, *op. cit.*, 60.   [6] *Ibid.*, 172.   [7] *Ibid.*, 106.
[8] *Ibid.*, 159.   [9] *Ibid.*, 241.   [10] *Ibid.*, 165, 241.
[11] *Maes* = "plain" in British (see Camden, 2, 325).
[12] Windle, *op. cit.*, 105.   [13] Evans, *op. cit.*, 342.

# 400 PHŒNICIAN ORIGIN OF BRITONS & SCOTS

Essex :
: *Cat*-wade, on Stowe, near Hedingham (2, 136-7).
*Chad*-well, near Romford, with prehistoric barrows[1] and Bronze Age remains.[2]
*Hat*-field Broad Oak, with Bronze Age remains[3] (2, 133).
*Had*-stock, with Briton coins.[4]
*Hed*-ing-ham, with Briton coins[5] and early Saxon remains (2, 137).

Somerset .
: *Cat*-cot, on Polden Hill, with *Burtle* Moor adjoining, with Bronze Age remains.[6]
*Cat*-cott, on River Brue, below Glastonbury.
*Cad*-bury, N. of Sutton Montis, with hill and castle and prehistoric "camp,"[7] and Roman remains, and tradition of Camelot of the Arthur legend (1, 78, 91-2).
*Cad*-bury Camp, near Tickenham, with prehistoric earthworks.[8]
*Cad*-bury Camp, near Yatton, N. of Barton, with earthworks.[9]
*Chat*-worthy, on Brendon Hill.
*Chedd*-ar and Cheddar Cliff, on Mendip Hills, below Barton and Priddy, with Neolithic and Bronze Age remains[10] (1, 108).
*Ched*-zoy, in Parret Vale, near Chid-ley Moat, with Roman Remains. (1, 99).
*Chid*-ley, near Bridgwater, with Roman remains (1, 98).
*Chut*-on, near Glastonbury (1, 82).
*Cot*-helston, in Quantock Hills, with Bronze Age remains[1] (1, 97).
*Cut*-combe and parish, on Bredon Hill (1, 90).
*Goat*-hurst and parish, in Parret Vale (1, 97).
*Goat* Hill village, at Millborne Port.
*God*-ney and *God*-ney Moor, at Glastonbury, with tradition of Joseph of Arimathea (1, 82).
*Hutt*-on, near Burton, w. of Axbridge.
*Yatt*-on, N.W. of latter.

Gloster :
: *Cotes* in Cotswold, with ancient earthworks (1, 413).
*Cottes*-wold Hills, modern "Cotswold" (1, 379, 383).
*Ched*-worth, N. of Cirencester, with Roman remains and barrows (1, 412).
*Goth*-ering-ton, with prehistoric earthworks and barrows (1, 407).
*God*-win Castle or "*Painswick* (Punic or Poenig ?) Beacon," with prehistoric barrows and Roman relics.[12]
*Sod*-bury, with prehistoric earthworks.[13]

Worcester :
: *Cothe*-ridge, west of Worcester, with *Bredi*-cott.
*Gad*-bury Bank, w. of Eldersfield, with prehistoric earthworks.[14]
*Kidd* Hill, on Severn, near *Pirton* and *Barton*.
*Kidd*-er-minster.

Shrops :
: *Chat*-ford, at Condover, with *Eaton* Mascot, in Combrook Dale of Severn.
*Quatt* and *Quatt*-ford, on Severn, on opposite bank to *Sid*-bury.
*Chett*-on, on pass into Severn Valley, opposite Quatt.

---

[1] Evans, *op. cit.*, 159.   [2] *Ibid.*, 104.   [3] *Ibid.* and *Proc. Soc. Antiq.*, 16, 327.
[4] *Evans, op. cit.*, 63, 344.   [5] *Ibid.*, 271, 422.   [6] *Windle, op. cit.*, 106.
[7] *Ibid.*, 245.   [8] *Ibid.*, 245.   [9] *Ibid.*, 245.   [10] *Ibid.*, 60.   [11] *Ibid.*, 106.
[12] *Ibid.*, 234.   [13] *Ibid.*, 234.   [14] *Ibid.*, 251.

# CATTI PLACE NAMES IN CUMBRIA, &c. 401

| | |
|---|---|
| Shrops (*contd.*) : | *Cott*-on (Weston-) and *Whitt*-ing-ton, near Parkington at Oswestry, with Bronze Age remains.[1]<br>*Sid*-bury, in Severn Valley.<br>*Shotta*-ton, N.W. of Shrewsbury.<br>*Whit*-cott Keysett, in *Clun* Valley, with menhir.[2]<br>*Eat*-on Constantine, near Little Wenlock, with Bronze Age remains.[3] |
| Hereford : | *Codd*-ing-ton, N. of Ledley.<br>*Hatt*-field, on Frome.<br>*Yatt*-on, on the Wye.<br>*Eat*-on, near Hereford on Wye, with " walls " and ancient camps (3, 74). |
| Monmouth : | *Cader* Arthur or Cadier Artur mountain, with Arthur's chair or seat, with peak Pen-y-*Gader* (3, 91, 110). |
| Glamorgan : | *Coity* castle, with remains of Caradoc's palace (3, 131).<br>*Ketti* Stones, the name of the chief cromlech in Gower,[4] and compare *Kits* Coty, in Kent. |
| Carmarthen : | *Cet*-guelli,[5] or *Cath*-welly, modern *Kid*-welly, and ruins of castle with tradition of founding by sons of " Keianus-the-Scot " (= Koronus *Caineus* ?) (3, 135, 137). |
| Pembroke : | *Coity* Artur, two rock stones near St. Davids (3, 151). |
| Merioneth : | *Cad*-van Stone of St. Cadvan, a British king and high priest at Towyn-on-shore, below *Cader* Idris (3, 172). |
| Montgomery : | *Kede*-wen's Gate, on the Severn, with Arthur's Gate and ancient remains (3, 165). |
| Carnarvon : | *Gwdir*, headland on coast. |
| Anglesea : | *Coed*-ana. |
| Cheshire : | *Cote*-brook, with barrows.[6]<br>*Cod*-ling-ton, with barrows.[7]<br>*With*-ing-ton, with barrows.[8]<br>*Setaia*, the Roman name for Chester Bay, implying that Chester (or its people) was anciently called " *Sete* " or " *Seteia*." |
| Lancashire : | *Cat*-on and *Caton* Mere, on Lune, above Lancaster.<br>*Catter*-all, on Wyre.<br>*Heaton*, near Bolton.<br>*Hutton*, near Preston.<br>*Wat*-lon, near Preston.<br>*Set*-anti, Roman name for Preston Bay, implying that Preston (or its people) was anciently called " *Set* " or " Set-anti." |
| Westmorland : | *Sed*-bergh, on Lune. |
| Cumberland : | *Cat*-land and *Cat*-land Fells.<br>*Cat*-gill, below Egremont, on Ennerdale Water.<br>*Coat* Hills village, near Eden, S. of Carlisle.<br>*Cutt*-erton, north of Penrith.<br>*Caude* or *Caud* River (modern Caldew),[9] rising in Cat-land Fells, at Carlisle, at end of Roman Wall in vale called *Cummers* Dale, with copper mines (3, 426, 427).<br>*Gates*-garth, *Gates*-gill and *Gates* Water.<br>*Sidd*-ick, at mouth of Derwent, below *Camer*-ton.<br>*Sit*-Murthy, on Derwent, above *Camer*-ton.<br>*Skid*-daw Mt., at Keswick.<br>*Hutt*-on, north of Penrith, near Cutterton. |

[1] Windle, *op. cit.*, 106.  [2] *Ibid.*, 202.  [3] *Ibid.*, 106.  [4] Rhys, *Hib. Lects.*, 192.
[5] Nennius' Chronicle, 14.  [6] Windle, *op. cit.*, 154.  [7] *Ibid.*, 154.  [8] *Ibid.*, 154.
[9] It is now called " Caldew," after the nearer Cald-beck Fells, whilst its further source is in the *Cat*-land Fells.

In Scotland we find the following series of these "Catti" Place, River and Ethnic names :—

Roxburgh : *Cat*-rail or "Fenced Ditch of the Catti," an earthwork rampart-trench extending from near the Pentlands to the Cheviots (4, 36), and separating Berwick from Strath-Clyde(?), and apparently following in part Watling Street.
*Ged*-worth,[1] the modern *Jed*-burgh, on Watling Street.
*Gade* River, the modern *Jed*.[2]
*Cadd*-roun Burn, head-water of Liddel at Catrail, with lower down "Arthur's Seat" near Bewcastle Fells.
*Gatt*-on-side, on Tweed, near Melrose, adjoining Watling Street and Cat-rail(?).
*Whitt*-on, adjoining Jed-burgh.

Selkirk : *Cat*-rail, as above.
*Cat*-slack, at site of Yarrow vale, inscribed monolith of about fifth century A.D., to a "*Ceti*" Chief, near Catrail and adjoining *Cat*-car-wood.

Peebles : *Cat*-rail, as above.
*Cade*-muir, with four ancient forts.

Lanark : "*Gad*-eni," tribe of Ptolemy, who occupied upper estuary of Clyde to about Dun Barton.
*Cadi*-cu, the modern "Cadzow,"[3] ancient name for Hamilton, the ducal capital of Clydesdale on the Clyde, above Glasgow.
*Cat* Castle, at Stonehouse, near Watling Street.
*Coat*-bridge.
*Kitt*-ock, rivulet in Clydesdale.
*Shotts*.

Passing from the Clyde Valley across the narrow waist of Scotland to the Forth, through the *Gad*-eni territory of Ptolemy and thence along the East Coast by Perth, the Don Valley to *Cait*hness and *Shet*-land, we find the following series of "Catti" names :—

Lanark : *Cadd*-er, on the Picts' (or Antonine's) Wall.
*Cath*-cart, a suburb of Glasgow (4, 85).

Mid-Lothian : *Cat*-cune castle, at *Borth*-wick on Esk, on Watling Street.
*Cat*-stane, at Kirkliston, with tumulus and early Latin inscription.
*Keith* (Inch-), also Inch *Ked*[4] or "Isle of the *Keiths*," in Forth, opposite Edinburgh or Dun-Edin, with Arthur's Seat.
*Keith* (Dal-), formerly "Dal-*Chat*" or "Dale of the *Chats* or Keiths," on Esk, opposite Inchkeith and south of *Pinkie* (Phœnice ?) on Watling Street.
*Seton* (Brit-), east of Edinburgh, with *Gos*-ford, not far distant.

Stirling : *Goodie* River, central tributary of Forth, and formerly probably in centre of Firth.

Perth : *Cotter*-town, with standing stone.[5]
*Sid*-Law Hills, from Perth, bounding Gowrie.

---

[1] Jedburgh was called "*Ged*-worth" in Ecgrid's time, 830–845 A.D. ; *Gorder Magazine*, 1922, 126.
[2] Its old name of "Gade" suggested to Baxter that that name was derived from the Gadeni tribe recorded by Ptolemy. Baxter wrote "Quid enim *Gadeni* nisi ad *Gadam* amnem geniti See R. Fergusson, *River Names of Europe*, 108.
[3] Or "Town of the Ced or Phœnicians" (see text).
[4] Skene, *op. cit.*, 416.   [5] F. R. Coles, *Proc. Soc. Antiq. Scot.*, 1907–8, 102.

# CATTI PLACE NAMES IN SCOTLAND

| | |
|---|---|
| Aberdeen : | *Cattie* villages in Don Valley, in neighbourhood of Newton Stone, see Map, p. 19, which adjoins many Pictish villages, bearing the prefix " *Pit.*" |
| | *Cattie* Burn, ditto. |
| | *Cot* Hill at *Hatter*-Seat, on coast, N. of Aberdeen. |
| | *Gadie* River, near Newton Stone (see Map, p. 19). |
| | *Keith*, on Banff border. |
| | *Hadds*, near Newton, and Hadds, at Newburgh. |
| | *Hatton*, several as prefix to village names. |
| Moray Frith : | *Cat*-boll or *Cad*-boll, on promontory N. of Inverness. |
| | *Cawdor* castle, near Nairn, on opposite side of Frith from above. |
| | *Chat* (Druim-), with vitrified fort at Knockfurrel, in Ross-shire. |
| Sutherland : | *Cattey* or *Cathy* (Norse, *Catow*), ancient name of Sutherland (4, 187). |
| Caithness : | *Cat*-ness or *Cattey*-ness (for *Kata*-ness of Norse), previously *Chat* of Pict Chronicle, and *Kata*-ib[1] (4, 187–190). |
| | *Watt*-en, on Wick river. |
| Orkney : | " *Ocetis* " is figured by Ptolemy as one of the Orcades. |
| Shet-land : | *Zet*-land is an older form of the modern name Shet-land (4, 536). |
| | *Khatti*-cu or *Xatti*-cu, name of old capital of Shetland (*see* p. 77). |

[1] *Calendar of Angus the Culdee* in ninth century, A.D.

## IV

### BRUTUS-THE-TROJAN AS THE HOMERIC HERO "PEIRITHOOS" AND HIS PHŒNICIAN ASSOCIATE CORINEUS AS "CORONOS CAINEUS," THE ASSOCIATE OF "PEIRITHOOS"

HOMER, I find, appears to mention repeatedly King Brutus-the-Trojan as the famous hero "*Peirithoos*," both in his Iliad and Odyssey, as one of the most famous of ancient classic heroes, as the conqueror of aboriginal tribes, the slayer of the Calydon boar, and as the associate of the Phœnician Hercules in the cruise of the Argo for the Golden Fleece; and Hercules, according to all tradition, visited Gades, beyond the Pillars of Hercules, which Phœnician port was, as we have seen, the half-way house of Brutus on his voyage to Britain. Though, as Peirithoos lived several centuries before the epoch of Homer, that immortal bard, with his usual poetic licence and anachronism, in gathering together into one romance all the galaxy of heroic names floating in Trojan tradition in his day, makes Peirithoos an Achaian hero, a generation before the Trojan war; for he could not, from Brutus' Trojan ancestry, as a descendant of Æneas, bring him in at all otherwise.

The resemblance between Homer's "Peirithoos" and Brutus-the-Trojan is so striking, not merely in the form of the name, but also in the numerous details of their respective traditional history and adventures, that it establishes the great probability that they were one and the same personage.

First as to their ancestry. We have seen that Brutus, the "*Briutus*" of the Irish Scot texts, was, according to the Ancient British Chronicles, the grandson of Æneas' son *Ascanios* and resided for a time in Epirus of Greece, where he married the king's daughter. Now Homer describes his hero *Peirithoos* (who also was for a time in Epirus he also went "marriage" hunting)[1] as "the son of the wife of *Ixiōn*."[2] Here "Ixion" seems presumably a dialectic or purposely obscured form of "Ascanios," the "*Isicon*" of the Scottish and Irish Scot versions of the "Briutus" tradition; and "son" is frequently used in the general sense of "descendant."

So great was the fame of the warrior Peirithoos, the "Pirithous" of the Roman writers, that he is figured alongside his companion Coronus, Caineus (the "Corineus" of the British Chronicles) on the Shield of Hercules,[3] and Homer makes Nestor say in chiding Achilles :—

"Yea, I never beheld such warriors, nor shall behold
As were *Peirithoos* . . . and [Coronus] *Caineus* . . . like to the Immortals.
Mightiest of growth were they of all men upon the earth;
Mightiest they were and with the mightiest fought they
Even the wild tribes of the mountain caves,
And destroyed them utterly."[4]

The picture of the hero Peirithoos was frequently painted in the interior of temples in Ancient Greece.[5] He is described as a slayer of the "*Calydon* boar,"[6] which may preserve a memory of his conquest of Caledonia, especially as Brutus is reported in the Chronicles to have conquered

---

[1] Pausanias, 1, 17.    [2] *Iliad*, 14, 317; and Strabo, 439 : 9, 5, 19.
[3] Hesiod, *Shield of Hercules*, 178.
[4] *Iliad*, 1, 262–268. From Lang and Leaf's translation; and see *Odyssey*, 11, 631.
[5] P.D.G., 1, 17 and 30.; 5, 10; 8, 45; 10, 29.    [6] *Ib.*, 8, 45.

N. Britain as far as the Forth. But his greatest achievement was his conquest of the wild marauding aborigines[1] of *Pelion* mountain, a name, which may possibly, as we shall see, be an adaptation of the name of " the rock-shotten isle of Albion," to fit a well-known classic Greek name, or it may connote the older name for Alban of " *Fel*-inis," though the British texts record that Brutus did actually occupy the Pindos region before coming to Alban. The Homeric record reads :—

" On that day when *Peirithoos* took vengeance of the shaggy wild folk,
And thrust them forth from *Pelion*, and drove them to the *Aithikes* (of *Pindos*)."[2]

It seems remarkable here that the " *Aithikes* " tribe of the *Pindos* mountain range is suggestive of the shortened " *Icht* " and " *Ictis* " title of the Picts of the numerous *Vente* places in Britain, and the *Pent*-land Hills in series with *Pindos*.

In his campaign against the shaggy wild folk, Peirithoos is assisted by *Corōnus Caineus*,[3] just as Brutus was assisted by *Corineus* ; and similarly Homer records that the sons of Peirithoos and Coronos Caineus, who had " jointly a fleet of forty black ships," ruled conjointly over the same wild people ;[4] so did the sons of Brutus and Corineus rule conjointly in Britain. Moreover, Peirithoos engaged in battle with the king of Epirus in North-western Greece and was confined on the banks of the *Acheron* river there,[5] just as Brutus, in the British account of his fighting against the King of Greece, had a battle on the bank of the " *Akalon* " river there, a name which is evidently intended for " Acheron." Further, it is stated that Peirithoos visited Epirus, " marriage-hunting,"[6] and was married on the borders of Epirus, just as Brutus married the daughter of the Grecian King of Epirus. In one of the frescoes in the ancient Greek temples Peirithoos is painted seated on the bank of the Acheron, and next him are the beauteous daughters of King *Pandureos*, one of whom was the famous " Clyte,"[7] who appears to have been the wife of Brutus, and, according to the British Chronicles, Brutus married the daughter of King " *Pandrasus*."[8] Still further, Epirus and the adjoining South Macedonia, were in part inhabited by a tribe called " *Parth-ini*,"[9] which was presumably the remains of the ruling tribe of Barats of Brutus, or the memory of his Barat or Brit-on tribe having formerly dwelt there, and in the Parth-ini region is the town " *Barat* " on the Devoli river. And on the northern or Macedonia frontier of Epirus was the town of " *Phœnice* " on the Xanthus river, thus attesting the ancient presence of Phœnicians there. For the classic Greek writers repeatedly state that Ancient Greece derived its letters and most of Higher Civilization from the Phœnicians. And lastly and significantly, *Peirithoos suddenly disappears from ancient classic Greek history, and I can find no reference anywhere to his death or tomb in Greece, nor of that of his kinsman Coronos Caineus*.[10] The last heard of him

---

[1] These people are called Kentaurs, but are the historical human wild tribe and not the half-horse, half-men of the later myth-mongers subsequent to Pindar. It is noteworthy that the territory of the *Cantii* tribe of Kent includes the site of London according to Ptolemy (*Geogr*., 2, 3, 12) and Brutus occupied that site and built there his capital ; and the form " *Canter*-bury " suggests a possible early form of " *Canter* " approximating " Kentaur."
[2] The *Aithikes* were a people of Epirus and Thessaly and occupied Mt. Pindos range. Strabo, 327 : 7, 7, 9 and 429 : 9, 5, 1.
[3] P.D.G., 5, 10.   [4] *Il*., 2, 746.   [5] P.D.G., 1, 17.   [6] *Ib*., 5, 10.
[7] *Ib*., 10, 28–30 ; and *Odyssey*, 19, 518. His wife in the *Iliad* bears the title of Hippodameia or " Horse-tamer," with the epithet " *Clytos*." *Il*., 2, 742.
[8] This historical marriage of Peirithoos to the daughter of King Pandureos, the Pandrasus of the British Chronicles, is presumably the historical source of the myth that Peirithoos tried to carry off the Queen of Hell, Persephone or Kore or Ellen (Pausanias, 3, 18). For, as Pausanias relates, Ancient Greek artists pictured the Acheron River of Etruria as the river of Hell and gave it the name of Acheron in Hades ; and hence, obviously, the myth of Peirithoos punished in Hell by the indignant husband of Persephone, Pluto, as described by Virgil and other myth-mongers.
[9] S., 327 : 7, 7, 8.
[10] The origin of the later myth that he raided Hell to carry off Proserpine and was captured by her enraged husband Pluto and condemned to infernal torture is exposed in above footnote [8].

presumably is that, according to the later myth of the Quest for the Golden Fleece, he sailed away on the good ship Argos with Herakles and Jason and their company of heroes on board, and is not heard of again. This traditional voyage of adventure from Greece seems also significant; and the inference in view of all the circumstances is that the British Chronicles are correct in recording that he came as Brutus or " Briutus " to Alban, assisted by " Coronos Caineus," and was the first king of the Britons in Britain.

The identity of the great Homeric hero Peirithoos with the " Brutus " or " Briutus " of the British and Irish Scot Chronicles will be more clearly seen when thus tabulated :—

*Identity of the Homeric Hero Peirithoos with Brutus, the Briton.*

| PEIRITHOOS of Homer. | BRUTUS OR BRIUTUS of British and Irish Scot Chronicles. |
|---|---|
| Son of *Ixion*. In Greece was a great warrior hero. Thrust the shaggy wild folk from their caves in *Pelion*. Drove them to the *Aithikes* in the *Pindos* mountains. | Son of *Ascanius* or *Isicon*. Went to Greece and became great warrior hero. Thrust the wild aborigines from their caves in Albion or " *Fel-inis*." Drove them across the " *Icht* sea " and to the *Vindo* and *Pent*-land Hills of the Picts or " *Ichts*." |
| Conquered Epirus and Thessaly of North Greece. | Conquered King of Greece. |
| Fought against King of Epirus with his friend Prince Theseus, son of Aigeus, and was confined by that king on the banks of the *Acheron*. | Fought against King of Greece with his friend, "the noble Greek prince Assaracus," and had engagement on banks of the *Akalon*. |
| Came to Epirus, " marriage-hunting," was married on borders of Epirus, and in frescoes is represented seated next the daughters of King *Pandureos*. | Married daughter of King of Epirus, *Pandrasus*. |
| Was aided in his fight against the shaggy folk by *Coronos Caineus*. | Was aided in his fight against the wild tribes of Aquitain and Alban by *Corineus*. |
| His son was joint ruler with son of Coronos Caineus. | His son was joint ruler with son of Corineus. |
| The *Parth-ini* tribe on frontier of Epirus with town of *Berat*, and within Epirus, town of *Phœnice*. | The "*Bart-on*" or " *Brit-on* " title of Brutus' ruling tribe of Barat Phœnicians. |
| He, along with Coronos Caineus, disappears from and does not seem to have died in Greece.[1] | Brutus with Corineus appear in Alban or Britain. |

This remarkable similarity between the traditions of the Homeric hero Peirithoos—the confederate of *Coronos* Caineus, the conqueror of aboriginal tribes, who went " marriage-hunting " to Epirus, slayed the *Calydon* boar and accompanied the Phœnician Hercules on a sea-voyage of adventure for the Golden Fleece—and King Brutus or Briutus " The Trojan "—the confederate of *Corineus*, who married in Epirus, and sailed with a fleet of Brito-Phœnicians on a voyage of adventure past the Pillars of Hercules to the Gold-and Tin-producing island of Albion, including *Caledonia*, and, conquering the aboriginal tribes, colonized and civilized it—suggests that Homer had heard from Phœnician sailors of the great exploits of Brutus in Britain over three centuries before his day, and had woven them into the form we now find them in his immortal romance.

[1] The legend of his death in captivity in Crete is only found in the later myth-mongering period.

## V

### FOUNDING OF LONDON AS "TRI-NOVANT" OR "NEW TROY" BY KING BRUTUS-THE-TROJAN, ABOUT 1100 B.C.

IT is not surprising that King Brutus-the-Trojan should have named his new city on the Thames in the new land of his adoption "New Troy," especially as the city on the old river Thyamis in Epirus, whence he came was also named "Troy."[1] The naming of this new "Troy" in Epirus by Helenus, the fugitive son of King Priam of Troy, is described by Ovid and Virgil. The latter says[3] :—

> "Skirting Epirus' coast, Chaonia's[4] port . . .
> That Helenus, Priam's son o'er Greeks
> Bore sway, succeeding to the throne and bed
> Of Pyrrhus[5] . . . Pyrrhus dead,
> Part of his realm to Helenus demis'd,
> Wno Chaonia's plain *by title new*
> '*Troy*' *Chaon called, and built him walls
> And ramparts on the steep whose names remind
> Of Pergamus and Troy.* . . . In pensive thought
> I traced the town, the miniature of Troy,
> Its yellow shrunken stream, its fort surnamed
> 'Of Pergamus.'"

This clearly shows that the Trojan colonists were in the habit of consciously and deliberately bestowing their treasured old Trojan names upon their new colonies, with the avowed object of "reminding" them of the old homeland of their Aryan ancestors. Besides this one, another new Troy is reported to have been founded by Æneas in the Tiber Valley[6] and still another by a Trojan colony near Memphis in Egypt.[7] And even the famous Troy of the Homeric epic appears to have been called "New Troy" in distinction presumably to the Old Troy underlying that site.[8] This old Trojan habit of naming some of their chief new colonial cities is analogous to that by which in modern times New York derived its name.[9]

The name "Tri-Novantum" could easily, as Geoffrey states, be "a corruption of the original word," for the city-name which was imposed by Brutus. That original word, which Geoffrey does not supply, may be presumed to have approximated the Gothic "*Troia-Ny*" or "Troia-

---

[1] It is named "Ilium" on later maps (see D.A.A., No. 11), that is the Latin spelling of *Ilien*, Homer's usual title for "Troy."
[2] *Metamorphoses*, 13, 721.   [3] *Æneid*, 3. 295, etc.
[4] The N.E. district of Epirus bordered by the Thyamis river. Virgil, by his use of the district name "Chaon" and "Xanthus" for the river, which I have rendered "yellow," presumably locates the city on the latter river and thus identifies this Troy with "Phœnice" there.
[5] Pyrrhus was son of Achilles, and consort of Andromache, wife of Hector, who was carried off by Achilles.
[6] *Livy*, 1, 1, 3.   [7] S., 808 ; 17, 1, 34.
[8] The "Nun Ilion" of Strabo, the so-called "Novum Ilium" of S.I., 19 and 38.
[9] "Troy" or Troia was named after *Tros*, the founder of the old city. New York was first named New Amsterdam (and thus in series with New *Troy*) when founded by the Dutch in 1624 ; but when seized in 1664 by the British, it was granted by Charles II. to his brother the Duke of York, after whom it received its present name ; and that name was derived from the old ducal city state in Britain, which Briton city, in its turn, as recorded by Geoffrey's Chronicle, was named after a descendant of Brutus.

Nyendi ";[1] and the "Tri-Novantes" of Cæsar are called "Tri-Noantes" by Ptolemy and Tacitus,[2] "Troia," the old Greek and Gothic name for the capital city of the Trojans could become "Tri" in British dialect, as seen in the Old English form of the word "Trifle" being spelt "Trofle,"[3] and "Tryst" is a variant of "Trust." Indeed, the Gothic form of "Troia-Ny" for this "Tri-Novantum" title of early London appears to be preserved in a Norse Edda which mentions "Troe-Noey" along with "Hedins-eyio" or Edin-burgh,[4] as furnishing a contingent fleet of "long-headed ships" for raiding their joint enemy, the Huns.[5]

As regards "Tri-Novantum" as a traditional name for early "London," it is remarkable that no modern writer, nor even Geoffrey or Nennius, appears hitherto to have equated that name to the well-known historical title of "Tri-Novantes" for the pre-Roman British people described by Cæsar as occupying the Essex or north bank of the Thames estuary, *including obviously the site of London City.*

Cæsar nowhere mentions the name London, for the obvious reason to be seen presently. The name "London" for the British "Lud-dun" or "Fort Lud" of the Cymric records is first mentioned in Roman history by Tacitus in 61 A.D., who described it as "the most celebrated centre of busy commerce,"[6] and he refers to it in such a way as to imply its time-immemorial existence as a city. And the historian Ammianus Marcellinus, of the fourth century, calls London (Londinium) "an ancient town towards which Cæsar marched,"[7] thus clearly implying that the ancient city was in existence in Cæsar's day.

The reason why Cæsar did not mention "Tri-Novantum" city, or "London," appears to be because he obviously did not pass through that city; and he was not in the habit of mentioning places unnecessarily in his very laconic journal ; and he does not even mention the names of the place or places where he landed and re-embarked on his two expeditions, nor the name of Cassivellaunus' stronghold, although it was the most important place which he stormed, and described by Cæsar as "admirably fortified," and the culminating place of victory in his British war—a fort which has been fairly well identified with Verulam at St. Albans.

Cæsar's avoidance of the capital city of the Tri-Novantes, or London, in his hurried brief campaign is apparent, it seems to me, from his own narrative. He states that at his second invasion of the S.E. corner of Britain, the Tri-Novantes were at war with Cassivellaunus, his chief enemy, and the paramount king of the Britons and leader of the confederated tribes,[8] and whose personal territory extended northwards from the north bank of the Thames, excluding the province of the Tri-Novantes, which comprised the petty kingdom now known as the eastern portion of Middlesex and Essex. Cassivellaunus, according to Cæsar's information, had slain the king of the Tri-Novantes some time previously, and the son of the latter, Mandubracius, had fled for protection and assistance to Cæsar in Gaul, and was accompanying Cæsar in his invasion and supplying him with auxiliary troops and information, so that he is called in the *Welsh Triads* "the betrayer of his country."

When Cæsar, with his veteran army of 30,000 infantry, besides cavalry, after driving back Cassivellaunus and his raw confederate forces from Kent to the Thames, forced the passage of the Thames at its lowest

---

[1] "*Troia*" was the old Greek name for the old capital city of the Trojans and that identical name for it is used in the Norse sagas of the thirteenth century (V.I.D., 642) ; and *Ny* and *Niuiis* are the Gothic originals of the modern English "New" in the Eddas and in Ulfilas' Gospel translations, corresponding to the Greek *Neos*, the Sanskrit *Nava* and Latin *Novus*.
[2] Tacitus, *Annals*, 14, 31.
[3] Piers the Plowman's *Creae*, 352 ; *Morte Arthure*, ed. Brock, 2932.
[4] Edinburgh was already called "Fort *Edin*" or "Fort *Eden*" (Dun-Edin or Dun-Eden) before the advent of the Anglo-Saxons, see S.C.P., cxliii and 10.
[5] "Helga-kvida Hundings Bana," see Edda. (N) 130, and V.P., 1, 134.
[6] *Annals*, 14, 33, 1.     [7] A.M.H., 27, 8, 7.     [8] D.B.G., 5, 5.

## FOUNDING OF LONDON ABOUT 1100 B.C.

only and difficult ford, which, on good evidence, is placed at Brent-ford opposite Kew,[1] despite the desperate resistance of his enemy who had planted sharp stakes in the river and along the bank, Cassivellaunus, despairing of success in a pitched battle with Cæsar's invincible legions, significantly resorted to the same tactics as ascribed to Brutus in Epirus, when attacked by the overwhelming forces of Pandrasus. He disbanded the greater part of his army, and for guerrilla war withdrew the people and their cattle into the recesses of the impenetrable woods, to which he retired himself with a small contingent—Cæsar says he retained " only about four thousand charioteers "—with which he harassed the detached foraging parties of the enemy and cut off stragglers, causing Cæsar to admit that " Cassivellaunus engaged our cavalry to their great peril and by *the terror which he thus inspired* prevented them from moving far afield."[2]

But on this sudden disappearance of Cassivellaunus' main force at Brentford, the Tri-Novantes, Cæsar tells us, were the first Britons to come to his camp (presumably at Brentford) and offer submission and beg protection for Mandubracius against Cassivellaunus. Cæsar demanded from them forty hostages for their good faith and corn for his army, and he notes, " They promptly obeyed these commands, sending the hostages to the number required and also the grain ; whereupon *the Tri-Novantes were granted protection and immunity from all injury on the part of the legions.*"[3] Thereupon the confederated tribes, and even part of Cassivellaunus' own tribe of Cassis, following the lead of the Tri-Novantes, deserted from Cassivellaunus and submitted to Cæsar, presumably won over by the latter through the agency of Mandubracius and by Commius, another exiled Gaulish Briton prince, who also was accompanying Cæsar and utilized by him to communicate with the Britons, obviously for the notorious Roman policy of weakening their antagonists by dividing them —" *Divide et impera.*"

Having thus isolated the heroic Cassivellaunus from his confederated Briton chiefs, Cæsar promptly pursued him to his stronghold at Verulam —which was almost due north of Brentford and by a good road, in great part the old " Watling Street, which by its name betrays its Gothic Briton origin[4]—and there forced him to surrender, and he eagerly patched up a peace with him, as we learn from the contemporary letters of Cicero, stipulating that Cassivellaunus would not invade the land of the Tri-Novantes, and he immediately hastened back to Gaul to quell the serious insurrections there, and disheartened, as the contemporary Roman writers relate, at the final failure of his attempt to conquer Britain. In his hurried pursuit of Cassivellaunus from Brentford to Verulam and his precipitate retreat to the port of his re-embarkation, in a campaign which lasted only a few weeks, it is clear that Cæsar did not enter the capital city of the Tri-Novantes (Tri-Novantum or " London ") at all, especially as he was debarred from so doing by his promise to prevent his legions from injuring or molesting in any way the Tri-Novantes, who had so largely contributed to the defeat of Cassivellaunus.

Cæsar's account of these events is generally confirmed by the indigenous

---
[1] One of the lowest, or the very lowest, fords over the Thames was formerly at Brentford, and it was " difficult," on account of its depth and the tides. Mr. M. Sharpe found from the Thames Conservancy that a line of stakes, of which some still remain " for about 400 yards below Isleworth Ferry," extended 45 years ago for about a mile up the river from " Old England," opposite the mouth of the Brent, and that " no other ancient stakes have been discovered in the lower river during dredging operations " (*Bregant-forde and the Hanweal*, 1904, 1, 22-7). The name " Brentford " itself, however, did not refer to this ford over the Thames, but to the small ford over the Brent at its junction with the Thames. And Brentford is about due south of Verulam by a good road, in part the " Watling " Road.
[2] D.B.G., 5, 8.   [3] Ib., 5, 8.
[4] A writer of the fourteenth century says Watling Street crossed the Thames to the *west* of Westminster. See H.A.B., 705.

account of his invasion preserved in the British Chronicles of Geoffrey,[1] which record the real name of "Mandubracius" as "Androgeus"—that is also the form of his name preserved by Bede,[2] of which "Mandubracius" is evidently a Roman corruption—and the real circumstances of the flight of that "Duke of Tri-Novantum," and his subordination to Cassivellaunus, the brother of that duke's father, King Lud of Tri-Novantum city, are therein fully recorded; also the fact that Cassivellaunus had magnanimously gifted the city of Tri-Novantum or Lud-Dun ("London") to that renegade, "the betrayer of his country," who had aided Cæsar with his own levies.

The remote prehistoric antiquity of the site of London, moreover, is evidenced by the numerous archæological remains found there, not only of the New Stone and Early Bronze Ages, but even of the Old Stone Age, thus indicating that it was already a Pictish settlement at the epoch when Brutus selected it for the site of his new capital of "New Troy."

The later name of "London" for "New Troy" appears to be a corruption of the late Briton name of "*Lud-Dun*" or "Lud's Fort," applied to it by Lud, the elder brother of Cassivellaunus, as recorded in the Chronicles; and "Caer-Lud" or "Lud's Fort" is still the Welsh name for London. This later Briton name for it is seen to survive in the modern names "Lud-gate Hill" and "Lud-gate Circus," which indicate that the old city or its citadel centred about St. Paul's; and that a chief gate appears to have been at Ludgate Circus on the banks of the old river Flete, the modern "Fleet," which in medieval times was a considerable navigable creek bordered by extensive marshes.[3] That creek obviously derived its name from its use as the old harbour of the naval fleet of those days—the "long headed ships of *Træ-Næy*" of the Norse Edda afore mentioned. That name "Fleet" is now seen to be derived from the Eddic Gothic *Fliota*, "to float, flit or be fleet,"[1] and secondarily *floti*, "a ship or fleet or number of ships,"[5] and cognate with the Greek *ploion*, "a hull or ship." The corruption of "Lud-dun" into "London" appears to have been due to the later Romans, who called it "Londinium." Yet it is noteworthy that the *o* in the modern city name is still pronounced with its old *u* sound.

London thus appears to have been founded as the capital city of the Brito-Phœnicians or Early Britons many centuries before Athens and the rise of historic Greece; and three and a half centuries before the traditional foundation of Rome.

[1] G.C., 3, 20.   [2] B.H.E., 1, 2.   [3] C.B., 1, 80.   [4] V.D., 161.   [5] *Ib.*, 161.

FIG. 76.—Archaic Hittite Sun Horse with Sun's disc and (?) Wings. From seal found at Cæsarea in Cappadocia.
(After Chantre C.M.C. Fig. 141)
It is carved in serpentine and pierced behind for attachment. The object above the galloping horse, behind the disc, is supposed by M.C. to be a javelin.

## VI

### Mor or "Amorite" Cup-marked Inscription with Sumerian Script on Tomb of an Aryan Sun-Priestess, of about 4000 b.c. from Smyrna, Supplying a Key to Cup-Mark Script in Ancient Britain.

("The Dean Hoffman Tablet.")[1]

This uniquely important archaic inscription, figured at p. 257 (Fig. 43), affords, through its explanatory Sumerian script, an additional key to the pre-historic Cup-mark script of Early Britain, etc.; and also attests the use of Cup-mark script by the Mors or Amorites, who are therein called *Ari* or "Ary-an." It, moreover, establishes still further the newly-found fact that a large proportion of *the words used by the Aryan Mors or Amorites, so early as about 4000 B.C., are radically identical in sound and meaning with common words in our modern English.*

The inscription is engraved on the stone in horizontal parallel lines in panels, as is common in Sumerian inscriptions, and shows the direction and sequence in which it is to be read, and in which I have read it. My reading thus differs from that of Prof. Barton, who read it cross-wise, inverted on its left side, and interpreted the Cup-marks as mere numerals, and so considered it to be a votive record of the gift of "a field of clay," of certain "cubits" measurement to a temple of the Sun-god, though he admits that his interpretation, the only one, apparently, yet made, gives a somewhat involved reading that does not make very good sense.[2] The form of this Sumerian writing is of the archaic type of about 4000 b.c., and this early date is confirmed by the word-signs being written erect, as in the very earliest documents.

My decipherment of the individual word-signs, made mainly through the sign values found by M. Thureau-Dangin,[3] is in general agreement with their values as read by Prof. Barton, excepting one or two minor signs; but the sequence of the signs, as now read in their orthographic direction, make sentences entirely different from his, and make good sense throughout.

In order to establish my reading, given at p. 257, I here supply the recognized transliteration of the Sumerian writing in roman type, and underneath have placed the literal meaning in English, word for word, with references to the authorities for the same. And I have adhered to the separate paragraphs as marked in the lines of the inscription.

### *Literal Translation of Hoffman Tablet, Word for Word.*

1st line  TUR    GAL      KUD.
          Tomb of the Girl  good.

MEŠ      XAL     UŠU         KI        DUG      QA.
Master hasten the Under-   to (this)   jug    (of thy) cue!
                  ground Sun         (vessel) (or assembly)

TU    TAŠ    ŠARU-TAŠ.
Thou Taš!  All-Perfect Taš!

[1] In Library of General Theological Seminary, New York.
[2] Jour. American Orient Soc. xxiii, 23, &c.    [3] T.R.C.

|  |  |  |  |  |  |
|---|---|---|---|---|---|
| 2nd line | GID | ZAL | TUK | NIR-A | ŠARU. |
|  | Caduceus (-holder) | of Sol, (Sun) | take up | O Lord | All-Perfect One. |
|  | NIN-A | MIŠ | TE | DA | TAŠ XAL WA. |
|  | Nina princess | (by) the Wood(Cross) | uplifted in (thy) hand. |  | O Taš hasten (thine)ear! |
|  | SIG | GI-BIL | ŠARU-A |  | TAŠ-A ARI. |
|  | The Sick-one | of Bil's Fire-Torch, | O All-Perfect |  | Taš, this Ari(lift up)! (Aryan) |
| 3rd line | AŠŠI[1] or ANŠE[2] | XAL | GIN | GI. |  |
|  | Horse(-man) hasten' the faithful one lift up! |  |  |  |  |
|  | KHAT | AZAG-A | TAŠ-A | MAD | ER-AS DU ŠA |
|  | Cut O Shining One, O Taš! the mud from her (in) mound within, |  |  |  |  |
|  | ŠARU | TAŠ. |  |  |  |
|  | All-Perfect Taš! |  |  |  |  |
|  | GID | ZAL | ŠARU | EŠ | TAX BID. |
|  | Caduceus (-holder) | of Sol! (Sun) | All-Perfect (in) | the house of | Tax (let her) bide! -the-Angel |

It will be noticed that this pathetic prayer is to Taš-Mikal for Resurrection from the Dead by the Wood-Cross. And the Horse-man Taš implored as "Horse" is the Sun-horse figured on the Briton coins, and on the archaic Hittite seals, on pp. xv. and 410.

The strikingly Aryan character and radical identity of the majority of these Amorite Sumerian words with those still current in modern English are here tabulated. The references for their values in the standard Sumerian lexicons of Brünow and Meissner are placed within brackets:—

*Gal* = " girl," slang " gal " (Br. 10906)
*Kud* = " good " (3338, and 3340)
*Meš* = " mas-ter," " majes-ty " (5953)
*Xal Khal*, or *Bulux* = " gall-op," " celer-ity," " veloc-ity;" Sanskrit *Cal* (78–79)
*Dug* = " jug," Akkad *Kannu* " a can,"
*Qa*, Akkad *Qu* = " cue " (1352, M. 791) (5891)
*Tu* = " thou " (Br. 10511 and 24)
*Gid* = Caduceus (7512)
*Zal* = " Sol," " Sol-an," Eddic " Sol," Shetland Sol-een " Sun " (7777)

*A* = O! Ah! (M. 8904)
*Tuk* = " take " (10545; M. 7968)
*Miš* = " mace "-wood (Br 5699)
*Sig* = " sick " (11869)
*Ari* = " Ary-an," Eddic " Harri " (M. 5328 · B.B:W., 316)
*Khat* = " cut " (Br. 5573, 5581)
*Mad* (or *Mat*) = " mud " or earth; Indo-Pers. *mati* (7386)
*Er* = " her " (M. 3719)
*Eš* = " house " (Br. 3814) Gothic and Old Eng. " Hus."
*Bid* = " bide," " abide "(Br. 6235)

We thus recover the actual Aryan words of this remotely ancient Amorite prayer, in series with those uttered by our Sun-worshipping Briton ancestors, in their prayers for Resurrection from the Dead in their Cup-mark inscriptions in prehistoric Britain about four or five thousand years ago.

[1] P.S.L. 34, which closely agrees with Sanskrit *Asva*, and the "*Aesv*" of the Briton Horseman Coins; and see Hittite representations on pp. xv. and 410.
[2] C.I.W.A., etc., in B.B.W. 211. Pinches reads the sign as *Ansu* " Ass," also " Horse " (M.D. 773), the word horse being originally of the ass tribe. The sign also reads *IZ-SA* or *ISSA*; cp. Br. 4984.

## VII

### THE AMORITE PHŒNICIAN TIN MINES OF CASSITERIDES OR CORNWALL (?) REFERRED TO ABOUT 2750 B.C. BY SARGON I. OF AKKAD, & KAPTARA OR "CAPHTOR" AS ABDARA IN SPAIN.

A CONTEMPORARY reference to the Amorite Phœnician tin mines in Britain appears probably to exist in the historical road-tablet of the great "Akkad" emperor Sargon I., about 2800-2750 B.C., recording the mileage and geography of the roads throughout his vast empire of world-conquest. The existing document is a certified copy in cuneiform script of the original record of Sargon I. It was found at the Assyrian capital of Assur, and was made by an official scribe in the 8th century B.C.[1]

The tablet details the lengths of the roads within Sargon's empire from his capital at Agade on the Euphrates, and records that "*the produce of the mines in talents*, and the produce of the fields to Sargon has been brought." And it states that his empire of "the countries from the rising to the setting of the sun, which Sargon the . . . king conquered with his hand," included amongst many other lands "the Land of Gutium," "the land of the Muru (or Amorites)" and "*the Tin-land country which lies beyond the Upper Sea (or Mediterranean)*."

This latter reference, which occurs in line 41 is translated by Prof. Sayce as follows:—

"To the Tin-land (KUGA-KI) (and) Kaptara (Caphtor, Krete), countries beyond the Upper Sea (the Mediterranean)."[2]

And Prof. Sayce remarks that "'The Tin-land beyond the Mediterranean' must be Spain, and so bears testimony to maritime trade at this early period between Asia and the western basin of the Mediterranean. It is unfortunate that the loss of the text on the reverse of the tablet prevents our knowing what the exact construction of the sentence was; but it would have been something like: 'The road led towards the Tin-land,' as well as other countries beyond the limits of the Babylonian empire."[3]

The word-signs in the tablet for "Tin-land," however, which are rendered "*Kuga-ki*" by Prof. Sayce, possess many other ideographic and phonetic values besides "*Kuga*" as selected by him; and an examination of these may help us to recover the real Sumerian or Amorite name for the land in question (— the affix *ki* or *gi* = "land," and is now disclosed as the Sumerian source of the Greek *ge* "earth," as already noted).

This Sumerian word-sign in Sargon's tablet for "Tin" means literally "shining, bright," and hence also "tin" and "silver";[4] and it has an unequivocal word-value of AZAG,[5] with the Akkad equivalent of *KAS-PU* or *GAZA-PA*,[6] which latter are probably cognate with the Greek word *Kassiteros* for Tin and "Cassiterides." The other Sumerian phonetic value of this Tin word-sign, although usually rendered *KU* or *KU-U*,[7] is very doubtful, because its two constituent word-signs have so many different values, the first having no less than 28 different sounds. Thus, besides KU-U, this word-sign may be restored amongst others as *KU-ŠAM*,

---
[1] Text is published in *Keilschrifttexte aus Assur verschiedenen Inhalts* 1920, No. 92.
[2] *Ancient Egypt*, 1924, 2.   [3] *Ib.* 4.
[4] But "silver" is usually distinguished by the addition of the sign for "Sun," on account of its superior brightness.
[5] Br. 9887.   [6] Br. 9891 and 4722.   [7] Br. 9888.

ÊS-U (? *Aes* bronze or copper ore), *BI-KUŠ, A-KUŠ* or *MU-KUŠ*, the latter two suggesting that *Ictis* or *Mictis* name applied by the Greeks to the Phœnician tinport at St. Michael's Mount in Cornwall, on the Sea of Icht.

There is probably, I think, another reference to this Western Tin-land in a subsequent line of this expanded paragraph. Line 47 of the tablet may be read, with literal translation, as follows:—

U MAD KUŠ-ŠA-IA I KI MI-ŠIR-ŠU ME

"*And the country of KuŠ-ša-ia, the captured*[1] *land* [*beyond*] *the frontier,*
 (*or* " *mud* ")    (*or Mi-sir,*
                    *i.e., Egypt*)
                    *as ordered.*"

This seems possibly to refer to "the Tin-land beyond the Mediterranean" as "The country of the *Kuššaia* or *Kašši* people," as captured by Sargon I., and as lying beyond the frontier of Egypt or "Misir." It thus would account for the name "Cassi-terides"; and *Kašši* is sometimes spelt with *u* in cuneiform script.[2]

The other captured Western land "beyond the Mediterranean," associated with this Tin-land in Sargon's tablet is named therein *Kaptara*, which is usually considered to be the "Caphtor" of the Philistines, of the Old Testament,[3] and conjectured to be Crete, as it is called therein an "island or sea-coast" by the Phœnician name " *ai* " (*i.e.*, the -*ay* or -*ey* place-affix in British coastal names. But the Cretans are held to be the "*Chereth*-ites" of the Old Testament, which thus excludes Caphtor from being Crete, which, moreover, could not be described as "beyond the Mediterranean." I venture therefore to suggest that this "Kaptara" is the ancient Phœnician mining-port of *Abdara* or "*Abdera*" in Spain, near the straits of Gibraltar, from which the initial *K* has latterly dropped out—like the *K* in "Khatti" to form "Hatti," in "Khallapu" to form "Hallab" or "Allepo," and the *G* in Gwalia, Gioln, Gwite, etc., to form "Wales, Ioln, Wight," etc. And the letters *t* and *d* are always interchangeable, as we have seen in Tascio, etc. In favour of this dropping of the *K* in Kaptara through the wear and tear of time, is the fact that since Strabo's and Ptolemy's day "Abdara" has now become shortened into "Adra." Abdara, as Ptolemy calls it, was a Phœnician silver mining seaport colony founded traditionally by Tyre.[4] And the Phœnicians had another "Abdera" port in Thrace, also with rich silver mines.[5] This Iberian Abdara has many coins bearing its name in Phœnician letters, along with a Sun-temple on the reverse; and the Roman coins repeat the Sun-temple and the Phœnician script, with the bi-lingual legend "Abdera."[6] And although a short distance inside the Straits, it was probably the Kaptara of Sargon's tablet, and a port of call of his subject Amorite merchants on their way to and from the outer Tin-mines of the Cassiterides of Cornwall about 2750 B.C., before the founding of Gades.

Regarding the tradition that "giants" occupied Britain before Brutus, and that "giants" were the builders of the Stone Circle, and megaliths and "giants' tombs," in Britain, Britany, Mauretania, Sardinia, and in other places colonized by the Phœnicians, it is significant that the Mor, Muru, Maruta or "Amorites" of Syria-Phœnicia-Palestine are called "giants" by the Hebrews in their Old Testament. They are, moreover, also called there "the sons of *Anak* (*Beni-anak*)."[7] Now "*Anak*" in Akkadian is a name for "Tin."[8] And Tarshish, which, as Tarz or Tarsus, we have seen

[1] Br. 3979.   [2] M.D. 444.   [3] Jer. 47. 4.   [4] Strabo, 3. 4. 3.   [5] Herodotus 6, 46-7.
[6] A.A.C. 16-17.   [7] Numbers 3, 28 f., Josh. 10, 5; 11, 21, etc.
[8] *Anaku*="Tin" also "lead" M.D. 70.

## AMORITE PHŒNICIANS IN CORNWALL     415

was a chief port of the Amorite Phœnicians, and which we know was actually visited and conquered by Sargon I., is thus celebrated in the Old Testament in connection with Tyre of the Phœnicians : " Tarshish was thy merchant by reason of the multitude of all kinds of riches ; with silver, iron, *TIN*, and lead, they traded in thy fairs."[1]

It would thus appear that the Tin which was imported into ancient Palestine, and which entered into the bronze that decorated Solomon's temple, and formed sacred vessels in that sanctuary, was presumably obtained in most part, if not altogether, from the Phœnician Tin-mines of Ancient Britain.

[1] Ezek. 27, 12.

# ABBREVIATIONS
## FOR CHIEF REFERENCES.

A.A.B.    Life in Ancient Britain. N. Ault. 1920.
A.A.C.    Ancient Coins. J. Y. Akerman. 1846.
A.C.N.    Antiquitates Celto-Normanicae. J. Johnstone, Copenhagen. 1786.
A.I.B.    Académie des Inscript. et Belles Lettres, Comptes Rendus. Paris.
A.L.    Tel el Amarna Letters : (W) ed. H. Winckler, 1896; (B) British Museum. 1892.
A.L.R.    Adamnan's Life of St. Columba, ed. Reeves.
A.M.H.    Roman History of Ammianus Marcellinus, Bohn's ed.
A.P.H.    Prehistoric Times. Lord Avebury. 1900.
A.Y.E.    Younger Edda (Snorri), tr. R. B. Anderson, Chicago. 1880.
B.A.S.    Anglo-Saxon Dictionary. J. Bosworth. 1901.
B.B.W.    Origin and Developt. of Babylonian Writing. G. A. Barton, Leipzig. 1913.
B.C.    Antiquities of County of Cornwall. W. Borlase. 1759.
B.E.D.    Egyptian Hieroglyphic Dictionary. E. W. Budge. 1920.
B.G.E.    Gods of Egypt. E. W. Budge. 1904.
B.H.E.    Hist. Ecclesiast. Gentis Anglorum. Bede ed. 1631.
B.H.S.    House of Seleucus. E. R. Bevan. 1902.
B.L.S.    Lives of the Saints. S. Baring-Gould. 1914.
B.O.I.    Ogam Inscriptions. R. R. Brash. 1879.
B.P.G.    Phœnizisches Glossar. A. Bloch, Berlin. 1891.
Br.    Classified List of Sumerian Ideographs. R. Brünnow, Leyden. 1889.
B.R.B.    Races of Britain. J. Beddoe. 1885.
C.A.F.    Cory's Ancient Fragments, ed. F. R. Hodges. 1876.
C.A.N.    Auraicept, etc. G. Calder. 1917.
C.A.S.    Trans. Cumberland and Westmorland Antiq. Society.
C.B.    Britannia. W. Camden ; ed. R. Gough, 2nd ed. 1806.
C.C.    Cyprus Researches and Excavs. L. P. di Cesnola. 1877.
C.I.S.    Corpus Inscript. Semiticarum : *Inscript. Phœniciæ.* Paris. 1887.
C.I.W.A.    Cuneiform Inscriptions of W. Asia. H. Rawlinson and T. Pinches.
C.M.C.    Mission en Cappadoce. E. Chantre. Paris. 1898.
C.M.M.    Mysteries of Mithra. F. Cumont, Chicago. 1910.
C.N.G.    New Grange and other Inscribed Mons. in Ireland. G. Coffey. 1912.
*cp.*    = compare.
C.P.N.    Personal Names of Cassite Period. A. T. Clay. 1912.
C.S.H.    La Glyptique Syro-Hittite. G. Contenau. Paris. 1922.
C.S.S.    Syrian Stone Lore. C. R. Conder. 1886.
D.A.A.    Dent's Atlas of Ancient Classic Geography.
D.B.G.    Cæsar's De Bello Gallico.

| | |
|---|---|
| D.C.O. | Cylindres Orientaux de la Bibliot. Nat. (B) ; du Musée du Louvre (L) 1920-23. L. Delaporte, Librairie Hachette. Paris. |
| D.E.M. | Early Man in Britain. Boyd Dawkins. 1880. |
| D.R.M. | Races of Man. J. Deniker. 1900. |
| E.B.I. | Ancient Bronze Implements. J. Evans. 1881. |
| E.C.B. | Coins of the Ancient Britons. J. Evans. 1864. |
| Edda. | Gothic Eddas (C) Codex Regius collotype. F. Wimmer & Jonsson. 1891. (N) romanized text by G. Neckel, Heidelberg. 1914. (VP) text in Corpus Poeticum Boreale by G. Vigfusson & Y. Powell. 1883. |
| F.C.A. | Life of Christ in Art. F. W. Farrar. 1901. |
| F.M.E. | Medallas de España. M. Florez. About 1818. |
| F.R.M. | Rude Stone Monuments. J. Fergusson. 1872. |
| G.A.C. | Hist. of Ancient Coinage, B.C 700–300. P. Gardner. 1918. |
| G.C. | Hist. Britonum. Geoffrey of Monmouth, tr. by A. Thompson, 1718, in " Old English Chronicles " by J. A. Giles. 1882. |
| G.D.B. | Dictionnaire Celto-Breton. J. le Gonidec. 1821. |
| G.D.F. | Decline and Fall of Roman Empire. E. Gibbon. |
| G.H. | Hieroglyphs. F. L. Griffith. 1898. |
| G.L.H. | Land of the Hittites. J. Garstang. 1910. |
| G.M.E. | Making of England. J. R. Green. 1897. |
| G.O.C. | Old English Chronicles. J. A. Giles. 1882. |
| G.R.V. | Hymns of Rig Veda. R. Griffiths. Benares. 1896. |
| H.A.B. | Ancient Britain and Invasion of Julius Cæsar. T. R. Holmes. 1907. |
| H.C. | Carchemish. D. Hogarth. 1914. |
| H.C.C. | Brit. Mus. Catal. Greek Coins of Cilicia, etc. G. Hill. |
| H.C.I. | Brit. Mus. Catal. Greek Coins of Ionia. H. Head. |
| H.C.P. | Brit. Mus. Catal. Greek Coins of Phœnicia. G. Hill. |
| H.E.R. | Encyclopœdia, Religion and Ethics, ed. J. Hastings. 1908–21. |
| H.F.F. | Faiths and Folklore. W. C. Hazlitt. 1905. |
| H.H.S. | Hittite Seals in B.M. D. Hogarth. 1920. |
| H.N.E. | Ancient Hist. Near East. H. R. Hall. 1920. |
| H.P.C. | Prehistoric Remains of Caithness. S. Laing and T. H. Huxley. 1866. |
| J.C. | Les Celtes. M. d'Arbois de Jubainville. |
| J.E.S. | Jour. Ethnological Society. |
| J.R.A.I. | Jour. Roy. Anthropological Institute. |
| J.R.B. | Religion of Babylonia. M. Jastrow. 1911. |
| J.S.D. | Etymological Dictionary of Scottish Language. J. Jamieson, ed. Metcalfe. 1912. |
| K.A.M. | Antiquity of Man. A. Keith. 1916. |
| K.B. | Hist. of Babylon. L. W. King. 1915. |
| K.H.I. | Hist. of Ireland. Jeof. Keating, ed. P. Joyce. Dublin. 1880. |
| K.M. | Man Past and Present. A. H. Keane. 1900. |
| K.S.A. | Hist. of Sumer and Akkad. L. W. King. 1916. |
| L.H.P. | Hist. of Penzance. W. S. Lach-Szyrma. 1878. |
| L.P.I. | Neue Phönizische u. Iberische Inschrift. aus Sardinien. W. F. v. Landau in *Mitt. d. Vorderasiat. Gesellsch.* 1900. 3. |
| L.S. | Stonehenge. N. Lockyer. 1906. |
| L.S.G. | Sumerian Grammar. S. Langdon., Paris. 1911. |
| M.B. | Mahā-Barata or Epic of the Great Barats. Calcutta text ; and (R) English translation. P. C. Roy. Calcutta. 1893. |
| M.C.T. | Coin Types. G. Macdonald. 1905. |
| M.D. | Dictionary of Assyrian Language. W. Muss-Arnolt. Berlin. 1905. |
| M.E.C. | Early Chronicles Scotland. H. Maxwell. 1912. |
| M.F.P. | Fians, Fairies and Picts. D. MacRitchie. 1893. |

# ABBREVIATIONS 419

| | |
|---|---|
| M.H.A. | Murray's Handbook to Asia Minor by C. Wilson. 1895. |
| M.I.S. | Races of Ireland and Scotland. W. C. Mackenzie. About 1910. |
| M.K.I. | Vedic Index. A. A. Macdonell and A. B. Keith. 1912. |
| M.O.B. | Origin and Character of the British People. N. C. Macnamara. 1900. |
| M.R.C. | Reich u. Kultur d. Chetiter. Meyer. Berlin. 1914. |
| M.S.D. | Sanskrit-English Dict. M. Monier-Williams. 1899. |
| M.V.M. | Vedic Mythology. A. A. Macdonell. 1897. |
| N.A.B. | Hist. Britonum by Nennius, tr. in " Old English Chronicles." J. A. Giles. |
| N.C. | Numismatic Chronicle. London. |
| N.P.E. | Pedigree of English People. T. Nicholas. 1868. |
| N.S.S. | New Statistical Acct. of Scotland. |
| P.A. | Formation of the Alphabet. W. F. Petrie. 1912. |
| P.A.B. | Ancient Britain. Beale Poste. 1857. |
| P.A.P. | Hist. of Art in Phœnicia. G. Perrot and C. Chipiez. 1885. |
| P.A.S. | Hist. of Art in Sardinia, Syria, etc. G. Perrot and C. Chipiez. 1880. |
| P.B.C. | Coins of Cunobelin and the Ancient Britons. B. Poste. 1853. |
| P.D.G. | Description of Greece by Pausanias. Bohn's trans. |
| P.E. | History of Egypt. W. F. Petrie, ed. 1912. |
| P.E.C. | Excavations in Cranborne Chase. A. Pitt-Rivers. 1886–1905. |
| P.G. | Ptolemy's Geography, ed. I. Ant. Aug. Patavino, St. Petersburgh. 1597. |
| P.G.G. | Galatie et Bithynie. Perrot and Guillaume. |
| P.M.M. | (a) Megalithic Monuments and Ancient Mines. (b) Distribution Megaliths in England. In Manchester Memoirs. 1915. No. 1. and 1921, No. 13. W. J. Perry. |
| P.S.A.S. | Proc. Soc. of Antiquaries of Scotland. |
| P.S.L. | Sumerian Lexicon. J. D. Prince. Leipzig. 1908. |
| P.V.H. | Vocabulaire Hiéroglyphique. P. Pierret. Paris. 1875. |
| R.C.B. | Celtic Britain. J. Rhys. 1904. |
| R.C.P. | Cities of St. Paul. W. M. Ramsay. 1908. |
| R.H.G. | Historical Geography of A. Minor. W. M. Ramsay. Roy. Geog. Soc. Supplementary Papers. 1896. |
| R.H.L. | Hibbert Lects. of 1886. On Celtic Heathendom. J. Rhys. 1892. |
| R.H.P. | History of Phœnicia. G. Rawlinson. 1889. |
| R.M.P. | Mission de Phénicie. E. Renan. Paris, 1864. |
| R.R.E. | Races of Europe. W. Z. Ripley. 1900. |
| R.V. | Rig Veda Hymns and Text of T. Aufrecht Bonn and M. Müller. |
| S.A.S. | British Archaic Sculpturings. J. Y. Simpson. 1857. |
| S.C.B. | Plates of Coins of Anct. Brit. Kings. Dr. Stukeley, F.R.S. Lond. 1765. |
| S.C.P. | Chronicles of Picts and Scots. W. F. Skene. 1867. |
| S.E.C. | Infl. Ancient Egyptian Civiliz. in East and America. G. E. Smith. 1916. |
| S.E.D. | Etymolog. Dict. of English Language. W. W. Skeat. 1882. |
| S.H. | The Hittites. A. H. Sayce. 1910. |
| S.H.L. | Hibbert Lects. for 1887 on Religion of Ancient Babylonians. A. H. Sayce. 1898. |
| S.I. | Ilios. H. Schliemann. 1880. |
| S.I.V. | Inscriptions of Van. A. H. Sayce in Jour. Roy. As. Soc. 1882. |
| S.M. | Mycenæ. H. Schliemann. 1878. |
| S.M.C. | Migrations of Early Culture. G. E. Smith. 1915. |
| S.S.S. | Sculptured Stones of Scotland. J. Stuart. Spalding Club, Aberdeen. 1856. |
| T.A. | The Alphabet. I. Taylor. 1883. |

| | |
|---|---|
| T.B.B. | Book of Buchan. J. F. Tocher. Peterhead. 1910. |
| T.O.A. | Origin of the Aryans. I. Taylor, ed. 1906. |
| T.R.C. | Recherches sur l'origine de l'Écriture Cunéiforme. F. Thureau-Dangin. Paris. 1898-9. |
| T.W.P. | Words and Places. I. Taylor. 1864. |
| V.D. | Icelandic-English Dictionary. G. Vigfusson. 1874. |
| V.P. | Vishnu Purana, trans. by H. H. Wilson, ed. F. Hall. 1864. |
| W.A.H. | Aberdeen and Banff County History. W. Watt. 1900. |
| W.E.H. | Empire of the Hittites. W. Wright. 1886. |
| W.F.S. | The French Stonehenge. T. C. Worsfold. 2nd ed. |
| W.L.W. | Lapidarium Walliæ. J. O. Westwood. Oxford. 1878-9. |
| W.P.A. | Prehistoric Annals of Scotland. D. Wilson. 1851. |
| W.P.E. | Remains of Prehistoric Age in England. B. C. Windle. 1904. |
| W.S.C. | Seal Cylinders of W. Asia. W. H. Ward. Carnegie Institute. Washington. 1900. |
| W.S.M. | Cylinders and other Oriental Seals in Library of J. P. Morgan. W. H. Ward. 1920. |
| Y.M.P. | Marco Polo. H. Yule. 1903. |

FIG. 77.—Pendant Phœnician Sun-Cross held in adoration. From Hittite seal of about 1000 B.C.
(After Lajard.)

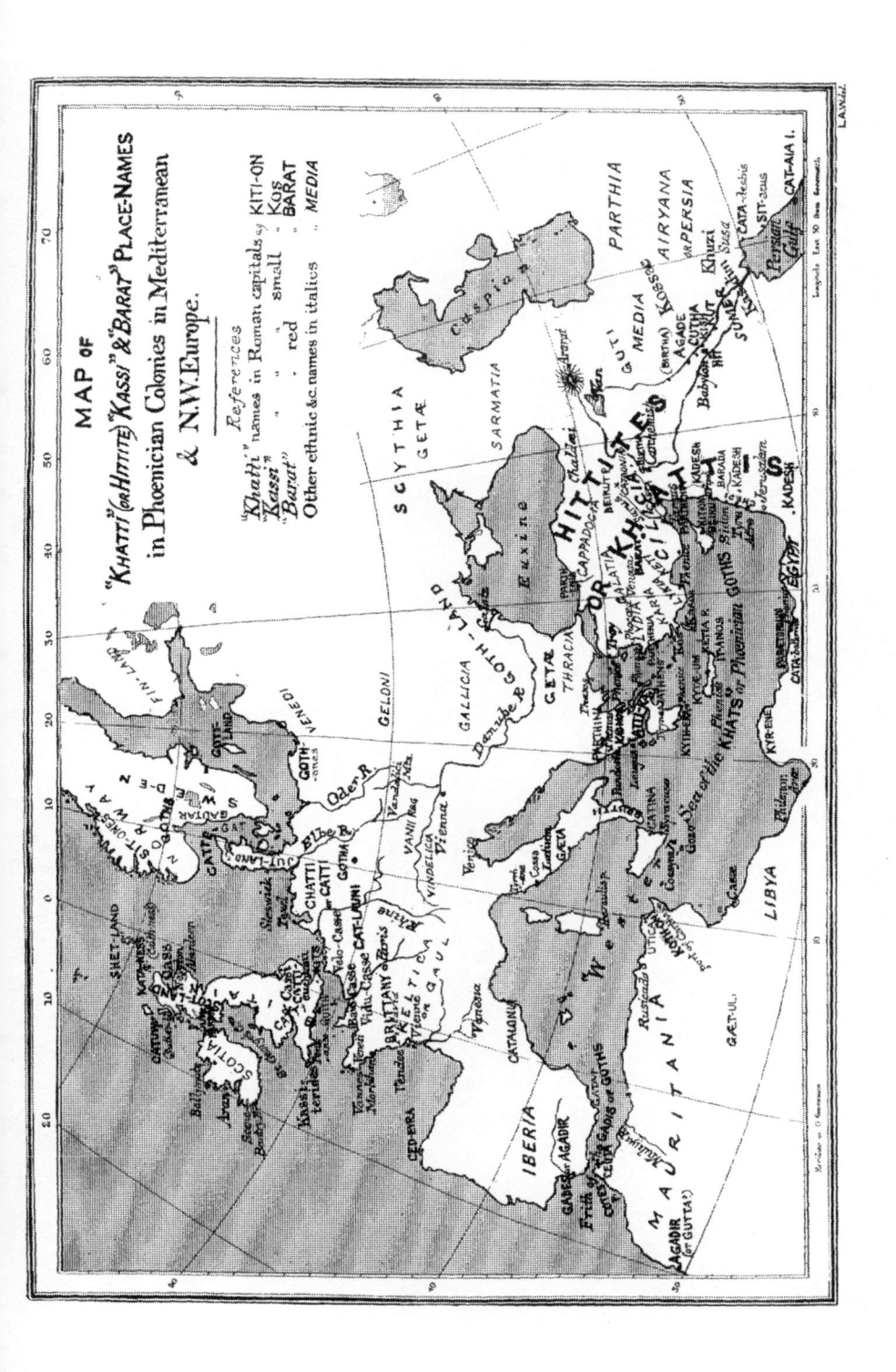

MAP OF
"KHATTI"(or HITTITE) "KASSI" & "BARAT" PLACE-NAMES
in Phoenician Colonies in Mediterranean
& N.W. Europe.

*References*
"Khatti" names in Roman capitals *eg* KITI-ON
"Kassi" " " small " KOS
"Barat" " " red " BARAT
Other ethnic &c. names in italics *MEDIA*

# INDEX

Abbreviations : A.B.=Ancient Britain ; n.=name.

Aberdeen, patron saint, St. Machar, a Phœnic. tutelary, 357-9 ; Phœnic. emblems in city arms, 357

Aberdeenshire, bronze sickles in, 183, 357 ; King Part-olon's Phœnic. inscripts. of 400 B.C. in Don Valley of, 1f., 16f. ; Pict underground villages in, 90, 199 ; prehist. sculptured stones in, 19 ; St. Michael's holy wells in, Phœnic., 341, 357f. ; Stone Circles in, sacred, 19, 235 ; Texali or Taizali A.B. tribe in, 357

Aborigines of Albion, not Britons, 103, 111, 120f., 168, 365 ; physical type of, non-Aryan, Iberian, Riverbed race, 103, 120-2, 134-5, 149, 365 ; as Picts, 95f., 111f. ; as Vans, Wans, Fenes or Finns, 93f. ; advent of, 98f. ; cannibalism of, 125 ; human sacrifice by, 183, 232 ; matriarchy of, 92f. ; Serpent worship of, 94f., 106f., 119, 124, 183, 271, 331 ; skin clad, 145 ; Stone Age sporadic Aryan type as straggler Amorite Phœnic. traders, 224-5

Aborigines of Ireland, as Van, Wan, Bian or Fen or Fene matriarchists, 91f. ; advent of, from Stone Age Albion, 92f., 122f.

Accad or Amorite Phœnic. tin traders in Albion about 2800 B.C., 160, 169-71, 216, 413f.

Ace, n. derived from Sumer, 240 ; see Words

Achaians, a tribe of Hitto-Phœnicians, 177, 246, 331 ; and the Goat symbol, 325, 331 ; n. Sumer, 331

Adam, " Son of God," of Sumerians, 239, 253

Addedo-maros (Aedd-mawr), A.B. coins of, with Phœnic. (Adad) solar emblems, 285, 339, 393

Adder, worshipped by aborigines in Albion, 105f. ; 110, 124-5, 183, 310f. ; 331

Aedd the great, father of Prydain or Brutus, 170, 190

Ægean culture, in Crete, introd. by Phœnicians, 27, 63-4, 161 ; spiral ornament in, Hitto-Phœnic. source and meaning of, 182, 247

Æneas, ancestor of A.B. kings, 148-9, 151 ; Trojan emblems of, as in Britain, 149

Æsv legend on A.B. coins, Hitto-Sumer source of n., 284-5, 413

Æthel, Ethel or Œdl, Sumer source of Gothic n., 182

Affixes to Brit. place names, Hitto-Sumer or Phœnician, 43, 171, 203-4 ; to Pict place-names, 204

Agadir, Phœnician port, re Cudder Point, and Penzance 68, 172, and see Gades or Agadir or Gadeira, 172

Agathyrsi, re Agadir, n. for Partolon's tribe, 68, 394f.

Agenor, Phœnician king, descendants of, in Britain, 161, 167

Agriculture, era of, instituted by Aryans, 49, 345, 361 ; in Britain, introduced by Phœnics., 170, 357 ; patron saint of, 345f. ; Phœnic. tutelary of, worshipped in A.B., 348f. ; see Corn Spirit ; a sacred rite of Aryans, 49 ; see Corn Spirit and Plough

Aire, Irish-Scot and Gaelic =Aryan, 191

Aken-aten, art of, Aryan Phœnician, 220f. ; art religious motives of, in A.B., 333-6, etc. ; solar cult of, Phœnician, and reflected in A.B., 221, 265-6f.

Alban, early n. of Albion, 87, 97, 103, 163 ; meaning of n., 103f.

Alban, Silvanus, colonization of Albion about 1150 B.C. by, 162-4, 168

# 422 PHŒNICIAN ORIGIN OF BRITONS & SCOTS

Albania n. for Scotland, 104, 157
Albans, St., anc. Verulam, cap. of Cassivellaunus, 408f.
Albion, early n. for Britain, 155; aborigines of, 103f.
Al-Clyde, Al-Clutha, Celtic n. for Dun-Barton, 197
Alfred, King, translates Briton law-codes for Anglo-Saxons, 181, 385-8
Alpha and Omega, God n. derived from Sumer, 252
Alphabet, Aryan Phœnic. origin of, 27-8, 31-34; Ogam, Phœnic. Fire-cult origin of, 35-7; Semitic Phœnic., 27, 33, 53.
Alpine or Round-headed race in Britain, 134-6, 141, 365f.
Amber trading Phœnicians in A.B. and Baltic, 171, 218-9, 222
America, U.S., Briton racial elements and civilization in, 377
Amor-ites, in Albion about 2800 B.C. as Tin traders, 160, 167, 169, 171, 190, 216, 413f.; a Semitic n. for Mar, Martu or Muru Hitto-Phœnics., 13, 216; as Aryans, 224-5, 257-8, 411-2; as "giants" of Early Albion, 153, 155, 160, 167-9, 171, 216f.; as "giant" rulers of pre-Israelite Palestine and Jerusalem, 216, 274, 417; as "sons of Anak," 417; Bronze Age introd. A.B. by, 161, 183; cup-marks used by, 257; physical type of, 224-5; Stone Circles in A.B. erected by, 167, 169, 183, 216f.; Sun-priestess of, Resurrection prayer and Cross of, 257, 411-2; Tin mines of, in Cornwall, 190, 216, 413f.; Moray, Moridun, More-cambe Bay, West Mor-land, etc., with prehist. mines and Stone Circles re Mors or Amorites, 217
Amulets in A.B., Cross as, 378; Cross and other Sun emblems on Hitto-Sumer Phœnic. and Trojan, as in A.B., 238f.; snake-stones as aboriginal, 125
Anak, sons of, in Britain, 417
Anatolia or Hittite Asia Minor, abode of Magi or "wise men of the East" at Epiphany, 279
Ancient Aryan place and river names in A.B., bestowed by Phœnicians, 188f.

Ancient Britons of Aryan race and highly civilized, see Briton
Ancient Names as sources of history, 189
*Ando*, n. on A.B. coins, variant of Andrew, 317, 336,
Andrew, variant of Hitto-Sumer god-name Indara or Indra, 246, 315f.
Andrew, St., incorporates Hitto-Sumer Indara worship, 246, 315f.; Cross of, in Hitto-Sumer and Phœn. seals, etc., as Indara's hammer, 316f., see Andrew Cross; festival of, in England, 327; Goat or Unicorn and, 332f., see Goat; patron of Goths, Scyths, etc., 315f.; pre-Christian worship of, in A.B., 259f., 315f., 320f., 326f.
Andrew, the apostle, an Aryan Hitto-Phœnic. or Goth, 315f., 321f.
Andrews, St., pre-Christian Indara shrine at, 321, 326; sculpture of Indara tearing the Lion (antagonist of Sun) at, 327
Angel gold coins of Early England, of Phœnic. type and legend, 360
Angel of the Lord, The, of O.T. is Phœnic. Tas-Michael (worshipped in A.B.), 275, 344
Angels, Aryan origin of idea of, 342f., worship of, in A.B., see Coins, Monuments, Archangel
Angles, a branch of Britons, 44, 186-7; as Yngl-ing Goths of Eddas, 186
Anglo-Saxon, modern term coined for language, 186; language of Briton origin, 179f., 186f., 370
Anglo-Saxons, a branch of Britons, 14, 44, 186-7; adopted Briton law-codes, 181, 385-8
Animals, sacred, of Hitto-Phœnic. in A.B.; see Eagle, Goat and Deer, Goose, Hawk, Horse, Bull and Sun-cult
Antenor, Phœnic., descendants of, in A.B., 160-1
Anthropomorphic god, in A.B., 259f., 266f.; Hitto-Sumer origin of, 245f., 342f.
Apostles Andrew, Bartholomew, Peter and Philip as Aryan Phœnicians, 82-3, 281, 323f.
*Ap*, prefix in Cymric names, 88
Aquitania, Picts in, 118, 154, 374

# INDEX

Aran holy isles, off Ireland, Sumer source of n., 65, 191, 199
Arch, Gothic, in early Scythic sculptures, 70, 303; Gothoid in Hittite, 70
Archangel Michael, Hitto-Phœnic., in A.B., 246, 341f., see Michael, St.
Argonauts as Phœnician sailors *re* Early Albion, 359, 406
*Ari*, Amorite for Aryan, 257
Arianism of Goths, Hittite origin of, 301, 303; of Early Christian Church at Tyre and Sidon, 323
Armorica, Amorites in, 216; Phœnician Sun-cult in, 269; megaliths in, 216-7; Sun and Fire worship in, 26; see Morbihan
Arran and Holy Isle and Goat Fell, with Stone circles, 197-9, 208
Arreton Downs, Stone Circles and Bronze Age remains in, 357
*Arri*, Hitto-Sumer for Aryan race or tribe, 6, 191, 235, 345f., 361, 394
*Arriya*, Mede (or Mitani) for Aryan, 14
Art, in A.B., 181-2, 325; Celtic, is Brito-Phœnic., 182; decorative, key patterns, spirals, etc., as Hitto-Phœnic., 182, 249, 285f., 295, 335f.; Egyptian " New " as Phœnician with parallels in A.B., 182, 220-1, 335; high, of Hitto-Sumers, 245f.; Phœnician motives in A.B., 182, 221, 249, 285, 295, 335f., 347f.; superiority of A.B. over medieval and Anglo-Saxon, 182
Arthur, legendary king, Gothic Eddic Heria-Thor, 195, 198, Cadbury camp and trad. of, 400; oven (Fire temp.?) of, 198; seats of, 196, 198
*Arya*, Indo-Aryan title of Aryan, 5-8, 12, 132
Aryan, a racial title essentially, vi, 5, 132, 257, 345f., 361; used by Hitto-Phœnic., 6, 14, 257; by Indo-Aryan and Medo-Persians, 8, 14, meaning of n., 191, 345f., 361; n. in Cymric Irish-Scot, etc., 191, 394; physical type of, 134f., 365; Phœnicians of A. type, 12; languages derived from Hitto-Phœnics., 132f.; Aryan Phœnician script, 26, 33

Aryans, The, origin and cradle-land of, discovered, 8f.; Agriculture established by, 49; " chosen people of God," 11, 324, 363; civilizers of world, 11, 324, 363; enter Albion, 142f., 169f.; Hittites, the primitive, 8f., 14-15; intermarriage with aborigines, 363f.; physical type of, 133f., 365; plough invented by, 348; script of, 26f., 33
*Asa*, Gothic title of God, derived from Sumerian, 240
Asia Minor, homeland of Aryans, formerly called Kur, Kuur or Syria, 12, 305
Astronomical theories of Stonehenge and other Stone Circles, 225f.
Astronomy, proficiency of Early Britons in, 216f.
*Aswin*, Twin Sun-horsemen of Vedic Aryans on Briton coins, 58-9, 285-6
Aten worship as, Phœnician, 265f.
Atrebates tribe in S. Britain, 213
*Att* legend on A.B. coins of Catti as Hatt or Hittite, 6, 203
Atte-cotti tribe of N. Britain, 45
Avon, river n., Phœnician, 174
Axe emblem of Catti or Hitt-ite and Saxon in A.B., 320f.; double in A.B., 320f.
Axe, river n., Trojan, 173f.
Axes, bronze, in A.B., of Hittite type, 183
*av* affix of Gothic isle and shore names, as Phœnician, 43

Baal, Semitic for Sun-god Bil or Bel, 42, 267; Jehovah as, 268, 276; Jupiter as, 244, 281
Babylonia, Cassi or Kassi ruling clan of A.B., in, 49, 291; Phœnicians in Early, 11, 13f.; Sun symbols of, in A.B, 294-5f.; Tin-mines of, in A.B., 160, 413f.
Bahika, Sanscrit n. for Picts(?), 201
Bairthy, Egyptian n. for Britannia, 60f.
Ballymote, key to Ogam script in book of, 22, 74-5, 91
Baltic and Cattegat, Phœnician trade in, 171, 218, 222
Ban, Van or Fene, pre-Briton aborigines of Brit. Isles and Asia Minor, 91f.; matriarch priestess

of, in Ireland, 94-5, 99, 104f., 123; tribe in Alban, 95-7, 103; see Van
Ban-bha, n. of Hibernia, 91
Baptism, Hitto-Sumer Sun-cult rite, non-Judaist, 273f.; introduced into A.B. by Phœnic. Goths, 273f.
Barat or Bārat or Brihat, patronym of Early Aryans and Phœnicians and source of " Briton," 1-8, 15, 38, 52f., 188f.; in place-names in Britain, 65, 118, 188-199; in Ireland, 199; n. on Phœnician coins, 9; origin of n., 188, patronym of Cassis, 53; Syria-Phœnicians the chief, 188
Barates, n. on A.B. monument of , a Syrio-Phœnician, 71-2
Bārati, early n. of Britannia as tutelary of Phœnicians, 58f.
Barats or " Brits " or " Brit-ons " in A.B., 52f., 169f.; in Carthage, 9; in Cilicia, 54-55; in Italy, 214; in Sardinia, 53; " chosen people of God," 1, 363; Phœnics., chief clan of, 188; as Sun-worshippers, 292; see Briton
Bar-clensis, Phœnic. clan in A.B., 78
Barley, cultivation in A.B. introd. by Phœnics.(?), 155; on A.B. coins, 6, 289, 338f.; on Phœnic. coins, 213f.; and the Corn Spirit in A.B., 338f., 390; see Corn
Barrow tombs, long, of Brito-Phœnics., 204, 224f., 365; see ead-form
Barter trade of Phœnicians, with A.B., xiii
Barthol Chapel nr. Part-olon's mon., 19, 81-2
Bartholomew, St., an Aryan Phœnician(?), 82-3; festival of, in Britain, 82-4
Barton Mere and Bronze Age remains, 193
Basques and the Picts, 118, 154, 374
Bath, fire-temple at, 387; founding of, about 870 B.C., 387
Beads, blue glazed Phœnic., in A.B. abt. 1400 B.C., 219-20
Beaker-men, race of, in Britain, 134f., 141, 365, and see Alpine and Hun
Beards, long, with clean upper lip, of early Aryans and Hitto-Phœnics., 239, 245, 247

Beirut, or Biruta, Barat port of Phœnicia, 71, 173; coins of, with legends as in A.B., 354; relations of, with Brit., 71-3
Bel (or Bil) Father-god of Phœnicians, 2, 13, 32, 42, 61, 267f.; of Sumerians, 267; Fire festival of, in Britain, 263, 269f., 271, 281, 282f.; and John-the-Baptist, 273f., as Jehovah, 268, 276; as Jupiter, 244, 281; inscriptions in A.B., 32f., 356; as personal n. in A.B., 42, 89; do. of Phœnicians of Cilicia, Tyre, etc., 42; and see Bil
Belgae, immigr. of, to S. Brit. and Wales, 264
Beltane or Summer solstice Fire festival in Britain, 269-71; in Brittany, 269-73; in Ireland, 270; in Phœnicia-Palestine, 270; in Spain, 273; on May Day, 271; n. origin and meaning, 269
Belerium, old n. for Cornwall, 281
Bennachie Mt., at Phœnic. monument at Newton, 17-19, 39; St. Blaze at, 268
Beowulf's Anglo-Saxon, 180
Berouth, Phœnic. n. for Britannia, H.C.P., xlvi
Berth, n. for Perth, 198
Berytus, Greek n. for Beirut
Beyrout, see Beirut
Bharat, see Barat
Biana, n. of pre-Aryan aborigines of Van, 98, 123-5
Bil, or Bel, Father-god; cult of, in A.B., 1, 32f., 46, 262f., 273; n. and meaning, 267-8; n. in A.B. inscripts., 1, 32f., 356; personal n. in A.B., 42, 89; see Bel
Bili, personal n. of Briton kings, 89
Bird men in A.B., 362; in Sumer seals, 253; Sun- in A.B., 251f.; see Sun-bird
Biridiya (Barat or Brit) personal n. in Syria-Phœnicia, 53
Blaze, St. of Cappadocia, worship of, in Britain, 40, 268; at Bennachie, 40, 268
Bleezes, 40, 268, St., see above
Blue leg, tribe of aborigines, 95, 109; in Ireland, 109; re Picts, 117
Boann, matriarch, of R. Boyne, 94
Boats, skin-, of aborigines, 104; and see Ships

# INDEX

Boghaz Koi anc. capital of Catti, Hitt-ites or Early Goths, 7, 70, 78
Boots of Hittites of Gothic type, 7, 340
Brain, developt. of frontal lobes in Aryan, v. " Celts," 122, 134–5f.
Brennus, (Brian), Briton king of Gaul, sacks Rome about 390 B.C., 34, 387, 389
Bretons, Sun Fire cult amongst, 216
Bride, St., or Brigit, and her serpent, 106f.
Brigit, St., or Frigg, matriarch of Gothic Eddas, 106f.
Brihat, form of n. Brit or Brit-on, 1, 53
Britain, or Britannia, origin and meaning of n., 52, 65, 169; n. given by Brutus, 142, 155, 168–9; Anglo-Saxon variations in spelling n., 66; former names of, 190, mixed races in modern, 363f.
Britain, Ancient, aborigines of, not Britons, 103, 111, 120–1, 125f., 168, 365; arrival of Britons in, 142f.; Amorites about 2800 B.C. in, see Amorites; affixes to place-names in, Hitto-Phœnician, 43, 171, 203f.; agriculture introd. by Phœnicians in, 170; Cross in, 289f.; destruction of monuments of, 35; Goths in, 179f.; Hitto-Phœnic. Sun-cult in, 262f.; ladies in, 71–3, 185, 245, 388; Part-olon's conquest of N., 67f.; Phœnics. in, 159f.; Phœnic. civilization and penetration of, 188f., 200f.; Phœnic. inscripts in, 32f., 43, 355f.; Phœnic. place and r. names in, 172f., 188f., 200f.; Resurrection belief in, 256f.; Sumerian inscripts. in, 227f., and see cup-marks, 238f.; trade with Gades, 147, 222; Trojan place and r. names in, 172f.; Trojan symbols in, 149, 294f.
Britain, Modern, Phœnician influence in, 363f., 380f.
Britanni tribe on Somme, 186
Britannia tutelary, Phœnician origin of n. and form of, 55f.; as Phœnician Barat or Barati, 55, 58; on coins of Carthage, 9, Cilicia, 55, Sidon, 57; in Egypt, 59–60; in Vedas, 58–9; on Roman coins, 56; as Bêrouth in Phœnicia, H.C.P., xlvi; re Diana, 45; her Cross, 55, 57, 61; her Fire-torch (re lighthouse), 58; helmet, 59; her son Neptune, 58
Britenden, and Ogam script, 44
British " camps," prehistoric, 191f., 205f., 397f.
British Chronicles, traditional, historicity of, 147–8f.
British, Hitto-Phœnic. origin of n., 52, 65; modern non-racial use of term, 371;
Brito-Martis, title of Britannia, 63–4
Briton, n. of Hitto-Phœnic. origin, 1, 8f., 14f., 52, 65; n. given by Brutus, 142, 155, 168–9; coins, see Coins; n. in personal names, 215; n. in place-names, 188f., in Ireland, 199; kings, list of early, 385; language of Sumerian origin introd. by Brutus is basis of English, 175f.; mod. use of term, 371; war-chariots of Hitto-Trojan type, 145
Britons, or Barats, a branch of Aryan Hitto-Phœnicians, 2, 5, 15, 38f.; false views about, 144f.; not aborigines of Albion, 111f., 127f.; arrival in Albion, 142f.; Anglo-Saxons, a branch of, 44, 186–7; agriculture introd. by, 170; art of, 181f.; Bronze Age introd. by, 183; chronicles of, 142f.; civilization of, 71f., 142, 151f., 184; clans of, see Tribes; coins of, 6, 144, see Coins; colonization of, 186f.; cup-mark inscriptions of, 236f.; home-land of, 8f, 14, 142f.; in Denmark, 186; in France, 186; in Germany, 186; Ireland, 67f.; Italy, 214; king-lists of, 385f.; language of, basis of English, 178f., 190; law-codes of, 181f.; physical type Aryan, 134f.; settlements sep. from aborigines, 203–4; ships of, 408; religion of, 262f.; roads of, 187, 191f., 204f.; Stone-Circles of, 216f.; Trojan elements in, 142f., 177f.; war chariots of, Hitto-Trojan, 145, see Barat, Briton and Britain Ancient
Brittany, Cassi tribe in, 389; Phœnician Sun and Fire festivals in, 103, 216, 273; megaliths in, 103, 216
Briutus, var. of Brutus, 404
Broch, towers of Hitto-Phœnic. style, 171; and n. Hittite, 171

Bronze Age in A.B. introd. by Phœnicians, 183 ; settlers of, in Don Valley, 183, 357 ; and see Art
Bronze chariots in A.B. graves, 145
Brow, narrow, of pre-Briton aborigines, 120, 122, 134f., 140
Brude or Bruide title of kings of Picts, 85f.
Brut, var. of Brutus, 190 ; the, of Layamon, 143, 319, etc.
Bruteport, 172, 193
Bruttii tribe of Italy, 214, of Greece, 357
Brutus-the-Trojan, 1st king, " First Dynasty " in Britain, 142f. ; ancestry of, 148, 151 ; arrival in Albion, 155 ; associate Phœnicians of, 154, 159f. ; banishes Sylvius Alba, 162f. ; cause of coming, 167 ; civilizes aborigines, 155, 168f. ; conquers " giants " (Amorites), 155 ; Cornwall allotted to Duke Corineus by, 155, 165 ; cultivates land, 155 ; date of arrival of, 165-7, 385f. ; fleet of, 152 ; founds London, 156, 407f. ; at Gades, 154 ; in Greece, 151, 407f. ; gives n. to Britain, 155 ; gives Phœnician and Trojan place and river names to Britain, 173f. ; houses built by, 155 ; identity of, with Homeric Peirithoos, 163, 404f. ; identity with Prydain, 190 ; iron introd. by(?), 183 ; as law-giver, 156 ; Phœnicians of Cilicia, Tyre and Sidon accomp., to Albion, 161 ; Stone of, at Totnes, 162 ; vision of, 153, 158f. ; voyage to Albion, 152f., 157f.
Buildings in A.B., 155, 170 ; wooden architect. of Hitt-ite or Gothic type, 69f.
Bull emblem of Indara or Andrew in A.B., 250, 317
Burial in A.B., solar orientation, 225 ; re Resurrection, q.v., red pigment in early, 224 ;
Burriton or " place of the Barats," n. of Penzance, 164, 193, 201
—*bury* or -*burg*, town affix is Hittite, 171
Button amulets of Sun-cult in A.B., 239f., 378 ; of Hitto-Sumerian and Trojan type, 239

Cabeiri, Phœnic. pigmy luck-gollywogs as Picts or Pihta (Ptah) Tin-miner and galley slaves 267
Cac legend on A.B. coins, 48 and cp. E.C.B. 353
Cad, title of Phœnics. and Britons, var. of Cat, Gad or Kad, 19, 71f., 180, 200, 203f., in A.B. placenames, 200, 205-7, 397f.
Cad-bury, with Briton " camp " and Phœnic. remains and Arthur legend, 174, 192, 398, 400
Cadeni or Gadeni tribe, 396
Cadiz, Phœnician port in Iberia, re Britain Tin trade, 160f. ; see Gades
Cadmeian, Phœnic. script, 34
Cadmon, 180, see Caedmon
Cadmus, Phœnician king as Sea colonist, 41, 202
Caduceus, n. and emblem derived from Sumerian, 239, 242, 245, 252
Cad-van's, St., stone of, 196
Cad-wallon, Cymric form of Cassivellaunus' n., 69, 71, 207, 394
Cad-zow, as Phœnician town, 78, 308 ; pre-Christian Cross of Hittite type at, 308
Cæd-mon, properly Cadmon, as Brito-Phœnician, 179 ; Briton dialect of, 179-80
Cær, Cymric fort, Sumer origin of n., 175
Cær-Leon or Isca, and Arthur legend, 195
Cær-Lud or London, q.v.
Cær-Marthen, re Morites or Amorites, 217
Cæsar (Julius), on Briton civilization, 113, 144 ; conflict with Cassivellaunus, 408 ; and London, 408 ; on Picts, 113, 144-5 ; on War-chariots of Britons, 145
Cæsarea in Hitto-Cappadocia, art of Briton type, 307, 410
Cait, ancestor of Part-olon, as Cathluan, 396
Caith Briton tribe and Caithness, 78, 87, 200, 209
Caithness early skulls at Keiss, Cassi or Mor (?), 210
Caiy Stone, cup-marks on, near Edinburgh, deciphered, 237
Caledonia, origin and meaning of n., 117f.
Caledonians as " Kelts," 117, 121, 140 ; re Picts

# INDEX 427

Cambri n. for Cymri tribe, 157
Cambria n. for Wales, Cumberland and Strath-Clyde, 143, 156
Cambreis n. for Britain, 143, 191; n. for Strath-Clyde, 112
Candlemas festival as fire-rite, 40
Cannibalism in British Isles, 271
Canonization of heroic Early Aryan kings 348
Canterbury, founding of, about 900 B.C., 386
Cap, horned of Hitto-Sumers, Goths and Britons, 239, 245, 247, 250; Phrygian of Hittites, Goths and Britons, 246, 247, 250
Caphtor, the Phœnician port of Abdara in Spain, 415
Cappadocia, central prov. of Hittites, 7, 70; home of St. Blaze, 40, 268; home of St. George of England and his Red Cross, 40
Caratacus, coins of king, with Phœnic. emblems and legends, 389, 392-3
Carlisle, founding of, about 940 B.C., 386
Caractacus, see Caratacus
Carthage, A.B. trade with, 147; coins stamped Barat, 9; date of founding, 166; pre-Christian Crosses at, like Briton (C.I.S. many); worship of Phœnician archangel Dashup-Mikal (or Michael) at, 341 (f.n. 2)
Cas (= Cassi) n. on A.B. coins with Hitto-Phœnic. Sun-emblems, 48, 211-2
Casse (Cassi) tribe in France, 389, see map
Cassi, title of Briton kings and their clan, 48, 211; a clan title of Hitto-Phœnic. Barat Fire-worshippers, 47-8, 209; a branch of Hittites, 47, 274; in Babylonia, 49-50, 53; in A.B., 201, 209, 416; in Don Valley, 32f.; in Epirus, 202; in France, 389; in India, 47-8; in Mediterranean ports, 202 and see map; in Palestine, 274; in Shetland, 77; coins of, in A.B., 48, 211; Cross of, in A.B., 51, 77, 295f.; n. in place-names of A.B., 200f., 209f.; n. of King Part-olon's clan, 32f., 47f., 211; in modern personal names, 215
Cassibellaun, or Cass-wallon, Cymric name, romanized as Cassivellaunus, 207
Cassiobury, city of Cassivellaunus and his Catye-uchlani tribe, 209
Cassi-ope. n. of Phœnic. ports, 202
Cassi-terides, Tin Islands of Phœnic., off Cornwall, 160, 201-2, 209, 415f.; Amorite kings in, 160f.; Amorite Coss-ini tribe at, 202; origin and meaning of n., 201f.; Pytheas on, 202; Sargon 1., relations with, about 2800 B.C. (?), 413f.
Cassiteros, Greek n. for Tin, 201
Cassi-vellaun, n. of Phœnic. origin, 69, 71f.; paramount Briton king, 145, 166, 210-2; defeat of, by Cæsar, 145-6, 408-10; war chariots of, 145; site of capital, 408-9
Cas-wallon, Cymric form of above n., 207
Cat, variant of Catti tribe n., 200f., 209, 403; in Brit. place names for Catti, 203f., 397f.
Cat-ness, old n. of Caithness, 209
Cat-rail, Briton earthwork, 402; Cetiloinn tribe inscript. near, 70f.
Cat-stanes, monoliths, 216, 224, 402
Cat-alonia, Phœnic. prov. in Spain, 71
Cat-alauni or Catuellani tribe, in Britain, 213, 394; on the Marne, 186, 389
Cataonia in Cappadocia, 45, 65
Cathluan, k. of Picts v. Part-olon, 90, 395f.
Catte-gat or "Gate of Catte," 180, see Baltic
Catti, title of Briton kings and their clan, 6, 200f.; title of ruling Hittites or Khatti including Phœnics., 5-8f., 200f. and see Khatti; coins of, with emblems as on Hittite seals and Phœnician coins, 5, 211f., etc.; origin and meaning of n. "Cutters" or axe-sceptre wielders, i.e., rulers, 8, 200, 209, 294-5 (b), 305, 320f.; in place-names in Britain, 200f., 397f.; do. in Don Valley, 19, 199, 403; in modern personal names, 215; and see Khatti
Cattedown cave remains, 173, 207
Cattuellauna tribe of Britons, 212, 396, see Caty-euchlani
Catuv, n. of Sutherland, 78

Catuvellaunus, form of Cassivellaunus, see Cassivellaun
Caty-euchlani tribe of A.B., 68, 200-2, 207, 210-12
Cauldron of Hell, of Serpent cult of aborigines, 94-5, 104-6
Cave gravings, prehistoric, in A.B., of Trojan and Hitto-Phœnic. emblems, 198, 335, 350
Ceasair, prehistoric Irish matriarch, 91, 93-4, 101-5
Cedi, n. for Getae or Phœnician Goths, 168, 262
Celt, origin and meaning of n., 99; misuse of term, 127, 139; modern introd. of n. to British Isles, 127f.
Celts or Kelts, confused racial use of terms, 127-30, 134-7; British, 127f.; re Caledons, 117, 125; re Culdees, 117; Gaulish, 129f.; re Khaldis, 99, 125, 139f.; re Picts, 139-41; physical type of, 133f.; 140; psychology of, 375
Celtic, art of Bronze Age is Brito-Phœnic., 182; Cross is Hitto-Phœnic., 334f. and see Cross; language, dialect of British Gothic 180; question, the, 127f.; race-type in Britain, 139f.
Centaur, v. Canterbury, 405
Cephalic index, of races, 134-6; of Aryan, 134
Cet-gueli, or Kid-welly, ancient port of Catti, 71
Ceti, form of n. Getae, Goth, Scot and Phœnics. (Cedi), 71, 168, 209, 262
Ceti-loinn tribe n. on Yarrow stone, near Cat-rail earthwork, 72
Chaldee (and Culdee) origin of n., 99
Chals, Gypsy or Chaldee of Van, 117
Chat-ham, 203
Channel, English, ancient n. Ictis or Icht, 116, 121, 163f., 201, 405
Chariots, War-, of Britons of Hitto-Trojan type, 145; buried with Briton chief, like Syrians in Egypt, 145
Charms, in A.B., see Amulets and Cup-marks; horse-shoe for luck, reason of, 287
Chattan clan, 208
Chatti tribe in Germany, 186
Cheddar caves and Bronze Age remains, 400

Chedi or Cedi, title of Phœnics., 262
Chiltern Hills and Celts or Kelts, 117
Christ, visits coast of Phœnicia and works miracles there, 323; Phœnicians early followers of, 323; "wise men" at Epiphany of, Hitto-Phœnic. *Magi* or Fire-worshippers, 279
Christianity, early centre of, in Phœnicia, 323; Arianism in Phœnician, 323, Arianism in Gothic, 301-3; Cross symbol introd. into, by Goths, 301f.; Phœnician elements in British, 383
Christmas or Yule, winter solstice festival, 69
Chronicles of Early Briton kings, historicity of, 146f.; King Lists in 385f.
Cilicia, homeland of Brito-Phœnic. Part-olon, 32, 41-2, 45; Barats of, 55; Britannia and, 55-8; clans of Phœnicians of, 159; in A.B., 41, 43, 61; coins of Briton type in, 43, 55, 346-7; colonization by, in A.B., 43; in Carthage and Sardinia, 42; in Sleswick, 44; Phœnicians of, accomp. Brutus to Albion, 161
Cimbri (or Cymri) in Jut-land, 186
Cimmerians, as Cymri, 19 f.
Circles, on A.B. coins as on Greco-Phœnician, and on Hitto-Sumer and Trojan amulets, 237f.; re Cup-marks as sacred script, 237f.; concentric on A.B. monuments and bronze shields and tools, solar-cult as in Hitto-Sumer, 237f.
Circles, Stone, as Solar observatories of Amorite Phœnics., 216, see Stone Circles
Cists, Stone, of A.B., cup marks on and their meaning, 237f.
Citi-um or Kition, Phœnic. port of Cyprus, Phœnic. factories at, with amulet seals, as in A.B., 178, 220
City states of Phœnicians, 55, 212
Civilization in A.B., 146-7; introduced by Brito-Phœnics., 168f., 181f.
Clans, see Tribes
Clās Merddin (or Diggings of Merd, Marut or Amorites) early n. for Albion, 190, 216

# INDEX 429

Cluny, Hitto-Phœnician n. var. of Gioln, 72
Clyde, Clwydd, Clutha, Cald, river names, Sumerian meaning of, 117, 197
Clytie, w. of Brutus (?) 405
Coins of A.B. with Phœnic. legends, Aesv, 284f.; Ando, 317, 336; Att, 6; Cas, 48, 212; Catti, 6, 212; Inara, 317; Tasci, 212, 339, etc., etc., with symbols, as in Phœnician coins, 6, 284f., 339f., 346f., 349; Circles on, 237; Crosses on, 6, 237, and see Cross; Hercules on, 347; St. Michael on, 347f.; pellets on, 284; rosettes on, 284f.; Macedonian theory of, 212f., 284; Tin, of Cornwall, 335f.
Col, or Coil, king of Britons, 185
Coldrum megalithic monument (giant's tomb), 121
Colonies, British, Briton elements in, 377
Colour, complexion re race in Britain, 133f., 371
Conn-the-hundred-fighter, solar hero of Irish Scots, 109 = (?) deified solar hero Khanu of Sumers
Cor Gawr, Cymric n. of Stonehenge, 192
Corineus, Phœn. Duke of Cornwall about 1100 B.C., 154, 160-70; as Homeric Coronos Caineus, 214f., 404f.
Corn, cultivation established by Aryans, 49; introd. to A.B. presumably by Phœnics., 170; ear of, on A.B. Catti coins, 6, 213; as on Hitto-Sumer seals and Phœnic. coins, 213-4; as Cross on A.B. coins, 214, 289, 339; assocd. with goat as in Phœnic. coins, 346
Corn Spirit of Hittites worshipped in A.B., 338f., 342f.; Briton represent. of., like Hitto-Phœnic., 339f., 346f.; Origin of discovered, 340f.; Hittite origin of Dionysos as 339f.; and see Tascio
Cornwall and Cassiterides, Tin-mines of Phœnics. in, 160, 201f.; Bel-Fire rites at, 281f.; coins of Cilician and Phœnic. type in, 212f., 335f.; Tin-port of Phœnic. in., 160, 164f.; Amorite Tin-land of Sargon I. (about 2800 B.C.), as 160, 167-71, 216, 413f.; Tin A.B. coins in, 335-6
Corunna and Phœnic. trade with Britain, 170; and Hercules, 170
Coss-ini tribe in Cornwall, 202
Cotentin port of Brittany, Stone Circles and Sun-cult of, 103, 216
Cotswold Hills, 400f.
Cowrie Shells at Stonehenge, 219
Cradle-land of Aryans, Britons, Goths and Hitto-Phœnics., 8, etc.
Craig Narget stone with pre-Christian Crosses and solar emblems, 15
Cranial form in diff. races, 134f.
Creator title of Father-god in Hitto-Sumer, 252, 265
Cremation in A.B. a solar rite, 365
Crescent and Sceptre symbol, meaning of, 355
Cresset stone for sacred Fire production in Britain, 272
Crete colonized and civilized by Phœnicians, 27, 63, 161
Crô-Magnon race, of Aryan type in Wales (Gower), 224-5
Cross, in A.B., pre-Christian of Hitto-Phœnic. origin, 6f., 278, 289f., 294f.; name C. also Sumer, 290, 314; origin and meaning of C. discovered, 290f.; is invincible *Fire-sceptre* symbol of Sun-god, 250, 262, 290f.; on prehistoric A.B. monuments, 295f.; on A.B. coins, 6, 285, etc.; True C. *not* the Crucifix, 299f.; introd. into Christianity by Goths, 301f.; Resurrection by C. in A.B., 259f.
Cross, as Crucifix, only medieval, 290f., 301f.
Cross as Devil and Death banisher in A.B., as with Hitto-Sumer and Phœnics., 255f., 293f., 303, 305f., 344f.
Cross as Sceptre of Aryan Hitto-Sumer kings, 262, 290; and Sun-priests, 278-9
Cross and pre-Israelite Hittite temple of Jerusalem, 278
Cross and Resurrection in A.B., 259f., as among Amorites, Hitto-Sumers, Phœnic. and Trojans 255f., 289f.
Cross and St. Andrew, 338f.
 ,,  ,, Constantine, 300f.
 ,,  ,, St. George, 291, 304f.
 ,,  ,, St. John-the-Baptist, 273, 279f.

# 430 PHŒNICIAN ORIGIN OF BRITONS & SCOTS

Cross and St. Michael, 334f., 349f., 360, and see Tascio
„ „ St. Patrick, 327-8
„ „ Hercules (or Dionysos), 335, 339f., 346f.
„ „ Tascio, see Tascio
Cross and Sacred Animals in A.B., as in Hitto-Phœnic. Eagle, 349; Goat and Deer, 334f., 346f., Goose, 349-50; Hawk and Phœnix, 349f.; Horse, 6, etc., 285f., 339f.; Wolves and Lions, *re* 308, 334f.
Cross, Forms of, in prehistoric A.B., as with Hitto-Sumers, Phœnics. and Trojans, 290f., 294f.; Andrew's or God Indara's, 316f.; Anthony's, 299; Cassi, 49, 51, 77, 294f.; Celtic, 294f., etc.; Hittite origin, 298f.; Corn, 49, 295, 339f.; Egyptian, 250, 293f, 314; Fiery, and why so-called, 290f., 303f., 350-1, 360; St. George's, and why so called, 291f., 304f.; Gothic or Runic, 291f., 298; Grain, or Harvest, 295, 49, 339f.; Greek, 291; High, of Hitto-Sumer and Trojans, 294f., 299; Hittite, 294f., 314; Key-pattern, 295, 321; Latin, 294f., 299; Maltese, 293f.; Phœnic., 294f.; Red, 290f., 303f., 350-1f.; Resurrecting, 298f.; Revolving Sumer, 294f.; Swastika, 297f., 316f., 333.
Cross, Wood-, of Hitto-Sumer, 255f., 278-9, 291f., 311, 344f., 412
Crucifix not the True Cross, 299f.
Cruithne n. for Briton, 86; misuse for Pict, 86
Cudder (Gadir) Point in Penzance Bay, 172, 200, 207
Culdee n. of Columba's miss. to Picts and Celts, 125
Cumber or Cymr = Sumer (?), 190, 195, 228
Cumber-land, Land of Cumbers, Cymrs or (?) Sumers, 190, 228
Cumber-nauld, 198
Cumbrae Isles, 197, 208
Cunobelin, coins of, 213, 385, 391; as Belinus III., 388; as sun-worshipper, 262
Cup and ring marks in A.B. 258-9
Cup markings, prehistoric, in A.B., 15, 236f., 258f., 308; key to script of, 238f., 242-6, 253-8, 261; prayers of A.B. in., 258f.,

261; on Amorite tablet, 257-8 411-2; on Hitto-Sumer seals, 238f., 303; in Palestine, 223, 260; in Phœnic. graves, 260; on Trojan amulets, 237-8, 254-6; script of, 241f., 258-61; as source of A.B. prehistory, 236f.
Cymbeline, 143; see Cunobelin
Cymry, people of Wales and Cumberland, 190, 195, 228, 371, = (?) Sumer, or Gomer, and see Cumber
Cynewulf's Anglo-Saxon, 160
Cyprus, Phœnicians in, 175-8; Phœnic. amulet symbols in, as in A.B., 294, 316, etc.
Cyrus, St., as Phœnic. St. George, 326

Danes, a branch of Britons, 75, 186
Daniel and the Lions in A.B., Hitto-Sumer source of, 334-5, 358
Dartmoor Tin-mines *re* Phœnics. and Stone Circles, 218
Dašap Mikal, Phœn. title of Tachab, Michael Corn-Spirit in A.B. xv., 249, 341f., and see Resef.
Daši, for Tascio or Dias Corn Spirit, xv, 338, 354
Daxa, Vedic n. for Taš or Tasc, or Tax, 249, 352-4
Dead, solar orientation of face of, in A.B., 225
*Deas*, form of n. Dias or Tascio on A.B. coins, 339
Deasil, Sumerian rite in A.B., 282-3
Death, figured as Dragon, 344; as Lion, 331f.; Serpent or Wolf, 331f.; prayers for Resurrection from, in A.B., 259; wolf and lion as emblem of, 308, 334-5
Decorative Phœnic. designs in A.B. and in mod. British art, see Spirals and Key Patterns
Deer sacred in Hitto-Phœnic. as in A.B., 334f.
Demons, worshipped by aborigines, 183; banished by Aryan Cross, 305, 344f.
Diana (or Peratheа) form of Phœnic. tutelary Britannia, 45; temple of, on Ludgate Hill, 64, 184
Diarmait, solar hero of Irish Scots 109
*Dias*, n. of Phœnic. archangel on A.B. coins, xv, 338-9, 346, 353f.; on Sumer seals, XV, 353

INDEX 431

Di-Caledon, title of Picts, 117
Din-sol, n. of Michael's Mount, 281
*Dioc*, n. of Dias or Tascio of A.B. on Phœnician coins, 354
Dionysos, Corn Spirit, worshipped in A.B., 70, 339f., 347f.; by Goths, 70; by Phœnics., 70, 346f.; Hittite origin of representn., 340; Sumer orig. of n., 354
*Dks*, *Dsk* n. of Dias or Tasc of A.B. on Phœnic. coins, 249, 346, 354
Dolmens *re* Phœnics., see megaliths
Don Valley prehistoric Briton monuments, 18f.
Door, The, title of Phœnic. St. Michael, 351
Dorians as Trojans, 177f.
Doric lang. as British Gothic, 177–81
Dragon, as coalesced totems of aborigines symbolizing Death, 331, 348; as Serpent in A.B., 311; figured in Hittite seals, 344; Indara as slayer of, 319f.; Indra as slayer, 315, 324, 343, 363; St. Andrew as slayer, 319; St. George, 319–360; St. Michael, (or Tascio), 319f., 343, 359f.; Taś or Marduk as slayer of, 359
Dress, of A.B. and Goths of Hittite type, 7, 46, 113, 239, 335; hornheaddress of A.B., Goths and Anglo-Saxons of Hitto-Sumer type, 239, 245, etc.; Early Gothic or Hittite ladies' d., 7, 245, 248, etc.
Druid Circles, misnomer for Stone Circles, 225
Druid origin of trilithon temple at Stonehenge, 232; and of Keswick Circle " temple," 228
Druid religion of aborigines, lunar and antisolar, 232; human sacrifice in, 232–3; Britons proper were non-Druids, 184
Drums, prehistoric sculptured stone, with solar emblems, as Sun-wheels for rolling rite, 272
Dual cup-marks for Sun in A.B. as in Hitto-Sumer, 246f., 249f.
Dumuonii tribe of *Ceti* in A.B., 72, 173, 282
Dun, a fort or town, Sumer orig. of n., 281
Dun-Barton or Fort of Bartons or Britons, 143, 159, 170, 197, 281; seat of Brit. king Bili, 87; of Br. king Gawolon 143; of Gildas 143; found. of, abt. 990 B.C., 386; see St. Patrick
Dun-Edin (Edinburgh), 198, 408
Dwr, Cymric " Water " from Sumer. Duru, 324, and cognate with Persian Darya
Dyaus, Vedic god in A.B., 244
Dyce and its Stone Circle *re* Tezal; or Texali tribe, 357

Ea or Ia (Jah) god n. of Sumers, invoked in A.B., see Ia
Eagle, Hitto-Sumer Sun-bird in A.B, 251, 284, 349; and see Hawk; on A.B. coins, 211, 284, 349
Ear, of Barley on Catti coins as in Phœnician, 6, 339, etc.; to ear (the ground) n. derived from Sumer, 345, 361
Écossais, origin of n., 49, 215
Eddas, The, epics of British and Norse origin, 179; historicity of, 179, 410
Edinburgh, Hedins-eyio of Goths, 408; and see Dun-Edin
Euphrates r. mentioned in Vedas *re* Indra (or Andrew), 324
Egypt, Aryan kings in ancient, 12; Britannia in, 60f.; Cross in, 295, 351; Flight to, to Sun-temple of Phœnix, 280; Fire-drill n. is Sumer, 62–3; Michael-Tascio (Makhial-Reseḟ) in, 350f.; New Syrian art in, is Phœnic., 220; Phœnicians in, 39, 60–1
Egyptian origin theory of Stone Circles, 217f.
*Eisv* legend on Sun-horse A.B. coins as Sumer, 285
English, language based on British Gothic, 178f.; and remotely on Sumerian, xi., see Words; people, not a race, 138; of mixed origin, 371; see Anglo-Saxon
*Eppi*, or *Erri*, legend on A.B. coins, 261
*Er* legend on A.B. coins *re* Erakles, 349
Erc, family n. of King Part-olon or Ikr, 50, 68, 396
Eremon n. of tribe in Ireland, 395
Erin, Aryan meaning of n., 199
Esk, Exe or Isca, river n. of Trojan origin, 173–4, 198, 208

Ethel, n. derived from Sumerian, 182
Ethics of A.B. summarized in Welsh Triads
Europe, Phœnician influence on modern, 379f.

Fan, dial. for Van or Fen tribe, 99
Fates, Three, Sumer origin of n. and function, 243, 248
Father-God in A.B., see Gods in A.B.
Fel, Isle, early n. of Albion, 190, 405
Female line of descent of Picts and aborigines of Albion, 113f., 122f.
Fen, dialectic for Van and Van wolf tribe, 93
Fenes, Feins, and Fians, aboriginal origin of n., 93–5
Festivals in A.B. of Hitto-Phœnic. origin: Bel-Fire, 269f.; St. Blaze day or Candlemas, 40; St. George's Day, 306; St. John's Day, 273f.; Harvest, 341; Lammas, 354; Michaelmas, 341; Yule (or Christmas), 69
Fiery Cross in A.B., origin and meaning of, 291, 304
Fin, Finn variant of Van, 95; Finn-men in A.B., 97; place-names in Britain, 97; in Ireland, 94
Fin-land, migration of Vans to, 100f.
Fire, Bel-, in A.B., 269f.; -Cross symbol formed by crossed firesticks, 291–2; -festivals in A.B. (see Festivals); Need-F. in A.B., 271–2; Perpetual F. in A.B., 272; -priests chiefly Barat Phœnic., 3, 292, and see Magi; production of sacred F. in solar cult in A.B., 271f.; Red Cross of, 291, 304; -sticks for sacred f. by friction, 37, 271, 291f.; -torch in Part-olon's homeland, 45; -worship in A.B., 40, 184, 262f.
Fish, sacred, of resurrecting Sun in A.B., as in Hittite, 251, 308
Fish-man as god of Waters, 247, and see Neptune
Five, sacred number of Tascio St. Michael in cup-marks in A.B., as in Hitto-Sumer, xv., 6, 237, 249f., 261, 339, 347, etc.

Fleet, of Brutus, 152; of Part-olon, 76; of Phœnics., 387; of Britons in R. Fleet, 408
Flint factories "Neolithic high-grade" in A.B., Phœnic., for mining tools, 183, 218, 366
Fomor aborigines (Vans or Fenes) of Ireland, 107
Forty days' fast re Michael, 359
Fortuna goddess, as Britannia, 57, 59
France, Aryan Briton elements in, 186, 389; Cassi tribe in, 389; Catalauni in, 186, 389; Celtic elements in, 129f.; lang. in, based on Sumer, see Words, and see Brittany and map
Furniture in A.B. tombs, 145
Future Life, belief in, by A.B., as by Hitto-Phœnics., 225, 257f.

Gad, title of Phœnicians, 18, 74f., 160, 180, 197, 200f.; G. place and r. names in Britain, 200f., 397f.
Gadeni, Briton tribe, 163, 180, 197, 308, 402
Gades, or "House of Gads," Phœnic. tin-port in Spain (Cadiz), 68, 74, 159–60; as Agadir, 171; as Gadeira, 171; Brutus at, 154, 159; Duke Corineus and his Phœnician kinsmen at, 160; Hercules visited, 159; .perpetual fire at, 272; Geloni Phœnic.- Goths related to, 395; trade with A.B., 147, 222
Gadie, r. at site of Part-olon's monument in Don Valley, 17f., 403; Gadi or Gade r. names in Brit., 203, 397, 402f.
Gaditani Fretum or Frith of Gads, Roman n. for Gibraltar Straits with Pillars of Hercules, see map
Gaels or "Celts" v. Picts, 136–140; Iberian type of, 136f.
Gaelic lang., branch of British Gothic, 180
Galatia, province of the Vans or Khaldis, 99, 100–2
Galatic n. for Gaul of the Kelts or Celts, 99, 117
Gates of Night, figured on A.B. monuments and coins, as in Hitto-Sumer, 247–9, 285 (a), 308
Gawolan, Brit. king of Dunbarton, 143

# INDEX

433

Geat, var. of Goth, 180
Geleoin, clan of Part-olon " Gioln," 67-8, 170, 394f., see Geloni
Gelon, son of Hercules, 70
Geloni tribe of Goths from Gelon, 70, 395 ; worship Dionysos (Tascio), 70, 395
Genealogies of A.B. kings, 385f.
Geoffrey of Monmouth, historicity of, Chronicles of, 74, 141f., 150f.
Geographic Distribution of Phœnic. settlements in A.B. from anc. place-names with remains, 188f., 200f.
George, Sumer orig. of n., 305
George, St., of Cappadocia, of Hittites, and England, 7, 304f.; association with England discovered, 305f.; n. of Hittite Father-god Indara or Bel as slayer of Dragon by the Cross, 305-6; legend imported into A.B. by Hitto-Phœnics., 306; Red Cross of, figured and invoked in A.B., 204f. (see Cross) ; Red Cross of, in pre-Israelite Hittite temple in Jerusalem, 278 ; festival of, in A.B., 306 ; as Heavenly Husbandman, 306, 345 ; as Horus, Sun-god, 306 ; as Indara or St. Andrew, 318f.; as Geor or Gothic Indri-Thor, 320
German head-form, 134-5
Germanic " race " non-Aryan, 134f.; in Britain, 136f., 141 ; lang. derived from A.B. Gothic, 132, 157, 180f.
Germany, colonized and civilized by early Britons about 950 B.C., 157, 186 ; Aryan racial elements in, 135, 186, and see Chatti, Goth; Runic mons., absent in, 180
Getae or Goths, 8, 70, etc., 301
Giants, predecessors of Brutus in Albion as Amorites, 153f., 169, 414; in Palestine, 414; see Amorites
Giants' tombs, at old Phœnician sites, in A.B., 223, in Sardinia, 223; Stone Circles and, see Stone Circles
Gilian n. of Cassis in Babylonia, 71
Gioln or " Hitt-ite " an Amorite n. of clan of Part-olon, 32, 67f., 395
Glasgow, as Hittite n., 78 ; Cayttis' dyke at, 209; St. Mungo and sacred Fire, 272

Glass beads, Phœnic. of about 1400 B.C. at Stonehenge, etc., 219f.
Glastonbury aborig. lake-dwellings, 136
Goat, as sacred solar animal in A.B., as in Hitto-Sumer and Phœnic., 250, 286, 330, 333, 335f., 347f.; as Cymric mascot totem, 251, 333 ; as Gothic totem, origin of, 331, 333 ; as rebus for " Goth," 251, 320, 330, 332, 345f.
Goat, and Achaians, 321, 325 ; in Aken-aten's art reflected in A.B., 221, 333 ; and St. Andrew, see Unicorn
Goat and Cross in A.B., as in Hitto-Sumer and Phœnic., 308, 333-7, 347f.; in Hitto-Sumer and Phœnic. seals, 334, etc. ; on Phœnic. coins, 346 ; and Daxa of Vedas, 352-3 ; and Hittites, 7, 334, 345f. ; and Indara, 243, 251f., 334f., 346f. ; and Indra, 286, 332f., 344 ; Michael (Tas), 333f., 346f., 352 ; and Phœnician, 346f. ; and Resef (Michael), 350-3 ; and Sun, 332f. ; and Tascio, 334f., 340f. ; and Thor, 320, 330 ; and see Unicorn
Goat horns in head-dress of Goths and Hittites, 340 ; and of Tascio, 350-3
Goat, name, Sumerian, 330-1, 333
Goat Fell, with Holy Isle of Goths and Stone Circles, 197, 208
God, Aryan origin of idea of One Universal, and current in A.B., 237f., 241f., 258f., 264f., 289f., 341f. ; as Alpha and Omega 252 ; Archangel of, in A.B., 246, 341f., and see Michael; Barats, the chosen people of, 1, 262f. ; as Creator, 342f. ; Cross as symbol of, 289f. ; as Disease curer, 343f. ; Father-, of Hitto-Sumers, and Phœnics. as Bil (Bel), Ia or Iahvh or Jove, or Indara (Indra, Andrew), 2, 42, 241f., 263f., 343f., 363 ; names of, in A.B., Gothic, Greco-Roman and Sanscrit of Hitto-Sumer origin, 244f. ; 342f. ; names in Cup-marks, 241f. ; prayers to, for Resurrection, in A.B., 259f. ; 343f. ; in pre-Israelite Hittite Jerusalem, 274f. ; as Rock of Ages, 342 ; sons of, Early Aryan title, 239, 253, 348 ; Sun as symbol of, 262f.

Gomer, Hebrew n. for Sumer and Cimmerian, 193, n. in Britain, 195
Goose, sacred Sun-bird of Hitto-Phœnics. and A.B., 284-6; eating tabooed in A.B., 341; on A.B. mons., caves and coins, 284; with Cross in A.B., 350; with Cross and St. Michael on Phœn. coins, 348-9; assoc. with Michaelmas, 341
Got, proper n. for Goth, 333
Goth, properly Got, or Guti, synonym of Gad, Kud, Catti, Khatti or Hitt-ite primitive Aryans, 7, 46, 70, 179-80, 186, 330f. n. of Hitto-Sumer origin, 330-1. Goat as rebus for, 251, 320, 346; Goat-horns worn by, 340; in place-names in Brit., 205f., 397f.
Gothic, arch. and architecture, Hittite, 70; Eddas mainly British, 179
Goths, as Early Aryans, Catti or Hittites, 7, 8; Arianism of, 301, 303, 323; dress of Hittite, 7, 46, 239f., 340; horn head-dress of, 239, 245f., 340; hymns of, to the Sun, 313; introd. Cross symbol into Christianity, 301f.; language of, derived from Sumerian, and basis of English, 179, 240f., see Words; physical type of, Aryan, 136; St. Michael as defender of, 346, Indara or Andrew as Defender of, 320f.
Got-ini and Goth-ones, tribe of Goths on Rhine, 186
*gow* affix in A.B. place-names, Hittite, 78, 308
Gower, of Arthur legend, and its megaliths, 195
Gowrie, Carse of, and its megaliths, 198
Grahams', or Picts', dyke, 197, see Grime
Grain Crosses in A.B., 214, 339f.
Grain tutelary of Hitto-Sumers in A.B., see Corn Spirit
Grammatical structure of English and Gothic based on Sumer, 35, 77, etc.
Graves, Chariots interred in, A.B., 145
Greek (Hellenic) lang., a branch of Hittite or Ilannu, 177, and see Words; Cross as Hitto-Phœnic., 291
Grim's, or Grime's (= Hun's) dyke, or ditch, 197; graves, as Stone Age Huns', in Norfolk
Guad-alquivir, r. of Phœnic. prov. in Spain, 118
Guti title of Goths in Early Mesopotamia, 179, 331
Gwalia n. for Wales, 140, 203
Gyaolownie, or "Hittite," title of Part-olon in Phœnic. inscript., 32, 67f.
Gyron Cross of British heraldry, Hittite origin and n. of, 306-7

Hafr, Eddic title of Gothic soldiers, of Hittite origin, 331
Hair, colour of, of A.B. Aryan, Britons, 134, 371; of beard, 239, 245, 247; of Celts and Iberians 134; in modern Britain, 371; ladies' coiffure (Hittite) of A.B., 7, 245, 248, 250
Hammer of Indara or Indra is Andrew's "Cross," 318f.; at St. Andrew's, 326; is Thor's H., 318, 320-1
Hand of Sun-god, ceremony of taking, in Hitto-Sumer, 46, in Gothic Eddas, 47, in Vedas, 47
Hare-Stanes, megaliths, Aryan meaning of n., 235
Harri, Gothic and Hittite for "Aryan," 235
Harvest Festiv. in A.B., 341.
Harvest Spirit in A.B., as in Hitto-Sumer. 338f., 350f.; -Cross in A.B., see Corn; and St. Michael, 350f.
Harvester of Life, Aryan god-title, 256
Hat or Hatt in Brit. place-names for Khatti, Hatti or Hitt-ite, 203f., 397f.
Hatti, Semitic for Khatti or Hittite, 203
Hatton, place n. in Brit., 203f., 397f.
Hawk, Sun-, on A.B. coins, 251, 284-6, 349-50; and see Eagle
Head-form, as index of race, 133f.; of A.B., 135f., 224f., of Phœnicians as Aryan, 12, 365
Heaven, Gothic n. Himin derived from Sumer, 243, 251
Hebrides *v.* Hiberia or Iberia, 137
He-Goat n. for Father-god, 243, 251
Helena, empress, reputed Briton princess, 185

# INDEX 435

Heraldic animals and emblems, British, as sacred animals and emb. of Hitto-Phœnicians, see Animals, Cross, Gyron, Unicorn, etc.

Hercules, the Phœnic., worshipped in A.B., 44, 335, 339, 347, 349, 391; a canonized human Phœnic. hero, 266; ancestor of Geloni Goths, 70, 395; as defender of Goat (or Goth), 334-5f., 346-7; as Dionysos, 340, 346; as Lord of Tarsus, 346; as St. Michael, 334-5, 359; as Tascio on A.B. and Phœnic. coins, 339f., 346f., see Tascio; on A.B. monuments, 335f.; on Hitt-seals and mons., 334, 340; Lion of, as vanquished Death totem of aborigines, 331f., 334f., and Ogam script, 37; Phœnic. statues of, 266; Pillars of, 27f., re Britain, 147; Point of, in Severn, 195; sailings of, 406; n. on A.B. coins (?) 261, 347, 349

Heremon (? German), opponent of Part-olon in Don Valley, 395

Heria Fædr, Eddic Gothic title of human King Thor as "Aryan Father" for Heria Thor or Ar-Thur, 195, 198

Herodotus on A.B. and Phœnician Tin mines, 160

Het-land n. of Shet-land, 209

Hett or Heth or Hitt, Hebrew for Khatti (or Hitt-ite), 8, 203, 222

Hibernia v. Hiberia or Iberia, 137

Himlico, Phœnic. admiral on A.B., civilization about 500 B.C., 147

Hit or Hitt in Brit. place-names for Khatti, 8, 203f., 397f.

Hitt-ite, European coined term for Khatti, ancient imperial ruling race of Asia Minor and Syrio-Phœnicia Palestine, 5-8, 200f.; Ilannu synonym for, 69; Khilaani (or A.B. Gyaolownie or Gioln) synonym for, 67f.

Hitt-ites, or Khatti or Catti, as Arri or primitive Aryans, 6-9, 12-15, etc., see Aryans; as Amorites, 224f., see Amorites; as Ancient Britons, 15f.; as Goths, 6f., see Goths; as Indo-Aryans or Khattiyo Barats, 8f.; as Phœnicians, 8-12f.; as Sumerians, 11f.; as world-civilizers, 200, 363; worshipped Vedic gods, 14f.

Hoffmann Tablet, archaic Amorite or Ari, with key to Cup-marks, 257-8, 411f.

Hor Mazd, Sun-god n. and function and representation derived from Sumer, 242

Horned head-dress of A.B., Anglo-Saxons, and Goths derived from Hitto-Sumer, 239, 245, 250f.; origin of, in rebus or totem Goat for "Goth," 331f.

Horse, Sun-, of Hitto-Phœnic. on A.B. coins, 6, 48, 213, 347, etc.; on Phœnic. coins, 9, 347f.; Thor or Odinn's, in Brit., 286-7; -shoe for luck, solar meaning of, 287

Horse-man on A.B. coins, 213 f with legend Aesv, Eisv, 284-5, etc.

Horus, Sun-god, Aryan Sumerian n., 306

House-building in A.B. introd. by Aryan Catti-Phœnicians, 70, 170f.

Houses in A.B. of wood (Hittite Khilaani type), 69f., 170f.

Hu or Ho, dedicates Bel monument at Logie, Don Valley, 356

Hu-Gadarn, leader of 1st Cymri migration to A.B., 190, 356

Hugh, Sumer origin of n., 356

Human sacrifice in A.B. by pre-Briton aborigines, 183, 271, 331; by Druids of lunar cult, 232-3

Hun, invasion of Britain about 1070 B.C., 157; racial type, 134f., 141; in modern Britain, 136, 365

Hymns to Sun, Sumer-Phœnician, 312; Brito-Gothic, 313

Hythe or Hith, 203, 205

Ia (Iahvh or Jove) or Indara, Hitto-Sumer Father-god worshipped in A.B., 259f.; as Induru, 323f.

Iberian race-type of aborigines of Albion, 93, 119, 134f.

Icar or Ikar, personal n. of King Part-olon in his inscrip., 32, 56; a common pers. n. among Cassis of Babylonia, 50

Icht, sea of (re Ictis and Picts), 116, 121, 139, 164f., 201, 405

Ictis, Phœnician tin-port in Cornwall, 116, 164f., 201, 414

Ier, n. of Hercules (?) on A.B. coins, 347

Ikar, pers., n. of Part-olon on inscrip., 32f., 50
Ilannu or "Hittite" *re* Briton clan Uallaun or Wallon, and in Part-olon's title, 69 ; personal n. of Cassis of Babylonia, 69
*Inara* legend on A.B. coins, as Indara or Andrew, 317, 384
Indara, Father-god and Sun-god of Hitto-Sumers, worshipped in A.B., 13f., 239, 244f., 259f., 315f. ; *re* St. Andrew, 315f. ; see Andrew ; or Bel, 318 ; as Creator, 252, 315, 320, 330 ; "Cross" of, is Andrew's Cross and hammer of Thor, 315f. ; as Dragon-slayer, 315f. ; as Ia, Iahvh, or Jove, 242f., 318, 323f. ; as Indra, 315f., 320, and see Indra ; as Induru, 323f. ; as lion slayer or tamer, 326f. ; name in cup-marks, 242, 244f.; Barats, chosen people of, 1 ; Deer and, 334f. ; Goats and, 251, 334f. ; see Goat ; as Rain and Water bestower, 245, 250, 315f., 324 ; River-garlanded, 245, 324
India, Aryanized and civilized by Hitto-Phœnics., 6, 8–10, etc. ; Arya n. derived from Hitto-Phœnics., 6–8, etc. ; Aryan language in, derived from Hitto-Sumer, 6f., see Sanskrit ; Bārat title of ruling race in, identical with Brit-on, 8f., 188f. ; clan and tribal titles Bārat, Cedi, Kāśi, Khattiyo, Kshatriya or Khatri, Kuru, Panchāla, Sakya, etc., are Hitto-Phœnic., 11–14, etc. ; epics of, as source of early Aryan history, 9f. ; late civilization of, and date, 5, 11 ; Stone Circles in relation to ancient mines in, 218 ; Vedas and Vedic gods of, derived from Hittites, 10–15, etc. and see Daxa, Indra, Maruta, Nasatya, Sura, etc,
Indo-Aryan, physical type, Nordic, 132
Indo-European or Aryan languages derived from Hitto-Sumerian, 132f.
Indo-Germanic, a misnomer for Indo-European, 132
Indo-Persian, a branch of Aryan race, 136
Indra, Father-god and Sun-god of Indian Vedas, is Indara of Hitto-

Sumers, 14, 245f., 315f., and see Indara ; as Creator of Sun, 265 ; Dragon-slayer, 315 ; Lion-slayer, 332 ; Goats of, 320, 332f. ; River-garlanded, 324 ; water bestower, 315 ; as Andrew of A.B., see Andrew
Indri, title of Gothic Father-god Thor, 265, 316
Induru, Sumer n. for Father-god Indara, Bel or Ia (Iahvh or Jove) or Indra, worshipped in A.B. 242, 323f. ; n. on A.B. coins as Inara and Ando *q.v.*, and see Indara
Inscriptions in A.B., see Aryan Phœnic., 1, 16f. ; Barates, cup-marks, cipher script, 255f.; Keswick, Logie and Newton Stones, Ogam, Phœnician, Sumer, 227f., 255f.; Yarrow, 70, etc., and see Coins.
Invasions of Early Britain, by Brutus about 1103 B.C., 142, 386 ; by Huns about 1070 B.C., 157, 386 ; by Mor or Amorite Phœnics. about 2800 B.C., 415f. ; by Part-olon about 395 B.C., 1, 32f., 387 ; by Silvanus Alba about 1150 B.C., 163f.
Invasion of Ireland by Part-olon about 400 B.C., 75, 91f.
Ionic column in Hittite architect. before 1200 B.C., 334
Iran, Aryan meaning of n., 199
Ire-land or Ir-land or Erin, Aryan meaning of n., 199 ; aborigines of, 91f. ; Fins or Fens in, 94f. ; first peopling of, 91f. ; Barat place-names in, 199 ; Matriarchy in, 93f. ; New Grange or Tara prehist. solar sculptures of, 249 ; Ogam inscripts. in, 35, 75 ; Part-olon king of Scots invades, 67, 74f. ; Picts in, 122f. ; Serpent-cult in, 94f., 106f. ; Scotia, a former n. of, 112
Irish-Scots, trad. history books of, 92f.
Iron introd. into A.B. by Brutus (?), 183
Isca or Esk or Exe r. names as Trojan, 173f. ; I. names in Britain, 173, 198, 208
Italy, Phœnician Barats in, 148f., 215 ; and see Sardinia

Jah, Jahvh (Jehovah) or Jove of Aryan Sumer origin of idea and n., 239, 244–6, etc.

# INDEX

Janus type of Sun-god, 239, 247, 252; and dual Sun in A.B., 249, etc.
Jebusites, pre-Israelite Aryan Hitto-Amorite Sun-worshippers at Jerusalem, 274, 280
Jed-burgh A.B. cup-marked stonecist inscript., near cyclopean masonry, 237, 402
Jerusalem, an Aryan Hittite or Catti pre-Israelite "holy city" of Sun-god and Cross, 274f.; Amorites of, 274f.; Cross in pre-Israelite temple on Mt. Moriah, 278; Fire and Sun worship in Solomon's temple at, 276f.; Hittite or Catti temple on Mt. Moriah, 274f., 280; n. is Sumer, 274f.; pillars of Solomon's temple of Phœnic. Sun temple type, 276; Phœnic. Sun-cult image in Solomon's temp., 276; St. George and Red Cross in ancient, 279; St. John and, see John the Baptist
Jet, amulet Crosses in A.B., 378; Phœnician trade in, in A.B., 182, 222
Jews, indebtedness to, for preserving ancient scriptures, 381
John the Baptist, St., presumably an Aryan Phœnician of Sun-Cross cult, 273; baptism rite of, Aryan Sumerian and non-Judaist, 273; Bel-Fire rites on Day of, 273, 281; Cross of Sun-cult carried by, 273, 279, 288; his father Zacharias an Aryan Fire-priest at Jerusalem, 273, 277-8
Jove or Ju-piter, Sumer origin of n. and representation, 244
Ju-piter pluvius, Sumer origin of, 244; as Bel, 244-5, 324
Jute, tribal n. dialectic of Khat, Xat, Xud or Goth; branch of Catti Britons, 186
Jut-land as Goth-land, 186

Kad, title of Phœnician, dialectic of Khad or Khat, 74, 78, 173-4, 180, 200, 351, etc.
Kadesh or Qadesh, or "House of the Kads," Phœnic. city n., see Gades
Kadisha, r. of Tripolis in Phœnicia, 18; and *cp*. Gadie, Gade, etc.,

river n. in A.B., and Guad-al-quivir, near Gades, 118
Kāsi, Aryan dynastic clan of Bārat Phœnicians, 47f., 274, etc.; dynasty in Babylonia, 48f., 211; in A.B. and Don Valley, 32f., and see Kassi and Cassi; in India, 47f.
Kassi or Cassi (dialectic of Kāsi) in A.B., Europe, Mediterranean, Palestine, etc., 201f., 413; see map; a branch of Hittites or Catti, 47f., 274; Crosses of, in A.B., 51, 295f.; place-n. in A.B., 209f., see Cassi
Kassi-terides Isles, Phœnic. tin-mines in, in A.B., 161, 201f., 413-4
Kāst, city n. of Part-olon, 32, 45f.
Kasta-bala, city of Part-olon and its Fire-cult in Cilicia, 45
Kastīra, n. for tin, 201, 413
Kata-onia or Cata-onia, prov. of Cilicia, 45
Katy-euchlani, A.B. clan, 68
Kazzi, dialectic of Kassi, title of Part-olon, 32, 211
Keiss, A.B. chief's skull at, 210, 224f., 365
Keith, dialectic of Khatti or Catti, in place and personal n. in Brit., 198, 200f.; n. of earl marischal of Scotland, 185; Inch-, isle of, 198
Kelt origin of n., 99, see Celt
Kentigern, St., makes sacred fire by Phœnic. solar mode, 272, 292
Kent's Cavern, with "palæolithic" art, 121
Kerry, landing place of Part-olon at, 74, 76, *re* Garrioch
Keswick, with copper mines, Stone Circle at, 223, 226f., n. as "Abode (wick) of Kassi," 235, "Druid temple" at, 228, observation stone of circle, 226f., Sumer inscript. at, 228; Sun-rise sighting at, 230
Key patterns of Phœnics. in A.B., 182, 249, 295, etc.
Khaldis, Children of, matriarchist title of aborigines of Van, 99f., 116f., 139f., *re* Kelt and Culdee
Khatti (Catti), Xatti or "Hatti," title of imperial Hitt-ites as "cutters" or "rulers," or Axe-sceptre holders (Khatti), 8, 200, etc., see name of; as primitive Aryans, 6f., 12-15, etc.; as Arri or Aryans, founders of

GG

# 438 PHŒNICIAN ORIGIN OF BRITONS & SCOTS

Agriculture, 345f. ; Amorites, a clan of, 258, see Amorites ; as ancestors of Catti kings and rulers of A.B., 6, 8, 47f., 188f., 200f. ; Barats or Brihats, leading subtribe of, 52f. ; Cedi or Chedi, dialectic of n., 168, 262 ; as Goths, 7, 179f., 186, 315, etc., and see Guti ; Harri or Aryan title of Ilannu, syn. of, 69 ; Kassi, a clan of, 47f., 200f., see Kassi ; Khilaani (Gioln) syn. of, 69f. ; Kurus or Syrians, clan of, 12f., 188 ; Mitani or Medes, a clan of, 14, 222 ; Phœnicians leading clan of, 12, 188 ; as White Syrians, 6 ; Cappadocia chief prov. of, 70 ; Cross emblem of, 294 ; cup-marks used by, 239 ; George and Red Cross of, 304f. ; Goat emblem of, 250f., see Goat ; language Aryan, 8, etc. ; n. of, origin and meaning, 8, 200, 290, 294–6(*b*), 305, 320f., and in Indian Pali and Sanscrit, 8f., 200 ; physical type of, Gothic or Nordic Aryan, 136 ; sacred seals of, represented in A.B., 334–5f. ; Sun-worshippers with symbols as in A.B., 262f. ; Unicorn emblem of, 7, and see Unicorn ; warchariots as in A.B., 145 ; worshipped Vedic gods, with Indara and Tashup (Tascio) as in A.B., and see Catti

Khattiyo, Indian Pali form of Khatti, Catti, or Hitt-ite, 8, 200

Khilaani, synonym of Hitt-ite, source of Part-olon's clan title of "Gioln or Gyaolownie," 69, 170, 395 ; an Amorite word, 69 ; in personal and place n. in Brit., 71f.

Kidwelly or Cet-gueli, port of Ceti, Catti, or Scots, 71–2

Kil-bride, meaning of n., 107

Kil-Chattan and megaliths, 208

Kil-Martin *re* Morites or Amorites, 217

Kil-Michael and standing stones, 208

Kilikia, see Cilicia

Kings, Early Briton, Lists of, 385f. ; *ex-officio* high-priests, see Priestkings, 152f., 184, etc. ; prayers for, by Early Aryan Sumers, 312

Kition, see Citium

Kit's Coty dolmen, as Catti or Khatti, 191, 203

Kubl, Gothic n. for barrow grave as Phœnic., 54

Kumreyar or "Cumbraes" Norse n. for Arran, 197, 208

Kur, anc. n. for Asia Minor, and Syria, 12, 13

Kuru-Panchāla, Sanscrit n. for Syria-Phœnicians, 12, 13 ; as leading Bārats, 188

Kwast, or Kāst, n. of Part-olon's home in Cilicia, 32, 45


Ladies, in Anc. Britain, 71–3, 185 ; coiffure and dress of, early Aryan or Hitto-Phœnic., 3, 7, 245, 248, 250

Lake dwellings in A.B., see Barton Mere, and Glastonbury

Lake Van, as cradle-land of Vans or Wans, primitive matriarchic aborigines of Albion, 91f., 98f. ; in Wales sacred to a goddess, 96

Language, Anglo-Saxon, based on British Gothic, 179–80 ; Aryan, in Britain, introduced by Amorites, 160, 167f., by Brutus, 175f. ; Aryan, in Europe, introduced by Hitto-Phœnics., 27f. ; Aryan Phœnician script in A.B., 26f., 175 ; Briton, or British Gothic, 178f. ; Celtic, 180, Cymric, a dialect of Sumer, 190f. ; Doric, 177f. ; English, based on Sumerian, through Briton Gothic, xi., 178–81, 190, and see Words ; German, derived from Briton, 157, 186 ; Gothic, a branch of Catti or Hittite, 35f., 178f. ; Greek, br. of Hitto-Sumer, 177, and see Words ; proto-Aryan, Latin, etc., derived from Sumer, see Words ; Phœnician, Aryan, 12f. ; Sanskrit, derived from Hitto-Sumer, 8f., 11f., and see Words ; Scandinavian, or Gothic and Anglo-Saxon deriv. from Sumer, see Words ; Sumerian as proto-Aryan, and basis of English xi., 178f., 190, and see Words ; Trojan as Hitto-Phœnic., 155, 178

Language and Race, 137–8

Law codes of Ancient Britons translated by King Alfred for Anglo-Saxons, 181, 385–8 ; Roman L. based on Hitto-Sumer, 181

Laws, Brutus makes, for Britons, 175, 181

Lear, king, date of, 387
Leicester, founding of, about 850 B.C., 387
Lion, as death totem of non-Aryan aborigines, in Old World, 331 ; in Hitto-Phœnic. religion and representations as in A.B., 334-5f. ; antagonism of, with Unicorn in Brit. heraldry, meaning discovered, 329f. ; antagonist of Sun-cult, of God (Indara) ; see Indara ; sculptures of Indara (Andrew) tearing Lion, at St. Andrews, 327
Logie Stone, with votive inscription to Bel, 20 ; Ogam inscript. deciphered, 356 ; prehistoric Hitto-Phœnic. sculptures on, explained, 20, 309, 355
Loki (or Lug), Gothic Lucifer, 109 ; Sumer origin of n. and function, 344f.
London early n. of, 407f. ; founding of, by Brutus, abt. 1100 B.C., 156, 175, 407f. ; in Cæsar's day, 408–10 ; Gothic ships of, 408 ; modern, named after King Lud, 156, 410
Long Meg, Stone Circle, observation stone of, 234
Lucifer, Sumer origin of n., 344
Luck, horse-shoe for, Hitto-Gothic solar reason for, 287 ; righthanded sun-wise direction for, 287 ; wood-touching for, Hitto-Phœnic. reason for, 312
Lunnasting, pre-Christian Catti Cross monument, 77, 179
Lycaonia Barats (Phœnicians) of Cilicia, 55

Ma, mother, Sumer origin of n., 243, 248-9
Macedonia, Barat or Brito-Phœnic. colonies in ancient, 213, 405
Macedonian theory of A.B. coinage, 212f., 284
Machar, St., of Aberdeen, Phœnician tutelary, 358
Magi, Sun and Fire priests of Hitto-Sumer, 279 ; carried the Cross symbol as mace, 279 ; n. Sumer, 279 ; as The Wise Men at Epiphany, 279
Magic cauldron of Van, Wans or Fenes, 93
Maiden Stones, 107

Maltese Cross, Hitto-Phœnic. Sun-Cross, 293 ; in Pre-Christian A.B., 295
Man-God, title of Tascio, worshipped in A.B., 243 ; and see Tascio
Mar, or Mer, n. for Mor-ites or Amorites, 216, 260 ; and Amorite source of Mar and Mer names in A.B., 217, etc.
Mar or Marr, prov. between Dee and Don
Marash or Marasion, Hitto-Phœnic. city in Asia Minor, 172 ; Ogamoid inscripts. at, 36, 172
Marasion or Marazion, n. of town at Phœnic. tin-port in Cornwall, 172f., 281
Marches, riding of, re city-states, 209
Mar-duk, Hitto-Sumer deity, worshipped in A.B., 259f., 343, and see Tascio-Michael
Market Crosses, of pre-Christian Hitto-Phœnic. origin
Marriage, introduced by Aryan Hitto-Sumers, 123
Marru, variant of Mar, Muru or Amorite, 216, etc.
Martin, v. Morite or Amorite, 217
Martu, variant of Mar or Amorite, 216, 243
Maruta, or Marutu, variant of Mar or Amorite, 216, 243, 343 ; identical in Vedic Sanscrit for sea-going storm spirits and Sun-worshippers, 243
Mascots in A.B., see Animals, sacred
Matriarchy of aborigines, in Albion, 97, 103 ; in continental Europe, 103 ; in Ireland, 92f. ; of Picts, 87f., 123 ; of Vans or Wans or Fins, 93f., 98, 103f. ; in Wales, 96
Matrilinear succession among aborigines in A.B., 122f.
Mauretania, as "Land of Maruts" or Amorite Phœnicians, 216 ; Catti and Cassi place-names in, see map
May (Maia), mother-goddess of aborigines, Sumer n., 243, 249 ; May Day alignments in Stone Circles, 226, 234 ; May Day transfer of Bel-Fire rites, 271
Mazda, Ahura-, or Hor-mazd, n. of Sumer origin, 242
Mediterranean, race or Iberians, in A.B., 134-6 ; Phœnic. and Barat

Cassi and Catti colonies in, see map; straits of, as "Frith of the Gads" or Phœnics., 159 and see map
Megaliths, re Phœnic. mine-workings in A.B., 217f.; in Brittany, 216; in Phœnicia and Palestine, 222f.; spread by Phœnics, 217f.; see Stone Circles
Mer, dialectic for Mar, Martu or Amorite, 190, 216, 243, 260; cup-marked tombstone of prehistoric, in A.B., 260; Diggings of the, early n. for Britain, 190, 216
Mercury's rod derived from Sumer, 239, 242, 245, 412
Merddin, Clās-, or "Diggings of Merd, Maruts, Mer or Mars, ancient n. for Albion, 216
Merlin and Stonehenge tri-lithon temple, 232f.
Metapontum, Bruttii Phœnics., 214; Corn on coins of, as in A.B., 214
Mesopotamia, Phœnicians in early, 13
Michael, St., the Archangel, worshipped by Sumers, Hitto-Phœnics. and Trojans, as in A.B., 249f., 334-5f., 349; blessing of, invoked by Phœnics. and Britons, as by King Alfred and English Prayer-book, 341, 343, 351f., 360-1; Cross of, in Hitto-Phœnic. Trojan and A.B., 357f.; Door of Heaven title of, in Sumer, 351, 359; Dragon-slayer in Hitto-Sumer, as in A.B., 319-20, 343; saves Goats as "Goths" from Lion and Wolf tribe totems in A.B., as in Hitto-Phœnic., 334-7, 352f.; Goose of, in Phœnic., as in A.B., 359f.; Phœnic. n. Miklu and Dashup-Mikal, 249, 338f., 341; Resurrector of Dead title of, in Hitto-Sumer, Trojan and A.B., 255f., 259f., 359, 412; Phœnix, Sun-bird of, in Phœnicia and A.B., 349-50, saves by Cross in Hitto-Sumer, Troj. and A.B., 256f., 360; Spear of, 354f.; shrines, prehistoric of, in A.B., 360; Wells, sacred, of, 341, 357f., 360; and see Tascio
Michaelmas, Hitto-Sumer origin of, and of n., 341; pre-Christian festival of, in A.B., 341f.

Michael's Mount, St., Tin port of Phœnics. in Cornwall, 164-5; Fire festivals at, 281; Ictis n. of, 164f., 414; Sun-temple at, 281
Mictis, n. for Phœn. Tin-port in A.B., 414; see Ictis
Midsummer Day, Hitto-Phœnic. solar festival of, in A.B., 225
Migration, prehistoric, of Vans or Fens from Asia Minor to Albion, 98f., 104f.; to Ireland, 91, 104f.
Miklu, n. of Michael on Phœnic. coins, 349
Mines of Phœnic. and Stone Circles, 218f.
Minos, king of Crete, a Phœnic., 161
Minting in A.B., 144, see Coins, and Segon, Selsey, Verulam, etc.
Mitani, Mittani or Midtani·, or Medes, as Arri or Aryan confederates of Hittites, 14, 222
Mithra, Sun-cult in A.B., 46, in Cilicia, 57
Mixing of races in British Isles, 141
Monotheism, idea of, origd. by Aryan Hittites, 263f., 303f., of A.B., 183f.; of Phœnics., 1, 13, 183, 263f.; of Aken-aten as Phœnician, and in A.B., 221, 265f.
Monuments, destruction of pre-Christian Briton, 35
Mor, dialectic of Mar, Marru, Muru or Martu, or "Amorite," 216, 257, etc.; in place-names in Britain, 216-17
Moray Firth and Morites, 217
Mor-bihan (or Little Mor) in Brittany, with megaliths and Sun-cult (Amorite), 103, 216
More-cambe Bay and Morites, 217
More-dun and Mori-dun and Moriton, 217
Moriah, n. of Palestine and Mt. of Jerusalem, as Amorite or Aryan, 274f.
Mor-Maer, clan chiefs in Moray and Aberdeen, re Mors
Morocco, mod. n. of Mauret-ania or Land of Maruts or Amorite Phœnic., with megaliths, 216
Morton, 217
Mungo, St., see Kentigern, 272
Murray, pers. n., re Marru or Muru, Amorite, 217
Muru, or Amorite, 257f.; Cup-marked tombstone of, in A.B., 260

# INDEX

Names, persistence of, anc. ethnic and place, 189; surnames in Brit. derived from Phœnic., 215
Nas-atya, Vedic n. of dual Sun from Sumer, 242 ; and represented in A.B., 237, 242, 249
Nazir, or devotee, Sumer origin of, 273
Necklaces of Phœnic. beads in A.B. about 1400 B.C., 220
Need, sacred Fires, in Brit. produced by Hitto-Phœn. way, 37, 271f.
Nennius' (Ninian's) Briton Chronicle, 74, 143
Neolithic high-grade Flints and culture introd. by Phœnics., 183, 218, 366
Neptune, Hitto-Phœn. origin of idea, n. and represent., 58
Newton Stone, Phœnic. inscripts. on, 1, 16, 28f. ; date of, 33f. ; decipherment of, 26f. ; Ogam inscriptn. on, 30f.
Night, Gates of, pictured in A.B. coins and monuments as in Hitto-Phœnic., 247-9, 308
Nina, Aryan Amorite sun-priestess, prayer of abt. 4000 B.C., with Cup-marks, as in A.B., 257f., 411f.
Nine Maidens, origin of, 106-7
Nin-girsu, n. for Taši or Tascio of A.B., 354
Nordic race as Aryan or Gothic, 134f.
Normans, branch of British Goths, 215
Norse and Swede, Aryan Gothic type of, 135
Norse relations with prehistoric Brito-Phœnics. re amber trade, 171, 218
Northumbrian dialect of Anglo-Sax. as Briton dialect, 179-80
Numbers, occult values of, in Cup-marks, etc., 242f.
Numerals, English names of, derived from Sumer, 240f.
Nursery rhyme, English words of Sumer origin, 242

Oannes, Phœnician Noah, in Cornwall(?), 193
Observation table-stone in Stone Circles in Brit., 226f., 231f. ; Sunrise sighting by, 230

Observatories, solar, of Phœnics. in A.B., 216f.
Oddendale, Stone Circles, 234
Oddin's or Thor's horse, the Sun-horse of Hitto-Phœnics., 286-7
Ogam, a Phœnic. solar script, 37 ; inscripts. at Brittenden, 44 ; in Ireland, 35 ; at Logie, 20 ; at Lunasting, 77, 179, 209 ; at Newton, 30f. ; at Silchester, 44 ; in Wales, BOI., 98 ; origin of, 35f. ; Sumerian affinity of, 36
Ogamoid inscript., in Hittite, 36
Olon or Aulaun or Wallon, A.B. tribal and pers. n. as "Hittite," 69f.
Omega, n. derived from Sumer, 252
Ope (Lat. *oppidum*), Cassi affix for town(?), 202
Orientation, of avenues of Stone Circles, 225 ; of faces of A.B. dead, 225, 262 ; of Observation Stone in Circles, 226f.
Orkney and A.B. Phœnics., 35, 76
Ottadini tribe in A.B., 163
Ouse, river n. of Phœnic. origin, 174

Panch-āla, Vedic n. for Phœnics., 1, 12f., 188
Pani, Vedic n. for Van, Fen or Biani aborigines of Van, 99
Palestine or "Land of Moriah or Amorites," Aryan Hittites or Amorites as rulers in pre-Israelite. see Amorite, Moriah and Jerusalem
Paradise, solar, of the Amorites, Sumers and Trojans, as in A.B., 257-60, 412
Parat, or Part, n. for Phœnic. Barat, 53
Parthenia, n. for Tarsus, 54, 58
Parthini tribe, in Macedonia, 158, 213, 405
Parthenos, n. for Britannia or Diana, 64
Partholoim, 82, see Part-olon
Part-olon, Aryan Phœnician "King-of-the-Scots" about 400 B.C., 2, 32, 38f., 52f., 67, 74 ; date of arrival in Brit., 387 ; date of inscription of, 33f. ; Bar-clensis title of, 78 ; as Bel worshipper, 1, 32f. ; as Briton and Scot, 2, 32, 52, 67, 74, 86 ; as Cassi clan, 47f. ; as Cath-luan, 394f. ; as

Cilician, 2, 32, 41f.; civilizes N. Brit., 67, 79, 81; at Garrioch, 76, 84; conquers and civilizes Ireland, 67, 74f., 91f.; Kastabala, birth place of, at, 46f.; n. a clan title, 52f., 57f.; personal n. Ikar or Icar, 50; monument of, at Newton, 16f., 32f.; in Orkneys, 75f.; Prat or Prwt. title of, 32f.; as Phœnic., 38f.; Sera or Sru title of, 78; local survival of n., 81f.; swastika of, 29f.

Pataikoi, Greek, n. for Picts *re* Phœnics., 267

Patrick, St., the Scot of Dun-Barton, 106, 328; Cat title of (= Catti), 106; Cross of Hitto-Phœnic. type (not a crucifix), 327; St. Michael and, 360; Serpent, banishing of, 106, 328; Sun and Fire worship of, 328

Paviland cave, Crô-magnon man of, proto-Aryan, 224

Pegasus, Sun-horse of Phœnics. on A.B. coins, 6, 213, 285; and see Horse of Sun

Peirithoos, Homeric hero, as Brutus the Trojan, 404f.

Penicuik, 198

Pent, or Pett, n. of Picts, 96f., 116

Pent-land or Pett-land, n. of Scotland of the Picts, 96f., 116

Penzance n. *re* Phœnician, 164; anc. n. Burriton, 164; tin mines of, seat of Bel-Fire cult, 282

Perathea, n. of Britannia or Diana at Part-olon's birth-place, 45

Persian Fire Cult and A.B., 184

Personal British surnames derived from Phœnician Catti or Gad and Mor titles, 215

Peru, Phœnic. solar cult in, 298

Peter, St., as an Aryan Sidonian Phœnician, 322–3

Philistines, a branch of Phœnicians, 309; swastika on coins of, of A.B. type, 30–10

Phœnice n., as general n. for Phœnic. ports in Mediterranean, 146, and see map

Phœnician, origin and meaning of n., 12f., 39f., and *cp.* Phœnix Sun-bird as rebus n., 211, 251, 349–50

Phœnicians, Arri or Aryans in race, 1, 12f.; as Amorites, 13, and see Amorites; as leading Barats or Brihats, 1, 32, 53, 188; as Cassi, Catti, Khatti, Cedi, Gad, or Goths, variants of " Hittite," see these heads; as Sumerians 13, 33, 190

Phœnicians, arrival of, in Albion, 160, 167, etc.; agriculture in A.B. estab. by, 170; art motives of, in A.B., 221, and see A.B. Coins and Monuments, Crosses, Key-patterns, Spirals; beads of, of 1400 B.C., in A.B., 219f.; Bel-cult of, in A.B, see Bel; Bronze Age in A.B. introd. by, 183; Bronze monopoly of, 201; Coins of, represented in A.B., with legends and symbols, 6, 284f. 339f., 346f., 349; Fire (sacred), making of, in A.B., 292f.; Flint factories, Neolithic, high grade of, in A.B., 183, 218, 366; house-building in A.B. by, 69, 170f.; inscripts. in A.B., 26f., 30f., 43, 356; and see Cup-marks and Sumerian; language of, Aryan, 26f., 32f., etc.; n. for Picts, 267; physical type of, Aryan, 12, 365; script of, Aryan, 26f.; " Semitic " script of, 27

Phœnicians, erect Stone Circles in A.B., 217f.; as leading Sun-worshippers, as in A.B., 13, 262f.; as Tin-workers in A.B., 159f., and see Amorites, Cassiterides and Tin

Phœnicians as World Civilizers, 1, etc.; and world-distributors of culture, 217f.

Phœnix Sun-bird on A.B. coins and monuments and in place-names, 39f., 211, 251, 348f., and *cp.* 286f.n.

Phrygian cap of A.B. and Goths is Hittite, 6–7, 47, 247, 340

Pict, n. 114f., 117f.

Pictavia, and Picts, 118, 139, 154; a n. for Scotland, 118

Picts, as Iberian aborigines of British Isles, 90, 111f., 119f.; as primitive Basques, 115, 154; as " Blue-Legs," 115; as " Celts," 113; as Khaldis, 116f.; as Vans, Wans, Vend, Fen, Fenes or Finns, 115f., 125f.; Fidga, n. of, 119f.; Icht, Ictis or Victis, n. of, 121f.; Cruithne v. P., 86; in Don Valley, 90; in England, 118–20; in Ireland, 119f.; in

INDEX 443

Scotland, 118 ; in Spain, 115 ; in Scythia, 395 ; Brude kings of P. as Aryans, 85f., 394 ; matriarchy of, 113f., 122f. ; Phœn. n. for, 267
Picts, origin of, 111f., 117f. ; cave-dwellings of, 90, 101–113f. ; disappearance of, 113f. ; physical type of, River-bed or Iberian, 119f. ; place-names of, 114, 116–23, 199, 203–4 ; settlements of, sep. from Britons, 203–4 ; wall or dyke of, 97, 197 ; and see Wans' dykes
Pixies, as Picts, 113f., 125, 168 ; grindstones of, 125
Place-names as sources of history, 189 ; see Barat, Cassi, Catti, Mor, Pict, Sumer and Van place-names ; and river-names
Plough, n. in Old Eng. "ear" is Hitto-Sumer, 345, 361 ; invented by early Aryan Hittites, 49, 340, 348, 354f. ; a sacred place of sanctuary in A.B. (G.C., 3, 17), and of the Cross, 49 ; n. Ar is basis of title Arri or Aryan (q.v.) and Corn-Spirit, 345, etc. ; Tascio as patron of, 361, and see Tascio
Ploughing, originated by Aryans and introd. into A.B. by Phœnics., 170 ; a sacred rite under the Cross of Sumerians and Cassis, 49, 214 ; and see Corn Crosses on A.B. coins, 214f., 339 : Phœnician tutelary of, in A.B., 338f. ; and see Corn-Spirit
Polyandry in A.B. among aborigines, 113
Pottery, decorated "Celtic," is Brit.-Phœnic., 182
Prat or Prydi, a Phœnic. form of Barat or Prydain or Briton, 32, 52f.
Prayers by prehistoric Britons, 258f., 261 ; for kings by Early Aryans, 312
Pretanikai, n. for Brit. Isles, 54, 146 ; Pretan-oi, n. for Britons, 54, 146
Priests, Kings ex-officio, in A.B. as with Hitto-Sumers, 152, 155, 184, 292, 340
Prydain, Cymri for Barat-on or Brit-on, 53, 170, 191
Psychology of Aryans, Iberians and Celts, 375–6

Public works of A.B., 182, 191f., 204f.
Pytheas, Phœnic. mariner, on A.B. civilization, about 350 B.C., 146–7

Q. and P. "Celts," 86
Qadi, variant of Kad or Gad for Phœnicians ; Qadi, n. of Goths in Moravia, 186
Qass, variant for Cassi, in Partolon's Ogam inscrip., 32, 211
Queens in A.B., 386–8 ; Queen Martia's code of A.B. Law, abt. 350 B.C., 388
Querns in late Neolithic Age in A.B., Phœnician (?)
Quicken (or Life-giving) Ash, or Rowan, sacred wood of Gothic Sun-Cross, 311

Ra, Egyptian Sun-god n., derived from Sumer, 242, 246 ; Ra-vi Sun-god of Vedas, 247, from Sumer
Race, Aryan, physical type of, 134f. ; Briton, 134f. ; Celtic or Alpine, 134f., 138f. ; "British Celtic," 133, 139 ; Germanic in Britain, 134f., 136, 365 ; Iberian, 134f. ; Pict, 111f. ; River-bed 134f. ; and Civilization, 168, 363, 381 ; and Language, 133, 137–8
Raven, evil spirit of Hittites and Goths, 344
Red Cross of St. George in A.B., 304f.
Red hair, as Aryan trait, 134, 371
Red Man of Gower, 224
Red Sea Shells (Phœnician ?) at Stonehenge Circle
Regni, A.B. tribe at Chichester, Sussex, 391, and see Ricon
Religion, Aboriginal, in Albion, animistic demonolatry of matriarchist Serpent-cult, 94, 107f., 124, 183, 271, 311, 331 ; cauldrons (witches') in, 94–5, 104–6 ; human sacrifice in, 183, 232f.
Religion of Ancient Britons, Aryan monotheism with Sun symbols of Hitto-Phœnician and Trojan type, 183f., 262f., 287f., 315f., 338f., see God (Aryan), Cross and "Sun-worship" ; Baptism in, 273 ; Corn-Spirit as Archangel Michael of Hitto-Phœnics. in,

338f.; and see Archangel and Corn-Spirit and Tascio-Michael; Cross as symb. of God in A.B., and devil and death-banisher, see Cross; Father-god in A.B., 264f., and see God, Bel, and Indara; Future Life, belief in, in A.B., 225, 257f.; God names in A.B. identical with Hitto-Phœnician, 241f., 317, 336, and see Michael; Orientation of Dead in A.B., 225, 262; Prayers of prehistoric Britons, 258f.; Resurrection from Dead by Cross in, 258f., 308f., 343, 359; Righteousness an ideal of, 262, 312; symbols of, identical with Hitto-Phœn. and Trojan, 262f., 289f., 315f.; Sts. Andrew, George, Michael in A.B., see these names, and Bel, Cross, Indara and Tascio, Paradise and Sun-worship

Resef, Egyptian n. for Tascif of A.B., 339, see Tascio

Resurrection from Dead in A.B., belief in, 256f., 308f., 343, 359

*Ricon*, Tascio-, n. on A.B. coins, 385, 391, *cp.* Rigg

Rigg, or Ric, British Gothic n. for Rex, Raja or king, 227; Castle R., n. for Keswick Stone Circle, 226

Rings, concentric, and cups, as prehistoric rock and stone marks, 258f., 287

Rings, concentric, on coins and monuments, 237-9, 341f.

River-bed race, as Picts, 120-2, 134-6; physical type of, 134f.

River names, Aryan, in A.B. conferred by Hitto-Phœnics., 172-4; and see Avon, Esk, Ouse, Tamar, Thames, Usk, Clyde, etc., 117, 197

Roads, so-called Roman, as A.B., 182, 191f., 204f., and see Watling St., etc.

Roman Cross, of Hittite origin, 299

Roman invasion of Britain, Cæsar's, *re* A.B. civilization, see Cæsar

Roman roads, as Briton, 182, 191, 204f.; ships inferior to Brittany and (?) British, 103

Rome, sacked by Briton king Brennus of Gaul, 34, 389

Rood-loft and screens, *re* pre-Christ. Gothic Cross, 311

Rosettes on A.B. coins and mons., 284

Rowan or Quicken Ash as Tree of Life of Hittites and Goths, 311; as devil-banishing wood of Sun-Cross, 311

Rufina, Briton lady in Roman society, 185

Runes, Gothic script allied to, and Phœnic., 178; common in Britain and Scandinavia, 180; non-Teutonic, absent in Germany, 180

Ruthwell Cross with Sun-hawk and Solar emblems *re* Cadmon, 180

*Rvii*, n. on A.B. coins, 392


Sacæ or Sakai Goths as Sax-ons, Hittite origin and meaning of n., 331, and see Zag synonym of Khat or Khatti

Sacred Fire produced in A.B. by Hitto-Phœnic. mode, 271f.

Sacred wells of St. Michael in A.B., Phœnician, 341

Sacrifices, human, by aborigines of Albion, 183, 232, 271, 331

Sægon, A.B. clan, worshippers of Hercules, 44; coins of, 261, 391

Sagas, Hitto-Amorite tribe in Syria Phœnicia (as Sax-ons ?), 331

Saints, patron, etc., see Andrew, Bartholomew, Blaze, Britannia, George, John, Michael, Patrick, Peter

Sakka, Vedic god in A.B., 244, and see Sig

Sakya, clan of Khattiyo, Catti, Aryans, of Buddha, as Sacæ or Sax-ons, 331

Sanctuary rights in A.B. at a Plough (G.C. 3, 17) *re* Hittite St. Michael-Tascio and Cross, 49, 340f.

Sanskrit, derived from Sumer, xi., 8f., etc., and see India, Vedas and Words

Saras R. of Cilicia, of Tarsus delta, the Vedic Saras-wati R. of the Barats and Barati, or Britannia 58

Sardinia, Amorite Phœnic. colony, Barat tombs in, 52f., giant's tombs in, 223; Stone Circles, 223

Sargon I. of Akkad, abt. 2800 B.C., and Tin mines of Cornwall, 160, 169, 171, 216, 413f.

# INDEX 445

Sarmatians as proto-Germans, 139
Satan of Hitto-Sumers, as Loki or Lucifer, 344
Saxons as Sacæ, Scyths or Goths, 331; as branch of Britons, 186; n. has battle-axe symbol Khat or Zag for Catti or Scyth, 320
Scandinavians or Sit(-ones) as Cati or Catti Goths, 186
Scot, meaning of n. discovered, as Xat or Khat (or "Cutter, Scotcher" or "Axe-Sceptre Wielder," i.e., rulers), 8, 200, 209, 290, 294-6(b), 305, 320f.; dialectic variants of, Cat, Caith, Catti, Cet, Ceti, Got or Goth, Hat, Het, Hit, Khat, Keith, Kit, Scyth, Shet, Sit, Xat, Zet, see these names; as Ecossais or Cassi, 49f.
Scotia, n. for Ireland, 122
Scotland for N.B., late origin and date of n., 113
Scots, properly so-called (Aryan) relatively few, 371; modern so-called, largely mixed and non-Aryan, 374; identity with Cassi and Catti Aryans, 34; first appear. under n., in classic hist., 112; in Scotland abt. 400 B.C., 34, 81f., etc.; in prehistoric England as Catti, (q.v.); as civilizers of Ireland, 91f.; Phœnic. orig. of, 39, 67f., etc.; relations of, with Picts., 89f.
Script, Aryan, 27f.; Aryan Phœnician, 26f.; Ogam as Hitto-Phœnician, 35f.; Runic or Gothic in Britain and Scandinavia, 178, 180, and absent in Germany, 180; Semitic Phœnic., 27, 33; Sumerian as proto-Aryan, 27f.
Scyths or Skuth-oi, as Goths, 8, 322f.; Indo-, Gothic arch of, 2nd cent. A.D., 70; St. Andrew, apostle and patron saint of, 315f.
Sea-faring aptitude of Phœnics. inherited by Britons, 383; -ports of Phœnics., 44, etc.
Segon, Sægon or Segonti, A.B. clan, worshippers of Hercules, 44; coins of, 261, 391
Seal-cylinders, sacred, of Hitto-Sumers and Phœnics. as sources of A.B. history, 244f.; with Cross and Sun symbols on wrists of dead, as amulets for resurrecon paralleled in A.B., 254f.

Selgovæ, A.B. tribe of Galloway as Cilician Phœnics., 44, 97
Selsey, Phœnic. inscribed coin of, 43-4, 174
Serpent, as totem of pre-Briton aborigines of Albion and Ireland, 106f., 125, 183; of Picts, 119, 124; of Vans, Wans or Finns, 94, 104f.; -rod, see Caduceus; St. Brigit and, 106; St. Patrick and, 106, 328; symbol of Death, 311
Settlements of Early Britons separate from aborigines, 203-4
Shap, Stone Circles of, 225, 234
Shepherd, title of early Aryan kings, and n. of Sumer origin, 262
Shet-land, meaning of n., 77, 209; Khatti or Xatti inscripts. at, 77, 209
Ships, hundred-oar, of early Phœnic., 13; Brutus' fleet of, 152; Part-olon's fleet of, 78; Phœnician fleets of, 387; Long, of Briton Goths, 408
Sibyl, Sumer origin of n., 243, 248
Sidon, Arianism (Gothic) of Early Christians at, 323; Coast of Tyre and S., visited by Christ with miracle, 323; followers of Christ from Tyre and, 323; Phœnicians accompany Brutus to Albion, 160; Sts. Andrew and Peter of(?), 322
Sig, Gothic n. for Father-god, from Sumer, 244, 330
Silchester, cap. of Segonti tribe with Hercules mon., 44
Silik title of Cilician Phœnics., 42; equivalents in A.B., 42f.
Silures A.B. tribe re Phœnics., 50-1
Silvius Alba, dominates Albion about 1150 B.C., 162f.
Sit-ones, n. for Scandinavians, 186
Skin-clad aborig. of Albion, 113, 168
Skiri-Jōn, Gothic n. for John-the-Baptist, 273
Sles-wick (of Angles and Jutes) as Phœnic. colony, 44
Sol, n. for Sun, derived from Sumer, 242, 247, 412
Solar cult, symbols, etc., see Sun
Solomon's temple, Phœnic. Bel pillars of, 276; Sun-worship in, 276f.
Somerset re Sumers, 195, 208
Solstice, mid-summer, and Bel-Fire festivals in A.B., 225; Stone Circles as observatories for fixing date of, 225f.

Spain, Phœnic. clans in, *re* A.B., 160 ; Early Phœn. trade of, with A.B. in Tin, Copper, Amber and Jet, 222 ; and see Gades, Caphtor and Cat-alonia

Spectacles, emblem of A.B. monuments, its Hitto-Phœn. solar meaning, 20, 247, 309, 355

Spiral ornaments, origin and solar meaning disclosed, 247f., 287, 307-8

*Ssil*, Phœnic. leg. on A.B. Coin, 43

St. Michael's Mount, Tin port of Phœnicians in A.B., see Michael's Mount

Stone Circles, as Amorite Phœnician Solar observatories, 167, 169, 216-9, 222-4 ; avenues orient. of, 225 ; burials in, 225 ; in Amorite Palestine, 222 ; in Brit., 216, 219 ; in India, 218, 223 ; in Persia, 223f. ; in Phœnicia, 222f. ; in Sardinia, 223 ; in Tripoli, 223 ; date of, 224 ; Egyptian theory of, 217 ; May Day alignment in, 226, 234 ; observation stones in, 226f. ; purpose of, 225f., 234 ; relation to anc. Phœn. mines, 218f. ; relation to Barat, Cassi, Catti and Mor names, 224 ; sacred as Law Courts, 235 ; Sumerian marks on observ. stones, 228, 231-2 ; Summer Solstice alignt., 225f. ; Sunrise sighting of, 230f. ; see Keswick, Long Meg, Shap, Stonehenge, Don Valley, 20, 309; Michael's Mount 281, etc.

Stone drums, prehist., graved with Solar symbs. in A.B., 272

Stonehenge, Stone Circle, 192 ; Friar's heel at, use of, 233-4 ; mode of Sunrise sighting at, 230 ; observation stone at, 231-2 ; Phœnician beads of 1400 B.C. at, 219-20 ; Trilithon temple at, Druidical, 232-3 ; Tyrian Shells at, 219

Strath-Clyde, or Cambreis, A.B. kingdom of, 112

Subterranean dwellings of Picts, 90f. ; of Vans, Wans, Bians or Fens, 101f.

Sumer, a n. of Early Mesopotamia 190 ; as n. Cumber or Cambreis in A.B., 190f.

Sumerian, a title for civilizers of Early Mesopotamia, 11f. ; a branch of Aryan Khatti or Hittites, 13f., 33, etc. ; as Amorites, 13f. ; as Cymri in A.B., 190f. ; as Early Phœnicians, 13f. ; as Gomer in A.B., 193-5 ; language as proto-Aryan and basis of English, xi., 27f., 411-2 ; and see Words ; n. in A.B. placenames, 190, 195, 197-8, 208 ; script in A.B., 227f., 249, and see cup-marks, 238f.

Sun, adored in A.B. as by Early Aryans, Hitto-Sumers, Phœnics. and Trojans, and by same names, 262f. ; anthropomorphic, 2, 46, 239f. ; as Bel in A.B., as in Hitto-Sumer, 1f., 32f., 309f. ; dual form in A.B. as in Hitto-Sumer, day and night, 247f. ; Gates of Night of, in A.B. as in Hitto-Sumer, 247-8 ; hymns and prayers to, in A.B. as in Hitto-Sumer and Trojan, 259f., 312f. ; Resurrecting, invoked for Resurrect. from Dead in A.B. as in Hitto-Sumer and Trojan, 249, 259f., 289f. ; son of the, title, 47 ; Symbols of, in A.B. as in Hitto-Sumer, Phœnic. and Trojan, see Bel, Sun-bird, coins A.B., Cross Circles, Fire, Goat, Horse, Spectacles, Spirals, Swastika, symbols, Tascio and Wheel

Sun Bird in A.B. as in Hitto-Sumer and Phœnic., see Eagle, Goose, Hawk, Phœnix

Sun-Crosses in A.B., see Cross, Fiery C. and Red C.

Sun-god, Bel, 3, etc., see Bel and Sun

Sun heroes in A.B., see Tascio ; in Ireland, 124

Sun horse, see Horse

Sun-priests, see Magi, Priest-kings ; -priestesses, Amorite and Phœnician, 3, 411f.

Sun symbols, see Symbols

Sun-wise lucky direction in A.B. as in Hitto-Phœnic., 282-3

Sun-worship, so called, in A.B. as with Hitto-Phœns., 183f., 258f., 261f. ; in Brittany, 103, 216 ; in Don Valley, 20, 29, etc. ; at St. Michael's Mount, (Phœnic. tin-port) of Phœn. type, 264f. ; on Coins (*q.v.*) ; Fire-production for, in A.B. by Phœnic. mode, 37, 271f. ; forbidden in A.B.

## INDEX

by Canute, etc.; introd. A.B. by Phœnics., 264; Sts. Andrew, Blaze, George, John and Patrick, and see names; Symbols of, see symbols
Surnames in Britain of tribal and racial significance, 215
Swastika, origin and meaning disclosed as Revolving Sun-Cross, 293f., 298f.; in A.B. as in Hitto-Sumer., Phœnic. and Trojan, 3, 294f., 340f.; on A.B. monuments and coins, 15, 29, 237, 295f., 308f.: forms of, 294-5f., 307f.; reversed as Resurrecting Sun, 238, 298f.; world-spread by Phœnics., 298
Symbols, sacred, on A.B. monuments and coins, as in Hitto-Phœn., see Bird-, Circles, Crescent and Sceptre, Cross, Cup-marks, Fire, Goat, Horse, Lion and Unicorn, Serpent, Spectacles, Sun, Swastika and Wheel
Syria (Kur), n. for Asia Minor of Hittites, 12f., 188, 195
Syrians, White, n. for Hittites, 6

Taboo of Goose in Sun-cult of A.B., 341
*Tachab*, n. of Hittite Corn-Spirit Tashab in Ogam inscript. in Don Valley, 20, 309, 355
Taizal, n. of A.B. tribe in Aberdeenshire, 357
Tamar R., a Phœnic. n., 173
Tara, ancient Irish-Scot cap. n., dual Hitto-Phœnician Sun signs at, 249; Solar Hitto-Phœn. spirals at, 187, 249; Sun Crosses of Hitt. Phœns. at, 187; Sun and the Gates of Night, of Hitt. type at, 249
Tarshish, Amorite Phœn. port as Tarsus, 41, 58, 68; relations with, A.B., 414
Tarsus, Amorite Phœn. port, 41, 58f., 68, 395; chief port of Barats, 58; coins (Phœnic.) of, of same type and legend as A.B., 259, 354, 346-7f.; home of Britannia or Barati cult, 58; Hercules as " lord of," 346; as Parthenai, 58; Traicia, of Part-olon's tradn. (?), 68
Tarz, anc. n. of Tarsus, 68, 394; Bel worship at, as in A.B., 346

*Tas*, n. of Hitt. Corn-Spirit in A.B., as in Sumer Tās and Tasi, 251, 353f.
*Tascif*, n. on A.B. coins for Hittite Corn-Spirit Tašap or Tashup, 339
*Tascio* and *Tasc*, legend on A.B. coins for Tās, Taši or Tax Corn-Spirit of Hitto-Sumers, 261, 339f., 342f., 346-8, 354-62, 389-391; on A.B. monuments, 335f.; as Archangel Mikal of Phœnics., see Michael; Dasap Mikal of Phœns., xv., 341f.; as Dionysos, (*q.v.*); as Hercules, 334-7, 391, and Cross, see Cross; in A.B. cup-marks, invoked, 243, 249-50, 259f.; in Egypt, 350f.; in Indian Vedas, 352-4; in Jerusalem 275; n. variation in spelling in A.B., 353; in Sumerian, 353-4; and Plough, 340, 343, and see Plough; Resurrector from Dead in A.B., 259, 343, 359; as St. Michael (*q.v.*); Worship of, in A.B., 338-362; worshipped by Cassis and Hittites, 340, 356; and see Dias
Tasciovanus, supposititious king of A.B., 389-91
Tašia, as " Man-god of Indara," or Intermediary angel, 243
Task, spirit n. in Scots = A.B. Tascio, 354
Tax, variant n. for Tascio
Teshub or Teshup, Semitic for Tašia, Taš-ub or " Tash of the Plough," see Tascio
Teutonic or Germanic, linguistic and racial misuse of term, 134; inapplic. to British and Scandinav. race and langs., 134f.
Texal, or Texalon, n. of A.B. tribe in Aberdeenshire, 357
Thames, R., n. derived from Thyamis R. of Brutus' prov., 174, 202; Caty-euchlani or Catuallauni A.B. tribe on, 200, 207, 210-2
Thor, Gothic Father-god in A.B., 316f.; Sumer orig. of n. as title of Bel, 318; as Indri or Eindri = Indara, 316f.; as Dragon slayer = Indara or St. George, 320f.; Goats and, *re* Indara (Indra) and, 243, 251, 331f., 344; hammer of, *re* Indra's or Indara's, 320; horse of, 286-7; Loki and = Indara's conflict with Lakh or Lucifer 109, 344; Sea-god title of, 316,

# 448 PHŒNICIAN ORIGIN OF BRITONS & SCOTS

Tiazi of Gothic Eddas in Hitto-Sumer Taši (Tascio), 251

Tks, Tkz, legends on Phœnic. coins = Tasc and Tascio of A.B., 346, 354

Timber houses of A.B., of Hitto-Phœn. type, 69f.; and see Ilannu and Khilāni

Tin, in A.B., Amorite, Mor, or Muru trade in, 159f., 165, 216, 413–5; Bel-fire rites in Tin mines in Cornwall, 269, 281; Cassiterides and Cornwall and Phœnicians, 160, 219f.; coins of Cornwall of Phœnic. type, 334–6; Midlands surface, in A.B., 218; mines of Phœnics. in A.B., 155, 159, etc.; n. in Sumer, Sanscrit and Greek, 201, 413; Phœn. monopoly of, 160; Phœn. Tin-port in Cornwall, 146, 164–5; Sargon I., see Sargon

Tombs, chariots interred in A.B., 145

Topography of Early Phœn. settlements in A.B., 189f.

Totnes, port of arrival of Brutus, 155; Brutus stone at, 162, tin mine at, 155

Towns of Early Britons separate from aborigines, 156, 203–4

Tracia, home of Britons, as Tarsus, 394

Triads, The Welsh, on prehist. invasions of A.B., 190, 408, cp. 143

Tribes or clans in A.B., Att (Catt), 6, 203; Atte-cotti, 45; Barclensis, 78; Briton (or Baraton), Caledon, 117; Cassi or Kazzi, 33, 48, etc.; Catini, 197; Catti (or Xattui) or Ceti, 6, 200f.; Catyeuchlani or Catuellauni, 68, 200, 212; Cossini, 202; Cymri, 190; Dumno-ni, 72, 282; Gadeni, 197; Gioln, 67f.; Myrd (Amorites), 190, 216; Ottadini, 163; Pehta or Pict, 90f.; Pœnig, 32; Prydain, 53f.; Regni, 391; Sægon, 44, 391; Selgovæ, 44, 97; Sera or Sru, 79; Setanti, Sidon, 161; Texal or Taizal, 357; Tyrian, 161; Vecturi-ones, 117; Xatti, 77, 269

Tri-Nova (or Troe-Noey) or "New Troy," anc. n. for London, 175, 407f.

Tri-Novantes, Roman n. for Londoners, 175, 408f.

Troe-Noey, or New Troy, Gothic n. for London, 175, 407f.

Trojan, amulets with Crosses and cup-marks as in A.B. coins and monuments, 237, 294–5, 378, Brutus the, and "Briton," conquers Albion, 167, see Brutus; Crosses, in A.B., 149, 237, 294–5, lang. re British Doric, 177–81; n., 177, 408; Phœnics. in A.B., 159; religion, as in A.B., 237f.; river names in Brit., 172–4; shrine from Brutus' birth prov., 149; Sumer inscripts. discovered at Troy, 149, 237f.; warchariots, as in A.B., 145

Trojans as Dorians, 177; as Hittites, 159f.; as Phœnics., 161f, 178.

Tues-day, Sumer origin of Gothic n., 354

Tuisco, god-n., re A.B. Tascio, 354

Tut-ankh-amen, art of, Phœnician, 220, with kindred relig. motive, in A.B., 333–6, etc.

Tychē, or Fortune, as Phœn. Britannia tutelary, 57f.; 249

Tyre, Arianism (Gothic) of Early Christians at, 323; coasts of T. visited by Christ and miracle worked, 323; clans of Phœnics. of, in A.B., 161; coins of, with analogous legends and symbs. as in A.B., 354; Hercules temp. at, 266; purple shells of, at Stonehenge, 219

Tyrrhenian Sea, title of Gulf of Gades, 159; of Gulf of Latium (Brutus' birth prov.) and Tuscany 159


Uchlani, Catye-, tribe in A.B. as Hittite Xilani or Khilani, or Gioln title of Part-olon, 67–9, 71–3f.

Udug's archaic Sumer Stone-bowl, with god-n. Zagg or Zeus, Gothic Sig and Ygg 244, 342

Unicorn, of Brit. heraldry as sacred totem of Hittites, 7, 334–5f.; assocd. with Indara, 334f., 336f.; assocd. with St. Andrew as with Indara, 329f.; misrepresented in Brit. heraldry, 332f.; in Scots Royal arms, 329; see Goat

Union Jack Crosses, as Hitto-Phœn. standards, 328f.

## INDEX 449

United States, Brito-racial elements and civilizn. in, 377
Usk, Esk, Exe river names as Trojan, 173-4

Van, Wan, Bian or Fen (or Finns), primitive matriarchist tribe of Asia Minor, 91f.; as aborigines of Albion and Ireland, 91f.; cap. of matriarch queen Semiramis, 98; cave-dwellings of, like Picts', 100; Eddic acct. of, 95; lake of, 98; do. in Wales with legend of goddess, 96; matriarchs of, 93f.; place-names of in Brit. and Ireland, 95f.; do. across Europe from Asia Minor, 102f.; Wolf totem of, as Fen Wolf of Gothic Eddas, 106f., 331f.
Vans, Wans or Fens as aborigines of Albion, 91f.; as Caledons, 117, Chaldees or Culdees, 97f.; as Finns, 97, 102; as Picts, 96f.; "Children of River," Khaldis, title of, 99, 116-7; Dykes of, in A.B., 95-6; matriarchs of, 93f.; physical type river-bed or Iberian, 99-103, 134; Serpent-cult of, 94, 104-5, 109
Vectis or Ictis, tin-port of Phœnics. in A.B., 116, 121f. 414
Vecturi-ones, n. for Picts, 116
Vedas (Indo-Aryan scripts),, gods of, invoked in A.B.; see Bārati, Daxa (Daksha), Dyaus, Indra, Maruta (or Sakra), Sakka, Sura, gods of, invoked by Hittites, 14; tribes of in A.B., see Arri (Arya), Bārata, Cedi, Kāśi, Khsatriya, Kuru, Maruta, Panchāla, Pani; lang. of, Sumerian origin of, xi, 2-14, etc., and see Words
Vend, or Vent, place-names in A.B., Europe and Asia Minor as Van, 96f.
Venedocia, n. for Wales, 96
Veneti, marine tribe of Brittany, 103
Venice, as Phœnic., 160
Verulam (mod. St. Albans), cap. of Cassi-vellaunus, 408f.
Victis, Phœn. tin-port of A.B., 116, 121f., 139, 414
Vienna and Vans or Vends, 103
Vindia hill in Galatia-Cappadocia of Vans, 100, 102
Vit or Vitr, n. of Picts, 115
Vortigern, and the Jutes, 112

Wales, or Gwalia, 140; "Celts" of, 139; Cymry as Aryan and Sumers, 190, 208; Cambr, Gomer and Somer n. in, 190, 195; 208; Catti names in, 401; Gower and Arthur legend, in, 195; Isca in, 195; Triads of, 190, 408; summarize A.B. ethics; Van and Vent n. in, 96f.; Went n. for, 97
Wallon, Cymric form of Ilannu. or Khilani, Gioln, Hittite, 69
Wan or Van tribe in prehist. A.B., see Van; place n., in Brit., 95f.
Wans' Dyke, or Ditch, or Picts' Dyke, 95-6f.
Watling Street as pre-Roman Briton road, 182f.; Barat and Catti place-names along, 191f., 205f., 399f., 409; in Scotland, 198
Weems or Caves, as Pict dwellings, 120
Wells, holy, in A.B., associated with St. Michael as Phœnic., 341, 357, 360; worship of, forbidden to Early Christians by Canute and others
Wemyss Cave-gravings of Hitto-Phœnic. type, 198, 335, 350
Wends as Vans, 96f.
West Mor-land and More-cambe Bay, with prehistoric mines and Stone Circles re Mors, Muru or Amorites, 217
Wheeled or "Celtic" Cross of Hittitte origin, 298f.
Wheels, prehist. Stone graved in A.B. of Sun-cult, 272, see Drums
White Syrians, n. for Hittites, 12
Whorls, Trojan, as Solar amulets, represented in A.B., 237f., 253
Wight, Isle of, n. re Goth, 72
Winchester, founding of, about 900 B.C., 386
Winged angels of Hitto-Sumers on A.B. coins and mons., 250f., 334-5, 347-9; goat (Sun), in A.B of Hitto-Sum. type, 347; horse (Sun), do. and see Tascio-Mikal
Wise Men of the East, The, at Epiphany as Hittite Magi Sun-worshippers, 279; w. woman of aborigines, 94
Witches, as priestesses of aborig. in A.B., 94, 115; cauldron of, in A.B., 104-5f.; three, as oracles

of Fate with Sumer origin of n., 248 ; nine, of Gloster *re* nine maidens, 106
Wither-shins ("against Sun '), and unlucky direct., 282-3
Woad dye *re* Picts, 116
Wolf totem of Van or Fen tribe in A.B., 106, 109, 331f., 335f. ; as Loki, Lugh of Irish Scots (from Sumer *Liki*, a dog), emblem of Death, 109, 331f., 344
Wood Cross, in A.B., Devil banishing as in Hitto-Sumer, 255f., 293f. ; invoked for Resurrection from Dead, 255f., 298f., see Cross
Wood, Touching, origin and meaning of Superstition, 312
Wooden buildings in A.B., 69f., 155, 170f., 395.
Words, some English critical, incidentally occurring in text, derived from Sumerian (their Gothic, Anglo-Saxon, Sanscrit, Greek and Latin cognates are usually cited at same page) : abyss, 273 ; ace, 240 ; arable, 345 ; ass, 285 ; bad, 248 ; bar, 278, 291 ; berry, 307 ; bide, 323, 412 ; blaze, 268 ; -bury, -boro (town affixes), 171 ; caduceus, 242, 252 ; can (dish), 412 ; celerity, 412 ; cereal, 351 ; cross, 290 ; cue, 412 ; cut, 8, 351, 412 ; deuce, 282 ; dual, 240 ; deer, 328 ; divine, 354 ; ear (to plough), 345, 361 ; eight, 241 ; fate, fatal, Three Fates, 243, 248 ; fire, 291, 296 ; flash, 268 ; fortune, 59 ; gallop, 412 ; George, 320 ; girl, 258, 412 ; goad, 342, 351 ; goat, 330-1 ; good, 258, 412 ; gore, 319 ; gully, 117 ; gyron (heraldic), 307 ; her, 412 ; hero, 274 ; hill, 103 ; hoop, 202 ; house, 412 ; ' inn, 320 ; jar (gar), 240 ; jug, 412 ; Lucifer, 344 ; ma (mother), 249 ; mace, 278, 412 ; magic, 279 ; magnify, 252 ; majesty, 412 ; major, 252 ; May, 243 ; mere (sea), 243, 260 ; mother, 243, 249 ; much, 252 ; nod, 77 ; my, 275 ; neath, 77 ; mud, 412 ; O ! 412 ; one, 65, 240 ; papa, 318 ; pyre, 291 ; quart and quarter, 241-3 ; raise, 35 ; rove, 249 ; Scot, to scotch or cut, 8, 412 ; scour, 273 ; scythe, 412 ; see 228 ; seed, 351 ; seven, 241 ; shepherd, 262 ; sibyl, 243, 248 ; sick, 412 ; six, 241 ; sol, solar, 242, 247f. ; take, 412 ; thou, 412 ; tinder, 269 ; town, 281 ; two, 240 ; unity, 240 ; velocity, 412 ; ween, 77 ; were (A.S. for " man "), 274 ; Yule, 69
Writing current amongst Britons from earliest period in A.B., 175

Xat, Xatti, Sumer variants of Khat, Khatti (or Hitt-ite), 200, 320, etc.
Xatt, n. of Catti tribe in Shet-land, 77, 209
Xattui Cuh or " City of the Xatts." n. of anc. cap. of Shetland, 77, 209
Xilakku, Babylonian n. for Cilicia, 41

Yarrow mon. of Ceti-loinn clan, 70, 72
Ygg, Gothic n. for Father-god Sig, derived from Sumer, 244
York, founding of, about 980 B.C., 386
Yngl-ing Goths, as early Angles, 186
Yule, Sumer origin of n., 69 ; Yule tide, fire festival of Winter solstice, 272

Zag (or Axe) Sumer synonym of Khat, as source of n. Sacæ or Saxon, 331
Zet-land or Het-land, variants of Shet-land, 209
Zeus, Sumer origin of name, idea and representation, 244, 342-3 ; worship of, in A.B., 244f., 259f.

Herzlichst!
Julia von Brenchen
(Pseudonym)
Autorin!
Jetta Collignon,
Mai 08

Julia von Brencken

Doktorhut und Weibermütze

Julia von Brencken

# Doktorhut und Weibermütze

Dorothea Erxleben – die erste Ärztin

Biographischer Roman

Verlag Ernst Kaufmann

*Bibliographische Information Der Deutschen Bibliothek*
Die Deutsche Bibliothek verzeichnet diese Publikation in der Deutschen
Nationalbibliografie; detaillierte bibliografische Daten sind im Internet über
http://dnb.ddb.de abrufbar.

4. Auflage 2003
© Eugen Salzer-Verlag, Heilbronn 1992
© Verlag Ernst Kaufmann, Lahr 2000
Dieses Buch ist in der vorliegenden Form in Text und Bild urheberrechtlich
geschützt. Jede Verwertung ist ohne Zustimmung des Verlags Ernst Kaufmann
unzulässig und strafbar. Dies gilt insbesondere für Nachdrucke, Vervielfältigungen, Übersetzungen, Mikroverfilmungen und die Einspeicherung und
Verarbeitung in elektronischen Systemen.
Printed in Germany
Hergestellt bei Ebner & Spiegel GmbH, Ulm
ISBN 3-7806-5306-0

## Inhalt

Frühe Wißbegier . . . . . . . . . . . . . . . . . 7
Etwas will hoch hinaus . . . . . . . . . . . . . . 12
Mit dem Lehrbuch am Kochtopf . . . . . . . . 21
Gehilfin des Vaters . . . . . . . . . . . . . . . . 31
Auf der Flucht . . . . . . . . . . . . . . . . . . 41
Erste eigene Verantwortung . . . . . . . . . . 52
»Aus der Feder eines vernünftigen
  Frauenzimmers« . . . . . . . . . . . . . . . . 63
Des Königs Antwort . . . . . . . . . . . . . . . 69
Die Sintflut . . . . . . . . . . . . . . . . . . . . 77
Die Base Jakobine . . . . . . . . . . . . . . . . 83
Der Heiratsantrag . . . . . . . . . . . . . . . . 89
»Du wirst eine Doktorin, versprich mir das!« . . . 97
Die Attacke . . . . . . . . . . . . . . . . . . . 107
Der Gegenschlag . . . . . . . . . . . . . . . . 117
»Alle Wetter, Mut hat sie!« . . . . . . . . . . . 129
Endlich nach Halle . . . . . . . . . . . . . . . 141
Antrittsbesuch beim Dekan . . . . . . . . . . 150
Die Prüfung . . . . . . . . . . . . . . . . . . . 159
In der Weibermütze kehrt sie heim . . . . . . . 166
Ein Gang nach Canossa . . . . . . . . . . . . 174
Tod der Herzogin . . . . . . . . . . . . . . . . 181
Launen . . . . . . . . . . . . . . . . . . . . . 187
Einquartierung . . . . . . . . . . . . . . . . . 191
Stiller Abschied . . . . . . . . . . . . . . . . . 204
Das Ende des Weges . . . . . . . . . . . . . . 211

Die Gesetze der ärztlichen Ethik gehen zurück auf den griechischen Arzt Hippokrates, den man auch den Begründer der wissenschaftlichen Heilkunde überhaupt nennen kann. Vor mehr als zweitausend Jahren faßte er in Worte, was als Ärztegelöbnis bis heute gilt, nämlich den sogenannten Hippokratischen Eid.

Vielleicht schwört heute niemand mehr *bei Apollon und ruft alle Götter zu Zeugen,* aber der moderne Arzt nimmt ebenso die Verpflichtung auf sich, Leben unter allen Umständen zu erhalten, jedem Kranken nach bestem Wissen und Gewissen beizustehen und über dessen Leiden und Gebrechen gegen jedermann Stillschweigen zu bewahren, so wie es Hippokrates als Voraussetzung zur Ausführung der Heilkunst forderte.

In die lange Reihe derer, die dazu ein geordnetes Studium samt Abschlußprüfung an einer Universität absolvierten, gehört im 18ten Jahrhundert erstmals eine Frau: *Dorothea Christiane Erxleben.*

## Frühe Wißbegier

»Nenne mir die Namen der zwölf Apostel!« fordert energisch Doktor Leporin und geht gewichtig in der Stube auf und ab. Die Arme hat er auf dem Rücken verschränkt, und seine Hände umklammern den Rohrstock, als habe er ein ganzes Auditorium vor sich und nicht nur einen einzigen Schüler, nämlich seinen Sohn Christian.
Dieser sitzt am Pult, die Stirn gekraust, hilflos die braunen Augen auf den Vater geheftet.
»Petrus... Johannes...« versucht er sich tastend der Jünger Christi zu erinnern, streicht eine Locke von der Schläfe, die dem Zopfband entschlüpft ist, und fügt zögernd Jakobus hinzu mit dem Bemerken, daß es deren zwei gab, nämlich Jakobus, den Älteren, und Jakobus, den Jüngeren.
»Gut so!« lobt Doktor Leporin und erwartet acht weitere Namensnennungen. Doch nichts kommt. Erleichtert über das errungene Lob läßt der Junge die braunen Augen über Kaminsims, Standuhr und verblaßtem Tapetenmuster zum weit offenen Fenster wandern. Sommer ist's, und im Garten blüht's in Fülle. Träge summt eine Hummel vorbei, besucht Malve, Wicke und Löwenmaul, auf dem Pflaster der Gasse zanken sich Spatzen. Die Katze des Nachbarn führt ihre Jungen aus, und vom Dachfirst klappert ein Storch seinen Gruß. Das alles ist für einen elfjährigen Jungen viel interessanter als die Namen erster Heilsverkünder. Doch der Vater drängt.

»Weiter, Christian, weiter mein Sohn.« Leporin junior reißt sich los vom verlockenden Geschehen vorm Fenster, aber sein Geist vermag den Bogen über eintausendsiebenhundert Jahre Kirchengeschichte nicht zu schlagen.
»Judas...« fällt ihm noch ein, »Judas Ischariot!« Wer weiß schließlich nicht, daß er es war, der um zwanzig Silberlinge den Herrn verriet.
»Gut, Christian, weiter«, ermuntert der Vater.
Aber Christian schweigt, den Blick auf seine gefalteten Finger gesenkt. Sie sind tintenverschmiert, immerhin liegen schon zwei Stunden Rechnen und Schönschreiben hinter ihm, während der er in ständigem Kampf mit der kleksenden Gänsefeder lag. Auch der Vater merkt, daß der Junge ermüdet ist, daß Konzentration und Stillsitzen seit dem frühen Morgen ihn überfordert haben.

Christian Polykarp Leporin ist Doktor der Medizin, also Arzt, hat es aber, weil er auch sonst gelehrt und belesen ist, übernommen, seinen Ältesten selbst zu unterrichten. Einerseits besitzt er ein Gespür, wann einem Kinde das Lernen verleidet ist, andererseits sind ihm Strenge und Konsequenz die vornehmsten Gebote jeglicher Erziehung. Längst entschlossen, den Jungen gleich laufen zu lassen, hinaus in den Garten oder mit der Angelschnur hinunter zum Weiher, besteht er zuvor auf der vollständigen Beantwortung seiner Frage.
»Nun, mein Sohn, ich höre...«
Der Doktor lauscht vergeblich. Christian läßt den Kopf noch tiefer hängen, kein Evangelist kommt mehr

über seine Lippen. Da ertönt statt seiner von der Tür her ein helles Stimmchen:
»Andreas, Philippus, Bartholomäus, Mattäus, Thomas, Thaddäus und Simon!«
Vater und Sohn blicken auf. Im Türrahmen steht ein kleines Mädchen, barfuß, im langen Hemd; die gleichen widerspenstigen Locken, wie Christian sie hat, quellen unter einem Häubchen aus weißem Leinen hervor. Und braun wie die des Bruders sind die Augen des Mädchens, die, wie um Entschuldigung bittend für die Kühnheit, das es sich erlaubt hat, dem Vater entgegensehen.
Doktor Leporin ist einen Augenblick ratlos, was er davon halten soll, daß sein achtjähriges Töchterchen so unvermutet als kleiner Besserwisser in seinen Unterricht schneit. Also reagiert erst einmal der Arzt in ihm.
»Dörtchen, Kind! Du sollst doch zu Bette sein, da du das Fieber hattest!«
»Ach, Papa, liebster, bester Papa«, bettelt und schmeichelt Dorothea – nur sie durfte sich diese Anrede dem Vater gegenüber erlauben – »wenn du nur wüßtest, Papa, eine wieviel schlimmere Krankheit die Langeweile ist.« Schon muß Leporin schmunzeln, und Dorothea, in der Gewißheit damit halb gewonnen zu haben, setzt mutig gleich zum nächsten Schritt an. »Bitte, Papa, darf ich nicht ein wenig bleiben und zuhören? Ich kann auch manche Antwort geben, wenn du mich nur fragen willst!«
»So, so«, brummt der Doktor, überrascht vom Vorstoß seiner Tochter, die hustend und fiebernd im Wechsel mit Bleichsucht und Schwäche seit Wochen seine ganze

ärztliche Kunst und Sorge in Anspruch nimmt. Kaum hat er ein Symptom gebannt, befällt sie ein nächstes, als wolle die Natur ihr das Leben nicht gönnen. Und tatsächlich war Bettruhe seit Wochen seine einzige Anordnung gewesen.

»So, so und woher die plötzliche Gelehrsamkeit, mein Kind?«

»Aus deinen Büchern, Papa!« erklärt Dorothea und lacht selbstbewußt. »Latein, Botanik, Anatomie und natürlich die heilige Schrift! Sie alle waren meine Bettgenossen, und wenn ich auch nur wenig verstand, im Lesen war ich immer flink, wie du weißt...«

Ja, das wußte Leporin. Fast ohne Anweisung hatte Dorothea bereits als Vier- und Fünfjährige lesen und schreiben können, als sei es ihr in die Wiege gelegt. Und wenn er bedachte, mit welch hartnäckigen Fragen, aber auch geduldigem Zuhören dies Kind ihn schon in Erstaunen versetzt hatte, so schien es nur natürlich, sie am Unterricht des Bruders teilnehmen zu lassen. Nur zeitweise und gelegentlich versteht sich, denn warum dem Mädchen Flausen in den Kopf setzen, die es nur von ihren späteren Pflichten als Hausfrau und Mutter ablenken.

Das Betteln im Gesicht Dorotheas wie ein erwartungsvolles Leuchten in dem des Bruders geben schließlich den Ausschlag.

Am Ende lernt mir der Bursche besser, wenn die Schwester mittut, sagt sich Leporin im stillen und laut zu Dorothea:

»Also gut, setz dich mit auf die Bank, Dorothea, und merk gut auf!«

»Nicht im Hemd und mit nackten Füßen!« ruft eine

Stimme von der Tür her, und diesmal erscheint die Mutter im Türrahmen, Anna Sophia, geborene Meinecke, Tochter des früheren Pfarrers von Sankt Nikolai. In die Falten ihres Kleides drückt sich Johannes, der jüngste Leporin, dem die Furcht vorm gestrengen Vater anzusehen ist. Und hinter den beiden taucht ein zweites Mädchen auf, größer als Dorothea, frischer die Gesichtsfarbe, aber sonst ihr gleichend wie ein Ei dem anderen.

»Geh, Maria«, weist Frau Leporin sie an, »geh, hol deiner Schwester die Pantoffeln! Sie wird sich sonst erkälten«, räsoniert die Mutter weiter und legt ihr eigenes Schultertuch dem Kinde um, »sie wird erneut das Fieber kriegen, Leporin, und dann steckst du sie mir wieder wochenlang ins Bett.«

Sie nennt den Eheherrn bei seinem Nachnamen, weniger aus Respekt und Ehrfurcht, sondern weil es unter Bürgersleuten Brauch ist. Der Liebe tut das keinen Abbruch, denn, wie man sich's im Städtchen Quedlinburg und drumherum erzählt, im Doktorhause herrscht Eintracht und eheliche Harmonie. Auch jetzt schwingen Stolz und Zärtlichkeit in Leporins Worten, als er seiner Frau zunickt.

»Das sind sie nun, unsere vier, einander so ähnlich und doch so verschieden! Christian, Schwärmer und Träumer, Maria, ein Hausmütterchen, Johannes noch am Schürzenband, unsere Dorothea aber will scheinbar hoch hinaus, am Ende einen Lehrer heiraten oder gar einen Apotheker!«

»Walte Gott, es ist ein guter Mann«, nickt seine Frau zurück, »das wiegt alle Gelehrsamkeit der Welt nicht auf!«

## *Etwas will hoch hinaus*

Seit diesem Tag nahm Dorothea Christiane Leporin regelmäßig am Unterricht teil und zeigte sich dabei von schier unermüdlichem Lerneifer. Durch ihre Gegenwart war auch Christian emsiger bei der Sache und stellte sich dem Wettstreit mit der Schwester. Beide hingen förmlich an den Lippen des Vaters, welches Thema dieser auch anschlug.
Leporin mischte die Themen wohlweislich, sprang über von Botanik zu Historie, von Religion zur Anatomie. Eben noch von Adam und Eva sprechend, fragte er zum Beispiel sein Schülerpaar:
»Wie viele Rippen hat der Mensch?«
Während Christian verdattert seinen mageren Körper betastete, um von dort eine Antwort zu bekommen, gab Dorothea blitzschnell Auskunft.
»Der Mensch hat zwölf Rippen auf jeder Seite, sieben davon sind vorn am Brustkorb verbunden, die fünf untersten aber nicht.«
»So, so«, kam es vom Vater wie stets, wenn das Wissen seiner Tochter ihn überwältigte. »In welchem meiner Bücher hast du das denn wieder nachgelesen?«
»In keinem, Papa, in keinem! Ich besah mir die Wandbilder in deiner Ordination, und da kann man deutlich sehen...«
»So, so«, unterbrach Leporin ärgerlich, »dann hast du sie also auseinandergerollt! Und das ohne meine Erlaubnis!«
Diese Wandbilder hielt der Doktor nämlich eifersüch-

tig vor jedermanns Blick verborgen, teils die Patienten nicht zu schrecken, teils aber auch um Gerede und rückschrittlicher Verdächtigung vorzubeugen. Immerhin waren es Abbildungen von Mann und Frau, nicht nur unbekleidet, sondern zeichnerisch noch der Oberhaut beraubt, um dem Betrachter lehrreichen Einblick auf Knochengerüst und innere Organe zu vermitteln. Diese Tafeln waren Leporins ganzer Stolz. Gewöhnlich forderte es die Schicklichkeit, daß er ein Leiden durch bloßes Betasten des Kranken durch dessen vollständige Bekleidung hindurch diagnostizieren mußte. Nicht selten frischten dann die Abbildungen des bloßgelegten menschlichen Körpers sein Wissen wieder auf. Warum derlei Hilfsmittel der Heilkunde noch immer verteufelt wurden, während die Kirche im Rahmen religiöser Kunst viel freizügigere, ja grausige Darstellungen des nackten, gar verwesten Körpers erlaubte, das war und blieb Leporin unverständlich.

Eher verärgert darüber als über die Neugier seiner Tochter, ging er mürrisch zum nächsten Fach über: Latein.
»Christian, nenne die lateinischen Stammformen von ›loben‹ und sehen wir, ob du dir ein Lob damit einheimst!«
Christians Wangen überzogen sich mit hektischer Röte, aber brav brachte er sein ›laudare, laudo, laudavi, laudatus‹ bis zu Ende durch.
»Gut«, lobte tatsächlich der Vater, »und nun das unregelmäßige Verb ›fühlen‹!«
»Sentire – sento – senti –«
»Falsch!« unterbrach Leporin ungnädig und noch ehe er

mit dem Finger auf Dorothea zeigen konnte, schnurrte diese herunter:
»Sentio, sensi, sensus...«
»Na also...« triumphierte Doktor Leporin, und sein Zeigefinger schwenkte wieder auf den Filius.
»Christian! Ich stehe... ich habe gestanden...!«
»Stare... sto... stadi...« war sich diesmal Christian seiner Sache sicher gewesen, so wurde er von der Schwester vorlaut korrigiert.
»Stare, sto, stiti, status!«
Tatsache war, daß Dorothea im Lateinischen den Bruder bald so weit überflügelte, daß es Leporin unsinnig erschien, sie in diesem Fach weiterhin gemeinsam zu unterrichten, ja daß gar seine eigene Kenntnis nicht mehr ausreiche, um die Tochter zu fördern. Aber noch wußte er sich keinen Rat, was stattdessen zu tun sei.
Auch in anderen Fächern wurde dem Doktor der stetig wachsende Wissensdurst seiner Tochter unheimlich. Ihre Gesundheit hatte sich eher stabilisiert, seit ihr hungernder Geist so reichlich Nahrung fand. Zeigten sich gelegentlich dennoch Bleichsucht, Blutarmut und Schwachheit der Brust, so ertrug sie diese sichtlich besser. Doch die Frage, wieweit dem Hunger des Geistes nachzugeben und ob solch Appetit bei einem Mädchen natürlich sei, bereitete Leporin große Sorge.

Was tut ein Mann, der Sorgen hat? Er trägt sie gern ins Wirtshaus, um sie am Stammtisch mit Freunden zu diskutieren oder bei einem Glas oder Humpen zu vergessen.
Auch Doktor Leporin machte sich, wie allwöchentlich, auf den Weg zum ›Bären‹, dem ersten Haus am Platze.

Längst war es Herbst geworden, hatte ein kräftiger Wind letzte Blätter von den Bäumen gefegt, lauerte hinter Mauern und Hausecken und sprang gelegentlich in frischen Böen auf. Schon lag der Geruch von Schnee in der Luft, den der Wind dann, sobald die ersten Flocken fielen, spielerisch vor sich hertreiben mochte. Leporin wählte des Wetters wegen einen festen Lodenumhang und drückte den Dreispitz aus braunem Filz tief ins Gesicht. So ging er von seinem Haus im Steinweg 51 durch dunkle Gassen, von Fachwerkhäusern flankiert, hinter deren Fenstern hier und da ein Licht schimmerte, bis hin zum Markt, dessen Geviert nicht einfach nur ein Platz war. Der Markt war den Quedlinburgern vielmehr ein Symbol für ihr Stadt- und Handelsrecht seit siebenhundert Jahren, gleichwertig anderen Städten wie Köln, Mainz oder Magdeburg.

Leporin betrat die Wirtsstube, in der es laut und lebhaft zuging. Dort hielt er sich nicht auf, warf nur dem Wirt einen fragenden Blick zu, der hinter dem Schanktisch Krüge mit schäumendem Bier füllte. Der nickte und wies mit dem Daumen zur Tür des Hinterzimmers.

»Der Herr Doktor sind spät dran«, tadelte er, »die Herren sind alle da, wie jeden Freitag!«

Noch ehe Leporin die Tür zum Hinterzimmer öffnete, wußte er ziemlich genau, wen er da treffen würde. Neben dem Herrn Bürgermeister, dem Herrn Rats-Apotheker, dem Konsistorialrat Meene von Sankt Benedikt, den Herrn Gottlieb Heinrich Klopstock, Advokat der Stiftsverwaltung, und gelegentlich sogar auch den Herrn Stiftshauptmann von Plotho, wenn er sich denn vom Schloß herabbemühte. Sicher aber wäre sein enger Freund und Vertrauter da, Rektor des Gymna-

siums, Tobias Eckhard, und dessen Ko-Rektor Prillwitz, mit denen Leporin heute abend gern ein Wörtchen in Ruhe sprechen wollte.
Doch erst einmal empfing ihn im Hinterzimmer Lärm und Stimmengewirr einer hitzigen Debatte.
»Welch eine Schmach!« hörte man durch die noch geschlossene Tür.
»Ein Urteil wie im finstren Mittelalter!« empörte sich eine andere Stimme, der beifällige Ausrufe folgten.
Leporin drückte die Klinke und trat ein.

An langem Tisch saßen die Herren, die er zu sehen erwartet hatte. Vor jedem stand ein Humpen Lichtenhainer Bier, eine Platte mit Speck, Schinken und Wurst in der Mitte, ein Laib Brot dabei, dem ein gutes Stück fehlte, wie man sich auch vom Geselchten schon bedient hatte. Stattdessen war man zum Tabak übergegangen, schmauchte jeder sein Pfeifchen, langstielige, wie sie aus Holland kamen, oder kurzstielige wie die Engländer, unmäßigen Qualm verbreitend, wie es der König zu Potsdam in seinen ›Tabakskollegien‹ zu halten pflegte. Und mit ihm beschäftigte man sich eben auch, als Doktor Leporin das Hinterzimmer des ›Bären‹ betrat.
»Ich versichere Sie, meine Herren«, ließ von Plotho sich vernehmen, »Seine Majestät wird in Warschau schärfsten Protest einlegen!«
Doktor Leporin, nicht ganz auf dem laufenden, sah von einem zum anderen.
»Was ist geschehen?« fragte er und zog den Dreispitz vom leicht ergrauten, streng frisierten Haar. »Um was geht es, meine Herren?«

Statt einer Antwort las Klopstock jetzt laut aus dem Zeitungsblatt vom November 1724:
*Das heute beim Königlichen Assessorial-Gericht zu Warschau gefällte Urteil in Punkto des Aufruhrs zu Thorn lautet: die Stadtoberen Rösner und Zernick werden enthauptet, ihr Vermögen zu Gunsten der Gesellschaft Jesu konfisziert. Sechzehn weitere lutherische Verursacher haben ihr Leben zu lassen, nachdem dreien von ihnen zuvor die rechte Hand abgeschlagen werden soll...*
Klopstock ließ das Blatt sinken.
»Und das alles nur, weil sie als Lutheraner nicht das Knie beugen wollten, als eine Prozession zu Ehren des heiligen Jakob vorüberzog!« endete er in tiefem Groll.

Ein Protest des preußischen Königs an den König von Polen war in einem Brief tatsächlich ergangen.
*... so können wir nicht umhin, Eurer Majestät freundbrüderlich bekannt zu geben, in welchem Maße Uns das harte Urteil gegen gut protestantische Bürger der Stadt Thorn wegen dort unglücklicherweise entstandenen Tumults empört! Unter dem Vorwand, die Ehre Gottes zu rächen, werden meine treuen Glaubens-Genossen daselbst mit Feuer und Schwert verfolgt und alles Einvernehmen der Katholischen mit den dortigen Evanglischen Einwohnern über den Haufen geworfen...*
Ohne ein Echo auf diese Zeilen war das Urteil bereits ausgeführt worden und ging schon damals als ›Thorner Blutgericht‹ in die Annalen der Geschichte ein.
Einen Augenblick herrschte betroffenes Schweigen im Hinterzimmer des ›Bären‹, dann löste sich die Stimmung in vermehrtem Qualmen und Paffen und in einem bedächtigen Schluck aus dem Humpen.

Erst jetzt kam Leporin dazu, die Herren im einzelnen zu begrüßen.

»Einen schönen guten Abend, verehrter Herr Bürgermeister!« rief er mit leichter Verbeugung, »desgleichen dem verehrten Herrn Konsistorialrat!« Die steife Höflichkeit der Anrede leugnete nicht die Tatsache, daß all die Herren, die hier um den Tisch saßen, langjährige Freundschaft verband. So kam denn der nächste Gruß des Doktors auch weniger formell. »Nun, Klopstock, was macht denn dein Gottliebchen?«

Der Herr Advokat, ganz stolzer Vater, strahlte übers ganze Gesicht.

»Oh, der ist schon ein richtiges Krabbelkind, dazu pausbäckig wie ein kleiner Posaunenengel.«

»Und die Frau Gemahlin, deine Klopstockin? Hat sie sich vom Kindbett gut erholt?« Und da jetzt Klopstock ein wenig bedenklich den Kopf wiegte, versprach der Doktor weiter: »Ich komme bald einmal am Schloßplatz vorbei und sehe nach ihr.«

So war es abgemacht, ehe Leporin sich grüßend an den Rest der Runde wandte.

»Eckhard«, sagte er endlich und winkte den Schulmeister beiseite, »Eckhard, ich bitt' dich auf ein Wort, mein Freund!«

Umständlich zündete sich der Doktor ebenfalls ein Pfeifchen an und berichtete dann dem Freund ausführlich seine Sorgen.

»Vielleicht tue ich das Falsche«, klagte er außer Hörweite der Tischrunde, »einem Frauenzimmer das Latein beizubringen!«

Eckhard lachte auf.

»Da magst du recht haben, Leporin! Der König hat

Kollega Dühan mit Ohrfeigen traktiert, als er ihn dabei erwischte, mit dem Kronprinzen Latein zu üben!«
Leporin lachte auch.
»Dann sind mir Stockschläge gewiß«, scherzte er, »denn ich will dich eben bitten, meine Lektionen zu erweitern...«
»Hm«, machte das Oberhaupt des Quedlinburger Gymnasiums, »wenn deine Dorothea wirklich so hoch hinaus will ... ich kann sie natürlich nicht zu meinen Buben in die Klasse setzen, aber einen Weg gäbe es schon...«
Der Vorschlag Eckhards lautete dann, die neunjährige Dorothea auf schriftlichem Wege zu unterrichten, und zwar derart, daß er ihr Blatt für Blatt die Aufgaben entsprechend der Tagesleistung seiner jüngsten Lateiner ins Haus schickte und zu Korrektur und Zensur wieder abholen ließ.
Der Pedell des Quedlinburger Gymnasiums wurde also ein regelmäßiger Gast im Steinweg 51, aber auch Tobias Eckhard selbst erschien hin und wieder, seine jüngste Schülerin zu examinieren. Mit Schlapphut und Stutzperücke, den schwarzen Halbrock über senffarbener Weste, kam er daher, schwenkte den Elfenbeinstock schon von weitem, und wenn Leporin keine Patienten hatte, hielt er nach ihm Ausschau und oftmals ging dem Examen ein Gläschen Roter oder ein selbstgebrannter Kräuterlikör voraus. Dorothea hielt sich dann wohlpräpariert wartend im Nebenzimmer auf, bis sie endlich zu den Herren hineingerufen wurde.
»Ah, da ist sie ja, unsere kleine Gelehrte!« rief Eckhard fröhlich, ging jedoch sogleich ans Werk. »Wie steht es mit der Deklination von Substantiven? Amicus...«

»... Amici, amico, amicum, amico!« kam es von Dorothea ohne jede Scheu.
»Gut so, mein Kind! Und jetzt ›die Freundschaft‹!«
»Amicitia, amicitatis, amicitati, amicitatem, amicitate«, brachte die Schülerin wie ein Uhrwerk hervor.
Rektor Eckhard beugte sich zu dem Kind hinunter und verharrte einen Augenblick lauschend, als könne er noch mehr hören als die fehlerlose Aufzählung. Dann legte er bedächtig eine Hand auf Dorotheas Kopf, sprach aber nicht zu ihr, sondern zum Doktor hin gewandt.
»Hier drinnen, lieber Freund, steckt etwas, das hoch hinaus will ... vielleicht höher, als wir beide ahnen ... höher jedenfalls, als wir in unserem begrenzten Denken einem Frauenzimmer zugestehen ...«
»Du schreckst mich, Eckhard«, rief Leporin, und wirklich malte sich Schrecken auf seinem Gesicht, »du triffst genau den Zweifel, der mir die Ruhe raubt! Soll man das Pflänzchen gießen, daß es gedeiht, oder ist es ein Unkraut, das beizeiten ausgerottet werden muß?«
Eckhard nahm seine Hand von Dorotheas Kopf und legte stattdessen einen Arm um ihre kindlich schmale Schulter.
»Was mich betrifft, Freund Leporin, werd' ich das Pflänzchen, wie du es nennst, mit allen meinen Kräften hegen und pflegen, daß es wachse und gedeihe ... zu welchem Ziel und Frommen, das mag Gott bestimmen.«
Leporin sagte nichts, aber in seinem Innern sprach er ein leises ›Amen‹.

## *Mit dem Lehrbuch am Kochtopf*

Etliche Male war der Storch vom Dach gegenüber nach Süden gezogen und wieder heimgekehrt, hatte mit Frau Storch das Nest vom Vorjahr ausgebessert, Hochzeit gefeiert und eine neue Generation Storchenkinder aufgezogen, um im Herbst erneut nach Süden zu ziehen.
Während all der Zeit hatte Dorothea Christiane Leporin nicht nachgelassen, zu lernen und zu studieren.
Im Latein hatte sie es bald soweit gebracht, daß Rektor Eckhard ihr Übersetzungen aufgab wie beispielsweise Caesars klassische ›Commentarii Belli Gallici‹. Der Pedell brachte den für den Tag ausgewählten Text in den Steinweg: GALLIA EST OMNIS DIVISA IN PARTES TRES, QUARUM UNAM INCOLUNT BELGAE, ALIAM AQUITANI, TERTIAM, QUI IPSORUM LINGUA CELTAE, NOSTRA GALLI APPELLANTUR ... Und wenn er den Bogen zurückbrachte, sauber und fehlerlos mit Dorotheas Handschrift versehen: *Gallien im Ganzen ist in drei Teile geteilt, deren einen die Belgier besiedeln, einen anderen die Aquitanier, den dritten die, die in der eigenen Sprache Kelten, in unserer Gallier genannt werden*, dann freute Eckhard sich so sehr, daß er ihr lobende und ermutigende Briefchen schrieb.

*Nicht ohne Vergnügen habe ich deine lateinischen Übungen, auch die bündige Sprache der deutschen Übersetzung gelesen. Ich habe diese so gut gefunden, daß sie die jungen Männer, die bekanntlich darauf bedacht sind, daß nur sie sich mit*

*Wissenschaft jeglicher Art befassen, einmal zu einem Wettstreit mit dir reizen könnte.*

Und ein anderes Mal:

*Ich bewundere die Fähigkeiten deines Geistes, auch die Begierde, dich mit wissenschaftlichen Dingen zu befassen und bewundere deine Fortschritte!«*

Oder auch:

*Wenn ich über irgendetwas verfüge, wodurch dein Drang nach Wissenschaft wie dein großer Fleiß unterstützt werden können, so wird es immer zur Hand sein! Ich halte es in jedem Falle für Unrecht, ein so lobenswertes Streben, ein Zeichen größter Tüchtigkeit, nicht zu fördern.*

Durch Eckhards Vermittlung hatten sich zu Dorotheas Unterweisung zwei weitere Lehrer hinzugefunden, und zwar Co-Rektor Prillwitz für die Fächer Französisch und Mathematik, und gelegentlich ein junger Diakon von Sankt Nikolai namens Erxleben, um ihr Einblicke in Religion und Geschichte zu geben.
Gegen Erxleben als Mentor seiner Tochter hatte Leporin zu Beginn etwas einzuwenden.
»Er scheint mir viel zu jung, um Stunden, wenn auch bei gelehrsamem Gespräch, mit ihr allein zu verbringen!«
Doch Pfarrer Meene konnte den Doktor beruhigen.
»Keine Sorge, Leporin, so jung ist er gar nicht, hat schon die Dreißig hinter sich. Und zudem kenne ich Erxleben als Amtsbruder zur Genüge. Wäre nicht

schon sein Charakter Garant in jeder Hinsicht, so doch die Tatsache, daß er sich soeben mit einer ganz jungen Frau verheiratete und seine Sophie so liebevoll wie eifersüchtig über ihn wacht.«

Arzt und Pfarrer schmunzelten in stillem Einverständnis, wußten sie doch beide, was eine energische Eheliebste auszurichten vermochte, wenn es um Wahrung von Sitte und Ordnung ging.

So war es Leporins Eheliebste, die immer wieder gegen die wachsende Gelehrsamkeit Dorotheas vorstellig wurde.

»Du machst unsere Tochter zum Gespött der Leute, Leporin!« protestierte Anna Sophia, »was soll denn werden, wenn sie einem Haushalt vorstehen soll und nicht einmal ein Ei zu kochen versteht, geschweige denn Brot zu backen, Gänse zu rupfen oder Marmelade einzumachen!«

Der Vorwurf stand in ihrem noch immer schönen Gesicht geschrieben, zumal das Recht auf ihrer Seite schien. Heirat und Hausfrauenpflichten waren nicht nur nach ihrer Ansicht unverrückbare Ziele im Leben einer Frau, und so stand es ganz außer Zweifel, daß auch Dorothea diesen Weg gehen würde. Was nützten ihr da Latein, Französisch und Mathematik? Ein paar Brocken gewiß, um das Kauderwelsch der Obrigkeit besser zu verstehen, auch das eine oder andere Wort Französisch, um Gruß und Kompliment den Damen vom Stift zu entbieten, wenn diese sich in die Stadt herabwagten. Addieren und Subtrahieren tat Not, um auf dem Markt nicht betrogen zu werden, aber niemals nutzten einer Frau und Mutter mathematische Gleichungen und geometrische Kunststückchen!

»Ja, ja«, wehrte Leporin jedes Mal von neuem, »du magst ja recht haben, Liebste, was in der Regel Bürgersleuten ansteht, aber unser Kind ist eine Ausnahme! Glaub mir nur...«

»Du meine Güte!« fuhr die Mutter stets dazwischen, »Ideen hast du, Leporin! Ist der Schaden nicht schon groß genug, den du im Kopf des Kindes angerichtet hast!«

Zornig wandte sie sich ab, fuhrwerkte laut klappernd in der Küche zwischen Töpfen und Pfannen und ließ ihren Zorn an diesen aus.

»Nicht eine Mahlzeit würde sie zustande bringen, nicht einen Flicken auf das Kleid setzen!« schalt sie vor sich hin, »ein Beispiel sollte sie sich nehmen an ihrer Schwester, die so fleißig mir zur Seite steht... an Maria hab' ich eine wahre Hilfe! Aber wenn sie den Kramer-Wirt heiratet und fortgeht...«

Nicht daß der Leporinsche Hausstand der töchterlichen Hilfe bedurft hätte, seit langem gab es eine Magd, der Familie zugehörig und vom frühen Morgen bis zum späten Abend redlich zugange. Ein männliches Faktotum, im Kopf ein bißchen schwach, doch ehrlich und verläßlich, sorgte für Garten, Hof und Stall. Dort stand ›Schnecke‹, eine braune Stute, die ihrem Namen alle Ehre machte. Vor Jahren angeschafft, gewann das hübsche Tier zwar bald die Kinderherzen, brachte den Doktor aber oft in Rage, weil es trotz Zuruf und Peitsche nur selten in Trab zu bringen war. Manch ein Patient, weit am Stadtrand wohnend und verzweifelt ärztlicher Hilfe bedürftig, hat dieser Stute wegen schon manche Stunde unnötig Schmerzen leiden müssen.

Für Quedlinburgs rund 15000 Einwohner waren noch

drei weitere Ärzte niedergelassen, aber ihre Zuständigkeit nicht starr nach Bezirken aufgeteilt. Diese regelte sich nach Erfolg und Beliebtheit unter den Patienten, so fielen Doktor Leporin neben Kranken im nahen Umkreis, die er leicht zu Fuß besuchen konnte, auch etliche zu, die weitab, ja bis hinaus zur Taubenbreite oder im Brühl verstreut wohnten.

Hinzu kamen die Damen des Stifts, die sämtlich bei Bedarf den Doktor Christian Polykarp Leporin riefen, zumal dieser rechtens den Titel eines Leibarztes der jeweiligen Quedlinburger Äbtissin führte. Ganz klar also, daß zur Führung seiner Praxis Pferd und Wagen unabdingbar nötig waren.

Den Streit, welchen Anteil Dorothea an den häuslichen Pflichten im Elternhaus haben solle, schlichtete sie dann endlich selbst.

»Schon gut, schon gut«, rief sie, als der Disput sich gerade wieder neu erhitzen wollte, »ich werde mich dem Wunsch der Mutter beugen und alles lernen, was eine Hauswirtschaft verlangt.« Und da die Mutter eben darob triumphieren wollte, schnitt sie ihr, sich an den Vater wendend, kurz das Wort ab. »Und du, liebster Papa, sorg dich nicht! Meine Studien sollen nicht darunter leiden, das versprech' ich dir.« Und dabei zwinkerte sie, die gewöhnlich mehr zu stillem Ernst und Würde neigte, dem Vater listig zu.

»Rühr die Suppe, knete den Teig!« hieß es nun montags, »lies die Erbsen und schabe die Möhren!« am Dienstag, mittwochs gar »hilf deiner Schwester das Zinn putzen!« und so fort die Woche durch. Seife kochen, Wäsche wringen, Laken säumen, Mutter Leporin wünschte, daß ihre Tochter wirklich alles lernte, was eine tüchtige Hausfrau wissen mußte. Selbst wenn der Herrgott ihr einen reichen Mann bescheren sollte, so war es gut, wenn man Mägde sachgerecht anweisen konnte. Nur dann war man ihrer Achtung sicher, so meinte die Mutter, nur dann hatte eine Frau Anrecht auf Respekt.

Zu ihrer großen Erleichterung fand sie in Dorothea eine geduldige und gelehrige Schülerin. Folgsam nahm die Tochter jede Arbeit hin und zeigte sich dabei weder ungeschickt noch säumig. Wo allerdings es immer möglich war, verrichtete sie eine Sache einhändig mit der rechten Hand und hielt in der Linken ein Buch, in dem sie las. Waren unabdingbar beide Hände für eine Tätigkeit erforderlich, so lag das Buch aufgeschlagen vor ihr auf dem Tisch, und sie las ebenfalls darin, und zwar so konzentriert und hingegeben, daß Schnee von Eiweiß, den sie gerade schlug, so weiß und steif wurde wie noch nie, oder das Zinn, das sie gedankenverloren rieb, wie helles Silber glänzte.

Auf die Gewohnheit von der Mutter angesprochen, biß diese auf Granit.

»Aber Kind, ein Buch in der Küche! Was soll der Humbug?«

»Liebste Mutter«, kam es dann mit unbeirrtem Blick aus braunen Augen, »ich finde es sehr wohl möglich, während verschiedener häuslicher Geschäfte gleicherzeit mit Nutzen ein Buch zu lesen. Nur so läßt sich, was im Studieren durch derlei versäumt wurde, wieder einbringen.«

Wollte die Mutter ärgerlich auffahren und weiter etwas Tadelndes vorbringen, so änderte sie plötzlich ihren

Sinn und schwieg. Anna Sophia Leporin, einzig in überkommenen Vorstellungen von Ehrbarkeit und weiblicher Tugend erzogen, war eine kluge Frau. Die Grenzen zwischen ihrer Auffassung der Dinge und der offenbar vorbestimmten Prägung ihrer jüngeren Tochter wurden ihr immer klarer, und sie wußte, daß sie soeben schmerzhaft an eine geschlossene Schranke gestoßen war. Wieviel mehr hätte es sie aber beunruhigt, wenn sie die Autoren und Titel der Bücher hätte deuten können, die Dorothea auch während der Hausarbeit nicht aus der Hand ließ. Nur dem Vater waren sie ein Begriff, gelehrte Namen wie Stahl, Alberti, Juncker und Heister, und nur er wußte, mit was ihre Werke wie: THEORIA MEDICA VERA oder COMPENDIUM ANATOMIAE sich befaßten. Und händereibend freute sich Leporin:
»Jetzt also hat sie es auch mit der Arzneygelahrtheit, meine Dorothea! Ich werde ihr alles beibringen, was die Medizin nur weiß!«

In einem ganz anderen Punkt, der Dorothea betraf, war allerdings auch er beunruhigt.
Wie stets pünktlich zur vereinbarten Stunde läutete die Hausglocke. Anstelle der Magd, die gewöhnlich öffnen ging, sprang Dorothea, wie es schien allzu bereitwillig, auf.
»Laß nur, Trine, ich gehe selbst zur Tür! Es wird der Herr Diakon sein zum Unterricht.«
Im schwarzen Habit, weißer Halsbinde, den schwarzen Dreispitz unterm Arm, stand der Herr Diakon Erxleben vor der Tür. Sein Gesicht, von frischer Morgenluft gerötet, schien freudig aufzuleuchten.

»Ah, Demoiselle Leporin, einen schönen guten Morgen«, grüßte er und trat an Dorothea vorbei ins Haus.
»Aber Herr Diakon«, beklagte sich Dorothea statt eines Grußes, »seit wann denn ›Demoiselle‹? Bisher war ich immer Dorothea für Sie! Sie kennen mich seit Kindertagen und haben mich niemals anders genannt.«
»Das ist wahr, Dorothea, aber du bist mit Riesenschritten dabei, erwachsen zu werden, und seit der Konfirmation im letzten Jahr dacht' ich mir...«
»Was dachten Euer Gnaden?« gab seine Schülerin keck zurück.
»...ich dachte mir, es wird Zeit, dich als Erwachsene ernstzunehmen und daß du es vielleicht gerne hörst...« Diesmal unterbrach der Herr Diakon sich selbst. »Du hast recht, Kind, lassen wir den Unsinn!« Er lachte hell auf und nahm mit beiden Händen die ihre, die sie ihm nun versöhnt zum Gruß entgegenstreckte. Was der Herr Diakon nicht sagte, war, daß die Förmlichkeit der Anrede, die er sich vorgenommen, ihn selbst bewahren sollte vor allzu großer Vertrautheit seinem Schützling gegenüber. Längst hatte Erxleben bemerkt, daß die Jahre nicht nur Dorotheas Geist und Intellekt hatten blühen und reifen lassen, sondern auch alle sonstigen Merkmale, mit denen der Herrgott ein erwachsenes Frauenzimmer schmückt. Was den Diakon daran schreckte, war das Ausmaß des Wohlgefallens, mit dem er sie wahrnahm, und andererseits eine gewiße atemlose Begeisterung, die Dorothea ihm gegenüber an den Tag legte. Diese konnte natürlich dem Unterricht gelten, der Freude am Lernen, aber Erxleben, achtzehn Jahre älter als Dorothea, wußte, wie leicht Grenzen des Gefühls sich verwischen. Zum Glück hatte Pfarrer

Meene mit der Beurteilung Erxlebens recht. Sein Charakter war ein Garant, so sicher wie der Fels in der Brandung, und auf besonders eindrucksvolle Weise traf derzeit auch der zweite Teil der Gewähr zu.
Gerade als der junge Geistliche seinen Hut aufhängte, streckte Doktor Leporin den Kopf aus der Tür seines Ordinationszimmers.
»Wie geht es Ihrer Frau, lieber Erxleben?«
»Danke, Doktor, ich denke, es ist bald soweit! Die Arme leidet sehr...« Der Diakon machte eine weitausholende Gebärde des Bedauerns.
»So, so... dann werde ich lieber noch einmal nach ihr sehen... Sie wissen, Ihre Sophie ist nicht gerade die kräftigste!«
Erxleben bedankte sich aufrichtig, dann begann der Unterricht.
Der Diakon verstand es, trockene Historie mit Sagen und Histörchen so zu vermischen, daß durch das eine das andere im Gedächtnis haftete, vom alten Rom bis zur Heimatkunde.
»Warum, Dorothea, glaubst du, hat unsere Nikolai-Kirche zwei Türme?«
Dorothea wollte eben zur Antwort geben, daß ja auch die viel ältere Stiftskirche oben auf dem Schloßberg zwei Türme habe, da zuckte es auch schon um die Lippen des Lehrers.
»Ja, das war nämlich so, daß der Bau, der endlich auch der Neustadt außerhalb der alten Wehrmauer eine Kirche schenken sollte, auf sumpfigem Grund stand. Es mußten so viele große Baumstämme eingerammt werden, daß der Bau viel teurer wurde, als geplant. Das Geld reichte einfach für keinen Turm mehr. Da fanden

die Hunde eines alten Schäfers auf den Wiesen vor Quedlinburg eine Truhe mit Gold. Der brave Schäfer lieferte ehrlich den ganzen Schatz ab und behielt keinen einzigen Heller für sich. Nun hatte die Stadt so viel Geld, daß sie gleich zwei Türme bauen konnten!«
Soweit die alte Sage, die für den heutigen Tag das Pensum alter Welfen-Herrlichkeit belebte.
Die Uhr zeigte Mittag, als wiederum der Doktor den Kopf zur Tür hereinstreckte, diesmal in die zum Garten hin gelegene Studierstube.
»Erxleben, ich mache mir Sorgen um Ihre Frau! Sie ist recht blutarm, wie mir scheint. Rühren Sie ihr Ei in Rotwein, ein paarmal am Tage. Und Erxleben, sprechen Sie ihr um Gottes willen Mut zu! Sie ist nicht gebaut zum Kinderkriegen!«
Dorothea sah ihren Vater besorgt den Kopf schütteln. Der Diakon schlug sofort sein Buch zu und erhob sich.
»Dann werde ich gehen«, sagte er wie schuldbewußt und ließ noch einen kurzen Blick über seine Schülerin gleiten, über das dunkle Blond quirliger Locken, über kluge braune Augen, Stirn und Wangen voller Anmut, den festen Mund und ein spitzes, kleines Kinn. Aber seine Gedanken waren nicht bei ihr, nicht mehr im Haus am Steinweg, sondern bei seinem Herrgott, den er um Schutz und Beistand für seine Frau bat.
Dorothea war ebenfalls aufgesprungen und wollte den Diakon zur Tür begleiten. Ein Wink ihres Vaters hielt sie zurück.

In dieser Nacht brachte Sophie Erxleben ihr erstes Kind zur Welt, dem jedes Jahr ein weiteres folgen sollte.

## *Gehilfin des Vaters*

Während all dieser Jahre war auch Christian Leporin nicht müßig gewesen. Herangewachsen zu einer Größe, die jedes Potsdamer Regiment entzückt hätte, waren seine Studien soweit gediehen, daß er nun die Universität besuchen sollte. Bestens rekommandiert vom Rektor des Quedlinburger Gymnasiums sollte er als Student nach Halle gehen, und das schon binnen weniger Wochen. Dorothea reagierte auf das bevorstehende Ereignis recht eigen. Sie wurde immer schweigsamer, und ihr hübsches Gesicht verdüsterte sich wie vor Ausbruch eines Unwetters.
»Du mußt dir die Trennung von Christian nicht so sehr zu Herzen nehmen«, suchte die Mutter zu trösten, »Halle ist nicht aus der Welt!« Damit aber deutete sie Dorotheas Gefühle völlig falsch.
»Die Trennung von Christian?« echote Dorothea verständnislos, um dann bitter aufzulachen. »Oh, die ist es nicht, die mich schmerzt! Ihm tut sich ja ein Himmel auf! Er darf alle jene Lehrer wie Lehren in natura hören, die ich mir mühsam aus Büchern zusammenlesen muß! Georg Ernst Stahl, sein Thema ›Medizin und Seele‹! Und gar Professor Hoffmann, Rektor daselbst, und seine Theorien über Bäder und Kuren!« Fast war Dorothea ein wenig laut geworden, ihre Stimme jedenfalls hart und vorwurfsvoll.
Tadelnd schaltete darum der Vater sich ein.
»Dörte, Kind, mißgönnst du all das etwa deinem Bruder?« fragt er mild, aber Dorothea fuhr erst recht auf.

»Ich bin es doch, der etwas mißgönnt wird!« rief sie. »Warum kann ich nicht mit ihm nach Halle und gleich ihm lernen und hören...«

»Du? Ein Mädchen...?« entsetzten sich beide Eltern, Leporin ahnungsvoll bedauernd, seine Frau schockiert über die neueste Anwandlung ihrer exaltierten Tochter.

Christian selbst sah einzig das Groteske an der Vision seiner Schwester.

»Mademoiselle Studiosa!« lachte er dröhnend, »ich sehe sie schon beim Kommers, die Pfeife qualmt, das Bier schäumt, und eine Zote jagt die andere...!«

»Das genügt, Christian!« fiel ihm der Vater ins Wort. »Um ernsthaft zu studieren, muß man sich nicht unbedingt gemein machen. Wenn ich erwäge, wieviel tausend alberne Leute zu den Akademien laufen und albern wieder heimkommen, warum dann nicht einmal ein weiblicher Student?«

Ihm tat es leid, daß Dorothea sich zurückgesetzt fühlte. Ihre Leistungen kamen in jeder Hinsicht denen ihres Bruders gleich, wenn er diesen auch in praxi mehr herangezogen hatte. Christian half dem Vater bereits seit geraumer Zeit bei der Behandlung von Patienten, machte Handreichungen und begleitete ihn bei seinen Hausbesuchen. Auch hier wirkten Brauch und Vorteil sich gegen Dorothea aus. Nicht im Traum war es Doktor Leporin bisher eingefallen, auch seine Tochter ein gebrochenes Bein schienen zu lassen, in ihrer Gegenwart einen eitrigen Verband zu wechseln oder sie gar in eine der ärmlichen Hütten zu einem Siechen mitzunehmen. Das, so nahm er sich vor, sollte jetzt anders werden. Ohnehin würde ihm die gewohnte Assistenz fehlen, und daß es ein Rock war, der nun an seiner Seite erschien, das zu akzeptieren würden seine Patienten schon lernen.

Schnell genug kam der Tag, an dem Christian Leporin einen Platz in der ›Ordinari‹ nach Halle hatte reservieren lassen. Die Einschreibgebühr im Postamt war schon vor Tagen bezahlt, in der Hoffnung im meist überfüllten Wagen einen leidlichen Platz zu bekommen, sich nicht neben Paketen, Körben oder sonstiger Fracht einzwängen zu müssen oder freibalancierend auf dem Kutschdach zu sitzen. Als dann aber der Studiosus in spe seinen Reiseschein abholte, auf dem Name, Tour und Abfahrtszeit vermerkt standen, war die Sitznummer doch nur für einen Platz hoch oben auf dem Bock gültig eingetragen.

»Nun, wenigstens das Wetter verspricht gut zu werden«, tröstete Dorothea, die am frühen Morgen den Bruder zum Postwagen begleitete. Damit sollte sie wohl recht haben. Schon jetzt zur Stunde, da die Quedlinburger kaum aus den Federn waren, schien die Sonne warm vom Himmel, und wenn Christian in den anderthalb Tagen der Reise nicht befürchten mußte, naß zu werden, so doch vor Staub und Hitze förmlich auszutrocknen. Eine Freude waren derlei Fahrten selten. War der Postillon nüchtern und die Löcher der Straße nicht zu groß, konnte man schon froh sein, brachen weder Rad noch Deichsel, schliefen die Pferde weder ein noch gingen sie durch, war die Sache fast perfekt. Hatte man dann noch eine Nacht der Ungewißheit verbracht, nämlich darüber, ob man eine Strohschütte in der Station fand oder der Postillon durchfuhr, um verlorene Zeit einzuholen, hatte man zweimal glücklich die Anhalt'sche Grenze passiert ohne allzuviel Ärger mit dem Zoll, dann konnte man erleichtert, wenn auch mit zerschlagenen Gliedern am Galgenberg vorbei in die Stadt Halle hineinrollen.

»Du wirst es schon überstehen, Christian«, tröstete Dorothea noch einmal und hievte ein Bündel Bücher zum Bruder hinauf, der schon über die Vorderräder auf den Bock geklettert war, »und denk immer daran, welches Glück dir beschieden ist, überhaupt studieren zu dürfen!« Wie gern wäre sie an seiner Stelle gewesen und hätte doppelt und dreifach die Strapazen solcher Reise auf sich genommen, um aus berufener Quelle ihren Durst nach Wissen stillen zu können!

»Ach, laß nur, Schwesterchen«, rief Christian von oben herunter und lachte herzlich, »ich bin zwar ein Mannsbild und darf studieren, dafür bildet dein Geschlecht die Zierde der Menschheit!«

Dann Winken, eine Kußhand, der Postillion stieß in sein Horn, und die Pferde zogen an. Die Räder ächzten auf und rollten kollernd über den Marktplatz, dann bog die Kutsche ums Rathaus in die Breite Straße ein und war nicht mehr zu sehen.

Dorothea blieb mit einem tauben Herzen zurück. Plötzlich war ihr trotz der Sonne kühl, zog sie ihr Schultertuch enger um ihr Mieder, raffte mit der anderen Hand den buntgestreiften Rock und wandte sich durch Schuhhof und Hölle wieder dem Steinweg zu. Sie war sicher, Bruder Christian war von nun an der freieste und froheste Mensch auf Erden, ein Student, ein Scholar, ein Jünger Äskulaps! Aber soweit war es noch nicht. Auch ihm legten sich Hindernisse in den Weg, die mit List und Tücke überwunden werden mußten.

Nach 1727 hatte der König ein Gesetz zur Aushebung von Rekruten erlassen, das sogenannte ›Kantonalsystem‹. Danach durfte jedes Regiment in einem ihm zugewiesenen Bezirk seinen Nachschub an Soldaten ausheben und auf Zeit oder bei Bedarf lebenslänglich für sich verpflichten. Die ›Kantonisten‹, also die zur Wehrpflicht in Augenschein genommenen, hatten gleich nach ihrer Konfirmation den Eid auf ihr Regiment zu leisten. Dabei wurde ihnen deutlich gemacht, daß der Staat das gesamte Vermögen ihrer Eltern einziehen werde, falls sie desertieren sollten. Der Rückgriff auf diese bereits vereidigten Aspiranten richtete sich dann im Bedarfsfall jeweils nach deren körperlichen Größe, Gesundheit wie dem allgemeinen Erscheinungsbild.

Alljährlich vor der offiziellen Frühjahrsbesichtigung gingen ein Regimentsoffizier und ein Zivilbeamter von Haus zu Haus und sahen nach dem rechten. Gefiel ihnen ein Mann, wurde er als ›disponibel‹ erklärt und hatte unmittelbar seinen Dienst anzutreten.

Christian Leporin, wie auch sein Bruder Johannes waren auf diese Weise in den Listen des 21. Infanterie-Regiments von Marwitz festgehalten. Das Interesse des Regiments am kerngesunden, hochgewachsenen Christian war äußerst lebhaft.

Kaum wurde also dessen Abreise nach Halle bekannt, lief der Einberufungsbefehl ihm hinterher. Einer möglichen Freistellung zum Studium wollte das Marwitzsche Regiment – mit Standort Halberstadt – um jeden Preis zuvorkommen. Halle aber widersprach der Einberufung, die Immatrikulation sei bereits perfekt. Damit war das Regiment keineswegs zufriedengestellt, legte seinerseits Einspruch ein, und es begann ein Tauziehen, dessen Hin und Her monatelang durch anwachsende Aktenberge beidseitiger Kanzleien nicht mehr durchschaubar war. Der Student Leporin blieb jedenfalls in Halle.

Friedrich Wilhelm I. von Preußen, wenn auch als ›Soldatenkönig‹ bekannt, war dennoch derjenige König auf preußischem Thron, der am wenigsten Krieg führte. Seine Armee, vorzüglich gerüstet und ausgebildet, stand gewissermaßen nur ›Gewehr bei Fuß‹. War es deswegen oder weil die Herren der Universität Halle im Recht waren, jedenfalls ruhte der Anspruch des Marwitzschen Regiments an seinem Rekruten Leporin einstweilen. Einstweilen! Es sollte schlimmer kommen, jedenfalls was Christian anbetraf.
Dorothea hingegen und ihrem insgeheimen Wunsch, dem Bruder auf die Universität folgen zu können, bot sich unterdessen eine ungeahnte Chance.

Wie erwartet fehlte Doktor Leporin die Assistenz Christians in seiner Praxis sehr. So geschah es immer häufiger, daß der Vater, wenn Dorothea gerade in Haus und Küche der Mutter zur Hand ging, sie von Herd und Waschtrog wegrief.
»Rasch, Dorothea, du mußt mir helfen! Der Geselle vom Müller ist mit den Fingern ins Räderwerk geraten! Wir müssen amputieren...«

Dann ließ die Tochter den Kochlöffel fallen und reichte stattdessen die Bestecke zur Operation des Müllergesellen. Als habe sie ihr Lebtag nichts anderes getan als solch blutiges Handwerk, war Dorothea ganz in ihrem Element. Bald hielt sie das Becken, wenn der Doktor die Frau Bürgermeisterin zur Ader ließ, beruhigte ein Kind, dem er ein Geschwür schneiden mußte oder mixte Tränke nach Anweisung und Tinkturen zur ambulanten Behandlung alltäglicher Leiden. Dabei vernachlässigte sie ihre Pflichten der Mutter gegenüber nicht und schlug auch jede freie Minute ihre Bücher auf, war es doch ihr Grundsatz: *daß alle wohlgesittete junge Frauenspersonen in denen Studiis ebenso fleißig, als in Dingen, die Haushaltung betreffend, müßten unterwiesen werden.*

Und eines Tages war es soweit, daß der Vater, wie es seine Art war, den Kopf ins Zimmer hereinstreckte: »Dorothea, nimm dein Cape um! Du begleitest mich heut auf Hausbesuche!«
Meist war die Schnecke schon angespannt, und kaum war Dorothea auf den Wagen geklettert, klapperten die Hufe des Pferdchens gemächlich von Haus zu Haus, von Patient zu Patient. Manch einer war wohl erstaunt, daß hinter dem Arzt seine Tochter das Krankenzimmer betrat, auch wenn dort im Bett Vater, Mann oder Sohn lagen, die der Hilfe bedurften.
»Jungfer Dorothea? Ich bitt' sehr ... wenn die Jungfer doch besser drüben in der guten Stube ...«
»Es ist schon recht, Frau Schreinermeisterin, die Dorothea ist meine Gehilfin! Sie versteht's grad so gut wie der Christian!«

Und damit – unerhört – schlug Leporin das Deckbett zurück, unter dem der Schreinermeister lag, und begann dessen schmerzenden Leib abzutasten, Dorothea derweilen stellte die schwere Arzttasche auf den Tisch, und bereitete auf den Wink des Vaters in aller Seelenruhe ein Klistier vor.

Ein andermal kündete Leporin an:

»Heut geht's hinauf zum Schloß, die Frau Äbtissin hat wieder das Reißen; wir werden ihr Senfpflaster auflegen.«

Dorothea kannte die derzeitige Stiftsherrin gut. Sie war eine Prinzessin von Holstein-Gottorp, eine stattliche liebenswürdige Dame, der die Töchter Leporin schon mehrfach ihre Aufwartung hatten machen dürfen und die auch schon Gast im Arzthause gewesen war.

Mühsam kämpfte sich die Schnecke die Brandgasse zum Schloßberg hinauf, durch das alte Doppeltor hindurch. Dorothea ließ ihren Blick über die gewaltigen Quader des Mauerwerks und die steilen Wände des Wehrgangs gleiten.

»Mich schaudert's, Papa«, rief sie leise und zog wirklich wie schaudernd die Schultern hoch, »dies Stück des Wegs kann einem das Fürchten lehren!«

»Kein Grund zur Furcht, mein Dörtchen«, kam es tröstend vom Doktor, »doch Ehrfurcht mögen sie uns schon einflößen, diese alten Steine! Sie haben noch den Sachsenkönig einreiten sehen mit seinem ganzen in Eisen gerüsteten Gefolge. Sie haben die Jubel- und Hochrufe gehört, wenn er siegreich daherkam, aber auch das Schweigen, als man seinen Sarg den gleichen Weg hinauftrug, um den großen Heinrich für immer in der Krypta seiner Königsburg zu betten.«

»Ich sch' das Bild deutlich vor mir«, rief Dorothea jetzt mit Begeisterung, »die Pferde in schwarze Schabracken gehüllt, das Volk barhäuptig auf Knien...«

»Die Sage sagt«, fiel der Doktor wieder ein, »an diesem Tag senkte sich die Sonne vom Himmel und quoll den Bürgern der Stadt wie Blut in die Fenster ihrer Häuser...«

Unwillkürlich schmiegte sich Dorothea näher an den Vater. Wenigstens schien heute die Sonne fröhlich vom klaren Maienhimmel herab und suchte den letzten Winkel des ehrwürdigen Gemäuers zu wärmen.

»Ah, Doktor, Sie bringen mir Ihre liebe Dorothea mit«, begrüßte die Prinzessin herzlich ihren Retter aus Schmerzensnot und küßte Dorothea nach deren ehrfürchtigem Knicks auf beide Wangen. Selbst weltaufgeschlossen sah es die Frau Äbtissin nicht als verwunderlich an, daß Dorothea sich einem so männlichen Interessensgebiet wie der Medizin widmete, ja bestärkte sie in dem Wunsch, ihr Wissen und Können an der Universität zum Abschluß zu bringen, so wie es jedem anderen Studenten freistand.

»Persistez, mon enfant!« rief sie auf französisch, »lassen Sie nicht nach, Ihr Ziel zu erreichen!« Und während Dorothea geschickt das Senfpflaster auf die schmerzende Stelle ihres Rückens plazierte, fuhr die Äbtissin fort: »Es wird wahrhaftig Zeit, wenigstens eine Bastion männlichen Geistes für uns Frauen zu erobern! Man sollte vielleicht...«

»Vergebung, Hoheit«, unterbrach Dorothea ebenfalls französisch den tastenden Gedankengang der Prinzessin, »sitzt das Pflaster so richtig? Spüren Euer Hoheit schon die wärmende Wirkung?«

»Ja, mein Kind, ja, perfekt! Aber was ich sagen wollte...« Noch immer schien die Äbtissin zu überlegen, machte dann aber einen geradezu zündenden Vorschlag: »Man sollte sich an den König wenden!«
Leporin, bisher mehr im Hintergrund der Szene, trat lebhaft einen Schritt vor.
»Hoheit meinen wirklich...?« schaltete er sich enthusiastisch ein, um aber sogleich mutlos hinzuzusetzen: »Seine Majestät sind äußerst ablehnend gegen jede Art von gelehrten Frauenzimmern!«
»Das ist mir bekannt, lieber Doktor«, nahm wieder die Äbtissin den Faden auf, »aber ebenso weiß man, wie sehr der Kronprinz anderen Sinnes...« Sie vollendete den Satz nicht. Sonst hätte sie hinzusetzen müssen, daß der König krank und sicher nicht mehr lange am Leben sei und daß dann eine andere Art von Herrschaft erwartet würde, aufgeklärt und menschenwürdig, den Wissenschaften zugeneigt... Sie sagte es nicht. Leporin verstand sie auch so. Dorothea aber, scheinbar nur wortloser Zuhörer, senkte sich der Gedanke tief in die Seele.

*Auf der Flucht*

Der König ist tot, es lebe der König! Im Juni 1740 legt der Kronprinz im verspielten Landschloß von Rheinsberg den seidenen französischen Rock ab.
»Messieurs, die Possen haben nun ein Ende«, erklärt er seinen Freunden, und im schlichten blauen Tuch eilt er nach Potsdam, dem Vater das letzte Geleit zu geben. Als Friedrich II. besteigt er den preußischen Thron. Die Berliner bejubeln ihren jungen König, die Vertreter der Stände huldigen ihm nach altem Brauch.
Zu gleichem Brauch fährt Friedrich im Juli nach Königsberg, Krönungsstadt der Hohenzollern, nicht sich krönen zu lassen, was er für unnötig und aufwendig hält, sondern lediglich um die Erbhuldigung entgegenzunehmen. Sein Großvater war noch mit 1800 Wagen und 30000 Pferden zur Krönung gereist, Friedrich reiste in drei schlichten Kutschen, für sich, für zwei Offiziere seiner Begleitung und für das Gepäck.
Auch in den preußischen Teilen Westfalens zeigt sich der neue König persönlich, aber in allen Städten seines Landes höchstselbst den Treueeid entgegenzunehmen, ist ihm natürlich nicht möglich. Es hätte Monate, vielleicht Jahre gekostet und den König von wichtigen Regierungsgeschäften abgehalten.
Um auch anderwärts der Form Genüge zu tun, wurden deshalb Kommissarien unterschiedlicher Zusammensetzung gebildet, die bis zum Herbst alle preußischen Provinzen bereisten.
Für den 24. November sagte sich der Regierungskom-

missar von Lüderitz beim Stiftshauptmann von Plotho an, so daß Quedlinburg eine der letzten Städte war, die zu den Feierlichkeiten einer Erbhuldigung rüsteten.

Ein Fackelzug war geplant, ein neuer Brauch, seit die Studenten von Königsberg spontan mit ihren Fackeln am jungen König vorbeigezogen waren. Die Zeremonie selbst sollte schlicht gestaltet werden, das Vorsprechen des Eides und die Bestätigung durch den Rat, von den Stufen des Rathauses herab eine Ansprache des Herrn Regierungskommissars an die Bürger, kurz und bündig.

Ein Festmahl zum Abschluß ließ sich die Stadt aber nicht nehmen, und dabei sollte exquisit getafelt und getrunken werden. Als es dann soweit war und der Herr von Lüderitz in einfacher schwarzer Kutsche, selbst ohne jeden Pomp, nur wie ein Beamter gekleidet, eintraf, gab es drei Personen in der Stadt, die, den kühnen Gedanken der Frau Äbtissin im Kopf, die günstige Gelegenheit beim Schopf zu packen suchten.

Doktor Leporin zog den Herrn Stiftshauptmann beiseite:

»Ach, lieber Plotho, Sie wissen doch, glauben Sie nicht, man könnte...?«

Und Plotho, mit der Familie vertraut und gut Freund, raunte bei nächster Gelegenheit dem Herrn von Lüderitz zu:

»Leporin, ein vorzüglicher Mann, nicht nur ein ausgezeichneter Arzt, sondern in jedweder sonstigen Weise honorig und beliebt! Dieser hat eine Tochter, die wahrhaftig das Zeug hätte...« Der Rest kam noch leiser, so als mute er Lüderitz etwas ganz Unglaubliches zu.

Selbstverständlich hatte der Regierungskommissar

Quartier oben auf dem Schloß, und dort sprach ihn auch die Frau Äbtissin an.

»Ich bin sicher, lieber Lüderitz, Sie werden einen Weg finden, Seiner Majestät plausibel zu machen ... man sagt, er habe die Pressefreiheit eingeführt, die Freimaurer unterstützt, öffentliches Reden gestattet, wie wird er da nicht einem Frauenzimmer das Studieren erlauben!«

Lüderitz war neugierig geworden und verlangte, Dorothea kennenzulernen.

»Gewiß«, versicherte Plotho, »ich werde Ihnen die Demoiselle Leporinin vorstellen lassen.«

»Aber, aber, lieber Plotho, wo bleibt Ihre Galanterie«, lachte Lüderitz, »ich bin es, der der Demoiselle vorgestellt zu werden wünscht!«

Die Frau Äbtissin machte dann bei dem geplanten Treffen den Chaperon. Als Dorothea im gelbgeblumten Rock mit grünem Überkleid, die Locken unter gelbbebänderter Haube, eintrat, lag sogleich ein wohlwollendes Lächeln auf Lüderitz' breitem Gesicht. Ehe er ein Wort an Dorothea richtete, sagte er laut zur Äbtissin gewandt:

»Aber Hoheit, sie ist doch viel zu hübsch, um sich unter die Wölfe wagen zu wollen!«

»Ah, Lüderitz, machen Sie mir das Kind nicht verlegen!« rief die Prinzessin und drohte ihm lachend mit ihrem Elfenbein-Fächer.

»Die Demoiselle möchte also nach Halle?« wandte sich Lüderitz an Dorothea.

»Ja, Euer Gnaden«.

»Und da möchte Sie studieren?«

»Ja, Euer Gnaden.«

»Grad wie ein Mannsbild?«
»Ja, Euer Gnaden.«
»Und ausgerechnet die medizinische Fakultät hat Sie sich gewählt?«
»Ja, Euer Gnaden.«
»Die Wissenschaft der Medizin ist nicht immer delikat! Und schon gar nicht für ein Frauenzimmer...!«
»Ja, Euer Gnaden.« Dorothea hob den Kopf und ihre Stimme wurde fester. »Euer Gnaden wissen, mein Vater ist Arzt...«
»Dennoch. So ein Studium dauert Jahre...«
»Es bedarf nicht des ganzen Studienganges an der Universität, Euer Gnaden, bin ich doch in Theorie und Praxis wohlvorbereitet durch meinen Vater. Wenngleich ich den einen oder anderen der hohen Professoren hören möchte, so ist es zuvörderst der graduelle Abschluß, den ich mir erbitte.«
Das klang recht selbstbewußt, und Lüderitz, den väterlich jovialen Ton fallenlassend, antwortete eine Spur kühler.
»Mach Sie eine schriftliche Eingabe, Demoiselle Leporin, ein Gesuch direkt an Seine Majestät gerichtet, und sende Sie mir das nach Potsdam!« Dann wieder wärmer und mit einem Kopfnicken zur Äbtissin hin: »Ich werde Sorge tragen, daß das Schriftstück dem König unter die Augen kommt.«
Dorothea versank erneut in einen Knicks gegen den Regierungskommissar und küßte der Prinzessin die Hand.
»Meinen untertänigsten Dank Euer Gnaden! Eure Dienerin, Hoheit!«
Damit verließ sie über das spiegelnde Parkett rück-

wärtsschreitend den Salon. Draußen begann sie zu laufen, atemlos, schwerelos, im Innern jubelnd. Ein Schreiben an den König! Ich werde meine Worte sorgfältig wählen wie Juwelen. Mein ganzes Herz werde ich hineinlegen in dieses Gesuch nach Potsdam, so schwor sie sich.
Daß Potsdam für lange Zeit nicht die rechte Adresse sein sollte, den König von Preußen eilends zu erreichen, das wußte Dorothea Leporin ebensowenig wie der Regierungskommissar von Lüderitz.

Seit Friedrich II. die Macht in Händen fühlte, nutzte er sie, um Schlesien für sich zu beanspruchen. Diesem Anspruch Nachdruck zu verleihen, brauchte er seine Truppen. Die Kontingente sollten nicht nur auf ihre volle Stärke gebracht werden, sondern auch jene ›Überkompletten‹ aktivieren, die die Reserve bildeten.
In den Städten und Städtchen Preußens dröhnt das Kalbfell, ziehen Trommler durch Straßen und Gassen: Alarm! Wer schon Soldat und wie üblich in Privatquartier untergebracht ist, eilt zu seinem Regiment. Wer in den Regimentslisten verzeichnet ist, meldet sich, den einstigen Eid zu erneuern und den Waffenrock anzulegen. Der eine tut es gelassen, der andere fluchend. Auch unter den Studenten brodelt es. Manche eilen begeistert zur Fahne, andere murren und sind ängstlich. Wird die Freistellung sie noch schützen?
»Ruhig, meine Herren, seien Sie ganz beruhigt!« beschwichtigt in Halle Pro-Rector Juncker seine Studenten und liest ihnen laut den Bescheid des Königs vom 1. Dezember 1740 vor, darin es heißt: ...*daß alle auf*

*hiesiger Universität sich befindende, auch ab- und zureisende Studiosi nicht allein von aller Werbung und Zwingung zum Soldaten gäntzlich befreyet seyn, sondern auch denjenigen, welche in letzten Jahren zu Soldaten angeworben sind, aber ihre studia continuiren wollen, die Päße abgenommen und sie losgelassen werden sollen.*

Damit, so sollte man meinen, sei jeder Student sicher, sein Studium ohne jeden militärischen Dienst weiterführen zu können. Auch Christian Leporin wollte seine ›studia continuiren‹, aber ein martialisch aussehender Korporal des Regiments von Marwitz erschien in Halle und hielt ihm eine gesiegelte ›Rückberufung‹ unter die Nase. Das Regiment ging also davon aus, Leporin sei bereits unter Dienst gestanden und erkannte somit den in Aktenbergen verschwundenen Einspruch der Universität einfach nicht an.
Unter dem Vorwand, seine Siebensachen zusammenzupacken, bat Christian den Korporal um ein paar Minuten Aufschub.
»Nur die Spanne eines Schoppens, Herr Unteroffizier und ein Gläschen dazu«, sagte er bereitwillig und schenkte dem Mann ein.
»Bloß noch Abmeldung bei meinem Vorgesetzten und ich stehe zur Verfügung«, versprach Christian weiter und erklärte lachend: »Ja, ja, so etwas gibt es hier bei uns nämlich auch.« Das stimmte zwar nicht, entsprach aber der Vorstellung des Korporals, so daß dieser den Aufschub ganz natürlich fand. Christian aber, kaum daß er die Tür seines Quartiers hinter sich hatte, lief, was er laufen konnte die Straße hinunter, versteckte sich bis zur einbrechenden Dunkelheit und machte sich

noch in der gleichen Nacht zu Fuß auf, die hier ja nahe Grenze ins Sächsische zu erreichen.
Von dort aus klärte er dann seine Vorgesetzten, den Senat der Friedrichsuniversität, über den Sachverhalt auf, und der Streit zwischen Halle und Halberstadt in Sachen Leporin flammte erneut auf.

Ein ähnliches Schicksal traf derweilen auch Johannes Leporin. Er war, wie gesagt, an Statur weit weniger imposant als Christian, und gesundheitlich von klein auf so labil, wie es Dorothea zu Beginn auch war. War diese unterdessen widerstandsfähig und kräftig geworden, ja hatte zwischen Haushalt, Büchern und neuerdings medizinisch praktischer Assistenz gar keine Zeit, eigene Beschwerden auch nur zu bemerken, so neigte Johannes ein wenig zu Hypochondrie und reichten Energie und Lebenswille nicht eben weit. Für ihn fand Doktor Leporin eine Stelle bei einem ehrbaren Quedlinburger Kaufmann namens Hentschel, und seitdem rechnete Johannes im Hinterzimmer eines Ladens Zahlen zusammen oder wog Tee und Gewürze ab. Johannes war mit seinem Leben zufrieden und daher entsetzt, als das Marwitzsche Regiment auch nach ihm die Hand ausstreckte. Im ersten Anlauf konnte Leporin den schlechten Gesundheitszustand seines Sohnes bezeugen und Befreiung vom Militärdienst erreichen. Doch dabei sollte es nicht bleiben.
An einem bitterkalten Tag Mitte Dezember läutete es energisch an der Haustür des Leporinschen Hauses. Zufall oder nicht, Leporin öffnete selbst, vielleicht weil er das wiederholte Ziehen der Glocke für den Notruf zu einem Patienten hielt. Vor ihm stand aber ein Offizier

des Infanterie-Regiments Nummer 21, blauer Rock, rote Aufschläge und strohgelbe Weste, die ihn aber wohl nicht recht wärmen konnten, denn seine Wangen waren rot angelaufen vor Kälte.
»Um Himmels willen, kommen Sie herein«, forderte daher der Doktor, noch ehe er wußte, um was es ging.
Der Offizier dankte und trat in den Hausflur. Hinter ihm tauchte jener martialische Unteroffizier auf, der in Halle den vergeblichen Besuch bei Leporin junior gemacht hatte. Der Ärger über die Schlappe, die er sich dort geholt, stand noch auf seinem Gesicht, doch ließ er seinem Vorgesetzten das erste Wort.
»Wo ist Ihr Sohn, Leporin?« begann dieser sofort wenig freundlich.
»Ich habe deren zwei«, erwiderte der Doktor leutselig, »der eine studiert in Halle, wie Sie wissen ...«
»Das tut er eben nicht«, konnte sich der Korporal nicht mehr enthalten zu unterbrechen, »er ist uns entwichen! Desertiert! Ins Ausland geflüchtet!« Der Zorn schien ihm jeden Respekt, und sei es auch nur vor seinem Offizier, genommen zu haben. Drum hob dieser beschwichtigend die Hand und schlug auch einen etwas höflicheren Ton an.
»Es ist wahr, Doktor, Ihr Sohn entzog sich der Dienstleistung!«
»Mein Sohn ist freigestellt«, korrigierte Leporin noch immer verbindlich, »grundsätzlich vom militärischen Dienst freigestellt wegen seiner Studien ...«
»Im Kriegsfall gilt diese Freistellung nicht, Doktor, und wir befinden uns im Krieg ... oder zumindest können uns befinden ... jeden Tag ...«

»Des Königs eigener Befehl widerspricht dieser Auffassung, Herr Hauptmann!«
»Und ich bringe Ihnen den schriftlichen Befehl vom Obristen Lieutnant von Wagner, Kommandeur unseres Standorts. Sie haben binnen acht Tagen Ihre beiden Söhne herbeizubringen...«
»Meine beiden Söhne? Auch der zweite ist freigestellt wegen körperlicher Untauglichkeit!«
»Zum Packknecht beim Troß taugt er uns jedenfalls! Also acht Tage, Leporin, andernfalls... lesen Sie selbst, welche Maßnahme dann verfügt wird.«
Damit zog der Hauptmann ein Schreiben aus seiner Manschette und übergab es mit theatralischer, wie gleichfalls drohender Gebärde.
»Acht Tage also!« wiederholte er statt eines Grußes und verschwand samt seinem Korporal.
Sofort brach Leporin das Siegel und begann zu lesen.

Aus Küche und Studierzimmer kamen seine Damen angelaufen und sahen dem Vater über die Schulter.
*... Im Falle die Frist verstrichen, ohne die beiden erwähnten Rekruten ihren Dienst ordnungsgemäß angetreten, der Vater, Doktor Leporin, statt ihrer in die Wache geworfen werden solle...*
Das war hart, zumal Doktor Leporin nur vermuten konnte, was sich in Halle abgespielt hatte.
»Christian muß irgendwo im Sächsischen sein, hatte er doch kaum eine viertel Meile bis dort!«
Und weiterdenkend fiel Dorothea ein:
»Johannes als Packknecht! Eine Absurdität! Auch er muß fort!«
»Du hast recht, Kind, er sollte gewarnt werden, noch

ehe die Marwitzschen ihn auf der Gasse abfangen! Sie wissen genau, zu welcher Stunde er gewöhnlich heimkommt..."

"Geh du einkaufen, Maria", fiel Madame Leporinin ein, "nimm Trine mit, ihr kauft Brot beim Bäcker und holt zwei Pfund Rindfleisch unten an der Ecke, damit es natürlich aussieht, dann geht ihr beim Laden vorbei und verlangt für einen Kreuzer Minze! Das wird euch Gelegenheit geben, mit Johannes zu reden!"

"Der Plan ist gut", bestätigte Leporin, "und besser noch, wenn er gar nicht mehr hierher nach Hause käme. Vielleicht schafft er über Nacht Braunschweig oder Anhalt. Hier, gib ihm dies!"

Damit fingerte Leporin ein paar Silbermünzen aus seiner Börse, die ohnehin nicht gerade prall bestückt war.

Maria rief Trine, und beide in warmen Kapuzen machten sich auf den Weg. Johannes Leporin kam diesen Abend nicht ins Elternhaus zurück, sondern nahm wie sein Bruder den nächtlichen Weg in ein fremdes Herrschaftsgebiet.

Die Familie wartete derweilen ab, was das Schicksal ihnen bescheren würde. Sie warteten den ersten Tag, den zweiten, dritten und vierten. Der König sei in Schlesien einmarschiert, hieß es.

Aber es hieß auch, eine königliche Kabinetts-Order habe beide Söhne Leporin offiziell zu Deserteuren erklärt. Und noch ehe die volle Woche um war, wurde der Vater aufgefordert sich auf der Wache zu melden.

"Grundgütiger Gott!" rief die Mutter und rang die Hände.

»Das kannst du nicht riskieren, Vater!« beschwor Dorothea ihn, »sie lassen dich nimmermehr los, und du bist kein junger Mann mehr!«
»Du hast recht, Dörtchen, ja, ich fürchte du hast recht...« Leporin kratzte sich den grauen Kopf und überlegte. »Da werd' ich wohl auf meine alten Tage noch zum Vagabunden werden müssen, in der Fremde heimlich und geduldet wie meine Söhne...«
»Du hast Freunde in Leipzig, Vater!«
»Ach, Kind, Freunde in der Not...«
»Nimm die Schnecke und den Wagen, Vater.«
»Dann wird's nicht grad eine rasante Flucht«, lächelte der Doktor wehmütig.
»Man wird glauben, du besuchst Patienten über Land.«
Und so wurde es dann auch gemacht. Mitten am Tag, ohne den Schutz der Nacht, nur mit seiner Arzttasche versehen und in einen dicken Pelz gehüllt, verließ der Doktor sein Haus, machte im Brühl noch einen unverfänglichen Krankenbesuch, und hielt sich dann auf der Straße nach Süden. Zurück ließ er Frau und Töchter ohne jeden leiblichen Unterhalt, womöglich hochnotpeinlicher Befragung und Verfolgung ausgesetzt, als einzig männlichen Beistand einen etwas geistesschwachen Knecht.

## *Erste eigene Verantwortung*

In einer kleinen Stadt wie Quedlinburg braucht ein Gerücht nur wenige Stunden, um sich zu verbreiten, eine Vermutung kaum weniger, und eine Nachricht erreicht von Mittag auf Abend jedes Haus. Doktor Leporin ins Sächsische geflohen, seine beiden Söhne desertiert! Tochter Dorothea Samariterin oder mit dem Teufel im Bunde, das zu entscheiden war man sich noch nicht recht im klaren. Da ging ein Gewisper von Mund zu Mund, hinter vorgehaltener Hand, hinter verschlossenen Türen.
Auch Dorothea wußte nicht, wie die Menschen reagieren würden. Die Praxis würde sie wohl schließen müssen. Der Himmel wußte, wovon sie leben sollten, wenn kein Heller mehr einging.
Im Sparstrumpf hatten die Leporins nie etwas, weil der Doktor die Armen meist umsonst behandelte und, die Reichen zu mahnen, ihm nicht einfiel.
Obwohl die Jüngste im Hause, wurde Dorothea instinktiv klar, daß sie jetzt der Haushaltsvorstand war. Mutter und Schwester reagierten eher hilflos. Wie blind taten sie weiter, was sie immer getan hatten.
»Soll ich diese Woche auch Apfelkuchen backen, Mutter?« hörte Dorothea ihre Schwester zwar fragen, aber dann die Mutter naiv und ahnungslos antworten:
»Aber ja, mein Kind, Vater ißt ihn doch so gern!«
Hatten die beiden denn nichts begriffen von der Gefahr, in der sich nicht nur der Vater, sondern auch beide Brüder befanden? Noch ehe der Wagen mit der langsa-

men Schnecke die Grenze erreicht hatte, konnten Patrouille oder Posten ihn anhalten, den Doktor vernehmen und ganz nach Willkür seine Angaben glauben oder nicht. Und Leporin – das wußte Dorothea – war ein schlechter Lügner. Wenn aber die Flucht nach Plan gelang, hieß das dennoch außer Landes warten, bis der Krieg beendet, die Söhne begnadigt waren. An Apfelkuchen daheim war auf lange Sicht nicht zu denken.
Nach schlafloser Nacht trank Dorothea ihren Morgenkaffee. Vor ihr lag ein langer, leerer Tag. Stunde um Stunde würde er sich dehnen zu nichts als Grübelei und Trübsinn.
Wie gern hätte sie jetzt den Vater befragt:
»Was tun, Papachen? Wie soll es weitergehen?«
Aber von Papa würde keine Antwort kommen, nicht heute, nicht morgen und auch nicht übermorgen.
Seufzend schenkte sich Dorothea eben eine zweite Tasse ein, als die Magd eintrat.
»Sie müssen sich beeilen, Fräulein, es wird höchste Zeit!«
»Zeit zu was, Trine? Und warum die Eile?«
»Nun, ist dies ein Doktorhaus oder ist es das nicht«, brummelte die Alte und wollte das Geschirr abräumen.
»Ein Haus ohne Doktor ist es, Trine, und daher habe ich alle Muße, meinen Kaffee zu trinken.«
»Die Patienten warten, Fräulein«, setzte mürrisch die Magd hinzu, »seit einer Stunde schon.«
Patienten? Sollte es sich bei dem einen oder anderen noch nicht herumgesprochen haben, daß der Vater fort war? Dorothea wollte diesen wenigen ein paar Worte der Erklärung sagen und sie dann nach Hause schicken.

Rasch trank sie den Kaffee aus und lief über den Flur zum Wartezimmer. Schon ehe sie an der Tür war, hörte sie Stimmengewirr. Es mußten etliche sein, dort drinnen, die die Nachricht nicht vernommen und nun enttäuscht sein würden, daß kein Doktor sie verarzten konnte. Mancher würde grollen, daß er wieder gehen mußte, ein anderer vielleicht Vorwürfe machen, daß er den weiten Weg gemacht. »Da ist nun nichts zu ändern«, sagte Dorothea still bei sich: Und entschlossen öffnete sie die Tür. Das Wartezimmer war brechend voll, mehr als zwei Dutzend Gesichter sahen ihr erwartungsvoll entgegen.

»Guten Morgen...« grüßte sie beklommen, »ich fürchte... ich muß Ihnen allen...« Man ließ sie nicht ausreden.

»Ach, bitte, Demoiselle, ich brauche einen neuen Verband!«

»Ein Fläschchen Medizin, Demoiselle, die gleiche wie letztes Mal.«

»Ein Furunkel, Dorothea, das kannst du mir doch schneiden.«

»Ich fühl' mich heute so hartleibig, Jungfer Dorothea.«

»Mein Bub, der Fabian, hat sich die ganze Nacht erbrochen. Kannst du Nachmittag kommen, Dörte, nach ihm zu sehen?«

»Ich fühle ein Fieber, Demoiselle, und der Kopf schmerzt...«

So ging es fort, und Dorothea begriff, daß sie alle von des Doktors Flucht wußten und einzig gekommen waren, ihr beizustehen. Dankbar erneuerte sie den Verband, schnitt das Furunkel, mischte Medizin. Sie half und hantierte Stunde um Stunde, behandelte, wo sie nur konnte, machte Besuche am Krankenbett, erteilte Rat, sprach Trost, aber sie kannte auch die Gesetze. Wer immer in die Hand eines Arztes gehörte, den schickte sie fort.

»Tut mir leid, Mutter Bertram, ich darf Euch nicht heilen! Geht zu Doktor Grasshoff, aber sagt ihm, der Schmerz sitzt in den Nieren!« So gab sie einen Hinweis, verstieß aber nicht gegen das ärztliche Gebot.

»Sie ist schwanger, liebe Schulzin, im dritten Monat! Aber wenn die Blutung wiederkommt, geh Sie zum Doktor Herweg!«

Am Ende dieses Tages war sie rechtschaffen müde, die Dorothea Leporin, und insgeheim mächtig stolz.

»Ach, liebster Papa«, sagte sie leise für sich, als sie am Abend die Lampen in der Ordination löschte, »wo immer du jetzt bist, liebster Papa, ich glaube, du wärst zufrieden mit mir...«

Sie verließ die Ordination, um über den Hausflur wieder die Wohnräume zu betreten, da sah sie vor dem Spiegel der Mantelgarderobe ein paar Münzen glänzen. Näher hinsehend war es eine gute Handvoll Kreuzer, darunter gar ein paar Silberstücke. Alle Patienten hatten unaufgefordert und sofort ihr vermeintliches Honorar hinterlegt. Die Hilfsbereitschaft dieser Menschen überwältigte Dorothea. Und am kommenden Tag, an dem das Wartezimmer erneut von Ratsuchenden angefüllt war, sollte sie noch von ganz anderer Seite Hilfe angeboten bekommen.

Ein langer arbeitsreicher Vormittag lag bereits hinter Dorothea, als es wieder hieß:
»Der Nächste bitte!«

Eine hohe Gestalt im schwarzen Habit trat ein.
»Guten Tag, Dorothea«, sagte eine tiefe Stimme. Dorothea, eben noch damit beschäftigt, eine Pinzette zu säubern, sah auf.
»Oh, Erxleben!« rief sie, als käme die Erinnerung von weit her, und sie verbesserte sich sogleich zu schicklicherer Anrede. »Guten Tag, Herr Diakon!« Sie hatten sich lange nicht gesehen, der Diakon und seine Schülerin. Seinem Unterricht war Dorothea längst entwachsen, und wenn man von Begegnungen in Amt und Würden absah, hatte anscheinend auf beiden Seiten eine gewisse Absicht bestanden, sich gegenseitig aus dem Weg zu gehen. Jetzt stand er in voller Größe vor ihr, und Dorothea ordnete ihn, Verlegenheit oder Abwehr, als weiteren Patienten ein.
»Wo fehlt es denn, Herr Diakon? Sie wissen ja, mein Vater ist...«
»Ja, ich weiß, Dorothea, und ich bin kerngesund...«
»Ist es bei Ihrer Frau wieder einmal soweit? Sie wissen, ich darf ihr nicht beistehen, da muß schon eine Hebamme her...«
»Nein, nein, auch das ist es nicht... ich bin gekommen... ich wollte wissen...« So wenig er von der Kanzel herab ins Stocken geriet, so schien er jetzt nach den rechten Worten zu suchen.
»Kann ich irgendetwas für dich tun, Dorothea? Für dich und deine Familie?«
Eben noch aktiv und tapfer, überkam Dorothea mit einem Mal eine innere Schwäche, die sich einzugestehen sie mit Entsetzen erfüllte. Alle Verantwortung abzuschütteln, sich gegen die Schulter dieses Mannes zu lehnen, hilflos, ängstlich, verzagt, einzig von ihm Kraft

und Trost zu empfangen, das erschien ihr für einen Augenblick als das köstlichste Glück. Die Versuchung war groß, fast überwältigend. Etwas davon trat wohl auf ihrem Gesicht in Erscheinung, ein Schimmern der Augen, ein Beben der halb geöffneten Lippen.
Erxleben faßte die ehemalige Schülerin am Ellenbogen und zog sie unmerklich eine Spur näher zu sich.
»Du bist verändert, Dorothea, mein Gott ja, du bist eine richtig erwachsene Frau...«
»Ich war im letzten November fünfundzwanzig!«
Der Druck seiner Finger verstärkte sich, ihre Blicke lagen lauernd ineinander, dann ließ er sie plötzlich los.
»Also, wenn wir irgendwie helfen können – Sophie und ich...«
Der Augenblick zerriß, der Zauber war verflogen.
»Besten Dank, Herr Pfarrer,* der Frau Pfarrerin meinen Gruß!« sagte Dorothea, wieder ganz gehorsames kleines Mädchen, und strich eine vorwitzige Haarsträhne unter den Rand ihrer weißen Leinenhaube.
»Ich werde es ausrichten«, bestätigte Erxleben trocken und ging zur Tür. »Soll ein nächster Patient eintreten?«
An ihm vorbei hatte sich schon eine alte Frau gedrängt, ein weinendes Kind an der Hand.
»Ach sehen Sie nur, Frau Doktor, mein Enkel ist gestürzt! Er blutet, sehen Sie nur, an beiden Knien!«

---

* Bis zum Jahre 1833 waren Stellung und Anrede ›Diakon‹ und ›Pfarrer‹ wie auch ›Pastor‹ absolut identisch. Nur wenn es auf einer Stelle zwei Pfarrer gab, nannte man denjenigen ›Diakon‹, der das geringere Gehalt bekam, also auch meist der jüngere war. Erst 1833 änderte sich die Bedeutung des ›Diakons‹ vor allem dadurch, daß dieses Amt nun auch ein Laie bekleiden durfte, der sich u.a. mit Krankenpflege befaßte. (Daher auch ›Diakonissen‹)

»Zuerst, gute Frau, Doktor bin ich nicht!« stellte Dorothea sofort richtig, wandte sich dann aber dem Kind zu. »Na, das werden wir gleich haben, kleiner Bub, und was hältst du von einer schönen bunten Zuckerstange gegen deine Tränen?«

Acht Wochen blieb der Vater fort. In dieser Zeit hatte Dorothea Leporin viel gelernt, ganz einfach weil die Menschen ihr vertrauten, mit ihren Schmerzen und Leiden zur ihr kamen, und sie versuchte, ihnen mit ihrem Instinkt und ihrem Wissen zu helfen.
Jeden Tag war das Sprechzimmer voller Patienten; ihre Beschwerden von unterschiedlichster Art und Schwere. Nur selten flammte bei einer Anweisung oder Anwendung Dorotheas einmal Mißtrauen gegen ihr Geschlecht auf.
»Ei, sieh nur einer an, was so ein naseweises Frauenzimmer schon wissen will!« begehrte wohl einmal der eine oder andere auf, wurde aber zumeist von den Umsitzenden beruhigt:
»Ah was, tut sie doch nur, was sie vom Doktor gelernt und abgeguckt hat! Und das seit sie ein ganz kleines Kind war! Nein, nein, unsere Demoiselle, die weiß mehr als so mancher Medikus!«
Und wenn dann Dorothea ihre Verordnungen so bestimmt wie liebenswürdig hervorbrachte, war solcher Widerstand meist rasch überwunden.

Irgendwann zwitscherte ein Vogel dem Doktor Leporin im fernen Leipzig zu, daß das 21. Infanterie-Regiment vollzählig nach Schlesien abkommandiert sei. So schirrte er die Schnecke vor den Wagen und lenkte sie heimwärts.

An einem Tag im März des Jahres 1741, einem Tag voller Frühlingsahnung, den ein strahlend blauer Himmel überdachte und eine goldene Sonne wärmte, kam das Wägelchen in die Stadt gerollt, durchs Oeringer Tor just den Steinweg herauf. Die Leute zogen den Hut und wünschten einen guten Morgen, als sei nichts gewesen, schickten aber im Laufschritt die Nachricht ins Haus Nummer 51 »Der Doktor kommt! Der Doktor kommt!« Die Damen jubelten:
»Der Vater kommt, der Vater kommt heim!« Dorothea und Maria liefen Arm in Arm die Gasse entlang, wo man schon das träge Hufgeklapper der Schnecke näherkommen hörte.
»Vater, Vater!« rief Maria und sprang aufs Trittbrett des Wagens.
»Papa, liebster Papa!« Dorothea erklomm gar im Fahren den Kutschbock, um den Heimkehrer herzlich zu umarmen.
In der Haustür stand dann die Mutter.
»Willkommen, Leporin!« sagte sie fest, die Hände unter der Schürze verbergend.
Tränen in ihren Augen zeigten, daß sie sich weit klarsichtiger gesorgt hatte in diesen Wochen, als der Anschein es hatte glauben lassen.
»Na, wie seid ihr zurecht gekommen ohne mich?« wollte Leporin nach dem ersten Willkommen wissen.
»Zurechtgekommen ja...« meinte Dorothea zögernd, »aber gefehlt hast du uns, Papachen, an allen Ecken hast du uns gefehlt!« Damit war Doktor Leporin eigentlich recht zufrieden und liebevoll schloß er alle drei noch einmal in seine Arme.
»Die Gefahr ist aber noch nicht vorüber, ist es nicht so,

Leporin?« sorgte sich seine Frau weiterhin. »Unsere Söhne sind noch immer Deserteure, und du solltest keinem vom Regiment begegnen!«

»Ach, die haben jetzt andere Sorgen!« rief der Doktor fast fröhlich, »die müssen erst einmal ihrem König Schlesien bewachen. Erobert war es schnell, aber jetzt heißt es aufpassen, Posten aufstellen in jeder Stadt, in jedem Dorf, damit der Feind sich nicht unversehens zurückholt, was er so überraschend verlor.«

Damit hatte Leporin keineswegs unrecht, so leisteten die Festungen Glogau, Brieg und Neiße noch immer verbissenen Widerstand. Friedrich kehrte, seinen Feldmarschall Graf Schwerin als ›Wachhabenden‹ in Schlesien belassend, nach Berlin zurück und hob noch einmal 30000 Mann aus, davon allein 20000 aus der Mark Brandenburg, um die unerwarteten Blitzerfolge seines ersten Krieges abzusichern. Und eben jetzt war der König erneut im Schlesischen und zwang das stolze Glogau in die Knie. Zwar brauchte er jeden verfügbaren Soldaten seiner Armee, aber Streitigkeiten seiner Regimenter um einen Studioso hier und einen schwächlichen Kaufmannslehrling dort konnten ihn derzeit wenig interessieren, schon gar nicht die Bürgschaft eines alten Medikus für seine beiden Söhne.

Doktor Leporin hatte tatsächlich der Familie während seiner Abwesenheit an allen Ecken und Enden gefehlt. So hatte Dorothea beispielsweise mehrfach versucht, den Text für ihr Gesuch an den König aufzusetzen, aber ohne die Erfahrung des Vaters in solcherlei Dingen wollte keiner ihrer Versuche gelingen. Jetzt nahm dieser sich Zeit, die Aufgabe mit ihr gemeinsam zu lösen.

»Na, laß doch mal sehen, mein Kind, was du schon geschrieben hast!«

Dorothea öffnete die Lade ihres Schreibschranks und holte ein paar Bogen Geschriebenes heraus. Das war noch nicht viel, was da notiert und gestrichen und wieder neu entworfen stand, allenfalls der Grundgedanke ihrer Bestrebungen, die bescheiden gefaßte Bitte, ihr eine solche Ausnahme zu gewähren, die Versicherung ihrer Dankbarkeit und Ergebenheit.

»Nun, ich dachte daran, auch noch die Gnade um Loslassung meiner Brüder vom Militär zu erbitten... was meinst du, Vater, sollte ich das noch anfügen?« Und ehe Leporin antworten konnte, bekräftigte sie: »Immerhin waren beide ja schon einmal freigestellt aus Gründen, die nach wie vor bestehen...« und da der Vater noch immer schwieg: »Es wird höchste Zeit, so meine ich, daß Johannes heimkehrt, kränklich wie er ist, und ebenso, daß Christian mit seinen Studien fortfährt... zumal ich ohne seine Gegenwart in Halle mich selbst nun doch nicht nach dorthin wagen würde...« Ein Seufzer folgte, der recht verzagt klang, und gleichermaßen verzagt fügte Dorothea an: »Schon den Herrn von Plotho aufzusuchen, das Schreiben – so es denn fertig gewesen wäre – an Herrn von Lüderitz weiterzuleiten... er hätte mir Fragen stellen können... nach dir und den Brüdern... nein, Vater... der Mut hätt' mir gefehlt!«

Absichtlich hatte Leporin seine Tochter reden lassen und schweigsam sich dabei in ihr Mienenspiel vertieft. Da hatte es gewettert und geleuchtet, war auf der Bühne ihres empfindsamen Gemüts ein Aufzug dem anderen gefolgt. Kühnheit und Stolz wechselten zu

Zweifel und Furcht. Leporin erkannte, seine Tochter war aus tiefster Überzeugung entschlossen, hoch oben einen schmalen Grat zu wandern, aber schwindelfrei, das war sie keineswegs.

Noch im gleichen Monat leitete der Stiftshauptmann von Plotho Dorotheas, nun mit Hilfe des Vaters fertiggestelltes Gesuch an Herrn von Lüderitz nach Potsdam weiter, nicht ohne selbst handschriftlich nochmals eine Befürwortung angefügt zu haben, und für den Fall der Genehmigung die Bitte um einen Frei-Tisch und Erlaß sämtlicher Gebühren... *inwiewohl der Doktor Leporin ein guter Medikus und sonst habil, von zeitlichem Vermögen aber vollständig entblößet ist...*

## »Aus der Feder eines vernünftigen Frauenzimmers«

Wann war es nur gewesen, daß Dorothea begonnen hatte, auch anderes zu schreiben? Genau wußte sie das selbst nicht, jedenfalls enthielt die Lade ihres Schreibschrankes mehr als jene Versuche zur Abfassung des Gesuchs an den König. Die ersten Bogen, die Dorothea dort verwahrte, noch mit kindlichen Schriftzügen bedeckt, schilderten ihr Entsetzen, als sie – im Jahre 1727 oder 1728 – auf offener Straße einem Marktschreier lauschte. Er nannte sich ›Doktor Hummel‹, und die Stadt hatte ihm erlaubt, öffentlich ein Schaugerüst aufzuschlagen, von dem herab er seine verschiedenen Tinkturen anpries, die rein alles vermochten, den Menschen gesund, reich und glücklich zu machen. Ja allen Ernstes empfahl er einen Sud aus Menschenkot als heilend gegen allerlei Gebrechen, vor allem gegen das ›wilde Feuer‹, wobei er sich auf die ›Land- und Hauß-Apotheca‹ eines Sincerus Hydrophilus bezog. Was seinen Empfehlungen an Glaubwürdigkeit mangelte, mußten die Darbietungen eines Hanswursts wettmachen, der in buntem schellenbestückten Gewand einen Purzelbaum nach dem anderen schlug. Weiterhin sorgte das Krächzen eines grünen Papageis und das Gekreisch eines Äffchens in roter Weste für genügend Zulauf von Schaulustigen.

Dorothea, seit frühester Kindheit vom wissenschaftlich aufgeklärten Geist ihres Vaters beeinflußt, widerten diese *Diskrepanz zwischen verantwortlichem ärztlichen*

*Handeln und mittelalterlichem Aberglauben* an, und genau so schrieb sie es auch nieder.
Tiefen Eindruck machte die Verurteilung einer Kindsmörderin auf die schon etwas ältere Dorothea. Agnes Fricke, eine Magd aus dem Nachbarort, hatte ihr Neugeborenes zuerst erwürgt und dann, um seines Todes sicher zu sein, auch noch im reißenden Gewässer der Bode ertränkt. Gestellt und in Gewahrsam genommen, schwor sie, ihr Kind zu lieben, es aber, von ihren Wirtsleuten außer Hause gejagt und vom Vater des Kindes verlassen, nicht ernähren zu können. So stünde dem armen Wurm, versicherte die junge Frau, der Tod besser an als Schmach und Schande.
Das Urteil für Agnes Fricke lautete Enthaupten auf öffentlichem Richtplatz. Obwohl die Quedlinburger dazu herbeiströmten wie zur alljährlichen Kirmes, verbot Doktor Leporin seiner Familie, das Haus zu verlassen. Er selbst, in seiner Eigenschaft als Arzt, wurde amtlicherseits bestellt, Zeuge des Vollzugs zu sein. Dorothea traf diese Seite der Medizin wie ein Schock. Mit Bitterkeit notierte sie:
*Mein Glaube war, daß Ärzte Leben bewahren sollen, und das um jeden Preis, wie es der Eid des Hippokrates fordert.*

Auf weiteren Blättern macht Dorothea Leporin sich, erst zögernd, dann energisch, Gedanken über die Gleichberechtigung der Frau. Mutig fragt sie:
*Warum sollten Frauen nicht die Fähigkeit zur Verwaltung öffentlicher Ämter besitzen?*
Auch ihre Hoffnung, selbst eine Universität besuchen zu dürfen, und das natürlich als Studentin der medizinischen Fakultät, bringt sie zu Papier.

*Es würde schon genügen, wenn ich dadurch mehr Gelegenheit bekommen würde, meine eigenen Gedanken zu ordnen, was ich für eine so nötige wie nützliche Bemühung halte.*
Und: *Mir persönlich fiele ein Studium nicht allzu schwer, weil ich einen gut Teil des Lehrstoffs schon intus habe und mir meine Erfahrungen dabei zur Hand gingen.*

Weitere Blätter zeigen bereits einen gewissen thematischen Zusammenhang, und zwar nach Abschnitten unterteilt, die sie nach Paragraphen beziffert und die sich mit den gängigsten Vorurteilen *gegen* ein Frauenstudium, speziell gegen ein Frauenstudium der Heilkunst befassen. Sie nennt alle diese doppelzüngig und widerlegt sie nach persönlicher Meinung und Ansicht. Unter ›§ 18‹ führt sie an:
*Gelehrsamkeit schicke sich nicht für das weibliche Geschlecht, weil dasselbe nicht fähig sey, etwas tüchtiges darin zu leisten.* Und widerspricht dem recht lakonisch: *Ich finde hierzu keine Ursache, daran zu zweifeln.*
Gemeint ist natürlich der Zweifel an der Tüchtigkeit. Und Zweifel ist auch gemeint, als ihr ›§ 21‹ anführt:
*Ob das weibliche Geschlecht auch diejenigen Kräfte besitze, die um Gelehrsamkeit zu erlangen nicht zu entrathen stehen?*
Dem setzt sie sehr entschieden gegenüber:
*Die erforderlichen Kräfte sind die Kräfte der vernünftigen Seele, besonders die des Verstandes, den man auch meinem Geschlecht nicht absprechen kann, da kein Unterschied in der Seele des Geschlechtes bestehe. Sie ist Anteil des Ebenbildes Gottes, den auch das weibliche Geschlecht empfangen und davon nicht mehr eingebüßt hat als die Männer.*
Und zum weiteren Vorwurf: *Die Weiber hätten zwar*

*Verstand empfangen, aber nicht im selben Grad wie die Männer* habe sie es nicht einmal nötig, zu widersprechen, denn: *es ist nämlich zweierlei, Verstand haben und ihn anwenden!*

So geht es fort, Bogen für Bogen, und als eines Tages diese aus purem Zufall dem Vater in die Hände fallen, ist es schon ein ganz schöner Packen.

»Welch eine Fundgrube an Aphorismen!« ruft er aus und ist begeistert, aber selbst in seiner Begeisterung liegt etwas von jener männlichen Überheblichkeit, die Dorothea angreift. »Diese Schriften, natürlich erweitert und vervollständigt, sind es wert, gedruckt zu werden! Weißt du was, mein gescheites Dörtchen, ich schreibe Kommentar und Geleitwort dazu, und wir geben es als Buch heraus!«

Dorothea, ohne Für und Wider, ließ den Vater gewähren, dieser machte sich mit Feuereifer daran, 54 Druckseiten Vorwort zu verfassen, denen er die selbstverfaßten Verse voransetzte:

*Der Weg zur Tugend steht für alle offen,*
*Auch Evas Töchtern lockt derselbe Ehrenpreis.*
*Kommt, sucht ihn, eilt, bemühet Euch mit Fleiß,*
*so habt Ihr tausend Lust zu hoffen.*
*Was hoffen? Dringt hinauf zu Pindus' edlen Zinnen,*
*so habt Ihr, was man kann auf dieser Welt gewinnen,*
*Ich schreibe nur noch eine Zeile:*
*Ach, hasset doch die die blinden Vorurteile!*

Als Titel des kleinen Bändchens war vorgesehen: *Reflexion über das Studieren und die akademischen Würden des Frauenzimmers.*

Kurz bevor es dann tatsächlich in Druck gehen sollte, meldete Dorothea Bedenken.
»Der Gedanke an die zu erwartenden Urteile schreckt mich, zumal schreibende Frauen in dem Ruf stehen, belehrend sein zu wollen.« Und vorsichtig war Dorothea Leporin, zumindest, was ihre Autorenschaft anging. Dem langatmigen Vorwort ihres Vaters folgt noch ein kurzes von ihr selbst, in dem sie unter anderem dem Leser versichert:
*Endlich muß ich auch mit denen mich unterreden, die da vermeinen werden, ob wäre dieses Werckgen nicht meine eigene Arbeit. Ich weiß mich ihnen nicht ehrlicher zu erklären, als wenn ich sie ersuche, mir solche Proben anzufordern, dadurch ich sie eines besseren überführen kann.*
Das Mißtrauen, aus dem Dorotheas Vorsicht hervorgeht, bestand in der Folge absolut zu Recht. Nachdem die Erstauflage 1742 auf Leporins Kosten in Berlin bei Johann Andreas Rüdiger verlegt und im Quart-Format, 343 Seiten stark, gedruckt worden war, fand das Buch ausgezeichnete Kritiken. Der Herausgeber der ›Leipziger gelehrten Zeitung‹ beispielsweise schrieb:
*Das Buch ist mit einer guten Belesenheit und angenehmer Schreibart abgefaßt, so daß der Leser begierig wird, auch die übrigen Schriften zu lesen, die die Verfasserin herauszugeben verspricht.*

Dann aber geschah Seltsames, das niemals ganz aufgeklärt wurde. War der Absatz der Schrift nicht befriedigend oder ergab sich ein sonstiger Anlaß, erhoffte sich am Ende ein Unbekannter Nutzen daraus, jedenfalls erschien der hauptsächliche Text sieben Jahre später ohne das einführende Vorwort und vor allem ohne jeden Hinweis auf den Autor nochmals, gedruckt in Leipzig unter dem Titel: *Vernünftige Gedanken vom Studieren des schönen Geschlechts.* Diesmal meldet sich eine Hamburger Zeitung zu Wort, die den schönen Titel trägt: ›Staats- und Gelehrte Zeitung des Hamburgischen unparteiischen Correspondenten‹. Sie verläßt sich auf ihr Erinnerungsvermögen und schreibt:

*Diese Schrift hat ihren Wehrt und verdient Beyfall, weil sie aus der Feder eines vernünftigen Frauenzimmers geflossen ist, und wir erinnern uns, damals schon davon geredet zu haben. Warum aber der Verleger die Käufer hintergehen will, da er seine noch etwa vorrätigen Exemplare mit Unterdrückung der Vorrede und des Namens der Verfasserin, mit einem neuen Titel und einer anderen Vorrede nur umschlagen hat, können wir nicht einsehen. Ob ein solches Verfahren erlaubt ist, überlassen wir dem kleinen Überrest seines Gewissens.*

Erst durch diesen Artikel erfährt Dorothea von dem Plagiat und setzt sich mit einer langen Gegendarstellung zur Wehr.

*...was kann niederträchtiger sein, als ernten wollen, wo man nicht gesät hat, und ohne Scheu den Nutzen einer fremden Arbeit sich anzumaßen?*

*Und: ...ich begnüge mich damit, daß vernünftige Männer schon damals meine Schrift gut beurteilt haben, nur kann ich nicht verhehlen, daß die jetzige, von Ihnen auch mit günstigem Gutachten versehene Schrift keineswegs eine neue von einem Unbekannten ist, sondern daß allein ich die Verfasserin bin...*

Doch die Schilderung dieser Vorkommnisse greift dem zeitlichen Ablauf vor. Kehren wir in das Jahr 1741 zurück.

*Des Königs Antwort*


Der Pulverdampf über dem Schlachtfeld von Mollwitz hat sich kaum gesenkt, da erreicht der neue Marschbefehl die Truppe. Er lautet: Brieg, die zweite der drei widerspenstigen Festungen Schlesiens, die endlich belagert und genommen werden soll. Der König selbst ist bereits unterwegs.

Allein im unscheinbaren, fast schäbigen Coupé, mit nur geringer Bedeckung, reist er nach dort. Die Pferde gehen im Schritt, der König hat Zeit. So rasch setzt sich eine Armee von 15000 Mann zu Fuß mit schweren Geschützen nicht in Bewegung, und vor ihnen anzukommen wäre nicht nur sinnlos, sondern gefährlich. Schon einmal wäre er ums Haar ein Gefangener der Österreicher geworden, als er ahnungslos am Stadttor von Oppeln Einlaß und Nachtquartier forderte. Sein Glück war einzig, daß das Tor nicht geöffnet, stattdessen aber österreichisches Gewehrfeuer aus der Stadt heraus ihn von der wahren Sachlage in Kenntnis setzte. Damals rettete ihn nur die späte Stunde und somit das Dunkel der Nacht.

Heute bewegt sich sein klappriger Reisewagen im hellen Licht eines warmen Apriltages.

Meine Kavallerie hat versagt, denkt der König erbost, ich muß ihr einen neuen Geist einblasen! Und weit freundlicher wenden sich seine Gedanken der Infanterie zu. Sie haben gestanden wie eine Mauer, die langen Kerls meines Vaters. Sie haben die Schlacht gewonnen. Und auf sie, seine Grenadiere unter den hohen Blechmützen, wartet er jetzt hier auf der Landstraße nach Ost.

Die Post kann ich durchsehen, denkt der König, und greift zögernd nach einem versiegelten Schriftstück. Einen ganzen Packen davon hat der Kurier von Potsdam her gebracht: Briefe, Gesuche, Petitionen, die seine Antwort fordern, Erlaße, Urteile, die seine Unterschrift benötigen. Der König blättert und liest. Den neumodischen ›crayon‹ in der Hand versieht er ein jedes mit Anweisungen und Randbemerkungen, denen sich später seine Sekretäre annehmen sollten. Jetzt kommt ihm ein Schreiben seines Regierungspräsidenten von Lüderitz unter. Friedrich bricht das Siegel, entfaltet den Bogen, aus dem ihm sogleich ein zweiter entgegenfällt. Voll Interesse haftet sein Blick auf der großen, schwungvollen, ein wenig schrägen Handschrift. Sie beginnt mit nachträglichen Glückwünschen zur Thronbesteigung, fährt mit der Versicherung tiefster Ergebenheit fort und kommt dann auf den seltsamsten Gegenstand zu sprechen, der dem König bisher untergekommen. Eine Demoiselle Dorothea Christiane Leporin zu Quedlinburg bittet um die Erlaubnis zu einem Studium der Medizin an der Universität Halle.

*... möchten Euer Majestät die Gnade haben, mich der medizinischen Fakultät zu Halle zum Examen zu sistieren wie darauf den Gradum Doctoris, um späterhin die Freiheit des Praktizierens zu erlangen ...* liest der König, und weiter:
*...das erheblichste aber meiner wehmütigen Angelegenheiten betrifft die Befreyung meiner Brüder, denn da ich gewiß bin, daß im Falle dieselbe nicht zu erhalten ist, ich mich auch meiner vor Kummer vergehenden Eltern bald beraubet sehen*

*werde, ich aber hingegen mit dem älteren meiner Brüder meinen Eltern noch das Vergnügen zu schaffen hoffe, mit demselben zugleich den Academischen Catheder zu betreten, und mit ihm pro Gradu mich zu legitimieren ...*

Dem beigefügt sind in der Handschrift des Herrn von Lüderitz die wärmsten Worte über das Erscheinungsbild der Demoiselle Leporinin, der zu begegnen er selbst im Beisein der fürstlichen Dechantin von Quedlinburg Gelegenheit gehabt hätte, wie auch die bereits erwähnte Befürwortung und Bitte um ›Frei-Tisch‹ aus der Feder des Herrn von Plotho, Stiftshauptmann daselbst.

Friedrich las das ganze zweimal, kopfschüttelnd, aber keineswegs abgeneigt. Er bewunderte Geist wie auch Initiative bei Frauen, fand man sie doch selten genug. Doch dann mußte er plötzlich lachen. Hatte er nicht soeben selbst in einem Anfall von Sarkasmus den Bibeltext zum Dankgottesdienst für den Sieg von Mollwitz ausgesucht, und zwar die Verse 11 und 12 aus dem 2. Kapitel des 1. Briefes von Paulus an Timotheus, wo es heißt:

*Ein Weib lerne in der Stille mit aller Untertänigkeit. Einem Weibe aber gestatte ich nicht, daß sie lehre, auch nicht, daß sie des Mannes Herr sei, sondern stille sei.*

Soweit wird es mit der Quedlinburger Demoiselle wohl nicht kommen, schmunzelte der König, war der Spruch von der Kanzel herab ja auch nicht auf sie, sondern auf meine teure Cousine, die Kaiserin in Wien, gemünzt.

Friedrich II. schien noch immer amüsiert, als er auch das Gesuch aus Quedlinburg mit einer Randbemerkung versah:

*Genehmigt. Die Herren in Halle davon in Kenntnis setzen!*

Am 15. April 1741 bereits erging ein königlicher Erlaß an die Universität Halle und ein Schreiben an den Stiftshauptmann von Plotho, die sich gleichlautend so anhören:
*Seine Majestät verfügt, daß die ihm zu Gnaden empfohlene Leporin der medizinischen Fakultät in Halle bezüglich vorzulegender Promotion rekommandiert sein solle, sobald sie sich dieserhalb weiterhin melden würde.*
Nur wenige Tage darauf erreichte die gute Nachricht auch das Doktorhaus.
»Hör nur, hör nur, Dörte, mein Kind! Wir haben einen Sieg davongetragen, wie ihn ein Feldherr nicht größer erringen kann!« frohlockte Doktor Leporin. Du bist die erste, mein Dörtchen, die erhobenen Hauptes die Phalanx männlichen Vorrechts durchbrochen hat!« Die Freude stimmte den alten Mann poetisch, und feuchten Auges setzte er hinzu: »Die erste Frau, die promovieren wird!«
Dorothea, nicht weniger stolz, reagierte jedoch nüchterner.
»Nein, Vater, die erste kann ich nicht mehr sein. Laura Bassi promovierte in Bologna, und das bereits vor neun Jahren!«
»Aber nicht als Medizinerin!« rief Vater Leporin und verwehrte so der Italienerin ihren Rang, »Physik, Philosophie ... was ist das schon?«
Dorothea blieb sachlich.
»Immerhin erhielt die Bassi nicht nur den Doktorhut, sondern ihrerseits einen Lehrstuhl an der Universität,

von dem aus sie den Studiosi Newtons Gravitationsgesetz verständlich macht.«

»Newton hin, Newton her!« machte Leporin verächtlich, »du wirst Menschen heilen, Leben bewahren, Dorothea, ist das nicht viel mehr?«

Über das Gesicht der Tochter huschte ein zärtliches Lächeln, als sie sich in den Arm schmiegte, den der Vater um ihre Schulter legte.

»Ja, Papachen, ja, für dich ist es viel mehr, ich weiß es. Deine Liebe und dein Glaube machen es dazu, und so soll es auch bleiben.«

Und doch war die Freude der beiden Leporins, Vater wie Tochter, nicht ungetrübt. Das Schreiben des Königs hatte die Bitte um Befreiung der Brüder vom Militärdienst unberücksichtigt gelassen. Beide galten also weiterhin als Deserteure, die preußischen Boden nicht betreten konnten, ohne sich im feingeknüpften Maschennetz von Denunziantentum und Kopfgeldjagd zu verfangen. In den Städten bespitzelte einer den anderen, um nicht selbst bespitzelt zu werden, auf dem Lande verdiente sich ein Bauer für jeden gemeldeten oder gar gefangenen Deserteur 6 bis 12 Thaler. Nichts war so gefürchtet wie der Kanonenschuß vom Stadtwall, der die Hatz auf fahnenflüchtige Soldaten eröffnete. Die Erfolgsquote belief sich bei hundert Entflohenen auf achtundneunzig Aufgegriffene, denen ein höchst unangenehmes Los sicher war. Die Strafen für Desertion schwankten zwischen Spießrutenlaufen und dem Strang.

Am 3. Mai des Jahres machte Doktor Leporin eine zweite Eingabe an den König, die sich nur auf die

Freilassung seiner Söhne bezog. Er legte noch einmal den ganzen Sachverhalt dar, und zwar, daß ja beide, Christian wie Johannes, bereits freigestellt waren, der eine wegen des Studiums, der andere wegen körperlicher Untauglichkeit, daß sie also im eigentlichen Sinne keine Deserteure seien. Auch dieser Eingabe fügte von Plotho ein paar Worte an, dergestalt, daß er den Leumund des Doktor Leporin nochmals hervorhob, aber auch wagte, den Wert des königlichen Erlasses vom 15. April für den Fall, daß Christian Leporin nicht rehabilitiert wird, einzuschränken: ... *immaßen seine Tochter alleine nach den Halleschen Universitäten sich nicht getrauet* ...

Diesem zweiten Gesuch wird ebenfalls stattgegeben, beide Brüder sind nun frei. Ein letzter Punkt allerdings bleibt unberücksichtigt: Der Antrag auf ›Frei-Tisch‹, sprich Gebührenfreiheit in allen Stücken. Die Familie Leporin ist arm. Als vorzüglichem Arzt, aber wenig begabtem Geschäftsmann, war es dem Doktor nie gelungen, nennenswerte Rücklagen zu machen, aber seit er beschlossen hatte, Dorotheas Schriften auf eigene Kosten drucken zu lassen, waren letzte Reserven an den Berliner Verlag gegangen. Dazu kam, daß der Gesundheitszustand des Doktors seit seiner Flucht, immerhin zu winterlicher Zeit, sehr gelitten hatte. Was nach seiner Rückkehr als vorübergehende Erschöpfung gegolten, die nur der Ruhe und Erholung bedurfte, entpuppte sich als hartnäckige Beeinträchtigung der Luftwege. Leporin selbst suchte es mit Humor zu nehmen und sprach von seiner »baufälligen Leibes-Hütte«, aber seine Tochter sah tiefer und machte sich berechtigt

Sorgen. Immer wieder war der Vater bettlägerig, mußte Dorothea wie während seiner Abwesenheit die Praxis allein versorgen, blieben die Einnahmen auf hier und da ein Scherflein beschränkt.

Doch endlich wurde auch die Gebührenfreiheit im Falle des Studiums der Geschwister gewährt, nämlich:

*... daß wir gedachte Candidaten beyderley Geschlechts der Universitaet dahin recommendiren, sich ihrer anzunehmen, ihnen zum Frey-Tisch zu verhelfen, und denenselben in allen übrigen zu ihren Vorhaben dienenden ohne Endgelt beförderlich zu seyn.*

Alles war geregelt, nichts, so schien es, konnte Dorotheas Plänen mehr im Wege stehen.

Der Sommer ließ sich dieses Jahr ganz besonders heiß an. Tag für Tag wartete Dorothea auf ein Zeichen von Christian. Johannes war unterdessen heimgekehrt und wog wieder im Laden vom Kaufmann Hentschel Tee und Kräuter ab. Die Schwester, Maria Elisabeth, hatte endlich ihren Kramer-Wirt geheiratet und zum Kummer der Mutter das Elternhaus verlassen. Im Bemühen, Küche wie Kranken gleichermaßen gerecht zu werden, war Dorothea vom ersten Hahnenschrei bis lang nach Vesperläuten auf den Beinen, stets dem Tauziehen zwischen Vater und Mutter ausgesetzt.

»Dorothea, begleite mich auf den Markt. Die Leute sollen sehen, daß du deiner Mutter beistehst.«

»Dörte, mein Kind, rasch die Arzneitasche! Die alte Wagnitz liegt in Krämpfen!«

Dorothea weiß kaum, wo ihr der Kopf steht.

»Gewiß, Mutter, aber nicht heut! Hör doch, der Vater ruft! Morgen ist auch noch Markt, Mutter, morgen komm' ich mit dir, und die Leute werden zufrieden sein!« Und zum Vater: »Gleich, Papachen, ich komme, Papachen! Nur noch rasch die Tasche geholt!«

So geht es fort, die eine Woche und die nächste, den Mai und den Juni und den ganzen Juli hindurch. Der August bringt einen Brief von Christian aus Halle.

*Allerliebste Schwester und Kommilitonin! Reise nach hier, so schnell du nur vermagst. Man wird dir Blumen unter die Füße werfen und dich durch die Gassen tragen. Mag sich auch manch Neider unter die Menge mischen, achte ihrer nicht! Halle und die gute alte Alma Mater erwarten dich, wie auch dein Bruder Christian Leporin.*

Dorothea ist glücklich. Schon packt sie Koffer und Reisetasche, verspricht der Vater, sie höchstselbst mit Pferd und Wagen ans Ziel zu bringen.

»Es wird ein bißchen langsamer gehen als mit der Postkutsche, aber ist die brave Schnecke mit mir bis nach Leipzig gekommen, wird sie es auf ihre alten Tage auch noch nach Halle schaffen.«

Um nichts in der Welt hätte der Doktor sich entgehen lassen wollen, die Tochter bis ans Tor des Tempels der Wissenschaften zu begleiten, und auch seinen Ältesten wiederzusehen liegt dem alten Mann am Herzen.

Doch da bricht der Morgen eines Sommertages an, den die Stadt Quedlinburg nicht so schnell vergessen sollte.

## Die Sintflut

An diesem Morgen wollte es nicht Tag werden. Die Menschen spürten etwas Ungewisses, traten vor ihre Häuser, standen in den Gassen beieinander. Die Furcht ging um.
»Vergib uns, Herr, wenn wir gesündigt haben...«
Endlich dämmerte es schwerfällig von Ost, fingerte eine blaße Sonne nach den Hängen des Harzgebirges. Bis zum Mittag lag der Himmel bleiern grau über den Dächern und Türmen, ohne daß auch nur der leiseste Windhauch ging.
Dann kamen Wolken auf wie von Geisterhand, erst zart wie Federn, dann dichter und endlich von West her übers Harzgebirge eine schwarz aufquellende Wand, als dräue der Herrgott selbst mit geballter Faust. Hier und da ein Blitz, Donnergrollen von fern. Regen setzte ein, urplötzlich und windgepeitscht, mit Hagel vermischt, ein kurzer heftiger Schauer. Und dann kam die Bode daher; gewöhnlich ein kleines Rinnsal hatte sie jetzt auf ihrem Weg vom Brocken an Wassern gesammelt, was ihr das Unwetter aus Seitentälern und Steilwänden, rauschend und stürzend, nur zuführte. Binnen Stunden trat sie über die Ufer und ergoß sich dort, wo sie sich durch die Altstadt zwängte, in Höfe, Häuser und Gärten. Das Wasser stieg während des ganzen Tages, während der ganzen Nacht und auch am kommenden Tag. Als es endlich fiel, stand es noch immer in Kellern und Vorratskammern. So wie es angeschwemmt war, erdig und schlammig, mischte es sich

mit den Brunnen der Stadt, und als Sonne und Hitze zurückkehrten, alsbald modrig und faulig.

»Der Herr steh uns bei, wenn es zur Seuche kommt!« rief Doktor Leporin und warf seiner Tochter einen bedeutsamen Blick zu.

»Ja, das wäre schlimm«, gab Dorothea zurück, »dann hätten du und ich, Papachen, alle Hände voll zu tun!« Daß sie dabei mit Bedauern an ihre Abreise nach Halle dachte, war nur aus einem tiefen Seufzer zu erkennen, den sie insgeheim ausstieß.

Am nächsten Tag schon wurde der Doktor zu einem ersten Fieberanfall mit Erbrechen gerufen. Gleich drauf zu einem zweiten und dritten. Entlang dem Mummental und der Pölle lag fast in jedem Haus ein Kranker. Dorothea zog noch einmal das Buch von Professor Welhof aus Helmstädt ›Forschungen über Fiebererscheinungen‹ zu Rate, obwohl sie es schon fast auswendig kannte. Der Professor empfahl schlicht Salbeitee oder allenfalls einen Absud aus Kornrose, auch in Alkohol eingelegte Clematis, aber bei alledem, so schien es Dorothea, blieb dem Herrgott noch zuviel anheim gestellt, so der Mensch nicht endlich lerne, der persönlichen Hygiene mehr Bedeutung zuzumessen.

Bald gab es Tote, vor allem unter den Kindern. Auch das Ehepaar Erxleben traf es hart. Sie hatten ihr dreijähriges Hannchen zu begraben.

»Du solltest einmal im Pfarrhaus vorbeigehen, Dörte, mein Kind. Sie werden Trost brauchen, vor allem sie, die Erxlebin!«

»Ja, Vater«, sagte Dorothea eher gehorsam denn überzeugt.

»Als Kinder wart ihr viel beieinander, du und Sophie...«
»Ja, Vater.«
»Und obendrein ist sie deine Cousine, eine geborene Meinecke!«
»Ich weiß, Vater.«
»Ihr seid dann auch zusammen konfirmiert, du und Sophie...«
»Ja, Vater...« Er hatte ja recht, mußte Dorothea sich eingestehen, sie war mit Sophie fast eines Alters und außer der Verwandtschaft verband sie wohl einmal so etwas wie Freundschaft. Aber dann, als Sophie den so viel älteren, damals noch Hilfspfarrer zu Sankt Nikolai heiratete, und auch noch ins Pfarrhaus zog, der Kaplanei Nummer 10, das einmal ihrer beider Großvaterhaus gewesen, da wurde zwischen ihr und Sophie mit einem Mal alles so anders... War es im tiefsten Grund ihrer Seele Neid, Eifersucht oder sonst ein Groll, es zu untersuchen hatte Dorothea stets weit von sich geschoben, sich aber auch nie von der unerklärlichen Hemmnis befreit, die sie vom Pfarrhaus und seiner Pfarrerin fernhielt.
»Also, mein Dörtchen, du wirst dich um sie kümmern, nicht wahr?« wollte Doktor Leporin bestätigt haben. »Du mußt ohnehin dort nach den Kindern sehen, ob auch sie das Fieber haben.«
An ihre ärztliche Pflicht brauchte man Dorothea nicht erst zu erinnern.
»Ja, Papachen, ich sehe noch heut im Pfarrhaus nach dem Rechten!«

Wehmütig betrat Dorothea am Nachmittag dann den so anheimelnden Innenhof des Pfarrgebäudes, überdacht und von Efeu umwuchert die Treppe und der hölzerne Umlauf, von dem herab sie noch die freundlich auffordernde Stimme des Großvaters zu hören meinte: »Komm nur herauf, mein Dörtchen, deine Großmutter hat grad den Eierauflauf fertig, den du so gerne schleckst!« Wie glücklich war sie damals gewesen bei diesen beiden alten Menschen! Sie mußten auch etwas Besonderes gewesen sein, denn noch immer hatte der Name Pastor Meinecke in Quedlinburg einen guten Klang, und gern erinnerte man sich auch an seine Frau, eine geborene Heimburger.

Seufzend besann sich Dorothea der Gegenwart und nahm die Stiege nach oben in die Wohnräume der Erxlebens.

Sie klopfte an eine Tür, hinter der man lebhaftes Stimmendurcheinander hörte, so lebhaft, daß sie noch einmal klopfen mußte. Dann wurde die Tür aufgerissen, und vier blanke Augenpaare sahen neugierig zu ihr auf.

»Es ist die Doktor-Dörte!« riefen alle vier aufgeregt, »die Dörte vom Doktor ist's!«

Dorothea trat ein. Mit einem Blick nahm sie noch immer Vertrautes an Möbeln und Ausstattung wahr, dazwischen Kinderspielzeug, eine Wiege, leise schaukelnd, und im Hintergrund eine Ottomane, auf der die Erxlebin ruhte. Sie wirkte erschreckend blaß und abgezehrt. Die Geburt ihres sechsten Kindes lag gerade acht Wochen zurück.

Dorothea trat vor die Ottomane und deutete einen Knicks an.

»Guten Tag, Frau Diakonin«, sagte sie leise und gleich drauf: »Von Herzen Beileid, Frau Pfarrer!«
»Aber Dorothea! Nichts von Diakonin und nicht Frau Pfarrer! Ich bin Sophie! Einfach Sophie, wie ich sie immer war! Ach, Dorothea, wie ich mich freue, daß du kommst! Daß du endlich den Weg gefunden hast...«
Tränen rannen der jungen Frau über beide Wangen, die sich mit hektischem Rot überzogen. Tränen der Rührung, der Trauer und ganz offensichtlich auch der Schwäche.
Sophie streckte die Arme aus, um Dorothea an sich zu ziehen, fand aber nicht die Kraft dazu. So beugte Dorothea sich zu ihr herab und schlang ihrerseits den Arm um die Freundin aus Kindertagen. Doch plötzlich fuhr sie zurück.
»Um Himmels willen, Sophie... du glühst ja, du hast das Fieber! Ich werde dir...« Alle eigene Rührung verdrängend, fiel Dorothea wieder ganz in die Rolle ärztlicher Hilfe. Und die tat Not. Zum infektiösen Fieber, wie allerorten, kam hier die geschwächte Konstitution durch fast alljährliche Geburten. Dieser Körper brauchte nicht nur Heilung, er brauchte auch Stärkung, falls diese nicht schon zu spät kam.
»Bleib ganz ruhig, Sophie«, tröstete Dorothea die Kranke, »ich bereite zuhause Medizin für dich und komme zurück, so schnell ich nur kann!« Und mit Hinweis auf die fröhlich umhertobende Kinderschar: »Hast du niemanden, der für sie sorgen kann, Sophie? Du brauchst Ruhe, absolute Ruhe.«
»Ach...« kam es von der geplagten wie liebevollen Mutter, »sie sind zwar wild, aber allesamt artig...«

Angesichts einer eben zu Bruch gehenden Vase wegen eines allzu heftigen Ritts auf dem Schaukelpferd kamen Dorothea Zweifel, zumindest was die größeren Geschwister anbetraf. Und spontan schaffte sie Abhilfe, indem sie die Initiative ergriff.
»Ich nehme die Kinder mit mir«, erklärte Dorothea, und die Quedlinburger hatten mal wieder etwas zu gucken, als sie sie energischen Schritts, rechts und links je zwei Erxleben-Kinder, dem Doktorhaus zustreben sahen.

Sophie Erxleben verstarb am 22. September 1741. Sie hinterließ fünf unmündige Kinder und, untröstlich, ihren Mann, Johannes Erxleben, Pfarrer von Sankt Nikolai.

## Die Base Jakobine

Der Herbst zog ins Land und die vier Kinder Erxleben waren noch immer im Doktorhaus. Mutter Anna Leporin, anfangs wohl murrend und sich sträubend ob der vielen Arbeit, die sie machten, gewann bald alle vier lieb und war im Grunde froh, daß wieder Leben im Haus herrschte. Platz gab es ja zur Genüge in den drei Stockwerken des Steinwegs Nummer 51, waren doch auch vier Kinder Leporin dort aufgewachsen, nun alle – bis auf Dorothea – außer Haus. Aber auch sie noch immer fest entschlossen und auf dem Absprung, nach Halle zu gehen.
»Was soll nun werden, lieber Erxleben?« fragte Doktor Leporin in einem Gespräch unter Männern.
»Ich dachte mir... meine Base Jakobine könnte vielleicht...« überlegte der Diakon unsicher, »sie ist die Tochter von Pfarrer Wichmann aus Oschersleben... nicht mehr ganz jung, gewiß... aber einen Pfarrhaushalt gewohnt, wenn auch...« Gar nicht recht mit sich im reinen brach Erxleben ab.
»Wenn auch was?« forschte Leporin jetzt energisch, denn er wollte zu einem Ende kommen, war er doch selbst nicht bei vollen Kräften und Dorothea bald in Halle. Trotz allen Verständnisses für Trauer und Wehmut das Haus voll lärmender Kinder wurde im zuviel. Und der Diakon, wie es Leporin schien, war weit davon entfernt, Tatkraft zu zeigen und den Dingen ins Auge zu sehen. Ließ er als Geistlicher allzusehr den Herrn die Wege bestimmen, oder war es die verstor-

bene Frau Diakonin gewesen, die trotz ihrer Jugend dies Amt in seinem Leben übernommen hatte? Wer immer die Zügel in der Hand gehalten, sie schleiften jetzt im Sande, und man mußte ihn ordentlich rütteln, den Johannes Erxleben, daß er aus seiner Trauer erwache und sich seiner Pflichten als Vater besinne.

»Also, mein Lieber, was hat es mit der Base Jakobine Wichmann auf sich?«

»Kinder ist sie nicht gewohnt . . . war nie verheiratet . . . eine Jungfer noch, ehrbar und gerecht, wenn auch nicht gerade duldsam . . .«

»So, so«, machte Leporin und stützte sich auf seinen Knotenstock, ohne den das Laufen ihm neuerdings Beschwerden machte, »so, so! Scheint mir nicht grad das Zeugnis, das ein Frauenzimmer als geeignet ausweist . . .«

»Sie meinen, Mutterstatt an fünf Kindern anzutreten? Da mögen Sie recht haben, Doktor, und dennoch . . . ich werde nach ihr senden, der Base Jakobine, oder besser noch . . . ich werde selber reisen, sie zu holen!«

So geschah es denn auch. Der Doktor lieh dem Herrn Diakon die Schnecke und wies vorsorglich daraufhin, daß der Wagen ein Verdeck zum Schließen habe.

»Damit uns die Jungfer Base nicht naß wird, wenn ein Regen kommt!« fügte er eine Spur spöttisch an.

»Um Himmels willen, sie könnte einen Schnupfen kriegen!« ging Erxleben auf den Ton ein. Die beiden Männer verstanden einander.

An einem Donnerstag nach der Morgenandacht war Erxleben aufgebrochen und am Freitag zur Vesperzeit wieder heimgekehrt. Es dunkelte schon, als er Pferd und Wagen ins Arzthaus zurückbrachte. Er fuhr ins Hoftor ein und, da der Knecht auf sein Rufen nicht hörte, schirrte er selbst die Schnecke aus und brachte sie in den Stall vor ihre volle Futterkrippe.

»Ein Rennpferd bist du wahrlich nicht, dafür aber eine brave alte Dame.« Dankbar klopfte er das Pferdchen am Hals und verließ den Stall. Er überquerte den Hof und wollte eben zur Küchentür, als er Licht im Wohnraum schimmern sah. Er trat ans Fenster und sah hinein. Schon wollte der Diakon sich seiner Neugier schämen, aber dann blieb er wie gebannt stehen. Was er sah, rührte ihn mit einer Macht ans Herz, wie er sie lange Zeit nicht mehr gespürt hatte.

Er sah drinnen am Kamin Sophie ... nein, nein natürlich nicht Sophie – die war tot, das wußte er ja. Es mußte Dorothea sein, die er dort drinnen im hohen Ohrensessel am Kamin sitzen sah, das braune Haar rötlich vom flackernden Feuerschein, den Kopf beim Sprechen leicht geneigt, frei die fließende Nackenlinie, von der das Schultertuch gerutscht war, das Profil dunkel wie ein Scherenschnitt gegen das Licht der Flammen, deutlich die hohe Stirn, die grade Nase, der feste Mund ... wie schön sie doch war, seine Sophie ... seine Dorothea ... gleich, welche es war ... vielleicht die Inkarnation von Ehefrau und Weggenossin schlechthin, vielleicht aber auch Versuchung und verbotene Frucht.

Der Diakon wischte sich über die Augen, um dem Spuk seiner Gedanken ein Ende zu machen. Natürlich war es Dorothea, die er sah, auf ihrem Schoß das vierjährige Gustchen, Sophie, ein Jahr älter, lehnte sich gegen ihr Knie, Fritz, siebenjährig, lag bäuchlings, die

Ellenbogen aufgestützt auf dem Boden und endlich Magdalena, die älteste der Erxleben-Kinder, sah der jugendlichen ›Muhme‹ über die Schulter. Das Jüngste, das die Idylle hätte vervollständigen können, das erst wenige Monate alte Lorchen, war nicht im Doktorhaus, sondern bei einer Amme untergebracht.

Erxleben trat näher ans Fenster. Offenbar erzählte Dorothea den Kindern Geschichten und hörten diese ihr voller Interesse zu. Neugierig, was sie den Kindern wohl erzählte und auch weil er ja nicht ewig so stehenbleiben konnte, wandte Erxleben sich nun doch zur Küchentür und trat ein. Der Duft von Frischgebackenem hing in der Luft, und eine Katze sprang aufgescheucht vom Sims, als der Eindringling im Halbdunkel ungeschickt an ein paar blankgescheuerte Tiegel stieß. Endlich fand er seinen Weg und öffnete leise die Tür zum Wohnraum.

»... der ehrliche Schäfer lieferte den ganzen Schatz ab und behielt keinen einzigen Heller für sich...« hörte Erxleben Dorothea gerade sagen und freute sich.

»Das ist die Sage der zwei Türme von Sankt Nikolai, die sie einmal von mir lernte!«

Kaum, daß die Kinder den Vater entdeckten, stoben sie auseinander.

»Vater, Vater!« riefen sie und liefen ihm entgegen, als wäre er nicht zwei Tage, sondern Jahre fort gewesen. Sogar das Gustchen hangelte sich von Dorotheas Schoß herab und trippelte durch die Stube.

»Papa, Papa! Die Kirche hat zwei Türme, Papa, und das ist, weil der Schäfer Gold gefunden...« plapperte es, stolz auf sein neuestes Wissen.

Erxleben küßte die Kinder, eins nach dem anderen,

und unschlüssig, ob er Dorothea gleichermaßen begrüßen dürfe, blieb er vor dem Ohrensessel stehen.

»Guten Abend, Herr Diakon«, sagte Dorothea förmlich und sah zu ihm auf. Hinter ihrer Förmlichkeit aber verbarg sich ein ähnlicher Sturm, wie er Erxleben durchweht hatte, als er draußen vorm Fenster gestanden. Hatte Dorothea mehrfach bei Begegnungen mit Erxleben den Wunsch verspürt, sich schutzsuchend an ihn zu schmiegen, sich seiner Kraft und Überlegenheit zu überlassen, so verspürte sie jetzt, da er zu später Stunde, übermüdet und noch immer von Trauer gezeichnet ins Zimmer trat, den lebhaften Wunsch, sich ihm zärtlich zu nähern, aber diesmal um Trost zu spenden und die eigene Kraft mit ihm zu teilen, von der sie ein Übermaß zu haben schien.

Johann Christian Erxleben war unterdessen vierundvierzig Jahre alt, kein junger Mann mehr, aber immer noch von imposanter Erscheinung, mit ebenmäßigen, männlich wirkenden Gesichtszügen von großer Klarheit des Geistes, aber auch menschlicher Empfindsamkeit. Noch immer unsicher, wie er Dorothea zu begrüßen habe, beugte er sich schnell entschlossen zu ihr und küßte sie auf die Stirn.

»Du verstehst es wunderbar mit den Kindern«, sagte er schlicht, »ich danke dir.«

Dorothea fühlte ihre Wangen sich blutrot übergießen, zum einen, weil er ihr dankte, zum anderen des Kusses wegen, den ersten, den sie je von ihm erhalten.

»Nun, was ist?« fragte Dorothea endlich »ist die Base nicht mitgekommen?«

»Doch«, kam es kleinlaut von Erxleben, »sie ist im Pfarrhaus und werkelt dort seit einer Stunde, rückt

Möbel, sieht in Truhen und Schränke... eine Bestandsaufnahme nennt sie das...«
»Das klingt nicht gut.« Dorothea biß sich auf die Lippen. Ein Urteil stand ihr nicht zu. »Und wie war die Fahrt?« fragte sie stattdessen möglichst unverfänglich.
»O je«, machte der Diakon, »die ganzen vier Meilen\* hat sie gebraucht, Bedingungen und Forderungen zu stellen und mir ihre Vorstellung von der Führung eines christlichen Haushalts darzulegen, ebenso wie die Erziehung der Kinder...«
Jetzt half alles Lippenbeißen nichts, Dorothea lachte laut heraus.
»Armer Erxleben!« rief sie, und er lachte befreit mit.
»Das wird was werden, wenn ich's mir recht überlege...« Doch plötzlich ernst werdend: »Was sollte ich denn anderes tun, Dorothea? Sag, was sollte ich tun, statt die Base kniefällig zu bitten...?«
Auch Dorothea wurde wieder ernst. Auf seine Frage sagte sie nichts, obwohl eine Antwort darauf ihr schon längere Zeit im Kopfe spukte.

\* 1 preuß. Meile = 7,5 Km

*Der Heiratsantrag*

Die Anwesenheit der Base Jakobine Wichmann im Pfarrhaus von Sankt Nikolai wurde tatsächlich ein Fehlschlag und endete im Fiasko.
Die Kinder fanden von Beginn an keinen Zugang zu ihr. Schon das Äußere der Demoiselle Wichmann war nicht geeignet, ihnen die Scheu zu nehmen. Mitten im farbenprächtigen Rokoko trug sie nur graubraune Kleidung, weder Spitze noch Borte, und ihr Haar straffte sie in einen Knoten.
Jakobine war groß und hager, ihr Gesichtsausdruck grämlich, so als täte jedermann ihr Unrecht. Die Methoden ihrer Kindererziehung, auf die sie großen Wert legte, wurzelten nicht in liebevoller Anleitung, sondern in Mißgunst und Neid auf etwas, das Gott ihr versagt hatte. Sie verlangte Disziplin in allem und jedem, selbst da, wo Vier- bis Neunjährige weit überfordert waren.
»Halt dich gerade, Fritz«, hieß es bei Tisch, »falte die Hände, Auguste« beim Dankgebet, »sprich nicht ungefragt, Magdalena« während der ganzen Mahlzeit. So ging es von Befehl zu Befehl den lieben langen Tag. Schon witzelten Nachbarn über den neuen Ton bei den Erxlebens. »Der Soldatenkönig ist tot, aber seine Frau lebt noch – im Pfarrhaus nebenan!«
In Haus und Küche stellte Base Jakobine die Kinder zu Arbeiten an, für die diese schlicht zu jung waren. Putzen, kehren, kochen, und wenn dabei einmal Glas oder Schüssel zu Bruch gingen, setzte es Schläge.

Mit fröhlichem Spielen und ausgelassenem Toben war es im Pfarrhaus nun vorbei, aber auch mit besinnlichen Stunden, Märchenerzählen, Kinderliedern, Bilderbüchern.

Zu spät spürte Pfarrer Erxleben seine Autorität im Hause schwinden und erkannte, daß er nur noch den Vermittler zwischen Kindern und Base machte, um Schlimmeres zu verhüten. Er trauerte wie die Kinder nicht mehr allein um den Verlust der Frau und Mutter, sondern um alles mit ihr Verlorene wie Eintracht und Wärme, Liebe und Zärtlichkeit. Das Schlimmste aber war ihm, daß er keinen Grund mehr hatte, des öfteren ins Doktorhaus hinüberzulaufen.

Ähnlich empfand Dorothea. Nicht nur, daß es für sie keinen Anlaß zu Besuchen im Pfarrhaus gab, ja sie mied es geradezu, hatte doch die Demoiselle Wichmann nur allzu deutlich gezeigt, daß sie Dorotheas Erscheinen als Einmischung und Kontrolle zurückzuweisen gedachte.

»Die Kinder sind sauber und wohlgenährt«, pflegte sie zu sagen, »es fehlt ihnen an nichts.«

Jede weitere Vokabel war der Base unbekannt, also beschränkte Dorothea sich darauf, sonntags in der Kirche den Kindern zuzunicken, wenn diese kerzengerade wie Ladestöcke, aber mit betrübten Gesichtern in der Bank saßen, während ihr Vater von der Kanzel die Nächstenliebe predigte.

Der Winter kam mit glitzerndem Flockenwirbel, der sich zu weißem, weichem Schneepolster lagerte, aber kein Schneemann wurde gebaut, keine Schlittenfahrt unternommen. Der Schnee schmolz wieder, machte

Platz für Blüten, Blumen und ringsum neues Grün, aber kein Kind pflückte einen Strauß auf bunter Wiese, wand sich einen Kranz aus Akelei und Türkenbund, streunte am Zufluß der Bode oder träumte auf Moos unter Bäumen.
Längst hätte Dorothea jetzt ihr Studium in Halle aufgenommen, wäre es nicht so schlecht um die Gesundheit ihres Vaters bestellt gewesen. Wieder kümmerte sie sich um die Praxis, um Kranke und Sieche, die Hilfe für ihre Leiden suchten. Sie tat es zum einen aus ärztlicher Berufung, zum anderen aber aus bitterer Geldnot. Jeder Kreuzer, der gegeben wurde, war den Leporins willkommen, offiziell kassieren durfte Dorothea nicht. Natürlich galt es auch zu verhindern, daß die Patienten sich zu anderen Ärzten hin verliefen solang der Doktor krank war, und so die Praxis gänzlich zum Erliegen kam. Schon rühmte sich Doktor Grasshoff laut, daß er das Fräulein von Oppen auf dem Schloß oben behandle, das immerhin Hofdame Ihrer Hoheit, der Frau Äbtissin sei. Und Doktor Herweg ließ keine Gelegenheit aus, herumzuerzählen, die Frau Bürgermeister habe ihn zum Aderlaß gerufen.
So oft es eben ging, erschien Doktor Leporin selbst in der Praxis und sprach den im Ordinationszimmer Wartenden Mut zu.
»Sie kann euch genau so helfen wie ich«, sagte er und deutete mit dem Kopf zu Dorothea hin, »sie hat's von mir gelernt. Sagt nur, wo es weh tut, und sie gibt euch die rechte Arzenei!«
Manchmal legte Leporin noch schnell ein Pflaster auf oder tastete den gedunsenen Leib des Wirts vom ›Goldenen Lamm‹ ab, aber dann bedurfte sein schwaches,

gepeinigtes Herz meist wieder der Schonung, und er zog sich auf sein Krankenlager zurück. Dort war er dann geduldiger Patient der eigenen Tochter, und wenn diese liebevoll schalt:
»Halt du nur Ruhe, Papachen, und sorg dich nicht so viel«, dann war es schon ihre freundliche Stimme, die ihm tatsächlich half.

Hinter dem Doktorhaus, dort wo Hof und Garten zusammenstießen, stand eine Bank, rechts und links von ihr hochstämmige Rosenstöcke, die schon kräftig Knospen ansetzten.
Wann immer Wetter und Befinden es erlaubten, saß der Doktor hier, Nachbars Katze auf dem Schoß, die Augen geschlossen, das Gesicht der Sonne zugekehrt, und überdachte sein langes Leben. Er dachte an die Zeit, da auch er in Rede und Schrift für eine fortschrittliche Medizin und eine breitere Basis ihrer Lehre gekämpft, ähnlich wie es jetzt seine Tochter tat.
In den frühen zwanziger Jahren war eine erste Abhandlung erschienen, die nach damaliger Mode den ellenlangen Titel trug:
*Unmaßgeblicher Vorschlag, wie fast alle Städte gleichsam zu Akademien zu machen, und eben dadurch die Aufnahme derer Studien gar merklich könne befördert werden.*
Beruhend auf der Erkenntnis, daß die vorhandenen Universitäten längst nicht über genügend Möglichkeiten zur Ausbildung weiterer Kreise verfügten, schlug Leporin Punkt für Punkt vor:
Jede Stadt, auch diejenigen kleineren Ausmaßes, sollte Hochschulen beziehungsweise Lehrstellen errichten, an denen jedermann – möglichst gratis – eine umfassende

Allgemeinbildung erwerben kann. Wer dann ein Studium an einer der großen Universitäten wünsche, könne sich nach einer solchen Vorbereitung einer Kommission zur Prüfung seines Wissenstandes stellen. An derlei Hochschulen sollten prominente Dozenten zu wöchentlich drei Stunden unentgeltlicher Vorlesung verpflichtet werden, meinte Leporin in seiner Schrift. Besonderen Wert legte er darauf, daß Studenten bereits während des Studiums praktisch tätig wurden. So sollten Mediziner beispielsweise gemeinsam mit den sie ausbildenden Ärzten Krankenbesuche machen und in Siechenhäusern arbeiten.

Weiter suchte Leporin wissenschaftliche Bibliotheken der Öffentlichkeit zugänglich zu machen, ebenfalls gratis versteht sich. Er wünschte, Gelehrte und Professoren ohne Familie zu verpflichten, ihren Bestand an Büchern ausschließlich diesen öffentlichen Bibliotheken zu vererben. Durch alle diese Maßnahmen wollte Leporin vermeiden, daß in vielen Berufen Menschen tätig würden, die *kaum mehr als eine Schein-Wissenschaft erlangten.*

Doch bereits vorab resignierend schloß er seinen Aufruf mit den Worten:

*Ob indessen solche Vorschläge jemahls werden angenommen werden, solches ist wieder eine andere Frage, denn es muß offt unterbleiben, was möglich, nöthig, billig und nützlich wäre.*

Auch anderes hat er schriftlich festgehalten, so erinnert sich Leporin und blinzelt ein wenig in die Sonne, an einen Aufsatz *Nachricht vom Handschaden eines Knaben, so er bei der Losschießung einer Flinte bekommen.* Er muß sich ein wenig besinnen, wie es dazu kam, dann aber fällt's ihm wieder ein. Das war der große Streit mit Kollega Bollman, damals Stadtphysikus und seit der Sache unversöhnlicher Gegner. Dem Herrn Braunbehren sein Jüngster hatte mit einer Flinte gespielt und ein plötzlich abgehender Schuß riß ihm fast den Daumen von der Hand. Doktor Bollmann, behandelnder Arzt der Familie Braunbehren, war nicht zu erreichen, so rief man den damals jungen Doktor Leporin, soeben aus Aschersleben übersiedelt, und dieser, seiner Sache sicherzugehen, zog den Herrn Chirurgus Johann Osswald mit hinzu. Gemeinsam taten sie ihr Möglichstes, aber der Daumen, nur noch lose durch einen Hautlappen mit der Hand verbunden, war nicht mehr zu retten. Osswald nahm den Daumen ab, und beide Ärzte sorgten gemeinsam für ein sauberes Abheilen der Nahtstelle. Bollmann, der sich übergangen fühlte, zog nun zu Felde, nannte Leporin unerfahren und Osswald übereilt.

Der Artikel aus Leporins Feder, gedruckt und veröffentlicht, erklärte den Fall eingehend, begründete die getroffene Maßnahme und diente so der grundsätzlichen Rechtfertigung.

Bollmann verstärkte darauf seine Kritik nur noch und gebrauchte Ausdrücke wie ›Medikant‹, ›Ertz-Schelm‹ und ›Pfuscher‹.

»Ja«, seufzte Leporin auf der Gartenbank hinterm Doktorhaus, »das war nicht eben die Voraussetzung zu einem leichten Anfang damals in Quedlinburg...«

Ganz versunken in die Vergangenheit und vielleicht dabei auch ein wenig eingenickt, hörte Doktor Leporin Schritte, die sich näherten und spürte einen Schatten auf sich fallen. Mit einer Hand schirmte er die Augen gegen das flirrende Himmelslicht und erkannte seinen Besucher.

»Ah! Erxleben, mein Lieber, suchen Sie nach einem Ihrer verlaufenen Schafe? Sie finden es recht marode und erschöpft von mehr als fünfzig Lebensjahren.«

»Ein jeder darf einmal ausruhen, der allezeit so rührig war wie Sie, Doktor«, erwiderte der Pfarrer wohl gerade aus dem Gottesdienst kommend, da er noch Habit und Beffchen trug.

»Aber, verehrter Leporin, ich bin gekommen, eine andere Sache mit Ihnen zu bereden...«

Eine ganze Weile hatten die beiden Männer schon miteinander gesprochen, als die Tür zum Haus sich öffnete und Dorothea über den Hof gelaufen kam. Eine Schürze, die sie vorgebunden trug, zeigte deutlich Spuren der Arbeit eines ganzen Vormittags zwischen Kranken und Verletzten, zwischen Unglück und Gebrechen.

»Vater!« rief sie schon von weitem, »Vater, die Müllerin hustet schlimmer denn je! Geb' ich ihr vom Quittenschleim oder...« Gewahr werdend, welch seltener Gast da neben dem Vater auf der Bank saß, suchte Dorothea noch im Laufen die Schürze abzubinden und sie hinter ihrem Rücken zu verbergen »... oder geb' ich ihr Pappelblüten in heißem Zucker?« Ein wenig außer Atem, die Wangen gerötet, blieb sie stehen. »Guten Tag, Herr Diakon!« sagte sie artig.

Erxleben hatte sich erhoben und schien etwas sagen zu wollen, aber Leporin kam ihm zuvor.

»Komm her, Dörte, mein Kind. Den Husten der Müllerin kurieren wir später. Erst höre, was der Herr Pfar-

rer und ich dir zu sagen haben...« er streckte seine Hand aus und faßte nach der seiner Tochter, »...besser gesagt, wozu Pfarrer Erxleben meine Erlaubnis eingeholt hat, nämlich dich zu fragen, ob du seine Frau werden willst!«
In Dorotheas Augen trat ein Leuchten, das alle Antwort vorwegnahm.
»Ist das wahr, Herr Diakon?« rief sie. »Ist das wirklich wahr?«
»Ja«, sagte Erxleben und trat einen Schritt vor, »aber nicht mehr Diakon, hörst du... Johannes.«
»Johannes«, probierte Dorothea flüsternd und sah zu Boden, »Johannes... so ist es also endlich wahr!«

Die Hochzeit fand am 14. August 1742 statt, die Trauung vollzog Amtsbruder Meene in der Kirche von Sankt Nikolai.

## »Du wirst eine Doktorin, versprich mir das!«

Nun war sie die Frau Pfarrerin Dorothea Erxlebin und zog in die Kaplanei Nummer 10 ein, das einstige Großvaterhaus, in dem sie als Kind so gern ein- und ausgegangen war.
Alles im Leben muß seine Ordnung haben. So verzeichnet ein Übergabeprotokoll bis in alle Einzelheiten Einrichtung und Ausstattung des Hauses, in dem Dorothea als Pfarrfrau nun Herrin war.

*I. Unten auf der Diele im Hause,* so wird aufgezählt,
*1) Eine Hauß Thür nebst Schloß und Schlüßel, wie auch 4 Riegeln.*
*2) Eine Klocke an der Thür,*
*3) 3 Fenster auf der Diele nach der Gaße nebst eisernen Stäben.*
*4) Ein Klein Fenster über der Thür.*
*5) Ein großer Thisch.*
*6) Eine Kannrücke.*
*7) Eine Thür nach dem Hofe mit 2 Anwürffen und 2 Riegeln.*
*8) Eine Gitter Thür dafür.*
und so fort durch alle Zimmer, römisch beziffert, wie auch endlich:
*VI. Die Stube nach welcher man von der Wohnstube durch eine Treppe hinauf steiget, daselbst:*
*1) Eine Thür nebst Schloß und Schlüßel.*
*2) Eine Thür nach dem Gange nebst einem Drücker und 2 Riegeln.*

*3) Eine andere Thür davor nach dem Gange.*
*4) 4 Fenster nach der Gaße, mit so vielen Vorsetzladen und eisernen Riegeln.*
*5) Ein eiserner Ofen mit einem Aufsatze von schwarzen Kacheln.*

In ähnlicher Weise werden Hof und Garten festgehalten und ausdrücklich bescheinigt, daß dem jeweiligen Pfarrhaushalt das Recht der Ernte von Obst und Nüssen zusteht.

Kaum anders als ein Teil des Hauses, Tür, Fenster, Ofen oder ein Möbelstück vielleicht, zwar nicht im Protokoll vermerkt, gehörte eine Magd zum Pfarrhaushalt. Martha war ihr Name, eine fleißige Kraft, so still und selbstverständlich, wie es die Trine im Doktorhaus war.

Was Dorotheas Pläne hinsichtlich ihres Studiums an der Universität Halle betraf, dachte sie: Aufgeschoben ist nicht aufgehoben. Sie selbst drückt es schriftlich so aus:

*Ob ich gleich durch die Erfahrung überzeuget wurde, daß der Ehestand das Studieren des Frauenzimmers nicht aufhebe, sondern daß es sich in der Gesellschaft eines vernünftigen Ehegatten noch vergnügter studieren lasse, wurde dennoch die vorgehabte Promotion durch meine Heyrath vorerst verzögert, da die mir nunmehro obliegende Sorgfalt für die Erziehung fünf annoch unerzogener Kinder, deren Anvertrauen ich als das erste Pfand der Liebe meines Mannes anzusehen hatte, meine Abwesenheit nicht wohl verstattete.*

Zu den ihr ›obliegenden‹ Aufgaben gehörte weiterhin, zumindest teilweise, die Versorgung der väterlichen Arztpraxis und des Vaters selbst, der immer hinfälliger wurde. Hinzu kam sehr bald eine erste Schwangerschaft, die die Anzahl der Kinder im Pfarrhaus auf sechs erhöhen sollte. Am 22. Juni 1744 wurde Christian Polykarp Erxleben geboren, dessen Namenspate zu seiner größten Freude Vater Leporin war. Auch die Geburt eines zweiten Sohnes am 9. September 1746, Albert, konnte der Doktor noch miterleben. Dann aber begann das Licht seines Lebens zu flackern und immer mehr an Kraft zu verlieren.

Es ging auf und ab mit dem Kranken, Anfälle von Atemnot wechselten mit Gliederschmerzen und starkem Kopfweh, und jede Diskussion über Ursache und Maßnahme, in die sich auch vehement die Mutter mit einschaltete, endete mit einem Seufzer Leporins:

»Ist es denn so schwer zu begreifen, daß jedes Ding sich einmal abnutzt? Mein Herz, meine Nerven sind einfach verbraucht, da hilft alle Wissenschaft nichts mehr!«

Dorothea tat, was sie konnte, doch bald sah auch sie ein, daß alle Medizin nutzlos und nur noch Liebe und Beistand für die schwere Stunde gefragt waren. Frau Anna war da ganz anderer Ansicht.

»Du mußt einen anderen Arzt holen, Dorothea!« forderte sie, »der Kammerherr von Preen war letztes Jahr genau so schlecht dran, und der Doktor Grasshoff hat ihn bestens geheilt.«

»Um Gottes willen, Mutter, laß das nicht den Vater hören!«

»Und ob ich das werde!« rief die Leporinin ohne jedes Verständnis und wurde bei ihrem Mann gleichermaßen vorstellig.
»Doktor Grasshoff muß her, Leporin! Der macht dich wieder gesund, er kann...«
»Still, Frau, still! Alles, was der kann, das kann Dorothea auch...«
»Ach, du bist vernarrt in die Idee, in ihr das Genie zu sehen! Nimm doch Vernunft an, Leporin, und laß mich einen Arzt rufen! Wenn du den Grasshoff nicht willst, dann meinetwegen den Herweg oder...«
»Nicht einer meiner Herren Kollegen kommt mir über meine Schwelle!« rief Leporin derart erregt, daß ein schwerer Anfall folgte. Wütend ging Frau Leporin hinaus, und Dorothea tat alles, um den Vater wieder zu beruhigen. Sie schüttelte seine Kissen auf, trocknete ihm die Stirn und bot ihm einen Schluck Lindenblütentee. Dann hielt sie seine Hand und lauschte dem wenigen, das er zu sprechen vermochte.
»Dörtchen, mein Kind, gib niemals auf...«
»Nein, Papachen, gewiß nicht!«
»Dörtchen, zeig es diesen Gelehrten in Halle...«
»Ja, Vater, ja...«
»...du weißt mehr als sie alle!« Er hob die Hand, um jeden Einwand auszuschließen und sprach schneller, als würde die Zeit ihm knapp. »Und du wirst eine Doktorin, Dörte, versprich mir das...«
»Ich verspreche es, Vater, ja, so Gott mir helfe!«
Beruhigt durch das gegebene Versprechen schlief Leporin zufrieden ein. Schon fürchtete Dorothea, es

sei dies ein letzter Schlaf, als sie unten im Haus laute Stimmen hörte. Begrüßungsworte der Mutter waren herauszuhören und dann deutlich:
»Kommen Sie nur herauf, Herr Doktor!« Gleich drauf Schritte auf der Stiege und die Stimme der Mutter: »Er ist der größte Dickkopf, mein Leporin, aber ich bin sicher, Sie bringen ihn zur Vernunft, Doktor!«
Dorothea war aufgesprungen und an die Tür geeilt, um den ungebetenen Gast von der Kammer fernzuhalten. Aber zu spät. Mit weitausholender Geste ließ die Mutter Doktor Grasshoff eintreten, und dieser mit ironischer Verbeugung zu Dorothea hin, erkundigte sich süßsauer:
»Nun, wie geht es unserem Patienten?«
»Was Sie anlangt, Monsieur Grasshoff, so ist mein Vater keineswegs Ihr Patient!« entgegnete Dorothea sofort scharf und suchte ihm wenigstens den Zutritt zum Bett zu wehren.
»Aber, aber, mein Kind«, näselte der Arzt, »ich war so höflich, mich pluralis auszudrücken, da mir bekannt ist, daß Sie bereits an ihm herumpfuschen... und im übrigen hat Ihre Mutter mich nicht nur autorisiert, sondern dringend gebeten, mich des Falles anzunehmen! Ich muß Sie also bitten, mir den Weg zum Patienten freizugeben!«

Über dem Streit war Leporin nicht nur erwacht, sondern wie von Sinnen hochgefahren und saß nun luftringend aufrecht in den Kissen.
»Was ist?« rief er, »Wer ist da?«
Dorothea trat beiseite.

»Der Doktor Grasshoff ist's, Papa, die Mutter hat ihn gerufen«, meldete sie kleinlaut.

Den Augenblick nutzend, schob Grasshoff Dorothea beiseite.

»Ah, lieber Kollege, da wollen wir mal sehen...«

Das Gesicht des Patienten wurde dunkelrot vor Blutandrang, sein Atem ging schwer und röchelnd.

»Sie rühren mich nicht an, Grasshoff! Mein Arzt ist die dort!« Damit zeigte er mit zitternder Hand auf Dorothea. »Sie wird die erste Doktorin der Arzeney sein, noch ehe ihr Quacksalber es euch versieht! Und die beste wird sie sein, die allerbeste...« Seine Worte gingen in Keuchen über.

»Papachen, bitte...« versuchte Dorothea den Ausbruch zu lindern. Aber noch war Leporin nicht zu Ende.

»...ihr jagt mir die Patienten ab, obwohl ich noch auf Erden wandle! Ihr macht sie dumm mit euren Reden von Vorsehung und Gotteswille und kassiert für jedes Wort, das ihr sprecht, anstatt zu sagen, daß sie die Räume lüften und sich selber waschen sollen...« Er brach ab, sein Atem ging rasselnd. Zwar erschöpft hatte er doch endlich gesagt, was ihm so lange Zeit schon auf der Zunge lag. Hatte der Besuch des Kollegen einen Nutzen, so war es allein dieser. Darüber hinaus, so mußte sogar Grasshoff eingestehen, war die Wirkung verheerend. Der Röte des Gesichts folgte rasch fahle Blässe, die Augen schlossen sich erneut, die Brust rang verzweifelt um einen nächsten Atemzug, der Mund aber, halb offen, schien das Ringen bereits aufgegeben zu haben.

»Gehen Sie, Doktor Grasshoff«, sagte Dorothea, »gehen Sie jetzt!« Sie sagte es mit ruhiger Bestimmtheit, ohne Zorn, aber auch ohne jede Versöhnlichkeit weder dem Arzt noch der Mutter gegenüber, die beide gemeinsam die Kammer verließen.
Das Lebenslicht des Doktor Christian Polykarp Leporin glomm noch eine Weile vor sich hin, bis es am 30. September 1747 ganz erlosch.

Jetzt erst wurde man gewahr, in welchem Umfang die Finanzen der Familie Leporin tatsächlich zerrüttet waren. In den Akten des Amtes Sankt Nikolai fand man Schuldeintragungen bis zu einer Höhe von 70 Reichsthalern und aufgelaufene Zinsen von insgesamt 56 Reichsthalern. Anscheinend handelte es sich um ein Kapital, das seinerzeit noch Pastor Meinecke dem Schwiegersohn vermittelt, und um dessen Rückzahlung Leporin sich niemals gekümmert hatte. Nun war guter Rat teuer. Kirchenvorstand und Stiftskonsistorium setzten sich zusammen und stimmten einem Vergleich hinsichtlich der Zinsen zu, dergestalt, daß sie auf 30 Reichsthaler reduziert wurden. Aber 100 rth hatte die Familie noch aufzubringen. Aber wie? Bekannt ist aus den Akten, daß Anna Sophia Leporin, Witwe, effektiv bis zum 2. Januar des nächsten Jahres den Betrag zurückzahlte. Es ist nur zu vermuten, daß jeder in der Familie sein Scherflein dazu beitrug.
Anna Kramer jedenfalls war gekommen, um für einige Zeit wieder im Steinweg zu wohnen und sich der Mutter anzunehmen. So wird wohl ihr Mann, der Kramer, in die Tasche gegriffen und ihr einen

Batzen mitgegeben haben. Bruder Christian, der älteste Leporin, natürlich längst mit dem Studieren fertig, verdiente unterdessen als Stadtphysikus in Nienburg an der Weser. Sein Gehalt wird nicht üppig gewesen sein, aber dennoch hat wohl auch er zu den 100 rth beigetragen. Johannes endlich, der inzwischen längst dem Kaufmann Hentschel den Rücken gekehrt und im Braunschweigisch-Lüneburgschen als Hannöverscher Feldprediger diente, trug wohl nach Kräften zur Tilgung der väterlichen Schuld mit bei. Vor allem aber war es Erxleben, der von seinem ohnehin nicht reichlich bemessenen Einkommen einen Teil abzweigte, um die Eintragung im Kirchenamt Sankt Nikolai alsbald streichen zu können.

Dorothea war jetzt zweiunddreißig Jahre alt, hatte für den Pfarrhaushalt, sieben Kinder und einen Mann zu sorgen, dessen Gesundheit ebenfalls nicht die beste war. Dabei bedrückte es sie, daß ihr Mann ihrer Familie so tatkräftig aus peinlichster Verlegenheit half. Viel lieber wäre sie allein die Hilfreiche gewesen.
»Mach dir nichts draus, Liebste«, tröstete Johannes Erxleben dann wohl, »vor Gott sind wir jetzt eins, und Ihm ist es gleich, ob du mich trägst oder ich dich trage. Allein die Liebe zählt, und die, so scheint mir, wächst zwischen uns von Tag zu Tag wie ein Baum mit tausend Ästen und Ästchen.«
Er hatte recht. Die Ehe war gesegnet, nicht zuletzt eine neue Schwangerschaft im nächsten Winter sprach dafür.

Tatkräftig hatte Dorothea gleich nach dem Tod ihres Vaters dessen Praxis in eigener Regie weitergeführt. Der Neid der anderen Ärzte, die bereitstanden, die nun unversorgten Patienten mit offenen Armen aufzunehmen, war ihr gewiß.
»Sie ist keine Ärztin, sie hat kein Recht, Kranke zu behandeln!« riefen die Herren Doktoris und bangten um den Broterwerb, den sie ihnen streitig mache. »Sie bereichert sich an den Armen, streicht das Geld ein, wo sie nur kann«, zeterten sie, »soll sie doch Frau Pfarrerin bleiben und sich begnügen, was der Klingelbeutel bringt!«

Zum Glück kamen die Patienten aber wie bisher mit all ihrem Weh und Ach zu Dorothea, ganz gleich ob sie die Frau Erxlebin im Steinweg fanden, oder ob sie an der Tür des Pfarrhauses die Glocke ziehen mußten. Sie verlangten wie gewohnt nach Dorotheas Rat und Hilfe, und, ohne zu zögern, gewährte sie beides unermüdlich von früh bis spät. Niemals verlangte sie dabei ein Entgelt, wie sie es auch bisher nicht getan hatte, lag da aber ein Thaler oder ein Kreuzer im Teller, war er von Herzen willkommen.
Und dennoch war es nicht das gleiche wie früher. Wie sehr fehlten Dorothea jetzt Beistand und Rückhalt durch den geliebten Vater! Immer wieder ertappte sie sich dabei, zu denken: Das muß ich nachher Papa fragen oder: Vater soll sich diese Wunde noch einmal ansehen! Aber da war kein Vater mehr, der lobte, tadelte und beriet, der anwies oder untersagte, Maßnahmen fachlich beurteilte, kurz über

allem wachte. Zum erstenmal fühlte Dorothea gegenüber all den Leiden, die man ihr vortrug, nicht allein die ärztliche Herausforderung, sondern die volle Last eigener Verantwortung.
Und das war der Zeitpunkt, an dem die Quedlinburger Ärzte zum Schlag gegen die vermeintliche Konkurrenz ausholten.

## *Die Attacke*

Nachdem sie im März 1750 eine Tochter, Anna Dorothea, zur Welt gebracht hatte, sah sich Dorothea Erxleben mit siebenunddreißig Jahren das vierte Mal schwanger. Und dieses vierte Mal trug sie schwer an ihrem Zustand. Ihr Körper schien ausgelaugt von der doppelten Belastung des großen Pfarrhaushalts und der Fortführung der väterlichen Praxis, jedenfalls soweit es das Gesetz erlaubte. Immerhin hieß es in der preußischen Medizinalordnung eindeutig: *Jedem nicht approbierten Arzt ist das Kurieren innerlicher Krankheiten bei Strafe verboten.*
Beraten jedoch und Heilmethoden empfehlen, Wunden versorgen und Gliedmaßen richten, das durfte sie und hatte es Tag für Tag, von früh bis spät, seit des Vaters Tod vor vier Jahren getan. Das Resultat spürte sie. Sie war müde. Hinzu kamen die Sorgen, die sie sich über gewiße Veränderungen am eigenen Leib machte, und diesbezügliche Vermutungen, die sie mit niemandem teilen, geschweige denn mit einem ihr wohlwollenden Arzt diskutieren konnte.
Wohlwollend, das nämlich waren die drei Quedlinburger Ärzte der Erxlebin gegenüber wirklich nicht. Ganz im Gegenteil, neidisch sahen sie auf den Zulauf von Patienten, den sie hatte, und mehr noch auf ihre offensichtlichen Erfolge. Besonders mit Doktor Grasshoff hatte Dorothea es verdorben, seit sie ihn des Hauses verwiesen. Doktor Herweg fürchtete eine Schmälerung seines Broterwerbs und sammelte daher fleißig

Klagepunkte gegen die vermeintliche Konkurrenz. Und Doktor Zeitz, eher zu Nachsicht und Gerechtigkeit neigend, wurde von beiden Kollegen einfach überstimmt.

»Wo kommen wir denn hin, wenn schon ein Weibsbild uns ins Handwerk pfuschen kann!« donnerte dann wohl der eine, und der andere fiel händereibend ein:

»Jawohl! Genau nach dem Buchstaben ist das zu nehmen, denn eine Pfuscherin ist sie, die Erxlebin!«

»Ihre Kundschaft sind die Armen«, hielt Zeitz dagegen, »jene, bei denen für unsereiner nichts zu holen ist. Und sie ... sie nimmt nichts von ihnen ...«

»Aha, Kollega Zeitz, wie steht es dann mit der Frau Äbtissin und sämtlichen Stiftsdamen? Sie alle schwören auf die heilsamen Kräuter der Frau Pfarrerin und wollen von uns nichts mehr wissen!«

Das war wohl wahr, gestand selbst Zeitz sich ein, und auch daß es Zeit war, gegen derlei Machenschaften eines nicht studierten Frauenzimmers vorzugehen.

»Wenn sie aber das Studieren nachholt?« suchte er noch einmal einzulenken.

»Studieren mag sie, soviel sie will«, fuhr Grasshoff dagegen auf, »da es ihr von Natur einem Mann gegenüber an Mutterwitz fehlt, schafft sie das Examen nie!«

Und Herweg wollte sich gar ausschütten vor Lachen:

»Ist sie doch schon einmal gen Halle gefahren, damals mit ihrem Bruder, um sich den Doktorhut zu holen, und kam doch nur in der Weibermütze zurück!«

Wer das Gerücht aufgebracht, Dorothea sei je mit ihrem Bruder mitgefahren, bleibt ungeklärt. Daß sie noch immer die ›Weibermütze‹, nämlich die weiße Leinenhaube, trug, so wie es sich für ein Frauenzimmer

gehörte, das war unbestritten. Den ›Doktorhut‹ natürlich sprach Herweg nur symbolisch an.
Spott und Verleumdung fanden ihren Weg auch ins Pfarrhaus und kamen Dorothea zu Ohren. Sich dagegen zu rechter Zeit und an rechter Stelle zu wehren, war sie entschlossen, aber vorerst hatte sie nicht die Kraft dazu.
Verhangenen Blicks saß sie im hohen Lehnsessel am Fenster, horchte auf Hagel und Regenschauer, die, vom Wind gejagt, gegen die Scheiben prasselten. Sie horchte in sich hinein, in ihren schmalen Körper, in dem zweierlei wuchs, ein neues Kind und Wucherungen einer bösen Krankheit. Mutlos bedachte sie ihr ganzes bisheriges Leben, in dem sie immer für andere dagewesen, und eigenes hintan gestellt hatte: das Studium, den Doktor, das Recht zu praktizieren. Doch noch wollte sie nicht aufgeben. Noch nicht.
»Herrgott im Himmel«, betete sie leise, »gib mir noch eine Frist, daß ich vollende, was ich angefangen! Gib mir die Lebenskraft zurück, die ich brauche... für die Menschen, die mir vertrauen, die auf mich bauen, die Kinder, den Mann und die Kranken, die meiner bedürfen...«
Die Tür zur Stube wurde geöffnet, und die Magd der Pfarrei trat ein, in den Händen eine dampfende Henkeltasse.
»Zeit für Ihre Brühe, Frau Pfarrer«, mahnte sie leise, »ein paar Kohlen will ich auch auflegen, Frau Pfarrer.«
»Danke dir, Martha. Stell die Tasse nur ab, ich werd' die Brühe schon trinken. Hab' mir sie ja selbst verordnet.«
Der Regen war in Schneefall übergegangen, große

Flocken schwebten in der Dämmerung eilig vom Himmel, um Dächer, Gassen und Gärten weiß zu überpudern. Martha machte sich mit der Kohlenschütte zu schaffen und fachte die Glut des offenen Wärmebeckens an. Die Frau Pfarrerin sollte es warm haben. Und Ruhe sollte sie haben, ohnehin ein kostbares Gut in einem so kinderreichen Haushalt. Eben jetzt, zur Vesperzeit, waren sie alle mit dem Vater im Gemeindegottesdienst, und ehe sie wieder hereinstürmten und fröhlich lärmten, wünschte Martha keine Störung für die Herrin.

Ärgerlich hob daher die Magd den Kopf, als draußen die Hausglocke ging. Jemand schien recht ungeduldig, denn gleich drauf schellte es ein zweites Mal. Martha schlurfte hinaus, die Stubentür halb offen lassend. So konnte Dorothea den Disput anhören, der sich am Eingang entspann.

»Die Frau Doktor! Bitte rasch!« rief ein helle Stimme.

»Nichts da Frau Doktor! Und auch nichts da Frau Pfarrer! Sie ist selbst krank, kann jetzt nicht doktorn und nicht kurieren!« wehrte Martha entschieden ab.

»Nur sprechen möcht' ich mit ihr!« bat wieder die helle Stimme, »bin eigens den Weg von Neuendorf...«

Angesichts heftiger werdenden Schneefalls und rasch einbrechender Dunkelheit schien Martha ein Einsehen zu haben.

»Also, komm herein, Junge«, erlaubte sie mürrisch und ließ einen Halbwüchsigen ein, der ganz durchfroren schien.

»Was ist?« rief Dorothea von drinnen aus der warmen Stube, »was will der Bursche? Von wem kommt er?«

»Ich bin der Knechts-Sohn vom Bauer Wegener. Von

Neuendorf komm' ich..." gab selbst der Junge Auskunft und zog die Mütze vom Kopf.
»Komm herein«, forderte die Frau Pfarrerin ihn freundlich auf, »sag, was du auf dem Herzen hast.«

Es wurde eine lange Geschichte, die sich Dorothea anhören mußte. Die Mutter des Bauern war krank, wohl eine ganz Weile schon, die Schwiegertochter aber, die Bäuerin, wollte keinen Arzt holen.
»Ist nur hinausgeworfenes Geld für die alte Frau!« habe sie gesagt, und der Bauer habe nicht gewagt, seiner Frau zu widersprechen. Dem Gesinde hatte sie leid getan, die Alt-Bäuerin, im Bett auf der Strohmatratze, in eiskalter Kammer, weil ein Feuer im Ofen wohl auch nur ›hinausgeworfenes Geld‹ war, und kaum daß einer nach der armen alten Frau sah. Aber seit drei Tagen habe sie so seltsame rote und weiße Frieseln über den ganzen Körper. Die Kuhmagd habe es entdeckt, als sie ihr Suppe brachte. Und die habe es seinem Vater, dem Knecht, gesagt, und der habe ihn geschickt, den Buben.
»Die Frau Doktor muß her!« hätte der Vater gerufen. »Lauf ins Pfarrhaus, aber erst, wenn's dunkelt, daß der Bauer es nicht merkt!«
»Die Kammer ist ungeheizt?« wollte Dorothea nochmals wissen.
»Ja, Frau Doktor...«
»Nicht Frau Doktor, mein Junge! Noch bin ich's nicht.«
»Ja, Frau Pfarrer, kein Feuer im Ofen, die Wände feucht, und Kerzen im Leuchter werden auch gespart!«
»Und rote und weiße Frieseln sagst du?«

»Ja, Frau... Pfarrer. Die Kuhmagd hat's genau gesehen.«
»Das Fleckfieber also...« Dorothea sagte es mehr zu sich selbst als zu dem Jungen, der die Gefahren dieser Krankheit wohl kaum hätte abmessen können. Ärztliche Behandlung war unabdingbar nötig. Eine Behandlung, die sie selbst nicht gewähren durfte, schon gar nicht gegen den Willen des Bauern, der wohl, wie die Dinge lagen, schon ihren wohlmeinenden Rat ablehnen würde. Dieser lautete nämlich zumindest, die Mutter in eine warme und trockene Kammer zu verlegen, ihr stärkende Kost zu verabreichen und sofort einen approbierten Arzt zu konsultieren. Dies alles dem Jungen auseinanderzusetzen, schien Dorothea nicht opportun. Was sie stattdessen sagte und veranlaßte, stand absolut, auch unter späterer Betrachtung, im Einklang mit ihrem Gewissen.
»Hör zu, Junge! Ich selbst kann nach Neuendorf nicht kommen, mein Zustand läßt es nicht zu. Aber morgen, sobald seine Zeit es erlaubt, wird der Herr Pfarrer hinauskommen und mit dem Bauern das Nötige besprechen. Du nimmst einstweilen dies Fläschchen mit. Die Wegnerin soll gleich heut abend davon nehmen, noch einmal des Nachts, und gleich morgen früh wieder. Es sind Tropfen, die das Fieber lindern. Sie wird sich darauf besser fühlen.«
Genau so geschah es dann. Der Junge bedankte sich, lief den weiten Weg nach Neuendorf zurück und berichtete alles treulich und genau seinem Vater, und dieser der Kuhmagd, die der alten Frau nach Vorschrift die Tropfen eingab. Die Patientin fühlte in der Tat Erleichterung und hatte eine gute Nacht. Auch die morgend-

lichen Tropfen nahm sie noch ein, aber als Pfarrer Erxleben am Nachmittag auf den Hof kam, mit dem Bauern zu sprechen, war die alte Frau tot.
»Du hast die Frau behandelt, Dorothea!« rief der Pfarrer heimkommend eher sorgen- denn vorwurfsvoll aus, »es ist der erste Todesfall, den man dir anlasten wird.«
Dorothea bedauerte zwar den Tod der Frau, blieb aber hinsichtlich einer Schuldzuweisung ungerührt.
»Ich bin mir keines Versehens bewußt«, antwortete sie, »es ist ein großer Unterschied *bei* einer Kur zu sterben, als *durch* eine Kur zu sterben!«
»Damit magst du recht haben, Liebes«, gab Erxleben bereitwillig, wenn auch unverändert sorgenvoll zu, »jedoch wird es hart werden, für diesen Unterschied zu streiten, sofern deine Neider die gute Gelegenheit ergreifen, dir die zweite Möglichkeit zur Last zu legen.«

Und das taten sie denn eiligst. Der Frau Erxleben war eine Patientin gestorben, und das nach Übernahme der ärztlichen Behandlung durch sie. Jetzt war die Jagd offen.

*Euer Hochwohlgeboren und Hochfreiherrliche Exzellenz werden uns endunterzeichneten hiesigen Medizinae Doktoribus und Prakticis gnädigst erlauben, in untertänigem Respekt hiermit eröffnen zu dürfen, wasmaßen seit einigen Jahren hier praxis medica durch die starke Pfuscherei dermaßen totaliter ruiniert worden, daß kein rechtschaffener Medicus hier mehr auskommen kann...* So beginnt ein Brief an den Freiherrn von Schellersheim, der seit kurzem dem Herrn von Plotho auf dem Posten des Königlich Preu-

ßischen Stiftshauptmannes gefolgt war. Ein Bote hatte den Brief von der Stadt heraufgebracht, und zwar am 5. Februar 1753 genau zum Zehn-Uhr-Läuten.
... *indem nicht nur die meisten Feldscheren*, hieß es weiter in dem Brief, *sondern auch Baders und Barbiere, Hebammen und andere wie auch insbesondere des Herrn Diakonus Erxleben Eheliebste innerlich kuriert, wie die letztere mit einer unverschämten Verwegenheit in der medizinischen Pfuscherei sich sonderlich hervortut, da sie die Patienten öffentlich besuchet und sich ohne Scheu Frau Doktorin grüßen läßt, wie sie solches gleich jetzo an der Wegener in Neuendorf bewiesen, welche an Friesel krank gelegen und gestorben* ... So ging Protest und Anschuldigung fort bis hin zum Ersuchen auf Bestrafung erwähnter Erxlebenscher Eheliebsten.
*Nicht nur für die Pfuscher selbst, insbesondere die oben Genannte, fordern wir zehn Reichsthaler Strafe für jeden Fall sogenannter ärztlicher Behandlung, sondern den gleichen Betrag auch von jedem Bürger, der sich zu solchem Behufe mit einem Pfuscher einläßt.* Unterzeichnet war der Brief dreifach: *Doktor Grasshoff – Doktor Herweg – Doktor Zeitz.*

Kopfschüttelnd faltete Schellersheim das gewichtige Schreiben zusammen.
»Das sieht mir ganz nach einem Privatkrieg aus dort unten im Städtchen«, murmelte der Stiftshauptmann. Ihm waren die Verhältnisse unter den Quedlinburger Bürgern noch nicht derart vertraut, daß er sich ein Bild machen konnte. Ganz anders Frau von Schellersheim. Ihr hatte die freundliche Frau Pfarrerin schon manche Migräne vertrieben, und wann immer Madame Erxle-

ben aufs Schloß kam, um nach den Damen zu sehen, bestand Frau von Schellersheim darauf, auch bei ihr ein Stündchen hereinzuschauen.

»Eine reizende Frau«, hörte Schellersheim sie dann schwärmen, »so reif und doch noch mädchenhaft! Fromm ist sie, aber keine Betschwester! Man meint, sie dient ihrem Gott in der Hingabe an die Kranken... und an die Wissenschaft.«

»An die Wissenschaft?« Schellersheim meinte, nicht recht verstanden zu haben.

»Ja, sie weiß mehr als mancher Medikus. Hat viel studiert, wenn auch an keiner Hochschule, aber ihren Abschluß, den möcht sie gern noch machen...«

»Ihren Abschluß? Du meinst den Doktor gar?«

»Den Doktor gar! Konsens dazu hat sie schon, vom König höchstpersönlich! Aber die Pfarrei, die Kinder, die ständigen Schwangerschaften...«

Die Worte seiner Frau kamen Schellersheim wieder in den Sinn, und nachdenklich faltete er das Schreiben nochmals auseinander. Rundweg ablehnen konnte man die Vorwürfe der etablierten Ärzteschaft wohl nicht, untersuchen mußte man den Fall, das stand fest. Aber die Beschwerden der Herren waren vielleicht mit dem ureigentlichen Wunsch der Dame Erxleben zu kompensieren, so eine Art Flucht nach vorn... man könnte doch... Aber Seine Gedanken griffen der Pflicht vor. Er hatte der Klage nachzugehen, das war seines Amtes. Also griff der Stiftshauptmann von Schellersheim nach Tintenfaß und Gänsekiel, nahm einen frischen Bogen Bütten vor und schrieb. Nach einer halben Stunde streute er Sand über das Geschriebene, blies die Tinte trocken und läutete nach dem Stiftsdiener.

»Dies ins Pfarrhaus zur Madame Erxleben! Augenblicklich! Und daß Er mir nicht an jeder Straßenecke schwatzt und Zeit vertrödelt!«

»Sehr wohl, Exzellenz! Direkt ins Pfarrhaus! Keinen Schwatz unterwegs!« Den Brief im Wams, sich tief verneigend, verschwand der Diener.

Schellersheim schnippte einen Rest Streusand vom tressenbesetzten Ärmel und lehnte sich im Sessel zurück.

»So«, brummte er, »das war erst einmal ein wohlgesetzter Schuß vor den Bug. Wollen doch sehen, wie die Dame sich zu wehren weiß ... wenn meine Frau recht hat, ist sie dazu mehr als Manns genug!«

*Der Gegenschlag*

Der Himmel erhörte das stille Gebet der Frau Pfarrerin Erxleben und stellte ihre Gesundheit einigermaßen wieder her, aber nicht ohne der Familie neuerlich Sorge zu bereiten. Der Februar brachte große Kälte. Der Weißgerber Johann starb und sollte zu Sankt Nikolai beerdigt werden. Ein Wunder, daß die Totengräber überhaupt die Grube hatten ausheben können, so tief saß der Frost. Erxleben, in Ausübung seines Amtes, fror Stein und Bein. Feuchte Kälte drang ihm durch den dünnen Talar bis auf die Haut, doch er hielt treulich aus.
»Von Erde zu Erde, von Staub zu Staub...«
Windboen fegten über das offene Grab, grad so als wolle der Herrgott im wahrsten Sinne des Wortes die Seele im Sturm holen, noch ehe der Pastor sie ausgesegnet hatte.
Als Erxleben durch das Hintertürchen von der Kirche zum Pfarrhaus hinüberlief, nieste er ein paarmal von Herzensgrund. Abends hatte er hohes Fieber. Er war ernsthaft krank, wie seine ›praktizierende Eheliebste‹ sofort erkannte.
»Ich werde einen der Doktoren holen, den Herweg oder den Zeitz!« Grasshoff schloß sie im Gedanken an die Szene beim Tode ihres Vaters lieber gleich von der Wahl aus. Den hatte sie sich zum unversöhnlichen Feind gemacht, wie sie sehr wohl wußte. Aber auch dazu, einen der anderen beiden zu rufen, kam es nicht.
»Nichts da!« wehrte sich der Kranke, »ich habe den

Doktor im Haus! Den besten und geschicktesten, den man sich nur wünschen kann! Du wirst mich schon kurieren, Liebste!« Eine fieberheiße Hand hielt sie am Ellenbogen umklammert, »Gell, Dörte, du und kein anderer? Versprichst du's mir?«
Schon um den Kranken zu beruhigen, sagte sie es zu. Und still für sich sprach Dorothea Erxleben ein Stoßgebet.
»Du hast mich schon viele heilen lassen, Herr, wohl tausend Mal mich Fieber bannen lassen! Hilf mir auch jetzt!«
Es war ihre ureigenste Überzeugung, daß all ihr Wissen und Können nichts nutze war, wenn der göttliche Segen fehlte. Ihre Einstellung widersprach in keiner Weise der Aufgeklärtheit ihres Geistes. Streng selbstkritisch wußte sie, daß ihre Kunst zu Ende war, wenn die fieberhafte Entzündung die Lungenflügel erfassen sollte, und es sah sehr danach aus. Zwei Tage lag Erxleben auf den Tod, und zwei Tage und Nächte blieb Dorothea wachsam in seiner Nähe.
Konsistorialrat Meene von Sankt Benedikt erbot sich, in Vertretung Gottesdienst und Predigt zu halten, Küster Meffert sprang in alltägliche Verpflichtungen ein. Dorotheas Sorge brauchte also nur dem Kranken zu gelten, so nahm sie jedenfalls dankbar an. Aber ausgerechnet jetzt wurde ihr ein Schreiben des Stiftshauptmannes von Schellersheim zugestellt. Sie brach das Siegel, entfaltete den Bogen, dem ein zweites, weit gewichtigeres Schreiben beilag. Dorothea begann zu lesen, aber die Schrift verschwamm ihr vor den Augen.
Selbst kaum genesen, im siebten Monat schwanger,

von den Nachtwachen erschöpft, überkam sie eine Schwäche, derer sie einen Augenblick nicht Herr wurde. Sie tastete nach einem Stuhl und ließ sich darauf nieder. Die Schreiben glitten ihr aus der Hand und fielen zu Boden.
»Was ist Ihnen, Frau Pfarrer? Kann ich etwas helfen?« Besorgt fragte es Küster Meffert, der hereingekommen war, um ein Brautpaar zur Terminabsprache zu melden.
»Es geht schon wieder, danke Meffert!«
Der Alte bückte sich, den Brief aufzuheben.
»Draußen warten Brinkhoffs Liese und der junge Mellentin. Sie wollen heiraten. Sie...«
»Ach, Meffert, schick Er die beiden doch zu Pfarrer Meene! Wo immer der sie trauen mag, hier bei uns oder in Sankt Benedikt, dem lieben Gott wird's recht sein...«
»Nicht Pfarrer Meene, Frau Pfarrer. Das wollen die beiden nicht. Sie wollen nur von unserm Herrn Pfarrer getraut werden!«
»Ach, Meffert, da wird es wohl noch dauern... Er weiß doch, wie krank mein Mann ist!«
»Ja, ich weiß, Frau Pfarrer!« Der Küster schüttelte traurig den Kopf und legte die beiden zu Boden gefallenen Bogen auf den Tisch zurück. Der eine trug wenige Zeilen in großzügiger, eleganter Handschrift, der andere war eng bedeckt von sorgfältigen, kleinen Buchstaben, die schon in ihrer Anordnung spitz und gehässig wirkten.
Gestärkt vom Gedanken daran, daß zwei junge Menschen ihrer Gemeinde bereit waren, ihr gemeinsames Glück aufzuschieben, nur damit es von ihrem Mann

und keinem anderen gesegnet würde, machte sich Dorothea ans Lesen der beiden Schreiben. Gegenüber den haßerfüllten Anschuldigungen der drei Ärzte, wirkten die Worte des Stifthauptmannes sachlich und gelassen. Dorothea hatte das sichere Gefühl, an ihm eine Stütze zu haben im Kampf, den sie jetzt ausfechten mußte. Ihm nicht auszuweichen, sondern ihn zu bestehen, war sie trotz physischer Schwäche fest entschlossen.

»Dann ist also die Krankheit meines Johannes mir geschickt als Prüfstein, an dem ich meine ärztliche Kunst beweisen soll«, sagte sie still bei sich, »und bin ich nicht die Pfuscherin, als die sie mich hinstellen, die Herren Kollega, dann werd' ich es auch schaffen! Gott steh mir bei!«

Dorothea trat an das Krankenbett ihres Mannes. Dieser war nach ruhigem Schlaf erwacht und sah ihr klaren Blicks entgegen. Sein Atem ging gleichmäßig, seine Wangen zeigten statt Blässe oder fiebriger Röte ihre natürliche Farbe.

»Dörte!« rief Johannes Erxleben und streckte eine Hand nach ihr aus, »Dörte, du hast mir eine Wundermedizin gegeben. Ich fühle mich erfrischt und gut. Und keinerlei Schmerz mehr in der Brust.«

Gott war ihr also beigestanden, die Krise war vorüber, der Patient über den Berg.

»Nicht weinen, Liebste, nicht weinen, Dörte! Alles wird jetzt gut«, hörte Dorothea ihren Mann sagen. Sie hatte gar nicht gemerkt, daß Tränen der Erleichterung und der Dankbarkeit, aber auch erneuter Schwäche und Verzagtheit ihr über die Wangen liefen.

»Ach, Johannes...« brachte sie nur hervor und beugte

sich zu ihm nieder, »mein Johannes...!« Jetzt von der neuerlichen Sorge sprechen? Von den Anschuldigungen, denen sie sich zu stellen hatte, die vielleicht das Ende ihrer Heilkunst waren? Jener Heilkunst, die sie doch eben wieder unter Beweis gestellt hatte? Nein, um ihn mit diesen Dingen zu belasten, war Erxleben doch noch zu krank. Sie mußte allein damit fertig werden. So zauberte sie denn ein Lächeln auf ihre noch immer hübschen Züge und strich Johannes über das längst ergraute Haar.

»Ja, du hast recht, Liebster! Alles wird jetzt wieder gut!« sagte sie so zuversichtlich, wie sie selbst es erhoffte. »Ich koch' dir rasch noch einen Tee aus Gerste, Weizen und Zuckerkandel, und dann schläfst du noch einmal ein Stündchen!«

Während ihr Mann seiner Gesundung entgegenschlief, setzte Dorothea sich an ihren Schreibschrank, eine Entgegnung an Schellersheim zu entwerfen.

*Höchwürdig Hochgeborener Freiherr, gnädiger Herr! Es hat dem Doktor Grasshoff, Doktor Herweg und Doktor Zeitz gefallen, bei Euer Hochwohlgeboren und Hochfreiherrlichen Exzellence mich dergestellt abzuschildern, als wenn ich in die Zahl derer gehörte, welche nicht nur durch unverantwortliche Kuren ihrem kranken Nächsten Schaden tun, sondern auch dadurch Anlaß geben, daß kein rechtschaffener Medikus mehr subsistieren könne.*

Es ist nicht leicht für eine Frau und Mutter, sich auf eine derartige Arbeit zu konzentrieren, ein solch entscheidendes Schriftstück fertigzustellen. Alle Naslang wird da die Tür aufgerissen, stürmt eins der Kinder herein, erhebt die Magd Klage über irgendetwas, braucht der Küster Anweisung oder wird ein Kranker gemeldet, der der ärztlichen Hilfe bedarf.

»Sophie erlaubt nicht, daß wir Schlitten fahren!« entrüstet sich beispielsweise Albert mit der ganzen Rücksichtslosigkeit seiner fünf Jahre.

»Nun, sie wird ihre Gründe haben, deine Schwester«, beschwichtigt Dorothea und sucht damit die Autorität der Stieftochter zu wahren, die die Aufsicht über die Jüngeren führt.

»Gründe?« begehrt Christian Polykarp auf, der mit vor Empörung geröteten Wangen neben seinem kleinen Bruder auftaucht. »Ein Angsthase ist sie, Mutter! Nur weil der Hang zum Weiher hinab vereist ist, meint sie, wir würden zerschellen mit unseren Schlitten!« Mit seinen bald neun Jahren war er ganz Verachtung gegen das weibliche Geschlecht.

Geduldig schlichtete Dorothea diesen Fall zugunsten der Sicherheit der wagemutigen Rodler und wandte sich dann wieder dem Text ihres Schreibens zu.

*Es sei ferne von mir, daß ich zu denen gehörte, welche ohne den Menschen in seinem gesunden Zustand zu kennen, ohne Erkenntnis der Krankheiten, ihres Verlaufs und ihrer Ursachen, ohne Kenntnis der Mittel und der Art, wie dieselben anzuwenden sind, nur aus Gewinnsucht behandeln, ohne zu bedenken, daß sie eines Tages dem Herrn über Leben und Tod Rechenschaft ablegen müssen.*

Bis hier war sie gekommen, als Magdalene, die Älteste der Stiefkinder, den Kopf zur Tür hereinstreckte.

»Oh, Mutter, ich möchte dich nicht bei der Arbeit

stören, aber der Vikar aus Dreyleben ist da ... darf ich ihn bitten, zum Essen zu bleiben?«
Längst war Magdalene zu einem jungen Mädchen herangewachsen, dessen Interesse ganz und gar einer Runde romantischer Verehrer galt, im besonderen aber wohl jenem jungen Vikar aus Dreyleben, wie der hoffnungsvolle Blick verriet, den sie auf die Stiefmutter gerichtet hielt.
»Darf ich, Mutter, kann er zum Essen bleiben?«
»Aber ja, mein Kind«, stimmte Dorothea geduldig zu, »bitte ihn nur zu Tisch, den Herrn Vikar, und sag Martha, sie soll eine gute Flasche Wein für ihn öffnen.«
»Danke, Mutter, hab Dank!« Ein stürmischer Kuß auf die Wange der Mutter unterstützte diesen Dank, und schon war Magdalena zur Tür hinaus. Erneut suchte Dorothea sich zu konzentrieren. Immerhin hatte sie sich ja gegen erhebliche Anschuldigungen und am Ende gar gegen ein Verbot jeglicher medizinischer Tätigkeit zu verteidigen. Schon kratzte die frisch gespitzte Feder wieder eilfertig über das Papier.
*Von klein auf habe ich mich unter Anleitung meines seligen Vaters dem Studium der Medizin gewidmet...*
Weiter kam sie nicht. Ohne anzuklopfen kam Martha ins Zimmer geschlurft. Ihre Miene verhieß nichts Gutes.
»Was soll das heißen, Frau Pfarrer, kommt da mir nichts, dir nichts die Magdalena in meine Küche, ich soll eine Flasche vom guten Wein aufmachen! Und schon hält sie mir die Bouteille unter die Nase, die ich eigens für den Herrn Pfarrer aufgehoben hab', wenn er das Bett verlassen darf und das erste Mal wieder mit

unten bei Tisch sitzt, ich meine wenn der Herrgott und die Frau Pfarrer ihn wieder gesund gemacht...«
»Martha, bitte!« suchte Dorothea die Zornige zu unterbrechen, aber nichts da, der Fluß ihrer entrüsteten Rede war noch nicht zu Ende.
»...nun ja, Frau Pfarrer, und warum überhaupt vom guten Wein, wenn doch kein Sonntag ist und kein Feiertag, nur weil dieser Mensch, dieser Vikar, der nichts ist und nichts hat, sich einmal bei uns satt essen will...«
»Nun ist's genug, Martha!« unterbrach jetzt die Pfarrfrau mit einem Anflug von Strenge, »ich war es, die den Herrn Vikar zum Essen lud, und willst du nicht die beste Bouteille für ihn öffnen, so sei es eben die zweitbeste! Jetzt aber Martha wünsche ich Frieden und Eintracht im Haus! Der Kranke braucht Ruhe, und ich hab' zu arbeiten!«
Brummelnd schlurfte die Magd zur Stube hinaus, und Dorothea tauchte erneut die Feder ins Tintenfaß.

*...und habe es damit so weit gebracht, daß Seine Majestät der König am 24. April 1741 geruhte...* Gleichmäßig kratzte die Feder Zeile für Zeile übers Papier. *...meine Kuren als Pfuscherei zu bezeichnen ist unberechtigt. Zur Behandlung der Wegener, wegen der ich mich zu verantworten habe, habe ich folgendes zu sagen. Während die Herren Gegner nicht versäumen, meine sonstigen Kuren recht schwarz zu machen und vermeintliche Fehler namhaft machen, warum tun sie dies nicht im Falle Wegener? Sie melden nur, daß diese Frau verstorben sei. Nach Zeugnissen bedeutendster Ärzte verläuft Fleckfieber stets lebensgefährlich und gilt es eher als ein Wunder, wenn ein Patient derlei*

*Krankheit lebend übersteht. Wer unter meinen Gegnern behaupten kann, ihm sei niemals ein Patient an einer derart gefährlichen Krankheit gestorben, dem erlaube ich, den ersten Stein auf mich zu werfen...*

Erneut eine Störung. Jemand klopfte hartnäckig an die Tür, ohne aber auf ein ›Herein‹ sogleich einzutreten. Dorothea blieb nichts, als sich vom Schreibpult zu erheben und, so behende es die Last in ihrem Leib erlaubte, zur Tür zu eilen. Draußen stand der Küster Meffert.
»So komm Er doch herein, Meffert«, forderte Dorothea den Alten seufzend auf, »was hat Er Wichtiges zu melden?«
Daß es etwas Wichtiges sein mußte, war dem Gehabe des alten Küsters zu entnehmen. Mehrmals öffnete er den Mund und schloß ihn wieder, bis er der Worte mächtig war.
»Ach, Frau Pfarrer! Daß es soweit kommen mußte, Frau Pfarrer!«
»Wie weit kommen mußte, Meffert?« Schon tat der Alte ihr leid, wie er noch immer einem Fisch auf dem Lande gleich, mit dem rang, was er vorzubringen hatte.
»Ich komme soeben vom Marktplatz her...« keuchte Meffert. Außer daß es bitterkalt war, konnte Dorothea noch nichts Alarmierendes darin sehen, daß der Küster vom Markt her kam, dem Mittelpunkt des Städtchens, was Handel und Wandel, aber auch Neuigkeiten anlangte.
»Ein Aushang auf dem Amt, Frau Pfarrer! Jedermann kann ihn lesen! Ein Verbot des Kurierens betreffend!«

»Ja, Meffert«, reagierte Dorothea ruhig, fast gelassen, »ich weiß, ich habe den Text hier!« Damit tippte sie mit einem Finger auf das Schreiben des Stiftshauptmannes, der den Aushang, zu dem dieser amtlich sich verpflichtet sah, wie es hieß, genau zitierte. *»Nachdem beschwerend angebracht worden«*, las die Pfarrfrau ihrem Küster vor, *»daß Bader, Barbiere, Hebammen und andere sich der medizinischen Pfuscherei unterfangen haben...«*

»Und andere, Frau Pfarrer, genau das ist's! Die Leute stehen da, lesen und gaffen, und einer flüstert dem anderen zu, daß natürlich unsere Frau Pfarrerin gemeint sei und daß ihr eine Kranke weggestorben, weil sie...«

*»...die Gesundheit vieler Menschen in Gefahr gesetzt und mancher Patient vor der Zeit zur Grabe befördert wurde...«* las Dorothea weiter vom Blatt und ließ es dann sinken. »Auf stolze zehn Reichsthaler ist die Strafe festgesetzt, Meffert, genau der Betrag, den meine konzessionierten Neider fordern! Ach, Meffert, laß Er die Leute reden, wir können sie nicht hindern... derweilen werd' ich tun, was meine Schuldigkeit ist.«

Mit einer Kopfbewegung deutete sie auf den Schreibtisch hinter ihr, und Küster Meffert verstand und verschwand eilends.

Ach, er meint es ja gut, der Alte, dachte Dorothea bei sich und wollte sich nun endgültig an ihre Streitschrift machen. Doch blieb es nicht bei dieser letzten Störung. Der Kranke verlangte ein paarmal nach ihr, und sie hatte sich zum Abend nicht nur der Familie sondern auch gastlich des Herrn Vikars aus Dreyleben anzunehmen. Erst spät in der Nacht, als alle schliefen und sie selbst auch längst hätte im Bett sein sollen, fand Dorothea Erxleben die rechte Ruhe, alles niederzuschreiben, was sie den gehässigen Anwürfen der drei Doktores entgegen zu setzen hatte.

*Ich leugne nicht, Patienten besucht zu haben, wenn der Fall es erforderte, habe aber niemals den Kranken meine Behandlung aufgedrängt. Aber ich habe mich stets nach den Gesetzen der Nächstenliebe verpflichtet gefühlt, einen Patienten, der mich darum bat, zu besuchen, und zwar nicht heimlich, sondern, wie die Herren Gegner mir jetzt vorwerfen, in aller Öffentlichkeit. Die lächerliche Beschuldigung hingegen, daß ich mich Frau Doktor nennen ließ, zu berühren, kann ich mich kaum überwinden. Niemand kann behaupten oder nachweisen, daß ich diese Anrede je gefordert hätte, mannigfach aber, daß ich ausdrücklich einem jeden verwies, es zu tun.*

Es ging auf Mitternacht, die Kerze begann zu blaken. Dorothea schnitt den Docht nach und schrieb weiter.

*Die Behauptung meiner Gegner, daß ihnen durch mein Kurieren großer Abbruch geschehe, entspricht nicht den Tatsachen. Die größte Zahl meiner Patienten sind solche, die versichern, daß sie keinen Pfennig für die Gesundheit aufwenden können, und die ich glücklich geheilt habe, ohne je mehr als einen Dank dafür erhalten zu haben.*

Ganze sechzehn Seiten wurden es, in denen sie anbot: *Da meine abermalige, in kurzer Zeit zu vermutende Niederkunft mich hindert, sofort die Promotion nachzuholen, bin ich erbötig, mich vor meinen Herren Gegnern zu einem vormaligen Examen zu sistieren, jedoch nur, wenn sie alle drei erscheinen, dieses Examen selbst vorzunehmen.* Und in nicht zu überhörender Drohung schloß sie: *Im übrigen überlasse ich es deren eigenem Gutbefinden, ob sie von Personen, die demnächst mit ihnen eines Standes sein werden, behutsamer reden wollen, oder ob es ihnen vorteilhafter scheint, sich weiterhin solchen Personen gegenüber anzüglicher und schimpflicher Ausdrücke zu bedienen.*

Gerade noch konnte Dorothea Sand über das Geschriebene streuen, es zu bündeln, zu rollen und zu siegeln, fehlte ihr die Kraft. Morgen, dachte sie nur noch, morgen..., schob die losen Blätter beiseite, blies die Kerzen im Leuchter aus, und kaum zu Bett, fielen ihr auch schon die Augen zu.

## »Alle Wetter, Mut hat sie!«

»Alle Wetter, Mut hat sie, die Erxlebin! Das muß der Neid ihr lassen!« So lautete tags drauf der Kommentar des Herrn von Schellersheim, kaum daß er die Epistel zu Ende gelesen. »Ich hätte nicht übel Lust, Teufel mit Beelzebub auszutreiben, sie nach Halle zu schicken, damit ›Frau Doktor‹ es mal den Herren zeigen kann, was sie wert ist!«
Die drei Doktores hingegen, denen der Stiftshauptmann eiligst eine Kopie anfertigen ließ, reagierten mit beißendem Spott.
»Frauen finden doch immer eine passende Ausrede.«
»Die Entbindung, die kommt ihr gerade recht.«
»Das möcht' ihr so passen, aus dem Wochenbett unter den Doktorhut kriechen!«
Der Erxlebin Vorschlag, sich einer Prüfung durch die drei Ärzte zu unterziehen, lehnten sie rundweg ab.
»Was käme dabei schon heraus?« meinten sie, »gewiß nur leeres Gezänk und Gewäsch, wenn auch die Frau Pfarrer mit ihrem feministischen Verstand etwas geborgtes Latein und Französisch um sich werfen würde, um recht doktormäßig sich anzuhören!«
Nein, darauf wollten sie sich nicht einlassen, die drei, und einer verbarg wohl vorm anderen die Furcht, bei solcher Gelegenheit über dieser oder jener Frage und Antwort recht dumm dazustehen. Und um ganz sicher zu gehen, kleideten sie ihre diesbezügliche Absage an den Herrn von Schellersheim wiederum in gepanzerten Hochmut:

*Nunmehr wenden wir uns erneut an Ihre Hochwürden und Hochfreyherrliche Exzellence, unseren gnädigen Herrn, und erklären uns dahin, daß wir hinfort nichts mehr mit der Frau Diakonin Erxleben zu thun haben wollen, schon gar nicht in derley wie einen Disput oder Prozeß!*

Das kam Schellersheim gerade recht. In einem freundlich gehaltenen Schreiben vom 19. März 1753 fordert er Dorothea auf, sofern sie wünsche, weiterhin Patienten anzunehmen und zu behandeln, sich binnen drei Monaten an der Universität Halle zur Promotion zu melden. Füge sie sich seiner Anordnung, von der er annehme, daß sie ihrem ureigensten Wunsche entspräche, *so solle im übrigen kein fernerer Schriftwechsel in dieser an sich klaren Sache gestattet werden.*

Damit hatte Schellersheim dezent dafür gesorgt, daß die Dinge sich ganz in Dorotheas Interesse entwickeln sollten. Wahrscheinlich aber waren ihm die Begleitumstände einer Geburt wie auch des Wochenbetts einer bald Vierzigjährigen nicht geläufig. So sieht Dorothea sich gezwungen, vor Ablauf der gesetzten Frist um Aufschub zu bitten. Am 14. April bringt sie ihren Sohn Johann Heinrich Christian zur Welt und muß sich eingestehen, daß die Geburt sie außergewöhnlich geschwächt und mitgenommen hat. Kein Gedanke daran, daß sie eine Postkutsche hätte besteigen können, um in Halle den Professoren gegenüberzutreten, geschweige denn daß sie die dazu notwendige Dissertation hätte fertigstellen können.

Schellersheim räumt bereitwillig den erbetenen Aufschub ein und verlängert ihn sogar noch einmal, da die Frau Pfarrerin Erxleben diesmal begründet: *mehrfach*

*Anfälle ernster Art überstanden zu haben und mich in einem Zustand befinde, der mich außer Stand gesetzt, an ernstliche Arbeit auch nur zu denken ...*

Es wird endgültig Frühling, der Pfarrherr, längst genesen von hartnäckiger Lungenentzündung, versieht sein Amt wieder –, es wird Sommer, es wird Herbst, der letzte der Geschwister Erxleben wächst und gedeiht prächtig, es wird wieder Winter, und all die Zeit sieht man Dorothea fast nur am Schreibtisch sitzen. Sie schreibt ihre Doktorarbeit.
*Akademische Abhandlung von der gar zu geschwinden und angenehmen, aber deswegen öfters unsicheren Heilung der Krankheiten.*

Ähnlich wie bei ihrer ersten schriftlichen Veröffentlichung unterteilt sie die Arbeit in einzelne Abschnitte, beziffert diese aber nicht römisch, wie sie es damals tat, sondern spricht von ›Hauptstücken‹, also erstes, zweites, drittes Hauptstück und so fort bis hin zum ›achten Hauptstück‹, dem sie der Mode der Zeit entsprechend einen langen, aussagekräftigen Titel gibt:
*Von einigen Umständen, welche in der medizinischen Praxi öfters vorkommen, damit man das Ansehen habe, als habe man bald und auf angenehme Weise geholfen, dabei aber dennoch die Sicherheit des Patienten oft aus den Augen gesetzt wird.*
Dieser Titel und zugleich letzter Punkt ihrer ausführlichen Dissertation, zeigt die ganze Erxleben, wie sie geartet ist, wie sie handelt und verstanden sein will: bedächtig, gründlich, reell und stets dem Patienten als einem fühlenden Menschen verpflichtet.

»Ich bin fertig, Johannes!« verkündet sie voller Stolz an einem der ersten Tage des Jahres 1754. »Willst du das Manuskript noch lesen, ehe ich es dem Herrn von Schellersheim aufs Schloß hinaufschicke?«

Und ob Johannes Erxleben das wollte! Jede freie Minute, die er erübrigen konnte, saß er nun, den Sessel nahe ans Fenster gerückt, die Brille auf der Nase, und las die Dissertationsschrift seiner Frau. Das fahle Licht der Wintersonne fiel über seine Schulter auf große, selbstbewußte, ein wenig fliehende Lettern.

*Sehr viele und große Pflichten liegen nach dem einmütigen Geständnis derer, welche von der Heilkunst einen richtigen Begriff haben, einem Arzt ob...* las Erxleben, und *Der Arzt soll möglichst bald helfen, denn viele Krankheiten sind mit großen Schmerzen verbunden, die der Kranke weder lange aushalten kann noch mag. Schlimmer aber noch kann eine verzögerte Behandlung die Krankheit wesentlich verschlechtern. Der Arzt soll angenehm behandeln, das heißt, wenn zur Besserung einer Krankheit mehrere gleichwirksame Medikamente zur Verfügung stehen, solle er das auswählen, welches für den Patienten am angenehmsten ist.* Hier war sie wieder, Dorotheas von Herzen kommende Rücksicht auf den Kranken! Und weiter las er:
*Der Arzt soll sicher behandeln, das heißt er soll die Ursache der Krankheit finden und sich nicht mit der Behandlung einiger Symptome begnügen.* Soweit das noch allgemein gefaßte Vorwort der Arbeit, dann aber das ›Erste Hauptstück‹, das sich mit der *Erklärung der Begriffe und Einteilung der Abhandlung* befaßt. Das ›Zweite Hauptstück‹ handelt *Von Brech-, Purgir und schweißtreibenden*

*Mitteln,* wobei dem Pfarrer eine hervorgehobene Forderung besonders gefiel:
*Der Arzt soll versuchen, die natürlichen Funktionen des Körpers zu unterstützen, wenn sie durch Krankheiten in Unordnung geraten sind. Er soll sich aber von jedem Übermaß hüten.*

Das ›Dritte Hauptstück‹ behandelt abführende Mittel, deren Wichtigkeit der Mensch aus einer gewissen Scham gern vernachlässigt. Das ›Fünfte Hauptstück‹ spricht von der monatlichen Reinigung bei der Frau, das ›Sechste Hauptstück‹ widmet sich dem Gegenteil, nämlich den blutstillenden Mitteln. Das siebente endlich handelt von Opiaten und Beruhigungsmitteln und warnt eindeutig: *Man hält dafür, daß Mittel dieser Art alle Beschwerden sogleich hinweg zu schaffen vermögen, daher werden sie mit nachdrücklichen Lobsprüchen belegt. Sie sind aber in Wahrheit sehr gefährlich, weil sie die Krankheit nur eine Zeitlang unterdrücken, viele Patienten aber, welche solche Mittel nehmen, dadurch tumm werden, und alle Hurtigkeit und Munterkeit, die sie von Natur haben, verlieren.*
Das ›Achte Hauptstück‹ endlich faßt unter dem bereits genannten Titel nochmals zusammen, daß ein Arzt sicher, bald und angenehm helfen soll. Hierbei verwirft Dorothea ausdrücklich *verwirrende Verordnungen verschiedenster Arzeneyen, vor allem ausländische theure Mittel, wo zu der vorliegenden Krankheit vielmehr solche nötig wären, die unsere Gegend an die Hand gibt. Mancher Arzt will für sein Ansehen sorgen, indem er ihrer Wirkung nach ganz verschiedene Mittel in einem Rezept zusammenkneten läßt.* Aber schließt sie energisch *Keine Krankheit rühret*

*von so verschiedener Ursache her, daß ein so weitläufiges Mischmasch von Arzeneymitteln zu deren Cur nöthig wäre.*

Johannes Erxleben ließ die Blätter auf seinen Schoß sinken und blickte sinnend zum Fenster hinaus, wo die Menschen in Pelz und Schal durch die winterlichen Gassen eilten. Menschen, hochmütig in ihrer Kraft und Gesundheit, die ein Gott ihnen schenkte, aber wie schwach und hilflos, wenn Krankheit sie beherrschte. Welche Gnade dann, an einen Arzt zu geraten, der »sicher, bald und angenehm« zu heilen verstand und niemals den Menschen als Gottes Kreatur aus dem Auge verlor, einen Arzt, wie Dorothea Erxleben einer war! Der Pfarrer von Sankt Nikolai nahm die Brille ab und wischte sich mit der Hand über die Augen.
»Mein Gott«, murmelte er, »was für eine Frau hast du mir gegeben, was für eine wundervolle Frau!«

Auch Dorothea nahm Pelz und wärmenden Schal um, da sie beschloß, die fertiggestellte Dissertation dem Herrn von Schellersheim selbst zu überbringen. Der Aufstieg zum Schloßberg erschien ihr mühseliger als gewöhnlich, spürte sie doch zum einen die schlaflosen Nächte, die hinter ihr lagen und in denen sie, die Ruhe des Hauses nutzend, emsig am Schreibtisch gesessen hatte. Zum anderen fand ihr Fuß nur schlechten Halt auf dem groben Kopfsteinpflaster der steilen Gassen, wie auch auf den Stufen der überall angelegten Treppen. Eine dünne Schneedecke machte beides gefährlich glatt, und manches Mal mußte sie Halt suchen an den eisernen Geländern, die diese begleiteten.

Endlich oben angekommen, ließ Dorothea sich in den Amtsräumen der Königlich preußischen Verwaltung sogleich dem Herrn Stiftshauptmann melden. Kaum konnte der Diener die Meldung weitergeben, wurde die Tür zum Amtszimmer weit geöffnet und Schellersheim begrüßte sie in unerwartet herzlicher Manier.
»Madame Erxleben! Welch seltener Gast! Bei diesem Wetter! Und noch gar zu Fuß! Hätt' ich's nur gewußt, denn gerade wollte ich...«
Was er wollte, erfuhr Dorothea zunächst nicht. Erst einmal genoß sie die Wärme eines offenen Kaminfeuers und für ihre müden Beine den Stuhl, den Schellersheim ihr anbot, nachdem der Diener Pelz und Schal mit sich genommen.
»Ich bringe Ihnen meine Dissertation, sie ist fertig«, kam Dorothea gleich zur Sache, während Schellersheim sich einen Augenblick zu besinnen schien, worum es ging. Irgendetwas anderes mußte ihm wohl im Kopf herumspuken.
»Oh, ja, ja...« sagte er und rieb sich die Hände so nahe den Flammen, daß Dorothea schon für die zarte Spitzenkrause seiner Ärmelaufschläge fürchtete. »O ja, Ihre Dissertation, Madame, dann sind wir ja nahe am Ziel...« Er nahm das ihm gereichte Manuskript entgegen, schlug den Einband zurück und überflog den Titel. Aber noch immer erschien Schellersheim dabei irgendwie geistesabwesend. »Ach, Madame, da Sie nun einmal da sind...« begann er zögernd, »meine Frau würde sich sicher freuen, Sie auf eine Tasse Tee zu sehen...« Plötzlich ballte er seine rechte Hand zur Faust und hieb mit ihr in die Handfläche der Linken. »Madame! Es klingt vielleicht seltsam... ausgerechnet aus

meinem Munde, aber ich bitte Sie, nach meiner Frau zu sehen! Die Galle! Sie leidet unter starken Schmerzen und will keinen der anderen Ärzte zu sich lassen. Ihr ganzes Vertrauen gilt Ihnen, Madame Erxleben, und ich gestehe, Gnädigste, daß ich geneigt bin, mich diesem Urteil anzuschließen. Bitte, Madame...«
Damit machte er bereits auffordernd ein paar Schritte in Richtung der Privaträume seiner Dienstwohnung.
Dorothea war sofort bereitwillig aufgestanden.
»Selbstverständlich sehe ich gern nach Ihrer lieben Frau, Herr von Schellersheim«, sagte sie möglichst obenhin, so als sei nicht ausgerechnet von ihm, in seiner Eigenschaft als Stiftshauptmann, das Verbot jeglicher ärztlicher Tätigkeit an sie ergangen, und um ihm auch jede weitere Peinlichkeit zu ersparen, fügte sie hinzu: »Lassen Sie nur, ich finde den Weg alleine!«

Daß dem so war, brauchte Dorothea nicht weiter zu versichern, schließlich war sie nicht nur oft genug mit der liebenswürdigen Frau von Schellersheim beieinander gesessen, sondern waren ihr Schloß und Burg bis in jeden Winkel hinein seit frühester Kinderzeit bekannt. Wie oft hatte sie den Vater begleitet, wenn dieser seiner Pflicht als Leibarzt der Fürstin wie auch der Stiftsdamen nachkam, zuerst nur aus kindlicher Neugier, später wurde dem Vater ihre tätige Assistenz unentbehrlich und nach dem Tod Doktor Leporins waren es ihre eigenen medizinischen Kenntnisse wie ihr ärztlicher Rat, deren man auf dem Schloß bedurfte.
Eine halbe Stunde etwa blieb Dorothea bei Frau von Schellersheim in vertrautem Gespräch, machte ihr feuchtwarme Umschläge zur Erleichterung bei Gallen-

anfällen und verordnete zu gleichem Zweck schwarzen Rettichsaft und Sud aus Löwenzahn. Dann kehrte sie ins Amtszimmer zurück, wo sie Schellersheim über das ihm gebrachte Manuskript gebeugt antraf, in dem er wohl fleißig gelesen hatte. Jetzt hob er den Kopf, während er gleichzeitig mit dem Knöchel seines Fingers auf die aufgeschlagene Seite pochte.
»Großartig Madame! Ihre Dissertation, einfach großartig! Man muß nicht Mediziner sein, um dem so klar und verständlich Gesagten Beifall zu zollen! Wie werden also erst die Herren Professoren der Universität den Wert der Arbeit ermessen können. Madame, ich denke, Sie haben das Rennen schon gewonnen.«
Dorothea blieb, so sehr sie das Lob freute, reserviert.
»Ich habe immerhin noch die mündliche Prüfung vor mir, Exzellenz«, sagte sie ruhig.
»Ah, Madame, die nehmen Sie im Sprung!« wehrte Schellersheim im Jargon des Reitersoldaten. »Mit Hurra hinein und der Sieg ist Ihrer!«
»Das Examen wird von Männern durchgeführt, die das Wort einer Frau in aller Öffentlichkeit nicht gewohnt sind, ja denen es als unweiblich und inkompetent widerstrebt.«
»Nun ja...« meinte der Hauptmann lau, da sie ihm den Wind aus den Segeln genommen. »Jedenfalls, Madame, werde ich die Abhandlung so rasch wie möglich nach Halle weiterleiten und um einen Termin zur Zulassung bitten Allerdings...« Hier nahm er wieder einen dienstlichen Ton an. »Allerdings sehe ich mich genötigt, mich nochmals mit einem Gesuch an den König zu wenden.«
»Aber...« Diesmal war Dorothea die Enttäuschung an-

zumerken, und sogleich fiel ihr Schellersheim streng ins Wort. »Der Erlaß, mit dem Seine Majestät geruhten, die Genehmigung zum Erwerb des Doktorgrades zu erteilen, ist ganze zwölf Jahre alt, Madame! Sie müssen einräumen, daß ich nicht korrekt verfahren würde, wenn ich mich ohne Rückfrage in Potsdam auf die Gültigkeit des damaligen Entscheids verließe...«

»Der damalige Entscheid war an keinen bestimmten Termin gebunden! Er lautete ausdrücklich, sobald ich mich zur Promotion melden würde, mir keinerlei Schwierigkeiten in den Weg zu legen!«

Schellersheim wechselte wieder seinen Ton, rang die Hände und schien fast zu flehen.

»Aber Madame! Zwölf Jahre! Das kann und will ich nicht verantworten.«

Trotz aller Enttäuschung mußte Dorothea zugeben, daß Schellersheim Bedenken ihre Berechtigung hatten. Was war seither alles passiert! Zwei Kriege hatte der König inzwischen geführt und mußte schon wieder in Sorge um das daraus Gewonnene sein. Die Wünsche und Ideen eines Frauenzimmers, das sich unter die Studenten mischen wollte, und noch dazu denen der medizinischen Fakultät, mochten ihm längst ebenso absurd und lächerlich vorkommen, wie sie auch von anderen Vertretern der Männerwelt angesehen wurden. Selbst wenn der König solch einem Wunsch in der Hochstimmung seines Sieges bei Mollwitz einmal zugestimmt hatte, so würde er unterdessen vielleicht ganz anderer Meinung sein. Die Vorstellung, daß eine Frau Doktor seinen Soldaten einen Bauchschuß verband oder ein Bein amputierte, würde er sicherlich unpassend finden. Wozu sonst aber, so mochte der Kriegser-

probte denken, war ein Medikus gut? Ja, vielleicht hatte der Hauptmann von Schellersheim recht, vielleicht sollte man sicher gehen, daß die Genehmigung aus dem Jahre 1741 noch ihre Gültigkeit hatte.
»Nun gut«, lächelte also Dorothea entwaffnend, »versuchen wir das Schicksal noch einmal, Exzellenz, ich selbst habe es ja lange genug herausgefordert.«
»Nun gut«, sagte Schellersheim ebenfalls und erhob sich zum Zeichen, daß die Unterredung beendet sei. »Ich lasse Sie es wissen, sobald ein Prüfungstermin feststeht, Madame.«
Auch die Frau Pfarrerin erhob sich, zumal auf ein Zeichen seines Herrn der Diener Pelz und Schal hereinbrachte. Ein Blick zum Fenster sagte ihr, daß es draußen bereits dunkelte und zudem das Wetter sich verschlimmert hatte. Schneeflocken wirbelten gegen die Scheiben, die unter harten Windstößen ächzten. Der Gedanke, sich jetzt über rutschiges Pflaster und kaum beleuchtete Stiegen hinunterzukämpfen, ließ Dorothea gegen ihren Willen aufseufzen. Doch Schellersheim hatte vorgesorgt.
»Ich habe anspannen lassen, Madame, mein Wagen wird Sie in die Stadt zurückbringen.« Um seinen Schreibtisch herumtretend, geleitete der Herr Stiftshauptmann die Frau Pfarrerin zur Tür. Einen Augenblick sah es aus, als wolle er ihre Hand an seine Lippen ziehen, doch dessen ungewohnt zog diese sie rasch zurück.
»Ich danke Ihnen, Exzellenz«, sagte Dorothea und schlang den Schal schützend um ihr Haar.
»Für diesmal, Madame«, murmelte Schellersheim beziehungsvoll »bin ich es, der zu danken hat!«

Draußen stand das gedeckte Coupé mit dem preußischen Wappen am Schlag, und kaum daß Madame Erxleben eingestiegen, zogen die Pferde vorsichtig tastend an.

## Endlich nach Halle

Am 11. Januar 1754 ging das nochmalige Gesuch an den König von Preußen ab. Am 18. Februar veranlaßte der Königlich Preußische wirkliche Geheime Staats-Minister Freiherr von Danckelmann die Antwort im Namen des Königs dahingehend, daß
*dem Gesuch der Supplicantin stattgegeben wird, sie soll sich aber wegen des Erlasses der Promotionskosten mit der Fakultät in Halle selbst in Verbindung setzen.*
Die beigefügte Kopie eines Briefes nach Halle bestätigt das nochmals mit dem einschränkenden Zusatz: *wenn Ihr dagegen nichts Erhebliches einzuwenden habt.*

Die Herren Professoren von Halle hatten nichts Erhebliches einzuwenden, der endgültige Zulassungstermin wurde auf den 6. Mai 1754 festgesetzt.

Nun hieß es für Dorothea Erxleben warten und bangen, was ihr manches Mal besser, manches Mal schlechter gelang. Wie gut, daß sie in dieser Zeit einen so geduldigen wie verständnisvollen Ehemann an ihrer Seite hatte. Schwand Dorothea der Mut und sah sie Halle und das durchlaufende Examen wie einen himmelhohen Berg vor sich, den sie ohne Stab und Stecken zu erklimmen hatte, dann wandte sie sich an Johannes.
»Was ist, wenn ich es nicht schaffe?«
»Du schaffst es, Dörte, denn auf zwei Dinge kannst du dich stets verlassen: auf deine eingehende Kenntnis der

Arzeneiwissenschaft und auf das fast klassische Latein, das du so sicher beherrschst!«
Und kam Dorothea neidisches Gewisper unter ihren Geschlechtsgenossinnen zu Ohren, das ihr Ruhmsucht und bloße Eitelkeit nachsagte, und sie sich bei ihrem Mann dagegen empörte:
»Denk nur, Johannes, sie glauben, ich wolle mich nur hervortun und in aller Welt mit meinem Titel prahlen!«, dann hatte er guten Trost aus seiner Sicht parat:
»Unser Herr und Gott, Dorothea, der dir tief ins Herz sieht und vor dem wir keinen Gedanken verbergen können, er weiß, daß du ihm die Ehre gibst, wenn du auf solche Weise dir einen Namen machst vor den Menschen, denen allein dein Wirken gilt.«

Und noch jemand tauchte auf, eigens um ihr Mut zu machen. Dorothea und die älteren Töchter machten sich an einem ersten schönen Tag im Pfarrgarten zu schaffen, die Mädchen senkten Samen allerlei Küchenkräuter in die frühlingswarme Erde, und Dorothea kniete vor einer Beetreihe und las Unkraut zwischen frisch erblühten Stiefmütterchen, als ein Mann zu ihnen trat. Dorothea, die sich nicht die Mühe machte, aufzusehen, hielt ihn für Erxleben.
»Sehen sie nicht aus, als hätten sie Gesichter, Johannes? Ich möchte nur wissen, warum man sie ausgerechnet Stiefmütterchen nennt, was meinst du, Johannes?«
»Vielleicht hat man sie nach dir benannt, weil du so ein reizendes Stiefmütterchen bist!« sagte eine Stimme über ihr, die nicht die Erxlebens war, aber die sie zu kennen meinte. Und schon rief Sophie vom Küchenbeet her:
»Es ist nicht Vater, Mama, es ist ein Fremder!«

Jetzt sah Dorothea auf. Stimme und Gestalt fügten sich zusammen, und ihr Herz machte einen Freudensprung.

»Christian!« rief sie, »oh, Christian, du bist es!«

Ja, er war es, der Doktor Leporin, der Herr Chirurgus aus Nienburg an der Weser. Dorothea wischte sich die Erde von den Fingern und erhob sich schwerfälliger, als sie gern wollte.

»Sie ist älter geworden, unsere Dörte«, sagte der Chirurgus bei sich, »immerhin, im nächsten Jahr wird sie vierzig...«

Er faßte sie am Ellenbogen, um ihr aufzuhelfen, und dann lagen Bruder und Schwester sich in den Armen.

»Ach, Christian, daß du gekommen bist«, seufzte die Frau Pfarrerin Erxleben und war mit einem Male die kleine ›Dörte‹ von ehemals.

»Nun ja, ich mußte doch nach meiner gelehrten, kleinen Schwester sehen«, versetzte Leporin und strich ihr eine Träne von der Wange, die sich in der übergroßen Freude dorthin gestohlen hatte.

»Gelehrt hin, gelehrt her, Christian«, lachte Dorothea schon wieder, »erst am sechsten Mai wird sich's weisen...«

»Das ist also der Termin der Prüfung?«

»Ja, und ich bin schon ganz krank vor Furcht...«

»Na, na, so wie ich dich kenne, Dörte, wird es ein Triumph!«

»Oh, Christian, die Professoren, der Dekan, alles würdige Herren der Schöpfung!«

»Was den Dekan angeht, ich kenne ihn gut, hat er doch auch mich damals geprüft. Professor Juncker ist ein prachtvoller Mensch. Und ich bin sicher, er wird nicht wenig stolz darauf sein, als erster eine derartige Promotion durchzuführen, von der alle Welt sprechen wird. Und was dich als weibliches Wesen anbetrifft... er ist ein reizender alter Herr und durch und durch Kavalier.«

Sie waren im Reden, nachdem ›Onkel Christian‹ auch die Mädchen begrüßt hatte, ins Haus geschlendert, nahmen in der etwas altväterischen Wohnstube Platz, in der schon beider Großvater residiert hatte. So vieles erinnerte noch an ihn, ein ringsumlaufender Fries gottgefälliger Sinnsprüche, an der Wand Bilder seiner Vorgänger in riesigen Allongeperücken, und die alte Spieluhr im Eckschrank. Die Kindheit schien beiden wieder aufzuerstehen und sie fester aneinander zu binden.

»Mein Gott, Dörte, weißt du noch...?« sinnierte Christian.

»Vater und Großvater, wie fehlen sie mir beide!« fiel Dorothea ein. Doch kehrten sie alsbald wieder in die Gegenwart zurück. »Soll ich dir hier im Pfarrhaus eine Stube richten lassen?«

»Nein, nein, ich wohne im Steinweg in meinem alten Stübchen«, wehrte der Chirurgus.

»Hab's mir fast gedacht, Christian. Mutter und Maria lassen sich selten blicken in letzter Zeit!« monierte seine Schwester.

Christian lachte.

»Das will ich meinen! Die beiden bereiten eine Überraschung für dich vor und sitzen Tag und Nacht mit Nadel und Faden, aber das sollte ich dir eigentlich nicht verraten!« fügte er erschrocken an.

Wie nicht anders zu erwarten, wandte sich die Unterhaltung bald medizinischen Themen zu. Dorothea be-

richtete in groben Zügen von ihrer Doktorarbeit und den darin behandelten Themen.
»Ah, den Abführmitteln hast du also einen ganzen Abschnitt gewidmet?« nahm Christian Leporin interessiert den Faden auf. »Daran hast du recht getan, Dörte, ist dies Kapitel doch so viel wichtiger, als die meisten Menschen glauben. Ich bin zum Beispiel ein ausgesprochener Gegner rasch wirkender solcher Mittel! Soll die Natur doch langsam und lieber durch heilsame Bewegung oder Mäßigung bei bestimmten Speisen dem Körper helfen...«
Dorothea nickte zustimmend, und er fuhr dozierend fort:
»Und ebenso denke ich über die Fieberbekämpfung. Unterdrückt man diesen Zustand des kranken Körpers zu früh, so kann das Leiden sogar ärger werden als zuvor.«
Wieder nickte Dorothea.
»Genau so habe ich auch dieses Thema in meiner Arbeit erörtert und hoffe, mit dieser Meinung vor den hohen Herren in Halle bestehen zu können...«
»Darum ist mir nicht bange«, fiel Christian ihr lachend ins Wort, »schon damals, als Vater uns beide unterrichtete, wußtest du immer das Rechte zu sagen, Dörte!«
Im Gespräch der Geschwister, an dem abends bei einem Glas Wein auch Schwager Erxleben teilnahm, verging der Tag wie im Flug ebenso der nächste und übernächste. Und bald schon mußte Christian Leporin wieder abreisen.
»Kopf hoch, Dörte«, mahnte er liebevoll noch einmal, als die Schwester beim Abschied bittere Tränen vergoß.

»Ich hätte dich so gern an meiner Seite gewußt, Christian!« gestand Dorothea verzagt, »war es doch so von Anfang an geplant, du und ich gemeinsam in Halle...«

»Aber nun hast du ja einen anderen Beschützer, der dir zur Seite sein wird!«

Damit bezog Leporin sich auf Fritz Erxleben, der seit etlicher Zeit in Halle Theologie studierte. Ihr Quartier nämlich, so war es abgemacht, sollte Dorothea bei dem ältesten ihrer Stiefkinder nehmen.

*Meine Wirtin*, so hatte der in einem Brief nach Hause geschrieben, *ist einverstanden, wenn Mama bei mir wohnt. Sie läßt dazu eigens ein zweites Bett in meine Stube stellen, und selbst wenn wir ihr dafür einen Obolus geben, so kommt es billiger als im Gasthaus.* Wie gern hatte Dorothea diese Einladung angenommen, zumal die Frage der zu erlassenden Promotionskosten seitens der Universität noch nicht ganz geklärt war.

Die Geschwister nahmen herzlichen Abschied voneinander, und Dorothea war wieder dem Auf und Ab ihrer Stimmungen überlassen, was die Aussicht auf die mündliche Prüfung vor aller Öffentlichkeit anbetraf.

Je näher aber der Tag kam, an dem die Postkutsche sie das erste Mal in ihrem Leben aus Quedlinburg fortführen sollte, desto ruhiger wurde sie.

Die Überraschung von Mutter und Schwester, die Christian um ein Haar verraten hatte, war ein Kleid, das die beiden ihr für den feierlichen Auftritt geschneidert hatten. Dunkle Seide saß eng um den Oberkörper, eine Reihe schlichter Spitze um den gemäßigten Ausschnitt, und bauschte sich dann in herrlichen Falten bis auf die Füße.

Schließlich ruhte das Kleid im großen Reisekorb hoch auf dem gelben Wagen, gab es ein herzliches Adieu, Küsse und Winken von den Kindern, Umarmung und Segenswunsch von Johannes Erxleben, der seiner Frau über den hohen Tritt ins Wageninnere half.
Die Abfahrt der Postkutsche war jedesmal von neuem ein Ereignis. Etliche Neugierige hatten sich eingefunden, denen vielleicht auch zu Ohren gekommen war, die Frau Pfarrerin wolle nun endlich Ernst machen und sich der Doktorprüfung unterziehen.
»Kopf hoch, Liebes, du wirst es schaffen«, flüsterte Johannes durchs unverglaste, offene Fenster.

Der Postillion gab das übliche Signal, und die Pferde traten schwerfällig an. Ein wenig bang war es Dorothea schon, als es zum Oeringer Tor hinausging, die Bode überquerend, an der Rossmühle vorbei, südlich des Kalkberges nach Gersdorf, zur ersten Anhaltschen Grenzstation und damit weiter, als sie jemals gekommen war. Leise, nur die Lippen bewegend, sprach sie ein stilles Gebet um Kraft und Mut für diese erste Reise und alle Prüfungen, die ihr im doppelten Sinne des Wortes bevorstanden. Scheu sah sie sich dabei um, daß auch ja keiner der Reisegefährten, ein Tuchmacher aus Aschersleben, ein Kaufmann aus Ditfurth und zwei junge Studenten, die wohl den gleichen Weg hatten wie sie, etwas von ihrem Flehen bemerke.
»Herrgott, dir empfehle ich meinen Geist und meine Seele und bitte dich um deinen Schutz und dein Geleit«, schloß sie und warf noch einmal einen scheuen Blick in die Runde. Niemand hatte ihr Gebet bemerkt, zumindest nicht davon Notiz genommen.

»Wenigstens haben wir herrliches Wetter heute«, begann der Kaufmann stattdessen ein Gespräch.

»Da haben Sie recht«, fiel der Tuchmacher ein, »nicht so heiß und trocken, daß wir allen Staub der Straße schlucken und nicht so regennaß, daß wir in jeder Pfütze um ein Rad fürchten müssen!«

»Und dennoch, meine Herren, liegt Gewitter in der Luft«, nahm einer der Studenten die Gelegenheit wahr, das Gespräch auf die Politik zu bringen. »Kein Gewitter vom Himmel herab meine ich, sondern eines, das von Potsdam kommt.«

»Oder auch von Wien, Bruder, je nachdem wie du es siehst«, fiel sein Kommilitone ein.

»Ach was, Gewitter«, meinte wieder der Tuchmacher, »Schlesien ist unser, was soll es da noch gewittern?«

»Bisher ist es kaum mehr als eine Leihgabe, Ihr Schlesien!«

»Die Kaiserin wird es sich wiederholen, das werden Sie sehen, meine Herren!« Die beiden Studenten schienen sich einig, auch als der Kaufmann gut preußisch reagierte.

»Die Kaiserin? Pah! Wie will sie das denn schaffen so ganz allein?«

»So allein scheint sie mir nicht«, meinten beide Studenten, ohne preiszugeben, ob sie preußisch oder kaiserlich gesinnt waren, »sie buhlt schon lange um Paris und Dresden, und die Zarin nennt sich bereits ihre Schwester!«

Dorothea Erxleben nahm an dem Gespräch der Herren nicht teil. Deren Worte vermischten sich mit den monotonen Geräuschen klappernder Hufe und rollen-

der Räder, während sie ihren eigenen Gedanken nachhing:
Würden ihr Geist und ihre Kraft ausreichen, für alles einzustehen, für das sie seit Jahren gestritten? Würde sie die Welt überzeugen können, daß eine Frau dem Manne nicht nachzustehen brauchte, daß sie ein Recht habe auf jeden Platz, den sie sich erkoren, auf jedes Amt, das auszufüllen sie sich imstande fühlte? Es schien ihr an der Zeit, den Beweis zu erbringen.

## *Antrittsbesuch beim Dekan*


Das Tempo beziehungsweise die Langsamkeit der ›Ordinari‹, das heißt der gewöhnlichen Post im Gegensatz zur sehr viel teureren ›Extrapost‹, gab vielfach Anlaß zu Spott und Kritik. Zwar gab es offiziell Fahrpläne mit Ankunfts- und Abfahrtszeiten, aber die Gründe und Anlässe, diese nicht einzuhalten, waren zahlreich, und so blieb die Notwendigkeit von Rast und Übernachtung und damit die Dauer der Reise überhaupt dem jeweiligen Kutscher oder Postillion überlassen. Unter den Spöttern sagten die einen, das Reisen mit dem Postwagen sei geeignet für Botaniker, da diese leicht während der Fahrt nebenher gehen könnten, um ihre Kräuter und Pflanzen zu pflücken. Die anderen meinten, während eines Pferdewechsels, bei dem die Kutscher sich auch ein Bier genehmigten, könne sich der Reisende die Füße vertreten, indem er den Weg vorauslaufe. Binnen einer Stunde hole der Postwagen ihn nicht ein! Nicht selten sprach man von der preußischen wie auch sonst von der deutschen ›Schneckenpost‹. Nur den hochbezahlten ›Extra- oder Eilposten‹ sagte man eine Leistung von einer preußischen Meile pro Stunde nach, die Normalpost schaffte deren meist nur eine halbe. Hinzu kamen Unfälle, Wetterverhältnisse, Straßenzustand und immer noch Raubüberfälle. Las man doch im Vorjahr eine Verlautbarung der taxischen Reichspost, die die Postillione anwies, Geldsendungen in Futtersäcken zu verstecken mit der Begründung *dadurch alle etwaige Anreizung zu Beraubungen und Diebe-*

*reien möglichst zu vermeiden. Da es nämlich leider durch die immer mehr überhandnehmende Raubbegierde da hingekommen, daß seit etlichen Monaten die ›Ordinari‹ nicht nur in der Nacht, sondern auch bei hellem Tage, wie solches durchgehendst bekannt ist, von verwegenen Straßenräubern gewaltsam angegriffen und ausgeraubet wurden.*

Dorothea Erxleben schien auf ihrer ersten Reise dahingehend Glück zu haben. Jemand hatte wohl dem Postillion die Besonderheit ihrer Person und ihres Vorhabens erklärt und dieser zeigte nun Ehrgeiz, seinen wichtigen Gast der ehrwürdigen Stadt Halle baldmöglichst und bestmöglichst abzuliefern. Er ließ die Pferde fleißig traben, auch an Stellen, wo er sie sonst gewöhnlich Schritt gehen ließ, und öfter als sonst ließ er die Peitsche über sie hinknallen.
Bei anhaltend ungetrübtem Wetter an diesem 4. Mai 1754 passierte man Mehringen und Schackstedt, hielt eine Rast in Alsleben, die knapp für eine Suppe und ein Glas Milch reichte, und fuhr weiter über Trebnitz nach Könnern. Eines der Pferde hatte ein Eisen verloren, der Schmied mußte her, dann ging es weiter wie vom Satan gehetzt: Dornitz, Domnitz, Nauendorf, und doch herrschte schon tiefe Dunkelheit, als die Pferde endlich wieder Pflaster unter den Hufen hatten. Laut klappernd fuhr man in Halle ein. Dorothea nahm schemenhaft aufragende Häuserzeilen zur Rechten und zur Linken wahr, nur selten Licht oder Laterne. Die Stadt lag bereits in tiefem Schlaf. Da man von Nord einfuhr und auch weil es Nacht war, sah Dorothea nichts vom düsteren Galgenberg, den schaurige Geschichten umgaben. Wie hätte es noch vor wenigen

Jahren Dorothea erschreckt, daß am sogenannten ›Kniegalgen‹ die Namen entwichener Soldaten angeschlagen wurden zum Zwecke der Wiederergreifung und Bestrafung gleich dort. Wer weiß, ob der Anschlag einst nicht auch den Namen Christian Leporin getragen hatte?

Lärmend fuhr die Postkutsche die Dessauer Straße und die Große Steinstraße hinab und bog mit einem kurzen schmetternden Signal, das sicherlich manchen Bürger im Bette hochfahren ließ, auf den Marktplatz ein. Nach mehrfachem ›Brr‹ und ›Hooh‹ des Kutschers blieben die Pferde endlich erleichtert stehen. Ringsum Stille. Schon fürchtete Dorothea, daß Fritz Erxleben sie gar nicht abholen würde, da niemand die Kutsche zu dieser Stunde erwartete. Sie ließ sich aus dem Wagen helfen und den Reisekorb vom Kutschdach reichen und atmete erleichtert auf, als Fritz aus dem Schatten eines Hauses trat. Das ganze Ebenbild seines Vaters, dachte Dorothea, als er auf sie zueilte.
»Liebste Mama, willkommen in Halle!« rief er und zog sie freudig in seine Arme. »Hast du die Fahrt gesund überstanden?«
»Gesund ja, aber entsetzlich hungrig«, gestand Dorothea ein, und Fritz lachte dazu:
»Das trifft sich fein! In Gasthaus oder Wirtsstube bekommen wir jetzt nichts mehr, aber ich habe vorgesorgt. Käse, Brot und ein gutes Bier, damit du die erste Nacht gut schläfst!«
Käse und Brot verzehrte Mutter Erxleben dann mit Appetit im engen Dachstübchen einer Seitengasse, das jetzt, da es ein zweites Bett beherbergen mußte, noch

enger geworden war. Fritz machte derweilen Pläne für den nächsten Tag.

»Morgen werde ich dir die Stadt zeigen, liebste Mama«, versprach er, »die Marienburg, den Roten Turm, die alte Stadtbefestigung! Und natürlich die Moritzburg mußt du sehen, auch den Dom und Schloß Giebichstein mit dem berühmten Fachwerk-Taubenschlag!«

Dorothea freute sich schon auf den erholsamen Ausflug mit dem Stiefsohn, als dieser bedeutungsvoll ausholte.

»Zuerst aber, Mama, punkt elf Uhr dein Antrittsbesuch beim Herrn Dekan!«

»Antrittsbesuch beim Dekan?« entfuhr es Dorothea erschrocken, »Fritz, ist das wahrhaft notwendig? Schon der Gedanke macht mir mehr Angst als die Prüfung!«

»Mama, Mama! Wo bleibt die Würde der Frau Pfarrerin?« Lachend drohte er ihr mit dem Finger wie einem Kind, dann aber setzte er ernst hinzu: »Deine Furcht ist unbegründet! Was den Dekan angeht, so wird er dir gefallen, er ist ein reizender alter Herr.«

Das waren die gleichen Worte, wie Christian sie gebraucht hatte, ihr die Furcht vor dem gestrengen Herrn Rektor der medizinischen Fakultät zu nehmen. So mußte also, sagte sich Dorothea, ihre Angst wohl wirklich unbegründet sein, doch ein Rest blieb und nagte in ihrem Innern. Das Bier tat dann das seine und, ohnehin todmüde von der Reise, schlief die Kandidatin in spe im zusätzlichen Bett bald ein.

Das Dunkelseidene hatte Dorothea erst noch einmal im Reisekorb gelassen, stattdessen zum braunen Merinokleid gegriffen, das sie auf der Reise schon getragen hatte. Nun stand sie beklommen vor dem Haus Professor Junckers in der Berliner Straße, Fritz neben ihr, der schon die Glocke gezogen hatte. Weder Magd, Diener noch gar Majordomus öffneten, sondern ein Kind kam fröhlich vom Garten her um das Haus herum gelaufen.

»Sie wollen zum Großvater?« fragte es vertraulich, ohne im geringsten über den Besuch erstaunt zu sein, »nicht wahr, Sie sind die Dame, die Doktor werden will?«

»Ja, die bin ich«, gab Dorothea wahrheitsgemäß zur Antwort.

Das Kind winkte den Besuchern zu folgen, und so betraten Fritz und Dorothea das Haus von hinten her durch eine Art Gartensaal. Dort hieß es sie warten. Eine ganze Weile verging so zwischen Topfpflanzen und Kübelpalmen, und Dorothea fühlte bereits Beklemmung und Furcht sich ihrer erneut bemächtigen, als eilige Schritte zu hören waren. Eine Tür flog auf, und ein kleiner, beleibter Herr trat ein, in Hausrock und Perücke, auf den Lippen ein Lächeln, die Stirn aber in Kummerfalten gelegt.

»Ein Mißgeschick!« rief er und trat mit ausgebreiteten Armen auf Dorothea zu. Einen Augenblick sah es aus, als wolle er sie umarmen, dann aber nahm er nur ihre Hand in seine beiden und schüttelte sie fest. »Ein Mißgeschick! Ich wartete im Salon auf Sie, derweilen Sie hier...« Mit einer bedauernden Geste ringsum auf Töpfe und Kübel verstärkten sich Lächeln wie Falten. »Sie müssen verzeihen, meine Enkelin kennt sich mit einem angemessenen Empfangsprotokoll für Besucher eben noch nicht so aus!«

Durch das, was Professor Juncker, denn niemand ande-

res war der kleine Herr, ein Mißgeschick nannte und durch die treuherzige Art seines Bedauerns verlor Dorothea endgültig alle Scheu.
»Es war der reizendste Empfang, der mir je zuteil geworden ist, Herr Dekan!« lächelte sie zurück und folgte unbefangen ihrem gelehrten Gastgeber in einen exquisiten Salon, an dessen hellblauen Wänden verblichene Gemälde hingen und wo auf Meißner Zwiebelmuster ein leckerer Imbiß angerichtet war.
Binnen wenigen Augenblicken ging die Unterhaltung lebhaft hin und her.
»Wenn ich ehrlich sein soll«, begann der Dekan eben wieder und beugte sich weit über den Tisch, »so habe ich mir die angekündigte Frau Kandidatin eigentlich ganz anders vorgestellt...«
»Dann kann ich nur hoffen, verehrter Herr Dekan, daß die Tatsachen nicht allzusehr vom erhofften Bild abweichen«, entgegnete Dorothea mit einem ihr sonst fremden Anflug von Koketterie.
»Wissen Sie, Verehrteste, wir, ich meine die Fakultät hat ja ebenso wie der Herr von Schellersheim ein Schreiben Seiner Majestät empfangen, und wenn ich mir erlauben darf, den Schlußsatz zu zitieren...« Hier schmunzelte er wieder behäbig und las vom Blatt: »*Ist diese Madame Erxlebin männlichen Geistes, so soll sie's beweisen, ist sie jedoch nur ein Weib, so wird es ihre Natur belegen.*« Hier ging sein Schmunzeln in breites Lachen über. »Madame, die Worte des Königs stellen den männlichen Geist einer anscheinend minderen weiblichen Erscheinung gegenüber, ich aber weiß seit heute, daß ein mutiger Geist sehr wohl in einer um nichts geminderten weiblichen Hülle wohnen kann!«

Dorothea errötete wie schon lange nicht mehr. Sie war neununddreißig Jahre alt, hatte vier Kindern das Leben geschenkt, hatte sich jetzt und hier vor der Ehrfurcht gebietenden Amtsperson eines Dekans der Friedrichs-Universität zu Halle, in der einst ein Thomasius und ein Wolff lehrten, von Herzen gefürchtet, und was erntete sie stattdessen im verspielten Rokokosalon bei Kaffee und Leckerei? Charmante Komplimente aus dem Munde eines Kavaliers.

Dieser beugte sich jetzt noch weiter über den Tisch und faßte nach ihrer Hand.

»Sie haben doch keine Angst vor morgen, meine Liebe?«

»Nun, Angst vielleicht nicht, Herr Dekan«, meinte Dorothea und entwand ihm vorsichtig ihre Hand, »wohl aber Besorgnis, ob ich im gegebenen Augenblick die rechten Worte finden werde.«

»Das werden Sie, das werden Sie!« rief Doktor Johannes Juncker zuversichtlich und nahm noch ein Häppchen von der Gänseleberpastete. »Eine Frau, die den kaiserlichen Universitätsprivilegien die Stirn bietet, die findet auch vor einer Prüfungskommission, wie sie morgen zusammentritt, die rechten Worte!«

»Kaiserliche Universitätsprivilegien?« fragte Dorothea unsicher zurück. Sie wußte sehr wohl, daß sie es geschafft hatte, Verordnung und öffentliches Gesetz, wie auch das noch geltende römische Recht, die alle der Promotion einer Frau entgegenstehen, zu umgehen, aber was besagten die erwähnten Privilegien? Und schon kam die Erklärung:

»Die Kaiserlichen Universitätsprivilegien betonen, daß akademische Würden nur an Männer verliehen werden dürfen und daß das medizinische Praktizieren einer Frauensperson..." erklärte Juncker und konnte sich an dieser Stelle wieder eines Schmunzelns nicht erwehren "... den Gesetzen der Ehrbarkeit und Schamhaftigkeit zuwiderlaufe."

Nun erschrak Dorothea doch ein wenig.

"Sie brauchen kein so bestürztes Gesicht zu machen, liebe Erxlebin", tröstete der Professor, "nicht allein auf den Hinweis Seiner Majestät sind wir von der Universität zu dem Schluß gekommen, daß eine wohlverdiente Frauensperson, die durch eine hinlängliche Prüfung ihre Gelehrsamkeit bewiesen hat, keinesfalls von den akademischen Würden auszuschließen ist. Und wenn man die Menschen so ansieht, wie sie vor Gott dastehen, und man nach den Richtlinien Christi ein gerechtes Urteil fällen soll, so kann es in dieser Frage nur heißen: Hie ist weder Mann noch Weib. Allein die Bemühung, die Kräfte des Verstandes und des Willens zur Erlangung der Wahrheit und der Tugend einzusetzen, darf zählen. Und wir kamen zu dem Schluß, verehrte Kandidatin, Ihnen unser Ohr nicht zu verschließen..." Bis hier war Professor Juncker gewohnheitsmäßig ein wenig ins Dozieren geraten, aber jetzt setzte er mit einem kleinen Augenzwinkern hinzu: "...mögen Sie sich nun einer glatten und sicheren Zunge bedienen oder auch ein wenig ins Stottern geraten... da werde ich Ihnen dann schon helfend beispringen!"

Als er nochmals nach ihrer Hand griff, überließ Dorothea sie ihm für einen Augenblick mit dankbarem Druck.

Viel zu lange hatten die Erxlebin und ihr Stiefsohn sich im Hause Juncker aufgehalten. Die Uhr schlug zweimal, als Dorothea sich erhob und einen weit herzlicheren Abschied nahm, als der offizielle Anlaß forderte.
»Ich stehe schon jetzt in Ihrer Schuld, Herr Dekan«, versicherte sie, »meine Furcht vor dem morgigen Tag hat sich in Vorfreude gewandelt!«
»Letzteres fühle auch ich«, meinte der Dekan, »hinzu kommt rein fachliche Neugier, was Sie uns zu bieten haben werden.«
Draußen auf der Straße wollte Fritz, der sich bisher schweigsam verhalten hatte, endlich wissen:
»Nun, Mutter, bist du erleichtert?«
»Erleichtert, mein Junge? Entzückt bin ich über diesen liebenswürdigen alten Herrn!« Und damit hakte sie sich bei ihrem Stiefsohn unter. »Komm, du wolltest mir die Stadt zeigen«, sagte sie fröhlich.

## Die Prüfung

Am nächsten Tag wurde es dann hochoffiziell. Der große Hörsaal der Friedrichs-Universität zu Halle, in dem erstmalig eine weibliche Kandidatin sich der medizinischen Prüfung unterziehen sollte, war überfüllt. Ein solches Ereignis wollten sich selbst die Studenten anderer Fakultäten nicht entgehen lassen. Dicht bei dicht, Reihe für Reihe saßen sie und verhielten sich ausnahmsweise mucksmäuschenstill. Die berühmte Nadel hätte man zu Boden fallen hören können, als nun eine in schlichte dunkle Seide gekleidete Frau das Podest betrat, sehr aufrecht und allem Anschein nach in vollkommener Ruhe. Mit einem kurzen Senken ihres Kopfes begrüßte sie die versammelte Prüfungskommission, die ihrerseits dem feierlichen Anlaß entsprechend in vollem Ornat mit prächtig altmodischen Allongeperücken erschienen war. Da war der Rektor, Professor Doktor Johannes Juncker, in dessen Erwiderung des Grußes man ein winziges ermutigendes Augenzwinkern erkennen konnte. Da war der Prorektor Alberti, eine imposante Gestalt, da waren die Professoren Büchner und Boehmer und endlich Professor Hoffmann, der Sohn des vor zwei Jahren hier verstorbenen langjährigen Rektors, der auf dem Gebiet des Blutkreislaufs geforscht und die Theorie aufgestellt hat, daß alle Krankheiten auf Spannung und Erschlaffung, also Systole und Diastole des Herzens beruhe.

Auf dem Prüfungsplan, wie man der Kandidatin zuvor bekannt gegeben hatte, standen Anatomie, Diagnostik und vor allem die Behandlung von Krankheiten.

Die Fragen, in lateinischer Sprache gestellt, prasselten nur so auf die bereits ein wenig matronenhaft wirkende Doktorandin nieder, und keine einzige Antwort, ebenfalls in Latein abgefaßt, blieb sie schuldig.

»Zählen Sie uns die harntreibenden Stoffe auf.«

»Welche auswurffördernden Mittel sind Ihnen bekannt?«

»Was wenden Sie zur Fieberbekämpfung an?«

Und plötzlich kam von Hoffmann, dem Jüngsten der Kommission, etwas gespreizt die Frage:

»Pflegen Sie auch die von meinem Vater entwickelten Tropfen zu verschreiben? Und wenn ja, für was wenden Sie seine ätherhaltige Lösung an?«

Ein tadelnder Blick des Dekans ließ darauf schließen, daß Hoffmann seine Frage aus purer Eitelkeit zusätzlich stellte. Die Kandidatin ließ sich jedoch nicht einen Moment beirren.

»Ich wende diese Tropfen bei Magen- und Darmaffektionen an«, sagte sie sehr bestimmt, »ich habe sehr gute Erfolge insofern mit ihnen, als sie von den Patienten sehr gern genommen werden. Für deren Heilwirkung ist das allerdings keinerlei Beweis.«

Und sofort stieß Hoffmann nach.

»Die Kandidatin möge uns berichten, was sie bei einem ausgesprochenen Hypochonder zu unternehmen gedenkt, welche Medikamente, welche Anwendungen...« Er lächelte süffisant. Augenscheinlich hatte er es darauf abgesehen, die zu Prüfende aufs Glatteis zu führen. Erneut traf ihn dafür ein strafender Blick von Seiten Junckers, aber wieder kam die Antwort zügig.

»Bei Hypochondrie halte ich es für das beste, die von ihr befallene Person zu einer rechten Arbeit anzuhalten, auf daß es ihr an Zeit mangle, in sich hineinzuhorchen und den Tag müßig damit zu verbringen, an eingebildete Krankheiten zu denken.«

»Und wie verwenden Sie Theriak in solchen Fällen?« stieß Hoffmann sogleich nach.

»Überhaupt nicht. Theriak mag durch Opium und Baldrian, sofern darin enthalten, den Patienten ruhig stellen, hat aber auf sein Gebrechen keinen eigentlichen Einfluß. Theriak ist ein Brei, darin vielerlei Stoffe gemengt sind. Man mag in alten Zeiten an seine Wunderkraft geglaubt haben, doch meine Meinung ist, daß sie zu nichts nütze sind als von Quacksalbern auf dem Markt verschrien zu werden.«

Die Herren Prüfer waren sprachlos. Mon Dieu! Einem Hypochonder Arbeit zu verordnen! Welch geniale Idee! Jeder andere hätte es nach hergebrachter Weise allein mit Beruhigungsmitteln versucht.

Jetzt nahm Professor Juncker, schon um des jungen Hoffmanns Eigenmächtigkeiten zu unterbinden, die Zügel selbst wieder in die Hand.

»Was sagt Ihnen der Name Boerhaave, Frau Kandidatin?«

Das erste Mal zeigte sich die Spur eines Lächelns auf den Lippen der Befragten.

»Arzt und Lehrer an der Universität zu Leyden, daselbst vor fünfzehn Jahren im hohen Alter von siebzig Jahren verstorben. Er sah den Menschen als eine Art Maschine aus flüssigen und festen Teilen, die physikalisch ineinanderwirken. Funktioniert diese Maschine, so funktioniert auch die Seele und ist der Mensch ge-

sund, eine Umkehrung dieses Satzes erkannte er nicht an. Störungen im Funktionieren dieser Maschine sah er in überfüllten und damit verstopften oder ungefüllten, also leeren Gefäßen der festen Teile. Entzündungen traten nach seiner Meinung auf, wenn es zu Stauungen der Säfte an den Gabelungsstellen von Adern und Lymphgefäßen kam. Fieber, das er übrigens sorgfältig beobachtete, entsteht nach Boerhaave, wenn Schweiß und Harn Blutwasser mit sich genommen haben, das Blut also verdickt ist und Reibung, sprich Wärme erzeugt.« Mit einem Seufzer unterbrach sie sich, um sogleich fortzufahren. »Aber er mahnte auch, die Erkenntnisse der Wissenschaft in Demut christlicher Gläubigkeit hinzunehmen und wies auf ihre Grenzen hin. ›Die innersten Zusammenhänge der Schöpfung‹, so sagte er, ›sind und bleiben Geheimnisse Gottes‹«.
Das Schweigen, das diesem Vortrag folgte, drückte mehr Anerkennung aus, als Worte es konnten.
»Ein letztes noch, Frau Kandidatin«, ließ sich Junckers endlich vernehmen, »wir geben Ihnen jetzt Merkmale eines Falles vor und wünschen von Ihnen daraus resultierend eine vollständige Diagnose samt medizinischer und medikamentöser Verordnung.« Er gab seinem Beisitzer Büchner einen Wink, und dieser zählte genau auf, was der fiktive Patient für Beschwerden und welcherlei Schmerzen vorzubringen habe.
Die Doktorandin hörte aufmerksam zu.
»Ich bitte noch um Angabe der Temperatur des Patienten und die genaue Pulszahl«, forderte sie, ehe ihrerseits ein genauer Krankenbericht samt Behandlungsweise und genauer Dosierung verordneter Arzneien erfolgte.

Bisher war alles in fließendem Latein gesprochen worden, jetzt aber entfuhr es dem Herrn Dekan auf deutsch:
»In Ihren Händen ist man als Kranker gut aufgehoben, verehrte Kandidatin! Ich wünschte, wir hätten immer solche Doktoranden, dann wäre mir um die Patienten nicht bange.«
Damit erhoben sich die Herren Professoren und zogen sich zur Beratung zurück. Die ›studiosa‹ blieb allein am Prüfungstisch zurück und suchte nicht auf das Gewisper und Getuschel zu hören, das sich jetzt auf den Bänken erhob. Stattdessen hielt sie innerlich Zwiesprache mit einem, den sie in dieser Stunde am meisten vermißte.
»Vater! Lieber, guter Papa, wenn du nur hier wärst! Es wäre der schönste Lohn für alles, was du je getan hast, und auch für mich, die ich dir heute meinen Dank abstatte für alle deine Mühe, deine Liebe und deinen Glauben an mich...«

Schon hörte man Schritte, der Hochschuldiener öffnete die Tür zum Beratungsraum, und einer nach dem anderen traten die Professoren im feierlichen Ornat wieder ein und nahmen, außer dem Dekan, Platz wie zuvor. Professor Juncker trat bedächtig ans Pult und räusperte sich. Sofort erstarb jedes Geräusch unter den Zuhörern.
Nach ein paar einführenden lateinischen Floskeln, sprach Juncker in deutsch weiter:
»Unsere verehrte Doktorandin hat zwei volle Stunden hindurch die an sie gerichteten Fragen mit bewundernswürdiger Bescheidenheit, aber vor allem Fertig-

keit entgegengenommen, gründlich und deutlich beantwortet und eingeworfene Zweifel mit größter Überzeugungskraft ausgeräumt. Hierbei bediente sie sich eines so schönen und wohlgesetzten Lateins, daß wir glaubten, eine alte Römerin in ihrer Muttersprache zu hören.« Eine ganze Weile ging Juncker dann auf Einzelheiten der Befragung ein und kommentierte sie mit Worten wie ›vortrefflich‹ und ›ausgezeichnet‹.

»Wie die Dinge also liegen«, fuhr er fort, »könnte die medizinische Fakultät ihr sofort die Doktorwürde erteilen; weil diese aber ein ›casus sine explo‹ ist, ein Fall ohne Beispiel, dergleichen also auf keiner deutschen Universität bis dato geschehen ist, hat die Fakultät es für nötig befunden, einstweilen nähere königliche Anweisung abzuwarten, wie hierin vorzugehen sei...« Er wartete einen Moment ab, bis ein Raunen, das sich im Hörsaal erhoben hatte, wieder abebbte und sprach mit fester Stimme weiter. »Wir glauben aber sicher sagen zu können, daß Seine Königliche Majestät unserer Frau Kandidatin das Doktorat zuerkennen wird. Sobald die Bestätigung Seiner Majestät eingetroffen ist, wird die Fakultät ihr in aller Form und Öffentlichkeit die Doktorwürde verleihen.«

Brausender Beifall in den Rängen erhob sich, dem hier und da Rufe des Unwillens beigemischt waren, wie »Warum warten?«, »Gerechtigkeit für diese Frau« und »Warum versteckt Ihr euch hinter dem König?« Das Prüfungskollegium hielt es für ratsam, sich schleunigst zurückzuziehen. Nur Juncker war noch geblieben und trat zu seinem Schützling.

»Nur nicht verzagen, meine Liebe«, sagte er und zog eine Schulter hoch. »Ich mußte einigen Widerständen im Kollegium nachgeben. Leider. Aber seien Sie unbesorgt. In der Sache soll noch heute ein Sonderkurier nach Berlin abgehen. Wir sehen uns wieder, hier in Halle, und zwar bald, glauben Sie mir!« Er setzte ein schiefes, etwas hilfloses Lächeln auf und nickte ihr zu. Dann wandte er sich rasch ab, den Herren Kollega nach draußen zu folgen.

Dorothea Christiane Erxleben, geborene Leporin, hatte die Prüfung vor der medizinischen Fakultät der Universität Halle mit Glanz bestanden, aber ein Wermutstropfen blieb doch. Sie trat, ohne den Doktortitel erhalten zu haben, die Rückreise nach Quedlinburg an.

## *In der Weibermütze kehrt sie heim*

Da sie nicht vorbestellt hatte, erwischte Dorothea Erxleben diesmal nur einen Platz in der ›Ordinari‹ nach Aschersleben. Jedoch tat ihr nach der überstandenen Nervenanspannung eine Nachtruhe in der alten Stadt der Askanier recht gut. Eine Postverbindung für die letzten drei Meilen nach Quedlinburg fand sich dann bequem am Morgen, so daß, dort ankommend, der Postillion weit vorm Oeringer Tor Signal gab, noch ehe die Mittagsglocken läuteten.

Hatten vor ihrer Abreise vor drei Tagen nur wenige Neugierige Notiz genommen, so schien sich jetzt ganz Quedlinburg auf dem Marktplatz versammelt zu haben. Mit Hoch und Hurra wurde die vermeintliche Doktorin empfangen, als die Postkutsche hielt, Schusters Daniel eilfertig den Schlag aufriß und der Herr Pfarrer seiner Frau zum Ausstieg die Hand reichte.

»Willkommen, Frau Doktor!« sagte er so laut, daß alle es hören konnten, aber auch Dorotheas Antwort war deutlich zu vernehmen.

»Nein, Johannes, noch nicht Frau Doktor! Die Prüfung hab' ich zwar bestanden, mich wohl auch mit Bravour geschlagen, aber zur Verleihung des Titels muß ich noch einmal nach Halle, wenn...« Es folgte die ausführliche Erklärung der Gründe warum und wieso, die im enttäuschten Gemurmel der Umstehenden unterging.

Am Rande der Menge aber standen zwei, denen nicht

Enttäuschung im Gesicht geschrieben stand, sondern die blanke Schadenfreude.

»Hab' ich es nicht gesagt, Herr Kollega«, rief Doktor Grasshoff und rieb sich die Hände, »in der Weibermütze kommt sie zurück und nicht im Doktorhut!«

»Ja, ja«, fiel Doktor Herweg ebenfalls händereibend ein, »dabei hat sie drauf gelauert wie die Katze vorm Taubenschlag!«

Doktor Zeitz, der als Dritter dabei stand, teilte den schadenfrohen Triumph nicht.

»Warten wir es ab, meine Herren, der Baum fällt nicht beim ersten Hieb«, meinte er und wandte sich grußlos dem Heimweg zu.

»Er mag recht haben, der Kollege Zeitz«, überlegte Herweg, nachdenklich geworden, »es ist schon mancher in sein Glück gefahren, wie der Bauer in die Stiebel!«

»Na, na«, brummte Grasshoff in seiner Schadenfreude gestört, »eh es soweit ist, lassen Sie uns noch einen Schoppen nehmen!« Damit faßte er den Doktor Herweg unter und steuerte mit ihm auf den ›Bären‹ zu.

Auch der Pfarrer nutzte den kurzen Heimweg, seine ›Eheliebste‹ so gut es ging zu trösten.

»Trag es mit Fassung, meine Dörte, bist du denn kein Doktor geworden, so bleibst du doch die beste und treueste Gefährtin, die ein Mann sich zu seinem Glück nur wünschen kann ...«

Doch Dorothea sah verständnislos zu ihm auf.

»Hast du denn nicht verstanden, Johannes? Nichts ist verloren, die Verzögerung nur Formsache. Der König kann mir seine Zustimmung nach dem Stand der

Dinge kaum verwehren. Das hieße ja dreimal Hott gesagt und dann im Ziel den Zügel anziehen! Nein, Johannes, hast du so lange die Zuversicht mit mir geteilt, so teile sie auch jetzt noch mit mir, und du wirst sehen, wie schnell man mich erneut nach Halle ruft!«
Damit waren sie im Pfarrhaus angekommen.
Dort gab es einen recht lebhaften Empfang. Die Haustür flog auf, der zehnjährige Christian und Albert, der achtjährige, stürmten auf die Mutter zu,
»Nun, bist du eine Doktorin, Mama? Hast du bestanden in Halle?«
Und auch die Stieftöchter, Sophie mit der kleinen Anna Dorothea an der Hand, und Lore, den Jüngstgeborenen Johann Heinrich auf dem Arm, wollten wissen, wie es stand.
Die Nachricht, daß es noch einen Aufschub abzuwarten gab, konnte die frohe Laune im Haus aber nicht dämpfen. Wie hatte Dorothea das Lachen und Lärmen der Kinder vermißt. So kurz sie auch nur fort gewesen war, so war sie doch in einer fremden Welt gewesen, ja meinte fast von einem anderen Stern heimgekehrt zu sein.
In der Tür stand Martha, die Magd, griesgrämig wie eh und je und dennoch herzensgut.
»Hab's schon gehört! Es bleibt bei Frau Pfarrer!« rief sie zum Beweis, daß Gerüchte doch schneller die Gasse hinablaufen, als Füße es können »nun denn, Frau Pfarrer, mir gilt es gleich!« brabbelte sie weiter und wischte sich die Finger an der Schürze ab, »Kommen Sie nur herein, Frau Pfarrer! Reisen macht hungrig, denke ich mir, hab' einen Braten im Ofen, Klöße im Rohr, und die Suppe steht fertig auf dem Tisch!«

So willkommen geheißen, trat Dorothea dankbar ein und nahm geduldig noch einmal die Rolle der Pfarrfrau und Mutter auf sich, die Gewißheit im Herzen, daß es nur noch ein ganz kleiner Schritt sein würde, der sie vom endgültigen Ziel trennte.

Mit dieser Gewißheit ihres Herzens sollte Dorothea recht behalten. Nach außergewöhnlich kurzer Frist, nämlich schon nach vierzehn Tagen, kam Antwort aus Berlin. Der König sandte ein Reskript an die Medizinische Fakultät *als werdet Ihr gnädigst hiermit autorisiert, gedachter Erxleben gewöhnlichermaßen den Gradum in Eurer Fakultät nach ihrem petito zu erteilen.* Eigenhändig gezeichnet: *Friedrich.*
Professor Juncker, offensichtlich selbst hocherfreut, teilte dies sofort Dorothea in einem Brief mit und lud sie zum 12. Juni ein, wieder in Halle zu erscheinen. Als pikante Note verfügte er, daß die feierliche Verleihung des Doktortitels nicht öffentlich in Aula oder Hörsaal stattfinden sollte, sondern vor geladenem Publikum in seiner Privatwohnung.

So saß Dorothea Erxleben am 12. Juni 1754 wieder im hellblauen Salon des Hauses Berliner Straße in Halle, um nun endgültig Diplom und Doktorhut entgegenzunehmen.
Anwesend waren natürlich die Herren der Prüfungskommission, einige weitere Professoren und – wieder eine hübsche Geste des Hausherrn – deren Damen, alle in festlicher, fast höfischer Kleidung, gegen die sich das schlichte Seidene der Doktorandin abhob, allerdings für den, der Geschmack und Feingefühl hatte, nur zum

Guten. Das Bescheidene ihres Auftritts, die verhaltene Würde, der ruhige feste Klang ihrer Stimme, als sie nun aufgefordert wurde, den Eid zu sprechen, Wort für Wort nach dem Gelöbnis, wie es vierhundert Jahre vor Christi der griechische Arzt Hippokrates, der Begründer der medizinischen Wissenschaft schlechthin, ablegte:

*Ich schwöre bei Apollon, dem Arzt, bei Asklepios und Hygieia und rufe alle Götter zu Zeugen an ... ärztliche Verordnungen nur zum Nutzen der Kranken zu treffen, sie vor Gefahr und Schaden zu bewahren. Ich werde niemandem ein tödliches Mittel geben, wie keiner Frau zu einer Abtreibung verhelfen. Lauter und fromm werde ich mein Leben gestalten und meine Kunst ausüben. In alle Häuser will ich kommen und was ich während der Behandlung sehe und höre, werde ich als Geheimnis hüten.* Und endlich: *So ich diesen Eid nicht breche, sei mir Erfolg in der Heilkunst beschieden, auf daß ich bei allen Menschen für alle Zeit Ansehen gewinne ...*

Wie sie dort stand, die Hand schwörend erhoben, das Gesicht in feierlichem Ernst, ergab Dorothea Erxleben ein Bild, das sich tief in die Herzen der Anwesenden senkte.
Endlich trat der Herr Dekan vor, um, sichtlich gerührt, die Ernennung zu verlesen.
»Unter kaiserlicher und königlicher höchster Autorität erkläre ich die fürtreffliche Kandidatin Dorothea Christiane Erxleben, geborene Leporin, aus Quedlinburg, zu einem Doktor in der Arzneigelahrtheit und gestehe ihr die Freiheit zu, die Heilkunst auszuüben.«

Einen Augenblick war es ganz still im Raum, dann wurde ein Beifall laut, der den Rahmen des hellblauen Salons zu sprengen drohte. Hochrufe erschollen aus dem Hintergrund, wo doch noch studentische Jugend im letzten Augenblick Zutritt erhalten hatte. Der Jubel aus ihren Reihen galt neben der Person Dorotheas besonders dem Fortschritt, den sie im Durchbruch feministischen Anteils an der bisher rein maskulinen Geisteswelt sahen.
Sobald die Begeisterungsstürme einigermaßen verklungen waren, trat Frau Doktor Erxleben an das für diesen Tag eigens aufgestellte schmale Pult, um ihre Dankesrede in lateinischer Sprache zu halten.
»Quidquid virium mearum exiguitas, quidquid bene ac ornate dicendi defectus«, begann sie, was soviel heißt wie: »Sind auch meine Kräfte nur gering, mangelt es mir auch an der Kunst der wohlgesetzten Rede, zumal aus einem so ungewohnten Anlaß wie diesem, muß ich trotz aller dieser Hemmnisse doch um Redeerlaubnis bitten.« Ihr Blick war dabei wie fragend auf Professor Juncker gerichtet, und dieser, wenn auch rein formal, gab mit einem Kopfnicken die Erlaubnis zur Rede. »Ich will den Empfindungen«, fuhr also Dorothea fort, »eines dankbaren Geistes, der sich über empfangene Wohltaten herzlich freut, Ausdruck verleihen; freilich wird diese Freude durch das Bewußtsein der eigenen Mängel gedämpft.« Leises Murmeln im Raum widersprach höflich der allzugroßen Bescheidenheit. Und weiter perlten förmlich die lateinischen Sätze: »Heute, da ich mich zwischen verschiedene und geradezu gegensätzliche Gefühle gestellt sehe, weiß ich kaum, was ich tun, was ich lassen, wohin ich mich wenden soll. So

empfinde ich meine Schwäche, nicht nur die, von der sich kein Mensch frei glauben darf, sondern auch jene, die alle dem schwächeren Geschlecht nachzusagen pflegen.« Bis hier zollten ihre Worte noch einmal der unterschiedlichen Perspektive Respekt, in der ihr Zeitalter die Geschlechter sah, um nun sich zu einem der darüber stand, aufzuschwingen. »Zugleich aber bewundere ich in demütiger Ehrfurcht die weise Führung des Allmächtigen. Er hat von der Wiege an mein Geschick so gelenkt, daß ich dahin gelangen konnte, wohin zu kommen vor mir kaum einer Frau geglückt ist und woran ich selbst nicht habe denken können. Dieser Vorsehung gehorsam, nahm ich es mir stets zum Vorsatz, nichts ohne Überlegung und nichts mit Überheblichkeit zu tun; doch auch Ängstlichkeit schien mir unpassend...«

Weiter schildert sie nicht nur ihre medizinische Laufbahn, sondern läßt in geziemender Weise recht selbstbewußte Töne anklingen, ohne die, das ist klar, sie niemals hätte erreichen können, was sie zu dieser Stunde erreicht hatte. Und endlich schließt Frau Doktor Erxleben: »Sie, hochverehrter Herr Dekan, Sie alle, meine hochachtbaren Herren Professoren, Leuchten der ärztlichen Kunst, Zierden des Menschengeschlechts...«, nichts in ihrer Miene deutet auf Ironie, die man doch aus ihren Worten fast zu hören glaubt, »... meine gefälligen Gönner, Sie alle erwähne ich mit höchstem Lobe. Allen übrigen bekunde ich meine tiefe Verbundenheit für die mir erwiesene Gunst.« Mit ein paar Floskeln, die Gottes Segen auf Kaiser, König und auf die Friedrichs-Universität herabflehen, endet die Rede.

In fast weihevoller Stille trat nun Dekan Juncker neben sie, um ein kurzes Schlußwort zu sprechen.
»Ich bitte Sie, meine geneigten Hörer, diesem neuen Doktor in der Arzneigelahrtheit gewogen zu bleiben. Erbitten Sie mit mir zugleich vom höchsten Geber alles Guten, daß die Bestrebungen dieser Matrone und ihr Fleiß zur Ehre des Höchsten, zum Besten der Kranken, insonderheit derjenigen weiblichen Geschlechts, und zur Ehre und Zierde der medizinischen Fakultät gereichen mögen!«
Fast schien es wieder, als wolle der Fünfundsiebzigjährige die Matrone, wie er Dorothea genannt, vor aller Augen umarmen, und niemand hätte es ihm wohl verübelt, wenn er es getan hätte, aber ein herzlicher Händedruck tat stattdessen das seine.
Die Feierstunde ging über in nicht endenwollende Gratulation, dazu erlesene Bewirtung, bei der ein guter Tropfen nicht fehlte. Dorothea Erxleben war am Ziel ihrer Wünsche, stand hoch oben auf dem Gipfel jenes Berges, den zu erklimmen sie als Achtjährige schüchtern im Nachthemd, dem Krankenlager entschlüpft, in des Vaters Studierstube begonnen hatte. Und zu ihm, dem geliebten Vater gingen auch zu dieser Stunde wieder ihre innigsten Gedanken.
»Siehst du, Papachen, da bin ich! Ganz so, wie du es wolltest, als deine Doktorin Erxlebin, stets und immer aber in deiner Schuld, lieber Papa!«
Niemand jedoch hörte eines dieser Worte, die sie in stummer Zwiesprache in ihrem Herzen bewegte.

## Ein Gang nach Canossa

Noch bevor Frau Doktor Erxleben offiziell ihre ärztliche Praxis wieder aufgenommen hatte, wurde ihr ein Besucher gemeldet.
»Er steht draußen«, meldete Martha geheimnisvoll, »und will nicht reinkommen!«
»Will nicht hereinkommen?« wiederholte Dorothea, »ist es ein Patient? Oder werde ich zu einem Kranken geholt?«
»Keins von beiden«, brummelte die Magd und hatte offensichtlich Order, nicht mehr zu verraten.
»Also, wer ist es so spät am Abend?« forschte Pfarrer Erxleben weit weniger geduldig als seine Frau. Endlich hatte er sie nach all dem Trubel, all den Ehrungen, Empfangskomitees und öffentlichen Feierlichkeiten einmal ganz in Ruhe für sich, saßen sie in trautem Beieinander in der guten Stube bei einem Glas Wein, da wurden sie wieder einmal aufgescheucht und daran gemahnt, daß sie beide, jeder auf seine Art, eine Amtsperson waren und nicht eine Minute, Tag oder Nacht, Anrecht auf Privatleben hatten. Wer immer dort draußen stand, konnte in irgendeiner Form verletzt oder verzweifelt sein, Hilfe an Leib und Seele brauchen, für sich oder einen Nächsten, da durfte weder die Uhr noch das eheliche Glück etwas zählen.
»Ich werde nachsehen«, meinte Dorothea rascher entschlossen als ihr Mann, doch als sie aufstand, folgte er ihr, und beide traten gemeinsam vor die Haustür. Die süße Milde der Juninacht schlug ihnen entgegen, die

Sterne am Himmel schimmerten heller als die Laterne, die den kiesbestreuten Gartenweg beleuchtete. Von dort her hörten sie jetzt Schritte knirschen. Ein Mann kam zögernd auf sie zu. Er trat ins Licht und zog den Hut. Es war Doktor Zeitz.

»Entschuldigen Sie bitte die späte Stunde, Herr Pfarrer«, begann er, den Blick zu Boden gesenkt, schien dann aber allen Mut zusammenzunehmen, hob den Kopf und sah Dorothea voll an. »Und auch Sie, Frau Kollegin ... verzeihen Sie mir bitte ...«

»So spät ist es ja noch nicht, Doktor Zeitz, wir dachten noch lange nicht an Nachtruhe!«

Dorothea war bemüht, ihm den Gang nach Canossa, und ein solcher sollte es wohl werden, so leicht wie möglich zu machen. Und tatsächlich ging ein dankbares Leuchten über die Züge des Doktors.

»Oh, ich meine all das andere, das Sie mir verzeihen sollen, Kollegin Erxleben! Die Art und Weise, wie ich mit Grasshoff und Herweg gegen Sie konspiriert habe ...«

»Schön war sie gerade nicht«, sagte Dorothea nun doch eine Spur tadelnd. »Im Ton haben Sie sich jedenfalls vergriffen, das steht fest, auch bei der Wahrheit sind Sie nicht ganz geblieben ...«

»Ja, ja, ich bedaure es jetzt, habe ich mich doch von den beiden zu diesem Feldzug überreden lassen!« Scheinbar sehr erleichtert über seine Beichte, hob er die Arme gegen den nachtdunklen Himmel und bekannte fast theatralisch: »Ich bereue von Herzen, verehrte Kollegin, ich hätte es nicht zulassen sollen, aber ich hatte nicht den Mut ...« Erschrocken hielt er inne, da er Dorothea lachen hörte.

»Allzusehr brauchen Sie nicht zu bereuen, lieber Zeitz, im Grunde haben Sie mir nur einen Gefallen getan!«
Zeitz ließ die Arme sinken.
»Ich verstehe nicht...« Die Sache lief ganz anders, als er sich vorgestellt, zumal auch der Pfarrer jetzt vergnügt schmunzelte.
»Na, Doktor, kommen Sie erst einmal herein«, lud er den reuigen Büßer ein, »wir sitzen grad bei einer Flasche Wein, und ein drittes Glas wird sich noch finden lassen.«
Drinnen dann, in heimeliger Stube, und nach dem ersten Schluck Rotspon begriff Zeitz endlich, was gemeint war. Ohne den Angriff des Doktor-Kleeblatts, deren Beschuldigungen und Klage beim Amt hätte sich Dorothea, seit langem Pfarrfrau und als Mutter in täglicher Verantwortung für neun Kinder, niemals mehr aufgerafft, sich zur Doktorprüfung anzumelden. Nur die Herausforderung als solche und die im Hintergrund wohlmeinende Haltung Schellersheims hatten die Kettenreaktion ausgelöst, das Rechtfertigungsschreiben, die Doktorarbeit und endlich Prüfung und Promotion.
»Sie sehen, Kollege Zeitz«, meinte Dorothea und hob ihr Glas gegen den Gast, »ich habe Ihnen dankbar zu sein!«
Mit dieser Umkehrung der Dinge war Zeitz dann nicht ganz einverstanden.
»Um Gottes willen, nein! Sollte ich mir für die Zukunft Ihre kollegiale Freundschaft erhalten, so bin ich schon mehr als gut davongekommen!« rief er, stimmte aber durch den Wein beschwingt, gern in die frohe Laune des Ehepaares mit ein.

Die kollegiale Freundschaft war ihm gerne zugestanden, aber Zukunft blieb ihm keine. Doktor Zeitz verstarb noch im gleichen Jahr in Quedlinburg.

Die erste Patientin nach der neu aufgenommenen Tätigkeit der Frau Doktor Erxleben sollte eigentlich Frau von Schellersheim sein. Zum einen wollte Dorothea die Gelegenheit nutzen, sich bei dem Ehepaar zu bedanken, zum anderen machte sich die Galle der Frau von Schellersheim wieder recht störend bemerkbar. Zuvor aber bekam es Dorothea mit einem anderen Patienten zu tun. Auf ihrem Weg zu den Schellersheims hinauf kam Dorothea wie gewöhnlich auch am Klopstockschen Haus auf dem Schloßplatz vorbei.
»Dörte!« hörte sie sich beim Namen rufen, »Dörte!« Und sich umsehend, gewahrte sie Frau Klopstock unter dem schlanken Säulenvorbau ihres Hauses stehen und ihr winken. Dorothea kehrte um und trat näher.
»Ich darf dich doch noch Dörte nennen? Oder muß ich jetzt Frau Doktor sagen?« Die Frage kam ein wenig ängstlich, denn die Klopstocks gehörten zu jenen, die die Dienste einer ›Quacksalberin‹ lieber nicht in Anspruch genommen hatten.
»Gewiß nicht, Tante Klopstock«, beruhigte Dorothea die alte Dame, »ich bin seit eh und je die gleiche geblieben, Dorothea oder Dörte, wie du nur willst.«
»Ach, ich wußte es doch, wo Klopstock und dein Vater zeitlebens die besten Freunde waren!« triumphierte Tante Klopstock. »Bitte, Dörte, willst du nicht hereinkommen, ich hätte ohnehin heute nach dir geschickt, einmal nach unserer Meta zu sehen! Du weißt doch, daß unser Gottlieb geheiratet hat?«

Ja, das wußte Dorothea Erxleben, sie wußte auch, daß der um acht Jahre Jüngere eben dabei war, sich als Dichter einen Namen zu machen. Student der Theologie und Hauslehrer, Gast und Freund am dänischen Hof, waren schon etliche seiner Oden gedruckt und ließen die Welt aufhorchen.

*Mach, Gott, dies Leben, mach es zum schnellsten Hauch,*
*oder gib die mir, die du mir gleich erschufst,*
*ach, gib sie mir, die leicht zu geben,*
*gib sie dem bebenden, bangen Herzen,*
*dem heiligen Schauer, der ihr entgegenwallt...*

Gleich, ob seine Zeilen der einst angebeteten Base Marie galten oder schon Meta Moller, die er in Hamburg kennengelernt, dort vor zwei Wochen geheiratet und jetzt als Schwiegertochter heimgebracht hatte.
»Sie gefällt mir gar nicht«, raunte Frau Klopstock der Erxlebin zu, »ein liebes Ding, aber so zart und schwach und hustet viel zu viel. Man möchte doch schließlich einmal Enkelkinder haben.«
Das Mädchen, das Dorothea dann drin in der Stube fand, von einer Frau konnte man wirklich noch nicht sprechen, war in der Tat von reizend liebenswürdigem Wesen, hübsch anzusehen mit ihren schweren goldenen Flechten, Augen so groß wie Teetassen! Nachdem die Doktorin sie aber untersucht hatte, war sie nicht weniger besorgt als deren Schwiegermutter.
»Zum Kinderkriegen weiß Gott nicht gebaut«, sagte sie leise zur Klopstockin, »viel zum schmal an Brust und Becken!« Laut fügte sie dann hinzu: »Gegen den Husten müssen wir etwas tun. Ich empfehle gequollene

Zwetschgen, die lösen den Schleim, und zudem Kamillendämpfe zum Atmen! Und, Madame Meta, Sie müssen sich schonen, hören Sie!«
»Ach was, ich bin kerngesund!« wehrte die junge Frau Klopstock fröhlich ab, »was würde mein Gottlieb sagen, wenn ich die Kranke spiele!«
»Sagen würde er nichts«, meinte Dorothea ernst, »aber tun würde er alles für Sie, wenn er Sie liebt!«
»O ja, er liebt mich, mein Gottlieb! Hören sie nur, was er für mich geschrieben hat, ganz allein für mich!« Damit nahm sie ein Blatt auf, dem anzusehen war, daß es wohl hundertmal schon gelesen und zärtlich an die Brust gedrückt worden war. Und noch einmal las Meta Klopstock, geborene Moller:

*Im Frühlingsschatten fand ich sie;*
*Da band ich sie mit Rosenbändern.*
*Sie wußt' es nicht und schlummerte!*
*Ich sah sie an. Mein Leben hing*
*Mit diesem Blick an ihrem Leben!*

Wieder drückte sie das Papier an sich und warf einen fast überirdischen Blick an die getäfelte Decke der Stube.
»Ist er nicht herrlich, mein Gottlieb?« rief sie.
»Ja, ja«, bestätigte Dorothea trocken und dachte an den heranwachsenden Buben und späteren jungen Mann, der im Hause Leporin oft genug ein und ausgegangen, ohne daß ihm damals die Flügel des Pegasus schon anzusehen gewesen wären.
»Ich muß weiter«, entschuldigte sie sich, »will noch nach der Frau Stiftshauptmann sehen, die es mit der Galle hat!«

Aber den ganzen Weg dann zum Schloß hinauf ging ihr die junge Frau nicht aus dem Kopf. Wenn sie nur hier in Quedlinburg bliebe, dachte die Ärztin bei sich, ich würd' sie schon kurieren, aber Klopstock wird wieder mit ihr durch alle Welt reisen und wer weiß, ob sie allerorten die rechte Kur findet. Da bleibt nur noch der Herrgott, ein so zartes Pflänzchen zu hüten.

## Tod der Herzogin

Frau Doktor Erxlebin nutzte zur täglichen Praxis wieder wie früher die Ordinationsräume ihres Vaters im Steinweg 51, und jeden Morgen, wenn sie vom Pfarrhaus herüberkam, fand sie das Wartezimmer voller Patienten. Da gab es Wunden zu verbinden, Brüche zu schienen, Fieber zu lindern, Rezepte zu schreiben und natürlich auch Kranke zu besuchen, alles wie eh und je, nur daß sie nicht mehr zu verwehren hatte, wenn es Frau Doktor hier und Frau Doktor dort hieß.
Ihr nächster Patient bereitete Dorothea dann große Sorgen. Unerwartet hielt eines Mittags im Sommer 1755 der fürstlich Holstein-Gottorpsche Wagen vorm Hause Leporin.
»Frau Doktor möchten sofort zur Frau Äbtissin kommen!« rief der Kutscher, ohne erst vom Bock zu steigen.
Dorothea, eben einen Aderlaß beendend, band in aller Eile die Schürze ab, griff nach der Arzttasche und stieg ohne weiteres Fragen in die Kutsche. Wenn die Frau Äbtissin ihr schon den Wagen schickte, mußte es schlecht um sie stehen. Und richtig, oben angekommen, fand sie sie kerzengerade im Sessel sitzend, aber so schwer atmend, daß es einem Röcheln nahekam.
»Ach, Kind...« brachte sie nur hervor, »weißt du noch, wenn du und dein Vater...« Wie es alten Leuten oft ergeht, waren ihre Gedanken weit in der Vergangenheit, »ihr habt mir heißen Zimtwein gebraut, der mir immer so guttat...«

»Ich lasse sogleich welchen aufsetzen, Hoheit, und noch schwarze Johannisbeere hinzutun«, beeilte sich Dorothea zu versichern. Nutzte der Wein auch nicht mehr viel, so war er der offenbar Schwerkranken vielleicht ein Trost, der mehr wog als ärztliche Kunst hier noch vermochte.

Wenn sie nur, so überlegte Dorothea, die Kranke überreden könnte, die enge Kleidung, das geschnürte Mieder und das Korsett zu lockern!

»Ein paar Knöpfe nur, Hoheit, es würde Ihnen Erleichterung bringen!«

»Ach, Kind, du kannst mich altes Gerippe nicht mehr ändern. Einst haben Kavaliere mein Dekolleté bewundert, glaub mir nur, aber seit man mich in ein Stift steckte...«

»Erlauben mir Hoheit wenigstens das Fenster zu öffnen, draußen ist Juli!«

Tatsächlich lag eine Sonnenglut auf dem Schloßhof, die nur das Kaminfeuer in der Stube der Kranken noch an Hitze übertraf.

»Alte Leute frieren leicht, kleine Doktorin, das mußt du doch wissen. Ich hab' in der Tat grad nach Holz geschickt, man soll es noch auflegen!«

Dorothea faßte die Hände der Greisin, um den Puls zu suchen, und schrak zurück, so kalt fühlten diese sich an.

Fast war es, als habe das Leben sich schon aus ihrem Körper zurückgezogen, als arbeiteten nur noch Gedanken, die der Erinnerung dienten.

»Vous vous rapellez, mon enfant, le temps où...« fiel die Prinzessin plötzlich in das ihr gewohntere Französisch, das ja auch eine distanziertere Anrede verlangte,

»Erinnern Sie sich, mein Kind damals als...« Sie beschwor die Zeit herauf, da sie die ersten Pläne zu Dorotheas Studium und Promotion gemacht, da sie den Herrn von Lüderitz für ihr Vorhaben gewonnen, und gedachte wehmütig des Doktor Leporin, der zu früh abberufen wurde, um den nun erreichten Triumph mitzuerleben.
»Sicher sieht er nun alles von droben...«
Dorothea ließ die alte Dame reden, denn auch das erschien ihr im Augenblick besser als jede Medizin. Sie hielt nur weiter ihre Hand, diese kalte Greisenhand und ließ bei allem Wissen um die Arzeneygelahrtheit dies eine Mal Gott den Vortritt, zu entscheiden, was das rechte war.
Der Wein wurde gebracht, Dorothea hielt der hohen Frau vorsichtig den Becher an die Lippen, und diese trank in kleinen Schlucken.
»Ah, ma chère, c'est délicieux!« lobte sie und schloß genießerisch die Augen. Der Wein tat seine Wirkung, von Zimt und Johannesbeere konnte Doktor Erxleben es nur hoffen. Die Atmung ging immer noch schwer, aber da der Alkohol die Angst vorm unmittelbaren Ersticken linderte, war auch die Gefahr einer Verkrampfung der Luftwege gebannt. Die Patientin wurde ruhiger, ihr Bewußtsein glitt weiter und weiter zurück in die Vergangenheit.
»Man soll dafür sorgen, daß mein Edikt neuerlich auf dem Marktplatz angeschlagen wird!« befahl sie plötzlich energisch.
»Welches Edikt, Hoheit?« Dorothea, an sich vertraut mit den Wirrnissen alter Menschen, ließ sich einen Augenblick dupieren.

»Nun, wie können Sie nur fragen! Mein Edikt gegen die Werbemethoden des Marwitzschen Regiments natürlich! Daß sie mir nicht weiter meine Untertanen zu Soldaten pressen! Ich weiß genau, der Major von Wagner hat es abreißen lassen und dem Scharfrichter übergeben, damit der es öffentlich verbrenne! Ich will, daß es ersetzt wird! Rufen Sie Posadowsky, er hat mir dafür geradezustehen!«

Dorothea öffnete den Mund, um das durcheinander geratene Erinnerungsbild der Fürstin zurechtzurücken, doch ihr kamen Zweifel am Sinn einer solchen Korrektur. Das Ereignis, von dem die Kranke sprach, lag gut zwanzig Jahre zurück. Damals war Posadowsky tatsächlich Stiftshauptmann gewesen, und damals sprach man auch von ›Untertanen des Stifts‹, auch wenn diese bereits im Jahre 1698 dem Kurfürsten von Brandenburg den Treueeid geleistet hatten. Seither befand sich das Stift in einem eher formalen Kampf um seine Vorrechte der preußischen Krone gegenüber. Im Rahmen dieser Auseinandersetzungen hatte tatsächlich im Jahre 1733 der Obristleutnant Wagner als Kommandeur des Standorts jene farce aufgeführt, die das getrübte Gedächtnis der Fürstin in die Gegenwart verlegte. Ein Erlaß des Stifts, öffentlich am Tor des Rathauses angeschlagen, gebot den preußischen Werbern, sich jeglicher Tätigkeit innerhalb der Stadt zu enthalten. Das war deutliche Sprache und bedeutete, kein Quedlinburger Bürger sollte den blauen Rock eines preußischen Soldaten tragen. Hohnlachend ließ Wagner den Erlaß von der Rathaustür reißen, in feierlich inszeniertem ›Standgericht‹ aburteilen und ›zur Exekution dem Scharfrichter übergeben‹.

Heute nun war Schellersheim Stiftshauptmann und der Streich des Obrist-Leutnants Wagner längst vergessen. Wie tief mußte sich aber die Demütigung von damals in die Seele der herzoglichen Fürstin gegraben haben, daß sie jetzt, da Geist und Körper mit letzter Kraft gegen deren Loslösung kämpften, noch einmal bedrohlich Gestalt annahm! Warum also die alte Dame durch Korrektur solcherart in Verlegenheit setzen?
»Gern Hoheit«, ging daher Dorothea auf das Spielchen ein, »ich werde Ihnen Posadowsky rufen lassen, den Major von Wagner zur Verantwortung zu ziehen, aber bleiben Sie ganz ruhig Hoheit!«
Aber schon war die Vision aus längst vergangener Zeit wie eine Seifenblase wieder zerplatzt.
»Aber Dörte, liebes Kind, was redest du da? Posadowsky weilt schon an zehn Jahre nicht mehr unter uns! Von Schellersheim heißt unser Stiftshauptmann, seit auch der Plotho nicht mehr ist, und Major Wagner? Mein Gott, der! Hat der sich doch einmal die Kinderei erlaubt, eine meiner amtlichen Verordnungen dem Henker auszuliefern! Das war so anno ...«
Der Atem wurde ihr wieder schwer, die Phase gnädiger Verwirrung war vorbei.

Draußen war rotgolden die Sonne untergegangen, als Doktorin Erxleben sich zum Gehen rüstete. Ins letzte Glas Zimtwein mischte sie ein leichtes Schlafmittel und suchte die Kranke zur Bettruhe zu überreden, jedoch vergebens.
»Nein, nein, ein Weilchen will ich noch so sitzen, aber schieb mich näher ans Feuer!«
Dorothea ließ der Frau Äbtissin ihren Willen, faßte

noch einmal nach ihrer Hand, um den Puls zu ertasten, der kaum spürbar und unregelmäßig seine Pflicht tat. Ehe Dorothea die schmale, von blauem Geäder durchzogene Hand mit dem prächtigen Saphirring daran, wieder auf den Schoß der Fürstin zurücklegte, küßte sie sie in kindlicher Ehrfurcht.
»Ich komme gleich morgen früh wieder vorbei, Hoheit, und bringe noch eine Medizin mit, die Ihnen guttun wird.«
»Ja, Kind, geh nur, kleine Dörte... und Gott mit dir...«
Das waren genau die Abschiedsworte, wie sie sie vor dreißig Jahren oftmals der Leporin-Tochter nachgerufen hatte. War ihr Geist erneut auf der Reise in die Vergangenheit? Dorothea beließ es dabei. Sie zupfte noch das Tuch zurecht, das der Kranken wärmend um die Schultern lag, dann ging sie.
Draußen empfing sie eine sternenträchtige Sommernacht, nach der übertriebenen Hitze im Krankenzimmer angenehm kühl. Durch dunkle, schlafende Gassen trat Dorothea den Heimweg an. Mit einem Mal war ihr unbegreiflich bang ums Herz.

In dieser Nacht verstarb Maria Elisabeth Herzogin von Holstein-Gottorp, ehrwürdige Äbtissin von Quedlinburg. In ihrem Sessel sitzend fand man sie in den frühen Morgenstunden, zu ihren Füßen das Feuer im Kamin niedergebrannt und ausgelöscht, so wie ihr Leben ausgelöscht war.
Vier Wochen lang ließen sämtliche Kirchenglocken Quedlinburgs und umgebender Ortschaften zu Mittag eine volle Stunde ihr Trauergeläut hören.

## *Launen*

Ein Posten wie der einer Äbtissin des adligen Damenstifts von Quedlinburg sollte keinesfalls längere Zeit vakant bleiben. Das wußte auch der König. Unter seinen Geschwistern machte ihm derzeit die um elf Jahre jüngere Anna Amalie die größten Sorgen. Durch ihre niemals ganz bewiesene Affaire mit dem Freiherrn Friedrich von der Trenck so ziemlich um ihren guten Ruf gebracht, erhielt sie dennoch bedeutende Heiratsanträge. Zarin Elisabeth hatte für den Großfürsten Peter, ihren Nachfolger, angefragt und Ludwig XV. von Frankreich wollte die Preußenprinzessin gern für seinen Sohn. Beiden erteilte Friedrich eine Absage, weil zu jener Zeit weder eine französische Verbindung noch eine solche mit Rußland in seine politischen Pläne paßte. Anna Amalia gegenüber, die über beide Absagen bitter enttäuscht war, tat es ihm herzlich leid, und er hatte jetzt, nach mehr als zehn Jahren, noch immer das Gefühl, etwas an seiner Schwester gutmachen zu müssen. Warum sie also nicht zur Äbtissin von Quedlinburg erheben? Gesagt, getan!

In der zweiten Hälfte des Jahres 1755 rätselten die Quedlinburger noch voller Spannung, wer demnächst über sie herrschen solle, und als es dann gewiß wurde, daß sie zwiefach preußisch regiert werden würden, Stift und Schirmherrschaft, da gingen die Meinungen lebhaft auseinander, ob sie wohl gut beraten seien. Niemand wußte so recht etwas über Prinzessin Amalie. Die einen sagten, sie sei ihrem Bruder nachgeraten, so klug wie er, aber auch von gleichem oft sarkastischem Witz. Die anderen meinten, wo immer sie aufträte, lobe man ihre Schönheit und ihren Charme.

»Sie ist den Armen zugetan, geht in ihre Häuser, hilft, wo sie nur helfen kann!« sagten wieder die einen, dagegen die anderen:

»Sie sitzt nur am Spieltisch bei Whist und Tarock, hat schon ein ganzes Vermögen durchgebracht!«

Keiner von ihnen hatte Gelegenheit, in den Tagebuchnotizen der Gräfin Voß, langjährige Hofdame der Königinmutter, nachzulesen, die beispielsweise schreibt:

*Trotz ihrer Jugend war Prinzessin Amalie sehr boshaft und sehr gefürchtet und machte uns allen viel Not und Unannehmlichkeiten.*

Oder was der englische Gesandte, Lord Tyrconnel, über sie nach Hause berichtete:

*Sie ist keck und unternehmungslustig und würde alles mögliche anstellen, um Aufsehen zu erlangen. Sie ist klug, aber noch weit eher falsch, ihr politischer Einfluß wäre jedenfalls zu fürchten, denn bei ihrem ruhelosen Wesen würde sie viele Ränke schmieden.*

Der Kammerherr der Königin, Graf Lehndorff, der anfangs sehr für die Prinzessin eingenommen ist, bemängelt gar:

*Man klagt allgemein über Prinzessin Amalie, daß sie niemanden ansieht und daß sie von aller Welt übel redet. Es ist schade, daß diese Prinzessin ein so launisches Wesen hat.*

Immerhin gesteht er ihr ebenfalls eine gewisse geistige Tiefe zu: *Ich besuchte Prinzessin Amalie mitten am Vormittag und fand sie im Morgenkleide wie ein Gelehrter im Studierzimmer arbeitend bei ernster und solider Lektüre...*

und notiert, als er von ihrer Wahl zur Äbtissin hört,

weiterhin: *Bedauerlicherweise macht sie sich gar nichts daraus, bei den Leuten beliebt zu werden.*

All diese Äußerungen hätten die Quedlinburger Bürger besser auf eine Enttäuschung vorbereiten können, wie sie ihnen mit der Inthronisierung der Prinzessin Anna Amalia zur Äbtissin ihres Stifts alsbald bevorstand. Sorgfältig wurde alles vorbereitet, um am 6. April 1756 die ›Installation‹ mit allem Pomp feierlich zu begehen. Immerhin kam ein solcher Schritt einer Hochzeit gleich, bei der der Bräutigam, genau wie bei den Nonnen katholischer Klöster, Jesus Christus hieß. Aus Magdeburg schaffte man eigens sechs Kanonen herbei, aus denen während der anschließenden feierlichen Huldigung durch den Rat, eine dreimalige Salve abgefeuert werden sollte.

Die Prinzessin, in einem weißseidenen Kleid mit silbernen Blumen bestickt, erfreute wirklich durch ihr reizvolles Aussehen, was ihre Aufmachung anging wie auch die jugendlichen Züge ihres Gesichts. Ihre Figur aber enttäuschte, sie war klein und da sie sich bei Essen und Trinken keinerlei Zügel auflegte, recht pummelig. Immerhin ließ sie Treuegelübde, Festessen und endlose Ansprachen geduldig wie hoheitsvoll über sich ergehen, richtete aber ihrerseits kaum das Wort an jemanden. Gewissermaßen als Höhepunkt des Tages äußerte sie dann einen recht makabren Sonderwunsch. Sie wollte die Gruft der bisherigen siebenunddreißig Äbtissinnen besichtigen. Und damit nicht genug, verlangte sie auch noch, die Särge zu öffnen, ein Wunsch, den man ihr glücklicherweise nur zum Teil erfüllen konnte, da viele der Schrauben festgerostet waren und sich nicht öffnen ließen.

Als man der neuen Äbtissin dann ihr Logis im Schloß anwies, monierte sie die steinerne Treppe, die zu ihren Räumen führte als unbequem, ließ anspannen und fuhr noch am gleichen Abend die zwei Meilen nach Blankenburg, wo ihre Schwester, die Herzogin von Braunschweig, ein Schloß besaß, und übernachtete dort.
Am andern Morgen erschien sie wieder in Begleitung ihrer Schwester und in bester Stimmung. Gemeinsam durchstöberten Äbtissin und Herzogin die Abtei von oben bis unten, schienen sich für alles zu interessieren, sich dabei aber auch köstlich zu amüsieren. Den Stiftsdamen gaben sie eine kleine Teegesellschaft im Schloßgarten, und als störend ein Gewitter aufzog, schon Blitze über den verfinsterten Himmel zuckten, und die Damen ängstliche Gesichter machten, meinte die Frau Herzogin von Braunschweig süffisant:
»Ach, im Schutze unserer Heiligen Äbtissin wird uns schon nichts passieren!«
So verbrachten die beiden preußischen Schwestern ein paar vergnügte Tage in Quedlinburg, die Nächte aber im herzoglichen Schloß Blankenburg. Doch noch ehe die Quedlinburger sich so recht von ihrem Schrecken erholen konnten, befahl die neue Äbtissin, ihre Koffer zu packen und reiste endgültig wieder ab. Ihre Apanage ließ sie sich noch kurz vor der Abreise in bar auszahlen, kam davon zwar ihren Verpflichtungen den Bedienten und Beamten des Stifts gegenüber korrekt und großzügig nach, nahm aber einen stattlichen Rest mit sich. Schließlich warteten ja die Spieltische von Berlin und Potsdam auf sie.

*Einquartierung*

Drei Frauen regierten in der Mitte der fünfziger Jahre des 18. Jahrhunderts die Geschicke Europas: Maria Theresia vom Thron der Habsburger aus, Elisabeth vom Zarenthron, und in Paris bestimmte eine Frau die Politik, zwar nicht vom Thron, aber nicht weniger allmächtig vom Himmelbett Ludwigs XV. aus, die Pompadour. Fast könnte man sie die drei Schwestern nennen, so einig waren sie sich, vor allem in einem Punkt: in ihrem Haß gegen Friedrich II. von Preußen.
Sie beschließen den kriegerischen Angriff auf Preußen für das kommende Frühjahr, da die diesjährige zur Kriegsführung geeignete Jahreszeit schon recht fortgeschritten ist, der Sommer 1756 neigt sich immerhin dem Ende zu. Friedrich fängt Kuriere ab und unterhält auch sonst ein gut funktionierendes Spionagenetz, er erfährt von den Plänen der drei Unterröcke, wie er sie hämisch nennt.
»Warum warten?« sagte der König sich, »ich bin besser dran, wenn ich ihnen zuvorkomme!«
Am 29. August, den baldigen Herbst vor Augen, marschieren die Preußen mit 60000 Mann in Sachsen ein.
War Quedlinburg im Kriegsgeschehen um Schlesien verhältnismäßig unberührt geblieben, so rückte dieses jetzt bedrohlich in ihre Nähe.
Magdalena Erxleben, älteste Tochter des Diakon Erxleben, hatte längst ihren Vikar aus Dreyleben geheiratet und lebte mit ihm in Thale. Und obwohl nur anderthalb Meilen zwischen ihnen lagen, schrieben Stiefmut-

ter und Stieftochter sich Briefe. Die Briefe Magdalenas aus den nächsten Wochen und Monaten müssen wohl sehr kleinmütig geklagt haben, jedenfalls antwortete Dorothea Erxleben im Oktober 1756:

*Bist Du nicht Dein Lebtag in einem evangelischen Pfarrhaus gewesen und hast dennoch all Dein Rüstzeug verloren? Wenn wir nicht sollten in der Not standhalten, wer dann? Ich glaube, Du denkst zuviel an Dich. Gehe in die Häuser Deiner Gemeindeglieder! Du wirst finden, daß ihrer wenige sind, in denen es besser steht als im Pfarrhaus. Du bist an der Quelle, so schöpfe den Trost und reiche ihn weiter. Aber nimm ein Stückchen Geräuchertes mit und ein paar Äpfel für die Kinder. Stecke hier und dort ein Lichtchen an, wo es am dunkelsten ist, und vergiß nicht die Wundsalben und ein altes Linnen. Du kannst den Schmerz nicht aus der Welt schaffen, ebensowenig wie ich, aber lindern sollen wir ihn. So laß Deine Liebe spürbar werden, meine Tochter! Und klage nicht, denn vorerst ist, Gott sei herzlich Dank, wenig Grund dafür.*

Wohl kaum sonst ein Zeugnis kann besser belegen, was für ein Mensch Dorothea Erxleben war! Gottvertrauen, Nächstenliebe, Gutherzigkeit auf unkomplizierte und natürliche Weise, gleich benachbart praktischer Sinn im Handeln, alles das dezent und diszipliniert ausgelebt.
Und dann aus einem Brief im Dezember 1756:

*Wir haben Verwundete hier im Spital, die bei Lobositz zu Schaden gekommen sind, sie wissen aber auch nicht viel. Zu mehreren Malen hatten wir Einquartierung im Haus, es waren ordentliche Leute. Gott schütze uns aber vor Freischärlern! – So verlebt denn ein gesegnetes Christfest! In Liebe Deine treue Mutter Dorothea Erxleben.*

Was die Erxlebin damit meinte und mit Recht so fürchtete, waren die sogenannten Freikorps und Freibataillone. Sie standen in ihrer Organisation und Disziplin außerhalb der regulären Truppen. Ihre Rekruten wurden nicht von Werbern angeheuert, sondern von Mittlern oder Agenten, die ihre Dienste, nämlich das Pressen und Aufstellen zusätzlicher Einheiten, dem König gegen Geld anboten, und von diesem gern angenommen wurden, seit die regulären Truppen zusammenzuschmelzen begannen. Diese Glücksritter mit Namen le Noble, Mayr, d'Angelelli, von Kalben und, einer der erfolgreichsten unter ihnen, Collignon suchten und fanden ihr Material unter Räuberbanden, internationalen Söldnern, in Zuchthäusern und Gefängnissen. Demnach war ihr Standard an Moral, Recht und Ordnung ein anderer als sonst im preußischen Heer.

Am 5. September 1757 passiert es dann. Ein ungeregelter Haufen ohne Schritt und Tritt wälzt sich zum Oeringer Tor hinein und ergießt sich wie heiße Lava in die Stadt. Sechshundert Mann vom Fischerschen Freikorps auf Suche nach Quartier, einer warmen Mahlzeit und einer Magd für ihr Bett.

»Heda! Aufmachen!« hört man straßauf und straßab, und wo nicht gleich geöffnet wird, das Splittern von Holz und Klirren von Glas. Mit ihren Stiefeln treten sie die Türen ein, Fensterscheiben gehen unter den Schlägen ihrer Gewehrkolben zu Bruch.

»Ist Er bei mir eingewiesen?« fragt Bäckermeister Ledebur einen Soldaten und will den Quartierschein sehen.

»Nix da, Firlefanz und Federlesens!« ruft der und zieht dem Ledebur das Bajonett quer übers Gesicht.

Andere fackeln nicht lange, dringen in Hühnerstall und Taubenschlag, schlachten dem Schulzen das beste Schwein. Schreie des Schreckens, der Empörung und der Furcht brechen sich in den Gassen, und auf manchem Dach sitzt bereits der rote Hahn.

Es war ein Höllenlärm, und die verwirrten Bürger fragten sich tatsächlich, ob sie es mit Freund oder Feind zu tun hätten. Schon wollte der alte Meffert die Feuerglocke läuten, aber was hätte das geholfen? Wer wäre der Stadt zu Hilfe gekommen, da die Eindringlinge gut preußische Uniformen trugen, hellblau Weste und Hose, darüber dunkelblau das preußische Tuch, Dreispitz und schwarze Knöpfgamaschen, wichtiger aber noch den preußischen Adler auf ihren Fahnen.

Nein, man hatte sie zu dulden, solange sie in der Stadt lagen, ihnen zu geben, was sie ohnehin sich nahmen. Wohlgehütete Vorräte in den Vorratskammern der Bürger schmolzen dahin wie der Schnee an der Sonne. Wer einen gepflegten Weinkeller unterhielt, manchen edlen Tropfen für besondere Anlässe aufgespart hatte, konnte nur noch die Scherben zerschlagener Flaschen zusammenkehren. Töchter und Kinder, auch die der Erxlebens, wurden eilends aufs Schloß geschickt, wo einigermaßen Sicherheit geboten war.

Die Doktorin Erxleben bekam in der Praxis doppelt und dreifach zu tun. Wunden und Brüche, aus Willkür und Mißhandlung stammend, mußten versorgt wer-

den. Frauen und Mägde, denen Schlimmes geschah, brauchten neben ärztlicher Hilfe Trost und Zuspruch, die Dorothea ihnen aus der Wärme ihres Herzens zukommen ließ. Manch einer ging seelisch gestärkt nach Hause, dem sie nicht Tropfen und Pulver verordnet, aber etwas von ihrer eigenen Würde und dem Mut, Unvermeidliches zu tragen, vermittelt hatte.
Wenn Dorothea dann endlich die Ordination abschließen und sich todmüde auf den kurzen Heimweg machen konnte, war es längst später Abend. Die sonst zu dieser Stunde stillen Gassen hallten wider von trunkenem Gegröhl und lautem Fluchen. Das Pfarrhaus dann fand Dorothea trotz streng angesagter Sparsamkeit mit Licht und Kerze, hell erleuchtet vor. So waren also, wie erwartet, auch die Erxlebens nicht von Einquartierung verschont geblieben. Auf alles gefaßt trat Dorothea ein und richtig stieß sie gleich in der Küche auf die weinende Martha, außer sich vor Zorn und Angst.
»Zwei Kerle sind es!« rief sie, haben sich breit gemacht in allen Stuben! Und... und Frau Doktor...« die Empörung benahm der guten Magd fast den Atem »... befohlen haben sie mir, ich soll ihnen ein Omelette servieren, eines von einem Dutzend Eiern! Und Schinken dazu! Jedem ein gehörig Stück! Mit Wein haben sie sich selbst bedient, sind schon bei der dritten Flasche von unserem besten!«
Dorothea überlegte kurz. Erxleben war nicht im Haus. Er war in der Kirche. Dort verkündete er von der Kanzel herab Gottes Wort und spendete unermüdlich seit dem frühen Morgen Trost und Zuspruch den Verzweifelten, genau wie sie es getan hatte.
»Wo sind die beiden jetzt, Martha?« Einer Antwort

bedurfte es nicht, man hörte rumoren und poltern von oben, wo die beiden Freischärler anscheinend Schränke und Kommoden inspizierten.

»Hör zu, Martha«, begann Dorothea, die einen Plan gefaßt hatte, »du machst das Omelette, aber nicht von einem Dutzend, sondern von zwei Dutzend Eiern, und ordentlich Speck dazu! Und beeile dich, hörst du! Ich decke derweilen im Speisezimmer den Tisch.«

Und noch ehe die Magd sich vom Staunen erholte, wurde die Tür aufgerissen und Christian, Dorotheas Ältester, stürmte herein. Mit seinen bald dreizehn Jahren hatte er sich nicht mit den anderen auf dem Schloß verstecken lassen, sondern sich als Beschützer des Hauses gefühlt. Daß ihm das von seiten der beiden Freischärler, denen er tapfer den Einlaß verwehrte, zwei kräftige Ohrfeigen eingebracht, das war seinem rotgeschwollenen Gesicht noch anzusehen.

»Ich... Ich...« begann er, »ich hab' dich gesucht, Mutter!« Und damit es ja kein Mißverständnis gäbe, setzte er sofort hinzu: »Ich wollte dir auf dem Heimweg Geleit geben, Mutter, es ist nicht sicher für eine Frau...«

Um nichts in der Welt hätte Dorothea den Stolz ihres Sohnes verletzen wollen.

»Das ist aber lieb von dir, Christian, ich hätte deinen Schutz gut brauchen können!« Liebevoll fuhr sie ihm über den Kopf. »Nun aber, mein Junge, geh und hole den Vater, er wird hungrig sein, denke ich.« Und dann in gewichtigem Ton: »Sag ihm, mein Junge, ich erwarte ihn, wir haben Gäste zum Essen.«

Christian, von wacher Intelligenz, schien sofort zu begreifen.

»Ja, Mutter, ich gehe, ich hole den Vater!«
Als dann zwanzig Minuten später Erxleben, noch in Talar und Beffchen, sein Haus betrat, zog ihm nicht nur der verlockende Duft von Speck und gebratenen Eiern in die Nase, sondern fand er seine Frau am festlich gedeckten Abendbrottisch, silberne Leuchter auf weißem Damast, das gute Porzellan von Pfarrer Meinecke und roten Wein in geschliffenen Gläsern. Bei ihr saßen, verlegen mit hochroten Köpfen, zwei Unteroffiziere des Fischerschen Freikorps, die höflich aufsprangen, als sie des Hausherrn ansichtig wurden.
Auch Pfarrer Erxleben begriff sofort, was sich hier abspielte. Ein Sprichwort sagt: Schlechte Beispiele verderben die guten Sitten. Seine Frau versuchte eine Umkehrung des Sprichworts in die Tat umzusetzen, und sie hatte verblüffend guten Erfolg damit.
»Guten Abend, meine Herren«, begrüßte der Pfarrer seine Gäste ganz im Sinne des Experiments, »ich heiße Sie herzlich in meinem Hause willkommen!«
»Ihre Frau Gemahlin war so freundlich, uns...« stammelte der eine der beiden, ein blonder Riese, der ohne Frage schon einmal bessere Zeiten gesehen.
»Bon soir, Monsieur le curé... pardonnez mille fois...« echote der andere, ein kleiner dunkler Kerl in schmuddeliger Uniform. Es gab unter den Freischärlern eine Menge französische Deserteure, die das höhere Handgeld auf die andere Seite gelockt hatte.
Erxleben winkte den beiden, sich wieder zu setzen. Er und Christian setzten sich ebenfalls. Martha kam herein, eine riesige Schüssel auf den Tisch stellend, deren noch geschlossener Deckel für den Franzosen eine zu große Versuchung darstellte. Mit raschem Griff wollte

er ihn hochheben und sich aus der Schüssel bedienen, aber ein strafender Blick seines Kumpan traf ihn.

»Erst beten, Kamerad!« zischte der ihm zu, da Erxleben schon die Hände gefaltet hielt.

»Aller Augen warten auf Dich, o Herr«, hörten sie die Worte des Hausherrn, »Du gibst uns Speise zur rechten Zeit, Du öffnest Deine Hand und erfüllst alles, was lebt mit Segen.«

Brav senkten die beiden die Köpfe und warteten das ›Amen‹ ab, sobald dann aber ihre Teller gefüllt waren, schlangen sie die ersten Bissen mit bäurischer Gier. Gewiß, man sagte ihnen zu recht nichts Gutes nach, aber wer weiß auch schon, wie man sich fühlt, wenn nach drei Tagen Marsch, ständig nur die Knute grober Offiziere im Genick, die erste warme Mahlzeit vor einem auf dem Tisch steht.

Kaum aber war der erste Hunger gestillt, gaben beide Korporäle sich wieder Mühe, Manieren zu zeigen.

»Es schmeckt köstlich, Frau Pfarrer!« lobte der Blonde, und der Dunkle: »Délicieux, Madame!«

»Ja, unsere Martha kann kochen«, meinte Dorothea leichthin, »zuhause haben Sie sicher auch eine liebe Frau, die gut kocht, nicht wahr?«

Jetzt war die Begeisterung ganz auf Seiten des kleinen Franzosen.

»O ja, Madame! Meine femme! Marie Claire kocht wie ein Engel!« Dann mit lustig schwärmerischem Augenaufschlag: »Und sieht aus wie ein Engel!«

Der Blonde erzählte ebenfalls wehmütig von Frau und Kindern, die er habe verlassen müssen, weil man ihn mit Gewalt vom Hof schleppte.

»Ich mache mir Sorgen, wie sie allein zurechtkommen«,

sagte er kleinlaut und sah auf seinen leergegessenen Teller hinab.

»Auch meine femme allein«, fiel wieder der andere ein, »ich Brot stiebitzt bei Franzosen, und weil Angst vor Strafe zu Preußen. Aber auch nicht besser, auch kein Brot, nur Strafe.«

Ganz von sich aus kamen sie dem ureigensten Bedürfnis des Menschen nach, sich mitzuteilen oder eben auch zu beichten. Nach einem rauhen Soldatenleben, in dem sie sich den Maßstäben anderer anzupassen hatten, erlaubte man ihnen hier im Pfarrhaus mit einem Mal, sich menschlich zu geben. Die Reaktion war wie ein Aufatmen.

Nach vier Tagen, die die beiden Freischärler fast wie Söhne im Pfarrhaus zubrachten, zogen sie mit ihrer Einheit weiter. Dorothea fand die Kammer, in der sie genächtigt hatten, tadellos aufgeräumt, nichts war gestohlen, nichts zerbrochen oder zerstört.

Doch war dies ein Einzelfall, ermöglicht durch Mut und tiefe psychologische Einsicht. Dorothea hatte nicht nur die Umkehrung des erwähnten Sprichworts erreicht, sondern noch ein anderes bewiesen: ›Wie man in den Wald hineinruft, so schallt es heraus.‹

In anderen Häusern der Stadt war es weit weniger glimpflich abgelaufen. Raub, Gewalt und Unflätigkeit waren dort an der Tagesordnung gewesen, und so blieb alles in allem diese erste Einquartierung eine ebenso böse wie schmerzliche Erfahrung für die Quedlinburger.

Als nächstes war es dann wirklich der Feind, der sich Quedlinburg näherte. Der französische General d'Armentières bezog Lager außerhalb der Stadt auf der Hochebene nach Ditfurth zu. Lebensmittel schien er genügend zur Verfügung zu haben, denn er schickte lediglich seine Verwundeten und Kranken in die Stadt mit der höflichen Bitte, diese zu versorgen. In aller Eile rüstete man also Schulen und Scheunen zu Spitälern um und bettete die Schwerkranken, so gut es ging. Wer nur leicht lädiert war, fand hier und da Privatunterkunft und verhielt sich im großen und ganzen artig bescheiden. Kein Vergleich jedenfalls zu den Erfahrungen, die die Quedlinburger zwei Monate zuvor gemacht hatten.

Für die Ärzte aber, Doktor Erxleben, Doktores Grasshoff und Herweg, wie ein junger Arzt aus Halberstadt, gab es Arbeit bis zur Erschöpfung. Schußwunden, in die der Brand gekommen war, Amputationen, Kanoniere mit Gehörverlust, andere, die ihr Augenlicht verloren. Familienväter, junge Burschen, unter ihnen welche noch im Knabenalter. Und dennoch die meisten siegessicher und voll Zuversicht.

Den Preußen schien das Glück nicht hold, absolute Depression seit Kolin. Friedrich, den man schon ›den Großen‹ nannte, schien eben seinen Nimbus wieder zu verlieren.

Doktor Erxleben machte sich daran, in einem der behelfsmäßig eingerichteten Lazarette ein zerfetztes Augenlid zu nähen.

»Tupfer!« rief sie und streckte die Hand aus, aber der Sanitäter, der ihr assistierte, reagierte nicht. Ärgerlich hob Doktor Erxleben den Blick, und ihre Augen trafen sich genau mit denen Doktor Grasshoffs. Seit ihrer Promovierung waren die beiden sich nach Möglichkeit aus dem Weg gegangen. Wenn Grasshoff auch Hetzreden und Verleumdungen gegen Dorothea eingestellt hatte, so hatte er die Größe eines Doktor Zeitz doch nicht bewiesen. Sogar im Widerspruch zu Doktor Herweg, der längst seine Hand zu friedlicher Zusammenarbeit reichte, hatte Grasshoff die letzten drei Jahre in grollender Distanz verbracht.

»Hier! Tupfer!« rief er bärbeißig und reichte anstelle des Assistenten Doktor Erxleben das Gewünschte hin.

»Danke!« sagte Dorothea kurz, einzig auf die komplizierte Operation konzentriert. »Faden! Nadel! Schere!« verlangte Doktor Erxleben weiter, so wie die Arbeit fortschritt. Und Doktor Grasshoff reichte ihr exakt zu, wie es gefordert war.

»So, das wär's«, seufzte Dorothea und lehnte sich zurück, »den Rest muß die Natur tun!«

»Eine vorzügliche Leistung, Frau Kollegin!« sagte Doktor Grasshoff, jede Silbe betonend, als habe er Angst, die Worte nicht herauszubringen. »Ganz vorzüglich, ein Meisterwerk!«

Erst jetzt erlaubte sich Dorothea, Grasshoff richtig wahrzunehmen, und ganz gegen ihren Willen fühlte sie etwas wie Stolz und Genugtuung. Die letzte Bastion, dachte sie bei sich und mußte unwillkürlich lächeln. Laut aber sagte sie:

»Danke, Herr Kollege!« In einem Stalleimer wusch sie sich provisorisch die Hände und trocknete sie mit einem Leinenlappen, der bereits etliche Spuren ihrer heutigen Tätigkeit aufwies.

»Nicht gerade das, was der Göttin Hygieia gefallen hätte, aber geben wir uns die Hand, Grasshoff!«

Verblüfft über ihre offene Art und ohnehin zum Einlenken entschlossen, ging Grasshoff darauf ein. Herzlich schüttelten sie sich die Hand, und ihre Zusammenarbeit sollte sich noch viele Jahre als fruchtbar erweisen.

Für den Augenblick galt es, eine Rezeptur gegen die Kanonentaubheit zu finden.
»Ich habe gute Erfahrung mit Zwiebel und Kamille gemacht«, sagte die Erxlebin so selbstverständlich, als habe sie ihr Leben lang mit Grasshoff harmoniert, »man koche beides fest ein und sehe es durch. Erkaltet ein paar Tropfen in das Ohr tut Wunder bei Schwerhörigkeit, warum nicht also auch bei Taubheit?«
»Probieren wir es aus, Frau Kollegin, wenn Sie das Kochen übernehmen wollen! Ist Ihnen vielleicht auch ein Geheimnis bekannt, was wir mit den vielen Fieberkranken tun können?«
Tatsache war, daß immer mehr Kranke dieser Art eingeliefert wurden. D'Armentières, der Gefechtsübungen auf den Höhen des Sallerslebener Holz und des Lehhofs abhalten ließ, wurde von anhaltenden Regenfällen überrascht, dazu ein Wind, viel zu kalt für Mitte Oktober. Die Folge waren jene Fieberkranken mit Katharr, starkem Husten, ja sogar Entzündungen der Lunge.
»Ja, Grasshoff«, hatte Dorothea sogleich eine Antwort parat, »Salbei, Kümmel, Süßholz, Schafgarbe und Beifuß! Auch das herzustellen übernehme ich, bin ich doch als Frau eher in der Küche zuhause!« scherzte sie, ihre kurze Freundschaft besiegelnd.
Eben wollte Doktor Erxleben sich über den nächsten Patienten beugen, als sie sah, daß jemand sie aus dem

Saal winkte. Sie band ihre nicht mehr ganz blütenreine Schürze ab und folgte dem Wink.

»Was ist, Meffert?« fragte sie, als sie erkannte, wer es war.

»Ach, Frau Doktor... bitte, Frau Doktor«, stammelte der alte Mann, »Sie möchten in den Steinweg kommen... Ihre Mutter«

Anna Sophia Leporin, geborene Meinecke starb am 19. Oktober 1757 im Alter von siebenundsiebzig Jahren. Sie gehörte zu jenen, die der Karriere ihrer Tochter stets skeptisch gegenüberstanden. Daß eine Frau den männlichen Körper berühren und betasten solle, und sei es auch zu medizinischen Zwecken, war ihr nach wie vor suspekt. Nach Meinung der Pfarrerstochter und Arztfrau gehörte ein weibliches Wesen immer noch in die Küche, hatte Kinder zu kriegen und die Familie in christlichem Glauben zusammenzuhalten. Folgerichtig war die Beziehung von Mutter zu Tochter stets mehr von Zurückhaltung gekennzeichnet gewesen, denn von Anerkennung oder gar Stolz auf die außerordentlichen Leistungen Dorotheas. Dennoch wurde sie von dieser auf eine stille Weise sehr betrauert.

## *Stiller Abschied*

Die Siegessicherheit von General d'Armentière wie seiner Männer wurde vom ersten scharfen Novemberwind hinweggefegt. Die Preußen hatten eine Schlacht geschlagen, bei einem Dorf mit Namen Roßbach, fünf Meilen südlich Halle, und dabei einen glänzenden Sieg davongetragen. Knapp vier Wochen später gelang ihnen ein zweiter vernichtender Schlag bei Leuthen. Aus preußischer Sicht ging es wieder aufwärts.
Den Bürgern Quedlinburgs brachte das allerdings noch keinerlei Erleichterung, sondern einstweilen eher das Gegenteil.
In aller Eile zogen zwar die Franzosen ab, aber nur, um nachziehenden Einheiten Platz zu machen. Ein General Turpin löste den General d'Armentière ab, und dessen Methoden stellten die der glücklich überstandenen Freischärler noch in den Schatten. Ihnen wiederum folgten Österreicher voller Rachedurst. Sie legten ihre Leute in die Bürgerhäuser, nahmen gar Geiseln gegen Kontribution. Die Quedlinburger bluteten darüber fast aus, ihre Vorräte waren aufgebraucht, Bedrängnis und Demütigung fanden täglich ihre Opfer.

Dorothea Erxleben geht unbeirrt ihrer ärztlichen Arbeit nach, unterscheidet nicht, ob Feind oder Freund, wenn ihre Hilfe gefordert ist.

*Inzwischen sind in unserer Gemeinde sieben Kinder zur Welt gekommen*, schreibt sie an Magdalena, *bei vieren*

*stand ich den Müttern bei, und es gedieh alles zum Segen trotz mancher unglücklicher Umstände.*
Zu den unglücklichen Umständen mag sicherlich eine durch die Kriegszeiten ungeklärte Vaterschaft gehören.
Das übergeht Dorothea taktvoll, reagiert als Ärztin mit deutlich hörbarem Stolz, aber auch mit einer unterschwelligen Sehnsucht, die sich gleich aus dem nächsten Satz erklärt: *Wie gerne würde ich Deinen lieben Buben einmal in die Arme schließen!*

Sie ist Großmutter geworden; eine neue schöne Erfahrung. Wenn Magdalena, die Dorothea den ersten Enkel schenkte, auch nur ihre Stieftochter war, so machte es keinen Unterschied in Dorotheas Gefühlen, da sie ja auch als Mutter niemals einen Unterschied zwischen den bei ihrer Heirat übernommenen Kindern und ihren eigenen später geborenen gemacht hatte.
Großmutter zu sein, selbst auf anderthalb Meilen Entfernung, bedeutete Dorothea zweifellos ein großes Glück, eines, das sie gern mit jeder anderen Mutter dieser Erde geteilt hätte. Wieviel mehr muß es sie ausgerechnet jetzt berührt haben, was sie weiter an Magdalena berichtet:

*Denke Dir nur, die arme Tante Klopstock traf ich neulich in schwarzer Trauerhaube! Kaum, daß sie mich sah, schluchzte sie auf, so daß sie kaum sprechen konnte. Ihre Schwiegertochter, die Meta, sollte daheim bei ihren Eltern in Hamburg nun endlich niederkommen, aber hat die Geburt nicht überlebt! Ich hab es befürchtet, damals, als ich sie sah, so schmal und mit dem Husten! So schmal und viel zu zart! Aber kann*

*man warnen und hindern? Wir können nicht Schicksal spielen, auch wir Ärzte nicht!*
Dorothea bedauert, daß sie und Erxleben wegen der Unsicherheit auf den Straßen der Taufe nicht haben beiwohnen können.
*Daß Ihr ihn auf den Namen Johannes getauft habt, hat vor allem den Vater herzlich gefreut,* schreibt sie weiter, kommt damit aber auf eine neue große Sorge zu sprechen.
*Ich schrieb Dir schon zu Anfang, daß es ihm gar nicht wohl geht, aber er läßt sich nichts anmerken. Er wird nur immer stiller. Das heißt, des Sonntags predigt er noch mit demselben Feuer wie in früheren Jahren. Doch sein Herz ist hinterher sehr müde, und ich sorge mich um ihn. Mein Bruder Christian schrieb aus Nienburg und riet mir, zu Goldtropfen für Vaters schwaches Herz. Ich besorgte sie sogleich. Wenn sie doch nur helfen möchten!*

Es war wohl nicht nur das schwache Herz, das Pfarrer Erxleben zu schaffen machte. Er rieb sich seelisch an den Zeitläuften auf, an seinem Unvermögen, den Menschen in ihrer Verzweiflung zu helfen, wenn jetzt die vierte Welle der Einquartierung über sie hinging. Vielleicht rang er auch mit Zweifeln, die er nicht mit seinem geistlichen Stand in Einklang bringen konnte. Sicher aber war, er war alt geworden.
Immerhin achtzehn Jahre älter als Dorothea, ging er auf sein zweiundsechzigstes Jahr. Sein Haar war längst nicht mehr grau, sondern schlohweiß, seine Bewegungen waren zuweilen fahrig, Zittern konnte ihn befallen und schlagartige Müdigkeit, die mit hartnäckiger Schlaflosigkeit wechselte. Dorothea ahnte sehr wohl,

daß angesichts der rasanten Veränderungen in der Physis ihres Mannes ärztliche Kunst bald nichts mehr würde ausrichten können, daß ein anderer, ein Höherer, Verlauf und Zeitmaß bestimmen würde. Aber daran wollte sie einstweilen nicht denken. Ihre Gedanken kreisten um weitere ihrer vielen Sorgenkinder, und auch davon schreibt sie ihrer Stieftochter.

*Neulich wurde ich zum Fräulein von Oppen aufs Schloß hinauf gerufen, aber kann ihr kaum mehr helfen! Zu meiner Jugend war sie eine der anmutigsten Hofdamen der Herzogin gewesen. Nie sah ich eine schlankere Taille, nie zierlichere Füßchen als bei ihr. Und nun sitzt sie in ihrem Sessel, von Wassersucht und Gicht aufgeschwollen. Auch das Gesicht ist unschön geworden, nur die Augen blicken noch gütig wie ehedem und rühren darum das Herz. Diese Frau quält sich und möchte gern sterben, und dort in Hamburg mußte die lieblich junge Klopstockin fort, die noch so gern auf dieser Welt geblieben wäre,* klingt es fast wie Auflehnung, um aber wieder schicksalsergeben zu enden: *Ja, Gottes Wege sind nicht unsere Wege! Euch aber nehme unser himmlischer Vater in seinen Schutz, darum beten wir täglich. In Liebe Deine Mutter Dorothea Erxleben.*
*Quedlinburg, dem 3. Dezember 1758.*

In diesem Winter nahmen die Kriegsereignisse erneut eine bedrohliche Entwicklung. Keinerlei Aussicht auf Frieden. Im Gegenteil. Die Russen sind auf dem Plan erschienen, haben noch im Sommer Küstrin verwüstet, Ausgleich dafür bot der preußische Sieg bei Zorndorf, dem aber im selben Jahr Hochkirch folgte, mit Vorteil für die Österreicher. Im dritten Kriegswinter war der

König tief deprimiert, abwartend, aber entschlossen, der erdrückenden Übermacht im Frühjahr erneut entgegenzutreten.
Der Stadt Quedlinburg aber brachte der Winter die fünfte Einquartierung und damit die nahezu völlige Ausschöpfung ihrer Existenzmöglichkeit.

Endlich schmilzt der Schnee wieder, zeigt sich die erste Frühlingssonne. Im Pfarrgarten wie in anderen Gärtchen hinter Bürgerhäusern versteckt, pflanzt man nicht mehr Stiefmütterchen oder sonst Blumen, sondern baut Kohl und Rüben, sät Bohnen und Kresse. Nicht mehr der Tischschmuck in der Vase zählt, nur noch das, was in Topf und Terrine, gekocht und gesotten, den Hunger vertreiben kann.
Doktor Erxleben geht weiter ihren Pflichten nach. Am 25. März 1759, nachmittags, wird sie zu einem Patienten weit am entgegengesetzten Rande der Stadt gerufen. Sie nimmt ein Tuch um, wirft ihrem auf seinem Lieblingsplatz am Fenster sitzenden Mann ein Grußwort zu.
»Wart nicht auf mich, Johannes, es kann spät werden. Fühlst du dich müde, Liebster, leg dich ruhig schon schlafen!« sagt sie und macht sich in die sinkende Sonne hinein auf den Weg. In einem der ärmeren Häuser findet sie einen Fieberkranken, dem sie ein linderndes Mittel verabreicht. Und da sie dessen Wirkung abwarten will, wird es tatsächlich, wie sie vermutet hatte, spät. Wieder zurück findet sie Martha, mürrisch wie immer, zwischen Töpfen werkelnd, und am Küchentisch, über ihr Einmaleins gebeugt, die neunjährige Anna Dorothea.

»Ach, Martha, hast du wohl einen Löffel Suppe für mich? Und du, mein Mädchen, bist immer noch fleißig?«
So begrüßt sie beide und läßt sich müde auf einen Stuhl nieder. »Und die anderen? Alle schon zu Bett?«
Das Kind klappt sein Buch zu.
»Ja, Mutter, alle schon zu Bett!«
»Und der Vater? Ging auch er schlafen?«
Martha stellt abrupt einen Teller heißer Suppe auf den Tisch.
»Ja, Frau Doktor, gleich nach dem Abendläuten meinte der Herr Pfarrer, er sei müde und ginge zu Bett.«
»Dann sei leise, wenn du hinaufgehst, Anna, mein Kind, damit du den Vater nicht störst.«
»Ja, Mutter! Gute Nacht, Mutter!«
Anna geht hinauf, Dorothea ißt die Suppe. Dann erhebt auch sie sich.
»Gute Nacht, Martha, vergiß nicht, das Feuer zu löschen.«
»Ich lösche es jeden Abend, Frau Doktor«, kommt es mit Vorwurf von der Magd, aber dann wünscht auch sie der Herrin eine gute Nacht.

Dorothea nimmt die Kerze, die immer am Treppenfuß bereitsteht, und steigt die Stufen hinauf. Ehe sie die Tür zur Schlafkammer öffnet, hält sie eine Hand vor das Licht, damit sein heller Schein den Schlafenden nicht wecke. Alles ist still im Haus und in der Stube. Doch etwas beunruhigt Dorothea. Was nur? Sie horcht noch einen Augenblick. Dann weiß sie es. Es ist die Stille. Sie hört keinen Atem. Sie nimmt die Hand vom Licht und hält es hoch über ihren Kopf. Hell umgibt der Schein das Gesicht des Schlafenden. Seine Augen sind geschlossen, der Ausdruck tiefen Friedens liegt auf seinen Zügen. Und Dorothea, mit ärztlich geschultem Blick, weiß sofort, ihr Mann Johannes Erxleben schläft den einen Schlaf, aus dem es kein Erwachen gibt.

## *Das Ende des Weges*

Hatte Dorothea befürchtet, daß sie nach dem Tod ihres Mannes das Pfarrhaus würde räumen müssen, so fand sich zu ihrer Erleichterung eine andere Lösung. Der neue Pfarrer, jung und unverheiratet, erklärte sich damit einverstanden, einstweilen ins Küsterhaus zu ziehen, und so blieb für Dorothea und die noch daheim lebenden Kinder alles beim alten. Sie konnten weiter wie bisher in den Räumen wohnen und leben, die der Familie ja nun schon in dritter Generation vertraute Heimstatt waren. Zwar erschienen Dorothea diese jetzt oft trostlos leer, da Erxleben nicht mehr am Fenster saß, an seiner Predigt arbeitete, das Tagesgeschehen mit ihr besprach, vor allem aber ihr das Gefühl von Wärme und Geborgenheit, von unverbrüchlicher Liebe vermittelte. In dieser Zeit fand die Erxlebin eine ganz besondere Stütze an ihrem sechzehnjährigen Sohn Christian Polykarp. Groß für sein Alter und recht wohlgebaut, kurz ein hübscher Junge, schlug er ganz nach seiner Mutter. Und das nicht nur im Aussehen, sondern offensichtlich auch im lebhaften Interesse für die Wissenschaften. Waren es bei ihm eher die Physikbücher als die der Arzeneygelahrtheit, in denen man ihn ständig lesen und blättern fand – ähnlich der kleinen Dörte von damals –, so ging er dennoch seiner Mutter auch in der ärztlichen Praxis mit Geschick und Fertigkeit zur Hand. Fiel es Dorothea manches Mal schon schwer, die Medikamententasche zu tragen, wenn es auf Krankenbesuch ging, so sah man Christian

Erxleben munteren Schritts, die Tasche unterm Arm, an ihrer Seite.

»Wir müssen heut zum Münzenberg hinauf, Christian«, ordnete die Mutter an einem recht warmen Sommertag an, »bei diesen Armen der Ärmsten macht sich die Unterernährung bereits gefährlich bemerkbar.«

»Ja, Mutter, ich hab' es auch schon bemerkt«, teilte der Sohn ihre Sorge, »sie haben Kinder, die vor Schwäche einfach nicht laufen lernen.«

»Und die Frauen, rückständig wie sie sind, packen ihre Kinder bei diesem Wetter noch warm ein, anstatt Sonne an ihre kranken Gliedmaßen zu lassen!«

So im Gespräch durchquerten sie die Stadt, Dorothea einen letzten Vorrat Kandiszucker bei sich, Christian Huckepack einen Sack Fichtenzweige aus dem oberen Harz, vom einen den Kindern Sirup einzuflößen, vom anderen, wenn sie denn die Mütter dazu überreden könnten, kräftigende Bäder zu verordnen.

Dorothea blieb einen Moment im Schatten eines Hauses stehen, um zu verschnaufen. Sie bemerkte etliche Bürger in Gruppen und Grüppchen stehen und erregt diskutieren. Das sah ganz nach alarmierenden Neuigkeiten aus.

»Lauf hinüber, Christian, frag, was es gibt!« bat Dorothea und wischte sich die schweißnasse Stirn mit einem Spitzentuch.

Christian lief, wie ihm geheißen, und kehrte sogleich mit bedenklicher Miene zurück.

»Die Russen, Mama!« rief er achselzuckend »sie stehen schon an der Oder! Der Hof ist wieder nach Magdeburg geflohen!«

»Also alles noch einmal, genau wie im letzten Jahr!«

seufzte die Erxlebin, »Wir können nichts tun als unsere Pflicht. Gehen wir also, Christian!«
»Ja, Mama«, sagte Christian und nahm seinen Sack wieder auf, den er abgestellt hatte, »gehen wir.«

Die Mütter im Armenviertel der Stadt waren kaum zu überreden, ihre Kinder aus den warmwollenen Kleidern und Röcken zu schälen, sie im Hemd an der Sonne spielen zu lassen, geschweige denn Fenster und Türen ihrer Häuser zu öffnen, damit Licht und Luft eindringen können. Da die Kleinen weder stehen noch gehen mochten, schleppten sie ihre Drei- und Vierjährigen herum. Traurig war der Anblick ihrer vor Entbehrung aufgequollenen Bäuche. Wenigstens einen Aufguß vom mitgebrachten Kandis schleckten die Kleinen gern, während Christian den Sack Fichtenzweige wieder unverrichteter Dinge mit sich nehmen mußte. Ein Kind zu baden, unbekleidet in einen Bottich zu stecken, noch dazu im klebrigen Sud von Tannennadeln, das lehnten die Frauen vom Münzberg rundweg ab.
»Wir können es nur immer und immer wieder versuchen«, meinte Dorothea, als sie mit ihrem Sohn wieder bergab schritt, »aber der hartnäckigste Feind allen Fortschritts ist das dumpfe Beharren im Denken!«
Christian lachte.
»Eine höfliche Umschreibung der Dummheit, Mutter!«
»Sagen wir der Unwissenheit, mein Junge. Und der müssen wir den Kampf ansagen.«
Alsbald umfingen Mutter und Sohn wieder die Straßen und Gassen wohlanständiger Bürgerhäuser mit

ihren Giebeln und Erkern, aber die Armut wohnte jetzt, im fünften Kriegsjahr, auch hinter diesen Mauern. Wiederholte Forderungen an Kontribution und Douceurs hatten die Schatullen geleert, der Schmuck ihrer Frauen war verkauft und verpfändet, Räucherkammern, Getreideböden, Weinkeller, Warenlager blank ausgefegt bis aufs letzte Korn. Und wo in ihren Gärten etwas sproß und wuchs, wurde es geerntet, ehe es ganz reif war. Der Hunger ging um, kein Haus ohne Trauer um einen Sohn oder Vater, und niemand sah ein Ende ab.
Dorothea und ihr Sohn nahmen die Brücke über die Bode und bogen bei der Pölke in die Kaplanei ein.

Ein Jahr verging in verhältnismäßiger Ruhe, wenn man den Wechsel von immer wieder Einquartierung, Requirierung, von erneut Drangsal, Not und Ausbeutung überhaupt so nennen kann. Die letzten in dieser Reihe waren dann am 18. Oktober 1760 die zur Armee des Marschalls Broglio gehörenden 800 Dragoner unter ihrem General Stainville, die Unterkunft, Verpflegung, und ärztliche Versorgung forderten, letztere auf manches Mal recht ungewöhnliche Weise.

Eines Abends waren Dorothea und Christian noch spät in den Praxisräumen im Steinweg anwesend, ein reiner Zufall, denn normalerweise waren sie zu dieser Stunde beide längst wieder ins Pfarrhaus zurückgekehrt. Plötzlich wurde laut an den geschlossenen Fensterladen geklopft und dazu gerufen:
»Madame le docteur! Ouvriez!«
Wer immer dort pochte, hatte wohl den Lichtschein

hinter den Fensterläden gesehen und so auf Erfolg seines Verlangens gehofft. Wenn die Worte auch französisch waren, so keineswegs ihr Tonfall, und konnte man vermuten, daß die Stimme glauben machen wollte, sie gehöre einem Franzosen. Gleich wie, Christian öffnete die Haustür und ums Haar wäre er gestolpert über das, was man dort abgelegt hatte. Wer es abgelegt hatte, blieb buchstäblich im Dunkel, denn nur eilige Schritte von offenbar zwei Personen verloren sich in der Ferne.
Christian beugte sich nieder, den Fund zu betrachten und rief sogleich nach seiner Mutter.
»Ein Soldat, Mutter! Er ist bewußtlos!«
Doktor Erxleben trat mit einer Laterne vors Haus und stellte neben außerordentlicher Jugend des Soldaten eine bereits brandige Wunde an der Schulter fest.
»Er fiebert und hat viel Blut verloren«, sagte sie, »komm, wir müssen ihn reintragen!«
Das zu bewerkstelligen war nicht ganz leicht. Christian umfaßte den Leib, Dorothea hob ihn vorsichtig am Kopf und suchte die verwundete Schulter zu stützen.
Der Bewußtlose begann zu phantasieren und um sich zu schlagen.
»Nein, nein!« rief er, und »nicht mich, nicht mich!« In seiner vom Instinkt geleiteten Abwehr entwickelte er große Kraft und, noch ehe er sicher im Haus geborgen war, holte sein Arm aus und traf Dorothea mit voller Wucht vor die Brust. Sie stöhnte auf und fühlte ein Flimmern vor den Augen, aber wie es oft geschieht, wenn ein Schlag mit großer Kraft trifft, drang ihr der Schmerz nicht sogleich ins Bewußtsein.
»Was ist?« rief Christian, der im Halbdunkel nur eine

kurze Bewegung wahrgenommen hatte, aber nicht wußte, was passiert war.

»Nichts, nichts«, wehrte seine Mutter ab und kümmerte sich weiter einzig um die Versorgung des Soldaten. Erst als dieser verbunden und in einer der leerstehenden Kammern untergebracht war, wurde Dorothea sich eines dumpfen Schmerzes in der Brust bewußt, und dieser sollte sie von nun an niemals mehr gänzlich verlassen.

In den nächsten Wochen und Monaten mehrten sich die Anzeichen, daß der Schlag gegen die Brust der Erxlebin nicht ohne Folgen bleiben würde. Nach anfänglich starkem Bluterguß, hegte sie den Verdacht, daß Wucherungen, wie sie sie vor Jahren schon vermutet, wieder aktiviert waren. Dorothea wurde sich alsbald bewußt, daß sie sehr krank war. Sie glaubte auch zu wissen, welcher Art ihre Krankheit sei, hatte sie doch Patientinnen mit ähnlichen Merkmalen bereits behandelt. Schon dachte Dorothea daran, sich Doktor Grasshoff anzuvertrauen, verwarf diesen Gedanken aber alsbald wieder. Er würde, da war sie sich sicher, auch nicht mehr viel helfen können.

Wenn sie sich morgens im Spiegel sah, erschrak sie über sich selbst. Noch immer war es nicht gerade das Gesicht einer alten Frau, aber die Augen schienen erweitert, tief in den Höhlen liegend, und die Haut spannte sich eng um Kinn und Wangenknochen. Wenn sie mit den Kindern am Familientisch saß, spürte sie deren sorgenvoll beobachtenden Blick auf sich.

»Geht es dir nicht gut, Mutter? Hast du wieder

Schmerzen?« fragten sie bestürzt, doch Dorothea suchte zu beruhigen:
»Nein, nein, Kinder, ein wenig müde, sonst nichts.«
Martha brummte unzufrieden, wenn die Herrin von den mühselig zusammengestellten Mahlzeiten jeweils nur ein paar Löffelchen aß.
»Es schmeckt der Frau Doktor wohl nicht? Ich kann ja nichts dafür, daß es nur noch Rüben und Karfiol sind statt Braten und Würste!«
»Nein, nein, Martha, es schmeckt köstlich! Du hast wieder einmal gezaubert«, beschwichtigte die Erxlebin dann wohl, »ich hab' nur grad nicht so den rechten Appetit.«
Zum Winter hin schien sich ihr Gesundheitszustand zu bessern, aber Dorothea glaubte nicht an ein Wunder.
Die Schmerzen kehrten wieder, einmal stärker, einmal schwächer, und bald verordnete Dorothea sich selbst jene Opiate und Schmerzmittel, deren Anwendung sie stets in ihren medizinischen Schriften verurteilte.
Nur mit Mühe konnte sie ihrer Arbeit in der Praxis nachkommen, mehr oder weniger stillschweigend übernahm Doktor Grashoff den einen oder anderen Fall. Mehr als genug blieben jene Patienten, die keinesfalls die Hilfe eines anderen Arztes annehmen wollten. Ihnen widmete sich Doktor Erxleben mit letzter Kraft.

Das Frühjahr 1762 kam mild und lockend über die Stadt. Wie ein Wunder schien es Dorothea, daß noch einmal Wiesen und Gärten grünten und sich mit farbiger Blütenpracht schmückten. Nach immer häufigeren schlaflosen Nächten ließ sie sich tagsüber oben in ihrer

Kammer am weit offenen Fenster betten und blickte hinab auf ihre kleine Welt von schwellenden Baumkronen, Dächern und Gassen ihrer Heimatstadt Quedlinburg. Dann dankte sie Gott für alles, was sie hier hatte erleben und erreichen dürfen, pries seine Umsicht und Gnade.
»Du hast alles wohlgetan, Herr, schenke mir nur noch eins: Frieden auf Erden, Frieden in diesem Lande!«

Dieser Wunsch sollte der Erxlebin nur zum Teil noch erfüllt werden. Karl Peter Ulrich Herzog von Holstein-Gottorp, ein naher Verwandter der verstorbenen Äbtissin, ehemals Kronprinz von Schweden, bestieg nach Verzicht auf die schwedische Krone, als Peter III. den russischen Zarenthron. Er war ein schwacher, etwas verwirrter junger Mann, bei dem nur eines klar hervortrat: seine schwärmerische Bewunderung allen Preußentums, insbesondere der Person Friedrichs II. Kaum auf dem Thron, warf er das Steuer bisheriger Politik herum, ließ seine Truppen nicht gegen, sondern Seite an Seite mit den preußischen marschieren. Das führte am 5. Mai 1762 zu einem Separatfrieden zwischen Rußland und Preußen, dem sich am 22. Mai Schweden anschloß. Die weiteren Staaten, die sich mit Friedrich im Krieg befanden, Frankreich, Österreich und Sachsen, waren zu einem solchen Schritt noch nicht bereit. So erlebt Dorothea Christiane Erxleben einen gänzlichen Frieden nicht mehr. Sie schließt am 13. Juni 1762, erst sechsundvierzig Jahre alt, für immer die Augen.
Reichtümer hat sie nicht angesammelt, die Doktorin Erxleben, weder durch ihre Tätigkeit als Ärztin noch

als Pfarrfrau. Bis zum Ende blieb ihr die Armut treu. So vermerkt der Eintrag im Sterberegister von Sankt Nikolai nicht nur, daß Dorothea Christiane, geborene Leporinin, des Herrn Diaconi Johannes Christian Erxleben Ehegefährtin, auf der rechten Seite des Friedhofs begraben wurde, wobei mit der großen Glocke zweimal vorgeläutet und um drei Uhr nachmittags zum Hingang mit beiden Glocken geläutet wurde, sondern auch, daß Grab und Aussegnung ihr gratis zugestanden wurden.

Wir wissen nicht, was auf ihrem Grabstein stand, aber passend wäre das Wort gewesen, das Johann Wolfgang Goethe dreißig Jahre später in seinem ›Torquato Tasso‹ schrieb:

*Es bildet ein Talent sich in der Stille,*
*Sich ein Charakter in dem Strom der Welt.*

# *Biographien aus dem Salzer Verlag*

Mia Munier-Wroblewski
*Die Goldmacher*
Die Erfinder des Meissener Porzellans
Historischer Roman
ISBN 3-7806-5365-6

Die Erfindung des „weißen Goldes" – ein historischer Kriminalfall? Wie gelangte der im Ruf eines Goldmachers stehende Apothekergehilfe Johann Friedrich Böttger in den Besitz der geheimen Forschungsunterlagen des Gelehrten Ehrenfried Walther von Tschirnhaus? Die Autorin deckt in ihrem spannenden Roman die Hintergründe auf und erzählt das Leben dieser beiden faszinierenden Persönlichkeiten zur Zeit August des Starken.

Beate Klepper
*Tumult der Seele*
Lichtenberg und Maria Dorothea Stechard
240 S., geb.
ISBN 3-7806-5360-5

Sie war blutjung und hatte nicht viel von dem kargen Leben zu erwarten, in das sie hineingeboren wurde. Doch dann begegnete 1777 Maria Dorothea Stechard dem kleinen Buckligen mit dem gescheiten Kopf, dem Aufklärer, Aphoristiker und Physiker Georg Christoph Lichtenberg. Eine der bemerkenswertesten Liebesbeziehungen der deutschen Geschichte, geschildert aus der Sicht der jungen Frau.

**Verlag Ernst Kaufmann**
Postfach 2208 · 77912 Lahr · www.kaufmann-verlag.de

# Biographien aus dem Salzer Verlag

Antje Windgassen
## *Kasturbai Gandhi*
Eine Mutter für Indien
240 S., geb. · ISBN 3-7806-5356-7

Wer war die Frau an der Seite Mahatma Gandhis? Wie lebten die beiden miteinander? Wie stand sie zu Gandhis Idealen? Kasturbai Gandhi hatte viele Gesichter: das der aufopfernden Hindufrau, die den Ansprüchen ihres Ehemannes gerecht wurde, das der „Ba", die mit Verständnis für die Sorgen anderer jahrzehntelang ein entbehrungsreiches Leben im Ashram führte, das der Freiheitskämpferin und Nationalheldin. Von ihr lernte Mahatma Gandhi die Kunst des passiven Widerstandes, die er so erfolgreich gegen die Engländer anwandte.

Antje Windgassen
## *Alexandra David-Néel*
Auf der Suche nach dem Licht
Biographischer Roman
248 S., geb. · ISBN 3-7806-5350-8

1891 reiste Alexandra David-Néel als Dreiundzwanzigjährige zum ersten Mal nach Asien, in das Land ihrer Träume. Als bekannte Orientalistin, Journalistin und Schriftstellerin verbrachte sie ihr halbes Leben dort, wanderte mit ihrem späteren Adoptivsohn, Lama Yongden, durch Indien, Sikkim, Nepal und China. In Tibet lebte und studierte sie über ein Jahr bei einem buddhistischen Lama in einer Hütte auf 4000 Metern Höhe und wurde als einzige Europäerin in den Stand einer Lamina erhoben. Eine Reise nach Lhasa, Begegnungen mit dem Dalai Lama und Mahatma Gandhi machten Alexandra David-Néel weltweit bekannt.

**Verlag Ernst Kaufmann**
Postfach 2208 · 77912 Lahr · www.kaufmann-verlag.de

# Biographien
# aus dem Salzer Verlag

Fritz Streitberger
## *Der Freiheit eine Gasse*
Die Lebensgeschichte des Christian Friedrich Daniel Schubart
128 S., geb. · ISBN 3-7806-5015-0

Fritz Streitberger, ein Nachkomme der Familie Schubart, schreibt zu dem Buch:
Der Dichter, Musiker und Journalist *Christian Friedrich Daniel Schubart* (1739–1791) war einer der schwierigsten Männer im Schwabenland des 18. Jahrhunderts. Ein bekanntes Goethewort ist für ihn zutreffend: Er war kein ausgeklügeltes Buch, sondern ein Mensch mit seinem Widerspruch. Gerade deshalb scheint es mir lohnend zu sein, diesem ach so zwiespältigen und oft auch als rebellisch bezeichneten Schubart nachzuspüren und ihn neu zu entdecken. Dazu möchte mein Buch beitragen, zumal ältere Schubartbücher und Schubartschriften weitgehend vergriffen sind.

Edith Biewend
## *Lieben ohne Illusion*
Leben und Werk des Janusz Korczak
112 S., kart. · ISBN 3-7806-5017-7

Dem polnisch-jüdischen Arzt, Dichter und Erzieher Korczak wurde 1972, dreißig Jahre nach seinem Tod, der Friedenspreis des Börsenvereins des Deutschen Buchhandels verliehen. Sein Leben war erfüllt von helfender Liebe: 1942 begleitete er seine zweihundert jüdischen Waisenkinder ins KZ von Treblinka. Die eigene Rettung hat er abgelehnt. „Du bist jähzornig, sage ich zu einem Jungen, nun ja, dann schlag nur zu, aber nicht zu fest; brause nur auf, aber nur einmal am Tag. – Wenn ihr so wollt, habe ich in diesem einen Satz meine ganze Erziehungsmethode zusammengefasst."
Mit diesem Buch würdigt die Autorin Leben und Werk dieses großen Pädagogen.

**Verlag Ernst Kaufmann**
Postfach 2208 · 77912 Lahr · www.kaufmann-verlag.de

# Biographien aus dem Salzer Verlag

Charlotte Hofmann-Hege
*Alles kann ein Herz ertragen*
Die weite Lebensreise der Elisabeth Thiessen
192 S., geb. · ISBN 3-7806-5279-X

Elisabeth, ein unbeschwertes, fröhliches Mädchen, reist im Frühjahr 1912 als Haushaltshilfe mit der Familie ihres Onkels nach Russland. „Es ist ein wunderbares Land", schreibt sie in ihrem ersten Brief nach Hause, nicht ahnend, was sie erwartet und dass sie ihre Heimat erst nach 55 Jahren wiedersehen sollte. Unverschuldet gerät sie in die Mühle der europäischen Zeitereignisse, die sie u. a. über 30 Jahre in sibirischer Verbannung festhalten.
Kein bequemes, aber ein sehr nötiges Buch, das bei aller herben Sachlichkeit spannend geschrieben ist.

Charlotte Hofmann-Hege
*Alle Tage ist kein Sonntag*
Das Geheimnis um Rudolf Schock und die Schloßmagd
176 S., geb. · ISBN 3-7806-5299-4

„In den Sechzigerjahren, als mein Mann Pfarrer in Bonfeld war, munkelte man, dass die Schlosslina, die als Stallmagd täglich unverdrossen ihrer harten Arbeit nachging, viel Geld für teure Rosensträuße an den Kammersänger Rudolf Schock ausgebe. Was war an den Gerüchten um Lina Brandt? Nur sehr zögernd und ganz behutsam erfuhren wir die Hintergründe dieser außergewöhnlichen Beziehung und wurden so Zeugen einer der bezauberndsten und anrührendsten ‚Liebes'- und Lebensgeschichten, die ich je miterlebt habe. Erst jetzt, nach Linas Tod, darf ich ihr Geheimnis lüften."

**Verlag Ernst Kaufmann**
Postfach 2208 · 77912 Lahr · www.kaufmann-verlag.de